# UNDERSTANDING THE
# OF ASSIGNMENT

The practical importance of intangible personalty such as debt, bonds, equities, futures, derivatives and other financial instruments has never been greater than it is today. The same may be said of interests in intellectual property. Yet the assignment of these intangible assets from one legal entity to another remains difficult to understand. Assignments are often taken to operate as a form of transfer akin to conveyances of legal titles to tangible personalty. However, this conception does not accurately reflect the law of assignment as it has developed in the caselaw in England and Wales. This book sets out a different model of the workings of assignments as a matter of English law, one that provides an analytical, yet historically sensitive, framework which allows us to better understand how, and why, assignments work in the way the cases tell us they do.

C. H. THAM received his LL.B. from the National University of Singapore in 1994, and the B.C.L. and D.Phil. from the University of Oxford in 1998, and 2017, respectively. He joined the faculty at the Singapore Management University in 2001. He has been Professor of Law at the Singapore Management University School of Law since January 2019. He has written on a wide range of private law topics including contract remedies, cross-border insolvency, and equitable and statutory assignment, and these have been published in case notes, book chapters and peer-reviewed journals, such as *Lloyd's Maritime and Commercial Law Quarterly*, *Trust Law International* and *Law Quarterly Review*. His work has been cited by the UK Supreme Court and the Singapore Court of Appeal.

# UNDERSTANDING THE LAW OF ASSIGNMENT

### C. H. THAM

*School of Law, Singapore Management University*

# CAMBRIDGE
## UNIVERSITY PRESS

University Printing House, Cambridge CB2 8BS, United Kingdom

One Liberty Plaza, 20th Floor, New York, NY 10006, USA

477 Williamstown Road, Port Melbourne, VIC 3207, Australia

314–321, 3rd Floor, Plot 3, Splendor Forum, Jasola District Centre, New Delhi – 110025, India

79 Anson Road, #06–04/06, Singapore 079906

Cambridge University Press is part of the University of Cambridge.

It furthers the University's mission by disseminating knowledge in the pursuit of education, learning, and research at the highest international levels of excellence.

www.cambridge.org
Information on this title: www.cambridge.org/9781108475280
DOI: 10.1017/9781108636674

First published 2019

Printed in the United Kingdom by TJ International Ltd. Padstow Cornwall

*A catalogue record for this publication is available from the British Library.*

*Library of Congress Cataloging-in-Publication Data*
Names: Tham, Chee Ho, 1970– author.
Title: Understanding the law of assignment / Chee Ho Tham.
Description: Cambridge, United Kingdom ; New York, NY : Cambridge University Press, 2019. | Includes bibliographical references and index.
Identifiers: LCCN 2019003494 | ISBN 9781108475280 (hardback : alk. paper)
Subjects: LCSH: Assignments (Law)–England. | Choses in action–England. | Assignments (Law)
Classification: LCC KD1574 .T43 2019 | DDC 346.4207/7–dc23
LC record available at https://lccn.loc.gov/2019003494

ISBN 978-1-108-47528-0 Hardback

# CONTENTS

# FOREWORD

In 1919, Albert Einstein received a telegram informing him that one of the important predictions made by his general theory of relativity had been validated. Astronomers had observed that the sun's gravity caused light to bend. A student of Einstein's is said to have read the telegram and to have asked, provocatively, what Einstein's response would have been if the observations of astronomers had been inconsistent with his general theory. 'Then', Einstein said, 'I would have been sorry for the dear Lord because the theory is correct.'

One mark of a fine legal theory is that it can provide a new justification for a body of precedent that is philosophically coherent and that can explain the outcomes in future fact patterns. Sometimes the justification for a body of precedent can take a very long time to emerge. This might be because the decisions defy rational explanation. Or it might be because no one has looked hard enough.

The discovery of a rationale underlying an equitable doctrine is made more difficult by the way that equitable doctrine sometimes mimics the labels used by different common law rules. In doing so, equity gives the false impression that it is doing nothing novel. The true rationale is hidden by the nomenclature. For instance, 'equitable title' to a chattel is not title to the chattel. An 'equitable lease' over land is not a leasehold estate in the land. 'Equitable fraud' is not fraud. And, as Professor Tham brilliantly demonstrates, 'equitable assignment' is not assignment. It does not, in Professor Tham's words, violate a cardinal principle of morality, by assigning, or substituting, the rights of the assignor for the assignee without the consent of the obligor.

*Understanding the Law of Assignment* is a comprehensive and exhaustive analysis of hundreds of cases and legislative provisions concerning equitable assignment. It focuses upon English law but with an eye to numerous other jurisdictions. It is written beautifully. It develops or applies the thinking of many great legal theorists including Blackstone, Story and Hohfeld. Professor Tham's theory, that an equitable assignment involves the creation of a bare trust coupled with agency, is sophisticated and elegant. And, most valuably of all, it provides justification for a very significant body of law. It explains rules that have been incomprehensible to generations of lawyers, described only by the name of the case that created them. And it provides a justification for the operation of s. 136(1) of the Law of Property Act 1925, as building additional effects on to the equitable 'assignment', without substantial violation of the moral principle that new obligations should not be imposed on people without their consent. In these ways, and many others, Professor Tham's theory does not merely help us to understand why the law is the way it is. It also helps us to understand how it should develop.

**James Edelman**
*Judges' chambers*
*High Court of Australia, Canberra*
*10 December 2018*

# PREFACE

To see what is in front of one's nose is a constant struggle.[1]

George Orwell, 'In Front of One's Nose'
*Tribune*, London, 22 March 1946

This book grew out of having to teach the law of privity of contract. Among the thicket of 'exceptions' to the rule of privity was a particular thorn: assignment.

Despite its prevalence as an essential tool of modern-day commerce and finance, it seemed to me, at least, that most works on the subject shied away from discussing how this doctrine worked: it was enough to know that there was such an institution, without needing to explain its operation. Unfortunately for me, and probably those around me, this breezy approach merely piqued my curiousity, leading me to dive down a rabbit hole which I now know to be closer to the size of Mammoth Cave in Brownsville, Kentucky.

Over the course of more than ten years, my exploration has resulted in a number of papers and articles musing on how equitable assignment works. Along the way, I was fortunate enough to be supervised by Professor Robert Stevens between 2014 and 2016 while completing a doctoral thesis at the University of Oxford, and in Trinity 2017, Professor Louise Gullifer kindly invited me to spend a term as a visiting fellow at the Commercial Law Centre at Harris Manchester College, University of Oxford. All of that work has been refined and extended into this book. But just as it takes a village to raise a child, it took a constellation of mentors, colleagues, friends and family to bring this book into being. In particular, I owe an enormous debt to those who generously gave me the gift of their time as I went on (and on) about assignment in my

---

[1] 'In Front of Your Nose' by George Orwell (Copyright © George Orwell, 1946). Reproduced by permission of Bill Hamilton as the Literary Executor of the Estate of the Late Sonia Brownell Orwell.

journeying. In addition to Justice James Edelman (who also kindly agreed to write the Foreword to this book), they include: Adrian Briggs, Simone Degeling, Mark Findlay, Birke Häcke, Rachel Leow, Nico Leslie, Timothy Liau, David Llewelyn, Kelry Loi, Kelvin Low, Gerard McMeel, Ben McFarlane, Charles Rickett, Francis Rose, Alvin See, Duncan Sheehan, Hans Tjio, Tiong-Min Yeo and Man Yip.

Readers of some of my earlier work on assignment will find echoes of those pieces in this book.[2] Without the encouragement and comments provided by the editors and reviewers who patrol these intellectual safe harbours, I would not have had the opportunity to work through the issues and themes which I believe underpin the law of assignment as it developed in England and Wales. I would therefore like to express my deepest thanks to all of them for their invaluable aid as I plodded through this area of the law.

Work on this book would also have been impossible without the astonishing facilities and privileges granted to visitors to the Bodleian Law Library, University of Oxford. Digitization of academic treatises is all very well, but to get a headstart in understanding areas of law of which one has little prior knowledge, nothing beats a slow walk along the shelves of a well-stocked library. Thanks are therefore owed to the librarians at the Bodleian Law Library for their sterling work in keeping this resource available and accessible. Finally, thanks are also owed to the team at the Cambridge University Press, and all who laboured on the production of this book, whose patience and care helped me make light work of a challenging project.

This book reworks, expands and resolves my central concern: to explain *how* equitable assignment appears to violate a cardinal principle of morality, that voluntarily undertaken obligations by an obligor to an obligee ought not to be open to unilateral variation by the obligee without the obligor's prior assent.

This concern worried even the Romans. But, pragmatic as they were, they developed the device of the *cessio actionum* to overcome the problem, whilst still affording some recognition to the importance of the

---

[2] Notably, my contributions to *Exploring Contract Law* (J. W. Neyers, R. Bronaugh and S. G. A. Pitel, eds.), and *Contracts in Commercial Law* (S. Degeling, J. Edelman and J. Goudkamp). Parts of Chapter 5 were drawn from C. H. Tham, 'Exploding the Myth That Bare Sub-Trustees "Drop Out"' [2017] *Trust Law International* 76; and parts of Part III were drawn from C. H. Tham, 'Joinder of Equitable Assignors of Equitable and Legal Choses in Action' [2017] LMCLQ 467. Thanks are owed to Professor Francis Rose for kindly allowing me to reuse some of the analysis and discussion in that article in this book.

proposition. The hypothesis in this book is that that Roman conception, by coincidence or design, happens to be the best model to explain how equitable assignment *simulates* the effect of substitution of the assignee in place of the assignor, but without actually doing so.

In the parable of the blind men and the elephant, a band of blind men with no prior experience of an elephant come across one. Each man touches a different part of the elephant, and, each provides an account of what an elephant is, based on their individual experience. So the blind man who touched the elephant's trunk says, 'An elephant is like a snake.' Another blind man who touched the elephant's ear says, 'An elephant is like a fan.' And a third blind man who touched the elephant's leg says, 'You're both wrong. An elephant is like the trunk of a tree.' But an elephant is not like a snake, *or* a fan, *or* the trunk of a tree. It is like all of them, and more.

Some prior attempts to explain how equitable assignments work have concentrated on the 'trust' aspect of such assignments. But as in the fable of the blind men and the elephant, that is not a sufficient explanation of how equitable assignments work: the case law clearly shows that there is something more in play. In this book, it is suggested that a fuller explanation of the workings of equitable assignments requires an appreciation that alongside the 'trust' aspect there is also an 'agency' aspect.

By effecting an equitable assignment, the assignor encumbers herself to her assignee in a manner that is akin to that which would have bound a bare trustee to his trust beneficiary. But an equitable assignment also entails the assignor delegating to her assignee such entitlements as the assignor had in connection with the chose assigned in a manner similar to that of a principal granting authority to his agent, whilst simultaneously releasing the agent from the associated fiduciary duties to which the agent or delegatee would usually be subjected.

An equitable assignment is, therefore, a *sui generis* institution, bearing dual characteristics: it is, in its operation, a bare trust coupled with an unusual form of agency. It is therefore misleading to insist that an equitable assignment *literally* effects a transfer of the assignor's entitlements to her assignee, for that would entail a substitution of the assignee in place of the assignor – a 'substitutive transfer'. Rather, the better position is to regard such 'transfer' as a metaphor: but a metaphor which does no harm, so long as we are clear of what we are speaking.

With eyes thus opened, it was natural to turn to how Parliament has intervened to modify the operation of equitable assignment. In Part IV, this book reviews the operation and effect of the Law of Property Act

1925, s. 136(1), by which it is said debts and choses (or things) in action may be 'statutorily' assigned. It then compares its operation with the operation of other statutes which also deal with 'transfers' or 'transmissions' of other, more narrowly defined, subclasses of intangible assets.

This book seeks to provide an analytical, coherent and robust explanation as to the workings of the core institution of *inter vivos* equitable assignment of equitable and legal choses in action, and its statutory gloss, as a matter of English law. It leaves aside detailed discussion and analysis of other modes of dealing with choses in action (for example, under the law of negotiable instruments, subrogation, succession, bankruptcy or insolvency). But by adopting a narrower focus, a more penetrating light may be shone to dispel the fog surrounding this cornerstone of modern commerce.

**C. H. Tham**
*Singapore*
*December 2018*

# CASES

## A

## C

# D

E

## H

# K

# L

## M

# N

# Q

# R

# S

## T

## U

## V

## W

## Y

## Z

# LEGISLATION

## United Kingdom

### *Statutes*

## Subsidiary Legislation

## Hansard

## Australia

## India

# ABBREVIATIONS

| | |
|---|---|
| Anderson (2008) | R. G. Anderson, *Assignation* (Edinburgh: Edinburgh Legal Education Trust, 2008) |
| Ames (1887) | J. B. Ames, 'Purchase for Value without Notice' (1887) 1 Harv L Rev 1 |
| Ames (1890) | J. B. Ames, 'The Disseisin of Chattels – Part III' (1890) 3 Harv L Rev 337 |
| Ames (1909) | J. B. Ames, 'Disseisin of Chattels' in *Select Essays in Anglo-American Legal History*, vol. III (Cambridge: Cambridge University Press, 1909) |
| Ames (1913) | J. B. Ames, *Lectures on Legal History and Miscellaneous Legal Essays* (Cambridge, MA: Harvard University Press, 1913) |
| Ashburner (1933) | Walter Ashburner, *Ashburner's Principles of Equity* (Denis Browne, ed., 2nd edn, London: Butterworth & Co., 1933) |
| Bailey (1932) | S. J. Bailey, 'Assignments of Debts in England from the Twelfth to the Twentieth Century – Part III' (1932) 48 LQR 547 |
| Beale, Gullifer & Paterson (2016) | H. Beale, L. Gullifer and S. Paterson, 'A Case for Interfering with Freedom of Contract? An Empirically-Informed Study of Bans on Assignment' [2016] JBL 203 |
| *Bl Comm* | *Blackstone's Commentaries on the Laws of England* |
| Bowstead & Reynolds (2018) | P. Watts and F. M. B. Reynolds, *Bowstead and Reynolds on Agency* (21st edn, London: Sweet & Maxwell, 2018) |
| *Brandt's* | *William Brandt's Sons & Co.* v. *Dunlop Rubber Co.* [1905] AC 454 |
| Bridge (2013) | M. G. Bridge, *The Law of Personal Property* (1st edn, London: Sweet & Maxwell, 2013) |
| Bridge (2016) | M. G. Bridge, 'The Nature of Assignment and Non-Assignment Clauses' (2016) 132 LQR 47 |

| | |
|---|---|
| Bridge (2018) | M Bridge *et al.*, *The Law of Personal Property* (2nd edn, London: Sweet & Maxwell, 2018) |
| C3PA | Contracts (Rights of Third Parties) Act 1999 |
| Calvert (1847) | Frederic Calvert, *A Treatise upon the Law Respecting Parties to Suits in Equity* (2nd edn, London: William Benning & Co., 1847) |
| Chitty (2018) | Joseph Chitty, *Chitty on Contracts* (H. G. Beale, Gen. ed., 33rd edn, London: Sweet & Maxwell, 2018) |
| Clerk & Lindsell (2018) | J. F. Clerk and W. H. B. Lindsell, *Clerk & Lindsell on Torts* (M. A. Jones, Gen. ed., 22nd edn, London: Sweet & Maxwell, 2014) |
| CLJ | Cambridge Law Journal |
| CLPA1854 | Common Law Procedure Act 1854 |
| *Co Litt* | *Coke on Littleton* |
| Copinger (2016) | W. A. Copinger, *Copinger and Skone James on Copyright*, vol. 1 (Gillian Davies, Nicholas Caddick and Gwilym Harbottle, eds., 17th edn, London: Sweet & Maxwell, 2016) |
| Corbin (1926) | A. L. Corbin, 'Assignment of Contract Rights' (1926) 74 *University of Pennsylvania Law Review* 207 |
| Davies (2015) | Paul S. Davies, *Accessory Liability* (Oxford: Hart, 2015) |
| Derham (2010) | S. R. Derham, *Derham on the Law of Set-Off* (4th edn, Oxford: Oxford University Press, 2010) |
| Dietrich & Ridge (2015) | Joachim Dietrich and Pauline Ridge, *Accessories in Private Law* (Cambridge: Cambridge University Press, 2015) |
| Drewry (1841) | Charles Stewart Drewry, *The Law and Practice of Injunctions* (London: S. Sweet, 1841) |
| Edelman & Elliott (2015) | James Edelman and Steven Elliott, 'Two Conceptions of Equitable Assignment' (2015) 131 LQR 228 |
| Elphinstone (1871) | H. W. Elphinstone, *A Practical Introduction to Conveyancing* (1st edn, London: William Maxwell, 1871) |
| Goode (1976) | Roy Goode, 'The Right to Trace and Its Impact in Commercial Transactions – II' (1976) 92 LQR 528 |
| Goode (1979) | R. M. Goode, 'Inalienable Rights?' (1979) 42 MLR 553 |
| Goode (2003) | R. M. Goode, 'Are Intangible Assets Fungible?' [2003] LMCLQ 379 |
| Goode (2009) | Sir Roy Goode, 'Contractual Prohibitions against Assignment' [2009] LMCLQ 300 |

| | |
|---|---|
| Goode (2017) | Sir Roy Goode, *Goode on Legal Problems of Credit and Security* (Louise Gullifer, ed., 6th edn, London: Sweet & Maxwell, 2017) |
| Green (1984) | Brian Green, 'Grey, Oughtred and Vandervell – A Contextual Reappraisal' (1984) 47 MLR 385 |
| Guest & Liew (2015) | A. G. Guest and Y. K. Liew, *Guest on the Law of Assignment* (2nd edn, London: Sweet & Maxwell, 2015) |
| Handley (2009) | K. R. Handley, *Spencer Bower and Handley: Res Judicata* (4th edn, London: LexisNexis, 2009) |
| Harris (1975) | J. W. Harris, *Variation of Trusts* (London: Sweet & Maxwell, 1975) |
| Hart (1982) | H. L. A. Hart, *Essays on Bentham: Studies in Jurisprudence and Political Theory* (Oxford: Clarendon Press, 1982) |
| Hayton & Mitchell (2015) | Ben McFarlane and Charles Mitchell, *Hayton and Mitchell: Text, Cases and Materials on the Law of Trusts and Equitable Remedies* (14th edn, London: Sweet & Maxwell, 2015) |
| Hohfeld (1923) | W. N. Hohfeld, *Fundamental Legal Conceptions as Applied in Judicial Reasoning and Other Legal Essays* (W. W. Cook ed., New Haven, CT: Yale University Press 1923) |
| Holdsworth (1920) | W. S. Holdsworth, 'History of the Treatment of Choses in Action by the Common Law' (1920) 33 Harv L Rev 997 |
| Holdsworth (1925) | W. S. Holdsworth, *A History of English Law*, vol. VII (1st edn, London: Methuen & Co., 1925) |
| Holland (1924) | T. E. Holland, *The Elements of Jurisprudence* (13th edn, Oxford: Clarendon Press) |
| Holmes (1968) | O. W. Holmes, *The Common Law* (Mark DeWolfe Howe, ed., London: Macmillan 1968) |
| Insolvent Debtors Relief Act 1838 | see '1838 Act' |
| *Jacob's Law of Trusts* (2016) | J. D. Heydon and M. J. Leeming, *Jacobs' Law of Trusts in Australia* (8th edn, Chatswood, NSW: LexisNexis Butterworths, 2016) |
| Judicature Act 1873 | Supreme Court of Judicature Act 1873 |
| Judicature Acts | Supreme Court of Judicature Act 1873 and Supreme Court of Judicature Act 1875 |
| Kerr (1867) | W. W. Kerr, *A Treatise on the Law and Practice of Injunctions in Equity* (London: W. Maxwell & Son, 1867) |

| | |
|---|---|
| Oditah (1991) | Fidelis Oditah, *Legal Aspects of Receivables Financing* (London: Sweet & Maxwell, 1991) |
| Oditah (2009) | Fidelis Oditah, 'Recurrent Issues in Receivables Financing' in John Armour and Jennifer Payne (eds.), *Rationality in Company Law: Essays in Honour of D. D. Prentice* (Oxford: Hart, 2009) |
| Peel (2015) | Edwin Peel, *The Law of Contract* (14th edn, London: Sweet & Maxwell, 2015) |
| Pollock (1910) | Frederick Pollock, 'Contract' in *Encyclopædia Britannica*, vol. 7 (11th edn, Cambridge: Cambridge University Press, 1910) |
| Roughton, Johnson & Cook (2014) | Ashley Roughton, Phillip Johnson and Trevor M. Cook, *The Modern Law of Patents* (3rd edn, London: LexisNexis, 2014) |
| Salinger (2017) | Noel Ruddy, Simon Mills and Nigel Davidson, *Salinger on Factoring* (5th edn, London: Sweet & Maxwell, 2017) |
| Smith & Leslie (2018) | Marcus Smith and Nico Leslie, *The Law of Assignment* (3rd edn, Oxford: Oxford University Press, 2018) |
| Snell (2015) | John McGhee et al., *Snell's Equity* (33rd edn, London: Sweet & Maxwell, 2015) |
| Spence (1850) | George Spence, *The Equitable Jurisdiction of the Court of Chancery*, vol. II (London: Lea and Blanchard, 1850) |
| Stevens (2007) | Robert Stevens, *Torts and Rights* (Oxford: Oxford University Press, 2007) |
| Story (1836) | Joseph Story, *Commentaries on Equity Jurisprudence, as Administered in England and America*, vol. II (1st edn, Boston: Hillard, Gray & Company, 1836) |
| Story (1882) | Joseph Story, *Commentaries on the Law of Agency: As a Branch of Commercial and Maritime Jurisprudence, with Occasional Illustrations from the Civil and Foreign Law* (Boston: C. P. Greenough, ed., 9th edn, Little, Brown, and Company, 1882) |
| Story (1884) | Joseph Story and W. E. Grigsby, *Commentaries on Equity Jurisprudence* (1st English edn, London: Stevens and Haynes, 1884) |
| Sugden (1846) | Sir Edward Sugden, *A Practical Treatise of the Law of Vendors and Purchasers of Estates* (11th edn, London: S. Sweet, 1846) |
| Terrell (2016) | *Terrell on the Law of Patents* (Mr Justice Birss, Gen. ed., 18th edn, London: Sweet & Maxwell/Thomson Reuters, 2016) |

| | |
|---|---|
| Tham (2010) | C. H. Tham, 'Notice of Assignment and Discharge by Performance' [2010] LMCLQ 38 |
| Tolhurst (2016) | G. J. Tolhurst, *The Assignment of Contractual Rights* (2nd edn, Oxford: Hart, 2016) |
| Tolhurst & Carter (2014) | G. J. Tolhurst and J. W. Carter, 'Prohibitions on Assignment: A Choice to Be Made' (2014) 73 *Cambridge Law Journal* 405. |
| Trukhtanov (2010) | A. Trukhtanov, 'In Defence of the "No Discharge after Notice" Rule' [2010] LMCLQ 551 |
| Tudsbery (1912) | F. C. Tudsbery, *The Nature, Requisites and Operation of Equitable Assignments* (London: Sweet and Maxwell, 1912) |
| Turner (2018) | P. G. Turner, 'Prohibitions on Assignment: Intellectualism v. Law' (2018) 134 LQR 532 |
| Underhill & Hayton (2016) | D. J. Hayton, Paul Matthews and Charles Mitchell, *Underhill and Hayton: Law Relating to Trusts and Trustees* (19th edn, London: LexisNexis, 2016) |
| Watts & Reynolds (2014) | Peter Watts and F. M. B. Reynolds, *Bowstead and Reynolds on Agency* (20th edn, London: Sweet & Maxwell, 2014) |
| Wenar (2005) | L. Wenar, 'The Nature of Rights' (2005) 33 *Philosophy & Public Affairs* 223 |
| Zakrzewski (2005) | Rafal Zakrzewski, *Remedies Reclassified* (Oxford: Oxford University Press, 2005) |
| 1826 Act | Act of 7 Geo IV, c. 56, intituled 'An Act to amend and consolidate the Laws for the Relief of Insolvent Debtors in England' |
| 1838 Act | Act of 1 & 2 Vict, c. 110, intituled 'An Act for abolishing Arrest on Mesne Process in Civil Actions, except in certain Cases; for extending the Remedies of Creditors against the Property of Debtors; and for amending the Laws for the Relief of Insolvent Debtors in England' |

# PART I

Introduction

# 1

# Introduction

Choses in action are valuable assets. This has compelled (and been facilitated by) the development of legal devices such as equitable assignment to allow holders of choses to deal with them, *inter vivos*. Such dealings form the bedrock of much of modern-day financial engineering. So, as a matter of English law, large swathes of debt factoring, the syndication of loans in the secondary market, and the 'transfer' of interests in intermediated securities held by a custodian rest on the institution of equitable assignment when the requirements for 'statutory' assignment pursuant to s. 136(1) of the Law of Property Act 1925 (hereafter 'LPA1925') cannot be satisfied.

This book aims to uncover the operation (i.e. the mechanics) of the assignment of choses in action arising under English law.[1] It will concern itself with exposing the mechanisms underpinning two forms of assignment which are of general application: equitable assignment of choses in action and 'statutory' assignment of choses in action pursuant to LPA1925, s. 136(1).[2] It will also examine and rationalize the role which notice plays in the operation of equitable assignments.

## A Scope

Although it will concentrate on the general case, this book will also consider the operation of other statutes which deal with the assignment of certain types of intangible personalty. It will therefore also consider[3]

---

[1] Given the export of the common law across the Commonwealth, similar conceptions of assignment of choses in action are to be found in Australia, Hong Kong and Singapore (to name a few examples). That said, some Commonwealth jurisdictions (for example, New Zealand and India) have very different conceptions of assignment. To keep this book within reasonable bounds, it will concentrate on the law of England and Wales, being, in a sense, the 'source' material from which the common law of assignment may be drawn.

[2] The analysis of statutory assignments will be found in in Chapter 12.

[3] In Chapter 14.

the operation of the relevant statutes relating to transfers made pursuant to such statutes of interests in intangible personalty arising from policies of marine[4] or life[5] insurance, and also certain intellectual property rights.[6] However, in the interests of length, it will leave aside discussion of assignments by and to the Crown,[7] transfers of shares and corporate securities,[8] and transfers of the legal estate in leasehold property.[9] This book will also leave aside analysis of instruments (or 'documentary intangibles')[10] which were recognized to be transferable under the law merchant.[11] Nor will it embark on analysis of transfers of choses in action arising from operation of law by reason of subrogation,[12] bankruptcy,[13] or death.[14]

This book will not address the interesting but adjacent question concerning the circumstances under which dealings in choses in action may be rendered ineffective as being contrary to public policy, for example, where the dealing amounts to maintenance and/or champerty, and is thus rendered null, void and of no effect.[15]

---

[4] Marine Insurance Act 1906.

[5] Policies of Assurance Act 1867.

[6] See Chapter 14.

[7] See *Halsbury's Laws* (5th edn, London: Butterworths/LexisNexis, 2009), vol. 13, para. 16. See also *Breverton's Case* (1536) 1 Dyer 30.

[8] For an abbreviated list of the relevant statutory provisions, see *Halsbury's Laws* (5th edn, 2009), vol. 13, para. 18. However, the transfer of legal title in company shares is not merely an 'assignment'; rather, it is more appropriately understood to be a novation: R. R. Pennington, *Company Law* (8th edn, London: Butterworths, 2001), p. 399; M. S. Ooi, *Shares and Other Securities in the Conflict of Laws* (Oxford: Oxford University Press, 2003), paras. 3.12 and 4.06.

[9] See LPA1925, s. 52(1).

[10] R. M. Goode, *Goode on Commercial Law* (E. McKendrick, ed., 5th edn, London: Lexis Nexis, 2016), pp. 51–3.

[11] E.g., bills of lading and negotiable instruments such as bills of exchange and cheques. The negotiability of bills of exchange, cheques, as well as promissory notes is now regulated by the Bills of Exchange Act 1882. 'Assignment' of a bill of lading is regulated by the Carriage of Goods by Sea Act 1992. It may be noted that the conception of 'negotiation' as applied to negotiable instruments is conceptually distinct from assignment: Liew (2018), paras. 1-52 to 1-53.

[12] See C. Mitchell et al., *Subrogation: Law and Practice* (rev. edn, Oxford: Oxford University Press, 2007).

[13] See M. Hunter, *Muir Hunter on Personal Insolvency*, 2 vols. (London: Stevens & Sons, 1988).

[14] See *Williams, Mortimer and Sunnucks on Executors, Administrators and Probate* (A. Learmonth et al., eds., 21st edn, London: Sweet & Maxwell, 2018).

[15] See Smith & Leslie (2018), chapters 23 (maintenance and champerty) and 22 (other policy grounds). Alternatively, see Liew (2018), chapter 4.

In addition, this book will not delve too deeply into the question of what amounts to a chose in action. That is a difficult and distinct inquiry in itself which, logically, should be answered in advance of the question to be addressed in this work.[16] But it is enough for present purposes to simply accept choses in action to be whatever English law recognizes to be such.[17] Accordingly, subject to one clarification, this work adopts Channell J's working definition: '"Chose in action" is a known legal expression to describe all personal rights of property which can only be claimed or enforced by action,[18] and not by taking physical possession.'[19]

The point of clarification is this. Although Channell J's definition suggests that a chose in action may *only* be claimed or enforced by action, he does not assert that a chose in action may only be *realized* by claim or action. Where the underlying obligation has been discharged by precise performance, no claim or action is needed since the chose in action would have been realized by performance. Therefore, reading in what Channell J must implicitly have taken to be the case: '"Chose in action" is a known legal expression to describe all personal rights of property which can only be claimed or enforced by action, and not by

---

[16] See Holdsworth (1920). For a compendium of the various definitions that have been attempted, see H. W. Elphinstone, 'What Is a Chose in Action?' (1893) 9 LQR 311, 311–12. See also Marshall (1950), pp. 5–33.

[17] For a list, see *Halsbury's Laws* (5th edn, 2009), vol. 1, paras. 5–11. For a list of entitlements which have been held *not* to be 'choses' or 'things' in action, see para. 12.

[18] Traditionally, choses in action are such 'things' (or 'choses') as may be claimed or *reduced* into possession through the bringing of an action: see Holdsworth (1920), pp. 997–8. On this view, a 'chose in action' such as a debt arising out of a contract of loan, and the 'chose in possession' in the form of the cash tendered by the debtor to the creditor in repayment of his debt, are merely two states of the same 'thing'. One could draw a loose analogy with how, in the physical sciences, the molecule dihydrogen oxide (or $H_2O$) may be liquid (as water) or solid (as ice). Yet each comprises the same molecule (or thing), i.e. $H_2O$. So too with 'choses in action' and 'choses in possession', as traditionally conceived. However, on this traditional conception, intellectual property entitlements would arguably not be choses in action at all since such entitlements are incapable of being reduced into possession: when a copyright holder brings proceedings against a copyright infringer to 'enforce' the holder's 'copyright' those proceedings do not and cannot reduce the holder's copyright entitlement into possession in the same manner as an action in debt will reduce the creditor's 'chose in action' into possession. Such entitlements which are incapable of being *reduced* into possession but which may nevertheless be *enforced* through the bringing of an action would come within Channell J's broader conception of a 'chose in action'.

[19] *Torkington* v. *Magee* [1902] 2 KB 427, 427. In similar vein, see *Colonial Bank* v. *Whinney* (1886) 11 App Cas 426, 440 (Lord Blackburn): '[I]n modern times, lawyers have accurately or inaccurately used the phrase "choses in action" as including all personal chattels that are not in possession.'

taking physical possession, [*so far as such claim or action be required.*]'
Consequently, though all *causes* of action will give rise to *choses* in action
by reason of the secondary obligations which are imposed upon breach of
primary obligations which may have been voluntarily assumed by one
legal person to another, since choses in action also arise independently
of breach, the category of choses in action is broader than the category of
causes of action.

## B    Understanding Equitable and Statutory Assignments

This book makes two claims.

The first claim is this: equitable assignments are best conceived as a
*sui generis* institution created within the court's exclusive equitable
jurisdiction to permit a present *grant* of entitlements in connection with
presently existing choses in action.[20] Because equitable assignments
operate by way of grant, and not by way of undertaking (contractual or
otherwise), it is possible to make a perfectly valid immediate[21] equitable
assignment of a legal or an equitable chose in action without any need
for consideration, so long as certain substantive requirements as to the
intention of the grantor (the assignor), the subject matter of the assignment (the chose in action to be assigned), and the identity of the grantee
(the assignee) are satisfied.[22] In addition, though generally there are
no formal requirements for an equitable assignment to be validly
made, equitable assignments of subsisting equitable choses in action

---

[20] As opposed to 'future' choses in action – being choses which may (or may not) come into
existence at a future point in time – e.g. the 'future receivables' which a supplier of goods
or services might earn from goods or services it may (or may not) be contracted to supply
in the future. Such future choses, having no present existence, may not be presently
assigned since there is, as yet, nothing to be assigned. At best, attempts to assign such
future choses may be construed by the court to be *agreements* to assign such future
choses, as and when they arise. Such agreements may be enforced if supported by
consideration pursuant to the equitable doctrine of conversion, equity deeming as done
that which ought to be done. As to agreements to assign future choses, see Smith & Leslie
(2018), chapter 15, paras. 15.01–15.46; Liew (2018), paras. 3-21 to 3-24. For cases, the two
leading authorities are: *Holroyd* v. *Marshall* (1862) 1o HLC 191; *Tailby* v. *Official Receiver*
(1888) 13 App Cas 523.
[21] As opposed to an *agreement* or promise to assign a presently existing chose at some
future date – which, if supported by consideration, would take effect pursuant to the
equitable doctrine of conversion: see Liew (2018), paras. 3-19 to 3-20. For a counterexample where there was not such consideration, see *Re McArdle* [1951] 1 Ch 669.
[22] These requirements, i.e. the 'three certainties', are discussed below, at text to n. 27.

which do not comply with the formalities prescribed in LPA1925, s. 53(1)(c) are invalid.[23]

This grant operates through a composite of two conceptual mechanisms. First, an equitable assignment operates in a manner not dissimilar to the operation of a bare trust: this is the 'bare trust mechanism'. Second, an equitable assignment also operates in a manner not dissimilar to the operation of an atypical agency where the assignee/agent is authorized by the assignor/principal to invoke the entitlements of the assignor/principal[24] against the obligor to the chose assigned, as the assignee/agent pleases, free from the fiduciary duties which would typically arise in principal–agent relations. The assignee/agent is, by reason of this unusual form of principal–agent relation, privileged to invoke the powers which have been delegated to the assignee/agent by the assignor/principal, instead of being duty-bound to invoke them in the interest of the delegator as would otherwise typically be the case.

Given the conjunction of these bare trust and agency mechanisms, and leaving aside the question of any formalities imposed by statute,[25] an equitable assignment is, in effect, a 'trust *plus*'. It is thus unsurprising that

---

[23] *Grey v. Inland Revenue Commissioners* [1960] AC 1. However, facts permitting, it may be possible to construe the transaction as one where the parties had agreed to effect an equitable assignment. If so ('if' being the operative word), the equitable doctrine of conversion may be invoked, so long as there is consideration supporting the promise to assign: see *Oughtred v. Inland Revenue Commissioner* [1960] AC 205, 227 (Lord Radcliffe); *Re Holt's Settlement* [1969] 1 Ch 100, 116; *DHN Food Distributors Ltd v. Tower Hamlets KBC* [1976] 1 WLR 852; *Neville v. Wilson* [1997] Ch 144. For general discussion of the point, see Smith & Leslie (2018), paras. 15.23–15.30. See also Meagher, Gummow & Lehane (2015), para. 7-195. But see *United Bank of Kuwait Plc v. Sahib* [1997] Ch 107, 129 (Chadwick J, *dubitante*).

[24] These entitlements arising on account of the assignor being the obligee to the obligation of the obligor in question.

[25] Section 9 of the Statute of Frauds 1677 provided that all 'Grants and Assignments of Trust or Confidence shall be in Writing signed by the partie granting or assigning the same'. This provision was replaced by LPA1925, s. 53(1)(c), which mandated that 'dispositions' of presently existing equitable interests must be in writing duly signed by the disponor to be valid. Notwithstanding its derivation from s. 9 of the Statute of Frauds, it is accepted that 'dispositions' is to be generously interpreted (see *Re Danish Bacon Co. Ltd Staff Pension Fund Trusts* [1971] 1 WLR 248, 245; and also the statutory definition in s. 205(1)(ii), LPA1925): the 'dispositions' caught by s. 53(1)(c) are not limited to the 'Grants and Assignments' of s. 9: see e.g. *Grey v. Inland Revenue Commissioners* [1958] Ch 690, 723 (Ormerod LJ, dissenting), aff'd on appeal [1960] AC 1. Accordingly, the general consensus is that equitable assignments *are* dispositions within the meaning of the statute, and so equitable assignments of subsisting equitable interests such as equitable choses in action must be executed in a duly signed writing to be valid: see e.g. Liew (2018), para. 3-34; Smith & Leslie (2018), para. 13.75.

the requirements for a chose in action to be validly and effectively equitably assigned closely track the 'three certainties'[26] which must be established for an express trust to be validly constituted. Hence:[27]

> [j]ust as with the intention necessary to create a trust, the intention to assign a chose in action can helpfully be broken down into three 'certainties':
>
> (1) certainty of the intention to assign;
> (2) certainty as regards the chose that is the subject of the assignment;
> (3) certainty as regards the identity of the assignee.

But as will be shown in this book, the assignor's intention to assign entails two matters: (a) an intention akin to the intention of a settlor constituting a bare trust over the chose in question; and (b) an intention to delegate to the assignee the assignor's entitlements as obligee to the chose in question, whilst also releasing the assignee-delegatee from the fiduciary obligations that would otherwise typically be imposed. These are the dual mechanisms which underpin the operation of equitable assignment: a 'bare trust' mechanism and an unusual 'agency' mechanism.

For ease of exposition, where appropriate, this work will refer to the assignor as 'A', the obligor as 'B' (when the chose assigned is legal) or 'T' (when the chose assigned is equitable), and the assignee as 'C'. In addition, 'A' will generally be referred to as being feminine, whereas 'B', 'T' and 'C' will be referred to as being masculine.

On this conception, equitable assignments entail the generation of a new set of jural relations[28] between assignor (A) and assignee (C). This modifies the jural relations between the obligor (B or T) and the assignee (C), but leaves the jural relations between the obligor (B or T) and the assignor (A) largely intact and unchanged, unless the requirements for

---

[26] Smith & Leslie (2018), para. 13.06:

> The three certainties, in a trusts context, are:
>
> (1) certainty of intention to create a trust;
> (2) certainty of subject-matter; and
> (3) certainty of beneficiaries or objects [of the trust].

[27] Smith & Leslie (2018), para. 13.09.

[28] Though use of Wesley Hohfeld's conception of jural relations to aid in the analysis of the operation of equitable (and statutory) assignments is not unprecedented (see e.g. Smith & Leslie (2018), chapter 2), this book will make much more extensive use of it than has hitherto been the case. A summary account of this analytical approach is to be found in Chapter 2, Section B.

'statutory' assignments have been satisfied. Crucially, on this conception of equitable assignment, the seeming 'transfer' of the obligee's entitlements against the obligor to the assignee does *not* entail extinction of those very same entitlements. Instead, this conception of equitable assignment requires that those entitlements continue to be held by the obligee, or there would be nothing for the obligee to hold on trust for the assignee's benefit; nor could the obligee delegate to her assignee powers which the obligee no longer had. The conceptual model of equitable assignment proposed in this book is, therefore, additive, and not subtractive or extinctive in its operation, at least so far as jural relations between the obligor and the obligee(-assignor) are concerned.

The second claim in this book is as follows: all statutory assignments arising under what is now LPA1925, s. 136(1) are necessarily, inherently, equitable assignments. Thus, where an equitable assignment has been validly effected, and where the formal requirements of s. 136(1) are satisfied, the effect of s. 136(1) is also additive: the statute merely mandates certain statutory effects which supplement the effects arising from the equitable assignment. Consequently, s. 136(1) statutory assignments should not be viewed as a completely different species of assignment: they are not. Section 136(1) statutory assignments are merely equitable assignments with some additional, statutorily sanctioned characteristics.

Where a debt or other chose in action has been validly equitably assigned *and* the requirements in s. 136(1) are satisfied, the specific entitlements spelt out in ss. 136(1)(a), (b) and (c) will be passed away from the assignor and transferred to the assignee. That is, *those* entitlements are extinguished so far as the assignor is concerned. But that is only true as regards entitlements falling within those provisions, and the set of entitlements listed therein is not exhaustive. Consequently, where the statutory requirements in s. 136(1) are satisfied, *only* those jural relations specified in ss. 136(1)(a), (b) and (c) as between obligor and assignor are modified by Parliamentary decree, and no others. 'Statutory' assignments, therefore, are actually a subclass of equitable assignments to which a legislative gloss has been applied.[29]

The composite model of equitable assignment, and the clarification of the nature of statutory assignment, reduces confusion over their operation and effects. Although the model presented within this book is, admittedly, complex, that complexity is the result of the historical

---

[29] See Chapter 13.

development of the institution of equitable assignment itself. Equitable assignment was developed as a response to the common problem faced by both the courts of Chancery and at common law that, as the Romans had recognized, when one voluntarily undertakes a duty to another to perform something, that is a duty not just to do some*thing*, it is also a duty owed to some*one*.

As will be explained in Chapter 3, in equity and at common law, it was recognized that all aspects of a voluntarily undertaken obligation, whether it be specifications as to *what* was to be done (or not done), or to *whom* that duty was owed, were invariable or immutable without the obligor's assent. At common law this was reflected in the doctrine of novation, and in equity this was exemplified in the proposition that the court has no inherent power in its equitable jurisdiction to vary the terms of a trust even if it were convinced that such variation would be beneficial for the trust beneficiaries.[30] And even though that lack was subsequently modified with the enactment of the Variation of Trusts Act 1958, not only is that statutory power narrowly defined, but beyond its narrow confines the court still has no general power to vary the terms of a trust.

To overcome this common problem of invariability, the court of Chancery gradually recognized how certain *equitable* obligations could arise between an assignor and assignee, and how *notice* of such obligations could generate further equitable obligations as between the obligor and the assignee. It also gave effect to such equitable obligations by issuing equitable remedies against those who breached such duties[31] by, for example, assisting the assignor in breaching her duties to her assignee,[32] or otherwise taking advantage of such breach.[33] But, although the courts of common law came to recognize such equitable obligations between the obligor and assignee, they were generally not in a position to issue common law remedies when such equitable duties had been breached because, by definition, common law enforcement only lay with respect to obligations arising at common law.[34] Despite this, the courts of common law eventually developed a power to bar the availability of certain kinds of defences.[35]

---

[30] *Chapman* v. *Chapman* [1954] AC 429.
[31] See Chapters 7 and 9.
[32] See Chapter 11.
[33] See Chapter 12, Section E(i).
[34] See Chapter 8.
[35] See Chapter 12, Section E(ii).

The administrative difficulties generated by that split jurisdiction were gradually ameliorated by legislative changes in the mid-1800s (most significantly for present purposes via the Common Law Procedure Act 1854), culminating in the administrative fusion effected in 1875 when the Supreme Court of Judicature Act 1873 came into force. Thus, since 1854, a court acting within its common law jurisdiction *could* give effect to equitable principles, albeit by way of a defence to a common law action (pursuant to s. 83 of the 1854 Act),[36] or by way of a replication to a common law defence (pursuant to s. 85 of the 1854 Act),[37] a position which was preserved under the Judicature Act 1873 and which persists to the present day.[38] Given this intertwining of equity, common law and legislation, it is no wonder that the story of equitable assignment is equally tangled and complex.

## C   Other Conceptions of Assignment and Transfer

The 'trust *plus*' conception of 'transfers' by way of equitable assignment is, admittedly, not the only model. Others are possible. For example, the Scottish conception of assignment, termed 'assignation', is different. Scots law appears to accept that changes to the identity of the obligor do not amount to any change in the obligation, and so do not violate the 'rule' of invariability set out above. Scots law treats the process of assignation to be incomplete until notice (or 'intimation') of the assignation is given to the obligor to the chose in question.[39] Intimation is therefore a constitutive component for a debt to be 'transferred' by means of an assignation under Scots law:[40]

> Both an agreement to assign and the transfer agreement are often confusingly called an 'assignation'. But it is only with intimation that there is properly an assignation. Scots law is one of a number of legal systems in which debtor notification is a constitutive requirement.

The centrality of intimation or notification of the assignation to the debtor/obligor presents a key difference with the English law of equitable assignment: there is *no* assignation without intimation. So should

---

[36] See Chapter 6, Section D.
[37] See Chapter 12, Section F.
[38] See Chapter 6, Section D; Chapter 7, Section C; and Chapter 12, Section H.
[39] For discussion of the Scots law on assignation, see Anderson (2008).
[40] Ibid., pp. 119–20.

the assignor (termed the 'cedent' in Scots law) succumb to insolvency prior to intimation, that debt would remain part of the cedent's assets for distribution amongst her creditors.[41]

Nor is the Scots model the only alternative. There are others where the substitution of the assignee in place of the assignor is effective, even without notice to the assignee (e.g. as in Belgium, the Czech Republic, Germany and Spain),[42] and yet others where notice is not sufficient and more is required (e.g. as in Italy).[43]

Indeed, even within some jurisdictions within the common law tradition, different models of assignment exist. If one turns to accounts of the law of assignment in the United States, which, broadly speaking, 'received the English law of assignments as part of the common law',[44] assignment of contractual entitlements is conceived of as:[45]

> the act by which an assignor transfers a contract to an assignee . . . [where t]o transfer a contract right is, in essence, to take from the assignor (B) and to give to the assignee (C) the right to performance by the obligor (A). Put in another way, the transferor of a contract right extinguishes the assignor's right to performance by the obligor and gives the assignee a right to that performance.

It would appear, therefore that, despite its common law origins, the understanding of assignment in the United States would conform more closely to civilian conceptions, given observations such as the following:[46]

> Every assignment of a contract right, even a right to money, goods or land, *changes* the obligor's duty to some extent. The obligor must now render the performance to a different person, the assignee, and that person may be less lenient than the assignor. But courts have not regarded these slight burdens as sufficient to outweigh the arguments favouring free assignability.

There is, accordingly, no single way by which intangible personalty may be 'transferred', even if we leave aside the civilian traditions, and

---

[41] Ibid., paras. 6-10 to 6-12.

[42] *Report from the Commission to the European Parliament, The Council and the European Economic and Social Committee on the Question of the Effectiveness of an Assignment or Subrogation of a Claim against Third Parties and the Priority of the Assigned or Subrogated Claim over the Right of Another Person*, Brussels, 29 September 2016, COM (2016) 626 final (on file), fn. 22.

[43] Ibid., fn. 23.

[44] E. A. Farnsworth, *Farnsworth on Contracts*, 3 vols. (3rd edn, New York: Aspen, 2004), vol. III, §11.2, p. 66.

[45] Ibid., §11.3, pp. 68–70.

[46] Ibid., §11.4, p. 80.

confine ourselves to looking at jurisdictions which may be thought to fall within the 'common law' tradition. Rather, there are many different ways by which intangible personalty arising from voluntarily assumed obligations may be transferred *inter vivos*, and different legal systems exhibit different choices of the weight to be given to respect for the individual decisions made by an obligor as to whom he is to be taken to be duty-bound, and also the extent to which the obligee is to have power over the obligor in light of that duty.

Indeed, even within English law, there are multiple senses in which a property entitlement may be said to be 'transferred' from one holder to another. On the one hand, certain kinds of property entitlements may be 'transferred' as a matter of English law by way of 'substitution' of the transferee in place of the transferor. Such 'substitution' entails enabling the transferee, post-transfer, to invoke all of the transferor's entitlements as former holder of the entitlements in the property that had been transferred in place of the transferor. The transferor would, post-transfer, no longer have any such entitlement: post-transfer, the transferor's entitlements arising by reason of her interest in that property would have been extinguished. This has the important characteristic of permitting/resulting in the 'transfer' of both benefits *and* burdens.

One example of 'substitutive/extinctive transfer' as applied to intangible personalty may be found in the English law on transfer of the legal title to registered certificated shares. As has been pointed out,[47] when a change on the share register is made in response to a duly completed share transfer form, the company is, in effect, agreeing to the replacement of one registered shareholder with another: the 'transfer' operates, in essence, by way of novation. The effect of this is not only to transfer the benefits of such registered shareholding: it also transfers the burdens to the transferee. So, for example, where the transferor has not fully paid up her shares, upon registration of the share transfer the transferor is no longer obligated to the company to pay the unpaid balance: it is the transferee who has to pay the balance. At the same time, the benefits of registered shareholding are no longer the transferor's to exercise. For example, it is no longer possible for the transferor to vote at the company's general meeting. The transferor's entitlement to do so has been extinguished upon the registration of the share transfer. Simultaneously, the entitlement to vote in respect of the transferred shareholding would

---

[47] See Pennington, *Company Law*, p. 399; Ooi, *Shares and Other Securities in the Conflict of Laws*, paras. 3.12 and 4.06.

vest in the transferee. Consequently, should there be a call for the shares to be fully paid-up, following the registration of the share transfer it is the transferee's duty to ensure that the shares are paid-up. If they are not, it is the transferee who is exposed to legal liability for the failure, and not the transferor.

On the other hand, as a matter of English law, property entitlements may also be 'transferred' (in a manner of speaking) by encumbering the transferor with duties such that such she is no longer entitled to invoke her property entitlements for her own benefit. Unlike the 'substitutive transfer' model mentioned above, such 'encumbrance-based' transfer may *not* transfer burdens: so far as the property entitlement in question also required the original holder thereof to be responsible for the due performance of certain obligations, that obligation or responsibility would remain in place and the original holder may not wash her hands of that responsibility. On the latter model of transfer, the original holder remains duty-bound and liable as regards those responsibilities, whereas the transferee is not; and the key example of such 'encumbrance-based transfer' is, of course, the trust.

Where A holds the benefit of a contract with B on trust for the benefit of C, A is duty-bound to C not to invoke her entitlements against B as contractual obligee for her own benefit. By virtue of the trust, A is duty-bound in equity to preserve such chose in action until such time as she is called upon to fully execute the trust on which she holds the benefit of the contractual chose by her trust beneficiary, C. Importantly, though the beneficial interest in the contractual chose is 'transferred' to C, nothing is changed so far as A's common law relations with B are concerned. So far as B is concerned, as a matter of common law, A is still entitled to invoke her contractual entitlements against B: they have not been 'divested' by reason of the trust she had constituted. But at the same time, if the contract imposed obligations which A was duty-bound to ensure the fulfilment of, A remains duty-bound to B to ensure their fulfilment: if they are not fulfilled, B may seek judicial assistance against A for that failure.

The *simulation* of 'substitutive/extinctive transfer' permitted by encumbering the 'transferor' A through the interpolation of a trust between A and the transferee 'C' has a significant shortcoming. Although A may no longer freely invoke her entitlements by reason of her equitable duties and liabilities with regard to C, so that C could seek an injunction to restrain A from invoking those entitlements in a manner contrary to those duties, that necessarily entails A *having* those entitlements and the capacity to invoke them (albeit potentially in breach of her duties to C).

Alternatively, C may obtain a mandatory injunction to compel A to invoke those entitlements as C might direct. In either case, C may not directly invoke *A's* entitlements: if A does not voluntarily do so without court order, C must invoke the assistance of the court to compel A to act (or to restrain A from acting) consistently with A's duties under the trust.

As will be explained in the chapters which follow, considerable English caselaw recognizes that equitable assignments entail a trust. However, to the puzzlement of many, it is well-recognized that an equitable assignee of the benefit of a legal or equitable chose in action *is* able to invoke the assignor's entitlements as against the obligor to the chose assigned without any prior judicial assistance. This has caused many to doubt whether equitable assignments entail a trust at all, or, contrary to the caselaw, to suggest that although equitable assignments of a legal chose entail a trust, equitable assignments of an equitable chose do not.

This book suggests that clarity returns when it is recognized that an equitable assignment operates not *merely* by the same kind of mechanism as arises when a bare trust is constituted: it also engages a mechanism entailing a form of delegation. That is, an equitable assignment entails not just a trustee–beneficiary relationship between assignor and assignee, but a further principal–agent relationship between assignor and assignee where the assignee-agent has been delegated the assignor-principal's entitlements free from the typical fiduciary obligations that are usually imposed on an agent.

It follows that the model of equitable assignment which was developed as a matter of English law is significantly different from the models of assignment developed in some other jurisdictions. It is also distinct from other conceptions of transfer that prevail in certain other areas of English law. As this book will show, the caselaw and legislation reveal policy choices that place English law at, perhaps, one extreme of respect for the individual obligor's choice of obligee.[48] But it will be shown that the law of equitable assignment that has developed as a result is an entirely coherent 'working-out' of that choice.

---

[48] The German model of assignment of debts is, perhaps, closer to the other end, with the Scots model somewhere in between.

# 2

# A Conceptual Account of Equitable and Statutory Assignments

## A The Argument, in Miniature

Obligations arising from voluntarily assumed obligations arising at common law may be 'transferred' by means of novation or by equitable assignment. The obvious difference between the two is that equitable assignment is effective even without obligor assent. As a matter of English law, equitable assignments of choses in action (as opposed to choses in possession)[1] arising from voluntarily assumed private law obligations[2] are effective without need for obligor assent: it is not necessary for the obligor to assent at the time of such assignment, or in advance (e.g. where the obligor agreed from the outset to be obligated 'to the obligee or his/her assigns').[3] Nor does the efficacy of an equitable assignment depend on giving notice of the same to the obligor to the chose assigned.[4] But equitable assignment is by no means some equitable variant of common law novation. If it were, one might expect that the kinds of intangible personalty which are susceptible to equitable assignment would be limited to those capable of being 'transferred' via novation. But this is not the case: it is possible to equitably assign many more kinds of intangible personalty than may be novated.

An obligee may equitably assign the benefit of *primary* obligations[5] arising from voluntarily assumed obligations arising at common law

---

[1] '[I]n modern times, lawyers have accurately or inaccurately used the phrase "choses in action" as including all personal chattels that are not in possession': *Colonial Bank* v. *Whinney* (1886) 11 App Cas 426, 480. In this book, unless indicated otherwise, 'chose' and 'choses' shall refer to 'chose in action' or 'choses in action', respectively.

[2] Though obligations also arise as a matter of public and administrative law, in this book, unless indicated otherwise, 'obligations' will be used to refer only to obligations arising as a matter of private law.

[3] *Mulkerrins* v. *PricewaterhouseCoopers (a firm)* [2003] UKHL 41; [2003] 1 WLR 1937, [13].

[4] *Bell* v. *The London & North Western Railway Co.* (1852) 15 Beav 548.

[5] The language of 'primary' and 'secondary' obligations is drawn from J. Austin, *Lectures on Jurisprudence, or, The Philosophy of Positive Law* (R. Campbell, ed., 5th edn, London: John

(such as contract or covenant). Choses in action arising from voluntarily undertaken obligations (most often, contractual obligations)[6] may also be novated, if all parties to the chose assent. But equitable assignments may also be effected of choses in action which may not be novated. For example, an obligee may equitably assign the benefit arising from obligations of a trustee under an express trust, or those of an executor to a will, or the benefit of the chose in action arising when *secondary* obligations are imposed by law following the breach of primary contractual, tortious or equitable obligations: i.e. an assignment of a *cause* of action.[7] This difference in the scope of equitable assignments when compared with novation suggests that their manner of operation may well be different.

When a contract is novated, the obligor becomes obligated to a new and different obligee under a new and different contract.[8] Since no

---

Murray, 1885), lecture XLV. Though applied most prominently to contractual obligations (see e.g. *Photo Production Ltd* v. *Securicor Transport Ltd* [1980] AC 826, 848–9. *Moschi* v. *Lep Air Services Ltd* [1973] AC 331), Austin's analysis applies to obligations generally: P. Birks, 'Equity in the Modern law: An Exercise in Taxonomy' (1996) 26 *University of Western Australia Law Review* 1, 10.

[6] There appears to be no conceptual reason why the voluntarily assumed obligations of a covenantor arising under a deed may not be novated. If B has covenanted by deed that he will pay £10,000 to A, A can promise to release B from his duty under that covenant in exchange for his executing a deed by which he covenants to pay £10,000 to C. For that matter, A can promise to release B from his duty under that covenant in exchange for his promise that he will pay £10,000 to C. Either of these would operate by way of novation to 'transfer' from A to C the benefit of B's promise of payment.

[7] Formerly, it was believed that it was impossible to assign a cause of action (i.e. a 'bare' right of action), whether it be a cause of action at law for breach of contract, or for breach of a duty arising in tort. It is now clear, however, that there is no absolute conceptual bar, but, rather, such assignments may be rendered ineffective by reason of the policy against encouraging maintenance and champerty. So long as those concerns do not arise, there is nothing to bar the assignment of a cause of action. For discussion of the effect of maintenance and champerty, see Liew (2018), paras. 4-21 to 4-32. Over and beyond the policy to discourage maintenance and champerty, statute has rendered the assignment of certain types of chose void or unenforceable. Some of these are discussed in Liew (2018), paras. 4-17 to 4-21.

[8] 'As might be expected, there was no dispute as to the relevant legal principles. They can be summarized as follows: – (a) Novation involves the creation of a new contract where an existing party is replaced by a new party. (b) Thus, novation requires the consent of all parties, including in particular the party which is thereby accepting a new person as his debtor or as his counterpart under an executory contract. (c) The consent may be apparent from express words or inferred from conduct': *The 'Tychy' (No. 2)* [2001] 1 Lloyd's Rep 10, [65]; aff'd in *The 'Tychy' (No. 2)* [2001] EWCA Civ 1198; [2001] 2 Lloyd's Rep 403. And it is also for this reason that the *burdens* owed by an obligee to her obligor may be 'transferred' to a third party via novation, such that it is that third party who is to be responsible for the due performance of such burdens.

person may ordinarily become contractually bound without their assent,[9] novation entails obtaining the obligor's consent to a *new* obligation with a new obligee.[10] Novation, then, reflects a basic common law principle: voluntarily undertaken obligations ought not to be capable of being unilaterally varied without the assent of the obligor thereto.[11]

By contrast, an equitable assignment of the benefit of a contractual chose in action is effective as between the assignor and the assignee, seemingly regardless of the obligor's assent (or lack thereof). The benefit of a contractual chose may be equitably assigned even where the obligor has not, expressly or implicitly, agreed to be obligated to the obligee or her assigns. And as mentioned above, it is also possible to equitably assign the benefit of an accrued cause of action in tort, also without the tortfeasor's consent. Rather, equitable assignments are generally effective, unless assignment is prohibited by statute or the public policy against encouraging maintenance and/or champerty; or the assignment is ineffective because the obligation underlying the chose assigned is 'too personal', for example, where it involves an exercise of judgement, discretion or some element of skill personal to the particular obligee.[12]

Care should, however, be taken over the 'too personal' objection. A contract may be said to be 'too personal' in two senses. Where A contracts for B to $\Phi$,[13] where '$\Phi$' means 'act as A's valet', B's services as valet are 'personal' in that it is B, and only B, whose services have been engaged. The obligation to $\Phi$ undertaken to A by B is non-delegable.[14]

---

[9] For authorities, see references cited in *Halsbury's Laws* (5th edn, 2012), vol. 22, para. 604.

[10] *Scarf* v. *Jardine* (1882) 7 App Cas 345, 351.

[11] See e.g. *Wedlake* v. *Hurley* (1830) 1 C & J 83; *Williams* v. *Everett* (1811) 14 East 582, 597; *Yates* v. *Bell* (1820) 3 B & Ald 643.

[12] This is a matter of construction: *Davies* v. *Collins* [1945] 1 All ER 247, 249E. One way to signify that the entitlements in question are 'too personal' to be assigned may be to provide for an anti-assignment clause: see Chapter 15, Section A. See also Liew (2018), para. 4-33. But an entitlement may be construed to be 'too personal' from the context: e.g. the chose in action accruing to an employer as to an employee's services under an employment contract was, at common law, too personal to be assigned without the employee's assent: *Nokes* v. *Doncaster Amalgamated Collieries Ltd* [1940] AC 1014, 1020 and 1026. But now, see also Transfer of Undertakings (Protection of Employment) Regulations 2006, and Liew (2018), para. 4-33.

[13] Read 'phi'.

[14] As will be explained below, the obligation to $\Phi$ involves a Hohfeldian duty which is owed by B to A, the Hohfeldian claim-right holder. But since the act of performing $\Phi$ would lead to the discharge of that duty/claim-right jural relation, so far as B may cause A's jural relations with B to change by so performing $\Phi$, B's duty to $\Phi$ also entails a Hohfeldian

And yet the *benefit* to A of such 'personal' contract may still be equitably assigned to C.

This very possibility was recognized by Professor Corbin:[15]

> Let us consider a few specific cases. I. [B] contracts with [A] to act as [A]'s valet. Surely, it will be said, [A]'s right is so personal that it cannot be assigned. But no, the contrary is believed to be correct although no decision pro or con has been seen by the writer. By this statement it is not meant to say that the character of the service can in any way be changed by assignment. The right of [A] is that [B] shall act as [A]'s valet, not that [B] shall act as valet for whom it may concern. Anyone ought to know that serving as valet to a cross, ill, miserly, old curmudgeon is not the same performance as serving a happy-go-lucky, generous, young prince. Therefore, when [A] assigns his right against [B], he must assign it as it is. He cannot by assignment to C create in C a right that [B] shall act as C's valet. That would be a different right to a different performance. But [A] can assign to C the right that [B] shall serve as [A]'s valet; and if [B] shall commit a breach it will be C who gets the damages measured by the value of the promised service.

Corbin's insight in the above passage exposes the foundation stone on which this book rests: entitlements arising out of voluntarily assumed obligations have multiple dimensions. For example, where an obligee such as A with whom an obligor, B, has contractually agreed to perform a stipulated act, $\Phi$, B *must* perform $\Phi$ in order to discharge (i.e. bring to an end) that obligation. As a matter of common usage, however, there is *associated* with that obligation to perform $\Phi$ another kind of legal relationship.

In general, so far as B is *legally* (as opposed to morally) obligated to perform $\Phi$, B's *failure* to perform $\Phi$ will render him liable to be sued for having breached his obligation to perform $\Phi$. The question then becomes: *who* may bring such legal proceedings? By default, as a matter of English law, *because* B's obligation to perform $\Phi$ had arisen out of his contract *with A* (as opposed to C, D or any other 'non-A'), the discretion or *choice* whether to commence such proceedings against B for such non-performance is left with A. Or, to put it another way, *because* B is duty-bound to A to perform $\Phi$, A is given standing to seek

---

*power*. Where $\Phi$ means 'act as A's valet', the context would indicate that B's *power* to discharge his duty to $\Phi$ by it is non-delegable.

[15] This was recognized in Corbin (1926), p. 218. The distinction between 'what the obligor is duty-bound to do' and 'to whom the obligor is duty-bound' will be expanded on in Chapter 3.

the court's assistance if a dispute were to arise as to whether B had fully performed Φ.

Corbin demonstrates that when we speak of A equitably assigning the *benefit* of her contract with B under which B is to perform Φ, the subject matter of such assignment has nothing to do with the specification as to what B is to *do*, but rather targets A's associated entitlements, which include A's entitlement to commence legal proceedings against B should B fail to perform Φ. Once this point is grasped, we may begin to see how equitable assignment operates differently from novation.

When a contractual obligation between A and B is novated by A to C with B's assent, that novation affects B's obligation to A arising out of his initial contractual duty to A by *extinguishing* that obligation, replacing it with another obligation, now owed to C. The extinction of the original obligation also extinguishes the associated liability as might arise upon breach – and therefore, following the novation, B becomes both obligated *and* legally liable to C instead of A. But as this book will show, it is possible to achieve a similar effect whereby B becomes liable to C *without* having to extinguish the original obligation between A and B. Such liability may be generated indirectly through the constitution of a trust, or by way of delegation, or by way of an equitable assignment (which is, this book proposes, effected via a composite of trust and agency mechanisms).

Corbin's insight tells us that in order to preclude equitable assignment of the benefit of a contract by reason of the contract being 'too personal', the court would need to be convinced not that B's obligation to perform Φ was non-delegable by him, but that *A* was not entitled to delegate to another her entitlement to bring legal proceedings against B were B to fail to perform Φ. Which is to say, for the benefit of a contract to be 'too personal' as to preclude its equitable assignment, the obligor and obligee must have agreed, expressly or implicitly, that the obligor is to be liable[16] to the obligee *and only* to that particular obligee – as, for example, when there is an anti-assignment clause.[17] This begins to explain why the obligor's assent is irrelevant for the efficacy of an equitable assignment of the benefit of a contract as between the assignee and the assignor, even where an anti-assignment clause is in play.[18] Where there is no change to

---

[16] In the Hohfeldian sense: see discussion below in Section B of this chapter.

[17] See discussion in Chapter 15, Section A.

[18] As the House of Lords recognized in *Linden Gardens Trust Ltd* v. *Lenesta Sludge Disposals Ltd* [1994] 1 AC 85.

*what* the obligor is obligated to do, there is no need to obtain any assent for such non-existent change.

This concern to obtain the obligor's consent rests on an uncontroversial premise: contractual obligations once undertaken by an obligor should not be unilaterally changed by the obligee without the obligor's assent.[19] To freely allow this would insufficiently protect the obligor's liberty.[20]

When one turns to *equitable* obligations, we find similar rules of invariability in connection with voluntarily undertaken equitable obligations, like those undertaken by trustees to express trusts. So, although '[i]t is established by all the cases, that if the cestui que trust *joins* with the trustee in that which is a breach of trust, knowing the circumstances, such a cestui que trust can never complain of such a breach of trust',[21] the trust beneficiaries have no entitlement that their trustee so join with them. Unless the trust provides for some power of appointment to be vested in the beneficiaries to require the trustee to act as they demand, the beneficiaries of an express trust may not ordinarily require their trustee to perform in a manner not sanctioned by the terms of his trust: their only option is to bring the trust to an end, perhaps by invoking the doctrine in *Saunders* v. *Vautier*,[22] and then to reconstitute a new trust, with new, more biddable trustees.

Nor does the court have any overriding power to alter the terms of a trust. As Lord Simonds LC said in *Chapman* v. *Chapman*:[23]

> [I]t is the function of the court to execute a trust, to see that the trustees do their duty and to protect them if they do it, to direct them if they are in doubt, and if they do wrong, to penalise them. It is not the function of the court to alter a trust because alteration is thought to be advantageous to an infant beneficiary.[24]

---

[19] *Cowey* v. *Liberian Operations Ltd* [1966] 2 Lloyd's Rep 45, 50 (Block J).

[20] See J. S. Mill, 'On Liberty' in J. Gray and G. W. Smith (eds.), *J. S. Mill, On Liberty, in Focus* (London: Routledge, 1991), especially pp. 30–1 and 116. See also I. Berlin, 'John Stuart Mill and the Ends of Life' in J. Gray and G. W. Smith (eds.), *J. S. Mill, On Liberty, in Focus* (London: Routledge, 1991), p. 135.

[21] *Walker* v. *Symonds* (1818) 3 Swan 1 (emphasis added).

[22] (1841) 4 Beav 115.

[23] [1954] AC 429, 446.

[24] This is now qualified by the Variation of Trusts Act 1958 (as to the effect of which, see Harris (1975), chapters 3 and 4). See also Trustee Act 1925, ss. 53 and 57; Settled Land Act 1925, s. 64: see Harris (1975), pp. 9–14 and 19–25. Outside these areas, the court also has a power to approve schemes varying administration of charitable trusts under the *cy-près* doctrine now regulated by Charities Act 2011, s. 62; and a further jurisdiction to

Consequently, equity, too, recognizes that it is impermissible to alter voluntarily undertaken equitable obligations (such as those undertaken by a trustee) without the equitable obligor's assent. That being the case, it is unsurprising that there should be no equitable doctrine allowing for a unilateral overriding of common law bargains.[25]

## B    Terminology

Thus far, the language of 'obligation' and 'entitlement' has been used to refer to what the obligor is obligated to do, and what the obligee is entitled that the obligor do. These words, like the layperson's usage of 'duty' and 'right', may be distilled into narrower and more precise conceptions of the legal and equitable relations between legal persons. To describe more accurately the effects of an equitable assignment of a chose in action, this book will use, as far as is helpful, the vocabulary developed by Professor Hohfeld in two seminal articles published in 1913 and 1917.[26]

Hohfeld identified a number of linguistic confusions in the law which impeded understanding what the law was doing, and how it did it. One of the most egregious of such confusions lay in the indiscriminate use of the terms 'right' and 'duty' in legal discourse. Thus:[27]

> One of the greatest hindrances to the clear understanding, the incisive statement, and the true solution of legal problems frequently arises from the express or tacit assumption that all legal relations may be reduced to 'rights' and 'duties', and that these latter categories are therefore adequate for the purpose of analysing even the most complex legal interests, such as trusts, options, escrows, 'future' interests, corporate interests, etc.

To overcome these limitations, Hohfeld proposed a set of prescriptive conceptual constructions which he termed 'jural relations', drawn to a large extent from extant legal and judicial usage. Hohfeld conceived these

---

order resettlements of matrimonial property by way of matrimonial relief pursuant to Matrimonial Causes Act 1973, s. 24 (as amended).

[25] *Maynard* v. *Moseley* (1676) 3 Swans 651, 655: 'for the Chancery mends no man's bargain, though it sometimes mends his [deeds of] assurance'. So the record of the parties' bargain may be rectified, but the bargain itself may not be modified by the court.

[26] W. N. Hohfeld, 'Some Fundamental Legal Conceptions as Applied in Judicial Reasoning I' (1913) 23 *Yale Law Journal* 16; W. N. Hohfeld, 'Fundamental Legal Conceptions as Applied in Judicial Reasoning II' (1917) 26 *Yale Law Journal* 710. Both essays were reprinted in Hohfeld (1923), pp. 23–64 and 65–114, respectively.

[27] Hohfeld (1923), p. 35.

as 'fundamental' in the sense that they might be termed the 'lowest common denominators of the law' or the 'lowest generic conceptions to which any and all "legal quantities" may be reduced'.[28]

Hohfeld identified (but did not define, since they were, in his view, *sui generis*) eight fundamental jural relations, namely:

(I) 'Claim-right',[29] which is correlative to 'Duty';
(II) 'Privilege', which is correlative to 'No-right';
(III) 'Power', which is correlative to 'Liability'; and
(IV) 'Immunity', which is correlative to 'Disability'.[30]

The sense in which these jural relations may be said to be 'correlative' is not straightforward and requires careful reading of the source texts.[31]

---

[28] Ibid., pp. 63–4.

[29] Hohfeld himself did not use the term 'claim-right', preferring, instead, to use 'right' or 'claim' interchangeably to denote the correlative jural relation to 'duty'. Given the confusion engendered by the common, non-Hohfeldian usages of the word 'right', it has been thought advisable to avoid its use when the Hohfeldian usage is intended. Similarly, given the common, non-Hohfeldian usage of the word 'claim' in connection with the phrase 'legal claim' denoting an entitlement to commence judicial proceedings, it has also been thought advisable to avoid using 'claim' to denote the correlative jural relation to a Hohfeldian duty. As a compromise, in this book, the term 'claim-right' will be used to denote the correlative jural relation to a Hohfeldian 'duty'.

[30] Hohfeld also posited that these eight jural relations might further be 'opposed' with each other as follows:

(V) 'Claim-right' is opposed to 'No-right';
(VI) 'Privilege' is opposed to 'Duty';
(VII) 'Power' is opposed to 'Disability'; and
(VIII) 'Immunity' is opposed to 'Liability.'

'Opposed' is Hohfeld's own usage. It has been pointed out that Hohfeld's goal was to show how these pairings in (V) to (VIII) involved contradictions: i.e. it would be *contradictory* to speak of A as having both a 'claim-right' against B that B do Φ *and* a 'no-right' against B that B not do 'Φ', or that A might have both a 'privilege' as against B to do 'Ω' *and* a 'duty' as against B to not do 'Ω'. It has therefore been suggested that it would be preferable to refer to these oppositional pairings as being 'contradictories' rather than 'opposites': see e.g. M. H. Kramer, 'Rights without Trimmings' in Kramer, Simmonds & Steiner (1998).

[31] In particular, Hohfeld, 'Some Fundamental Legal Conceptions as Applied in Judicial Reasoning I'; Hohfeld, 'Fundamental Legal Conceptions as Applied in Judicial Reasoning II'; and W. N. Hohfeld, 'The Relations Between Equity and Law' (1913) 11 *Michigan Law Review* 537. All three are reproduced in Hohfeld (1923). For useful explanatory accounts, see Smith & Leslie (2018), paras. 2.15–2.30; J. Stone, *Legal System and Lawyers' Reasonings* (Stanford, CA: Stanford University Press, 1964), pp. 139–61. See also Wenar (2005).

But Hohfeld's distillation of the broad conceptions of 'right' and 'duty' into more discrete senses allows for a more sensitive portrayal of what occurs to the jural relations between legal persons when, say, legal title to realty or personalty is conveyed from a disponor to a disponee, when a trust is constituted over realty or personalty for the benefit of another, and when an agency relationship is created between a principal and her agent. Using these conceptions, we can more clearly see how control over property may be ceded in multiple ways. In other words, we can see how 'transfer' of such control may be effected in more ways than one.

What follows is an attempt to sketch out the bare bones of Hohfeld's vocabulary and grammar of jural relations which will be employed in this book.

Hohfeld's eight jural relations may be divided into two categories: first-order jural relations (comprising of classes (I) and (II), above), and second-order jural relations (comprising of classes (III) and (IV), above). The distinction between the two orders is that the second-order jural relations set out the parameters within which a legal person's first-order jural relations may be changed (power/liability) or not changed (disability/immunity) by another legal person.

The first-order jural relations may be understood to arise in connection with 'two fundamental forms of rights assertions: '"A has a right to phi" and "A has a right that B phi", where "phi" is an active verb'.[32] In the discussion below, 'phi' will be represented by its Greek symbol, 'Φ'.

When we say that 'A has a right that B Φ', we are saying that A has a *claim-right* that B Φ; or correlatively, that B has a *duty* to A to Φ. This means that B is not *privileged* as against A not to Φ. So far as A is concerned, B *must* Φ whether it pleases him to Φ, or not, and B has no entitlement to insist otherwise.

When we say, however, that 'A has a right against B to Φ', we are saying that A is *privileged* as against B to Φ. This means that A is under no *duty* to B to Φ: so far as B is concerned, A *may* Φ if it pleases her to do so, but B has no entitlement to insist that A Φ. Therefore, correlatively, we could say that B has *no-right* against A that A Φ.[33]

---

[32] Wenar (2005), p. 225.

[33] See Hohfeld (1923), p. 39: 'Thus, the correlative of X's [claim-]right that Y shall not enter on the land is Y's duty not to enter; but the correlative of X's privilege of entering himself is manifestly Y's "no-right" that X shall not enter.' In this passage, X holds the legal title to the land in question, and Y is a legal person who does not hold the legal title to the said land.

However, '[w]e have not only privileges and claims, but rights to alter our privileges and claims, and rights that our privileges and claims not be altered'.[34] Hence, we have second-order jural relations by which we have the *power* to alter privileges and claim-rights, as well as *immunities* from having our privileges and claim-rights altered.

Hohfeld explains the power/liability jural relation as follows:[35]

> Many examples of legal powers may be readily given. Thus, X, the owner of ordinary personal property 'in a tangible object' has the power to extinguish his own legal interest ([claim-]rights, powers, immunities, etc) through that totality of operative facts known as abandonment; and – simultaneously and correlatively – to create in other persons privileges and powers relating to the abandoned object – eg, the power to acquire title to the latter by appropriating it.

And as to the immunity/disability jural relation:[36]

> A [claim-]right is one's affirmative claim against another, and a privilege is one's freedom from the right or claim of another. Similarly, a power is one's affirmative 'control' over a given legal relation as against another; whereas an immunity is one's freedom from the legal power or 'control' of another as regards some legal relation.
>
> A few examples may serve to make this clear. X, a landowner, has, as we have seen, power to alienate to Y or to any other ordinary party . . . On the other hand, X has also various immunities as against Y, and all other ordinary parties. For Y is under a disability (ie, has no power) so far as shifting the legal interest either to himself or to a third party is concerned; and what is true of Y applies similarly to every one else who has not by virtue of special operative facts acquired a power to alienate X's property.

Thus, when we say that 'A has a *power* against B', we are saying that A is able to change B's jural relations with some legal entity or entities in some respect. Supposing A had lent B £10,000, and it was expressly agreed that B would repay £10,000 to A on 1 January 2018, B would be duty-bound to A to pay £10,000 to A on that date. But so far as B's act of tendering payment of £10,000 to A on 1 January 2018 would lead to the discharge of the duty/claim-right arising from that loan (assuming A accepted such tender), B may be said to have a *power* as against A to change that duty/claim-right jural relation.

---

[34] Wenar (2005), p. 230.
[35] Hohfeld (1923), p. 51.
[36] Ibid., p. 60.

As will be shown in the next chapter, that discharge can only arise if A cooperates by *accepting* a conforming tender of payment.[37] Accordingly, A will have a corresponding power against B to change the duty/ claim-right jural relation arising from the loan if B were to tender a conforming payment. Further, unless the context indicates otherwise, English law appears to recognize that powers may be delegated, that is, every holder of a power arising from a voluntarily assumed obligation is also empowered to delegate its exercise to another (i.e. an agent), it being presumed (unless the context indicates otherwise) that the party against whom such power might be exercised will have assented to such delegation. However, as mentioned above, certain kinds of powers in certain contexts will be taken to be 'personal' to the holder, and hence are non-delegable; and if the context were at all unclear, express words may be stipulated to make it plain that such powers are to be non-delegable.

There are situations, though, where A has the opposite of a power against B, i.e. where A is under a disability as regards B's jural relations with, say, A. For example, in some circumstances, we may speak of A being under a disability as regards B to change B's duty to A to Φ. Correlatively, we may speak of B being immune to A changing B's duty to A to Φ.

On the facts of the case where A had lent B £10,000 to be repaid on 1 January 2018, one disability/immunity jural relation as between A and B would have arisen in the following way. Once the contract of loan had been formed, though B would be duty-bound to A to Φ (where 'Φ' means 'pay A £10,000 on 1 January 2018'), A would be under a disability to B to change B's duty to Φ; or, correlatively, B is immune to A changing B's duty to Φ.

In plain language, A has no ability to unilaterally change any aspect of Φ, be it the amount to be paid ('£10,000'), the currency and mode in which it was to be paid ('English pounds in cash notes'), the time when it was to be tendered ('on 1 January 2018'), or the party to whom the money was to be tendered ('A'). Though A might authorize another entity to accept a conforming tender on her behalf, and so, in a sense, allow for tender to be made to someone *in addition* to herself, A may not unilaterally change the identity of the party to whom tender was to be made to the extent that tender *to A* would no longer be good tender *at all*, such that *only* tender to her nominee would be good tender.

---

[37] See Chapter 3, Section B(i).

That, however, is premised on the assumption that B would generally have assented to A having the power to delegate her other powers against B to be exercised by another. As mentioned above, it is possible for B to expressly provide to make it clear that he was *not* assenting to A being invested with such power of delegation. If such express provision had been made (or if the context otherwise indicated the impermissibility of such delegation), A would have a disability against B so far as delegation to, say, C, was concerned. Correlatively, B would have an immunity against A delegating exercise of A's other powers against B to a third party such as C.

Returning to the facts of our example of the loan by A to B of £10,000, suppose a third party, C, falsely led B to believe that A had equitably assigned the benefit of the contract of debt between A and B to him. Suppose that B had then tendered payment to C in the mistaken belief that C was A's equitable assignee, which tender C accepted. Such tender of payment to C would plainly be ineffective to discharge B's common law duty to A with regard to the debt.[38]

By reason of A's loan to B, B would have been duty-bound to A to tender payment to A; and A would have had the power as against B to accept such tender of payment. Such acceptance by A would have resulted in the discharge of B's duty to A: that duty would have been brought to an end. A's acceptance would, accordingly, have changed B's duty/claim-right jural relations with A by extinguishing the debt. But absent any equitable assignment by A to C (or any trust or agency relationship between them apart from such assignment), C plainly has no power to affect A's and B's duty/claim-right jural relations with each other. Not only is A immune to C changing A's duty/claim-right jural relation with B, B is similarly immune to C changing B's duty/claim-right jural relation with A. There is, accordingly, an immunity/disability jural relation as between B and C, absent an equitable assignment by A to C of the benefit of B's indebtedness.

Where the debt has been equitably assigned to C by A, if we pay close attention to the case law, we may discern two distinct effects. First, we may observe that C will have the ability to *indirectly* affect B's duty/claim-right jural relation with A in that A will be duty-bound to C to

---

[38] It may be the case that where C had been clothed with the requisite apparent authority by A, B might have a defence at law on grounds of such apparent authority were A to sue B for non-payment of the debt. But even so, such defence presupposes that B's tender to C would *not* have discharged B's indebtedness to A.

invoke her powers against B as C may direct: A would no longer be *privileged* against C to invoke her powers against B as she pleased. So if C directs A to execute a deed of release by which B would be freed from his duty to pay the debt, A is duty-bound to C to comply; and if she does not, an injunction may issue to compel her to do so.[39] Consequently, C will have the power to change B's duty/claim-right jural relations with A, albeit indirectly, through A.

Second, we see that C may 'leapfrog' or 'bypass' A so as to change B's duty/claim-right jural relations with A without A's intervention. For example, having been equitably assigned the benefit of the debt, were B to tender £10,000 to C on account of the loan from A, if C accepted such tender for that purpose, that act of acceptance by C would discharge B's duty/claim-right jural relation with A.[40]

Much of the difficulty in understanding how equitable assignments operate rests in the inadequacy of the language of 'rights' and 'duties'. Undifferentiated use of these words obscures the limited effect of equitable assignments in that it leaves the jural relations between obligee-assignor and obligor to the chose assigned entirely intact. When carefully analysed, an equitable assignment affects the jural relations between obligee-assignor and assignee, as well as the immunity/disability jural relations between the obligor and the assignee. But because equitable assignments leave the jural relations between obligor and obligee-assignor intact, and because English law accepts that, absent provision otherwise, an obligor will be taken to have assented to the possibility of his obligee subjecting herself to duties to another as to her invocation of her powers as against the obligor, and/or his obligee delegating to another her powers against the obligor, equitable assignment is able to achieve the effects we observe in the cases without any need to obtain the obligor's assent to such assignment, there being no relevant change to the jural relations between the obligor and the obligee-assignor require his assent to be effective.

---

[39] As Roskill LJ recognized in *Warner Bros Records Inc.* v. *Rollgreen Ltd* [1976] 1 QB 430, 443–4.

[40] As Lord Cranworth LC recognized in *Jones* v. *Farrell* (1857) 1 De G & J 208, 218. However, as will be explained in Chapter 11, payment of the sum owed to the assignee, when accepted by the assignee to be in repayment of the assigned debt with knowledge of the assignment, may give rise to liability for the equitable wrong of dishonest assistance. Further, if proceedings at law were brought against the debtor for having failed to tender payment to the assignee, the debtor would be barred from pleading the facts as would otherwise support the defence of payment: see Chapter 12.

That said, in the following chapters, for convenience's sake, the term 'obligation' will continue to be used as a catch-all for the duty, no-right, liability and/or disability which an obligor owes an obligee, when the context does not require a more precise identification of the nature of the obligation; and correlatively, the term 'entitlement' will continue to be used as a catch-all for the claim-right, privilege, power and/or immunity which an obligee is owed by an obligor, when the context does not require greater precision.

## C   The Structure of the Book

The fundamental proposition of the impermissibility of unilateral variations of obligations voluntarily undertaken by an obligor without the obligor's assent, and how the conceptual model of equitable assignment that is proposed in this work best conforms with that proposition is explained in Part II ('The Model').

Part III ('Joinder') examines when and why proceedings in the court's common law or equitable jurisdiction will, or will not, require joinder of the assignor of a chose to proceedings at common law or in equity against the obligor to such chose.

Part IV ('Notice') examines the role and operation of notice within equitable assignment. It will explain the rationale for the much-criticized 'rule' in *Dearle* v. *Hall*,[41] as well as explain why equities stop running against the assignee following such notice. It will also demonstrate that, when an obligor to a chose that has been equitably assigned receives notice of such assignment, such notice creates the conditions by which the obligor is made duty-bound in equity to the assignee to refrain from acting in such manner as dishonestly assists the obligee-assignor in committing a breach of her equitable duties (as assignor) to her assignee.

Part V ('Statutes') examines the operation of LPA1925, s. 136(1), and compares its operation with that under a number of other statutes. The proposition in Part V is that when a debt or chose in action is 'statutorily assigned' pursuant to LPA1925, s. 136(1), the debt or chose in action is *not* assigned by reason of the statute because it does not stipulate a mode of assignment which is distinct from the modes of assignment already extant at law or in equity. Rather, s. 136(1) 'regulates' the operation of

---

[41]   (1828) 3 Russ 1; aff'd (1828) 3 Russ 48 (Lord Lyndhurst LC).

such assignments as are otherwise recognized at law or in equity,[42] on satisfaction of its requirements that such assignment be 'absolute', in a signed writing, and that written notice be given to the obligor, by imposing additional statutory effects by way of supplementation.

Where a chose in action has been equitably assigned, and where the requirements in s. 136(1) are satisfied, the entitlements specified in ss. 136(1)(a), (b) and (c) will be statutorily transferred away from the assignor to the assignee, thereby extinguishing the assignor's ability to assert or invoke those entitlements. Such 'statutory' assignee then becomes *exclusively* enabled to assert or invoke them, and the trust and agency effects which would otherwise apply to those entitlements would be overridden.

However, this 'transfer' only arises with regard to the entitlements specified in s. 136(1), and not any others.[43] The entitlements listed in s. 136(1) do not exhaust the universe of entitlements as may arise in respect of every conceivable chose in action.[44] Any extraneous entitlements falling beyond those specified by s. 136(1) would *not* be 'transferred' by s. 136(1), and the trust and agency effects which arose when the chose in action was equitably assigned would still apply with regard to such extraneous entitlements.

Finally, in Part VI, some of the more obvious implications of the model of assignment proposed in this book will be set out. Not only are there gains in conceptual clarity, there are practical consequences as well, and certain assumptions as to the operation of limitation, discharge of obligations and priorities, to name just a few, may require rethinking.

---

[42] *Hockin v. The Royal Bank of Scotland* [2016] EWHC 925, [44] (Asplin J): '[S]ection 136 Law of Property Act 1925 does not create a statutory right of assignment in itself as much as regulates the effects of assignments which have taken place.' See also *Curran v. New Park Cinemas Ltd* [1951] 1 All ER 295, 299H.

[43] Examples of such entitlements as may be present in connection with a particular chose in action include the entitlements arising from: a contractual option; a contractual power of termination; a choice of jurisdiction clause; or an arbitration clause.

[44] The implications of this will be explored in Chapters 13 and 15.

# PART II

## The Model

# 3

## Invariability

This chapter will explain the major premises on which the model of equitable assignment proposed in this book is based. They are:

1 Private law obligations comprise two parts: (I) what the obligor is duty-bound to do; and (II) to whom the obligor is duty-bound.

2 A change to either (I) or (II) means making a new obligation. That is, a substitution of a 'new' obligee to the existing obligation is, in essence, the substitution of a new obligation with a new obligee.

3 It is impermissible at common law and in equity for one party to a voluntarily undertaken obligation to unilaterally replace it with another obligation without the counter-party's assent.

4 That said, an obligation may be framed so that the obligee to whom the obligation is owed is specified in an 'impersonal' manner. A good example would be the tort of trespass to land, where the primary obligation is owed by an obligor, being *such* legal person as does not hold the legal title to the parcel of land in question, to an obligee, being *such* legal person as *does* hold the legal title to the land, not to trespass on the land.

5 Such 'impersonally' drawn obligations are easily mistaken as instances where, without the obligor's consent, the obligee has been changed and a new obligation been imposed. But we may recognize that there is no change at all in the identity of the obligee, or a swap of one obligation for another, so far as the obligee in such impersonally drawn obligations is framed by reference to the contingent association between any legal person at any particular time with some*thing*. The obligation remains the same throughout.

6 The proposition in 3, above, is true of voluntarily assumed obligations at common law and in equity. As their rules on invariability of voluntarily assumed obligations without obligor assent are the same, the proposition 'equity prevails over the common law' has no application.

7 Given the above, the *sui generis* institution of equitable assignment
   cannot operate as an equitable form of novation which dispenses with
   obligor assent when varying the obligation. It operates in a distinct
   manner, entailing the constitution of a bare trust over the chose assigned
   *plus* an atypical agency in which the assignee is authorized to act as if he
   were the assignor, and who is also granted the authority to invoke such
   delegated powers without regard for the assignor's interests.

## A    'Equity Prevails over the Common Law'

As mentioned in Chapter 2, the operation of equitable assignments
remains obscure.

On one view, equitable assignment as a matter of English law changes
the identity of the obligee to the chose in action assigned, somewhat like a
novation, but without needing the obligor's assent. This will be referred
to in this book as the 'substitutive transfer' model of equitable
assignment.[1]

This book suggests that conceiving equitable assignment as a substitutive transfer is misguided. Instead, it will be shown that as a matter of
English law, equitable assignments effect a *virtual* transfer:[2]

> 'The wisdom and policy of the sages and founders of the law,' says Lord
> Coke . . ., 'have provided that no possibility, right, title nor thing in action,
> shall be granted or assigned to strangers, for that would be the occasion of
> multiplying contentions and suits.'[3] But, in regard to *choses in action*, as
> the same doctrine has been adopted in every other state in Europe, it may
> be doubted whether the reason, which has been the foundation of the rule
> everywhere else, was not also the reason for its introduction in this
> country; namely, that the credit being a personal right of the creditor,
> the debtor being obliged towards that person could not by a transfer of the
> credit, which was not an act of his, become obliged towards another; and
> the more especially as the mode of effecting a *virtual* transfer which was
> invented by the Roman jurisconsults, namely, by constituting the assignee
> the mandatory of the creditor . . . to sue for and recover the debt in the

---

[1] This alternative (and arguably more mainstream) conception of equitable assignment will
   be discussed at greater length in Chapter 4.
[2] Spence (1850), pp. 849–50, emphasis added; cited with approval: Ames (1887), p. 6, fn. 2;
   Ames (1913), p. 211, fn. 6 (reproducing the argument in Ames (1890), p. 339, fn. 2);
   Holdsworth (1920), p. 1003; Frederick Pollock, *Pollock's Principles of Contract* (Sir P. H.
   Winfield, ed., 13th edn, London: Stevens & Sons, 1950), p. 174.
[3] *Lampet's Case* (1612) 10 Co Rep 46b.

name of the creditor ..., has also been adopted in our system of our jurisprudence.

The starting point which suggests that the 'substitutive transfer' conception of equitable assignment is open to question is this: one does not owe an obligation; one owes an obligation *to* someone (as Section B, below, will explain). Hence, the identity of the obligee to whom an obligation is owed is part and parcel of the specification of that obligation.

Recognizing this, the common law rule is that voluntarily assumed obligations (e.g. contractual obligations) are invariable without the obligor's assent. Consequently, it should not be possible to vary such obligation by an *equitable* doctrine such as equitable assignment unless the rules of equity and common law diverge on the point; though *if* they diverged, subject to the qualification to be discussed below, 'equity prevails over the common law'.

Section 25(11) of the Judicature Act 1873 statutorily enshrined the position that had held since the decree of James I following *The Earl of Oxford's Case* by which precedence was given to the rules of equity over those of the common law, so far as they differed.[4] Where matters had not *otherwise* been provided for in ss. 25(1)–(10), if the rules developed by the courts of equity[5] over particular subject matter contradicted the rules developed by the common law courts over the same subject matter, then (and only then) would the rules of equity prevail. Two points follow.

First, as a matter of statutory interpretation, since the question of assignment of choses in action *is* a matter 'particularly mentioned' in sub-sections (1)–(10), given s. 25(6) which provides for additional statutory effects to override the effects that would otherwise arise on an assignment,[6] the proviso to s. 25(11), which reads 'in all matters not hereinbefore particularly mentioned', precludes the rules of equity from 'prevailing' over the rules of common law. And since s. 49 of the Senior Courts Act 1981 merely replaced s. 25(11) without making any substantive changes to the law,[7] the same

---

[4] (1615) 1 Chan Rep 1, 48.

[5] Both the court of Chancery and the court of Exchequer had an equitable jurisdiction, but the latter's equitable jurisdiction was removed by the Administration of Justice Act 1841.

[6] Judicature Act 1873, s. 25(6) is *in pari materia* with LPA1925, s. 136(1), the effects of which will be discussed in Chapter 13.

[7] Senior Courts Act 1981, s. 49(1), 'embodies, in a concentrated form, the fundamental objectives of the Judicature Acts 1873–1875': Sir Geoffrey Vos (editor-in-chief) et al., *Civil Procedure*, 2 vols. (London: Sweet & Maxwell, Thomson Reuters, 2018), Vol II, para. [9A.170]. Section 49(1) re-enacts s. 44 of the Supreme Court of Judicature (Consolidation)

must be true today, given the preservation of s. 25(6) of the Judicature Act 1873 within LPA1925, s. 136(1).

Second, and more fundamentally, there is no conflict between the *rules*[8] of equity and the common law[9] regarding unilateral variation of voluntarily assumed obligations without the obligor's assent. Both agreed that this was impermissible, as will be shown in the following sections. Consequently, since there was (and still is) no conflict between the rules of equity and the common law in respect of the invariability of voluntarily undertaken obligations without the obligor's assent, there is no reason to prefer the rules developed in equity over those developed at common law.

## B    Obligations, and Associated Hohfeldian Jural Relationships

Choses in action arise from obligations.[10]

'Legal' or 'common law' obligations are those recognized and enforced at common law (i.e. 'common law' or 'legal' obligations), breaches of which may be remedied by common law remedies such as an order of compensatory damages following the successful prosecution of an action for breach of contract or the commission of a tort, or an order to pay a fixed sum of money following the successful prosecution of an action in debt. As a matter of English law, many common law obligations are also recognized and enforced in equity. For example, breaches of common law obligations arising from a contract may also be remedied by orders of specific performance, or injunction, being remedies issued by the court acting within its equitable jurisdiction.

---

Act 1925 which, in turn, re-enacted s. 25(11) of the 1873 Act. As to the 'fundamental objectives' of the Judicature Acts, see *C. E. Heath Plc* v. *Ceram Holding Co.* [1988] 1 WLR 1219, 1229 (Neill LJ).

[8] As opposed to the remedy which might be granted: Meagher, Gummow & Lehane (2015), paras. 2-155, 2-175 and 2-185.

[9] As to what a 'conflict' between the rules of equity and common law might entail, before s. 25(11) of the 1873 Act be resorted to, see F. W. Maitland, *Equity: A Course of Lectures* (J. Brunyate, ed., 2nd edn, Cambridge: Cambridge University Press, 1936), pp. 16–17.

[10] As mentioned in Chapter 2, although obligations may also arise as a matter of public or administrative law, in this book, 'obligations' will be used to refer to obligations arising under private law.

There are also 'equitable' obligations.[11] Though these obligations are recognized at common law[12] and in equity, they are enforced *exclusively* in equity.[13] Equitable obligations are, accordingly, obligations whose breaches may be remedied *only* by remedies within the court's equitable jurisdiction such as orders of specific performance, injunction or equitable compensation.[14]

There are, in general, two aspects to every obligation: (I) *what* the obligor is obligated to do; and (II) *to whom* the obligor is obligated. This is generally the case whether the obligation be legal[15] or equitable,[16]

---

[11] Commonly encountered examples of equitable obligations include the obligations arising under a trust or a will, the obligation owed to creditors in a bankruptcy, and the obligations arising under vendors' and purchasers' liens. Some other examples are listed in Liew (2018), para. 1-07.

[12] The distinction between 'recognition' and 'enforcement' of equitable obligations by a court acting within its common law jurisdiction, as opposed to a court acting within its equitable jurisdiction, is analogous to the distinction between 'recognition' and 'enforcement' of a foreign penal or revenue rule by an English court, as opposed to how a court in that foreign jurisdiction from which that rule originated might do the same. This distinction is discussed and explained in Part III: Joinder. As to the recognition of equitable obligations by the common law courts, specifically, see Chapter 7, Section C.

[13] Leaving aside the statutory reforms of the mid-1800s leading up to the enactment of the two Judicature Acts, the common law courts did not have jurisdiction to grant common law remedies in respect of an obligation that was *solely* the creature of equity. For example, since the equitable obligation of a trustee arising under a trust falls within the court's exclusive equitable jurisdiction, the common law courts never had a concurrent jurisdiction in respect of such equitable obligations. Conversely, the courts of equity did have a concurrent jurisdiction to grant its remedies in respect of many obligations that were recognized at common law, for example, contractual obligations, or obligations arising from common law torts. These divisions were preserved following the reforms under the Judicature Acts 1873 and 1875, such that even today, the court may not award common law damages (which necessarily would have to be awarded in exercise of its common law jurisdiction) to remedy breaches of exclusively equitable obligations such as the fiduciary obligations of a trustee under an express trust. Breaches of such equitable obligations are to be remedied exclusively by the court in exercise of its equitable jurisdiction.

[14] These lists of equitable remedies are merely illustrative and are not exhaustive.

[15] The tort of public nuisance may be an exception. As to this tort, see Clerk & Lindsell (2018), paras. 20-03, 20-04 and 20-69.

[16] Save for obligations arising in respect of trusts for charitable purposes, and also certain narrowly defined non-charitable purpose trusts. See *Bowman* v. *Secular Society, Ltd* [1917] AC 406, 441 (Lord Parker). Some non-charitable purpose trusts are also valid, notwithstanding their lack of any beneficiaries. See *Re Endacott* [1960] Ch 232, 246 (Lord Evershed MR), 250–1 (Harman LJ). For a view that English law does not ordinarily recognize the validity of non-charitable purpose trusts, see Paul Matthews, 'From Obligation to Property, and Back Again?' in D. J. Hayton (ed.), *Extending the Boundaries of Trusts and Similar Ring-Fenced Funds* (The Hague: Kluwer Law International, 2002), refuting the contrary view in P. Baxendale-Walker, *Purpose Trusts* (London: Butterworths, 1999).

primary or secondary, voluntarily undertaken or imposed by operation of law.[17]

Concentrating, for now, on the Hohfeldian duty/claim-right jural relationship, where A has contracted for B to paint X's house in exchange for an advance payment of £1,000, B is duty-bound to paint X's house, and B owes this duty to A. Alternatively, putting it in terms of the correlative judicial relation, in these circumstances, A has a claim-right that B paint X's house, and A has this claim-right as against B. *If* B were to paint X's house, therefore, B would have done right by A: A would have no basis of complaint, as B would have discharged his *duty* to A to do so.

When we look at the cases, so far as private law obligations are concerned, one cannot be obliged in the abstract. In the ordinary case, one must be obliged to some*one*.[18] So the specification of the identity of the obligee in (II) is as much a part of the specification of that obligation as the specification in (I) as to what the obligor is obligated to do.

As has already been pointed out, an obligation is made up of multiple jural relations. A fuller range of these will be shown in Example 3.1.

---

**EXAMPLE 3.1**

A lends B £10,000.

---

When *A* lends B £10,000, B is duty-bound to A to do $\Phi$ where '$\Phi$' means, in this context, 'repay the loan *to A*'. Hence, A has a claim-right against B that B do $\Phi$.

---

[17] Obligations arising as a matter of public law fall beyond the ambit of this book.

[18] Hence, in respect of trusts, 'an use is a trust or confidence in some other ... as a thing collateral, annexed in privitie to the estate of the land ... *scilicet*, that *cesty que use* shall take the profit': Co Litt 272b. And in respect of contractual promises, 'The obligation of contract is an obligation created and determined *by the will of the parties*. Herein is the characteristic difference of contract from all other branches of law. The business of the law, therefore, is to give effect so far as possible to the intention of the parties ... But even where the law has to fill up gaps by judicial conjecture, the guiding principle still is, or ought to be, the consideration of what either party has given the other reasonable cause to expect *of him*': Pollock (1910), p. 38 (emphasis added). See also S. M. Waddams, *Principle and Policy in Contract Law: Competing or Complementary Concepts?* (Cambridge: Cambridge University Press, 2011), p. 53.

A's claim-right/duty jural relation that B so perform will ordinarily be associated with various power/liability jural relations.[19] Ordinarily, under English law, A will have the power against B to bring judicial proceedings against B should there be a dispute over the discharge of B's duty to A;[20] and A will also have the power against B to release B from his duty to A.[21] But there other powers, for example:

(a) A will have the power against B to effect a discharge by accepting payment; and
(b) A will have the power against B to 'insist on payment to herself or such person as she thinks fit'.[22]

These two powers of A's will be examined below.

### (i)   Power to Effect a Discharge by Accepting Payment

In Example 3.1, 'payment' is not an action that B may completely perform without A's cooperation.[23] As Gloster J observed:[24]

---

[19] This is not the place to engage with the ongoing debate as to whether the entailment between the claim-right/power jural relation and any associated power/liability jural relations is a logical necessity, or is merely the result of a policy choice. It is sufficient for present purposes to recognize that there is such an association as a matter of English law, whatever the reasons for that may be.

[20] Or, as Diplock LJ put it, where B had breached his duty to A, 'A has a cause of action against B for any infringement by B of a right of A which is recognized by law': *Letang v. Cooper* [1965] 1 QB 232, 246.

[21] Drawing on Hart's analysis, N. E. Simmonds suggests that at least one or other of these power/liability jural relations must accompany a claim-right/duty jural relation for that claim-right/duty jural relation to be a *legal* (as opposed to a non-legal, say, moral) right: 'To possess a right, on [Hart's] view, is to have control over a duty incumbent upon someone else. The right is not the rationale of the duty, nor its justification: it is the power to waive or to demand performance of the duty': N. E. Simmonds, 'Rights at the Cutting Edge' in Kramer, Simmonds & Steiner (1998), pp. 215–16. For Hart's own views on this, see H. L. A. Hart, 'Definition and Theory in Jurisprudence' in H. L. A. Hart, *Essays in Jurisprudence and Philosophy* (Oxford: Clarendon Press, 1983), p. 83; and 'Legal Rights' in Hart (1982), pp. 183–4 and 186–8.

[22] This appears to entail a unilateral power in A (as creditor) to change B's obligation. But as will be shown below, this is not the case.

[23] *Startup v. MacDonald* (1843) 6 M & G 593, 610.

[24] *Canmer Investment Inc. v. UK Mutual Steamship Assurance Association Ltd* [2005] EWHC 1694 (Comm), [53]. The proposition is supported both by common sense and by authority. As was recognized in Sir W. S. Holdsworth, *A History of English Law* (2nd edn, 12 vols., London: Methuen & Co. Ltd, 1937), vol. VIII, p. 79 (emphasis added): 'A payment was complete so that the money was at the risk of the payee, as soon as he

Payment is a consensual act and thus requires the accord of both creditor and debtor. Even if a tender[25] by a debtor to his creditor complies fully with the terms of the contract, and the creditor's refusal to accept the payment thus constitutes a breach of contract, the tender does not discharge the debtor's obligation, although the creditor may be prevented thereafter from claiming any interest or damages for late payment or for claiming damages for breach of the payment obligation.

Therefore, until A cooperates by accepting what B has tendered, 'either by expressly declaring its unconditional assent to the payment, or by acceptance or by treating the money as its own',[26] B's duty to A to do Φ is not discharged.

### (ii)   Power to 'Insist on Payment to the Creditor or Such Person as the Creditor Thinks Fit'

Apart from the above, English common law appears to have developed a rule that, unless otherwise provided for, a creditor would also have the power to nominate an alternate payee. Such a power was recognized in *Hodgson* v. *Anderson*, where Bayley J held '[t]here can be no doubt that a creditor has a right to insist on payment to himself, *or* to such person as he thinks fit'.[27]

In relation to this case, Bailey noted that:[28]

> [T]he common law recognized that 'every creditor has the right to insist on payment ... to such person as he thinks fit' ... but this rule gave no independent right of action to the assignee – it merely enabled the creditor to choose whom the debtor was to pay.

The last clause in Bailey's reading of *Hodgson* v. *Anderson* may be read to suggest that by invoking such power of choice, the creditor could *preclude* tender of payment to herself with the result that *only* tender of payment to her designated recipient would be an effective tender.

---

had *accepted* the coins', relying on the authority of *Canter* v. *Shepheard* (1699) 1 Ld Raym 330.

[25] The rules of tender are also ancient, having been summarized by Coke in *Wade's Case* (1601) 5 Co Rep 114a.

[26] *Canmer Investment Inc.* v. *UK Mutual Steamship Assurance Association Ltd* [2005] EWHC 1694, adopting the analysis of Hobhouse J in *TSB Bank of Scotland Plc* v. *Welwyn Hatfield District Council* [1993] 2 Bank LR 267 (Comm), 272–3.

[27] (1825) 3 B & C 842, 853–4 (emphasis added).

[28] Bailey (1932), pp. 549–50.

But that would be reading too much into Bailey's text and Bayley J's judgment.

Bayley J merely held that the creditor had a 'right' (i.e. a Hohfeldian power) to insist on payment 'to himself or to such person as he thinks fit'. The difficulty lies with the connector 'or'. Did Bayley J hold that having named an alternate payee, the debtor would have to tender payment to that alternate payee to the exclusion of the creditor? Had Bayley J done that, it would follow that the debtor would be duty-bound to tender payment *only* to that alternate payee. Tender to the creditor following invocation of such power of *substitution* would, indeed, be a nullity. But, perhaps, that goes too far. Though B might have been indifferent as to whether payment might, at his option, be tendered to C instead of to A, it is not immediately obvious that B would invariably be indifferent to having to tender to C with no option at all to tender to A.

As Bailey's commentary (reproduced above) on Bayley J's judgment recognized, when a creditor names another person to whom payment might be tendered (i.e. her 'assignee') by way of alternative, the debtor *remains* obligated (i.e. indebted) *to* the creditor, and not the alternate payee, to tender payment to the creditor *or* to her designated recipient. This particular entitlement as identified by Bayley J gives no *independent right of action to the assignee*. If a creditor names an alternate payee, and the debtor fails to pay such alternate payee (*or* the creditor), such debtor would have breached his obligation to the creditor, but will have breached no contractual obligation at common law to the alternate payee. Thus, it is still for the creditor to bring judicial proceedings at law against the debtor in respect of such breach: the *cause of action at common law* is still the creditor's, and not the alternate payee's.

So far as one might be analysing these cases from the perspective of a court acting within its common law jurisdiction, one might rationalize the creditor's 'power to insist' to be merely a power to make an offer to her debtor where, in consideration for the debtor either tendering payment to the creditor's nominee or promising to do so, the creditor promises to release the debtor from his duty to tender payment to the creditor.[29] The debtor may reject such offer by

---

[29] Cf. Trukhtanov (2010), p. 555.

choosing to tender payment to the original creditor;[30] or accept it by tendering payment to the creditor's nominee (in which case the creditor would be bound to release the debtor from his duty to tender payment to her). Or the debtor might accept by promising to do so (which would lead to the offer becoming irrevocable).[31] The modification of the debtor's duty (as to what he was duty-bound to do) would thus depend on the debtor *accepting* the offer of variation, which he may, or may not do. Further, this view would depend on whether the communications between the creditor and her debtor might be interpreted as evincing the requisite intentions to extinguish the prior obligation by which the debtor was duty-bound to the creditor to tender payment to her, with a 'new' obligation by which the debtor was duty-bound to the creditor to tender payment to her designated recipient.[32]

But suppose such an interpretation of the communications between creditor and debtor was not tenable, or could only be arrived at with great artificiality. An alternative way of looking at the matter might be this: the naming of an alternate payee could merely be an incident of exercising the power vested in every legal person to delegate. Save where the context precludes it,[33] the law allows for powers to be exercised by those who hold them, as well as their duly authorized representatives or agents. In Example 3.1, A would have the power to accept a conforming tender of payment. But A also has the power to delegate invocation of such power to a duly authorized agent – for example, C. If, having done so, she then tells B to tender payment to C, when B tenders payment to C, B will have duly performed his duty *to A* to tender payment *to A*.[34]

---

[30] If she could be found, it being the debtor's duty to find his creditor and to tender payment to her, wherever she might be so long as she was within the jurisdiction: see Co Litt 210b. This rule is suspended when the creditor is outside the jurisdiction: *Fessard* v. *Mugnier* (1865) 18 CB (NS) 286.

[31] *Hodgson* v. *Anderson* (1825) 3 B & C 842, 855.

[32] If the designated recipient were also party to the communications leading to the formation of the 'new' obligation, a novation would, of course, have arisen.

[33] Where the context makes it clear that the power in question is to be exercised by a particular entity in light of his or her peculiar personal characteristics, e.g. the powers to execute or to revoke a will are personal to the testator.

[34] As will be explained in subsequent chapters, although a court acting within its common law jurisdiction would not do so, a court acting within its equitable jurisdiction would recognize and give effect to the agency mechanism which underpins the equitable institution of equitable assignment without need for anything more. Consequently, when

Of course, B's act of tendering payment to C, and C's act of acceptance, will not be a literal satisfaction of what B was duty-bound to do. But given that the acts of an agent are to be taken to be the acts of its principal, so long as the agent acts within the ambit of the authority granted by its principal, A could not deny that C's act of accepting B's conforming tender of payment as her agent would have to be taken as if she had accepted it herself, since she had authorized C to perform that very act. In effect, therefore, B's *duty* to A would be to tender payment to A, and also to A's duly authorized agent, unless the context clearly indicated otherwise.

A modified version of the reasoning above could also be applied where C had not actually been authorized by A to act as A's agent to accept a conforming tender of payment from B in discharge of the debt owed by B, for when A requests that B tender payment to C, that request may cloak C with sufficient *apparent* authority to, in effect, precluding A from denying that C had actually been authorized.

Importantly, however, if C is to be taken as having either actual (or apparent) authority to accept a conforming tender of payment from B to enable B to be discharged from his duty at law in relation to the debt of £10,000, what B is duty-bound to do does not change: B may *still* tender payment to A. And if A were to accept such tender, the debt contract would *still* be discharged by reason of B's precise performance. On this account, A cannot lose her power to accept a conforming tender of payment, because if she no longer had such power, there would be nothing for her to delegate for C to invoke on her behalf. Agency reasoning necessarily requires the principal/delegator to retain such powers as the principal/delegator had authorized her agent/delegatee to invoke.

All that this agency reasoning permits, is an extension of the reach of A, such that A may act through intermediaries. But the intermediaries' acts are only acts 'in right of' A. They are acting and interacting as A's avatar, albeit in the real as opposed to the virtual world. There is, accordingly, no change of the duty/claim-right jural relation between A and B at all, on this conception of A's instruction to B that he should tender payment to C. Nor is there any change of the duty/claim-right jural relation between A and B in terms of what B is duty-bound to A to do: although B *may* discharge his duty to A to tender payment to A by tendering payment to C (as A's designated recipient and representative),

---

acting within its equitable jurisdiction, the court will recognize and give effect to the *delegation* of the assignor's powers to her assignee as part of this agency mechanism.

when C accepts such tender in exercise of A's power of acceptance which had been delegated to him, C's acts are taken as A's acts, and B will still have discharged his duty to A.

## C   Populating Hohfeldian Jural Relations

### (i)   A's Claim-Right against B that B Do Φ

Each of A's powers as against B mentioned in the preceding section is invested exclusively in A because it is A who has the claim-right against B that B do Φ. A has such claim-right against B because A was both party to the contract with B and provider of the consideration in exchange for B's promises within that contract. Hence A has the claim-right ('is entitled') to B's performance of Φ: it is *right* ('justified') so far as A is concerned that B do Φ. And in support of this, English law gives A a privileged status: A is given *standing* to seek the assistance of the Crown in the form of its courts to adjudicate over any disputes which A might have with B over B's performance of such duty.

### (ii)   A's Powers against B

A's claim-right against B populates the content of the four abovementioned power/liability jural relations between A and B in Example 3.1, and explains why they have arisen between *A* and B, and not as between, C, D or anyone else who is 'not A' and B. That is, *but for* A holding the claim-right against B that B do Φ, A would *not* have these powers against B.[35]

---

[35] This is not to say that power/liability jural relations may *only* arise in connection with an associated claim-right/duty jural relation. It is entirely possible for a particular power/liability jural relation to arise independently of any particular claim-right/duty jural relation. For example, where A and B have no prior dealings with each other, A has the *power* to make B an offer where she promises to pay him £10,000, if, in exchange, he promises to paint her house. Prior to receiving such an offer, B would have been under a disability (i.e. have had no power) as against A to subject her to a duty to him to pay him £10,000. But by reason of A's offer, A will have invested B with a power to subject A to such a duty, if he were to *accept* A's offer. So here we have a case where A had a power/liability jural relation with regard to A's power to make an offer to B to enter into a legally binding contract with B that does not pertain to any pre-existing claim-right/duty. The claim in the main text is merely that the four power/liability jural relations identified in the main text are tied to the claim-right/duty jural relation, at least as a matter of English law.

### (iii)  A's Privileges against B, C, D or any 'Non-A'

As to A's powers against B which have arisen because of A's claim-right against B that B do Φ, A is *privileged* against B to invoke each of these powers, or not, as she pleases.[36] B has *no right* to insist that A invoke them, nor does he have any right to insist that A *not* invoke them.

These twin privilege/no-right jural relations also exist in respect of other legal persons. Besides B, A is similarly privileged against C, D or anyone else who is 'not A'. We might therefore generalize: 'A is privileged against any "non-A" to invoke her powers against B, or not, as she pleases', keeping in mind that this is only a convenient mode of expression. The underlying reality is that A is *individually* privileged as against C, and also as against D, and so on.

### (iv)  A's Immunity against B, C, D or any 'Non-A'

These powers of A's against B are also A's to invoke. No one else has *such* powers to change A's jural relations with B arising from the contract of loan in Example 3.1.

It would be futile for B, C, D or anyone else who is 'not A' to execute a deed purporting to release B from his duty to perform or do Φ. Hence A has an immunity against B, C, D or anyone else who is 'not A', changing A's jural relations with B by invoking A's power to grant a release by executing a deed of release.

Similarly, it is not open to B, C, D, or anyone else who is 'not A', to bring legal proceedings against B, should B breach his duty to repay the loan. Only A may invoke such power, since none of B, C, D or anyone else who is 'not A' can be said to have been privy to and provided the consideration to B in contract arising in Example 3.1: only A has standing to bring such proceedings at law against B should a dispute arise over B performing or doing Φ.

So we may say that A has an immunity against B, C, D or anyone who is 'not A' changing A's jural relations with B by invoking A's power to commence judicial proceedings against B. And again, purely for convenience's sake, we may say: A is immune against any 'non-A' invoking A's powers against B as would change her jural relations with B in this manner.

---

[36] Hart would have termed these 'bilateral liberties': 'Legal Rights' in Hart (1982), pp. 166–7.

The point made above about the linkage between A's claim-right/duty jural relation with B, and the associated power/liability, privilege/no-right and immunity/disability jural relations, is underscored in Example 3.2.

## D   Modifying the Identity of an Obligee to a Voluntarily Assumed Obligation

None of the above jural relations is immutable as they depend on party agreement.

---

### EXAMPLE 3.2

A lends B £10,000.
   They also agree that B is to tender payment, not to A, but to C because A wishes to make a gift to C.
   A and B also agree that C is not to have any rights arising under the Contracts (Rights of Third Parties) Act 1999.[37]

---

In Example 3.2, B is duty-bound to A to do $\Omega$ where '$\Omega$' means, 'the act of tendering payment of £10,000 to C'.

Unlike her position in Example 3.1, A now has no power to accept a conforming tender of payment because the formulation of B's duty in Example 3.2 precludes there being such a power in A.[38] Since payment is now to be made *to* C, it is C who has to accept the tender of payment by B for payment to be completely and precisely performed. Thus the power to accept a conforming tender of payment to allow B to discharge his duty to do $\Omega$ by performance in Example 3.2 would be vested in C, and not A (although if B tendered payment to C, C might *refuse* to accept such payment so far as he was under no duty to anyone to accept such

---

[37] The effect of such an exclusion is that the statutory duties which B might owe C if the 1999 Act applied in C's favour do not arise: see s. 1(2).

[38] However, since B's duty to do $\Omega$ is owed to A, substantive English law accepts that A also has the power to make an offer to B to vary the obligation by replacing it with another one: say, for the payment to be made to A (i.e., to do $\Phi$). If A were to invoke such a power, giving B the power to extinguish his duty to do $\Omega$ and to replace it with a duty to do $\Phi$, the power to accept a conforming tender of payment would then necessarily revert back to A. But if no such offer to vary B's duty is made, and B's duty remains a duty to do $\Omega$, it follows from such duty that the power to accept a conforming tender of payment must lie in C, the payee as specified in $\Omega$.

payment but was a mere donee:[39] from C's perspective, this would amount to an unsolicited gift. In such cases, since the law recognizes that donees may reject gifts, C may refuse such a *gift* if so inclined).[40]

We see, therefore, that the nature of the power/liability jural relations as to acceptance of tenders of payment to permit B's duty to do $\Omega$ to be discharged will have changed because A's claim-right against B in Example 3.2 is differently framed. Unlike in Example 3.1, B is duty-bound to do $\Omega$, and not $\Phi$. So the power/liability to discharge/be discharged by acceptance will have likewise changed.

But although B is duty-bound to do $\Omega$, B still owes this duty to A, and not C. Again, this is because A (and not anyone else) had lent B the money as B had requested, and it was A's loan (and not anyone else's) which B was content to accept. Accordingly, even though what B is duty-bound to do in Example 3.2 is different from Example 3.1, in both, B remains duty-bound *to A*. This is the case because B voluntarily assumed a contractual duty to A, and not to anyone else,[41] given A's having furnished the consideration and A's willingness to be privy to the contract with B. And this is corroborated by the observation that it is A who has the power to release B from his duty to $\Omega$, A who has the power to bring judicial proceedings against B if there should be a dispute over his performance of $\Omega$, and A who has the power to make an offer to B, promising to release B from his duty to $\Omega$, in exchange for some alternative act or promise to perform some alternative act.

---

### EXAMPLE 3.3

In addition to the facts in Example 3.2, suppose A and B further agree that B would be liable to become duty-bound *to such person as A might name in writing as her assign* by a certain deadline, but if no one was named, then B would be duty-bound to A.[42]

---

[39] Though C would be presumed to assent to such a gift unless he clearly manifested his intention to disclaim it so long as that power of disclaimer had yet to be lost: see references in Chapter 4, n. 10.

[40] If this occurs, the contract between A and B would probably be discharged by frustration.

[41] S. A. Smith, 'Contracts for the Benefit of Third Parties: In Defence of the Third-Party Rule' (1997) 17 *Oxford Journal of Legal Studies* 643, 645.

[42] The wording of the hypothetical contract in Example 3.3 should not be taken to be mere academic fiction. Similar wording may be found in real-world applications. See e.g. Article 18 of the model private placement agreement released by the Euro PP Working Group in January 2015, focusing, in particular, on the wording in clause 18.3. A soft copy

In Example 3.3, B is also duty-bound to A to tender payment to C: B is still under a duty to do Ω. But the identity of the party to whom B is duty-bound is contingent on what A does, B having assented to A having the ability to *change* the identity of the party to whom B is duty-bound. In Example 3.3, we see that there is a further contractual *power* in A to change B's duty/claim-right jural relation with A.

From a duty to do Ω which was owed to A, once A 'named' C as her 'assign' by executing a document 'assigning' the benefit of her contract with B to C (assuming such acts would be construed to be a valid invocation of the contractually stipulated power vested in A to 'name an assign'), if B failed to do Ω, B would have breached his duty *to C* to do Ω. Conversely, if A did not make a nomination in writing within the stipulated period, B would then remain duty-bound to A, *and only to A*, to do Ω.[43]

A's invocation of the contractual power to substitute another in her place by 'naming' them as her 'assign' would have effected a substitution of the obligee to the contractual voluntary obligation undertaken by B in that, upon the exercise of this contractual power, B would no longer be obligated to A, but would only be obligated to such person as A had made her 'assignee'. But importantly, such substitution has been effected *as a matter of contract* with B's consent in advance: the substitution arises because of B's assent as part of that same contract and takes effect by way

---

of this model agreement may be retrieved from www.euro-privateplacement.com (last accessed 6 March 2019). Notwithstanding the references to 'assignments', the mechanism allowing for substitution of new lenders for old under these two agreements rests on the contractual terms on which the respective facilities had been granted to the borrowers thereunder. For a further example, see clause 24 on 'Changes to the Lenders' of the Loan Market Association's Multicurrency Term and Revolving Facilities Agreement, focusing, in particular, on the wording in clause 24.6 (*The ACT Borrower's Guide to LMA Loan Documentation for Investment Grade Borrowers* prepared by Slaughter and May for the Association of Corporate Treasurers in April 2013 reports that the wording in clause 24.6 was first introduced by the Association in April 2009 (at p. 132)). A soft copy of this Guide may be retrieved from www.treasurers.org/ACTmedia/ACT_guide_LMA_doc.pdf (last accessed 6 March 2019).

[43] The construction that, until A nominated someone or her power to nominate lapsed unused, B was duty-bound to no one is, it is suggested, untenable. Similarly, a construction that B would be duty-bound in an inchoate manner to either A or such person A might nominate within the time specified (if any) is, for similar reasons, unlikely. Neither construction is convincing since either construction would lead to a conclusion that *no* contract had been formed by reason of uncertainty of the terms and/or a lack of intention to create legal relations.

of a form of novation.[44] Accordingly, the substitution of C in place of A given the agreement in Example 3.3 would have occurred as a matter of common law doctrine, and not as the result of the institution of equitable assignment.[45]

Such plasticity in the specification of obligees to voluntarily assumed obligations at common law may also arise in connection with voluntarily assumed obligations in equity, as the following section will show. The following section will, in addition, show that such plasticity may also be found in certain kinds of obligations which are imposed by law. Such plasticity does not, however, detract from the proposition in this chapter, which is that voluntarily assumed obligations may not be unilaterally varied without the obligor's assent.

## E   The Different Ways of Specifying the Obligee to an Obligation

The Hohfeldian conception of the jural relations between obligors and obligees requires that there *be* such obligors and obligees, identifiable at

---

[44] As Ames recognized: 'When the substitution of duties is by consent, the consent may be given either after the duty arises or contemporaneously with its creation. In the former case the substitution is known as a novation, unless the duty relates to land in the possession of a tenant, in which case it is called an attornment. A consent contemporaneous with the creation of the duty is given whenever an obligation is by its terms made to run in favour of the obligee and his assigns, as in the case of annuities, covenants, and warranties before mentioned, or to order or bearer, as in the case of bills and notes and other negotiable securities. Here, too, on the occasion of each successive transfer, there is a novation by virtue of the obligor's consent given in advance; the duty to the transferror is extinguished and a new duty is created in favour of the transferee': Ames (1913), p. 212.

[45] It has been suggested that all equitable assignments of contractual choses in action operate by means of a contractual term to such effect, implied, if need be: Bridge (2016), p. 54. With respect, this is difficult. For one, the implication of terms in a contract or the construction of express terms in a contract is a matter of common law principle. These are not matters arising within *equity's* jurisdiction. Quite how such common law principle can explain the operation of an *equitable* doctrine such as equitable assignment is not obvious. Secondly, rationalizing equitable assignment by reference to contractual terms cannot explain what happens when intangible personalty other than contractual choses in action are equitably assigned. Since non-contractual choses in action (such as equitable choses in action, and those arising in connection with tortious causes of action or intellectual property entitlements) may also be equitably assigned, acceptance of Professor Bridge's analysis means accepting that there are different conceptions of equitable assignment within English law, depending on whether the chose assigned is contractual or not. Such a fragmented understanding of equitable assignment may not be necessary. This book shows that equitable assignment developed as a single conceptual entity which was sufficiently flexible to be applied to a wide range of intangible personalty, and was thus not limited to contractual choses in action.

the relevant point in time, and having legal personality.[46] However, Hohfeld's theory of jural relations does not dictate how such obligors and obligees are to be specified. That is a matter for the substantive law pertaining to the obligation in question.

In perhaps the simplest case, an obligee may be specified to be such by reason of his or her identity as such, without more; as when under the terms of a testamentary trust, T is vested with the legal title in the fee simple of Blackacre for the benefit of A. A is the obligee under such trust because A is the entity named as beneficiary in the will.

But an obligation may specify the obligee thereto in a more open-ended way. Borrowing the language used in the C3PA, an obligee may be expressly identified by name, as a member of a class, or as answering a particular description.[47]

---

EXAMPLE 3.4

Suppose T holds the legal fee simple in Blackacre on a testamentary trust for the life of such children of S's as have reached their majority at the date of S's death, *or such person or persons as each of such children might identify as their nominee or assign.*

---

The obligees (i.e. beneficiaries) to whom T is obligated as trustee of S's will in Example 3.4 are specified or defined in a more impersonal manner: they are identified by reference to their characteristics, namely, they must be either: (i) children of S's, who have reached the age of majority at the time of S's death; *or* (ii) the 'nominees or assigns' of such persons as satisfy all the requirements in (i). Consequently, only persons who meet the description by satisfying (i) *or* (ii) are 'beneficiaries' to whom T owes trust duties under S's will.

Suppose that S died, survived by his children, $A_1$ (aged twenty-five), $A_2$ (aged twenty) and $A_3$ (aged seventeen). Under the terms of S's testamentary trust, T would be trustee for $A_1$ and $A_2$ (because they each satisfy the requirements in (i)), but not $A_3$ (who does not). Nor does $A_3$ satisfy (ii).

But suppose $A_2$ executes a deed of assignment, assigning his interest as beneficiary under S's testamentary trust to $A_3$. $A_3$ would then become a beneficiary of that trust because she now satisfies requirement (ii)

---

[46] Hohfeld (1923), pp. 74–5.

[47] C3PA, s. 1(3), in respect of identifying third parties to whom the statute might be applied.

(assuming $A_2$'s execution of the 'deed of assignment' was such as to make $A_3$ an 'assign' of $A_2$ as a matter of construction of the terms of the testamentary trust), and T would be trustee for $A_3$ because, when T assented to be S's testamentary trustee, T had agreed *in advance* to be obligor to such person(s) as satisfied the requirements in (i), or such person(s) as satisfied requirement (ii). And T would be so duty-bound under the terms of S's testamentary trust, even in advance of his being notified of the 'assignment' to $A_3$.[48]

$A_3$'s entitlement as beneficiary under the terms of S's testamentary trust arises because she conforms with the description of the beneficiaries therein, independently of any other substantive effects generated by $A_2$'s equitable assignment. $A_3$'s position in Example 3.4, therefore, is analogous to the position of C in Example 3.3. In both, the respective obligors (T and B) are directly duty-bound to the respective obligees ($A_3$ and C) *independently* of the operation of the law on equitable assignment. The relevance of the law on equitable assignment, then, is only to provide the criteria by which $A_3$ and C become 'assigns' within the meaning of the phrase in the contract or the will giving rise to the testamentary trust in each example in this book.

Turning away from voluntarily assumed obligations, many obligations imposed by law specify obligees in a broadly similar way by setting out an 'impersonal' description. For example, the obligees to the primary obligations arising from the tort of trespass to land, or the tort of conversion of personal chattels are specified by reference to their association with a 'thing', namely, their association with the legal title to an estate in land, or the legal title in a particular item of tangible personalty, respectively.

Thus, the primary obligation 'not to trespass on Blackacre' is owed by such persons/person as do/does not hold the legal title to Blackacre *to* such persons/person as do/does hold the legal title to Blackacre. And similarly, the primary obligation 'not to convert a particular tangible chattel to one's own use' is owed by such persons/person as do/does not hold the legal title to that tangible chattel *to* such persons/person as do/does hold the legal title to that tangible chattel.

A subsidiary question will arise, of course, as to what 'holding of legal title' means in this context, but that need not concern us here. What is

---

[48] *Ward v. Duncombe* [1983] AC 369, 392 (Lord Macnaghten): 'The trustee of the fund is trustee for the persons entitled to the fund, whether he knows their names or not. ... [B]efore notice given he is just as much a trustee for the persons rightfully entitled as he is after he receives the notice'. These words could be read to also encompass the proposition set out in the main text.

important in the present context is that the identity of the obligee is ascertained in these circumstances by reference to how the obligation *describes* the obligee, and seeing whether the obligee answers the description.

These 'impersonally' drawn obligations which specify the obligees thereof by reference to impersonal and potentially non-unique characteristics are not the exclusive province of tort law. We find similarly impersonal obligees in the law of negotiable instruments where the drawer of a negotiable instrument is duty-bound to such legal person as the negotiable instrument may be negotiated to pay the sum indicated on the instrument if the drawee dishonoured the instrument. And, to give an even more commonplace example, it is entirely uncontroversial for a contract to be formed whereby the obligor promises to become duty-bound to such legal person as satisfies some stated criteria at some future point in time, as where B makes a unilateral offer to pay a reward of £1,000 to such person as finds and returns B's lost dog.

Though primary obligations which describe their obligees in this 'impersonal' manner would appear to entail the possibility of the obligee being changed without any assent on the part of the obligor, that is an illusion, for the obligee is actually the same throughout. Nor is there any swapping of one obligation for another. In these cases, there is *no* change in the obligee to whom the obligor's obligation is owed since the obligor is obligated in these cases to whomever answers the description specified in the obligation. As Holmes observed:[49]

> If A, being the possessor of a horse or a field, gives up the possession to [C], the rights which [C] acquires stand on the same ground as A's did before. The facts from which A's rights sprang have ceased to be true of A, and are now true of [C]. The consequences attached by the law to those facts now exist for [C], as they did for A before. The situation of fact from which the rights spring is a continuing one, and any one who occupies it, no matter how, has the right attached to it.

When dealing with the issue of the invariability of obligations arising at law and in equity, we need to take care when confronted with instances where there has been a seeming substitution of obligees to the obligation. We may discover that the obligees to such obligations are actually defined from the outset by way of a description, such that both 'original' and 'replacement' obligees may all answer that description, albeit at different

---

[49] Holmes (1968), p. 265.

points in time. Where such obligations are *imposed* by law, we may discern that there is, accordingly, no relevant change in the obligee's identity from one moment to the next: the obligor is duty-bound to the same obligee throughout, just that the obligee is such legal entity as answers the description specified in the obligation. Additionally, where such obligations are *voluntarily undertaken*, not only is there no relevant change in the obligee, the obligor would have assented to her obligee being specified in such a non-specific manner. In these cases, therefore, the obligor would have assented *in advance* that she would not be duty-bound to any specifically identified obligee, but would, rather, be duty-bound to whichever legal entity answered the description specified in the obligation.

## F  Invariability of Voluntarily Assumed Obligations Arising at Common Law

The proposition in this chapter is that, so far as voluntarily assumed obligations between an obligor and his obligee have two dimensions, namely: (I) *what* the obligor is obligated to do and (II) *to whom* the obligation is owed, neither (I) nor (II) may be unilaterally changed without the obligor's assent. Consequently, the Hohfeldian jural relationship pairings between obligor and obligee derived from (I) and (II) may not be changed without the obligor's assent, either.

This is embedded in the common law doctrine of novation, which shows the common law's acceptance of the proposition that, in general, legal obligations may only be varied in respect of (I) and/or (II) with the obligor's assent.[50] Given the facts in Example 3.1, if A wished to cause B to become duty-bound to C to tender payment of £1,000 to C[51] such

---

[50] 'I do not think it is necessary to say more than this, that it is not competent for a party to a contract to vary the terms of that existing contract by passing a notice': *Cowey* v. *Liberian Operations Ltd* [1966] 2 Lloyd's Rep 45, 50 (Block J); 'From the conception of a promise being valid only when given in return for something accepted in consideration of the promise, it follows that the giving of the promise and of the consideration must be simultaneous. Words of promise uttered before there is a consideration for them can be no more than an offer; and, on the other hand, the obligation declared in words, or inferred from acts and conduct, on the acceptance of a consideration, *is fixed at that time, and cannot be varied by subsequent declaration*, though such declarations may be material as admissions': Pollock (1910), p. 37 (emphasis added).

[51] If A only intended for C to be in a position to receive the money from B without needing to account to A for such receipt, a different mechanism could be invoked by A. A might simply: (i) authorize C to accept a conforming tender of payment from B on her behalf; and (ii) release C from the fiduciary duty that would usually arise in such agent–principal relations to account to A for such receipt. In such a case, though C would be empowered

that C would then be empowered to compel B at law to do so, A could offer to release B from his duty to tender payment to A[52] in exchange for B covenanting by way of a deed poll[53] that he will tender payment to C.[54] If B accepted A's offer and executed a deed poll with such covenant as stipulated in A's offer, the debt obligation between A and B would be discharged by mutual agreement. In its place would be a fresh obligation arising between B and C in which B was duty-bound to C (by reason of the covenant) to pay C £1,000.

Notwithstanding B's execution of the deed poll by which B covenanted to give C £1,000, C could still disclaim such gift[55] of money from B when tendered.[56] But failing such disclaimer, should B fail to perform his duty, C would then have the power to bring proceedings at law against B in respect of B's breach by reason of the deed that B had executed. Through this chain of acts by A, B and C, A would have novated her contract with B to C.[57]

---

to accept tender of payment from B, and such tender to A's duly authorized agent would certainly be a good tender, which, if accepted, would discharge B's duty to A, C would *not* have the power to bring proceedings against B for breach of that duty.

[52] If the consideration for the new agreement between A and B wherein A promised to release B from his obligations under the original agreement if B were to execute a deed in the form stipulated, covenanting to pay C, and B did so, the new contract would be validly formed. If C declined to accept payment by B under the covenant, as C would be entitled to do, so far as he was a mere donee, that obligation arising by way of covenant would not then be capable of being discharged by performance. But this would not lead to the frustration of the new agreement between A and B, since all that B was duty-bound to A to do under this new agreement was to execute the deed in favour of C, which B had performed in full.

[53] I.e. a deed poll which named B and C to be parties thereof. '[A] deed poll could always be sued on by any person with whom the covenant was made': R. F. Norton et al., *A Treatise on Deeds* (London: Sweet & Maxwell, 1906), p. 24. See, generally, R. J. Bullen, 'The Rights of Strangers to Contracts Under Seal' (1977) 6 *Adelaide L Rev* 119.

[54] It is possible for there to be a variation of the original agreement whereby B agrees to become duty-bound to a new promisee, C, in exchange for consideration furnished by C or under seal, but where A merely promises B not to invoke her power to bring proceedings at law against B for non-performance of his duties to her under the original agreement between them: see e.g. *Morris* v. *Baron & Co.* [1918] AC 1, *British and Beningtons Ltd* v. *North Western Cachar Tea Company Ltd* [1923] AC 48, 68–9 (Lord Sumner). But even such variation without discharge of the original agreement would still require the assent of the obligor to be duty-bound on the terms of the new contract.

[55] On the given facts, the deed was executed without any consideration from C. Consequently, B's covenant to pay C £1,000 would remain a promise to make a gift, albeit one enforceable at law.

[56] Such disclaimer of the gift would discharge the new contract as arose when B accepted A's offer by reason of frustration. That said, the law presumes that C would assent to such a gift unless he clearly manifested his intention to disclaim it.

[57] For an account of what novation entails, see *Linden Gardens Trust Ltd* v. *Lenesta Sludge Disposals Ltd* (1992) 30 Con LR 1, 13 (Staughton LJ).

A novation, therefore, extinguishes one of the jural relations between A and B (i.e. the claim-right/duty jural relation), leading to attendant changes to the other associated jural relations (i.e. the power/liability, privilege/no-right and the immunity/disability jural relations). At the same time, it creates a new claim-right/duty jural relation between B and C, leading to attendant changes to certain power/liability, privilege/no-right and immunity/disability jural relations between them as well.

To illustrate: prior to the novation, some salient jural relations between A, B and C would be as follows:[58]

1 B would be duty-bound to A (by reason of the loan of money given by A, which, when accepted by B, gave rise to the debt between them) to tender payment of £1,000 to A; and

2 Given 1, B would usually[59] be liable to A commencing proceedings at law before a court of competent jurisdiction to adjudicate any disputes which might arise between them over B's discharge of his duty in 1.

3 B would, however, be privileged against C not to tender payment of £1,000 to A *because* B is under no duty to C to do so;

4 Given 3, B would be immune to C commencing proceedings at law before a court of competent jurisdiction to adjudicate any disputes as might arise between B and C over B's carrying out of his duty *to A* to tender payment of £1,000 to A *because* B is under no duty to C to do so.

After the novation to C, however, the jural relations are different:

5 B is now duty-bound *to C* (by reason of the covenant by which B bound himself to C) to tender payment of £1,000 to C;

6 Given 5, B would now be liable *to C* commencing proceedings at law before a court of competent jurisdiction to adjudicate any disputes as might arise between them over B's discharge of his duty to C in 5.

7 However, B would now be privileged against *A* not to tender payment of £1,000 to C *because* B is no longer under any duty to A to do so;

8 Given 7, B would now be immune to A commencing proceedings at law before a court of competent jurisdiction to adjudicate any disputes as might arise between B and A over B's carrying out of his duty *to C* to

---

[58] There are other jural relations in play, but it suffices for the moment to just concentrate on how changes to a claim-right/duty jural relation affects one of the power/liability jural relations between the parties.

[59] Subject to any concerns as to limitation and/or formalities as would render breaches of the duty to be unenforceable.

tender payment of £1,000 to C *because* B is no longer under any duty to A to do so.

It would seem, therefore, as if A's place as obligee to the obligation between A and B arising under the *contract* between them had been taken by C. But C is obligee to B as regards B's duty to tender payment to C under a new and distinct obligation (arising in covenant), and not the original contractual obligation as between A and B. There is, therefore, no 'substitution' of C in place of A in respect of the *original* contract obligation. Instead, there has been an extinction of the original obligation, and its replacement with a new one. So if novation effects a transfer, it effects such transfer by substituting a new obligation (with a new obligee) in place of the old.

Crucially, we observe that such substitution of one obligation for another could not occur without the obligor's assent: not only must he assent to being released from the original obligation, he must also assent to becoming obligated under the *new* obligation which is to take the place of the original one, though of course, assent may be given in advance (as was the case in Example 3.3).[60]

### G   Invariability of Voluntarily Assumed Obligations Arising in Equity

As a general rule, equitable obligations are also not open to unilateral variation. This may be demonstrated by examining the central case of trust obligations, and considering how trust beneficiaries are sometimes said to have powers to vary them.

### (i)   'Varying' a Bare Trust by Bringing It to an End

The obligations of a bare trustee were defined in *Christie* v. *Ovington* as follows:[61]

> Who is a bare trustee is a question of general practical importance. Where there is a trustee whose trust is to convey, and the time has arrived for a conveyance by him, he is, I think, a bare trustee, whether considered in reference to the *Vendor and Purchaser Act*, 1874, s. 5, or in reference to the *Land Transfer Act* [1875], s. 48. Mr. Dart and Mr. Barber, in the 5th

---

[60] See also *Habibsons Bank Ltd* v. *Standard Chartered Bank (HK) Ltd* [2010] EWCA Civ 1335; [2011] QB 943, [22].

[61] (1875) 1 Ch D 279, 281.

edition of their Treatise on the Law of and Practice relating to Vendors and Purchasers of Real Estate, recently published [at p 517], have expressed their view that 'the Act does not define what is meant by a "bare trustee" in this and the preceding section; and the term is generally considered to be ambiguous; but it will probably be held to mean a trustee to whose office no duties were originally attached, or who, although such duties were originally attached to his office, would, on the requisition of his *cestuis que trust*, be compellable in equity to convey the estate to them, or by their direction, and has been requested by them so to convey it.' In my opinion the words 'has been requested by them so to convey it' are not an important or a necessary ingredient to a person being a bare trustee, but leaving out these words, I approve of the statement which I have read from their valuable work.

Consequently, one is a 'bare trustee' when one is compellable in equity to fully execute the trust by conveying the trust property as one's beneficiaries may direct, always remembering that a court in its equitable jurisdiction will only make such an order on terms that the trust beneficiary indemnify the trustee for any costs incurred by reason of such execution.[62]

In Hohfeldian terms, one is a bare trustee of trust property when one is obligated to the trust beneficiaries to fully execute the trust by conveying title to the trust property held on trust when the beneficiaries so direct. Like the secondary obligation to pay damages following a breach of a primary obligation at common law, this obligation is in present existence, and yet may not be performed in advance of such direction by the beneficiaries: it may only be performed *when* the demand is made. In Hohfeldian terms, then, this obligation to fully execute the bare trust on direction by the beneficiaries is a *liability*.[63]

This Hohfeldian liability to fully execute the bare trust on demand also entails an associated duty: it would be impossible for the bare trustee to fulfil his liability to fully execute the trust on demand unless he was simultaneously duty-bound to preserve the trust property *until* such a direction was given. A bare trustee, therefore, is always subject to a Hohfeldian *duty* to his beneficiaries to preserve the trust property,[64] until his beneficiaries invoke their Hohfeldian *power* to require him to fully execute his trust by conveying such title as he may have in the trust

---

[62] E.g. *Re Brockbank* [1948] Ch 206, 209.

[63] As to Hohfeldian liabilities, see Chapter 2, Section B.

[64] *Joseph Hayim Hayim v. Citibank NA* [1987] 1 AC 730, 748; cited with approval in *Parker-Tweedale v. Dunbar Bank Plc* [1991] Ch 12, 19.

property to their order.[65] And such hybrid duty-liability is part of the 'package deal' whenever one assents to take up the office of bare trustee.

It is also important to note what obligations a bare trustee is *not* subject to. As *Christie* v. *Ovington* explains, a bare trustee is *only* obligated in the manner described above: he is *not* obligated to his beneficiaries to do anything else. So if, in our example above, A had directed T to continue to act as bare trustee *for X instead of A*, such that X, but not A, would thereafter have the power to require T to fully execute the bare trust, T would be privileged to comply, or not, with such request.

---

EXAMPLE 3.5

T holds the legal title in 10,000 Black Co. Ltd ('BCL') shares. He constitutes himself bare trustee of his legal title in these shares for A's benefit. A, who is *sui juris*, accordingly acquires an equitable chose in action against T.

---

In Example 3.5, A has no power to require T to continue to hold his legal title on such terms. A may request T to do so, but T has no duty to A to comply. So in Example 3.5, in agreeing *only* to be a bare trustee for A's benefit, T would *not* have assented to A (or anyone else) being vested with any power of appointment – unlike T's position in Example 3.4.

Consequently, in Example 3.5, if A, as beneficiary of the bare trust, directed T to fully execute the bare trust by conveying his legal title in the shares to X, and T refused to do so, T would be in breach of his duty as bare trustee which he owed *to A*. There is nothing in A's status as beneficiary of this bare trust that allows A to unilaterally change the obligee (i.e. the beneficiary) to whom T is duty-bound.

---

[65] For discussion of the power/liability jural relations arising between trustees and their beneficiaries, see T. Cutts, 'The Nature of "Equitable Property": A Functional Analysis' (2012) 6 *Journal of Equity* 44. The proposition in this book is that a trust relationship *also* entails a claim-right/duty pertaining to preservation of the trust property in the interim, pending invocation by the beneficiaries of their power to require execution of the trust. Cf. J. E. Penner, 'The (True) Nature of a Beneficiary's Equitable Proprietary Interest Under a Trust' (2014) 27 *Canadian Journal of Law and Jurisprudence* 473. For further discussion of bare trusts, see P. Matthews, 'All About Bare Trusts: Part I' [2005] *Private Client Business* 266, and P. Matthews, 'All About Bare Trusts: Part II' [2005] *Private Client Business* 336.

*(ii)* *'Varying' a Special Trust by Invoking the Doctrine in* Saunders
v. Vautier *to Convert It to a Bare Trust*

Nor would the analysis be much different if T held trust property by way of a *special* and not a bare trust.[66]

Under English law, in general,[67] *sui juris* beneficiaries of a special trust who have been vested with and who hold between them the entirety of the beneficial interest in the trust property have the power under the

---

[66] Traditionally, 'a bare trustee ... is a mere passive repository for the beneficial owner, having no duties other than a duty to transfer the property to the beneficial owner or as [s]he directs. By contrast a trustee holding property on special trusts has active duties to perform, for example, in executing the trusts of a will or settlement, with administrative (and perhaps also dispositive) powers accompanying his active duties': Lewin (2015), para. 1-028; '[T]here is the *special* trust, where the active duties of the trustee go beyond the basic *Saunders* v. *Vautier* duty, but as a result of the trust terms themselves': Matthews, 'All About Bare Trusts: Part I', p. 268.

[67] The *Saunders* v. *Vautier* power to collapse a special trust into a bare trust may be unavailable as regards 'discretionary trusts' and 'unit trusts'. As to the former, see Jacob's Law of Trusts (2016), [23–15]. With regard to such discretionary trusts, given certain observations in *Gartside* v. *Inland Revenue Commissioners* [1968] AC 553, 605–6, and *Sainsbury* v. *Inland Revenue Commissioners* [1970] 1 Ch 712, 725, there is a view that, 'to say that as between all of them the objects enjoy beneficial ownership and therefore may, if all sui juris, invoke the rule in *Saunders* v. *Vautier*, is to envisage a group interest greater than the aggregate of individual interests by attribution to the whole of a character not possessed in any degree by any of its parts': *Jacob's Law of Trusts*, ibid. As each of the objects of a discretionary trust has only an entitlement that the trust be duly administered, including an entitlement that the trustee takes due consideration when exercising his discretionary power of appointment, it may be that the *Saunders* v. *Vautier* power may not be susceptible of being invoked by all extant objects of such power acting together. However, there is some English authority suggesting otherwise when the class of persons in whose favour the power might be invoked is closed: see e.g. *Re Smith (sub nom Public Trustee* v. *Aspinall)* [1928] 1 Ch 915, 918–19, following observations made in *Re Nelson* [1928] 1 Ch 920 (though reported in 1928, this decision was handed down in 1916); and *Re Beckett's Settlement* [1940] 1 Ch 279, 285. There is also some more recent Australian authority to similar effect: *Sir Moses Montefiore Jewish Home* v. *Howell & Co. (No. 7) Pty Ltd* [1984] NSWLR 406, 410–11; cited with approval in *CPT Custodian Pty Ltd* v. *Commissioner of State Revenue* [2005] HCA 53; (2005) 224 CLR 98; 221 ALR 196, [48]. This is also the position adopted in Lewin (2015), para. 24-016. Furthermore, it was held in an appeal from a striking-out application in *Orb A.R.L.* v. *Ruhan* [2015] EWHC 262 (Comm) that it was at least arguable that the *Saunders* v. *Vautier* power may be exercised by all extant objects even if the class was not completely closed where the trustee retained a discretion to select new objects to add to the class (at [118]). As for unit trusts, the High Court of Australia suggested in *CPT Custodian Pty Ltd* v. *Commissioner of State Revenue* (2005) 224 CLR 98; 221 ALR 196 (at [46]) that *Saunders* v. *Vautier* may also be unavailable to the holders of the units in the trust. It has been suggested that, at least while the unit trust is a going concern, since 'a unit trust deed is a contract, a party cannot terminate a unit trust unilaterally unless there is provision in it that empowers such a party to do so. The right of termination under *Saunders* v. *Vautier* is a rule of gift, not a

doctrine of *Saunders* v. *Vautier*[68] to collapse that special trust into a bare trust in favour of the beneficiaries identified by the terms of the special trust. As the High Court of Australia has recognized:[69]

> there is force for Anglo-American law in the statement that the rule in *Saunders* v. *Vautier* gives the beneficiaries a Hohfeldian 'power' which correlates to a 'liability' on the part of the trustees, rather than a 'right' correlative to a 'duty'.

Accordingly, this *liability* to become a bare trustee when the doctrine of *Saunders* v. *Vautier* is validly invoked is part of the 'package deal' whenever one assents to be a trustee under a special trust, and as bare trustee, one is liable to come under a duty to fully execute such bare trust should the beneficiaries thereof direct. But even under the doctrine of *Saunders* v. *Vautier*, unless the terms of the trust provide for it, the beneficiaries of a special trust have no power to require their trustees to do anything more.

---

EXAMPLE 3.6

Suppose T holds the legal title in 10,000 BCL shares for $A_L$ for her life, and $A_R$ as remainderman. T is therefore trustee for $A_L$ and $A_R$ under a special trust. Both $A_L$ and $A_R$ are *sui juris*, and together they hold the entirety of the beneficial interest in the legal title in the shares held on trust for their benefit by T.

---

Given the situation described in Example 3.6, $A_L$ and $A_R$ may jointly invoke the doctrine of *Saunders* v. *Vautier* to collapse the special trust into a bare trust.[70] $A_L$ and $A_R$ may then jointly direct T to convey his legal title in the 10,000 BCL shares to X to hold as trustee for the benefit of Y's life, and thereafter, for the benefit of Z. But the doctrine of *Saunders* v. *Vautier* invests no power in $A_L$ and $A_R$ to require T to *continue* to hold on the terms of the special trust, but for Y for his life, and for Z as remainderman. Thus, T's duties as special trustee may not be changed in such manner without his assent.

---

rule of contract. [Hence] it should not be applicable to unit trusts': K. F. Sin, *The Legal Nature of the Unit Trust* (Oxford: Clarendon Press, 1997), p. 183.

[68] (1841) 4 Beav 115.

[69] *CPT Custodian Pty Ltd* v. *Commissioner of State Revenue* (2005) 224 CLR 98; 221 ALR 196, [44].

[70] Indeed, if $A_L$ were to equitably assign the benefit of her life interest to $A_R$, it would open to $A_R$, alone, to collapse the special trust to a bare trust and, thereafter, require its full execution to $A_R$'s sole order: *Anson* v. *Potter* (1879) 13 Ch D 141.

Though the *Saunders* v. *Vautier* doctrine and the nature of the obligations of a bare trustee appear to suggest that equity is more amenable to the idea that the obligees to such trust obligations may be unilaterally changed without the need for assent by the trustees who owe those obligations, the better analysis is that these are cases where the said trustees had assented in advance to being liable in these ways, *but no more*. There is no *general* power in the beneficiaries of a trust to require their trustees to do anything more than bring a bare or special trust to an end. These powers are, therefore, analogous with A's power against B in Example 3.1 to effect a discharge by accepting payment from B. Just as A in that example had the power to bring the contract to an end, A in Example 3.5 and $A_L$ and $A_R$ in Example 3.6 have analogous powers to bring their respective bare and special trusts to an end.

Furthermore, we may note that T's position in Example 3.6 is distinct from T's position in Example 3.4. In Example 3.6, T did *not* agree to become trustee of a trust in which anyone had a power of appointment analogous to that which was set out in Example 3.4. Consequently, the only power which $A_L$ and $A_R$ are allowed as a matter of the general law is the *Saunders* v. *Vautier* power. But that is not the same kind of power as the expressly stipulated one in Example 3.4.

In Example 3.6, if $A_L$ and $A_R$ jointly invoked the *Saunders* v. *Vautier* power and required T to collapse the special trust over the BCL shares to a bare trust for their benefit, and then, as beneficiaries of that bare trust, directed T to fully execute it by conveying his legal title in the shares to X, if T refused to do so, T would have breached his duties to $A_L$ *and* $A_R$: T would *not* be in breach of any duty to X for failing to comply with $A_L$'s and $A_R$'s direction. All that the *Saunders* v. *Vautier* doctrine allows is for a special trust to be folded into a bare trust for the *same* beneficiaries, who may then require that bare trust to be fully executed. So there is nothing within the *Saunders* v. *Vautier* doctrine that would allow $A_L$ and $A_R$ to unilaterally cause T to become duty-bound to anyone other than themselves.

### (iii)  *'Varying' a Trust by Acquiescing to a Breach of Trust*

The beneficiaries of a trust have a further power: they may waive breaches of trust by their trustee. As Harris pointed out:[71]

---

[71]  Harris (1975), pp. 2–3.

The beneficiaries, if all *sui juris*, can dissolve a trust-settlement. They cannot, however, direct the trustees how to administer the trust so long as they allow the settlement to continue: (*In Re Brockbank*[72] ...). But, since no beneficiary can complain of a breach of trust to which he has expressly consented, they can collectively authorise the trustees to administer the trusts in a way not permitted by the trust instrument[73].

But the beneficiaries' power to 'vary' the trusts by acquiescing in a breach of trust arises only in a manner of speaking.

Absent an express grant of a suitably worded power of appointment in the trust beneficiaries, and unless some such power be granted to the beneficiaries by, say, statute, trust beneficiaries simply have no power against their trustees to unilaterally require their trustees to continue to hold the trust property on the same trust and yet act for the benefit of persons not specified as beneficiaries under the terms of that trust. Such a demand plainly goes beyond the *Saunders* v. *Vautier* power or the power of beneficiaries of a bare trust to require its complete execution. Indeed, compliance with such a demand would entail the trustees having *breached* their duties under the terms of that trust. Leaving aside statutory provision otherwise, the trustees *cannot* be obligated to comply with such a demand unless the trust provides for it, in which case compliance would no longer be a breach of their trust duties. But without such provision in the trust for the trustees to so act, the trustees cannot be obligated to so act since it would be an oxymoron to assert that they were obligated to act in *breach* of their trust duties.

The proposition that trust beneficiaries might unilaterally impose a new trust obligation (with new trust beneficiaries) on their trustees was specifically rejected by the Court of Appeal in *Morley* v. *Moore*:[74]

It is true that if called upon to do so the assured is obliged to sue or to allow the insurance company to sue in respect of the particular loss that

---

[72] *Re Brockbank* [1948] Ch 206.

[73] As authority, Harris cites *Re Kolb's Will Trusts* [1962] Ch 531, 540 (Cross J, whose decision was appealed against, but the appeal was compromised: (1962) 106 SJ 669); and *Re Druce's Settlement Trusts* [1962] 1 WLR 363, 369 (Russell J).

[74] [1936] 2 KB 359, 366 (Sir Boyd Merriman P, with whom Scott LJ agreed). *Morley* was a case of subrogation, but it has been recognized that subrogation and equitable assignment are closely affiliated concepts: *Hobbs* v. *Marlowe* [1978] AC 16, 39 (Lord Diplock). *Morley* was cited with approval and applied by Cairns LJ in *Hobbs* v. *Marlowe* [1978] AC 16, 24; aff'd on appeal to the House of Lords, which also held that *Morley* v. *Moore* was correctly decided: *Hobbs* v. *Marlowe*, 28–39 (Lord Diplock, with whom Lord Elwyn-Jones LC, Viscount Dilhorne, Lord Simon of Glaisdale and Lord Salmon agreed).

they have paid, and if the assured recovers it he is obliged to hand that sum over to the insurance company because it is impressed with a trust on their behalf; but putting that trust at its highest I am unable to understand how it can be said that the cestui que trust, that is the insurance company, by taking a particular course, which is not warranted by any independent contract, and by disclaiming their own right as a cestui que trust, can impose upon the assured as another cestui que trust the very person from whom at common law he is entitled to recover as damages that which is said to be the subject of the trust.

In similar vein, Vaisey J held in *Re Brockbank* that the beneficiaries of a trust are empowered to 'put an end to the trust if they like; nobody doubts that; but they are not entitled ... to arrogate to themselves a power which the court itself disclaims possession'.[75] Equity does not encroach on the autonomy of equitable obligors such as T who have assented to the office of trustee and thus have assented to the obligations arising by taking such office: there is no general rule in equity vesting a power in anyone enabling them to impose a new trust on the trustee without his assent.

This is corroborated by the fact that the courts have no inherent power to effect a variation of the terms of a trust: such power has had to be granted to it by statute.[76] First, as Farwell J said in *Re Walker*: 'I decline to accept any suggestion that the court has an inherent jurisdiction to alter a

---

[75] *Re Brockbank* [1948] Ch 206, 210. The specific holding in that case was legislatively overruled with effect from 1 January 1997 when s. 19 of the Trusts of Land and Appointment of Trustees Act 1996 came into force. See also *Stephenson (Inspector of Taxes) v. Barclays Bank Trust Co. Ltd* [1975] 1 WLR 882, 889; *Re Higginbottom* [1892] 3 Ch 132; and Lord Eldon LC's observations in *Goodson v. Ellison* (1826) 3 Russ 583, 593–4. However, it has been suggested, *obiter*, that trustees holding company shares on trust are duty-bound to vote at General Meetings of the company as their beneficiaries wish, and that if the beneficiaries could not come to an agreement as to how the trustees were to vote, the court could compel the trustee to vote as it thought proper: *Butt v. Kelson* [1952] Ch 197, 207. That proposition was doubted and not followed by Upjohn J in *Re George Whichelow Ltd* [1954] 1 WLR 5, 8, Further, the observations in *Butt v. Kelson* appear to be inconsistent with Lord Templeman's observations in *Joseph Hayim Hayim v. Citibank NA* [1987] 1 AC 730, 748.

[76] Given the court's lack of any inherent jurisdiction to do so, various statutes have empowered the courts to vary the terms of trusts in various circumstances. Prior to the enactment of the Variation of Trusts Act 1958 in response to the decision of the House of Lords in *Chapman v. Chapman* [1954] AC 429, more limited statutory powers to sanction variations to trusts had previously been vested in the courts pursuant to s. 57 of the Trustee Act 1925 (on application by the trustees or any party having a beneficial interest under the trust: s. 57(3)), and s. 64 of the Settled Land Act 1925. The effects of these two provisions and the degree to which they derogate from the proposition that the courts are not to rewrite trusts are discussed in D. Waters, 'The Variation of Trusts' (1960) 13 *Current Legal Problems* 36.

man's will because it thinks it beneficial. It seems to me that is quite impossible.'[77]

Secondly, although Lord Simonds LC identified four exceptions to the above statement in his speech in *Chapman* v. *Chapman*, he recognized that those exceptions did not extend so far as to entrench in the court any inherent jurisdiction to approve the variation of the terms of a trust where there was no dispute between the beneficiaries to the trust as to the manner by which the trustees were to administer the trust, but where they desired the beneficial interests thereunder to be rearranged with binding effect on infant beneficiaries as well as unborn persons who would be affected by such rearrangement.[78] In particular, Lord Simonds LC said:[79]

> It is the function of the court to execute a trust, to see that the trustees do their duty and to protect them if they do it, to direct them if they are in doubt and, if they do wrong, to penalize them. *It is not the function of the court to alter a trust because alteration is thought to be advantageous to an infant beneficiary.*

Certainly, if the trustees complied with such request, and if such request amounted to acquiescence by the trust beneficiaries to the resultant breach of trust, the trustees would have a prima facie defence should the acquiescing beneficiaries subsequently bring judicial proceedings against them.[80] But to say that the trustees have a defence in such circumstances is not also to say that they are duty-bound to act in such a way as would give rise to such defence. Consequently, leaving aside statutory innovations such as those in the Variation of Trusts Act, a trustee is privileged to decline to comply with requests to commit breaches of trust. No trustee is obligated to so act, though he may promise to so act (and such promise may well be binding in equity on

---

[77]  *Re Walker* [1901] 1 Ch 879, 885.

[78]  *Chapman* v. *Chapman* [1954] AC 429, 445.

[79]  Ibid., at 446. Lord Morton of Henryton agreed (at 461–2), and also concluded that the inherent power of the court to vary the terms of a trust were limited to those identified by the Lord Chancellor. Lord Asquith of Bishopstone agreed with Lord Morton. The Law Reform Committee observed that the position following *Chapman* v. *Chapman* was unsatisfactory: Law Reform Committee, *Sixth Report (Court's Power to Sanction Variation of Trusts)* (Cmnd 310, 1957), para. 12.

[80]  *Walker* v. *Symonds* (1818) 3 Swan 1, 64 (Lord Eldon LC); cited with approval in *Re Pauling's Settlement Trusts* [1962] 1 WLR 86, 107 (aff'd: *Re Pauling's Settlement Trusts* [1964] 1 Ch 303).

him, if supported by consideration). And if so, the parallel with novation in the preceding section becomes rather striking.

Given the facts in Example 3.5, if A proposed to T that he should convert the shares into money, and acquire other shares in substitution to be held on trust for A and X, though A would be acquiescing in a breach of T's duties as bare trustee, since such trust gave T no powers of investment, if T refused to comply with A's proposal, T would breach no duty owed to A. And, *a fortiori*, T would breach no duty to X either.

## H    The Rules at Law and in Equity

The rules at law and in equity regarding the variability of legal and equitable obligations are essentially the same. Unless otherwise agreed, the obligee to voluntarily assumed obligations arising from contract or trust has no power as against the obligor to unilaterally vary the obligor's duty to his obligee under that contract or trust. Given the absence of any power to effect a unilateral change, the obligee can only effect changes to her existing claim-right/duty jural relationship with her obligor with the assent of the obligor. Since every attempt to substitute new obligees for the existing obligees entails a substitution of new obligations in place of the old, it follows that there is no general rule, at law or in equity, which permits substitution of obligees without the obligor's assent.

The need for assent is essential because no one may be made duty-bound to do any*thing* and/or be rendered duty-bound to any*one* without their assent to the same, at least so far as one is concerned with voluntarily assumed obligations. To allow such unilateral imposition of duties would be an act of sovereignty over another, and would, in essence, change the basis or reason by which the duties arising from such obligation are given judicial recognition.

So far as one is concerned with voluntarily assumed obligations (as arise at common law from debt, covenant or contract, and in equity, the trust, to give some examples) the reason why the obligors to such obligations are held to them is, at least in part, because they were voluntarily undertaken by such obligors. It is no imposition on their personal autonomy to hold them to that which they had voluntarily undertaken.

If equitable assignment of a chose in action operated to extinguish the original obligation which an obligor had voluntarily undertaken, only to subject that obligor to a *new* obligation which he had *not* voluntarily undertaken, recognition of the latter obligation could no longer be justified on grounds of the obligor's voluntary undertaking in respect of the original obligation. This is not to say that no other justification would be possible – just that a fresh one would be required. And the normative challenge which proponents of the view that equitable assignments cause the obligor to be subjected to a new obligation in place of the old *without* his assent is, accordingly, to identify what such alternative justification might be, and then to show why that alternative justification might justifiably be accorded greater weight as to override concerns pertaining to preservation of the obligor's personal autonomy.

It is contended that such further justification is unnecessary so far as English law is concerned because equitable assignments in English law do *not* operate by changing the obligor's original obligation as owed to the obligee. Though the court of Chancery could have created an equitable doctrine that achieved *precisely* the same effects as a novation would have done, only without requiring the assent of the obligor, it did not do so. Instead, as the following chapter will show, it developed a *sui generis* institution which had the characteristics of a bare trust, coupled with an extended conception of agency. The effect of this *sui generis* institution was to change some of the jural relations between the obligee-assignor and her assignee, and those between the obligor and the assignee, whilst leaving the suite of jural relations between obligor and obligee-assignor *entirely* intact. The genius of equity, therefore, was its realization that one could *simulate* a transfer of control over the claim-rights and powers of an obligee-assignor as against her obligor *without* requiring their extinction and substitution with new claim-rights and powers between the obligor and the obligee-assignor's 'replacement'. Hence,[81] '[t]he informing idea behind equitable assignment ... is not that we do this at common law, and that in equity. It is rather that we *don't* do this at common law, and we *pretend* to do it in equity.'

---

[81] B. McFarlane, 'Understanding Equitable Estoppel: From Metaphors to Better Laws' (2013) 66 *Current Legal Problems* 267, 279 (emphasis in original).

# 4

# Different Models of Equitable Assignment

The goals in this chapter are as follows:

1 Having set out the basic premise that voluntarily assumed obligations, once undertaken, are invariable without the obligor's assent, this chapter will outline the two prevailing models of equitable assignment.
2 It will then note the deficiencies in each of the prevailing models.
3 Lastly, it will set out a composite model of equitable assignment which avoids those deficiencies.

## A Two Prevailing Models

There are currently two schools of thought on equitable assignments:[1] a 'substitutive transfer' model, and a 'partial' trust model.[2]

### (i) Substitutive Transfer Model

There is a view that equitable assignment extinguishes the claim-right/ duty jural relation between the assignor and the obligor, and replaces it with an 'equivalent' claim-right/duty jural relation between the assignee

---

[1] There are others. Holmes took equitable assignment to operate by analogy with the law of succession: Holmes (1968), chapters 11 and 12; whereas Dean Ames argued that equitable assignment was an extension of the 'power of attorney' reasoning used by the common law: Ames (1887), p. 6; Ames (1890), a later, revised version of which may be found in Ames (1909): the relevant pages are at 582–4. Ames' views appear to have been anticipated by Professor Holland, who noted the similarity between the operation of equitable assignment with the Roman conception of 'cessio actionum': T. E. Holland, *The Elements of Jurisprudence* (13th edn, Oxford: Clarendon Press, 1924), pp. 314–15, repeating a point first made in 1880 in the first edition of this work, at pp. 205–6. Professor Bridge has also recently suggested that equitable assignment rests on the implication of an appropriate contractual term in the chose assigned: Bridge (2016). But as explained in Chapter 3, n. 45, that view is difficult.

[2] 'Partial', because it appears to apply only to equitable assignments of *legal* choses in action.

and the obligor. In Professor Corbin's words, the effect of an equitable assignment is as follows:[3]

> Let us determine first what is meant by the assignment of a right. . . . Let us suppose that A has a right that B shall pay him $100. It is established law that A has power to assign this right to C. It is also established law that the assignment is operative without the consent of B. After the assignment B is under the same[4] duty as before; that is, he must still pay $100 at the same time and place specified. The correlative *right*, however, is no longer in A; it is in C. . . .
>
> If the foregoing is correct, an assignment of an existing right is an act of the possessor of that right which operates to extinguish the right of the assignor and to create an exactly similar right in the assignee. This definition is in terms of legal operation – of the effect of the assignor's act upon the action of organized society.

Similar views eschewing Hohfeldian language may be found in other secondary literature.[5] For example, in Professor Bridge's account of what happens when a debt (i.e. a legal chose) is assigned:[6]

> In this example, [B] is the debtor, [A] the assignor and C the assignee. Assignment means that [A] may *transfer* the debt, owed by [B], to C without obtaining the prior permission of [B]; C may then call upon [B] to pay him instead of [A]; and C may then give [B] a good discharge for payment of the debt initially owed to [A]. The effect of assignment is to *transfer* [A's] payment entitlement to C. In consequence, a relationship of debtor and creditor between [B] and C is *substituted* for the earlier debt relationship between [B] and [A]. The debt owed previously by [B] to [A] has been transferred by [A] to C in the same way as [A] might have sold to C an antique clock or a second-hand car earlier acquired from [B].

No distinction is made between equitable or statutory assignments in this passage. If these statements are taken to apply to equitable assignments, they would seem to posit that an equitable assignment of a chose in action operates in an *equivalent* manner to that which arises when legal title to tangible personalty is transferred. Accordingly, Bridge's hypothesis is that, like transfers of legal title to tangible personalty,

---

[3] Corbin (1926), pp. 208–9 (emphasis in original).

[4] The mis-step in Corbin's reasoning occurs here. As explained in Chapter 3, a change in the identity of the obligee to an duty is a change in that duty: it is *not* the 'same' duty at all.

[5] See also: J. G. Starke, *Assignments of Choses in Action in Australia*, (Sydney: Butterworths, 1972); Tudsbery (1912), p. 1.

[6] M. G. Bridge, *Personal Property Law* (Clarendon Law Series, ed., 4th edn, Oxford: Oxford University Press, 2014), p. 231 (emphasis added).

equitable assignment of a chose in action entails extinction of the assignor's entitlements against the obligor to that chose coupled with a regrant by operation of law to the assignee of the assignor's entitlements.

Nor is the usage of 'transfer' in an extinctive sense a purely academic usage. The language of 'transfer' as entailing some sense of extinction and regrant has certainly been used in the courts. For example, in *Co-operative Group Ltd* v. *Birse Developments Ltd*, Stuart-Smith J concluded that 'assignments and declarations of trust are different legal creatures, not least because an assignment transfers the legal and beneficial interest, but a trust does not'.[7] Given that a trust cannot operate by means of extinction and regrant, by contrasting assignment and trust in this manner Stuart-Smith J might be taken to have suggested that the former entails some form of extinction and regrant, although the latter does not.

Though attractive, not least on account of its apparent simplicity, when scrutinized more minutely, cracks begin to show in the hypothesis that the effects of an equitable assignment of a chose in action, and the effects of a conveyance of legal title to tangible property are *equivalent* to each other. This may be shown by Example 4.1.

---

**EXAMPLE 4.1**

B owns a copy of Bridge's *Personal Property Law* (the 'Book'). B hands it over to A, making it clear that he is giving and not lending it to A by saying, 'Here, take this. This Book is yours.' This transaction is witnessed by X who happens to be in the room.

---

As explained in Chapter 3,[8] the obligation arising from the tort of conversion as applied to the use and enjoyment of this Book may most appropriately be set out in the following form:

- All persons who do not hold the legal title to the Book
- are duty-bound to such person who holds the legal title to the Book
- to do Φ, where 'Φ' means 'the act of not converting the Book to his or her own use'.

---

[7] [2014] EWHC 530 (TCC), [2014] BLR 359, [88]. See also *Burton* v. *Camden London Borough Council* [2000] 2 AC 399, 408 (Lord Millett).
[8] Chapter 3, Section E.

Before the Book was gifted to A, X (being a person who did not hold the legal title to the Book at that point in time) was duty-bound to B (being such person who held the legal title to the Book at that time) to do Φ. It would also be accurate to say that A (being a person who did not hold the legal title to the Book at that point in time) was also duty-bound to B (being such person who held the legal title to the Book at that point in time) to do Φ. Conversely, it would also be accurate (if odd) to say that B (as holder of the legal title to the Book at that point in time), was *not* duty-bound to either A or X to do Φ.

But following the gift to A, X (still being a person who did not hold the legal title to the Book at that later point in time) would continue to be duty-bound to do Φ, though X would then be so duty-bound to *A*, as A had become owner of the legal title to the Book in place of B at that later point in time.

B's gift of the Book to A seems to have unilaterally varied X's claim-right/ duty jural relation arising in connection with the tort of conversion. But as explained in Chapter 3, this is illusory. The obligee to whom X is duty-bound is unchanged because X had always been (and remains) duty-bound to whomsoever holds the legal title to the Book. Consequently, B's action in divesting himself of his legal title in the Book has not changed X's duty: X is *still* duty-bound to such person as holds the legal title to the Book.

What, then, of A?

Following the gift to A, A would no longer be duty-bound to B to do Φ. What is more, X and B, as non-holders of the legal title to the Book, are now duty-bound to A as holder of the legal title to the Book, to Φ. So it seems that A's jural relations have been changed by B's actions. A's duty to B not to convert the Book to her own use has been eliminated, and A now has claim-rights against B and X that they not convert the Book to their use which A did not previously have. But these changes to A's jural relations with B and X are not achieved without assent by A.

English law recognizes that gifts may be disclaimed by donees: 'A person cannot be compelled to take what he does not desire to accept.'[9] Therefore, A's jural relations with B and X in respect of the tort of conversion as applied to the Book are contingent on A's assent to the gift. Though such assent may be presumed,[10] A may overturn that presumption by clearly disclaiming the gift once she comes to know

---

[9] *Halsbury's Laws* (5th edn, 2014), vol. 52, para. 250, and authorities cited therein.

[10] 'It was settled as long ago as the time of Lord Coke that the acceptance of a gift is to be presumed until his dissent is signified, even though the donee is not aware of the gift': *London and County Banking Co. Ltd* v. *London and River Plate Bank* (1888) 21 QBD 535,

of it.[12] Once this power to disclaim gifts is taken into account, we see that the change in A's jural relations with B and X by reason of A being vested with the legal title in the Book is contingent on A not invoking this power: the change to A's jural relations with B and X in connection with the legal title to the Book will only occur on A's sufferance. There is, accordingly, no *unilateral* change to A's jural relations, imposed without any concern as to A's preferences at all.

The above may be contrasted with what transpires when a chose in action is equitably assigned.

---

**EXAMPLE 4.2**

A has rented B her vintage car (the 'Car') for two years, and the rental agreement expressly provides that B is to pay a rental fee of '£200 per month to A'.

Two weeks later, A sells the Car to C. C agrees to take the legal title to the Car subject to the rental agreement with B. A also equitably assigns the benefit of her rental agreement with B to C. The assignment is effected orally and is not reduced into writing.[11]

B is informed of the equitable assignment, and B is also told that he should tender future payments of the monthly rental fee to C and not to A.

---

From Example 4.2, we may say that the obligations arising from the rental contract entail the following:

- B, having accepted A's offer of the rental agreement for the use and possession of the Car,
- is duty-bound to A, being the person who made the offer of the rental agreement for the use and possession of the Car which was accepted by B,
- inter alia,[13] to do Φ, where 'Φ' means 'the act of paying a monthly rental of £200, to A'.[14]

---

541. See also *Butler and Baker's Case* (1591) 3 Co Rep 25a, 26b–27a; *Thompson* v. *Leach* (1692) 2 Vent 198, 203; *Siggers* v. *Evans* (1855) 5 El & Bl 367 380–1; and *Standing* v. *Bowring* (1855) 31 Ch D 282, 290.

[11] LPA1925, s. 53(1)(c) formalities do not apply to equitable assignments of a legal chose in action. And since there is no written assignment, the effects mandated by LPA1925, s. 136 (1) do not apply either.

[12] *Standing* v. *Bowring* (n. 10), 288; *Mallott* v. *Wilson* [1903] 2 Ch 494, 501.

[13] There are probably other implicit duties, e.g. a duty to keep the car in reasonable repair, and a duty to return the car to A in roughly the same condition as when B received it at the end of the rental period (fair wear and tear excepted).

[14] Though the contract made no express mention as to whom rental was to be paid, by construction we may infer payment is to be tendered to A.

In addition, we may also say that B was *not* duty-bound to C to do Φ (at least to begin with).

Following the equitable assignment to C, if B had become duty-bound thereby to C to do Φ, that would mean the obligee to whom B was duty-bound had changed. As explained in Chapter 3, both the specification of what an obligor is obligated to do, and to whom he is obligated, are necessary components for there to be a private law obligation recognized at law or in equity. Since the specification of the obligee to whom the obligor is obligated is part and parcel of the specification of the obligation, there is *still* a change to the obligation for which it would seem B's assent should be obtained for it to be effective, and such assent is not to be presumed from the fact of notice, since the giving of notice is still a unilateral act.

In Example 4.1, no one had a jural relation with the Book since it is an inanimate thing without legal personality. One may have jural relations with other legal persons *in respect of* the Book (or more accurately, 'in respect of' the legal title to the Book), but that is something quite different. In contrast, in Example 4.2, though A might, loosely speaking, be said to 'own' the 'obligation' owed to her by B just as A 'owned' the Book following B's gift of the Book to her, we must not forget that the obligation 'owned' by A in Example 4.2 is really A's jural relation with B.

We cannot speak of the obligation 'owned' by A in Example 4.2 without recognizing that it is an obligation by which B is obligated to *A* since the obligation arose by reason of A (and not anyone else) having provided the consideration for B's promise to pay the monthly rental, and it being *A* (and not anyone else) that B assented to be obligated to. So if the effect of an equitable assignment of the chose in action arising from that obligation was to *modify* that obligation, B's assent must be sought for such modification to be effective. Since equitable assignments are recognized to be perfectly effective without such assent, it must follow that equitable assignments do *not* entail such modification.

No comparable concern arises with the conveyance of the legal title to the Book. This is because the Book is not an obligor owing duties to A. Since the Book has no legal personality, it is axiomatic that it cannot be duty-bound to A. So given the essentially different jural relations between Examples 4.2 and 4.1, though the two cases may well appear to be analogous in a general sense, it goes too far to suggest that the operations of equitable assignment of A's chose in action against B and a conveyance of A's legal title in the Book, following B's gift of the same to her, are equivalents.

Though, in a general sense, it may be helpful to draw comparisons between a conveyance of legal title to tangible personalty, and an equitable assignment of the benefit of a contract, we must be careful not to draw more from such comparisons than is useful given that we are comparing apples with oranges. As demonstrated above, the similarities between the conveyance of legal title to a tangible thing such as a book that has no legal personality, and the 'transfer' that is effected by an equitable assignment of the benefit of a chose in action arising out of duties owed by one legal person to another, can easily be overstated since the two processes relate to fundamentally non-equivalent sets of jural relations. We should not, therefore, be so quick to assume that the mechanisms in play when legal title in tangible personalty is conveyed are also those that apply when intangible personalty is equitably assigned.

Consequently, a different model of equitable assignment may be preferred: one which does *not* entail such 'substitutive transfer', but which leaves the claim-right/duty jural relation between obligor and obligee-assignor intact. This has led to what may be termed a 'partial' trust model of equitable assignment which analyses equitable assignments as involving a trust, at least in respect of *legal* choses in action.

### (ii) 'Partial' Trust Model

One alternative view conceives equitable assignments as entailing some form of trust, at least when legal choses are equitably assigned. This may be termed a 'partial' trust model, since its proponents restrict it to assignments of legal choses in action.

Authority for the proposition that equitable assignments of a legal chose in action entail the constitution of a trust is not hard to find. For example, in *Gorringe* v. *Irwell India Rubber and Gutta Percha Works*,[15] Fry LJ observed that by writing to the appellants that they would henceforth hold certain sums for the appellants' benefit until their indebtedness to the appellants was extinguished, the respondents had made themselves, 'trustee of the debt for the Appellants, and therefore it is equivalent to an equitable assignment'.[16]

Understanding equitable assignments of a legal chose in action as entailing some form of trust is inherently irreconcilable with the substitutive transfer model because the trust conception of equitable

---

[15] (1886) 34 Ch D 128.
[16] (1886) 34 Ch D 128, 136.

assignment does not entail any extinction or regrant of the claim-rights or any of the associated jural relations arising between the obligee-assignor and the obligor to the chose. Instead, it entails encumbering the obligee-assignor's powers associated with those claim-rights, with the result that the obligee-assignor becomes duty-bound to the assignee as to their exercise. On the trust model, the obligee-assignor loses her privilege against her assignee to invoke her powers against the obligor as she pleases. But importantly, the obligee-assignor will retain her privilege against her obligor to invoke those self-same powers.

To illustrate the difference between the trust and the substitutive models of equitable assignment, it is helpful to consider Example 4.3.

---

EXAMPLE 4.3

A lends B £10,000 to be repaid after twelve months have elapsed. One month later, A equitably assigns the benefit of B's loan to C.

---

On the substitutive transfer model of equitable assignment, A's equitable assignment to C would extinguish the creditor–debtor relationship between A and B, and replace it with an equivalent creditor–debtor relationship between C and B. B would then owe no duties to A as debtor, following the assignment, but would be indebted instead to C.

But conceived of in terms of a trust, A's equitable assignment to C would *not* extinguish the creditor–debtor relationship between herself and B. Instead, A would have created a new equitable relationship where A would be duty-bound to C to invoke her entitlements against B as though A had constituted herself trustee of the benefit of her legal chose against B for C's benefit.

On this model, C does not take A's place in the debtor–creditor relationship with B. A *remains* B's creditor, precisely as she had been before her equitable assignment of the debt to C; C remains a stranger to the debtor–creditor relationship between A and B; and no direct cause of action in debt arises between B and C.[17] Consequently, A is still empowered to bring proceedings at law against B should disputes arise over B's discharge of his common law obligations which are still

---

[17] See *M. H. Smith (Plant Hire) Ltd* v. *D. L. Mainwaring (t/a Inshore)* [1986] 2 Lloyd's Rep 244, 246 (Kerr LJ).

owed to A,[18] though A is herself subject to equitable obligations to C as to whether, and when, she is to invoke such power.[19] Furthermore, as noted above, although A would have thereby lost her privilege as against C to invoke her powers against B as she pleased, A would still be privileged against B to invoke those powers: B would still have no right against A to require A to invoke or to refrain from invoking those powers against him.

One advantage of the trust model over the substitutive transfer model is, since the debtor–creditor jural relations between A and B are unchanged by A's equitable assignment to C so far as such assignment is conceived as operating in the manner of a trust, there is no need to obtain B's assent to effect any changes to those jural relations as they would not have been changed at all: the state of affairs as between A and B (though not as between A and C, or B and C) would have remained exactly the same.[20]

Next: the effect of A allowing herself to become duty-bound to C as to her invocation of her powers against B will mean that C will have acquired, albeit indirectly, the ability to affect B's jural relations *through* A (since B would have had an immunity to C affecting those jural relations prior to A's creation of such duty). However, the case law tells us that such a change to A's claim-right/duty jural relations with third parties like C which might indirectly have an effect on B's immunity/disability jural relations with such third parties is, in effect, presumed to have been assented to by B, unless contrary provision had been made.[21]

---

[18] 'The only person who can enforce a right is the right-holder, and persons who suffer loss because of the infringement of someone else's right do not have standing to sue': Stevens (2007), p. 173.

[19] See e.g. *Bexhill UK Ltd* v. *Razzaq* [2012] EWCA Civ 1376; *Kapoor* v. *National Westminster Bank Plc* [2011] EWCA Civ 68, [2012] 1 All ER 1201; *Three Rivers District Council* v. *Governor and Company of the Bank of England* [1996] QB 292.

[20] Indeed, this provides an explanation as to why notice is not a constitutive requirement for an equitable assignment to be effectively made: just as with the constitution of a trust in favour of trust beneficiaries, the trust is validly constituted without need for any prior notification to the intended beneficiaries.

[21] This was implicitly recognized by the Court of Appeal in *Barbados Trust Company Ltd* v. *Bank of Zambia* [2007] EWCA Civ 148; [2007] 1 Lloyd's Rep 495, [30]–[43]. In that case, by recognizing that an appropriately worded 'anti-trusts' clause could preclude an obligee from validly constituting a trust over the benefit of an obligation owed to it, the Court of Appeal must be taken to have accepted that by *not* making such a provision, the obligor would be taken to have assented to such a possibility.

Most proponents of the trust model of equitable assignment suggest it only applies to equitable assignments of *legal* choses in action. For example, *Snell's Equity* distinguishes between instances where the whole of an equitable chose has been equitably assigned to an assignee, and cases where the assignment leaves some interest outstanding, as when there is an equitable assignment of part of a chose (whether legal or equitable), or in an equitable assignment of a legal chose, 'for in the latter case, even if the whole chose is assigned, the original creditor still owns the chose in law, holding it in trust for the assignee'.[22] However, where the whole of an equitable chose has been equitably assigned, 'equity has always permitted [the assignee of the equitable chose] to sue [the obligor to the chose assigned] in his own name without joining the original creditor [i.e. the equitable assignor]',[23] and 'the chose existed only in equity, and so equity was free to hold that the assignee was the sole owner and that no interest remained in the original creditor'.[24] So it appears that *Snell's Equity* endorses a 'substitutive transfer' conception of equitable assignment when equitable choses are assigned.

*Guest on Assignment* sets out a broadly similar position, accepting that although an equitable assignment of a legal chose would entail the engrafting of duties on the assignor in the exercise of her entitlements against the legal obligor,[25] an equitable assignment of an equitable chose would entail a 'transfer' of the right assigned.[26]

Smith and Leslie also accept that an equitable assignment of a legal chose in action is appropriately conceived as a trust over the benefit of

---

[22] Snell (2015), para. 3-023. They do not, however, express a view as to whether the trust is imputed by law (i.e. a constructive trust), or otherwise.

[23] Snell (2015), para. 3-022, following *Cator* v. *Croydon Canal Co.* [1843] 4 Y & C Ex 593, 594.

[24] Snell (2015) para. 3-022, following *McMurchie* v. *Thompson* (1906) OLR 637, 639. The correct citation for this case appears to be *McMurchie* v. *Thompson* [1906] 8 Ontario Weekly Reporter 637, 639, where Anglin J held that an equitable assignment of an equitable chose in action was valid, even if it had been made gratuitously: 'It stands ... as an equitable assignment of a chose in action incapable of legal transfer, for which neither writing nor any particular form of words is requisite, provided the intention to make a present transfer is satisfactorily proven ... As the assignment ... relates to property over which courts of equity had special jurisdiction, the assignee could sue in such courts in his own name.'

[25] Liew (2018), para. 3-06.

[26] Ibid., para. 3-05.

that chose.[27] However, they deny this where an equitable chose is equitably assigned:[28]

> Where the whole interest in an equitable chose has been assigned from asssignor to assignee, equity permits the assignee to sue in his own name without joining the assignor. This is because – provided the *whole* interest has been assigned – the assignee is the sole owner and no interest remains in the assignor.

This, it would seem, follows from their reading of a passage from the Lord Chancellor's judgment in *Cator* v. *Croydon Canal Co.*,[29] and also certain passages in *Fulham* v. *McCarthy*[30] and *Donaldson* v. *Donaldson*.[31] It also suggests that in a case where T holds certain assets on trust for A, if A were to equitably assign the entirety of the benefit of her interest in those assets as trust beneficiary to C by way of an outright gift, that equitable assignment would lead to A being *entirely* divested of her 'interest' in those assets. This, however, may go too far.

Where an equitable chose arising out of a trustee–beneficiary relationship between T and A has been equitably assigned, the proposition that A, by equitably assigning her equitable interest as beneficiary to an assignee, C, would have lost her 'beneficial interest' in the trust assets does *not* denote that the equitable assignor has no interest whatsoever following the assignment. By 'loss of beneficial interest', we denote that the assignor (A) is no longer privileged as against the assignee (C) to invoke her entitlements as against the obligor (T) to the chose assigned without regard for C's interests: rather, by reason of the assignment, A will have become duty-bound to C, *and only to C*, to invoke her entitlements in C's interests. But the equitable assignment to C does not change the jural relations as between A and all non-C's: notwithstanding the assignment to C, A remains privileged against all others (i.e. all non-C's) to invoke her entitlements against T as beneficiary of the trust without regard to the interests of every non-C.

Correlatively speaking, despite the equitable assignment to C, A remains under no duty to any non-C to invoke her entitlements

---

[27] Smith & Leslie (2018), paras 11.19–11.24. They appear to conclude, however, that that the trust is not an express trust, and so reason by elimination that it must be a constructive trust: para. 11.26.

[28] Ibid., para. 11.06 (emphasis in original).

[29] *Cator* v. *Croydon Canal Co.* (n. 23), 593–4.

[30] (1848) 1 HLC 708, 717–18, being an appeal from the Irish High Court of Chancery.

[31] (1854) Kay 711.

against T for the interest of any non-C. It is therefore open to A to validly create a further equitable assignment of the same equitable chose to, say, D. Such later assignment is not invalid on grounds that A had no interest whatsoever that might be equitably assigned to D. It is valid, so long as the 'three certainties'[32] (and any relevant formalities)[33] are satisfied. This is why in cases where an assignor effects multiple and inconsistent equitable assignments over the same equitable chose, the claims of the competing equitable assignees are not determined simply on grounds that the first assignee will take free of the subsequent assignments: instead, the 'rule' in *Dearle v. Hall* is applied.[34] Consequently, even on the terms set out by Smith and Leslie, the equitable assignment by A to C of the equitable chose arising out of T's trust would *not* entail a divesting of the '*whole* interest' with the result that 'no interest remains in [A]'.

Justice Edelman[35] and Elliott have also argued that the trust conception of equitable assignment applies to equitable assignments of legal choses in action, and may also be applied to equitable assignments of equitable choses in action, and statements to the contrary in some of the recent cases should be cause for concern. Although they concede that *Cator v. Croydon Canal Co.*, *Redman v. Permanent Trustee Company of New South Wales Ltd*[36] and *Fulham v. McCarthy* are commonly taken to suggest that the assignor of an equitable chose 'drops out',[37] they question the correctness of that view,[38] given their inconsistency with the views expressed by Lawrence Collins LJ (as he then was) in *Nelson v. Greening & Sykes (Builders) Ltd.*[39]

---

[32]  See Chapter 1, text to n. 27.

[33]  See LPA1925, s. 53(1)(c).

[34]  This is discussed further in Chapter 10.

[35]  Justice of the Supreme Court of Western Australia (as he then was).

[36]  (1916) 22 CLR 84. *Redman*, however, is not independent authority for the proposition since the sole reference on point was made by Isaacs J, *obiter* (at 22 CLR 95), relying on the authority on *Fulham v. McCarthy* (n. 30).

[37]  Edelman & Elliott (2015), p. 246.

[38]  Ibid., p. 246. Whether a bare sub-trust of an equitable interest entails the sub-trustee 'dropping out' is contentious. Though there are views that cases such as *Onslow v. Wallis* (1849) 1 Mac & G 506; *Re Lashmar* [1891] 1 Ch 258; and *Grainge v. Wilberforce* (1889) 5 TLR 436 dictate this, it has been argued that such a view is unprincipled, and that these cases have been misinterpreted, and Collins LJ's statements in *Nelson v. Greening & Sykes (Builders) Ltd* [2007] EWCA Civ 1358; [2008] 1 EGLR 59 would certainly be consistent with the latter view. These points are discussed further in Chapter 5.

[39]  *Nelson v. Greening & Sykes (Builders) Ltd* (n. 38), [57]. Those views, albeit *obiter*, formed part of his Lordship's reasoning, leading to his holding that there was no basis to say that

Lawrence Collins LJ's views will be considered in greater detail in a subsequent chapter.[40] But, as Justice Edelman and Elliott point out, Collins LJ's analysis suggests that there is something not quite right with the partial trust model of equitable assignment posited above in *Snell's Equity, Guest on Assignment*, and by Smith and Leslie. Indeed, as the following will show, the partial trust model is contrary to long-standing authority.

By 1808, it had become accepted that equitable assignments of equitable choses entailed the immediate constitution of a trust over the subject matter assigned. Without taking this step, the courts of equity would not have been able to recognize the validity of *gratuitous* equitable assignments of equitable choses given its general reluctance to lend its assistance to volunteers.

Gratuitous assignments of equitable choses had been conceded to be valid by the parties in *Lord Carteret* v. *Paschal*,[41] which was decided in 1733. But the point was clearly decided in 1808 in *Sloane* v. *Cadogan*,[42] where Sir William Grant MR held that a voluntary equitable assignment of an equitable chose was effective notwithstanding that no consideration had been given in exchange.

In *Sloane* v. *Cadogan*, William Cadogan ('A'), son of Earl Cadogan, had an equitable reversionary interest in a fund that had been vested in the trustees of the Earl's marriage settlement ('$T_1$'). Prior to his marriage, A assigned his equitable reversionary interest in the fund to other trustees ('$T_2$') on special trust for various volunteers, though certain powers of appointment were reserved for himself.

When A died without issue and without exercising these powers of appointment, Jane Cadogan, A's widow, commenced proceedings against $T_1$. She contended that A had failed to completely constitute a trust over his equitable interest in the fund arising from Earl Cadogan's marriage

---

the administrators of a deceased's estate were to be treated as if they had 'dropped out'. Those views have since been approved and applied in *Sheffield* v. *Sheffield* [2013] EWHC 3927 (Ch); [2014] WTLR 1039, [82].

[40] See Chapter 6, Section E.

[41] (1733) 3 P Wms 197.

[42] *Sloane* v. *Cadogan* (1808), reported in Sugden (1846), p. 1119. A summary of the facts and decision of Sir William Grant MR in this case may be found in Sir L Shadwell V-C's decision in *Beatson* v. *Beatson* (1841) 12 Sim 291, 291–4. Unfortunately, the learned V-C appears to have misapplied the principle on which *Sloane* v. *Cadogan* was decided: S. J. Bailey, 'Assignments of Debts in England from the Twelfth to the Twentieth Century – Part III' (1932) 48 LQR 547, 558, fn. 30. Shadwell V-C's reasoning in *Beatson* v. *Beatson* was not followed by the Court of Appeal in Chancery in *Donaldson* v. *Donaldson* (n. 31).

settlement because the assignment of that equitable interest to $T_2$ was ineffectual, being voluntary. If so, A would have failed to divest his interest in the fund during his lifetime, and that equitable interest would then have to go to A's widow in accordance with A's will.

Grant MR rejected the widow's argument:[43]

> The Court will not interfere to give perfection to the instrument, but you may constitute one a trustee for a volunteer. Here the fund was vested in trustees [of the Earl's marriage settlement]: [A] had an equitable reversionary interest in that fund, and he assigned it to certain trustees [$T_2$], and then the first trustees [$T_1$] are trustees for his assigns, and they [the assigns, $T_2$] may come here, for when the trust is created no consideration is essential, and the Court will execute it though voluntary.

Crucially, as Grant MR pointed out, the reason why $T_1$, the trustees of the Earl's marriage settlement, were 'trustees for his [A's] assigns' was because A had *already* constituted a trust[44] in respect of his equitable interest.[45] Since A had done nothing apart from execute the deed of assignment to $T_2$, that trust must have arisen by that same deed. For the gratuitous 'assignment' to $T_2$ to be valid, Grant MR must have recognized that A had constituted *himself* to be a trustee of the benefit of his equitable reversionary interest and so rendered himself duty-bound by such trust to his assignees, $T_2$, who were to hold their entitlements against A arising by reason of such trust, for the benefit of A's intended donees and not absolutely for their own benefit. And so far as one *has* constituted a valid trust, even if voluntary, a court in its equitable jurisdiction would enforce its terms.[46]

This reading of *Sloane v. Cadogan* was accepted and applied in *Kekewich v. Manning*, being 'the leading case on the subject'.[47] In *Kekewich v. Manning*, Knight Bruce LJ applied *Sloane v. Cadogan* and held that a voluntary deed equitably assigning an equitable interest was effective

---

[43] *Sloane v. Cadogan* (n. 42).

[44] Just over fifty years earlier, it had been held in *Tomlinson v. Gill* (1756) Amb 330 that a trust could be validly constituted over a presently existing chose in action.

[45] Corroboration that this reading of Grant MR's judgment is correct may be found in *Blakely v. Brady* (1839) 2 Drury & Walsh 311, of which an excerpt of the relevant part may be found in Spence (1850), vol. II, p. 903.

[46] '[T]he distinction is settled, that in the case of contract, merely voluntary . . ., this Court will do nothing: but if it does not rest in voluntary agreement, but an actual trust is created, the Court does take jurisdiction': *Pulvertoft v. Pulvertoft* (1811) 18 Ves Jun 84, 98–9. See also *Kekewich v. Manning* (1851) 1 De G M & G 176; *Meek v. Kettlewell* (1842) 1 Hare 464, 469.

[47] *Re Patrick* [1891] 1 Ch 82, 87 (Lindley LJ, with whom Bowen and Fry LJJ agreed).

upon its execution.[48] Critically for present purposes, Knight Bruce LJ observed that 'Fortescue v. Barnett ..., Wheatley v. Purr, and Blakeley [sic] v. Brady ... have, without question, followed Cadogan v. Sloane, and if it could require support supported it'.[49]

Of these three cases, Fortescue v. Barnett and Blakely v. Brady involved gratuitous equitable assignments of *legal* choses in action; Wheatley v. Purr did not.

Wheatley v. Purr[50] was a case where the holder of a deposit account with a bank had effected a gift of the legal chose so arising by constituting herself trustee of that legal chose for the benefit of her intended donee. Following the donor's death, the bank paid the sums standing in the account to her personal representative. Though the donor's actions were voluntary, Lord Langdale MR held that that did not preclude the valid constitution of a trust. Once validly constituted, the donor's trust devolved to the personal representative. Consequently, the donor's personal representative held the monies received in discharge of the bank's indebtedness on the same trust for the benefit of the donor's intended donee.

Fortescue v. Barnett,[51] however, involved a gratuitous equitable assignment in 1813[52] of the benefit of a life assurance policy by the assured to assignees to hold on trusts declared by the assured; whereas Blakely v. Brady[53] involved a gratuitous equitable assignment of a debt to assignees to hold on trusts specified by the assignor.

When the assured in Fortescue surrendered the policy, Sir John Leach MR ordered him to account to his assignees for the value of the policy that had been assigned together with all bonuses which had been, might be, or would have been declared, but for such surrender. Since the assured did nothing else apart from effecting the assignment to the assignees in question, this can only be explained on grounds that the assured had, by that very act, encumbered himself in a manner akin to the account-holder in Wheatley v. Purr who had constituted herself trustee of the benefit of her legal chose against her bank. Hence, just like

---

[48] (1851) 1 De G M & G 176, 201–2.

[49] Ibid., 194 (references omitted).

[50] (1837) 1 Keen 55.

[51] (1834) 3 My & K 36.

[52] Such assignment was necessarily equitable as assignments of the benefit of life assurance policies pursuant to s. 1, Policies of Assurance Act 1867, or of choses in action generally pursuant to s. 25(6), Supreme Court of Judicature Act 1873, still lay in the future.

[53] See n. 45.

the account-holder who had constituted herself trustee of her legal chose against her bank in *Wheatley* v. *Purr*, when the assured in *Fortescue* surrendered the life assurance policy, thereby bringing it to an end (that being an act which the assignees had not sanctioned), the assured was duty-bound to the assignees to account for the traceable substitutes of the legal chose arising from the policy. As *Re Patrick* subsequently explained: 'If once the conclusion is arrived at that the assignment of the [common law] debts was complete ... it follows that the settlor, having got in the debts himself, is accountable to the trustees of the settlement for the amount he so got in.'[54] Such assignments of legal choses are *complete* because, once the requisite intention to assign is manifested,[55] nothing more[56] is required for the *trust* that underpins such equitable assignment to be fully constituted.[57]

The point was even more obviously stated in the decision of the Irish High Court of Chancery in *Blakely*. When the administrator of the assignor accepted monies tendered by the debtor in discharge of the debt that had been assigned, Lord Plunket LC held that the administrator held such monies 'in trust' for the benefit of the assignee.[58] This can be simply explained on the basis that, as with *Fortescue*, when the assignor effected the assignment of the debt to the assignee, he, too, had encumbered himself in the manner described above. And when he died, the office of trustee which he had held would devolve to his personal representative (namely, the administrator of his estate). So devolved, the administrator of the deceased trustee's estate would be bound to hold the monies received in discharge of the debt (being the traceable substitute for the legal chose that had been assigned) for the benefit of the assignee.

---

[54] See also *Re Patrick* (n. 47), 87 (Lindley LJ, explaining *Fortescue* v. *Barnett* (n. 51): 'If once the conclusion is arrived at that the assignment of the [common law] debts was complete ... it follows that the settlor, having got in the debts himself, is accountable to the trustees of the settlement for the amount he so got in.'

[55] See Chapter 1, n. 27.

[56] There are no formality requirements for an equitable assignment of a legal chose, unlike the position with regard to equitable assignments of equitable choses: LPA1925, s. 53(1)(c).

[57] And, so far as an equitable assignment also entails the delegation of powers to the assignee, to invoke as the assignee pleases, such grant of authority must also, by parity of reasoning, have been 'complete' once the assignment was effected, requiring nothing further of the assignor – at least so far as a court of equity was concerned.

[58] *Blakely* v. *Brady* (n. 45), 328. This appears to have been accepted as an uncontroversial statement of English law in F. T. White and O. D. Tudor, *White & Tudor's Leading Cases in Equity: With Notes* (E. P. Hewitt and J. B. Richardson, eds., 9th edn, London: Sweet & Maxwell 1928), p. 797.

*Fortescue* and *Blakely* therefore recognized that a voluntary equitable assignment of a legal chose entails a trustee–beneficiary relationship between the assignor and the assignee. And since 'you may constitute a trustee for a volunteer',[59] equitable assignments of legal choses were effective without need for consideration *because* they entailed a trust. Yet these cases did not originate a distinct pattern of reasoning applicable to equitable assignments of legal choses.

As Knight Bruce LJ recognized in *Kekewich* v. *Manning*, these cases had followed the reasoning of Grant MR in *Sloane* v. *Cadogan*: that is, these cases concluded that voluntary equitable assignments of legal choses, like voluntary equitable assignments of equitable choses, were effective because, in both, a trustee–beneficiary relationship had arisen by reason of the equitable assignment between assignor and assignee; and since such trustee–beneficiary relationship could be validly created to benefit volunteers who had provided no valuable consideration, the lack of such consideration was immaterial.[60]

The pattern of reasoning was, therefore, that there was no distinction to be drawn between an equitable assignment of an equitable or a legal chose in action. The former entailed a trustee–beneficiary relationship which did not require consideration to be validly constituted, and so, too, would the latter.

Subsequent authorities which have held that gratuitous equitable assignments are valid also analyse such equitable assignments of equitable[61] or legal[62] choses as entailing the constitution of a trust over the chose in question. Suggesting, as some have done, that the trustee–beneficiary relationship only arises in connection with equitable assignments of legal choses but not with equitable assignments of equitable choses is therefore contrary to precedent. The 'partial' trust model which posits that only equitable assignments of legal choses in action entail a trustee–beneficiary relationship between assignor and assignee is, accordingly, contrary to authority.

---

[59] *Blakely* v. *Brady* (n. 45), 328, following *Sloane* v. *Cadogan*. One may equally delegate one's powers to be exercised by a duly appointed and authorized agent without need for consideration. The significance of such 'agency' effects will be discussed in the following section.

[60] See also *Nanney* v. *Morgan* (1888) 37 Ch D 346, 355 (Cotton LJ, with whom Sir James Hannen and Lopes LJ agreed).

[61] See, for equitable assignments of equitable choses: *Voyle* v. *Hughes* (1854) 2 Sm & Giff 18; *Harding* v. *Harding* (1886) 17 QBD 442; *Re Spark's Trusts* [1904] 1 Ch 451.

[62] *Richardson* v. *Richardson* (1867) LR 3 Eq 686.

The above is not, however, to take *Kekewich* v. *Manning* to be authority for the proposition that, 'equitable assignments of equitable choses and declarations of trust over those same choses are indistinguishable'.[63] The proposition that the two are 'indistinguishable' would require acceptance of the proposition that an equitable assignment of an equitable (or legal) chose merely entails a trustee–beneficiary relationship, *and nothing more*. But that would not be correct.

All that has been suggested thus far is that whether the chose assigned be equitable or legal, the institutional construct named 'equitable assignment' entails the constitution of a bare trust between the assignor and the assignee over the entitlements arising in connection with the chose assigned. This does not entail any suggestion that an equitable assignment is *only* a trust. Rather, as the following section will show, it is clear that an equitable assignment is *more* than a trust. Consequently, where the parties have intended that an equitable assignment be effected, but fail to comply with any requisite procedural requirements to effect a valid equitable assignment, the doctrine in *Milroy* v. *Lord*[64] will preclude the courts from re-characterizing the transaction to take effect by way of trust.

## B   Dualist 'Trust Plus Agency' Model

### (i)   *The Poverty of a Monist 'Trust' Model*

The challenge is to explain how, notwithstanding that equitable assignments of both legal and equitable choses in action entail the constitution of a trust, an equitable assignee may invoke the assignor's powers against the obligor directly without the assignor's involvement. For example, even prior to there being any question of breach of duty, '[I]n the case of an assignment of the equitable interest in stock standing in the names of trustees, ... the donee may go with that deed [of assignment] to the trustees, and say, transfer to me the interest in this sum of stock.'[65]

Numerous cases tell us that where an equitable chose has been assigned, should the duties associated with that chose be breached, the assignee may invoke the assignor's power to bring proceedings in equity against the obligor without needing to join the assignor.[66] But if an

---

[63]   Smith & Leslie (2018), para. 11.16.
[64]   (1862) 4 De G F & J 264.
[65]   *Donaldson* v. *Donaldson* (n. 31), 718–19. See also *Re Smith* [1928] 1 Ch 915.
[66]   E.g. *Goodson* v. *Ellison* (1826) 3 Russ 583; *Cator* v. *Croydon Canal Co.* (n. 23).

equitable assignment merely entailed a trustee–beneficiary relationship between the assignor and the assignee, this conceptual structure could not explain how the assignee might do so.

Part of the answer to the question why joinder of the equitable assignor of an equitable chose is not absolutely necessary lies in a proper understanding of the rules on joinder of parties in equitable proceedings.[67] But beyond the technical rules of joinder in equity, there is a further conceptual reason that explains why assignor involvement is unnecessary in both the pre-breach and post-breach contexts. That is, an equitable assignment is not merely a trust: it is a trust *plus* an agency of an atypical kind, akin to the Roman *cessio actionum*.[68]

The better analysis is that all equitable assignments (whether of legal or equitable choses in action) are underpinned by two effects.

First, an equitable assignment operates in the manner of an express bare trust:[69] that is, when a legal or equitable chose is equitably assigned, the assignor will be obligated to her assignee in just the same way as if she had expressly constituted herself a bare trustee of the chose for the benefit of her assignee. Second, an equitable assignment also entails the grant of authority to the assignee in an atypical manner: that is, having equitably assigned the chose to the assignee, the assignor will have authorized the assignee to invoke the assignor's powers in relation to the obligor to the chose as if he were the assignor, *and* will have further authorized the assignee to invoke those powers without regard to the assignor's interests.[70]

Given the unusual principal–agent relationship which is appended to every equitable assignment, just as 'every charge is not an equitable mortgage, though every equitable mortgage is a charge',[71] not every bare trust will amount to an equitable assignment, though every equitable assignment will entail a bare trust. Consequently, although it is certainly true, as Romer LJ observed in *Timpson's Executors* v. *Yerbury*, that:[72]

> [t]he equitable interest in property in the hands of a trustee can be disposed of by the person entitled to it in favour of a third party in any one of four different ways. The person entitled to it (1) can assign it

---

[67] This is explained in Chapter 7.
[68] Holland (1924), pp. 314–15. Broadly in agreement, see Ames (1887) and (1890); Ames (1913), p. 213, fn. 1; and A. Pretto-Sakmann, *Boundaries of Personal Property* (Oxford: Hart, 2005), pp. 158–63.
[69] The nature of a bare trust has been explained in Chapter 3.
[70] The question as to the revocability or otherwise of this 'agency' is addressed in Chapter 6.
[71] *Shea* v. *Moore* [1894] IR 158, 168.
[72] [1936] 1 KB 645, 664.

> to the third party, (2) can direct the trustees to hold the property in trust
> for the third party …, (3) can contract for valuable consideration to
> assign the equitable interest to him, or (4) can declare himself to be a
> trustee for him of such interest[,]

it goes too far to say that each one of these four techniques to 'dispose' of
the donor's beneficial equitable interest in property in the hands of a
trustee amounts to an equitable assignment.

As will be explained below, an equitable assignee is entitled to require
his assignor to act for his benefit, and is *also* empowered to act in right of
his assignor. This is because an equitable assignee is, in effect, both the
beneficiary of a trust over the assignor's entitlements against the obligor
to the chose assigned, *and* the delegatee of those self-same entitlements.[73]
However, although a donee who has been delegated a donor's powers is
usually duty-bound to invoke those delegated powers in the interest of
the donor, the manner of delegation inherent in an equitable assignee is
accompanied by a release of the assignee from such duties. The equitable
assignee is therefore privileged as against the assignor to invoke these
powers without having to take the assignor's interests into account. If
the equitable assignee does not encumber himself to anyone else as to
how he is to invoke such delegated powers (for example, by creating a
further sub-assignment), the assignee would be privileged as against the
assignor to invoke those delegated entitlements, freed from any duty to
invoke them for the assignor's benefit, and may invoke them as he
pleased. In contrast, where a trust *simpliciter* has been constituted over
a chose in action, such trust merely creates the former set of trustee–
beneficiary jural relations, without touching on the latter.[74]

---

[73] As will be explained in Chapter 6, the conjunction of the equitable proprietary interest
generated by the 'trust effect' in favour of the assignee, with the delegation of the
assignor's powers to the assignee, has led the courts to recognize that the assignee's
'authority' to act in place of the assignor in such circumstances is irrevocable.

[74] Conceptual coherence requires, therefore, that we abandon Marshall's proposition that
one may equitably assign a chose in action by *merely* constituting a trust over that chose:
Marshall (1950), p. 200. Marshall also suggested that an equitable assignment of a legal
chose arising of, say, a debt, could also be effected by getting the debtor to 'hold the chose
in trust for the assignee' (at p. 97). With respect, though such a request to the debtor, if
acceded to, could indeed effect a disposition of the creditor's entitlement to be paid such
sum, yet such disposition has nothing to do with the institution of equitable assignment.
The disposition of the creditor's entitlement to be paid in such circumstances arises *at
law* by reason of an accord and satisfaction. In exchange for the creditor's promise not to
pursue the debtor for non-payment, the debtor will have constituted itself trustee of
monies in its hands equalling the sum of the debt for the benefit of the 'assignee', thereby

Cases which discuss and analyse equitable assignments as entailing some form of trust cannot be taken to mean anything else. If they meant equitable assignments to be *no more than* trusts, it would be impossible to distinguish the institution of the trust from the institution of equitable assignment. But the cases are clear: the institutions of equitable assignment and the trust are so distinct from one another that the courts will not give effect to a failed disposition intended by the disponor to operate as an equitable assignment by recharacterizing it as a trust *simpliciter* because the intention to effect an equitable assignment is *not* the same as the intention to constitute a mere trust.[75]

So far as an equitable assignment involves the constitution by the assignor of a bare trust over the chose assigned for the benefit of the assignee, that 'trust effect' divests the assignor of her *beneficial interest*[76] in the powers associated with the chose: thereafter, she is longer privileged against her assignee to invoke her powers against the obligor to the chose without regard to the assignee's interests – rather, she is duty-bound to preserve her entitlements (i.e. she is duty-bound not to invoke them), until such time as the assignee might direct her to do so.

As has been observed in relation to what happens when a trust is constituted over the legal title to property:[77]

> The trustee has a legal title and access to common law courts and remedies, *but [she] is a driven vehicle for the superior rights of [her] beneficiary.* [She] litigates at common law in response to [her] equitable duties, and not to [her] common law rights, which have been subordinated. The trustee is now a manager in an institution which is a hybrid between the creation of an agency and the disposition of property.

---

providing executed consideration (the satisfaction) in support of the creditor's promise (the accord). Such a dealing can only be an 'assignment' in name.

[75] *Milroy* v. *Lord* (n. 64). See also *Pearson* v. *The Amicable Assurance Office* (1859) 27 Beav 229; *Richards* v. *Delbridge* (1874) LR 18 Eq 11; *Re Rose, Rose* v. *Inland Revenue Commissioners* [1952] 1 Ch 499; *Co-operative Group Ltd* v. *Birse Developments Ltd* [2014] EWHC 530 (TCC); [2014] BLR 359. This was also accepted by Eve J to be so in *Hill* v. *Peters* [1918] 2 Ch 273, leading him to conclude that the rule in *Dearle* v. *Hall* (see Chapter 10) would not apply to determine the priorities between the competing claims of a trust beneficiary and an equitable assignee, a view which Lord Reid agreed with in his speech in *BS Lyle* v. *Rosher* [1959] 1 WLR 8, 23, although Lord Kilmuir, Lord Morton of Henryton and Lord Cohen left the point open at 15, 17 and 24, respectively.

[76] Keeping in mind the limits of such language as noted in the main text to n. 31, above.

[77] Jeffrey Hackney, *Understanding Equity and Trusts* (London: Fontana Press, 1987), pp. 21–2.

By parity of reasoning, there seems no obvious reason why the position should be any different when the trust property is equitable in origin.

But if the assignor *intends* to equitably assign the chose in action instead of merely constituting a trust over it, such assignor will also *intend* to enable the assignee to 'leapfrog' or 'bypass' his assignor in his dealings with the obligor; and such intent is given effect to by means of an atypical agency[78] between the assignor and her assignee. Thus, every equitable assignment also entails the assignor authorizing her assignee to act as if he were her, *and* as without having to consider the assignor's interests. This 'agency effect' is part and parcel of the institution of an equitable assignment: when the assignor, A, effects an equitable assignment, as opposed to any other mode of dealing (say, the constitution of a trust, *simpliciter*), such equitable assignment necessarily entails such agency effect. The analysis is not, therefore, that equitable assignment involves some form of 'equitable' power of attorney paralleling a power of attorney at law: it is that this unusual kind of 'agency' is intrinsic to the institution of 'equitable assignment'. Accordingly, the absence of a grant of a power of attorney, over and beyond the equitable assignment per se, becomes immaterial,[79] so far as we are concerned with a court that would recognize and enforce the same.[80] The point is that once there *is* an equitable assignment, that institution entails the creation of the duty/claim-right jural relations between the assignor and assignee as one

---

[78] In the usual case, '[a]gency is a consensual relationship in which one (the agent) holds in trust for and subject to the control of another (the principal) a power to affect certain legal relations of that other': W. A. Seavey, 'The Rationale of Agency' (1919–20) 29 *Yale Law Journal* 859, 868.

[79] The 'difficulties' pointed out in Smith & Leslie (2018), para. 11.17, with the 'agency' analysis, therefore, would appear to misunderstand the argument. In addition, at para. 11.18, Smith and Leslie rightly point out that with an agency analysis, the assignor (as principal) would *not* be divested of the delegated powers. This, they suggest, is contradicted by the authority of *Fulham* v. *McCarthy* (n. 30). With respect, this reading of *Fulham* v. *McCarthy* may be misconceived. The case is discussed in Chapter 5.

[80] As will be explained in detail in Part III, the court of Chancery would and did recognize and enforce all aspects of the equitable institution of an equitable assignment: how could it not, given that it was a creature of its own creation? Hence, Chancery would give effect to both the 'trust' and 'agency' effects entailed by that institution, without further need for any distinct grant of authority to the assignee apart from the assignment per se. However, the courts of common law did not go so far: they would only recognize the institutions arising from the exclusive jurisdiction of Chancery. Consequently, courts acting within their common law jurisdiction would not give effect to the agency effect which underpins equitable assignment, and would require a further and distinct grant of authority to the assignee before it would give effect to such delegation of authority.

might find as between a bare trustee and the beneficiary to such bare trust, but coupled with a liability/power jural relation between the assignor and assignee as one might find as between a principal and her agent to whom various of the principal's powers had been delegated, but where the agent had been released from the usual duty to invoke such delegated powers for the principal's interests. The dualist model of equitable assignment conceives of equitable assignment as a distinct equitable institution, albeit one made up of two component parts which work in tandem: once hitched together, there will have been an equitable assignment. Consequently, so far as a trust *simpliciter* does not entail such 'agency' effects, the equitable institutions of equitable assignment and trust may be kept distinct from each other.

This proposition will be more closely examined in the following sections.

## (ii)  Dealing Directly with the Obligor

An assignee is empowered to deal directly with the obligor to the chose assigned in ways which go beyond his ability to bring judicial proceedings in equity without needing to join the assignor.

---

### EXAMPLE 4.4

Suppose T holds the legal title to 10,000 BCL shares on a testamentary trust 'for A's benefit'. The terms of the trust are that T is to pay the income generated from such holding to A until A turns forty-five years of age. It does not vest T with any power of sale or reinvestment, nor does it provide A with any power to require T to convey his legal title to her order.

A, aged thirty, subsequently equitably assigns her equitable interest in T's legal title in the shares to C by way of gift.[81]

---

By such equitable assignment to C, with or without notice to T, C would already have the power to require T to convey his legal title in the shares to C's order.[82] Though C may not exercise such power without informing T of the assignment, that is beside the point, the point being that if C (and not A) invoked the *Saunders* v. *Vautier*

---

[81] As mentioned above, such assignments are effective and valid notwithstanding the lack of consideration in support: *Sloane* v. *Cadogan* (n. 42).

[82] See *Donaldson* v. *Donaldson* (n. 31), 719.

doctrine to collapse the testamentary trust to a bare trust, and then directed T to fully execute that bare trust by conveying his legal title in the shares to C, T will have become a bare trustee by C's invocation of the *Saunders* v. *Vautier* doctrine. If T then failed to fully execute the bare trust as per C's request, T would breach his duties as such bare trustee, and proceedings might then be brought by C in respect of such breach.

Since the testamentary trust merely provided that T was to hold 'for A's benefit', no power of appointment having been reserved to A, A's equitable assignment to C did not turn C into a beneficiary of that trust on its own terms. And so far as an equitable assignment operates by creating a new trustee–beneficiary relationship between A and C, that trust effect *alone* would not make C any less a stranger to the testamentary trust between A and T. So analysing equitable assignment as entailing *merely* a trust relationship cannot explain how an assignee like C may validly invoke the *Saunders* v. *Vautier* doctrine to collapse T's testamentary trust for A's benefit into a bare trust.

For the above reasons, every equitable assignment of *any* chose in action (be it legal or equitable) entails an atypical agency *as well as* a trust, and though C (as assignee) remains a stranger to the testamentary trust, C is nevertheless authorized to invoke any and/or all of A's entitlements against T and, crucially, is also authorized to invoke such delegated entitlements as C pleases. But can an agent be authorized to such an extent?

### (iii)    The Acts of a Duly Authorized Agent are the Acts of His Principal

When dealing with the question of agency, our concerns most often lie with questions whether and when an agent's actions bind his principal in a contractual relationship with a third party. In other cases, we might be concerned whether a principal may be held vicariously liable for his agent's tortious acts. Neither of these preoccupations, however, spans the entire breadth of the operation of the law of agency.

*Bowstead and Reynolds on Agency* observes:[83]

> An agent may execute a deed, or do any other act on behalf of the principal *which the principal might himself execute, make or do*; except

---

[83] Bowstead & Reynolds (2018), para. 2-017 (emphasis added). See also Story (1882), §2. As authority, Story cites Co Litt 258a.

for the purpose of executing a right, privilege or power conferred, or of performing a duty imposed, on the principal personally, the exercise or performance of which requires discretion or special personal skill, or for the purpose of doing an act which the principal is required, by or pursuant to any statute or other relevant rule, to do in person.

Leaving aside instances where personal action by the principal is required,[84] if *sui juris*, whatever the principal is empowered to do, she may authorize another to invoke in her right and on her behalf. Insofar as such powers and entitlements are invoked by the agent within the bounds of his authority, such acts are the acts of the principal: '*Qui facit per alium facit per se*'.[85]

This includes the assignor's power to commence judicial proceedings. Hence, where such agency effect is recognized (as it would be by a court in its equitable jurisdiction), a court would permit an assignee to bring proceedings against an obligor even though the assignee was a stranger *because* it recognized the assignee to have been authorized to do so by the assignor, and was prepared to give effect to such delegation of power. Those proceedings would accordingly be treated as having been commenced by the assignor herself.

It is important to remember that such delegation to an 'agent' does not entail an impermissible unilateral change to the obligations arising between obligor and obligee-assignor. Those jural relations between obligor and obligee-assignor remain unchanged notwithstanding such 'agency'. And even though equitable assignment does displace the immunity/disability jural relations between the obligor and the assignee, as explained in Chapters 2 and 3, such change does not take place entirely without regard to the obligor's assent. This is because, so far as a voluntarily undertaken obligation may vest powers in an obligee, the obligor would be taken to have assented to their being invoked by delegatees on behalf of the obligee, unless the context indicates that such delegation was not, or could not have been, assented to.

Clear examples of such non-assent would, of course, be where the powers in question were *personal* to the obligee.[86] But otherwise, clear

---

[84] I.e. instances of non-delegable duties and powers.

[85] See 1 Bl Comm 417. It has been suggested that the principle which underlies it is simply a fiction of unity of identity between principal and agent, or master or servant: O. W. Holmes, 'Agency' (1890–1) 4 *Harvard Law Review* 345 and O. W. Holmes, 'Agency II' (1891–2) 5 *Harvard Law Review* 1.

[86] E.g. where the contract expressly stipulated that the powers arising thereunder were non-delegable.

words would be sufficient to indicate the withholding of assent – and indeed, express terms providing for an anti-assignment clause may well be indicative of such non-assent to the possibility that the obligee might delegate such powers as she might have against the obligor to be exercised on her behalf by another.[87] But outside these contexts, the obligor has no grounds to complain if the obligee delegates these powers to another to invoke as her 'agent'.

An assignee who has been equitably assigned an equitable interest in property held on trust for the sole benefit of the assignor may thus invoke the assignor's power to require such trust to be fully executed without needing the assignor to act personally;[88] and an assignee who has been equitably assigned the benefit of a contractual debt that was payable to the assignor may invoke the assignor's power to make an offer of release, on condition that the debtor tender payment to someone else.[89] Invocations of such delegated powers of the assignor are valid, without court order, though judicial proceedings may be brought by the assignee[90] if the obligors fail to comply with such invocations of the relevant delegated power.[91] And so far as the courts of equity (but not the courts of common law) would have recognized and given effect to such 'agency effect', an assignee may also invoke the assignor's power to initiate judicial proceedings *in equity* against the obligor to the chose to seek equitable judicial remedies, *without* any further involvement of the assignor, even though the assignee remains a stranger to the chose in question.[92]

---

[87] As will be explained in Chapter 15, Section A(ii).

[88] *Donaldson* v. *Donaldson* (n. 31), 718–19.

[89] I.e. the '*Hodgson* v. *Anderson*' power discussed in Chapter 3, Section B(ii). Consequently, as was accepted by Lord Cranworth LC in *Jones* v. *Farrell* (1857) 1 De G & J 208, 218: 'I think the only safe way for the debtor in such a case [where his creditor has assigned the debt to an assignee] would be to send at once to the assignee and pay him the debt. That would be a valid discharge. If my creditor tells me to pay A.B., and I accordingly pay A.B., and the creditor afterwards sues me, I have a good plea of payment.' See also discussion in Chapter 6, Section D.

[90] In the name of the assignor, if the action was brought within the court's common law jurisdiction. That said, as will be explained in Part III: Joinder, it is possible to bring proceedings against an obligor to a common law chose within the court's *equitable* jurisdiction, in which case the assignee may bring such equitable proceedings in his own name, unless there be practical reasons to require the joinder of the assignor.

[91] As in *Cator* v. *Croydon Canal Co.* (n. 23).

[92] This point will be elaborated on in Part III: Joinder.

## (iv)   Delegation of Powers with a Privilege to Invoke Them without Regard for the Delegating Assignor's Interests

As noted above, the 'agency' relationship which is coupled with the 'bare trust' within an equitable assignment is one where the assignor's entitlements against the obligor that have been delegated to the assignee may be exercised by the assignee as the assignee pleases, without regard for the interests of the assignor. In Hohfeldian terms, by virtue of the equitable assignment, the assignor would have also granted her assignee a *privilege* to invoke her entitlements against the obligor without regard for the assignor's interests.

In this connection, it should be kept in mind that no particular formalities are required *in equity* for the grant of such a privilege, at least so far as such a privilege is granted in connection with the manner by which a power is to be exercised by the donee of the power. This is clearly demonstrated from the cases which recognize that testamentary powers of appointment may be granted in either a fiduciary or a non-fiduciary manner, i.e. equity recognizes that powers may be granted to the holder on trust, or they may be granted to the holder to exercise as the holder pleases. In the latter situation, the grant would be of a 'mere power', as opposed to a power coupled with a duty (sometimes termed a 'trust power').[93] And there seems to be no principled reason why such a position is to be limited to powers of appointment arising from a will alone. Such reasoning has certainly been applied to other contexts.

Though this agency relationship is atypical so far as the delegated entitlements (inter alia, powers) of the assignor-principal against the obligor are delegated (i.e. granted) to the assignee for him to invoke without regard for the assignor's interests it is clear that such an expansive form of delegation is not conceptually impossible. If, in general, an agency relationship entails fiduciary claim-right/duty jural relations between principal and agent, the principal who is owed fiduciary duties by her agent has the power to release her agent from those duties, leaving the agent free to invoke those powers delegated to him by virtue of his

---

[93] For an example of a 'trust power' in the context of powers of appointment under a will, see *Burrough* v. *Philcox* (1840) 5 My & Cr 72. In the same context, for examples of a 'mere power', see *Re Weekes' Settlement* [1897] 1 Ch 289; *Re Combe* [1925] Ch 210; *Re Perowne* [1951] 1 Ch 785. Whether the power be granted in one or the other manner is a matter of, 'intention or presumed intention to be derived from the language of the instrument': *Re Scarisbrick's Will Trusts* [1951] Ch 622, 635 (Evershed MR).

appointment as agent without regard for the interests of the assignor. Not only is this logical, it echoes what the Romans recognized to be the case with a *cessio actionum*.[94] Consequently, neither the default position that *delagatus non potest delegare* nor the principle that an agent may not serve two masters stands in the way of this analysis.[95]

This atypical 'agency effect' is absent from a trust *simpliciter*, so consequently, as Waller LJ said in *Barbados Trust Company Ltd v. Bank of Zambia*, '[A] declaration of trust is not an equitable assignment'.[96] Yet we may still say that 'every equitable assignment is a trust' given that an equitable assignment is not *merely* a trust, but is a trust *plus*.

The proposition in this book, therefore, is that so far as a court in its equitable jurisdiction is concerned, there need not be any express words setting out the constitution of any trustee–beneficiary relationship between the assignor and the assignee; nor any express words of authority and release setting out the constitution of the atypical agent–principal relationship mentioned above. Rather, in concluding that the acts and/or words of the assignor have validly created an equitable assignment of a legal or equitable chose in action, the court in its equitable jurisdiction will have concluded that both such trust and agency effects will have arisen so far as they are necessary and sufficient entailments of the institution of equitable assignment. Conversely, if an obligor constituted herself express trustee of the benefit of an obligation owed to her by an obligee for the benefit of a third party, and also granted the third party the authority to invoke all of the obligor's entitlements as against the obligee as if the third party were the obligor *and* without being duty-bound to invoke such delegated powers for the obligor's interests, that combination of effects would give rise to an equitable assignment.

## C   Applying the Composite Model to Equitable Assignments of Choses in Action

It is convenient now to set out in greater detail how the composite model of equitable assignment works.

---

[94] As was pointed out in Holland (1924), p. 315.

[95] The unusual nature of the 'agency' relationship arising between assignor and assignee will be expanded and explained further in Chapter 6.

[96] [2007] EWCA Civ 14; [2007] 1 Lloyd's Rep 495, [45].

---

EXAMPLE 4.5

Suppose that A has lent B £10,000. A will have a legal chose in action against B in respect of the debt of £10,000. Accepting that this legal chose is property and can be dealt with, A tells C that she is giving the debt to him. For good measure, A makes this gift before independent witnesses. By such speech-act, A will have equitably assigned her legal chose in action against B to C[97] by way of gift.[98]

---

Unlike the example with B's Book in Example 4.1, the subject matter of the gift in Example 4.5 is no longer a thing with which no jural relations are possible. Rather, the subject matter of the gift is *itself* a set of jural relations encompassing claim-rights/duties, privileges/no rights, powers/liabilities and immunities/disabilities between A and B.

To begin with, A will have a claim-right against B that B repay £10,000 to A. Ordinarily, this claim-right will be associated with a number of powers. For the purposes of analysis, however, we will just consider one power, namely A's power against B to offer to release B from his duty to repay £10,000 to A if B tenders repayment to C, A's nominee, instead.

In Tables 4.1–4.3 in the following pages, '$\Phi$' means 'the act of repaying £10,000 to A'; and '$\Theta$' means 'the act of offering to release B from his duty to A to do $\Phi$ if B tenders repayment to whomever as A may name at a later date'.

Starting with the jural relations in Table 4.1, if an equitable assignment of the debt by A to C *substituted* C in place of A by extinguishing A's claim-right/duty jural relation with B, and substituting in its place a new claim-right/duty jural relation between C and B, such extinction and regrant would modify the entire suite of jural relations between A, B and C: the jural relations between A, B and C would be those set out in Table 4.2.

The difficulty with such unilateral extinction and revesting of the entire suite of A's jural relations with non-A such as B and C as in Table 4.2 is that it rests on the unilateral modification of A's claim-right/duty jural relation with B (which is impermissible as a matter of common law principle).

---

[97] An equitable assignment of a *legal* chose in action falls outside the ambit of LPA1925, s. 53(1)(c) (which only applies to dispositions of subsisting equitable choses in action). Since the legal chose in action in Example 3.5 relates to personalty, its assignment also falls beyond the ambit of LPA1925, s. 53(1)(b) (which only applies to the constitution of trusts over land).

[98] For authority that gratuitous equitable assignments of legal choses in action may be validly made, see the discussion in Section A(ii) above.

Table 4.1 *The Starting Point*

---

1.1  A has a claim-right against B that B do Φ;

1.2  A has a power against B to do Θ;[99]

1.3  A has a privilege against B to invoke her power against B to do Θ, or not, as she pleases: she is under no duty to B to invoke that power, or not; and

1.4  A has an immunity against B changing A's jural relations with B in that B has no ability to effectively invoke A's power against B to do Θ.[100]

Other jural relations also arise by reason of the loan between A and B. In particular, as between A and C, a third party to the loan:

1.5  A has a privilege against C to invoke her power against B to do Θ as she pleases, or not; she is under no duty to C to invoke it, or not; and

1.6  A has an immunity against C changing A's jural relations with B in that C has no ability to effectively invoke A's power against B to do Θ.[101]

---

Suppose, however, we were to distinguish between what B was originally obligated (i.e. duty-bound) to do (i.e. repay £10,000 to A); and to whom B was so obligated (i.e. to A). Might we then partially sidestep objections that one may not unilaterally change B's obligations, so far as we have not suggested in Table 4.2 that what B was duty-bound to do has changed?

As has been explained in *still* been changed because the other aspect of the obligation, 'to whom' he owed that obligation, has been changed. Changing *to whom* a duty is owed is just as much a change of the

---

[99]  If A invoked her power to do Θ, she would change B's jural relations with herself in that by making such offer, B would be granted a power against A he previously would not have had: the power to cause A to be duty-bound to B to release B from his duty to A to do Φ by accepting A's offer. B's power of acceptance is also a Hohfeldian power so far as A would, prior to B's acceptance, have a claim-right against B that B do Φ.

[100]  A's offer to release B from his duty to do Φ in exchange for his tendering payment to such person as A may name at a later date rests on A's power to release B from his duty by executing a deed of release. Since the latter power of release is for A to invoke, B's execution of such a deed (i.e. a forgery) would have no effect as against anyone other than himself, and anyone as might be claiming through him: *Re Cooper* (1882) 20 Ch D 611, 634 (Lindley LJ).

[101]  A's offer to release B from his duty to do Φ in exchange for his tendering payment to such person as A may name at a later date rests on A's power to release B from his duty by executing a deed of release. Since the latter power of release is for A to invoke, C's execution of such a deed (i.e. a forgery) would have no effect as against anyone other than himself, and anyone as might be claiming through him: *Re Cooper* (above, n. 100).

Table 4.2 *Effect of Substitution*

2.1 If the equitable assignment of the debt to C had the effect of substituting C in place of A, C will now have a claim-right against B that B do Φ;

2.2 Given the changes to B's duty, C now has a power against B to do Θ (i.e. release B from his duty to Φ);

2.3 Given the changes to B's duty, C now has a privilege against B to invoke *his* power against B to do Θ, or not, as he pleases: he is under no duty to B to invoke that power, or not; and

2.4 Given the changes to B's duty, C has an immunity against B changing C's jural relations with B in that B has no ability to effectively invoke C's power against B to do Θ.

As to the relations between A and C, on the supposition that equitable assignment extinguished the claim-right/duty jural relation between A and B and replaced it with an 'equivalent' jural relation between C and B, A would then become the third party to *that* 'new' obligation between C and B. Accordingly:

2.5 Given the changes to B's duty, C has a privilege against A to invoke his power against B to do Θ as he pleases, or not; and[102]

2.6 Given the changes to B's duty, C has an immunity against A changing C's jural relations with B in that A has no ability to effectively invoke C's power against B to do Θ.[103]

obligation as a change in what is to be done. So, in principle, a unilateral change as to whom B is duty-bound should not be permissible either. Yet the 'substitutive transfer' model of equitable assignment would seem to suggest that that is what equitable assignment does.

It is not true that the jural relations between A and C may only be changed by modifying the jural relations between A and B. There are other ways of achieving the former, while leaving the latter entirely unmodified. Suppose, as in Table 4.3, A constitutes herself bare trustee

[102] If B's duty to A had changed in the manner suggested by 'substitutive transfer' models of equitable assignment, A would no longer have any privilege against C to invoke her power against B to do Θ because she would no longer have any such power.

[103] If B's duty to A had changed in the manner suggested by 'substitutive transfer' models of equitable assignment, A would no longer have any immunity against C changing A's jural relations with B by invoking A's power against B to do Θ, because she would no longer have any such power.

of her legal chose in action against B for C's benefit, and simultaneously authorizes C to invoke her entitlements against B, as if he were her, and as he pleased. By such acts, A would have assented in advance to the possibility that C might change her jural relations with B by invoking such delegated powers, and A would be powerless to preclude C from doing so.[104]

Given the bare trust, without changing the claim-right/duty jural relation between A and B, A's privilege against a *certain* non-A (namely C, the beneficiary of such trust) to invoke her powers against B associated with her claim-right against B will have been lost since A will have become duty-bound and liable to C to invoke those powers in accordance with the bare trust she had constituted. A's constitution of the bare trust over the debt for C's benefit thus divests A of her beneficial interest in the debt whilst necessarily leaving her jural relations with B entirely intact.

The atypically broad grant of authority to C, meanwhile, would result in A losing her exclusive ability to effect changes in her jural relations with B (in that although she retains her powers against B in respect of the debt, she is no longer immune against C effecting changes to those jural relations with B when he invokes the powers she had delegated to him). Correspondingly, B, too, would no longer be immune against C effecting changes to his jural relations with A. But, as mentioned, B is presumed to have assented to such a possibility, unless B had exercised his power to preclude it by withholding his assent to the same through, perhaps, the inclusion of an anti-assignment clause in his debt contract with A.

We see, therefore, how it is possible to divest oneself of beneficial interest and *exclusive* control over the powers and liabilities arising from and associated with the claim-right and duty jural relation between A and B without having to effect any change to that underlying claim-right/duty jural relation or the associated power/liability jural relation. All we need is for A not only to authorize C to act in her place: but also to release C from the fiduciary duties that would normally accompany such grant of authority. Thus, we would have the set of jural relations shown in Table 4.3.

---

[104] As will be explained in Chapter 6, Section A, such authority, when coupled with an interest, is irrevocable and will survive even A's death.

Table 4.3 *Effect of Authorization Plus Release*

3.1 A has a claim-right against B that B do Φ;

3.2 A has a power against B to do Θ;

3.3 A has a privilege against B to invoke her power against B to do Θ, or not, as she pleases: she is under no duty to B to invoke that power, or not; and

3.4 A has an immunity against B changing A's jural relations with B in that B has no ability to effectively invoke A's power against B to do Θ.

3.5 By reason of the bare trust constituted in favour of C, A no longer has a privilege against C to invoke her power against B to do Θ as she pleases without regard for C's interests, or not; she is under a duty to C to invoke her power against B to do Θ, or not, in accordance with the terms of the bare trust; and

3.6 By reason of the authority granted to C, coupled with a release of his fiduciary obligations, A will no longer have an immunity against C changing A's jural relations with B in that C will now have the power against A to invoke A's power against B to do Θ, and as he pleased without regard for A's interests. That power is no longer for A, and A alone, to invoke; since A had authorized C to invoke such power as her agent. Furthermore, C is also privileged against A to invoke such delegated power against B as he pleases without regard for A's interests.

The argument is that equitable assignment should be conceived as operating through the combination of a bare trust plus an atypical agency in which the assignee is authorized to act as if he were the assignor, and without regard for A's interests,[105] leading to the results spelt out in Table 4.3.

Though Tables 4.1–4.3 have only mentioned one of A's powers against B, namely her power to release B from his duty, the analysis may be applied to any or all of A's powers against B arising in connection with her claim-right/duty jural relation with B by reason of the loan contract in Example 4.4. We may thus apply, *mutatis mutandis*, the composite conception of equitable assignment to explain how C may invoke A's power to release B from his duty to tender payment of £10,000 to A by way of outright grant without any quid pro quo, whilst also having the power to restrain A from acting in any way that would frustrate the efficacy of such release; or how C may invoke A's power to bring judicial proceedings against B, should there be a dispute over B's performance of

---

[105] See discussion at text to and following n. 78, above.

his duty, whilst also having the power to restrain A from invoking her power to release B from his duty, and so forth.

Consistently, too, with the proposition in this book that there is a singular conception of equitable assignment which applies regardless as to whether the chose assigned be legal or equitable, the analysis above applies equally well to equitable choses in action arising from equitable obligations such as the obligation arising between a trustee and his beneficiaries, or the obligation arising between the executors of a will and the beneficiaries under the will, to name just a few.

Suppose T holds legal title to 10,000 Black Co. Ltd ('BCL') shares on a bare trust for A, if A is *sui juris*, that trust entails A having a claim-right against T that T shall fully execute the bare trust by conveying his legal title in the shares to such person as A might name. This claim-right is, accordingly, associated with a variety of powers, amongst which would be A's power against T to name a person to whom T's legal title in the shares is to be conveyed to allow T to fully execute his duty as bare trustee.

If we take '$\Phi$' to mean, 'the act of fully executing the trust by conveying T's legal title to such person as A may name'; and '$\Theta$' to mean, 'the act of naming a person to whom T's legal title in the shares is to be conveyed to allow T to carry out his duty to do $\Phi$', we may see that the analysis above in Tables 4.1–4.3 will apply to similar effect. That is, the combination of the kind of trust and atypical agency described in Table 4.3 allows for a 'transfer' of control over the jural relations between obligor and obligee *without* needing to change any aspect of their jural relations *inter se*.

So in respect of T, A, and C, jural relations 3.5 and 3.6 in Table 4.3 may be restated as follows:

---

*3.5bis* By reason of the bare trust constituted by A in favour of C, A will be duty-bound to C not to invoke her power against T to do $\Theta$, save in a manner sanctioned by the terms of the bare trust for C's benefit (i.e. unless C directs her to do so).[106]

*3.6bis* By reason of the atypical authority granted by A to C, C will have the power against B to invoke A's power against T to do $\Theta$, and what is more, C will be privileged against A to invoke A's power against T to do $\Theta$, or not, as C pleases without regard for A's interests.

---

[106] See e.g. *Stephens* v. *Venables (No. 1)* (1862) 30 Beav 625, in which George Henry Venables, the beneficiary of a share in the residuary estate of his father under the terms of his father's will, had equitably assigned that share to Stephens by way of security for a debt of £1,000,

We should notice the functional similarity between jural relations 3.6 and 3.6*bis* with jural relation 2.5 from Table 4.2. That is to say, we can approximate the result in jural relation 2.5, without needing to effect any change to the claim-right/duty jural relations between A and T.

Comparison of jural relations 2.6 (from Table 4.3) and 3.5 or 3.5*bis*, however, reveal significant differences.

Jural relations 3.5 (or 3.5*bis*) set out the proposition that A is duty-bound to C not to invoke her power against B (or T) to do $\ominus$, unless C directs her to do so. But being duty-bound *not* to invoke her power against B (or T) to do $\ominus$ does not mean that A no longer has such power. She does, save she may not invoke it without prior direction by C. Accordingly, jural relations 3.5 (or 3.5*bis*) tell us that A may still invoke her power against B (or T) to do $\ominus$, even if no prior direction by C had been given: such invocation is valid *as against B (or T)*, albeit it will be a breach of her duty to C. Accordingly, C would *not* be immune to A changing C's jural relations with B (or T) (arising from his 'agency' under jural relations 3.6 (or 3.6*bis*) in that A, as 'principal', would necessarily retain her power to invoke *her* power against B (or T) to do $\ominus$.

This may be contrasted with the effect in jural relation 2.6: where the claim-right/duty jural relation between A and B had been extinguished, and a 'new' claim-right/duty jural relation between C and B had been constituted in its place, A would no longer have *any* power against B to do $\ominus$; that power would be exclusively (re-)vested in C. So C would thereafter be *immune* to A changing C's jural relations with B in that A has no ability to effectively invoke C's power against B to do $\ominus$.

This is significant, for the cases tell us that an equitable assignor may be restrained by injunction from acting contrary to the interests of her

---

notice of such assignment having been given to the trustees and executors of the father's will. At 30 Beav 627, Sir John Romilly MR held: 'The [assignees] insist that after the receipt of the notice of the charge given by George Henry Venables in their favor, the trustees could not, without their consent, be allowed any payment made to George Henry in respect of the testator's estate. ... This is also my opinion. When a trustee or executor receives notice that a legatee has charged his legacy in favor of a stranger, the trustee is bound to withhold all further payments to that legatee, unless made with the consent of the mortgagee of the legacy.' Hence, although the executors and trustees of the testator's estate certainly had the power by reason of the testamentary trust to make payments out of the estate to Venables, once they were given notice of the equitable assignment to the assignees, even if such assignment had been by way of security, the executors and trustees would have become duty-bound to the assignees *not* to invoke that power without their assent. On the facts of the hypothetical facts in the example in the main text, A, as assignee, would obviously be cognisant of her duties to her assignee, C.

assignee.[107] Such an injunction would be unnecessary (and would not issue, since 'equity does not act in vain'), if equitable assignments operated by way of substitutively transferring the assignor's claim-right/duty jural relation (as sketched out in Table 4.2). But such an injunction would make sense if equitable assignments operated by means of the composite trust and agency model sketched out in Table 4.3.

The combination of trust plus agency explains how the outcomes in the cases may be achieved, whilst respecting the inherent invariability of the obligation voluntarily assumed by the obligor. Through changes to the jural relations between assignor and assignee, we can *approximate* the effects as would otherwise have to arise by changing the claim-right/duty jural relation between obligor and obligee.

## D   Equitable Assignments of Choses in Action Arising from Obligations Imposed by Law

The analysis thus far has concentrated on the operation of equitable assignment of choses in action arising from voluntarily assumed obligations. If equitable assignments are conceptualized to operate by means of a bare trust coupled with agency, since those mechanisms work by leaving the jural relations between obligor and obligee-assignor entirely unchanged, seeking obligor consent for the assignment to take effect is unnecessary because, in essence, it is none of his business. And although such 'trust plus agency' does effect changes to the obligor's immunity/disability jural relations with regard to the assignee, as has already been mentioned, an obligor will generally be taken to have assented to such changes unless provision be made otherwise. It is not, therefore, that no

---

[107] See e.g. *Applin* v. *Cates* (1861) 30 LJ Chan 6: injunction granted on application of assignee of a contractual debt payable by instalments, to enjoin the assignor of the debt from accepting future tenders of instalments by the debtor; *Kekewich* v. *Manning* (n. 46): injunction granted on application of assignees (being trustees of a settlement in favour of volunteers) of an equitable remainder interest in certain funds, to enjoin the assignor from vesting that interest in the trustees under a later settlement. See also *Fortescue* v. *Barnett* (n. 51), where the assignor of the benefit of a policy of assurance who had received bonuses on the policies and had successfully invoked his powers against his insurers by surrendering his policy was ordered to pay to the assignee such sum as had been secured by the policy, the bonus declared, as well as such further sum as would be sufficient to answer all future bonuses as would have been payable, had the policy not been surrendered. Such order could not be made if equitable assignments operated in the manner described in Table 4.2 since on that conception of assignment, any dealings with the assignor by the obligor of the *new* claim-right/duty jural relation envisaged in that model would have been a nullity.

account is taken of the obligor's assent to changes as to his immunity/disability jural relation with the assignee at all. Account *is* taken, by granting the obligor the power to displace such assent, thereby stifling the obligee's power to so delegate.

As mentioned in Chapter 2, not all obligations are voluntarily assumed. Many obligations such as the secondary obligation at common law to pay unliquidated damages arising after a contract has been breached are imposed by law.

The primary obligation at common law not to commit, say, the tort of trespass, is also imposed by law. When that duty is breached, the law imposes a secondary obligation on the tortfeasor to pay unliquidated damages to such person as the law defines and specifies to be the party to whom the tort duty is owed, and who has the power to bring legal proceedings to recover such damages.

Some obligations imposed by law may be equitably assigned. For example, unless precluded by statute or policy (for example, the policy against encouraging maintenance and/or champerty),[108] it is now recognized that the chose in action arising from a contractual or tortious cause of action arising from a breach of contractual or tortious duties may be equitably assigned.[109] If equitable assignment operated by *changing* the jural relations between obligor and obligee, it would be difficult to explain how equitable assignments of *secondary* obligations arising in connection with causes of action might be normatively justified.

As mentioned above, any model of equitable assignment predicated on exposing the obligor to a new obligation should provide a normative justification why such imposition is justified. Yet the cases reveal no such concern. That suggests that, whatever equitable assignment is doing, it is not operating in such a way which demands such justification. And that is precisely what the composite 'trust plus agency' model of equitable assignment proposed by this book does. No new normative justification for the 'new' obligation as would necessarily have to arise if equitable assignment did operate by way of extinction and regrant is needed because equitable assignment does not so operate. Rather, because

---

[108] See Smith & Leslie (2018), chapters 22 and 23; Liew (2018), chapter 4.

[109] Authority for the proposition that tortious and contractual causes of action may be equitably assigned (assuming no issues of champerty or maintenance are made out) may be found in *King* v. *Victoria Insurance Company Ltd* [1896] AC 250 (PC); *Compania Colombiana de Seguros* v. *Pacific Steam Navigation Co.* [1965] 1 QB 101 (tortious causes of action); and in *Linden Gardens* v. *Lenesta Sludge Disposals Ltd* [1994] 1 AC 85; *Offer-Hoar* v. *Larkstore (Technotrade Ltd, Part 20 defendants)* [2006] EWCA Civ 1079; [2006] 1 WLR 2926 (contractual causes of action).

equitable assignments do not operate by way of extinction and regrant, equitable assignments do not change any aspect of the jural relations between obligor and obligee. Thus, when a cause of action is equitably assigned, there is no change to any aspect of the jural relations between the obligor and obligee to the secondary obligations connected with that cause of action, and there is no concern to establish any new normative justification for the effects which result from the equitable assignment.

Since no new duty/claim-right jural relation as between obligor and obligee is generated by the obligee's equitable assignment of the chose to her assignee, those normative reasons which justified the imposition of secondary duty/claim-right jural relations on such obligor (as party-in-breach or tortfeasor) vis-à-vis such obligee pre-assignment, would be sufficient to justify continued imposition of those secondary obligations on the obligor with regard to the obligee post-assignment. No new or further justification is required because, as matters stand between the obligor and the obligee, everything is precisely as it used to be.

Finally, it may be noted that the substitutive transfer model of equitable assignment that has been posited elsewhere provides no reasons for the truism that an equitable assignment may only 'transfer' the benefits of a chose in action, but not the burdens. That is to say, an equitable assignment may allow an assignee to take the benefit of the chose assigned, but the assignor remains obligated to the obligor to that chose to discharge any burdens arising thereunder: it is not possible for the assignor to be released from those burdens. But the question is: why should this be the case? If equitable assignment *did* entail a unilateral substitution of the assignee in place of the assignor by extinguishing the assignee's jural relations with the obligor and recreating them but with the assignor in place of the assignee, why should such substitution/extinction only operate with regard to the benefits but not the burdens? Beyond repeating that that is what the cases say,[110] and repeating the

---

[110] Given Lord Templeman's rejection in *Rhone* v. *Stephens* [1994] 2 AC 310 of the so-called pure principle of benefit and burden suggested by Megarry V-C in *Tito* v. *Waddell (No. 2)* [1977] 1 Ch 106. Where the chose assigned involves benefits whose enjoyment is preconditioned on the discharge of certain burdens, a 'transfer' of such burdens may, in a manner of speaking, arise in connection with the assignment of such a chose. Such burdens may, of course, be performed by the assignor or her assignee, so long as the performance is not stipulated to be personal to the assignor. Such burdens may, therefore, be 'transferred' to the assignee, but only in a very loose sense in that, so far as the assignee may be motivated to perform said burden so as to fulfil the precondition to the obligor's counter-performance, the benefit of which had been assigned to the assignee.

proposition that such transfer of burdens ought not to be allowed, proponents of the substitutive model provide little insight into why this is the case.

Conceived of in terms of the trust-plus-agency model proposed in this book, however, the reasons why only benefits but not burdens may be 'transferred' becomes apparent. Although an obligee to a chose in action may certainly hold the benefit of such chose on trust for another by constituting a trust over it, such trust cannot transplant any duties owed by such obligee to the obligor to her intended trust beneficiary: as a matter of trust doctrine, only the benefits are held on trust. Similarly, although a principal may certainly delegate and authorize her agent to invoke her powers and/or immunities as arise from a chose in action, the conception of agency does not allow for anything more. Even if performance of the principal's duties may be delegated, the 'burden' or *liability* for non- or defective performance still remains with the principal. The constraint that 'only benefits may be equitably assigned, but not burdens' becomes, consequently, the logical result of the twin mechanisms that underpin the operation of equitable assignment.

This composite trust-plus-agency model of assignment is, however, novel. Most commentators on the English law of assignment propose other models. But, as explained in this chapter, although these other models explain some of the caselaw on assignment, they struggle to explain other cases. In the chapter which follows, the misconceptions of the caselaw which some of the proponents of these other models appear to suffer under will be dispelled.

# 5

# Misconceptions

The composite conception of equitable assignment set out in the preceding chapter goes against the current of most contemporary accounts of equitable assignments. These tend towards either a wholesale 'substitutive transfer' model, or a 'partial' trusts model according to which equitable assignments of legal choses entail the assignor holding the benefit of the chose assigned on trust for her assignee, whilst conceding that equitable assignment of equitable choses take effect by means of a substitutive transfer. Neither of these approaches fully integrates the significance of the proposition that voluntarily undertaken equitable obligations, just as much as legal ones, are not generally capable of being unilaterally varied by the obligees thereto without the obligors' assent, whether such assent be given in advance, or at the time of such variation.

Proponents of the partial trusts model who concede that the 'trust' model is applicable only to equitable assignments of legal choses, but not equitable choses, appear to have adopted this position because of a rather literal reading of authorities such as *Cator* v. *Croydon Canal*.[1] They may also have been influenced by the proposition that where a bare sub-trust is constituted over an equitable chose, the bare sub-trustee 'drops out' so that the obligor to the chose assigned, the primary trustee, then holds on trust for the beneficiary of the sub-trust. Two specific points may be made in response.

First, although some cases do say that an assignor of an equitable chose retains 'no interest' post-assignment, such statements must be read contextually in light of authority and principle. The authorities discussed in Chapter 4 show that an equitable assignment of an equitable chose entails the constitution of a trust over such chose for the assignee's benefit. It follows that the assignor may not invoke or assert her interest or entitlements against the obligor as she pleases. She will have become

---

[1] (1843) 4 Y & C Ex 593. This and other cases which are usually relied on for the proposition are discussed below in Section A.

duty-bound to her assignee to invoke or assert her powers against the obligor according to the terms of that trust. So the assignor of an equitable chose retains her equitable interest, and the resulting entitlements against the obligor, but may no longer invoke or assert them *for her own benefit*. That is to say, the assignor loses her beneficial interest in the chose assigned.

This is corroborated by the universal acknowledgement that an equitable assignment, even of an equitable chose, is effective without notice to the obligor to the chose.[2] It is also universally accepted that an obligor who discharges his duties under that chose in ignorance of an equitable assignment of the benefit of that chose is exposed to no liability to either the assignor or the assignee for such acts.[3]

Thus, where a trustee, T, holds property on special trust for A, should A collapse that special trust to a bare trust by invoking the doctrine of *Saunders* v. *Vautier*, and then invoke her power as beneficiary of such bare trust to require its complete execution by directing T to convey his title to the trust property to A, notwithstanding that A had equitably assigned her equitable interest under the special trust to C beforehand, T's compliance with A's instructions *whilst he was ignorant of A's prior assignment to C* will extinguish his obligations arising under that special trust without exposing him to any liabilities, equitable or otherwise, to C.[4] That is so despite T's actions having destroyed C's beneficial equitable interest in A's equitable interest in the trust property that had been held by T on special trust for A's benefit. If equitable assignment of an equitable chose resulted in an extinction of the assignor's interest and a revesting of the same in the assignee, such a result would be impossible. The notion that such is the case must, accordingly, be mistaken.

---

[2] *Hobson* v. *Bell* (1839) 2 Beav 17, 23; *Donaldson* v. *Donaldson* (1854) Kay 711, 719; *Weddell* v. *J. A. Pearce & Major* [1988] Ch 26, 32–3.

[3] *Donaldson* v. *Donaldson* (n. 2) at Kay 719; *Low* v. *Bouverie* [1891] 3 Ch 82, 104; *Ward* v. *Duncombe* [1893] AC 369, 392 (Lord Macnaghten). For authorities holding that obligors in legal choses in action will be discharged of their legal obligations thereunder if they perform to their obligees in ignorance of their obligees' having equitably assigned such legal choses to assignees, see e.g. *Williams* v. *Sorrell* (1799) 4 Ves Jun 389; *Stocks* v. *Dobson* (1853) 4 De G M & G 11; *Herkules Piling Ltd* v. *Tilbury Construction Ltd* (1992) 61 BLR 111 (Comm).

[4] The effect of notice of assignment in generating a distinct and direct equitable obligation between assignee and obligor in connection with the equitable wrong of dishonest assistance will be explained in Chapter 11. Notice may also trigger the procedural bars to pleading certain common law defences which might otherwise be available to the obligor: this is explained in Chapter 12.

Second, there is also a view that even accepting that an equitable assignment of an equitable chose entails the constitution of a trust over that equitable chose, so far as such trust is conceived to be a *bare* trust, the assignor, as bare sub-trustee, will 'drop out', leaving the obligor to the chose obligated to the assignee. By way of response: a bare trust is still a trust. So if an equitable assignment of an equitable chose entailed the constitution of a bare trustee–beneficiary relationship between the assignor and assignee, such assignor would still be trustee (albeit a bare one) of the equitable chose, and such assignor would necessarily still have to retain her equitable interest over which such bare trust had been constituted in order for there to *be* a trust. So the 'dropping out' of such equitable assignor ought not to be possible either.

So far as the law is to be consistent with principle, then, it seems that an equitable assignment, whether of an equitable or a legal chose in action, cannot extinguish the chose which bound the obligor to the obligee-assignor, and replace it with some kind of equivalent between the obligor and the assignee. Nor may an equitable assignor of an equitable chose 'drop out' once it is accepted that such equitable assignments entail the creation of a bare trustee–beneficiary relationship between the assignor and her assignee. To assess whether such unprincipled results are what the cases dictate, the following sections will examine the caselaw which is often relied on in their support.

## A 'No Interest Whatsoever'

Smith and Leslie accept that where the chose assigned is legal, the assignment operates in the manner of a trust over the benefit of the legal chose in action.[5] However, '[w]here the whole interest in an equitable chose has been assigned from assignor to assignee, equity permits the assignee to sue in his own name without joining the assignor. This is because – provided the *whole* interest has been assigned – the assignee is the sole owner and no interest remains in the assignor.'[6] Thus, where the benefit of a legal chose in action is held by T as trustee for the benefit of A (who therefore has an equitable interest in the benefit of that legal chose

---

[5] Smith & Leslie (2018), para. 11.19–11.24, concluding that an equitable assignment of a legal chose in action has a substantive effect in divesting the assignor of her beneficial interest in that legal chose, and vesting it in the assignee.

[6] Ibid., para. 11.06 (emphasis in original).

in action), when A equitably assigns her equitable interest to C, Smith and Leslie suggest that '[t]he effect of the assignment is therefore to cause assignor [A] to drop completely out of the picture. [A]'s equitable (beneficial) interest passes to C, and [T] holds on trust for C rather than [A]. In these circumstances, there is no *substantive* reason for joining [T] to any proceedings brought by assignee C to enforce the chose.'[7]

As authority, Smith and Leslie cite a passage from Lord Lyndhurst LC's judgment in *Cator v. Croydon Canal Co.*:[8]

> It was said that, as these proceedings were instituted by the assignee, the assignor ought to have been made a party to the suit. It is quite clear that, where the assignor has a legal title and he assigns his interest, and any proceedings are taken by the assignee with respect to the property so assigned, the assignor must be a party to the suit, because, by his assignment, he does not part with the legal estate, and the person having the legal estate must be before the Court. But the principle clearly does not apply to the facts of this case. There was no sum awarded specifically to this gentleman, Mr Scott. All that he had was an equitable interest— – an equitable title to be paid the sum of money if he made out his title to the land. That equitable interest and right he assigned before the suit; he parted, therefore, with all interest, and, *having parted with all interest* of every description, of course it was not necessary that he should have been a party to these proceedings.

Smith and Leslie also rely on the authority of two other cases. First, they rely on *Donaldson v. Donaldson*, which provides:[9]

> In the case of an assignment of the equitable interest in stock standing in the names of trustees, the deed of assignment passes the whole equitable interest of the donor, and the donee may go with that deed to the trustees, and say, transfer to me the interest in this sum of stock; and I think that in such a case it would not even be necessary to make the donor a party to a suit to enforce a gift.

Next, they also rely on *Fulham v. McCarthy*, where Lord Cottenham LC said of the assignment before the court:[10]

> It is not an assignment of a legal right, it is an assignment in equity of a purely equitable interest; in which case, as Mr Turner very properly

---

[7] Ibid., para. 11.08 (emphasis in original).
[8] *Cator* v. *Croydon Canal Co.* (n. 1) at 4 Y & C Ex 593–4 (emphasis added).
[9] *Donaldson* v. *Donaldson* (n. 2) at Kay 718–19 (Page Wood V-C).
[10] (1848) 1 HLC 708, 717–18.

admitted at the bar, the course of practice of Courts of Equity is to file a bill, not by the assignor, who, if the assignment be valid, has no longer any interest in the property assigned, but by the party claiming as assignee.

By their own words, Smith and Leslie admit that when A equitably assigns her equitable chose against T to C, A merely 'loses' her beneficial interest in the equitable chose ('[A]'s equitable (beneficial) interest passes to C').[11] This undermines the proposition that such assignor 'drops out completely' since the 'loss' of the assignor's 'beneficial interest' merely denotes that A is no longer privileged as against C to invoke her entitlements as holder of that equitable interest for her own benefit. If A had indeed lost the *entirety* of her equitable interest in the equitable chose that she had assigned to C, it would be otiose to speak of A having lost her *beneficial* interest.

Given the cases which tell us that equitable assignments of legal and equitable choses, alike, entail the constitution of a trust, judicial statements that an equitable assignor of an equitable chose or interest retains 'no interest whatsoever' or has 'no equitable interest' following the assignment cannot be taken literally. Read in context, they should be taken to mean that post-assignment, the equitable assignor retains no *beneficial* equitable interest in the equitable chose or interest, such beneficial interest having passed to her assignee.

Indeed, the House of Lords in *Fulham* v. *McCarthy* alluded to this at another part of the judgment when Lord Cottenham LC[12] held that:[13]

> [i]f the assignees, that is, the trustees of the religious house, had filed a bill, then the defendant would have an interest in the question on the issue [as to whether the assignment to the assignees had been induced by their undue influence over the assignors], because every defendant has an interest in shewing that the party sueing [sic] him has no interest in the subject-matter of the suit; and it would be a perfectly valid course of defence to shew that this deed was not a deed which a Court of Equity could recognize as giving a *beneficial interest* to the party claiming under it.

---

[11]  Smith & Leslie (2018), para. 11.08.

[12]  Lord Cottenham was Lord Chancellor from 1836 to 1841 (when he handed down his decision in *Cator* v. *Croydon Canal Co.*), and then again from 1846 to 1850 (when he handed down his decision in *Fulham* v. *McCarthy*).

[13]  (1848) 1 HLC 708, 717–18 (emphasis added).

*Donaldson* v. *Donaldson* should be read similarly as it adopted and extended the reasoning of Grant MR in *Sloane* v. *Cadogan*,[14] a decision which rests on the proposition that an equitable assignment of an equitable chose entails the constitution of a trust. Reading the references in *Donaldson* to the assignor as literally having 'no equitable interest whatsoever' would be incoherent.

What, then, of Lord Cottenham LC's earlier speech in *Cator* v. *Croydon Canal Co.*,[15] on which Smith and Leslie also rely?

Unlike *Fulham* v. *McCarthy*, there is nothing in Lord Cottenham's speech in *Cator*[16] to indicate that he had in mind the extinction of the equitable assignor's *beneficial* equitable interest. Thus, many commentators, Smith and Leslie amongst them, have been content to take the Lord Chancellor at his word, that following the assignment of his equitable entitlement to compensation to the assignee, Cator, the assignor had, 'parted . . . with all interest', and so have accepted that such assignment had completely extinguished the assignor's equitable interest.

As pointed out above, however, so literal a reading of Lord Cottenham's words in *Cator* would necessarily entail acceptance of the proposition that equitable assignment would operate differently depending on whether the subject matter of the assignment was an equitable or a legal chose. But such a result is difficult, as the later decision in *Kekewich* v. *Manning* shows: *Kekewich* v. *Manning* reveals that the reason why it is possible to make a gift of an equitable or a legal chose is because *all* equitable assignments entail a trustee–beneficiary relationship arising between the assignor and her assignee.[17]

What is more, taking Lord Cottenham's speech in *Cator* at face value would be hard to reconcile with his later speech in *Fulham* v. *McCarthy*: if the equitable assignment did have the effect of completely extinguishing the equitable assignor's equitable interest, and not just her beneficial interest, there would have been no point in mentioning the latter in *Fulham* v. *McCarthy*. We have, therefore, two possibilities: either Lord Cottenham was using 'interest' consistently in both decisions to refer to *beneficial* interest, or he was not.

---

[14] *Sloane* v. *Cadogan* (1808), reported in Sugden (1846), p. 1119; and discussed in Chapter 4, text to n. 42.

[15] *Cator* v. *Croydon Canal Co.* (n. 1).

[16] Reproduced at text to n. 8, above.

[17] This was discussed in Chapter 4, Section A(ii).

Although it is certainly true that Lord Cottenham would not have been bound in *Cator* by Grant MR's 1808 decision in *Sloane* v. *Cadogan*,[18] it is striking that nothing in the Lord Chancellor's comments on the objection to non-joinder of the assignor in *Cator* reveals any concern that he might be departing from the position and reasoning that had been reached some thirty years previously in *Sloane* v. *Cadogan*. Nor is there anything in his later speech in *Fulham* v. *McCarthy* to indicate that he was resiling in that case from any contrary position he might have adopted previously, himself. To maintain consistency with Grant MR's analysis, as well as his own subsequent speech in *Fulham* v. *McCarthy*, it would seem that a more coherent interpretation of *Cator* would be to read Lord Cottenham as also having intended to refer to beneficial interests and *not* equitable interests per se.

But even if Lord Cottenham *did* intend to be taken literally in *Cator*, then clearly, when delivering the leading speech of the House of Lords in *Fulham* v. *McCarthy*, perhaps that earlier literalist position had been abandoned. If so, by the time *Fulham* v. *McCarthy* was decided, if an equitable assignment extinguished anything, it extinguished merely the assignor's beneficial interest: which means that the assignor *must* be taken to have retained her equitable entitlements pertaining to the subject matter of the assignment, although she would no longer be privileged to invoke them for her own benefit. In other words, by so equitably assigning, she would have become obligated to her assignee in a manner akin to that between a trustee and her beneficiary. With respect, commentators who have concluded otherwise on the basis of cases such as *Fulham* v. *McCarthy*, *Donaldson* v. *Donaldson* and *Cator* v. *Croydon Canal Co.* may thus have failed to fully appreciate the broader context within which the passages relied on should be construed.

Such 'dropping out' appears to involve an insuperable contradiction. The trust analysis requires that the assignor/trustee *not* 'drop out'. But is there something odd about 'bare sub-trusts'? This leads us to a second misconception that occludes understanding of the law of equitable assignment.

## B    'Dropping Out'

There is a view that where a primary trustee ($T_1$) holds property (e.g. an equitable interest in realty or personalty) on trust for a beneficiary ($T_2$),

---

[18] Discussed in Chapter 4, Section A(ii).

who then constitutes herself as bare sub-trustee of her equitable interest in the primary trust property for the benefit of a sub-beneficiary ('C'), $T_2$, as bare sub-trustee, 'drops out' of the primary trust with the result that $T_1$ becomes trustee for C.

Upjohn J assumed this to be so in his judgment in *Grey* v. *Inland Revenue Commissioners*;[19] and many commentators[20] read *Onslow* v. *Wallis*,[21] *Re Lashmar*[22] and *Grainge* v. *Wilberforce*[23] as supporting it, leading to the suggestion that because the bare sub-trustee of a subsisting equitable interest 'drops out', every constitution of such bare sub-trusts entails a disposition of that interest, and so must comply with the formalities prescribed by s. 53(1)(c), LPA1925 to be validly constituted.[24]

If bare sub-trustees 'dropped out' such that $T_1$ no longer owed $T_2$ any obligations arising from the primary trust between them, and $T_1$ became directly obligated to C, then so far as equitable assignments of *equitable* choses might be conceived of as entailing a bare sub-trust, equitable

---

[19] [1958] Ch 375, 382. That view has been doubted: see, e.g. P. V. Baker, 'Case Note on *Grey* v. *Inland Revenue Commissioners* [1958] 2 WLR 168' (1958) 74 LQR 180, 181–2; Gareth Jones, 'Section 53(1)(c) and (2) of the Law of Property Act 1925 – Recent Developments' [1966] CLJ 19, 22.

[20] See e.g. G. Battersby, 'Formalities for the Disposition of Equitable Interests Under a Trust' [1979] *Conveyancer* 17, 28; A. J. Oakley, D. B. Parker and A. R. Mellows, *Parker and Mellows: The Modern Law of Trusts* (9th edn, London: Sweet & Maxwell, 2008), para. 4-018; R. A. Pearce and W. Barr, *Pearce & Stevens' Trusts and Equitable Obligations* (7th edn, Oxford: Oxford University Press, 2018), pp. 124–5. The point was also made in D. J. Hayton, *Underhill's Law Relating to Trusts and Trustees* (13th edn, London: Butterworths, 1979), p. 170; D. J. Hayton, *Hayton and Marshall: Cases and Commentary on the Law of Trusts* (7th edn, London: Stevens, 1980), p. 54; and J. Glister and J. Lee, *Hanbury and Martin Modern Equity* (20th edn, London: Sweet & Maxwell, 2015), para. 6-014. However, current editions of these three works have retreated from the proposition, given Lawrence Collins LJ's *dicta* in *Nelson* v. *Greening & Sykes (Builders) Ltd* [2007] EWCA Civ 1358, [2008] 1 EGLR 59: see Underhill & Hayton (2016), para. 12.15; Hayton & Mitchell (2015), para. 3-082; and J. Glister and J. Lee, *Hanbury and Martin Modern Equity* (21st edn, London: Sweet & Maxwell, 2018), para. 6-015.

[21] (1849) 1 Mac & G 506.

[22] [1891] 1 Ch 258.

[23] (1889) 5 TLR 436.

[24] Both Green (1984), and J. E. Penner, *The Law of Trusts* (10th edn, Oxford: Oxford University Press, 2016), para. 6.22, suggest that even if it were true that bare sub-trustees did 'drop out' (which they also doubt), all instances of sub-trusts, whether special or bare, should fall within the language of 'disposition' in LPA1925, s. 53(1)(c), and so should require a suitably signed writing to be valid. This book proposes that an equitable assignment of an equitable interest, being a trust *plus* agency, is conceptually distinct from a mere trust over that same interest, and so the former, but not the latter, is rightly viewed to be a 'disposition' for the purposes of s. 53(1)(c).

assignments would seem to be effected by means of a form of substitutive transfer after all. However, if bare sub-trustees did 'drop out' in the manner some have supposed, the 'no look through' principle that participants within the various intermediated security-holding systems which have proliferated throughout the broader world of international corporate finance have assumed to apply to them would, to their surprise, not be applicable.[25] The systemic shock would, accordingly, be considerable. But fortunately, the view that bare sub-trustees 'drop out' is false as it simply misunderstands the cases.

*Onslow* decided that a trustee would be ordered to fully execute his trust by conveying to a sub-trustee who had duties to fulfil under the terms of the sub-trust.[26] In contrast, *Re Lashmar* merely decided that, when property is held on trust, the primary trustee will not be compelled to fully execute that trust by conveying his title therein to a sub-trustee whose sub-trust had failed. Therefore, these two cases do not support the proposition that, following constitution of a bare sub-trust, the equitable entitlements arising between the primary trustee and his beneficiary (now sub-trustee) are extinguished, and equivalent entitlements arise between the primary trustee and the sub-beneficiary, leading the bare sub-trustee to 'drop out'.[27] As for *Grainge* v. *Wilberforce*, that was a case of statutory overreaching pursuant to the Settled Land Act 1882.

### (i)   Onslow v. Wallis *(1849)*

In *Onslow* v. *Wallis*, legal title in a freehold property was held by the principal trustee ($T_1$) on trust for a beneficiary (A) absolutely. A executed a will, stipulating that on her death the legal title in the freehold was to be conveyed to testamentary trustees ($T_2$ and $T_3$) on a trust for sale,

---

[25] For discussion of the 'no look through' principle, and how the view that bare sub-trustees might 'drop out' would preclude its operation, see Ben McFarlane and Robert Stevens, 'Interests in Securities: Practical Problems and Conceptual Solutions' in Louise Gullifer and Jennifer Payne (eds.), *Intermediated Securities: Legal Problems and Practical Issues* (Oxford: Hart, 2010). McFarlane and Stevens also note how the cases, properly understood, do not support the view that bare sub-trustees 'drop out'. See also *Secure Capital SA* v. *Credit Suisse AG* [2017] EWCA Civ 1486, [2017] 2 Lloyd's Rep 599, [9]–[11].

[26] Green (1984), p. 397.

[27] As will be explained below, *Onslow* v. *Wallis* (n. 21) but not *Re Lashmar* (n. 22), was distinguishable from the reasoning of the Lord Keeper in *Burgess* v. *Wheate* (1759) 1 Eden 177. Consequently, '[*Re Lashmar*] simply decided that a party with no beneficial interest in property, and with no duties to perform as trustee of that property, could not claim that property from the party holding legal title to it': Hayton & Mitchell (2015), p. 96, fn. 99.

the proceeds from such sale to be used to pay A's creditors, and the balance to be distributed to legatees whose identity would be set out in a separate document.

A died a widow without any heirs. In her lifetime, she had not required $T_1$ to convey the legal title in the freehold property to her, though she could have done so, being the sole, *sui juris* and absolutely entitled beneficiary under a bare trust of that freehold. Accordingly, at her death, all A had was an equitable interest in $T_1$'s legal title in the freehold property which devolved to her testamentary trustees, $T_2$ and $T_3$.

$T_2$ and $T_3$ applied to $T_1$ to execute the trust on which he held the freehold so they could discharge their duties under A's testamentary trust, but $T_1$ declined, on grounds that the document identifying the legatees to whom the 'legacies' mentioned in A's will had been lost (those legacies had therefore failed), leaving only the creditors to A's estate, and $T_1$ was willing to pay those creditors out of other funds available to him. $T_2$ and $T_3$ then brought proceedings seeking an order to compel $T_1$ to convey his legal title in the freehold to them to allow them to carry out their duties to A's creditors. The Lord Chancellor granted the order applied for.

On these facts, notwithstanding the 'failure' of the 'legacies' because the document identifying the legatees had not been found, even if A's legatees could not yet (or perhaps ever) be established, A still had creditors who were ascertainable, and $T_2$ and $T_3$ were duty-bound to collect in the trust asset (i.e. the legal title to the freehold), sell it and use its proceeds to pay A's debts. *Onslow* was, therefore, distinguishable from the decision of the Lord Keeper in the case of *Burgess* v. *Wheate*[28] in which it was recognized that, as the law stood at the time, it was possible for a sub-trust to fail for want of beneficiaries and so come to an end, the doctrine of escheat having no application in respect of equitable interests in land.[29]

As to the question of the excess funds, if any, after paying the creditors, such excess funds would be held by $T_2$ and $T_3$ for the legatees if the document specifying their identities was ever located. But that was a matter between $T_2$ and $T_3$ on the one hand, and those legatees and their

---

[28] *Burgess* v. *Wheate* (n. 27). As to that decision: '[W]hatever opinion might have been originally entertained about *Burgess* v. *Wheate*, it has remained unreversed for more than eighty years; and, consequently, it must be considered as binding upon the Court. . . . The case was nothing more than this. A legal estate was vested in a trustee, in trust for A. who died without an heir; and it was held that the trustee might hold for his own benefit; the Crown having no equity to claim on the ground of escheat': *Taylor* v. *Haygarth* (1844) 14 Sim 8, 17 (Shadwell VC). See also Matthews (2012).

[29] *Onslow* v. *Wallis* (n. 21), 514.

successors-in-title, if they were ever to emerge, on the other; and $T_2$'s and $T_3$'s obligations to those legatees were no concern of $T_1$'s. As the Lord Chancellor noted: '[W]hether or not they [$T_2$ and $T_3$] have power afterwards to dispose of all the beneficial interest, is a matter with which the Defendant Wallis [$T_1$], as mere owner of the legal estate, has nothing whatever to do.'[30]

Consequently, the court ordered $T_1$ to convey his legal title in the estate to $T_2$ and $T_3$, thereby putting them in a position to perform their duties as trustees of A's will.

### (ii)   Re Lashmar (1891)

In *Re Lashmar*, $T_1$ and others held the legal title in a freehold property under P's will as trustees for certain life tenants, with remainder for the benefit of A absolutely. In turn, A left his estate to $T_2$ and $T_3$ on trust for A's widow for her life, with remainder over absolutely to A's illegitimate son, H.

P died in 1859; and A died in 1868, while some of the life tenants under P's will were still alive. Thus, on A's death, his reversionary equitable interest arising under P's will devolved to $T_2$ and $T_3$ to hold on trust for the benefit of A's widow for her life and, thereafter, for H.

In 1880, H died intestate and, without heirs or creditors. A's widow died in 1886 while some of the life tenants under P's will were still alive: the last of these life tenants only died in 1889.

When the last life tenant under P's will died, $T_2$ (being the sole surviving trustee under A's will) appeared to have gained the power to require $T_1$ (being the sole surviving trustee under P's will) to fully execute that trust under P's will by conveying his legal title in the freehold to $T_2$ for his own absolute benefit (since there was, by this time, no one to whom $T_2$ was duty-bound or liable under the trust under A's will). But when directed by $T_2$ to do so, $T_1$ declined on grounds that $T_2$ was no longer subject to any duties under the terms of A's will since A's widow had died, and H had died leaving no heirs or creditors.

$T_2$ applied for an order to compel $T_1$ to convey his legal title in the freehold to him. But the Court of Appeal dismissed the application. Bowen LJ agreed with Lindley LJ, who was persuaded to hold in favour of $T_1$ because:[31]

---

[30]  Ibid., at 515.
[31]  *Re Lashmar* (n. 22), 267–8.

[O]n the true construction of [A's] will, Moody [$T_2$], the trustee under it, having no duty whatever to discharge, and having nothing on earth to do with the property, cannot take the house in question from Penfold [$T_1$], who has got it. It appears to me that the true way to regard this will is to look through Moody [$T_2$] as nobody. So it comes to this, the property is in Penfold [$T_1$] on trust for nobody at all. Therefore, he keeps it.

To understand this passage, we need to appreciate the following: in *Re Lashmar*, when A died while the life tenants under P's will were still living, A's equitable remainder interest in $T_1$'s legal title in the freehold devolved to $T_2$ to hold on trust for the life of A's widow, and thereafter for the benefit of H, A's illegitimate son, as remainderman. At that instant, A's widow acquired an equitable life interest in $T_2$'s equitable remainder interest in $T_1$'s legal title in the freehold, whereas H would have acquired an equitable remainder interest in $T_2$'s equitable remainder interest in $T_1$'s legal title in the freehold. So when A died, the beneficial interest in $T_1$'s legal title in the freehold was dispersed between the life tenants under P's will still living, A's widow and H (though A's widow and H would have had to act through $T_2$, as trustee of A's will and not directly).

When H predeceased A's widow in 1880, leaving neither heirs nor creditors, that opened a gap in the allocation of the beneficial interest in $T_1$'s legal title in the freehold.[32] Accordingly, after H's death, $T_1$ was no longer liable to fully execute the testamentary trust. That could only arise if the life tenants, A's widow and H (or H's successors in title) had invoked the *Saunders* v. *Vautier* power in concert. But H had died leaving no heirs and no creditors, and in circumstances under which neither the doctrines of escheat nor *bona vacantia* to the Crown could operate. Thus, although $T_1$ was still not absolutely entitled, his liabilities had shrunk.

As to why neither escheat nor *bona vacantia* would apply on the facts:[33]

---

[32] The manner by which the gap in the beneficial interest arose in *Re Lashmar* (n. 22) is different from the hypothetical gap in the vesting of beneficial interests that was suggested by counsel in *Vandervell* v. *Inland Revenue Commissioners* [1967] 2 AC 291. In *Vandervell*, it had been suggested that the beneficial interest in the subject property (an option) might be 'in the air' until the terms of the trust were completely finalized, which suggestion Lord Wilberforce rejected (at 329). In *Re Lashmar*, however, the beneficial interest in $T_1$'s legal title in the shares was perfectly vested, at least to begin with: first in the life tenants of F's will, and in A, as remainderman, and later, following A's death, in the life tenants of F's will, A's widow and H. The 'gap' only arose in light of subsequent events.

[33] Lewin (2015), para. 8-013.

Before 1926, the general rule was that realty undisposed-of went to the heir and personalty undisposed-of went to the next-of-kin. If there was no heir, then the undisposed-of beneficial interest in realty, if the death occurred before August 14, 1885 [*sic*], sank into the land for the benefit of the trustee or legal tenant;[34] where the death occurred after that date but before 1926, it escheated to the lord as if the interest were a legal estate in corporeal hereditaments.[35] If there was no next-of-kin, the undisposed-of interest in personalty went to the Crown by the prerogative.[36]

H's equitable reversionary interest in $T_2$'s equitable reversionary interest in $T_1$'s legal title in the freehold was realty. So had H died intestate with an heir, that equitable reversionary interest of H's would have devolved to his heir. But H died without an heir, so it could not so devolve.

Nor could it 'revert' to the Crown by escheat or devolve to it by way of *bona vacantia*. As was held in *Burgess* v. *Wheate*,[37] escheat did not extend to equitable interests in land, and this was still the case in 1880 when H died because the statutory extension allowing escheat of equitable interests in land pursuant to the Intestates Estates Act 1884 had yet to be enacted. And at the time, the doctrine of *bona vacantia* applied only to ownerless *personalty*, as the statutory extension of *bona vacantia*[38] to also encompass realty lay decades ahead.[39]

---

[34] See e.g. *Burgess* v. *Wheate* (n. 27); *Taylor* v. *Haygarth* (n. 28); *Cox* v. *Parker* (1856) 22 Beav 168.

[35] 'Escheat' of equitable interests in land was eventually permitted by statute: Intestates Estates Act 1884, s. 4, which received the Royal Assent on 14 August 1884. Thus, in *Re Wood* [1896] 2 Ch 596, Romer J held that where the testatrix had devised her legal title in a freehold to trustees on a trust for sale, but had made no provision as to the residue of her estate by the will, the testatrix was to be taken to have died intestate as to the beneficial interest in the freehold and that it was escheated by reason of s. 4 of the 1884 Act. The 1884 Act was repealed vis-à-vis deaths after 31 December 1925: Administration of Estates Act 1925, s. 45(1)(d).

[36] That is, by reason of *bona vacantia*. As to how *bona vacantia* formerly applied only to personalty (as supplemented by the equitable doctrine of conversion), see *Middleton* v. *Spicer* (1867) 1 Bro C C 201; *Barclay* v. *Russell* (1797) 3 Ves Jun 424; *Taylor* v. *Haygarth* (n. 28); *Powell* v. *Merrett* (1853) 1 Sm & Giff 381; *Cradock* v. *Owen* (1854) 2 Sm & Giff 241.

[37] *Burgess* v. *Wheate* (n. 27); discussed exhaustively in Matthews (2012).

[38] The Crown's acquisition of property of an intestate by reason of *bona vacantia* was limited to the intestate's personal property until 1 January 1926, when Administration of Estates Act 1925, ss. 45(1)(d) and 46(1)(iv), and Law of Property Act 1922, s. 28 came into force. The commencement date for the 1922 Act was originally 1 January 1925, but it was postponed to 1 January 1926 by Law of Property Act (Postponement) Act 1924, s. 1.

[39] Had H died leaving a will directing that his realty be sold to pay his creditors, if any, on the authority of *Middleton* v. *Spicer* (n. 36), the Crown would have succeeded by the doctrine of *bona vacantia* to any such realty which would be treated as personalty by the doctrine of conversion.

Therefore, H's death in 1880 caused his 'share' in the beneficial interest in $T_1$'s legal fee in the freehold to 'sink into the land'. Accordingly, when H died in 1880, no one succeeded to H's power to act in concert with A's widow and the life tenants to require $T_1$ to fully execute the trust arising under P's will.

This is not to say that $T_1$ became completely free to invoke his entitlements as holder of the legal fee simple for his own benefit once H died: $T_1$ was still duty-bound to the life tenants, and also to A's widow (acting through $T_2$) as the remaining successor-in-title to A. So A's widow (acting through $T_2$) would have been entitled to require $T_1$ to restrain the life tenants from committing waste to safeguard her reversionary entitlement. And certainly, A's widow (acting through $T_2$) and/or the life tenants would have been entitled to restrain $T_1$ from dealing with his legal title in a manner inconsistent with the terms of P's will, for example, by selling his legal title to a third party.

When A's widow died while there were life tenants still living, her life interest in $T_2$'s reversionary interest in $T_1$'s legal title to the freehold would have ended. Accordingly, at this point, all beneficiaries to the trust arising from A's will would have been exhausted. As explained above, H left no successor in title. On the other hand, though A's widow could have had successors in title, none could have been devolved her life interest arising from A's will as that interest ended upon her death. $T_2$'s sub-trust had therefore come to an end through exhaustion of the beneficiaries.

The Court of Appeal decided as it did not because $T_2$ was a 'bare sub-trustee' who had 'dropped out'. It simply applied *Burgess* v. *Wheate*: $T_2$'s sub-trust had failed and ended for want of beneficiaries. Consequently, there was no reason for the court to assist $T_2$ by ordering $T_1$ to convey the legal title in the realty in question to him as $T_2$ no longer had any trust to carry out: following the death of A's widow, $T_2$ was trustee for no one.

As for $T_1$, had he required equity's assistance, he, too, would have been refused. But $T_1$ already held the legal title in the freehold: he did *not* need the court's assistance. Consequently, as $T_1$ no longer had any trust to perform either, $T_1$ was entitled to hold his legal title in the property for his own benefit.[40]

---

[40] *Cox* v. *Parker* (n. 34), 171 (Romilly MR): 'The question is, whether the devise took effect at all, for if it did the trustee must take the legal estate. Having taken the legal estate[,] there are no trusts to perform, and they are, therefore, entitled to hold the property.'

Thus, *Re Lashmar* cannot be understood as a case where the 'bare' sub-trustee 'drops out'.

### (iii)   Grainge v. Wilberforce *(1889)*

In *Grainge* v. *Wilberforce*, the defendant was tenant for life of certain estates in Sussex. As tenant for life, he had leased a dwelling house to the plaintiff. The plaintiff then contracted to purchase the house from the defendant. But a dispute arose as to the form of the conveyance.

The defendant's interest as tenant for life arose under a number of deeds of settlement, dating from 1863, 1864, 1865 and 1867. Under the 1864 deed, the house in question had been appointed to one Charles Lloyd to hold in trust, with power to raise up to £15,000 by mortgage. In 1865, Lloyd conveyed the legal title in the house to mortgagees, subject to a proviso that if the persons entitled under the deed of 1863 paid the mortgagees £11,500 plus interest, the mortgagees should reconvey the legal title in the house to the use of Lloyd, or other trustee or trustees under the deed of 1864, or as he or they should direct.

The plaintiff contended that the conveyance for the house he had purchased from the defendant ought to include Lloyd as a necessary party thereto. The defendant's view was that that was unnecessary. Being unable to agree as to the form of conveyance, in 1888, the defendant gave the plaintiff notice to quit the premises. The plaintiff then commenced proceedings seeking specific performance of the contract of sale to compel the defendant to execute a good and valid conveyance, and an injunction to restrain the defendant from dispossessing him.

Chitty J held: 'The defendant was clearly tenant for life, and even if he was so under the deed of 1867 his conveyance, having regard to section 20 of the Settled Land Act [1882], passed the property free from all estates and interests under the deed of 1867 and bound every one claiming under that settlement.'[41] Consequently, as Green has observed:[42]

> [*Grainge* v. *Wilberforce*] was simply a case where it was confirmed that a tenant for life under the Settled Land Act 1882 could successfully pass the legal estate to settled land without any need for the trustee of a sub-trust behind the settlement joining in the conveyance: an entirely justifiable

---

[41]  *Grainge* v. *Wilberforce* (n. 23), 437.
[42]  Green (1984), p. 397. See also Hayton & Mitchell (2015), p. 96, fn. 99; McFarlane & Stevens (2010), p. 48, fn. 55, crediting a suggestion made by Professor Paul Matthews.

result which owed nothing whatsoever to the fact that the sub-trustee was a bare trustee, and which would clearly have been the same even if the sub-trustee had had substantial outstanding active duties to perform.

In other words, *Grainge* v. *Wilberforce* was decided according to the doctrine of overreaching provided for by ss. 3 and 20(2) of the Settled Land Act 1882.[43]

After observing that any conveyance of the legal title of the realty in question by the defendant as tenant for life would overreach the interests of anyone else claiming an entitlement under the settlements giving rise to that tenancy for life, and that it would not therefore be necessary to join any other interest holders under the settlements to the conveyance for the sale of the property in question, Chitty J held that:[44]

> Lloyd had no interest whatever, or, if he had any, it was only an equitable right as trustee for the persons interested under the deed of 1867. *The case, therefore, fell within the principle that where A was trustee for B, who was trustee for C, A held in trust for C, and must convey as C directed.* B – in this case Lloyd – might therefore be left out even under the old strict rules as to parties – '*Head* v. *Lord Teynham*' (1 Cox 57). Therefore, Lloyd, or his heir, was not a necessary party to the conveyance, and the purchaser would be safe in completing without him.

Given the effect of ss. 3 and 20(2) of the 1882 Act, Chitty J's assertions as to A, B and C (emphasized in the quotation), plainly do not form part of the *ratio* of his decision. They were *dicta* whose derivation and justification were nowhere made plain. Beyond the fact that they were uttered judicially, their persuasiveness and weight is doubtful. But what, then, of the case of *Head* v. *Lord Teynham* itself, which Chitty J also referred to?

---

[43] Settled Land Act 1882. Section 1(3) of the 1882 Act provided that, unless otherwise provided for, this Act was to commence and take effect from 31 December 1882. The report of *Grainge* v. *Wilberforce* does not set out precisely when the contract of sale between the plaintiff and defendant was entered into, but it seems likely that it was entered into after 1882 (given Chitty J's application of the 1882 Act to the facts of the case) and before 24 June 1888, which is when the defendant wrote to the plaintiff giving the defendant notice to quit the premises. The modern-day equivalent to s. 20(2) of the 1882 Act may now be found in s. 72(2) of the Settled Land Act 1925. For an account of this form of overreaching, see Megarry & Wade (2012), p. 396. A fuller account of the operation of the 1882 Act may be found in the 5th edition of Megarry & Wade, pp. 317–24.

[44] *Grainge* v. *Wilberforce* (n. 23), 437.

### (iv)  Head v. Lord Teynham (1783)

It is unclear why Chitty J thought the issues in *Grainge* v. *Wilberforce* were analogous to those in the eighteenth-century decision in *Head* v. *Lord Teynham*, given that the former rested on the operation of a nineteenth-century statute.

In *Head* v. *Lord Teynham*, a bill was filed in the High Court of Chancery seeking an order to compel the trustees of a will ($T_1$) to fully execute the testamentary trust. Under the terms of the will, lands were limited to trustees for 500 years to raise a sum of £4,000 for distribution between the settlor's younger children (i.e. excluding the settlor's heir).

At his death, the settlor had six younger children. Two of these children 'assigned their shares of the £4000 to a trustee [$T_2$] for the benefit of two other of the children'.[45] Proceedings were then brought by the testator's children against the trustees of their father's will, $T_1$, to compel the due performance of the trusts under the will without joinder of the sub-trustee, $T_2$. $T_1$ objected on grounds that the suit ought not to be proceeded with without first joining $T_2$. But the objection was overruled. The report records as follows:[46]

> For plaintiff it was insisted that as the original trustees of the term who had the legal estate [$T_1$], and all the children who had the beneficial interest were before the court, there was no occasion to make the other trustee [$T_2$] a party, and the court would direct a sale of the term without his joining in the sale: and of that opinion was the court – and decreed accordingly.

This result, however, is not based on $T_2$ 'dropping out' on grounds that $T_1$ owed $T_2$ no equitable duties at all. This becomes clear when we consider *Fletcher* v. *Ashburner*[47] (yet another Chancery case), and examine how the requirement for joinder of necessary parties in equity works, the best account of which may be found in Calvert's *Treatise upon the Law Respecting Parties to Suits in Equity*.[48]

---

[45] *Head* v. *Lord Teynham* (1783) 1 Cox 57, 57.

[46] Ibid.

[47] (1779) 1 Bro C C 497.

[48] Calvert (1847), para. 6-11, repeating his analysis from the first edition (published in 1837). The significance of Calvert's insight was, unfortunately, missed by Story who, in his much more influential treatise on equity pleadings (first published in 1838), mentioned having read Calvert's analysis, but thought it unhelpful: Story (1838), p. 74, fn. 4. This has retarded understanding of the 'necessary party' doctrine: G. C. Hazard, 'Indispensable Party: The Historical Origin of a Procedural Phantom' (1961) 61 *Columbia Law Review* 1254, 1286–7.

In *Fletcher* v. *Ashburner*, by his will, John Fletcher devised his personalty and his burgage house in Kendall to trustees on trust to sell so much as sufficient to pay his debts, and then to permit his widow, Agnes, to enjoy the residue during her life, and after her death, to sell and dispose such residue as remained, deduct certain small sums by way of costs and honoraria, and then to distribute the balance of the money realized thereby equally between his son William and daughter Mary; but if either of them should die before his or her legacy became due, then to the survivor of them. The testator died, survived by Agnes, William and Mary.

The report states that by custom of burgage tenure in Kendall,[49] Agnes was entitled to hold the Kendall burgage house so long as she did not remarry, notwithstanding the provisions of the will. Agnes did not remarry, and survived both her children, each of whom died unmarried after having reached their majorities. When Agnes died, the heir at law of William and John Fletcher filed a bill against the trustees and personal representatives of the testator, John Fletcher, and also against the trustees and personal representatives of his widow, Agnes, seeking a declaration to have, in particular, the Kendall burgage house devised by John Fletcher's will conveyed to him. However, the representatives of Agnes contended that by reason of the direction that the realty be sold, it was to be treated as personalty by the doctrine of conversion, and so was to go to the personal representative of William, who had survived Mary, his sister.

When the matter came before Sir Thomas Sewell MR, an objection was taken that the personal representative of William had not been joined to the proceedings. The report records as follows:[50] 'But the Master of the Rolls was of opinion there were sufficient parties to sustain the question; that the personal representative [of William] was a mere *formal party*, and that, if he thought proper to make a decree, a personal representative might [then] be brought before the Master.' Sewell MR therefore proceeded to hear the merits of the dispute, holding over the objection on grounds of (possible) misjoinder.

Joinder of William's personal representative ultimately proved unnecessary because Sewell MR held that the realty was to be treated as personalty. Therefore, '[i]n the present case, William Fletcher, the son, had the whole beneficial title vested in him as money, subject to his

---

[49] For an account of burgage tenure, see Thomas Littleton, *Littleton's Tenures in English* (Eugene Wambaugh, ed., Washington, DC: J. Byrne, 1903), pp. 79–83.

[50] *Fletcher* v. *Ashburner* (n. 47), 498 (emphasis added).

mother's interest for life or widowhood. She was his sole next of kin, and her personal representatives are now entitled to the estate as money; the bill must therefore be dismissed without costs.'[51]

*Fletcher* v. *Ashburner* shows that parties with an interest in the subject matter over which Chancery litigation is brought need not *always* be joined before a final decision was handed down. Rather, what was critical was ascertaining the objective (or 'object', to use Calvert's terminology)[52] of such litigation, and whether the judicial order(s) which the litigation sought to obtain could, in justice and fairness, be made, given the parties who *were* before the court.

*Fletcher* v. *Ashburner* demonstrates that there may well be 'formal parties' who are 'interested' in the subject matter of the litigation before the court, yet not 'interested' in the objective or judicial remedy sought by such litigation, and who are thus not *necessary parties* who must be joined before the court comes to its final decision on the litigation in which that judicial remedy is sought. This view, as Calvert points out, is corroborated in many cases.[53]

Relying on these and other authorities, Calvert concluded as follows:[54]

> To select those persons as parties, *against whom a decree may be made*, or *against whom relief may be prayed*, or *who have an interest or power in the subject of the suit which requires to be bound by the decree*, or *who are interested in the question*, is to act upon the supposition that it is the mode in which the court is asked to deal with the subject of the suit; that, in other words, it is the object of the suit, which is the criterion whether any particular person is or is not to be made a party.
>
> If this distinction between the meaning of 'the subject of a suit', and that of 'the object of a suit', is borne in mind, it will be clear, that the word 'interest', when introduced into the rule concerning proper parties to a suit, means interest in its object, not interest in its subject-matter.

[51]  Ibid., 502.
[52]  See Calvert (1847), pp. 6–11. In similar vein, '[A]ll persons who may have in the object of an action in the Chancery Division an apparent interest or against whom the decree sought for will establish a right, or upon whom it will impose a duty, ought to be made parties either as plaintiffs or defendants': Arthur Underhill, *A Practical and Concise Manual of the Procedure of the Chancery Division of the High Court of Justice* (London: Butterworths, 1881), p. 44.
[53]  See *Smith* v. *Snow* (1818) 3 Madd 10, 11; *Lloyd* v. *Lander* (1821) 5 Madd 282, 288; and *Small* v. *Attwood* (1832) You 407, 458 (rev'd by the House of Lords on appeal, but not on this point: (1838) 6 Cl & F 232).
[54]  Calvert (1847), pp. 10–11 (emphasis in original).

Therefore: '[A]ll persons who have in the object or objects of the suit an interest or interests apparent upon the record, are necessary parties.'[55] Alternatively:[56]

> Another mode of expressing the general rule is, that under all circumstances, the question resolves itself into this, whether the relief sought in the bill, in other words, the equity of the bill touches any particular person, so as to obtain from him a benefit, or to fasten upon him a duty: that, if this question is answered in the affirmative, he is a necessary party.

This explains why $T_2$ did not need to be joined in *Head* v. *Lord Teynham*. It was not because $T_2$ had 'dropped out' of the picture. Rather, joinder of $T_2$ was unnecessary because $T_2$ had no interest in the objective or object of the proceedings that had been commenced by the plaintiffs.

By their bill, the plaintiffs in *Head* v. *Lord Teynham* sought a decree against $T_1$ to compel him to effect a sale of the term he had been granted and so raise the £4,000 for division between the younger children, precisely in conformity with the terms of the testamentary trust. With regard to such remedy, the joinder of $T_2$ was unnecessary since his entitlements against $T_1$ by reason of the sub-trust that had been constituted by two of the six younger children would not be affected by the decree being sought. Thus, $T_2$ had no interest in the *object* of the suit (and a broader 'interest', or curiosity about it, was not enough). $T_2$ was a merely 'formal party' (to use the terminology of *Fletcher* v. *Ashburner*) whose joinder was not necessary: his non-joinder would not mean that the decree of the court should be set aside for having been wrongfully made.

It follows that *Head* v. *Lord Teynham* is no authority for the proposition that an intermediate trustee 'drops out'. It is simply an illustration of the rule as to joinder of necessary parties in equity.[57]

It is fair to conclude that none of the cases usually relied on to support the point that bare sub-trustees 'drop out' actually stands for that proposition. And this is confirmed by Lawrence Collins LJ's *obiter dicta* in

---

[55] Ibid., p. 13. See also *Prosser* v. *Edmonds* (1835) 1 Y & C Ex 481, 496 (Lord Abinger CB).

[56] Ibid., p. 16. As further illustrations, Calvert cites *Hereford* v. *Ravenhill* (1839) 1 Beav 481; *Balls* v. *Strutt* (1841) 1 Hare 146; *Baring* v. *Nash* (1813) 1 V & B 551, 554.

[57] For further discussion of the proper scope of this rule, see Hazard, 'Indispensable Party' (n. 48), who discusses and demonstrates both the true rule, as well as how some later English (and American) authorities have gone astray.

*Nelson* v. *Greening & Sykes*,[58] statements which were cited with approval and applied by Judge Pelling QC in *Sheffield* v. *Sheffield*.[59]

In short, even with a bare sub-trust, it is wrong to speak of the bare sub-trustee *substantively* dropping out because for there to *be* a sub-trust, there has to be subject matter for that sub-trust to bite on. And when the subject matter of the sub-trust is the sub-trustee's chose against the primary trustee, it is conceptually impossible for the sub-trustee to be substituted by her sub-beneficiary.[60]

This is not to say that for *some* specific purposes it may be appropriate to short-circuit the analysis even whilst recognizing that there is no substitution of the assignee for the assignor. For example, in *Kapoor* v. *National Westminster Bank Plc*,[61] the Court of Appeal was concerned with a question of statutory interpretation, namely whether an equitable assignee of a part of a debt owed by a bankrupt to the assignor was a 'creditor' for the purposes of voting at a meeting to approve the bankrupt's proposed Individual Voluntary Arrangement under rr. 5.21 and 5.22 of the Insolvency Rules 1986.[62] The Court of Appeal held that an equitable assignee *was* to be taken to be a 'creditor' for such purpose, notwithstanding that the assignor was, in principle, *still* the bankrupt's creditor at law. But even so, it is an oversimplification to suggest that bare sub-trustees 'drop out'. Though it may seem that way, as with much in equity, appearances can be deceiving.

---

[58] *Nelson* v. *Greening & Sykes (Builders) Ltd* (n. 20), and reproduced at text to Chapter 6, n. 59).

[59] [2013] EWHC 3927 (Ch); [2014] WTLR 1039, [81]–[86].

[60] See also McFarlane & Stevens (2010), pp. 47–8.

[61] [2011] EWCA Civ 68; [2012] 1 All ER 1201.

[62] Insolvency Rules 1986, SI 1986/1925.

# 6

# Combination

As explained in Chapter 5, a bare sub-trustee does not 'drop out'. Therefore, so far as an equitable assignment of an equitable chose is conceived of as entailing the constitution of a bare sub-trust over that equitable chose, the assignor does not drop out either. But if the equitable assignee does not replace the assignor as obligee to the equitable chose assigned, how is such assignee able to deal directly with the obligor to the chose, as the cases tell us he is?[1]

The answer, as explained previously, lies in conceiving equitable assignment as also entailing the atypical agency effect mentioned in Chapter 2. This explains how an assignee of an equitable interest arising out of a trust is enabled to invoke the assignor's powers against the trustee to require full execution of that trust; and also how an assignee of a debt may invoke the assignor's powers against the debtor to accept a conforming tender of payment.

Since the 'agency effect' means the assignee is authorized to invoke any and all of the assignor's powers, an assignee will also be authorized to invoke the assignor's powers to commence judicial proceedings against the obligor. So far as such agency effect is recognized and given effect to by the courts, it would be 'as if' such proceedings had been commenced by the assignor herself.[2] Not only might the assignee, a stranger to the

---

[1] See *Donaldson* v. *Donaldson* (1854) Kay 711; *Goodson* v. *Ellison* (1826) 3 Russ 583; *Re Smith* [1928] 1 Ch 915. The same was accepted to be the case in *Cator* v. *Croydon Canal Co.* (1843) 4 Y & C Ex 593, so far as the court there recognized that the assignees in that case had validly required the Croydon Canal Co. to fully execute the constructive trust on which they held the funds in question and could bring proceedings in equity against the Croydon Canal Co. for its failure to do so in their own names without needing to join the assignor.

[2] A striking illustration of this may be found in *Bates* v. *Pilling and Seddon* (1826) 6 B & C 38. That was not a case of equitable assignment, but a simpler case where a judgment creditor granted actual authority to his solicitor to commence execution proceedings against his judgment debtor. The solicitor wrote to the judgment debtor, informing him that if the judgment debt was not satisfied by a certain date and time, he would commence execution

obligation between assignor and obligor, be thereby enabled to commence proceedings in relation to that obligation by such 'agency', taken together with the rules of *res judicata*, a final decision as would bind the assignor could be handed down, and so, in many circumstances, it would not be necessary as a matter of principle to join the assignor to such proceedings.

This may be illustrated by the facts of *Cator v. Croydon Canal Co.*.[3] In that case, the assignor ('A') was entitled to be paid a sum of money for damage to and compulsory acquisition of his land. The entitlement arose by way of a constructive trust constituted over a fund of money held by the Croydon Canal Co. ('T') for the benefit of affected land owners.[4] A, therefore, had an *equitable* chose in action against T that it execute its trust by paying the compensation sum in accordance with the terms of the trust.

A sold and transferred his legal title to the land in question, and also equitably assigned such interest as he had against T, to Cator ('C'). C then brought proceedings in equity against T seeking to compel it to fully execute its trust over the fund.

Although A was not party to the proceedings, C succeeded, having shown that he was assignee of A's equitable interest in the compensation sum and that such assignment was not void for maintenance or champerty (since it was in support of his legal title to the land in question).

proceedings as instructed by the judgment creditor. The judgment debtor paid the judgment debt to the judgment creditor within the stipulated deadline, but the judgment creditor failed to inform his solicitor of the same; so the solicitor instructed bailiffs to seize the judgment debtors' chattels in execution of what, to the solicitor's knowledge, was an unsatisfied judgment debt. The judgment debtor then brought proceedings in detinue against the judgment creditor for having wrongfully detained his goods, through the actions of his duly authorized agent. The action succeeded, on grounds that so far as the solicitor was acting within the scope of his authority, his acts in commencing execution proceedings against the judgment debtor were to be taken to be the acts of his principal, the judgment creditor: *qui facit alium facit per se.*

[3] *Cator v. Croydon Canal Co.* (n. 1).

[4] Under the terms of the statute which empowered the Croydon Canal Co to acquire the affected lands to effect the construction of the proposed Croydon Canal, if the compensation monies could not be immediately paid out because of doubts over the claimant's title to the land in question, those monies should have been paid into Court pending resolution of such doubts. In the assignor's case, instead of complying with that requirement, the sums to be paid in respect of the assignor's land were retained by the Croydon Canal Co. in its accounts. Consequently, a constructive trust was imposed on those monies for the benefit of such person as would satisfactorily establish his title to the land in question: *Cator*, ibid., at 419.

That is, C successfully invoked A's powers to commence proceedings in equity against T in his own name as A's assignee, *and* obtained final judgment, without joining A, the assignor, even though C remained a stranger to the constructive trust that had been imposed on T in A's favour.

This would be inexplicable if equitable assignments were merely bare trusts. Even on Calvert's pre-Judicature Acts conception of the rule of joinder in equity,[5] since the order sought required T to fully execute the constructive trust on which it held the compensation sum, A would be a 'necessary' party being 'interested' in the 'object' of such proceedings since T's compliance with such order would extinguish A's claim-right against T arising from that constructive trust.

Neither may cases like *Cator* be rationalized to be cases of derivative actions brought by trust beneficiaries because the trustee would still have to be joined to the proceedings, albeit as defendant.[6] Thus, in *Meldrum v. Scorer*[7] (a case involving a derivative action in respect of breaches of equitable duties owed by a testamentary trustee to the trustees for the derivative claimant) and *Roberts v. Gill & Co.*[8] (which was concerned with a derivative action in respect of breaches of common law duties owed by a solicitor to the trustees for the derivative claimant), the trustees holding those choses in action in trust for their respective beneficiaries had to be joined to the proceedings.

To explain how a stranger to the obligation may have the *standing* to bring proceedings against the obligor, a partial answer may be had in the 'agency effect' which has been suggested underpins the operation of equitable assignments. This, together with the operation of the rules of *res judicata*, explains why joinder of the assignor is not required when equitable proceedings are brought against an equitable obligor by an assignee before a final decision is handed down in those proceedings.

Discussion of the rules and effect of *res judicata* will, however, be held over for now.[9] Given the important role which the agency effect plays, over and beyond when judicial proceedings are brought, the remaining sections in this chapter will examine its irrevocability, how such assignees conceived of as 'agents' may nevertheless have the power

---

[5] See Chapter 5, text to n. 54.
[6] Lewin (2015), para. 43-012.
[7] (1887) 56 LT 471.
[8] [2010] UKSC 22; [2011] 1 AC 240.
[9] They will be discussed in Part III.

to subdelegate, how substantial damages may be recovered by an assignor in light of such trust and agency effects, and how problems of double liability are resolved on the dualist, composite model of equitable assignment advanced here.

## A    Irrevocable Grants of Authority

The composite model of equitable assignment proposed in this book rests on an atypical form of agency where the assignee is authorized to invoke the assignor's powers against the obligor without redard for the assingor's interests. So he may act as if he were the principal (the assignor) *and* he is privileged against all others (even against the assignor who granted him such authority) to invoke such delegated powers as he pleases.[10] Conceiving the 'agency' arising by reason of equitable assignment in this manner has interesting consequences.

Generally speaking, agents owe their principals fiduciary obligations,[11] and their agency is freely revocable.[12] And yet:[13]

> There are ... cases where authority is actually conferred in terms that purport to make it irrevocable, and the law recognizes the irrevocability as such. ... These cases are usually in English law referred to as cases of 'authority coupled with an interest'. The interest is that of the agent in carrying out the authority; and herein lies the organizing idea of this part of the law. We are here really not in the general law of agency at all. The central idea of agency is that of someone who acts on behalf of another

---

[10]  These unusual chacteristics of the 'agency' relationship between equitable assignor and assignee arising from the equitable assignment were discussed in Chapter 4, Section B.

[11]  Bowstead & Reynolds (2018), para. 1-001.

[12]  The discussion below applies independently of the provisions of the Powers of Attorney Act 1971, ss. 1 and 4 which provide that where a power of attorney has been created in an instrument complying with the formalities required in s. 1, such power, if expressed to be irrevocable, and if given to secure a proprietary interest in the power's donee or the performance of an obligation owed to the donee, so long as the donee retains that interest or the obligation remains undischarged, such power may not be revoked by the donor without the donee's consent; nor will such power be revoked by the donor's death, incapacity, bankruptcy or, where the donor was a body corporate, its winding up or dissolution. However, statutory irrevocability conferred under the 1971 Act is 'co-extensive with and does not abrogate the rules of common law relating to powers of attorney coupled with an interest': N. P. Ready, *Brooke's Notary* (14th edn, London: Sweet & Maxwell, Thomson Reuters, 2013), para. 8-42.

[13]  F. M. B. Reynolds, 'When Is an Agent's Authority Irrevocable?' in Ross Cranston (ed.), *Making Commercial Law* (Oxford: Clarendon Press, 1997), p. 260 (emphasis added). See also Bowstead & Reynolds (2018), paras. 10-007 and 10-010. The point was first made in 1976 by the editors of the fourteenth edition of *Bowstead* at p. 436.

and in that other's interest: it is for this reason that agents in general owe fiduciary duties and their authority can be revoked. But in these cases of authority coupled with an interest the agent acts, and exercises his authority, *in his own interest*. We have therefore a case where agency reasoning is deployed to achieve a different effect from the paradigm cases at which it is directed. It is a standard technique of law to use reasoning in this way.

And outside the law of assignment, that an agency relationship may well be irrevocable has also recently been affirmed by the Supreme Court:[14]

> 6 The general rule is that the authority of an agent may be revoked by the principal, even if it is agreed by their contract to be irrevocable. . . .
>
> 7 The main exception to the general rule is the case where the agent has a relevant interest of his own in the exercise of his authority. The exception applies if two conditions are satisfied. First, there must be an agreement that the agent's authority shall be irrevocable. Secondly, the authority must be given to secure an interest of the agent, being either a proprietary interest (for example a power of attorney given to enable the holder of an equitable interest to perfect it) or a liability (generally in debt) owed to him personally. In these cases, the agent's authority is irrevocable while the interest subsists.

Since an equitable assignment entails the conferring of authority by the assignor on the assignee whereby the assignee is also privileged to invoke such delegated powers self-interestedly without regard for the interests of the assignor, and such agency is twinned with an equitable interest in the subject matter which the equitable assignment has also vested in him, the 'agency effect' which underpins equitable assignment would seem to be a paradigm example of an agency that would be irrevocable *inter vivos*,[15] if it were accompanied by the requisite agreement that it be so[16] (which the Supreme Court in *Angove's Pty Ltd* v. *Bailey* recognized need not

---

[14] *Angove's Pty Ltd* v. *Bailey* [2016] UKSC 47; [2016] 1 WLR 3179, [6] and [7].

[15] *Smart* v. *Sandars* (1848) 5 CB 895; *Gaussen* v. *Morton* (1830) 10 B & C 731. See also: W. A. Seavey, 'Termination by Death of Proprietary Powers of Attorney' (1921–2) 31 *Yale Law Journal* 283, 283.

[16] As authority for the proposition that there must also be agreement that the agency be irrevocable for the court to hold it to be so, in *Angove's Pty Ltd* v. *Bailey* (n. 14, at [8]), Lord Sumption relied on two Privy Council decisions, namely *Esteban de Comas* v. *Prost and Kohler* (1865) 3 Moo NS 158, and *Frith* v. *Frith* [1906] AC 254. At (1865) 3 Moo NS 179–80, the Privy Council made it plain that the agreement as to the irrevocability of the agency relationship need not be express, but may be inferred from the facts of the case.

be express, but might be inferred from the context).[17] If so, such irrevoc-able agency may survive the bankruptcy of the donor of the power.[18]

But what if the 'principal' dies?

In general, agent–principal relations cannot survive the principal's death.[19] And it is often said that the grant of an authority coupled with an interest will not survive the death of the principal either, following *Watson* v. *King* where Lord Ellenborough rhetorically asked: 'A power coupled with an interest cannot be revoked by the person granting it; but it is necessarily revoked by his death. How can a valid act be done by a dead man?'[20]

It is not clear that the courts of common law were entirely *ad idem* on the point. In *Shipman* v. *Thompson*,[21] Fortescue J (whose decision was ultimately upheld by Willes CJ in the Court of Common Pleas) observed as follows:[22]

> It is said that the defendant had an authority by letter of attorney to receive the testator's rents, that this authority did not determine with the testator's death, and that therefore, as the defendant received it by the authority of the testator it is money had and received to his use, and it shall not be presumed to have been received by the consent of the executor. But I think as this is a naked authority and not coupled with any interest it could not subsist after the testator's death.

[17] See n. 14, at [8].

[18] See *Alley* v. *Hotson* (1815) 4 Camp 325 (Lord Ellenborough). It has been suggested that an authority coupled with an interest granted by corporation would similarly survive the corporation's winding up or dissolution: Bowstead & Reynolds (2018), Article 118, Rule (3), and references cited therein.

[19] *Wallace* v. *Cook* (1803) 5 Esp 117 (Lord Ellenborough). This is, 'an ancient and well-settled doctrine of the common law': Story (1882), §488. Equity appears to have adopted the same position: *Mitchell* v. *Eades* (1700) Prec Ch 125, so far as one was concerned with a *mere* power of attorney, but not where the power of attorney was granted together with an interest: see cases discussed below.

[20] (1815) 4 Camp 272, 274, maintaining consistency with Lord Ellenborough's decision in *Wallace* v. *Cook* (n. 19). It has been suggested that Lord Ellenborough's decision in *Watson* v. *King* was impelled by the need to comply with Lord Liverpool's Acts (26 Geo III, c. 60, 1786 and 34 Geo III, c. 68, 1794): see M. C. McGaw, 'A History of the Common Law of Agency with Particular Reference to the Concept of Irrevocable Authority Coupled with an Interest' (D.Phil. thesis, University of Oxford, 2005), pp. 261–2.

[21] The appeal to Willes CJ from Fortescue J's decision is reported at *Shipman* v. *Thompson* (1738) Willes 103; whereas Fortescue J's decision in the court below is reported at note (a) to Willes 104. The reasoning of Willes CJ (and, implicitly, Fortescue J) was explained and accepted to be correct by Romilly MR in *Lambarde* v. *Older* (1853) 17 Beav 542, 546.

[22] *Shipman* v. *Thompson* (n. 21), 105.

So it seems there may have been a view at common law that although the grant of a 'naked authority' not coupled to any interest would not survive the testator's death, matters were otherwise where the authority *was* coupled with an interest.

In any event, equity's rules were different, given *Dale* v. *Smithwick*,[23] which was followed in *Lepard* v. *Vernon*,[24] *Gurnell* v. *Gardner*,[25] *Spooner* v. *Sandilands*[26] and *Kiddill* v. *Farnell*,[27] all decisions of the High Court of Chancery. Thus, *Meagher, Gummow and Lehane* states that '[a]t law a power of attorney, although coupled with a grant to a donee of an interest, was necessarily revoked by the death of the donor, even if the donee had no notice thereof, but semble in equity it was not so revoked'.[28]

*Dale, Lepard, Gurnell, Spooner* and *Kiddill* suggest that, where an equitable interest has been created and where the creator of that equitable interest pairs it with an agency relationship thereby enabling the beneficiary of that equitable interest to enjoy the benefits of his entitlement without having to act through the creator of that equitable interest, equity imposes a duty on the donor of the authority (and her personal representatives) *not* to revoke that authority. And *Shipman* v. *Thompson* arguably tells us that the judges in the Common Pleas were prepared to recognize that that was the case in Chancery.

These cases tell us that where an authority is, upon its grant, coupled with an interest, the donor of the authority is duty-bound in equity to the donee of that authority *not* to invoke her power to revoke it.[29] Consequently, the donee's authority becomes irrevocable so far as such donee could obtain an injunction in equity to prevent the donor from revoking that authority, if the same was threatened; and so far as such authority *had* already been revoked by the donor, the donee would have the power in equity to require the donor to reinstate the donee's authority,[30]

---

[23]  (1690) 2 Vern 151.

[24]  (1813) 2 V & B 51.

[25]  (1863) 4 Giff 626.

[26]  (1842) 1 Y & C C C 390.

[27]  (1857) 3 Sm & Giff 428.

[28]  Meagher, Gummow & Lehane (2015), para. 2-085(i), contrasting the positions arrived at in equity (in *Lepard* v. *Vernon* (n. 24)) and at common law (in *Watson* v. *King* (n. 20)).

[29]  See *Stephens* v. *Venables (No. 1)* (1862) 30 Beav 625, discussed in Chapter 4, n. 106.

[30]  One could hazard a guess that this lies at the root as to why equity came to view grants of authority coupled with an interest to be irrevocable. Supposing A had constituted herself trustee of the benefit of a debt owed to her by B for the benefit of C, and A had also executed a deed granting C a power of attorney, under which C was empowered to invoke

*with retrospective effect*, if necessary.[31] And where the donor had died, such *equitable* duties would be exigible against the donee's personal representatives by reason of the equitable interest that had been granted.[32]

So far as the rule in equity diverged from the rule at law, s. 25(11) of the Judicature Act 1873,[33] now, recast as s. 49(1) of the Senior Courts Act 1981,[34] tells us that the rules of equity are to prevail over those of common law (if different), so far as no provision otherwise had been made within ss. 25(1) to (10) of the 1873 Act.[35] Thus, where a chose in action has been equitably assigned, by reason of the interplay of the trust and agency effects which underpin the operation of such assignment, the assignee obtains, in effect, an irrevocable power to act as if he were the assignor, and such power will survive the assignor's death (and, by analogy, where the assignor is a corporate entity, the dissolution of such corporate form). Through the combination of trust (which vests in the assignee a proprietary equitable interest) and agency (which allows the assignee to bypass the assignor), the institution of equitable assignment allows for the 'transfer' of control over an equitable chose *without*, however, jeopardizing the personal autonomy of the obligor to the chose.

## B  Subdelegation and Making Further Assignments

The release of the assignee from the usual fiduciary obligations arising on the grant of authority by a principal to her agent is important in another respect. Besides rendering such authority irrevocable, it also enables the assignee to effect further assignments of the chose in question by

---

all of A's entitlements against B as C pleased, including A's power to bring an action in debt against B on the debt. Suppose, then, that A purported to revoke such power of attorney. Even assuming such revocation *was* effective at law to bring that power to an end, recalling A's duties to C pursuant to the trust A had also constituted, C would be entitled in equity to demand that A fully execute her trust, say, by re-granting C such authority to invoke A's power to sue B at law as A had just revoked; and if A failed to to so, C might certainly obtain a mandatory injunction in equity to compel A's compliance. Coupled with the doctrine of ratification, A's earlier revocation of the power of attorney would be rendered otiose.

[31]  This would be an application of the doctrine of ratification of authority.

[32]  Since such personal representatives would, necessarily, be mere volunteers.

[33]  Supreme Court of Judicature Act 1873, s. 25(11).

[34]  Senior Courts Act, s. 49(1).

[35]  As noted in Chapter 3, Section A; and see Meagher, Gummow & Lehane (2015), para. 2-085(i).

permitting the assignee to constitute further trusts over that chose, and to further subdelegate such authority as he had been delegated by the assignor by reason of the equitable assignment.

In a typical agent–principal relationship, by reason of the default fiduciary obligations which are imposed on an agent, it would be impermissible for such agent to subject himself to any additional duties to a third party to invoke his delegated powers in a manner which would conflict with his fiduciary duty to his principal: a man cannot serve two masters. Hence, an agent may not constitute himself trustee of the powers he had been delegated by his principal for the benefit of a third party. Doing so would lead the agent to become obligated to two masters and expose him to the possibility of being put in a position of conflict. So far as the agent is subject to fiduciary obligations to his principal as to his manner of exercising his delegated powers, it would follow that those duties also entail a duty that he not put himself into a position of conflict of interest: this is the 'no-conflict' fiduciary duty.

At the same time, in the usual case, because the agent is to invoke his delegated powers for the benefit of his principal, it is implicitly accepted that the principal will be relying on the judgement and good sense of *this* agent to carry out his fiduciary duties. So unless the context clearly shows otherwise, an agent is not ordinarily authorized to subdelegate, that is, to delegate to another such powers as had been delegated to him: *delegatus non potest delegare*.

As Professor Mechem put it:[36]

> The selection of an agent in any particular case is made, as a [general] rule, because he is supposed by his principal to have some fitness for the performance of the duties to be undertaken. In certain cases his selection is owing to the fact that he is considered to be especially and particularly fit. . . . [U]nless the principal has expressly or impliedly consented to the employment of a substitute, the agent owes to the principal the duty of a personal discharge of the trust. . . .

---

[36] §§305–6, F. R. Mechem, *A Treatise on the Law of Agency: Including not only a Discussion of the General Subject, but also Special Chapters on Attorneys, Auctioneers, Brokers and Factors*, vol. I (2nd edn, Chicago: Callaghan, 1914). See also Bowstead & Reynolds (2018), para. 5-002. As to the constraints posed by the Trustee Delegation Act 1999, since the assignor would have had, at the point of assignment, no beneficial interest in the chose assigned, those constraints would not apply, either (see s. 1(1)). The constraints posed by the Trustee Act 2000, ss. 11–23, are also irrelevant because they constrain the ability of trustees to delegate their powers *qua* trustees. The delegation arising from cases of assignees effecting a reassignment entails delegation of the powers that had been delegated to them *qua* agent.

> Hence it is the general rule of the law that in the absence of any authority, either express or implied, to employ a subagent, the trust committed to the agent is presumed to be exclusively personal and cannot be delegated by him to another so as to affect the rights of the principal.

However, the agency relationship proposed in this book is atypical. It entails not only authorizing the assignee to invoke the assignor's powers against the obligor, but also entails a simultaneous release of the assignee from the typical fiduciary duties associated with the creation of an agent–principal relationship. So far as there are *no* duties owed by the assignee 'agent' to the assignor 'principal', the basis for the general rule of *delegatus non potest delegare* falls away.

Given the above, an assignee can equitably assign to a third party that which had been equitably assigned to him, and so on and so forth down a chain of multiple assignees.[37]

## C   Recovery of Substantial Damages in Right of the Assignor

If, as has been argued, the substitutive transfer conception of equitable assignment does not sufficiently reflect its operation, it cannot be that where damages at law are sought against a common law obligor to a common law chose by an equitable assignee, the court, acting within its common law jurisdiction, would seek to assess the assignee's losses arising by reason of the obligor's breach. In such actions, the assignee is plainly suing the obligor in the name of and in the right of the assignor to whom the obligor is *still* duty-bound, breach and assignment notwithstanding. This is why, in cases where there has been an equitable assignment of a common law chose in action, a 'black hole' problem may arise. This may be illustrated by Example 6.1.

On the facts in Example 6.1, it would appear that B will have breached either express or implied terms in his contract with A as to the quality of the paint supplied and used by B. In relation to B's breach of contract, compensatory damages would appear to be the most pertinent judicial remedy. But, given the express authority which A had granted in favour of C, although C may certainly bring proceedings within the court's common law jurisdiction against B for B's breach of his contractual

---

[37] The effect, therefore, *approximates* what occurs when legal title to realty or tangible personalty is conveyed. The discussion in the text should be distinguished, however, from the trust and sub-trust arrangements which underpin indirect holdings of securities in which no question of delegation of powers normally arises. The effect of anti-assignment provisions is discussed in Chapter 15, Section A.

---

### EXAMPLE 6.1[38]

A contracts for B to rustproof and respray C's car for £1,000. This is because A wished to make a gift to C, and C had asked for this as opposed to a simple gift of money. The contract between A and B expressly stipulates that B is to apply a reputable rustproofing treatment and to respray using a suitable brand of paint so that the car will not need to be repainted for at least another five years. A pays B the fee for his labour and materials, and B commences work.

Shortly after completion of the work, as part of her gift to C, A equitably assigns the benefit of her contract with B to C. The document setting out the assignment also includes a clause by which A authorizes C to bring legal proceedings against B if there should be any dispute over B's performance of the contract. No *written* notice of the assignment is ever given to B, so such assignment is not 'statutory'.

Within a few months, the paint applied by B begins to flake and peel. The evidence reveals that this is because B used a brand of paint which was incompatible with the rustproofing treatment. The car will now have to be repainted at a cost of £1,800.

---

duties under the contract with A, C will plainly be recovering *as A's agent*. That is to say, C will be recovering *in right of A*.

In Example 6.1, given that B was duty-bound to A to use a suitable paint to repaint the car, when that primary duty was breached, as Hohfeld pointed out, B would then become secondarily duty-bound to A to pay her damages for *her* losses arising from breach of that primary duty that had been owed to her. So, where there has been a breach of a primary contractual duty arising between A (as claim-right holder) and B (as duty-bound party):[39]

---

[38] The facts in Example 6.1 are loosely drawn from *Darlington Borough Council* v. *Wiltshier Northern Ltd* [1995] 1 WLR 68, with two substantial differences. In that case, the assignment was a statutory one complying with the requirements of LPA1925, s. 136 (1). Secondly, the contractual promise-assignor had entered into the contract with the promisor-builders for the promisor-builders to build on land owned by the assignees, Darlington Borough Council, in order to satisfy a contractual obligation owed by the assignor to the assignees. But under that contract, liability to the assignees should the work performed by the promisor-builders be substandard or defective had been excluded. This case is discussed further in Chapter 13, Section F.

[39] W. N. Hohfeld, 'Nature of Stockholders' Individual Liability for Corporation Debts' (1909) 9 *Columbia Law Review* 285, 293–4.

[t]he latter, as a consequence of the breach of his primary duty, is now under a remedial duty to make *non-specific* reparation, that is, a duty to pay to A damages . . . and, correspondingly, A has a remedial right. . . .

[And i]f [B] fails to act under his remedial duty, A has *ab initio* the power, by action in the courts, to institute a process of compulsion against [B].

The equitable assignment of the benefit of the contract by A to C (coupled with the express authority to sue in A's name) has no effect on any of this. As noted above, the express authority merely empowers C to bring proceedings within the court's common law jurisdiction against B; but those proceedings are, even so, still brought in right of A. Hence, the damages which may be awarded by the court in light of B's breach of contract, if established, would be awarded in respect of the losses sustained by A, and not C.

Since damages for breach of contract are usually quantified as at the date of breach,[40] the starting point for quantification would be to ascertain A's loss (if any) which was caused by B's breach of contract at the time of such breach. Arguably, this would have occurred the moment B applied the paint in question to the car. But, as the facts in Example 6.1 make plain, although the breach occurred before A had effected her equitable assignment to C of the benefit of the painting contract with B by way of gift, that gift exposed A to no contractual or other obligation to indemnify C for C's losses by way of expenses incurred to make good B's defective contractual performance. Further, since the car was never A's to begin with, A could never have suffered any loss in respect of expenses to make good B's defective contractual performance. Finally, on the facts in Example 6.1, the C3PA would be of no use to C, since the contract between A and B was plainly beyond its ambit.

It might then appear that A would have sustained no substantial loss, since the car was never hers, A had breached no common law duty to C, and A was under no common law liability to C to pay for B's poorly done work to be made good. The loss *to C* caused by B's breach by reference to the expense of making good B's poorly done work would, seemingly, have gone down a 'black hole' because, even though C could bring proceedings at law against B in A's name, A would seemingly have suffered no loss (or, at least, no loss by reference to the cost of rectifying

---

[40] *Leigh* v. *Paterson* (1818) 8 Taunt 540; *Gainsford* v. *Carroll* [1824] 2 B & C 624; *Phillips* v. *Ward* [1956] 1 WLR 471; *Miliangos Ltd* v. *George Frank (Textiles) Ltd* [1976] AC 443, 468; *Johnson* v. *Agnew* [1980] AC 367, 400–1.

the problems caused by B's defective performance of his contractual duties). Therefore, the damages, if any, would not encompass such 'loss'.

The result above is not dependent on the fact that in Example 6.1 A had expressly authorized C to sue at law in her name, if need be. The same 'black hole' problem would materialize without such express authorization.

In the absence of such express authorization, as a mere equitable assignee, C would not be able to bring proceedings within the court's common law jurisdiction his own name. But suppose A was willing to cooperate with C, and performed as she was duty-bound in equity to C to do: namely, she was willing to lend her name to C to commence such proceedings. Given modern-day practice pursuant to the *Vandepitte* procedure,[41] A could join with C as co-plaintiff against B. Even so, the same 'black hole' problem would still arise, so far as the equitable assignment between A and C would *not* have the effect of changing the claim-right/duty jural relation between A and B arising from the painting contract that had been formed between them. So far as that primary jural relation remains one as between A and B, then the secondary remedial jural relations would also arise solely between A and B.

There are a number of possible resolutions to this 'black hole' problem, namely, by application of the 'narrow' or 'broad' grounds of recovery set out in *Linden Gardens Trust Ltd.*[42] But apart from these two grounds, the 'black hole' problem which would ensue when an equitable assignment of a legal chose in action is effected might also be addressed in a separate way. So far as an equitable assignment entails a relationship between assignor and assignee akin to that between a bare trustee and a beneficiary of such bare trust, the assignor would be duty-bound to her assignee to preserve the chose in action assigned. But where the 'chose' is a contract which, by its very nature, is not a static 'thing', given that the point of a contract is for it to be discharged by due performance by the contractual promisor, the subject matter of the assignor's duty of preservation is not just the contractual chose per se, but the promised outcome. That is, an equitable assignor of the benefit of a contractual chose in action is duty-bound in equity to her assignee to ensure that whatever was promised under the contract would be done, *is* done.

---

[41] The operation and basis of the *Vandepitte* procedure will be discussed in Chapter 8, Section B.

[42] [1994] 1 AC 85. Admittedly, the 'narrow' ground would probably not be of any assistance to resolve the 'black hole' problem arising in Example 6.1 as its requirements would not be satisfied.

Turning back to the facts in Example 6.1, given the express authority that A had given C to bring proceedings at law against B, it is clear that C may bring proceedings against B for B's breach of contract as A's duly authorized agent. But even supposing such words had been left out, C could still bring proceedings against B at law by reason of the equitable assignment alone, so long as A was joined as co-plaintiff or co-defendant in line with the *Vandepitte* procedure.

The conclusion above, that A might be taken to have sustained no substantial loss so far as A was under no obligation to C to reimburse C for any expenses incurred by C to make good B's defective work only focusses, however, on the lack of any *common law* duties as between A and C: it ignores the *equitable* duties owed by A to C by reason of the equitable assignment which A had effected in favour of C. But that ought not to be the case.

As Channell J recognized:[43]

> The Court of Equity would undoubtedly have recognized his [the assignee's] right, and would have treated the assignor as being trustee for his assignee, and they would have given to the assignee all the rights and remedies as against his assignor which they gave to a cestui que trust against his trustee, and would have given to him [the assignee] against the other party to the contract all the rights and remedies which they gave to a cestui que trust against a third person dealing with his trustee in reference to the subject of the trust after notice of the trust.

It has been suggested elsewhere[44] that when a trust is constituted over the benefit of a contract, the trustee holding the benefit of such contract will come under an equitable duty to her beneficiary to preserve the trust asset. Where the trust asset is a contractual chose in action, the 'asset' is, by its very nature, not a static 'thing', but a promise by the contractual promisor to achieve some stated end. So the trustee's duty to 'preserve' such non-static asset must, as was said above, go beyond maintaining the status quo.

It has been suggested that in this context where the contractual chose is created in order for the benefit thereof to be held by the obligee on trust for a third-party beneficiary, the trustee-obligee's duty to 'preserve' the trust asset translates into a duty to ensure that that which the obligor promised would be done *is in fact done*. And if the obligor failed to

---

[43] *Torkington* v. *Magee* [1902] 2 KB 427, 431–2.
[44] C. H. Tham, 'The "Trustee Exception" in *Lloyd's* v. *Harper*: Loss, Liability, and "Black Holes"' (2016) 132 LQR 148.

perform that which he had promised would be done, the trustee-obligee would have to ensure that that state of affairs which should have resulted had the obligor duly performed his promise does in fact ensue.[45]

Applying the above to the facts in Example 6.1: when A equitably assigns the benefit of her contract with B to C, she will have come under an *equitable* duty to C to preserve the trust asset (by reason of the trust effect which underpins equitable assignments). Given the nature of the trust asset (a contractual chose in action), A will be duty-bound to C to ensure that that state of affairs which had been promised by B would in fact come about.

When B breached the contract by using unsuitable paint, B caused A to breach this equitable duty to C, and therefore caused A to become liable to C in equity for breaching such duty. C could seek a remedy in equity against A, requiring A to do her equitable duty, if A did not do so voluntarily without judicial compulsion. As a result, A would have to expend funds to put the car into the state it should have been in. That quantum of loss arising from A's equitable liability to C serves to mark the magnitude of A's substantial (and not nominal) loss arising from the damage to her interest in B's due performance of the contract with A.[46]

It might be thought that one possible constraint upon A's recovery of substantial damages from B in light of her equitable liability to C would be the question of remoteness of loss: it might be argued that so far as B did not know (and could not have known) that A would sell the car to C and bind herself to C by way of assignment subsequent to her contract with B, such loss attributable to her equitable liabilities to C would be too remote, and therefore irrecoverable.

This objection should not hold.

As noted above, A is equitably liable to C because of her duty to ensure that that which B had promised would be done was in fact done. This means that A is liable to C to incur costs to make good such deficiencies in performance resulting from B's breach of contract, which is to say, A will be liable to C (in equity) to incur costs of curing the faults arising from B's breach of contract. It is not difficult to see that so long as such

---

[45] Ibid., 152.

[46] The result may be different if the contract between A and B contained an anti-assignment clause which precluded A from effectively assigning the benefit of the contract to B: see *Linden Garden Trust Ltd* v. *Lenesta Sludge Disposals Ltd* [1994] 1 A 85, 110 (Lord Browne-Wilkinson): 'One party to a contract cannot be liable for damages flowing from the doing of an act by the other party which the contract itself expressly forbids.'

costs of cure A would be liable to incur fall, nevertheless, within the losses as would arise in the 'natural course of things' following from C's breach, being costs A would have incurred had the car not been sold to C, and the cause of action not been assigned to C,[47] it would not matter that A was *equitably* liable to C to incur them. The point is that so long as such 'cost of cure' falls within the ambit of the 'ordinary or natural course of things' arising from B's breach, such loss would amount to a 'normal' or 'ordinary' type of loss which would not be 'too remote' by reason of their coming within the first limb of *Hadley* v. *Baxendale*.[48] Accordingly, it does not matter that B did not and could not have known when he was contracting with A that the car was not A's, but C's, and that the benefit of his contract with A would be assigned to C. Such knowledge is irrelevant so far as A's claim against B pertains to a *type* of loss which falls within what B would be taken to have known at the time of contract, since such loss would be *normal* loss.

But what, then, of mitigation? This issue does not arise in Example 6.1. However, suppose the car was A's to begin with, but, following B's completion of the contracted-for works on A's car, A then sold the car (and equitably assigned the benefit of the contract with B) to C for full value on an 'as seen, as is' basis?

Although losses which have actually been avoided may not be recovered, even if such loss-avoiding steps could not have been required of A by way of mitigation,[49] whatever 'loss' A had averted through ridding herself of the car would be matched by an equivalent 'loss' by reason of her equitable duties and liabilities to C. Furthermore, since such 'loss' arising from A's equitable liability vis-à-vis C would mirror her 'loss' in making good the defective paintwork had she not entered into the subsequent dealings with C, they do not *worsen* her position and do not violate her 'duty' to mitigate.

## D   Double Liability

The dualist model of equitable assignment in this book proceeds on the basis that where a debt has been equitably assigned, the assignment

---

[47] Echoing the qualifications put forward by Staughton LJ in *Linden Gardens Trust Ltd* v. *Lenesta Sludge Disposals Ltd* (1992) 30 Con LR 1, 17; cited with approval in *Offer-Hoar* v. *Larkstore Ltd* [2005] EWHC 2742 (TCC), [51].

[48] (1854) 9 Ex 341.

[49] Chitty (2018), vol. I, para. 26-103.

effects no change to the common law obligation arising from the debt in any way, and although there is a change to the obligor's immunity/disability jural relations with the assignee, absent prior agreement otherwise, the obligor will usually be taken to have assented to the possibility of such change.

As a result, if the duty/claim-right jural relation as between the debtor and his creditor remains unchanged, as is the associated power/liability jural relations between them, for the debt to be discharged at law by precise performance, payment must *still* be made in precise conformity with the original terms of the debt contract. Hence, if A lent B £10,000 on terms that B was to repay £10,000 to A in one year's time, even if A had equitably assigned the debt to C and notice thereof had been given to B, discharge of that debt obligation at law by precise performance would still entail B tendering payment *to A*, at least so far as the common law was concerned.

Accordingly, if B tendered payment to C on being satisfied that C had indeed been duly assigned the benefit of A's contract with B, B would *not* have discharged his obligations under that debt contract at law by precise performance, and so might seem liable to be sued by A for failing to do so. In other words, B might face the risk of having to pay a second time should A sue at common law for non-payment of the debt.

Fortunately for B, there is an answer to this conundrum. As Lord Cranworth LC observed in *Jones* v. *Farrell* in 1857:[50]

> I think the only safe way for the debtor [B, who has been informed that the benefit of his debt has been assigned] would be to send at once to the assignee [C] and pay him the debt. That would be a valid discharge. If my creditor tells me to pay [C]. and I accordingly pay [C]. and the creditor afterwards sues me, I have a good plea of payment.

The basis as to how such 'good plea of payment' arose is, however, more complex than Lord Cranworth's terse judgment suggests.

*Jones* v. *Farrell* was a decision handed down by the Court of Appeal in Chancery in 1857, prior to the administrative fusion of 1875 when the Judicature Act 1873 came into force. By this time, however, Parliament had already enacted the Common Law Procedure Act 1854. But even so, at common law, C's status as equitable assignee would not be given effect to so far as C would *not* be recognized by a court acting within its common law jurisdiction to have been delegated A's powers with regard

---

[50] (1857) 1 De G & J 208, 218.

to C. But a court acting within its equitable jurisdiction would not be so constrained.[51]

Where B had received notice of an equitable assignment to C (regardless as to whether such notice had originated from C, A, or any other reliable source), and where B had then tendered payment to C as A's equitable assignee, C's acceptance of such tender would be taken by a court acting within its equitable jurisdiction to have been the exercise by C of A's power at common law to accept a conforming tender of payment. Thus, such tender to and acceptance by C, as A's equitable assignee, would amount to a good discharge by way of payment, *so far as the court when acting within its equitable jurisdiction would be concerned.* Consequently, if B were sued by C or A within the court's equitable jurisdiction, the suit in equity would fail as the court, when acting within its equitable jurisdiction, would recognise and give effect to the agency mechanism underpinning the equitable assignment to C and would, accordingly, treat the tender to and acceptance by C of the payment by B to be equivalent to a tender to and acceptance by A, given the delegation by A to C of her powers vis-à-vis B arising from the common law debt between them. C would thus have a good plea of payment *in equity.*

That said, as at 1857 when *Jones* v. *Farrell* was decided in the Chancery courts, the position of a court of common law would be slightly different, leaving aside certain legislative changes which had been introduced by Parliament in 1854. To begin with, the substantive common law principles set out in the case law would establish that B's tender of payment to C and C's acceptance thereof could not amount to a precise performance of B's duties at common law: only tender of payment to A, and A's acceptance of such tender, would do. And, although a court in its equitable jurisdiction would give effect to an equitable assignment by treating B's tender of payment to C, and C's acceptance thereof, to be equivalent to B having tendered payment to A, and A having accepted it, because of the 'agency effect' underpinning the equitable assignment, a court of common law would not go so far: it would only recognise, but would not give effect to, equitable institutions such as equitable assignment which had arisen within the Chancery's exclusive jurisdiction. Thus, if A commenced proceedings at law against B on the debt, B would not be able to rely on the fact of his having tendered payment to C, and C's acceptance of the same, to support a plea of discharge by payment.

---

[51] The difference between recognition and enforcement of equitable assignments in equity and at common law is discussed at greater length in Part III.

B could, however, seek injunctive relief from the court of Chancery. Where A had directed B to pay her assignee, or where A had caused B to be directed to pay her assignee, it would plainly be unconscionable for A to go back on such direction by bringing proceedings at law on the debt against B where B had complied with such direction, especially since the debt would have been regarded in equity as having *already* been 'discharged' by the tender of payment to C. Indirect relief could, therefore, be afforded to B through the device of a common injunction against A, enjoining her from continuing with such proceedings at law against B.[52]

By 1854, however, Parliament enacted legislation which further enhanced the position of a debtor such as B:[53]

> LXXXIII. It shall be lawful for the Defendant or Plaintiff in replevin in any Cause in any of the Superior Courts in which, if Judgment were obtained, he would be entitled to Relief against such Judgment on equitable Grounds, to plead the Facts which entitle him to such Relief by way of Defence, and the said Courts are hereby empowered to receive such Defence by way of Plea; provided that such Plea shall begin with the Words 'For Defence on equitable Grounds', or Words to the like Effect.[54]

In *Jones* v. *Farrell*, Lord Cranworth LC spoke of how a debtor ('B') who had paid the equitable assignee ('C') of the debt on the instruction of his creditor ('A') who had effected such assignment would have a 'good plea of payment' were proceedings at common law to be brought against the debtor.[55] Although Lord Cranworth did not refer to it, s. 83 would apply to allow a debtor like B to plead a good defence of payment, had common law proceedings been brought.

Given s. 83, B would have been entitled to plead by way of a 'defence on equitable grounds' the facts pertaining to (i) A's equitable assignment of the benefit of the debt to C; (ii) B's having received notice of said assignment; and (iii) his having tendered payment to C on A's

---

[52] See Kerr (1867), pp. 14–15. The power to issue common injunctions to preclude proceedings after they had been commenced was abrogated by Judicature Act 1873, s. 24(5).

[53] CLPA1854, ss. 83 and 85 were repealed by the Statute Law Revision and Civil Procedure Act 1883, but subject to the saving now found in the Supreme Court of Judicature (Consolidation) Act 1925, s. 209.

[54] See e.g. *Wodehouse* v. *Farebrother* (1855) 5 El & Bl 277, 287; *Jeffs* v. *Day* (1866) LR 1 QB 372. Such defence was only available where a court of equity would have granted relief unconditionally: *Gee* v. *Smart* (1857) 8 El & Bl 313, 319; *Flight* v. *Gray* (1857) 3 CB (NS) 320, 323.

[55] *Jones* v. *Farrell* (1857) 1 De G & J 208, 218.

instruction. Thus, B would have a good defence derived from the 1854 Act were an action at law brought by A against him on the debt, without needing to incur the additional expense and trouble of obtaining injunctive relief from the court of Chancery.

In light of the above, Lord Cranworth LC's statements in *Jones* v. *Farrell* would therefore appear to be a statement of its time. But do they have any relevance today? It would seem that they do.

The operation of CLPA1854, s. 83, was explicitly duplicated in the language of Judicature Act 1873, s. 24(2):

> If any defendant claims to be entitled to ... relief upon any equitable ground against any deed, instrument, or contract, or against any right, title, or claim asserted by any plaintiff or petitioner, or alleges any ground of equitable defense to any claim of the plaintiff or petitioner in such cause or matter, the said Courts respectively, and every Judge thereof, shall give to every equitable ... ground of relief so claimed, and to every equitable defense so alleged, such and the same effect by way of defense against the claim of such plaintiff or petitioner, as the Court of Chancery ought to have given if the same or the like matters had been relied on by way of defense in any suit or proceeding instituted in that Court for the same or the like purpose before the passing of this Act.[56]

Although the Judicature Act 1873 was itself repealed, s. 38 of the Supreme Court of Judicature (Consolidation) Act 1925 was broadly *in pari materia*. And although the 1925 Consolidation Act has itself been replaced by the Senior Courts Act 1981, it would seem that s. 19(2) of the 1981 Act has preserved the earlier position, so far as there is no indication that Parliament intended to make any substantive changes despite the simplification in wording.

As a result, it is still possible to say that a debtor who tenders payment to an assignee following notice of the assignment 'has a good plea of payment' even so far as would concern a court acting within its common law jurisdiction. However, the basis for such plea of payment is *not* that such tender of payment amounts to a precise performance of the common law debt obligation in accordance to the caselaw derived principles. The basis for such 'plea of payment' lies in a complex interplay of the equitable remedy of common injunction, the statutory co-option of such power by the courts of common law and the preservation of such statutory empowerment within the High Court of today.

---

[56] The wording in Supreme Court of Judicature (Consolidation) Act 1925, s. 38, is *in pari materia* with CLPA1854, s. 83.

## E   Combining the Trust and Agency Effects

And so it comes to this. The combination of trust and agency supplies[57] the defects of each doctrine standing on its own.

Where T holds the legal title in 10,000 BCL shares on bare trust for A, and where A has subsequently constituted herself to be a *mere* bare sub-trustee of her equitable interest in T's legal title in the BCL shares for C, C has no direct recourse against T.[58] Though A has the power to require T to execute the bare trust by conveying his legal title in the shares in accordance with her directions, and A is duty-bound (by virtue of the sub-trust she had constituted) to C to invoke such power at C's direction, should C wish T to convey his legal title in the shares to, say, C, C must give effect to such wish by going *through* A: C must direct A to require T to execute the bare trust by conveying his legal title in the shares to C, as A had instructed; and if C were to attempt to bypass A and direct T to execute the bare trust, though T *may* do so, T is by no means obliged to C to do so – a point which Lawrence Collins LJ made clear in his judgment in *Nelson* v. *Greening & Sykes (Builders) Ltd*:[59]

> It is also true that in *Grey* (affirmed [1960] 1 AC), at p. 715, Lord Evershed MR (dissenting, but not on this point) said that where a person who is the owner beneficially of property (and the legal estate is vested in another as trustee for him) makes a declaration of trust, the practical effect would seem ... to amount, or be capable of amounting, to the 'getting rid of' a trust or equitable interest then subsisting. It is said in *Snell's Equity* ((31st ed) McGhee, 2005), in para 19-11, that 'where property is transferred to T "on trust for B absolutely" ... [i]f B in turn becomes a bare trustee of his equitable interest for C, T will hold directly in trust for C ...', citing *Head* v. *Lord Teynham* (1783) 1 Cox Eq 57 (which holds only that where trustees and the beneficiary are before the

---

[57] In the sense of 'making up for a deficiency or fulfilling a want or need': Lesley Brown, *The New Shorter Oxford English Dictionary: On Historical Principles* (4th edn, 2 vols., Oxford: Oxford Universty Press, 1993), vol. II, p. 3152.

[58] *Joseph Hayim Hayim* v. *Citibank NA* [1987] 1 AC 730 (PC), 748F–G (Lord Templeman). This passage was referred to with approval by Nourse LJ in *Parker-Tweedale* v. *Dunbar Bank Plc* [1991] Ch 12, 19, and in that case, Purchas LJ also noted (at 25) that in most cases, '[t]he beneficiary's rights are against the mortgagor as trustee upon whom there is a duty to take reasonable care to preserve the assets of the trust but this does not extend to give a right of action directly to a beneficiary against a third party who has, or may have, caused a loss to the trust assets.' See also *Bradstock Trustee Services Ltd* v. *Nabarro Nathanson (a firm)* [1995] 1 WLR 1405.

[59] [2007] EWCA Civ 1358; [2008] 1 EGLR 59, [56]–[57] (Collins LJ, with whom Wall and Ward LJJ agreed).

court, an intermediate trustee of the equitable interest need not be made a party).

These authorities do not bind this court to hold that, as a matter of law, an intermediate trustee ceases to be a trustee. I accept the submission . . . that saying (as Lord Evershed MR said) that the practical effect would seem to amount to, or be capable of amounting to, the 'getting rid' of the trust of the equitable interest then subsisting, is not the same as saying that, as a matter of law, it does get rid of the intermediate trust. What he was saying was that in the case of a trust and sub-trust of personal property, the trustees may decide that, as a matter of practicality, it is more convenient to deal directly with the beneficiary of the sub-trust.[60]

But C would not need to act through A if C had been *authorized* to invoke A's entitlements against T as though C were A, and where A had granted C the privilege against all non-C to invoke those entitlements as C pleased.

If, as is contended, when A equitably assigns her equitable chose against T to C, C is empowered and privileged by A to invoke A's entitlements against T as if he were A and as he pleased without regard for A's interests, T would be liable to C 'changing' T's duty (to A) to preserve his legal title in the shares to a duty to convey his legal title in the shares in accordance with the directions given by C (as A's 'agent' given the 'agency effect'). And if T failed to do so, T would then be liable to C (as A's 'agent', given the same 'agency effect') bringing proceedings in equity against T in respect of his breach of his duty to fully execute the trust by conveying his title in the shares in accordance with the directions issued by C as A had authorized him to do.

Next, although '[t]he dominant assumption in the cases is that a grant of authority is of its nature revocable',[61] so that agent–principal relations are generally revocable *inter vivos* by the principal, or automatically upon the principal's death, given Lord Ellenborough's rhetorical question in *Watson* v. *King*: 'How can a valid act be done in the name of a dead man?',[62] we may quote Professor Powell's riposte that that decision 'overlooks the fact that an authority coupled with an interest is really a

---

61 Bowstead & Reynolds (2018), para. 10-007. See also *Angove's Pty Ltd* v. *Bailey* [2016] UKSC 47; [2016] 1 WLR 3179, [7].

62 (1815) 4 Camp 272, 274 (reproduced above at text to n. 20).

transfer of property'.[63] The extinction of such authority would not apply in respect of C's 'agency', above, since the *trust* effect which also underpins A's equitable assignment would have simultaneously vested C with the requisite interest as would render the agency to be irrevocable.[64]

Though such trust and agency effects would not have been given effect at common law, it suffices that they would have been both recognized and given effect by courts acting within their equitable jurisdiction. A court of equity would have granted a common injunction to restrain an action at law brought in disregard of these effects. And given the effects of ss. 83 and 85[65] of the Common Law Procedure Act 1854, which have been preserved by s. 49 of the Senior Courts Act 1981, those facts as would have given rise to a common injunction may now be pleaded by way of defence to an action at law brought in disregard of these same effects, or by way of reply to a defence at law which similarly disregarded such effects. Consequently, through the combination of the trust and agency effects, equity *simulates* (though only approximately) the result when legal title in tangible personalty is conveyed, without needing the assignor's entitlements against the equitable obligor to be extinguished and then reconstituted or revested in the assignee.

This dualist, composite conception of equitable assignment is more consistent with the authorities applying the same trust-based analysis to equitable assignments of legal or equitable choses in action alike.[66] It is also more respectful of the principle that the obligor's voluntarily undertaken obligations may not thereafter be unilaterally varied or altered without his assent.[67] So far as we understand how an equitable assignment effects a 'transfer' by means of this simulation, no intellectual damage is done. But we forget this at our peril.

---

[63] Raphael Powell, *The Law of Agency* (2nd edn, London: Sir Isaac Pitman & Sons Ltd, 1961), p. 388, fn. 5.

[64] See Bowstead & Reynolds (2018), para. 10-007: 'Authority *can* be irrevocable; but this is only where the notion of agency is employed as a legal device for a different purpose from that of normal agency, to confer a security or other interest on the "agent". In such a case it is intended that the agent use the authority not for the benefit of his principal but for his own benefit, to achieve the objects of the arrangement.'

[65] The operation of CLPA1854, s. 85 is discussed in Chapter 12.

[66] As sketched out in Chapter 4.

[67] As sketched out in Chapter 3.

# PART III

Joinder

# 7

# Joinder of Assignor in Equitable Proceedings

In this and the following two chapters, it will be shown why, given the composite, dualist conception of equitable assignment, joinder of the equitable assignor to proceedings brought by the assignee against the obligor to the chose assigned before a final decision is handed down is necessary in some cases, but not others.

## A    Joinder of Assignor to Equitable Proceedings when the Chose Assigned Is Equitable

As Calvert explained:[1]

> [U]nder all circumstances, the question [of joinder of necessary parties in equitable proceedings] resolves itself into this, whether the relief sought in the bill, in other words, the equity of the bill touches any particular person, so as to obtain from him a benefit, or to fasten upon him a duty: that, if this question is answered in the affirmative, he is a necessary party.

Where an assignee of the benefit of a trust brings proceedings against the trustee to compel the trustee to fully execute the trust by conveying such title as he has in the trust property to the assignee, the assignor would be 'interested in the object of such suit' since such an order, if complied with, would 'obtain from [the assignor] a benefit', namely, the assignor's equitable interest in that trust property. If so, the assignor should, of necessity, be joined before a final decision is handed down by the court. But this is not what the cases tell us. Repeatedly, we see that when an assignee of an equitable chose brings proceedings (necessarily in equity) against the obligor, joinder of the assignor is not required as a rule, though the assignor *may* be joined if there be some good reason to do so.[2]

---

[1] Calvert (1847), p. 16. The point has been discussed more fully in Chapter 5, Section B(iv).

[2] *Goodson* v. *Ellison* (1826) 3 Russ 583; *Cator* v. *Croydon Canal Co.* (1843) 4 Y & C Ex 593; *Donaldson* v. *Donaldson* (1854) Kay 711, 719.

Although joinder of the assignor would seem to be necessary by reason of her interest in the object of such suit, such joinder is rendered unnecessary because of the combination of the trust and agency effects underpinning the assignment.

First, the assignor's power to bring judicial proceedings will have been delegated to the assignee. So far as such agency effect will be recognized by the court in its equitable jurisdiction, the assignee may commence such proceedings against the obligor-trustee notwithstanding that the equitable assignment does not make the assignee any less a stranger to that obligation (leaving aside cases where the obligor undertook to be obligated to the obligee or her assigns, as in Example 3.3).

Second, the assignor will be bound by the decision of the court, notwithstanding her non-joinder. For *res judicata* purposes, the principal–agent and/or the trustee–beneficiary relationships between assignor and assignee are sufficient to bind assignor and assignee to the decisions of a court in proceedings brought by either of them.[3]

This is not to say that an assignee of an equitable chose may always bring proceedings in equity against the obligor without needing to join anyone else. That depends on the nature of the remedy sought, and whether anyone else, apart from the assignor, might be affected by the object of such proceedings.

## B    Being 'Bound' by a Decision: Estoppel by *Res Judicata*

To illustrate how joinder of the assignor is not necessary in such equitable proceedings, and when joinder of others might still be required, we may consider Example 7.1.

---

**EXAMPLE 7.1**

T holds the legal fee simple in Blackacre on trust for '$A_L$ for his life and $A_R$ as remainderman'.

$A_R$ equitably assigns her equitable remainder interest in T's legal title in Blackacre to C absolutely by way of gift.

C and $A_L$ subsequently agree to bring the special trust to an end. Invoking the doctrine in *Saunders* v. *Vautier*, they order T to fully execute the trust by conveying his legal title in Blackacre to X.

T refuses, on grounds that he holds his legal title in Blackacre absolutely for his own benefit.

---

[3]  See discussion in Sections B(iii) and (iv), below.

On the facts in Example 7.1, should it be desired to bring equitable proceedings against T for an adjudication whether:

**I** T was duty-bound to $A_L$ for his life and $A_R$ as remainderman by reason of the special trust; and

**II** T was in breach of his duties under that trust when he refused to comply with the directions of $A_L$ and C, as $A_R$'s assignee,

must $A_L$ and/or $A_R$ be joined?

As explained above, by reason of the 'agency effect', C may commence these proceedings against T even though C is a stranger to the trust on which the proceedings are brought. But it seems clear C may not bring such proceedings alone.

In principle, $A_R$ should be joined to these proceedings since she is plainly interested in their object. If C succeeded in obtaining the order prayed for, T's compliance with such order by conveying his legal title in Blackacre to X would extinguish $A_R$'s equitable remainder interest in that legal title. But, as will be explained below, so far as $A_R$ and C may be treated as one and the same party ('identity of parties') by reason of their principal–agent relationship, *or* to be in 'privity of interest' by reason of their trustee–beneficiary relationship, $A_R$ would not need to be joined as a party to be bound by such final decision as might be handed down in her absence.

The same, however, cannot be said of $A_L$. Being interested in the object of the suit, $A_L$ is a necessary party to these proceedings, and a final decision may not be made without joining $A_L$.

The wisdom of staying proceedings against T until $A_L$ be joined follows from the rules of *res judicata*,[4] in particular, the doctrine of 'issue estoppel'.[5]

Suppose that C brought proceedings in equity against T in his sole name, without joining either $A_R$ *or* $A_L$. Suppose also the court proceeded to final judgment and decided that in respect of issue **I**, T was *not* trustee of the legal title in Blackacre for the benefit of $A_L$ for life, and $A_R$ by way of remainder. The consequence is that the court would not need to decide on issue **II**. Accordingly, the court dismissed C's application for an injunction.

---

[4] Estoppel by *res judicata* is a substantive right, and is not merely a rule of evidence or public policy: *Johnson* v. *Gore Wood & Co. (a firm)* [2002] 2 AC 1, 59E (Lord Millett); *Associated Electric and Gas Insurance Services Ltd* v. *European Reinsurance Co. of Zurich* [2003] UKPC 11; [2003] 1 WLR 1041, [15].

[5] 'Issue estoppel may be a comparatively new phrase, but I think that the law of England – unlike the law of some other countries – has always recognized that estoppel per *rem judicatem* includes more than merely cause of action estoppel': *Carl Zeiss Stiftung* v. *Rayner & Keeler Ltd (No. 2)* [1967] AC 853, 913.

If $A_L$ was not made party to C's proceedings against T, $A_L$ would not be party to the decision on **I**. Therefore, $A_L$ would not be bound by that decision, and no estoppel by reason of *res judicata* may be asserted against him by T should $A_L$ re-litigate the same issue in subsequent proceedings, leading to the possibility of conflicting findings.

### (i)    Requirements

T may raise *res judicata* as an estoppel against any subsequent claim in which issue **I** is to be re-litigated as long as T can show that:[6]

(i)   the [prior] decision, whether domestic or foreign, was judicial in the relevant sense;

(ii)   it was in fact pronounced;

(iii)   the [prior] tribunal had jurisdiction over the parties and the subject matter;

(iv)   the [prior] decision was –
   (a) final;
   (b) on the merits;

(v)   it determined a question raised in the later litigation; and

(vi)   the parties [in the later litigation] are the same [as the ones in the prior litigation] or their privies,[7] or the earlier decision was *in rem*.

### (ii)    Decision In Rem or In Personam?

The court's decision on issue **I** is not a decision *in rem* for *res judicata* purposes. As *Spencer, Bower and Handley* explain: 'A decision *in rem* conclusively determines the status of a person or thing; that is its jural relation to persons generally, not just parties and privies. ... It would have been clearer if decisions had been classified *inter omnes*, and *inter partes*.'[8] And for *res judicata* purposes:[9]

> Status is the 'legal position of the individual *in or with regard to the rest of the community*'; 'the condition of belonging to a class in society to which

---

[6]  Handley (2009), para. 1.02.

[7]  '[T]here is no doubt that the requirement of identity of parties is satisfied if there is privity between a party to the former litigation and a party to the present litigation. ... It has always been said that there must be privity of blood, title or interest': *Carl Zeiss Stiftung* v. *Rayner & Keeler Ltd (No. 2)* (n. 5), 910E, 910G (Lord Reid).

[8]  Handley (2009), para. 10.01.

[9]  Ibid., para. 10.05 (references omitted, emphasis added).

the law ascribes peculiar rights and duties, capacities and incapacities', *and* 'a condition attached by law to a person which confers or affects or limits a legal capacity of exercising some power that under other circumstances he could not or could exercise without restriction.

The court's decision on issue **I** merely decided there was no *in personam* relationship of trustee and beneficiary between T on the one hand, and $A_L$ and $A_R$ on the other. Thus, the decision on issue **I** is not a decision *in rem* as to T's status as a person for *res judicata* purposes because it is not a decision as to T's legal position 'in or with regard to the *rest of the community*': it is simply a decision as to T's legal position with regard to $A_L$ and $A_R$, whether he was duty-bound to either of them in his ownership of the legal title in Blackacre in the manner of a trustee.

Neither is the decision on issue **I** a decision *in rem* on grounds that it 'conclusively determines the status . . . of a thing'. As mentioned, the decision on issue **I** was that T was *not* in a trustee/beneficiary relationship with $A_L$ and $A_R$. It was not, therefore, a decision as to the status of a *thing*. Thus, the court's decision on issue **I**, so far as it concerns $A_L$'s relationship with T, is only a decision *in personam*.[10] It was a decision as to the *in personam* relations between T, on the one hand, and $A_L$ and $A_R$, on the other.

### (iii)   Identity of Parties

T may only successfully invoke issue estoppel to bar re-litigation over issue **I** if he can satisfy the six requirements listed above. It is clear that T will be able to satisfy the first five requirements. And if subsequent proceedings were brought by C to re-litigate issue **I**, there would be

---

[10] Although the court's decision on issue **I** is a decision *in personam* so far as $A_L$ is concerned, should $A_L$ attempt to bring further proceedings against T in respect of the same issue, it is not *invariably* a decision *in personam* for everyone, and for all purposes. The court's decision on issue **I** is a decision *in rem* so far as may concern, say, Z, to whom T had contracted to sell his unencumbered legal title in Blackacre. If Z repudiated the contract, and T brought proceedings against Z for his repudiatory breach, Z would be barred by reason of issue estoppel if he sought to justify his repudiation on grounds that T did *not* have unencumbered title to Blackacre, but held it on trust for $A_L$ and $A_R$. In *that* context, the court's decision in the proceedings brought by C on issue **I** would be a decision *in rem* as would bind the whole world; so far as regards such a defence by Z, it would be a decision as to the status of a thing, the thing being T's legal title in Blackacre. Hence, '[t]here is no reason why an order should be characterized as either wholly in rem or wholly in personam . . . The extent (if any) to which an order operates in part in rem and in part in personam is a matter of analysis': *Pattni* v. *Ali* [2006] UKPC 51; [2007] 2 AC 85, [37].

identity of parties as would allow those subsequent proceedings to be barred by reason of issue estoppel.

Next, $A_L$ is obviously not C. And although the courts have treated a principal who had instructed an agent to bring judicial proceedings in the agent's own name to be the 'real' party for whose account or benefit the party on record was suing or defending for the purposes of estoppel by *res judicata*, causing subsequent proceedings by the 'real' party to be issue estopped by treating such 'real' party and its agent as one and the same, if C was not acting on $A_L$'s instructions when he commenced his suit in equity against T, C and $A_L$ may not be regarded as one and the same party for *res judicata* purposes.[11] So T may not successfully invoke issue estoppel on this ground should $A_L$ bring subsequent proceedings against T re-litigating the same issues as had been decided in C's suit against T.

But what of $A_R$?

In *Re McArdle*, Jenkins LJ made the point that where an equitable assignment had been made, 'the assignee is entitled to demand payment from the trustee or holder of the [trust] fund, and the trustee is bound to make payment to the assignee, with no further act on the part of the assignor remaining to be done to perfect the assignee's title'.[12]

Although one could explain this on grounds that the equitable assignor of an equitable chose 'drops out' or retains 'no interest' following the assignment, as has already been explained, such language is merely metaphorical at best and should not be taken at face value.[13] Rather, as explained elsewhere in this book, this is arguably because equitable assignment entails a 'trust effect', *and* an 'agency effect'.[14] Hence, so far as a court acting within its equitable jurisdiction was concerned, the very fact of the equitable assignment entailed empowering or 'authorizing' the assignee to invoke the assignor's entitlements against the obligor to the

---

[11]  If T established that $A_L$ knew of the proceedings brought by C, but had been 'content to stand by and see his battle fought by someone else in the same interest' (*Re Lart* [1896] 2 Ch 788, 794 (Chitty J)), the courts may be prepared to treat $A_L$ as party to those earlier proceedings: see Handley (2009), para. 9.12. But on the facts of Example 7.1, since C had kept $A_L$ in the dark throughout, this concession would not apply to T.

[12]  [1951] 1 Ch 669, 677. See also *Kekewich* v. *Manning* (1851) 1 De G M & G 176, which held that where an equitable interest in certain funds held by principal trustees had been assigned to assignees to hold on trust for the benefit of certain donees, such assignees were entitled to require the principal trustees to fully execute the trust without further order of court.

[13]  See discussion in Chapter 5.

[14]  See also C. H. Tham, 'The Mechanics of Equitable Assignments: One Engine or Two?' in Simone Degeling, James Edelman and James Goudkamp (eds.), *Contract in Commercial Law* (Sydney: Thomson Reuters, 2016).

chose assigned as the assignee pleased. Consequently, as Wood V-C noted in *Donaldson v. Donaldson*:[15]

> [I]n the case of an assignment of the equitable interest in stock standing in the names of trustees, the deed of assignment passes the whole equitable interest of the donor, and *the donee may go with that deed to the trustees, and say, transfer to me the interest in this sum of stock*; and I think that in such a case it would not even be necessary to make the donor a party to a suit to enforce the gift.

Accepting that equitable assignments necessarily entail such 'agency effect', so far as a court acting within its equitable jurisdiction was concerned, $A_R$ would have 'authorized' C (albeit in advance) to invoke $A_R$'s entitlements against T, including $A_R$'s power to commence proceedings in equity against B, thus enabling C to sue T, and as C pleased. Thus, C's bringing of equitable proceedings against T without $A_R$'s direct involvement was something for which $A_R$ was responsible as 'principal'. So $A_R$ and C may be taken to be the same party for *res judicata* purposes, and T could successfully invoke issue estoppel against $A_R$ if $A_R$ were to re-litigate issue **I**.

However, even if this 'agency effect' be denied, as has been shown in Chapter 3, an equitable assignment also entails a trustee–beneficiary relationship as between assignor and assignee. As the next subsection will show, such trustee–beneficiary relationship is enough to create a 'privity of interest' between them as would also trigger issue estoppel.

### (iv)  Privity of Blood, Estate or Interest

As the caselaw recognizes, the equitable assignor of an equitable chose owes the same kinds of obligations to the assignee as a bare trustee would owe to the trust beneficiary.[16] By reason of this 'trust effect', $A_R$ would hold its equitable remainder interest in Blackacre for C's benefit, resulting in a 'privity of interest' between $A_R$ and C, over and beyond an identity of persons by reason of the 'agency effect'.

As Megarry V-C held in *Gleeson v. J. Wippell & Co.*:[17]

---

[15]  (1854) Kay 711, 718–19 (emphasis added).

[16]  See e.g. *Roberts v. Gill & Co.* [2010] UKSC 22; [2011] 1 AC 240, [68]. It may be noted that Lord Collins did not distinguish between assignments of legal or equitable choses.

[17]  [1977] 1 WLR 510, 515G; cited with approval in: *Johnson v. Gore Wood & Co. (a firm)* (n. 4), 32E (Lord Bingham); *Barakot Ltd v. Epiette Ltd* [1998] 1 BCLC 283, 287–8. For general discussion, see Handley (2009), para. 9.44.

> [H]aving due regard to the subject matter of the dispute, there must be a
> sufficient degree of identification between the two to make it just to hold
> that the decision to which one was party should be binding in proceedings
> to which the other is party. It is in that sense that I would regard the
> phrase 'privity of interest'. Thus in relation to trust property I think there
> will normally be a sufficient privity between the trustees and their benefi-
> ciaries to make a decision that is binding on the trustees also binding on
> the beneficiaries, and vice versa.

Consequently, re-litigation of issue $I$ in subsequent proceedings by $A_R$ against T would be issue estopped. But as $A_L$ and C share no such relationship, they have no privity of interest.

In Example 7.1, if T refused to comply with the direction to convey his legal title in Blackacre to X voluntarily without order, C would have to join $A_L$ to any proceedings seeking the requisite order. This would entail two equitable suits wrapped up in one. First, a suit by C compelling $A_R$ to bring proceedings, alongside $A_L$, against T; and second, a suit by $A_R$ (so compelled) and $A_L$ forcing B to convey to X. However, though both $A_R$ and $A_L$ are interested in the ultimate object of such proceedings, $A_R$'s privity of interest or identity of person with C means her joinder is unneces-sary as she would still be bound by such decision as might be handed down in proceedings brought by C and $A_L$ against T without being joined.

## C   Joinder of Assignor to Equitable Proceedings when the Chose Assigned Is Legal

Similar concerns as to the impact of *res judicata* arise when certain legal choses in action are equitably assigned and proceedings in equity are then brought to adjudicate disputes over the associated common law obligations.

For example, when a common law obligation arising from contract is breached, in most cases the remedy of damages awarded by a court within its common law jurisdiction would be an adequate remedy. But if such remedy in a particular case be inadequate, the court's concurrent equitable jurisdiction to award an equitable remedy such as specific performance may be resorted to.

If the obligee to such contractual obligation had equitably assigned the benefit of such contract to an assignee, the assignee may bring proceed-ings against a defaulting obligor in the court's concurrent equitable jurisdiction. Though the assignee would be a stranger to the contract between the obligor and the obligee-assignor, when the assignee brings such proceedings within the court's equitable jurisdiction, the court would recognize the agency and trust effects which underpin the equitable assignment, and would give effect to the assignee's authority to bring such equitable proceedings.

Because of the agency and trust effects, joinder of the assignor to those equitable proceedings is excused even if the assignor might be interested in the object of such proceedings. This is reinforced by the operation of *res judicata* on the assignor: that decision *would* bind the assignor by reason of her being treated as if she were the same party as her assignee by reason of the principal–agent relationship, or her privity of interest with the assignee because of their trustee–beneficiary relationship. Thus, the assignor would be barred from re-litigating the issue before the court within its equitable jurisdiction for the reasons explained above,[18] *mutatis mutandis*. However, unlike the case where proceedings are brought in equity in respect of an *equitable* chose in action, proceedings in equity in respect of a *legal* chose in action derived from a *common law* obligation invariably entail an additional complication.

Pre-Judicature, disputes concerning such common law obligations could also be brought before a court of common law. As the Judicature Acts merely fused the administration of the courts of common law and equity within the Supreme Court of Judicature, even today contractual obligees may still, in principle, bring proceedings before the court within its equitable or common law jurisdiction.

Example 7.2 illustrates the complication.

To obtain an order of specific performance, apart from satisfying the court of the inadequacy of common law remedies, in Example 7.2, C would need to establish that:

**III** a contract had formed between A and B;
**IV** that B had failed to fully perform his duties under that contract;
**V** that there was no excuse for such failure; and
**VI** that A had validly equitably assigned the benefit of such contract to C.

Suppose the court decides issues **III**, **IV** and **VI** in favour of C, and holds that a contract *had* been validly formed between A and B. However, as to issue **V**, it decides against C, holding that on the true construction of the contract, B had a contractual power to prematurely terminate it, which power B had validly invoked, thereby releasing himself from any further duty to complete the works. Accordingly, specific performance would not be ordered, there being no outstanding contractual obligation.

---

[18] See Sections B(iii) and (iv), above.

---

EXAMPLE 7.2

A enters into a contract with B, an electrician, for B to rewire A's mansion on Blackacre which A runs as a boarding house.

B starts work, but A then sells the legal title to Blackacre to C. As part of the sale, A also *equitably* assigns the benefit of her contract with B to C.

The rewiring work goes very slowly, and months after completion of the sale of Blackacre to C, more than half of B's work is still undone. This means C is unable to run the mansion as a boarding house as, until the work is done, the premises are not fit to be used for that purpose.

Eventually, however, B repudiates the contract and tells C that he will not be finishing the job.

C makes enquiries as to the possibility and cost of getting in an electrician to carry on from where B had left off. Because of the complexity of the project, C finds that hardly anyone is willing to pick up where B had left off, and that those that might agree to do so would charge as much, if not more, than just starting from scratch. But if the works were started again from scratch, that would mean a further delay to C's boarding-house business.

Given this, C elects to reject B's repudiatory breach, affirms the contract whilst commencing proceedings in equity for an order of specific performance against B. Importantly, C elects *not* to seek assistance from the court within its common law jurisdiction at all, making this plain by not claiming for damages.

---

If C re-litigated issue **V** in subsequent proceedings within the court's equitable *or common law* jurisdiction, B could successfully invoke issue estoppel against C, all requirements to raise such estoppel[19] having been satisfied. And if A re-litigated issue **V** in subsequent proceedings within the court's *equitable* jurisdiction, B could also successfully invoke issue estoppel against A, even if A had not been made party to those earlier proceedings.

As explained above, a court exercising its equitable jurisdiction would recognize the trust and/or agency effects underpinning A's equitable assignment of the contractual chose to C, *and* give effect to them by granting equitable remedies as needful. Borrowing terminology more commonly encountered in private international law contexts, a court in its equitable jurisdiction would both 'recognize' and 'enforce'[20] the

---

[19] See text to n. 6.

[20] A. V. Dicey, *A Digest of the Law of England with Reference to the Conflict of Laws* (London: Stevens and Sons, 1896), p. 30:

> A Court recognises a right when for any purposes the Court treats the right as existing. . . .

equitable principles and rules pertaining to the equitable institution of equitable assignment. But the distinction between recognition and enforcement is not limited to the realm of private international law,[21] and the distinction may also be applied to domestic principles and rules. Indeed, this very distinction was embedded within the Supreme Court of Judicature Act 1873 (hereafter, the '1873 Act'). For example, s. 24(4) provided that the judges of the High Court were to 'recognise *and take notice of*' equitable matters, whereas s. 24(6) provided that the judges of the High Court were to 'recognise *and give effect to*' a range of matters arising outside of equity.[22] Given such recognition and enforcement of equitable principles and rules by a court acting within its equitable jurisdiction, A and C would be taken by such court to have sufficient privity of interest or identity of persons for *res judicata* purposes.

But what if A were to bring subsequent proceedings *at law* against B?

If A were to bring subsequent proceedings at law against B, although the earlier proceedings brought by C against B in the court's equitable jurisdiction would satisfy the first five of the six criteria required for *res judicata* to be successfully raised, so far as the court's decision in its equitable jurisdiction as to issue **V** is merely a decision *in personam* and not a decision *in rem*, to raise *res judicata* against A in such subsequent proceedings at law, B would need to show that A and C were to be regarded for *res judicata* purposes to be the same entity (identity of persons), or that A and C were to be regarded for *res judicata* purposes to be in privity of blood, estate or interest.

For the reasons set out in the preceding section, it is most unlikely that the court's decision on issue **V** would be characterized as an *in rem* decision. But taken as a decision *in personam*, A and C could not be regarded at common law to have identity of persons by reason of agency, or to be in privity of interest by reason of trust, since the court, when

---

A Court enforces a right when giving the person who claims it either the means of carrying it into effect, or compensation for interference with it.

It is plain that while a Court must recognise every right which it enforces, it need not enforce every right which it recognises.

For a modern-day statement, see A. V. Dicey, J. H. C. Morris and L. Collins, *Dicey, Morris and Collins on the Conflict of Laws* (15th edn, London: Sweet & Maxwell, 2012), r. 41 and paras. 14-002 to 14-006.

[21] See *Geyer v. Aguilar* (1798) 7 TR 681, 695–6 (Lord Kenyon CJ, adverting to the recognition of Exchequer judgments by the court of King's Bench.

[22] For further discussion of these provisions, see text following n. 36, below.

acting within its common law jurisdiction, could not give effect to (i.e. 'enforce') the equitable assignment *at common* law.[23]

Although the pre-Judicature court of Chancery would recognize and enforce equitable institutions such as equitable assignment, the courts of common law would not go so far. The courts of common law would certainly *recognize* the equitable interest arising from an assignment or a trust in certain contexts. For example, since *Scott* v. *Surman*,[24] the courts of common law had recognized that only property that was beneficially held by a bankrupt would pass to his assignees in bankruptcy pursuant to the bankruptcy legislation in force at the time. But the courts of common law declined to grant common law remedies so as to give effect to these institutions devised by equity. They viewed enforcement of such equitable institutions to be a matter exclusive to the equity jurisdiction.[25] Consequently, no court of common law would, for example, award common law damages to compensate a trust beneficiary for losses caused by her trustee's breach of his duties arising under a voluntary trust.

Post-Judicature, the same division was retained. Parliament did not enact that the Supreme Court of Judicature (comprising the High Court and the Court of Appeal) was to have a single jurisdiction in which the rules and doctrines as developed by the courts of common law and equity should be 'blended and united'.[26] As Sir John Coleridge A-G made plain when the bill was sent to the Commons,[27] the primary purpose of the 1873 Act was not fusion of the substantive rules at law and in equity.[28] And Lord Selborne LC said nothing to the contrary before the Lords.[29]

Parliament's primary goal was to eliminate the administrative problem of litigants being sent from pillar to post, seeking remedies in one court

---

[23] This issue is discussed further in Chapter 8.

[24] (1742) Willes 400. See also *Winch* v. *Keeley* (1787) 1 TR 619, 623 (Buller J). For further discussion, see L. D. Smith, 'Tracing in *Taylor* v. *Plumer*: Equity in the Court of King's Bench' (1995) LMCLQ 240, 241–8.

[25] *Winch* v. *Keeley* (1787) 1 TR 619, 622–3; *Sinclair* v. *Brougham* [1914] AC 398, 420 (Viscount Haldane LC). See also *Re Diplock* [1948] 1 Ch 465, 519; aff'd on other grounds: *Ministry of Health* v. *Simpson* [1951] AC 251.

[26] That had been a feature of the High Court of Justice Bill (as amended), PP 1870, clause 9. Although that bill was passed by the House of Lords, it was withdrawn before debate in the Commons. For a summary of some features of that bill, see S. M. Waddams, 'Equity in English Contract Law: The Impact of the Judicature Acts (1873–75)' (2012) 33 *Journal of Legal History* 185, 186–7.

[27] HC Deb 9 June 1873, vol. 216, cols. 644–5

[28] Ibid. (emphasis added).

[29] HL Deb 13 February 1873, vol. 214, col. 339.

which another could not grant.[30] To achieve this, s. 16 of the Judicature Act 1873 merely enacted that each of the jurisdictions of the superior courts, in particular the court of Chancery and the courts of common law, were to be transferred to the Supreme Court of Judicature (comprising of the High Court and the Court of Appeal).[31] Thus, the Judicature Act 1873 effected, broadly speaking, 'a fusion of courts, not a fusion of law'.[32] So notwithstanding s. 25(11) of the 1873 Act providing for equity to 'prevail' over the common law by which the courts were often tempted by counsel to 'favour a new extension, restriction, or qualification of the former law, whether that earlier rule was from common law or equity, as a result of 'fusion into one law'[, o]n the whole, however, they resisted such invitations, adhering to the standard answer … that the new judicature was only a matter of court administration'.[33]

Matters could not be otherwise, given the diktat in s. 23 of the 1873 Act:

> The jurisdiction by this Act transferred to the said High Court of Justice and the said Court of Appeal respectively shall be exercised (so far as regards procedure and practise) in the manner provided by this Act, or by such Rules and Orders of Court as may be made pursuant to this Act; *and where no special provision is contained in this Act or in any such Rules or Orders of Court with reference thereto, it* [i.e. each jurisdiction transferred via s. 16] *shall be exercised as nearly as may be in the same manner as the same might have been exercised by the respective Courts from which such jurisdiction shall have been transferred, or by any of such Court.*[34]

This section was subsequently re-enacted *in pari materia* in s. 32 of the Supreme Court of Judicature (Consolidation) Act 1925 (hereafter, the '1925 Act').

---

[30] See also Meagher, Gummow & Lehane (2015), paras. 2-110 and 2-115; A. W. B. Simpson, 'The Modification of the Structure of the Courts' in J. Thornley and P. Allsop (eds.), *Then and Now, 1799–1974: Commemorating 175 Years of Law Bookselling and Publishing* (London: Sweet & Maxwell, 1974), p. 65. For judicial authorities, see *Salt* v. *Cooper* (1880) 16 Ch D 544, 549 (Sir George Jessel MR); *Ind, Coope & Co.* v. *Emmerson* (1887) 12 App Cas 300, 309 (Lord Watson).

[31] Judicature Act 1873.

[32] Patrick Polden, 'The Judicature Acts' in Sir John Baker (Gen. ed.), *The Oxford History of the Laws of England* (vol. XI, Oxford: Oxford University Press, 2010), p. 770. For similar sentiments, see A. Underhill, 'Changes in the Law of Property' in *A Century of Law Reform* (London: Macmillan & Co., 1901), p. 319.

[33] Polden, 'The Judicature Acts' (n. 32), p. 771 (references omitted).

[34] Emphasis added.

Though neither s. 23 of the 1873 Act nor s. 32 of the 1925 Act were unqualified, nothing in the Rules of Court or other pertinent provisions[35] of the 1873 or the 1925 Acts substantially contradicted the position set out above. If anything, they reinforced it.

For example, s. 24(4) of the 1873 Act instructed judges of the High Court to:

> recognise *and take notice* of all equitable estates, titles, and rights, and all equitable duties and liabilities appearing incidentally in the course of any cause or matter, in the same manner in which the Court of Chancery would have recognised and taken notice of the same in any suit or proceeding duly instituted therein before the passing of this Act.[36]

No mention was made of *enforcement* of such equitable matters by judges of the High Court. None was needed since, when acting within the equitable jurisdiction of the High Court, their enforcement within that jurisdiction followed as a matter of course from the instruction in s. 23. In effect, s. 24(4) preserved the pre-Judicature position as to courts of common law: so far as a judge in a pre-Judicature court of common law might 'recognize' and 'take notice of' equitable titles or interests but would not have issued any common law remedy to enforce such equitable titles or interests, so, too, a judge of the High Court when acting within its common law jurisdiction.

In contrast, s. 24(6) of the 1873 Act instructed judges of the High Court to:

> recognise *and give effect* to all legal claims and demands, and all estates, titles, rights, duties, obligations and liabilities existing by the Common Law or by any custom, or created by any Statute, in the same manner as the same would have been recognised and given effect to if this Act had not passed by any of the Courts whose jurisdiction is hereby transferred to the said High Court of Justice.[37]

Thus, so far as courts of common law or the court of Chancery would each, pre-Judicature, 'recognize' and 'give effect to' common law entitlements within their respective jurisdictions, so, too, would judges of the High Court when acting within its common law or equitable jurisdiction, respectively. For example, if a judge in the pre-Judicature court of Chancery would recognize and enforce a contractual promise supported

---

[35] E.g. ss. 36–44 of the 1925 Act (restating ss. 24(1)–(7) and 25(11) of the 1873 Act). The effects of ss. 24 and 25 of the 1873 Act are discussed in M. Leeming, 'Equity, the Judicature Acts and Restitution' (2011) 5 *Journal of Equity* 199, 213.

[36] Re-enacted *in pari materia* in s. 40 of the 1925 Act (emphasis added).

[37] Re-enacted *in pari materia* in s. 42 of the 1925 Act (emphasis added).

by consideration by issuing an order of specific performance, so, too, a judge of the High Court when acting within its equitable jurisdiction. And if a judge in a pre-Judicature court of common law would recognize and enforce such a contractual promise by ordering that common law damages be paid by way of compensation, so, too, a judge of the High Court when acting within its common law jurisdiction.

This is still the position today, though we have to read between the lines of the Senior Courts Act 1981 (hereafter the '1981 Act') to perceive it. Despite the repeal of the 1925 Act by the 1981 Act (itself a consolidating Act), the continuity of the High Court's jurisdictions is clear.

First, s. 19(2)(b) of the 1981 Act provides that:

> (2) Subject to the provisions of this Act, there shall be exercisable by the High Court – . . .

> (b) all such other jurisdiction (whether civil or criminal) as was exercisable by it immediately before the commencement of this Act (including jurisdiction conferred on a judge of the High Court by any statutory provision).

Next, though s. 19(2)(b) is qualified by s. 49, as Lord Hailsham LC explained in Parliament, s. 49 merely 'states in a more economical fashion the fusion of equity and law . . . which was originally contained in nine successive sections of the old Judicature Acts',[38] the 'nine successive sections' mentioned therein being ss. 36–44 of the 1925 Act, which restated and re-enacted ss. 24(1) to (7) and 25(11) of the 1873 Act. The 'administrative fusion' of the 1873 Act thus remains intact despite the new wording.[39]

Returning to Example 7.2: acting within its common law jurisdiction and applying legal principles, the High Court would conclude that A and C shared neither privity of interest, nor identity of persons. So far as the court, when acting within its common law jurisdiction, would be applying and giving effect to *legal* and not equitable principle, it could not take A and C to share privity of interest or identity of persons without going beyond recognition of equitable interests, to enforcing them. And the latter was where the common law courts had stopped short. Parliament having preserved that position under the Judicature Acts, attempts by

---

[38] Hansard, HL Deb 18 December 1980, vol. 415, col. 1214.

[39] That said, nothing in the 1873 Act (or its successors) bars 'fusion by analogy': J. Edelman, 'A "Fusion Fallacy" Fallacy' (2003) 119 LQR 375, 377; though caution may be advisable: M. Leeming, 'Equity, the Judicature Acts and Restitution' (2011) 5 *Journal of Equity* 199, 222–7.

A to re-litigate issue **V** *at law* would *not* be barred by issue estoppel: A would not be bound by any decision previously handed down by the court in its equitable jurisdiction.

But suppose A had been joined to C's earlier equitable proceedings. If so, the risk of conflicting decisions caused by re-litigation at law of issues previously decided in equity would evaporate as A's lack of privity of interest or identity of persons at law would no longer matter.[40] This, accordingly, is the source of the so-called rule of practice requiring joinder of the assignor of a legal chose in action to proceedings brought in the court's equitable jurisdiction, and not necessarily as a matter of course, so as to bind the assignor to the court's findings in those equitable proceedings and preclude their re-litigation at law.[41] Hence, as Chitty LJ noted:[42]

---

[40]  A point recognized in *Ardila Investments NV* v. *ENRC NV and Zamin Ferrous Ltd* [2015] EWHC 1667 (Comm); [2015] BCLC 560, [23].

[41]  See *Performing Right Society Ltd* v. *London Theatre of Varieties Ltd* [1924] AC 1, 14; cited with approval in *Roberts* v. *Gill & Co.* [2010] UKSC 22; [2011] 1 AC 240, [65]. Given the analysis in the main text, there may be a corresponding rule of practice at common law where the final decision of the court in its common law jurisdiction in proceedings brought by the assignor of a legal chose in action ought not be handed down without the *assignee's* joinder to those proceedings. This would ensure that if equitable proceedings were brought subsequently by or against the assignee, issue estoppel might be asserted against such assignee, so binding him to the prior decision reached by the court in its common law jurisdiction. Alternatively, because a court acting within its common law jurisdiction would recognize (though not enforce) the assignee's equitable entitlements arising from an equitable assignment, such recognition would be enough to support a stay of the proceedings (pursuant to the power originally granted in s. 24(5) of the Judicature Act 1873, re-enacted *in pari materia* in s. 41 of the Supreme Court of Judicature (Consolidation) Act 1925, but now encapsulated within s. 49(3), Senior Courts Act 1981). This may explain Etherton LJ's observations in *Kapoor* v. *National Westminster Bank Plc* [2011] EWCA Civ 1083; [2012] 1 All ER 1201, [30], that 'the assignor [of a debt] cannot bring proceedings to recover the assigned debt in the assignor's own name for the assignor's own account. The assignor can sue as trustee for the assignee if the assignee agrees, and, in that event the claim must disclose the assignor's representative capacity. *In any other case, the assignor must join the assignee, not because of a mere procedural rule but as a matter of substantive law in view of the insufficiency of the assignor's title*' (emphasis added), as well as the result reached by the majority in *Three Rivers District Council* v. *Governor and Company of the Bank of England* [1996] QB 292, 313G: 'If, unusually, the assignor sues, he will not be allowed to maintain the action in the absence of the assignee.' Cf. A. Tettenborn, 'Equitable Assignment and Procedural Quibbles' (1995) 54 CLJ 499, 501.

[42]  *Durham Brothers* v. *Robertson* [1898] 1 QB 765, 769–70 (emphasis added). A. L. Smith and Collins LJJ agreed with Chitty LJ on this point.

[A]n ordinary debt or [legal] chose in action before the Judicature Act was not assignable so as to pass the right of action at law, but it was assignable so as to pass the right to sue in equity. *In his suit in equity* the assignee of a debt, even where the assignment was absolute on the face of it, had to make his assignor, the original creditor, party in order primarily to bind him *and prevent his suing at law,* and also to allow him to dispute the assignment if he thought fit.

The application of issue estoppel rules by a court acting within its equitable jurisdiction explains why the assignor of a legal chose may be required to be joined to those equitable proceedings as a matter of procedural convenience because otherwise such assignor would not be bound by the decisions handed down in such equitable proceeding. Joinder of the assignor to such equitable proceedings, though not absolutely necessary, would obviate the risk of conflicting proceedings at law involving the assignor being brought subsequently. But where such risk was negligible, or, as in *Brandt's*,[43] if the obligor was prepared to take the consequences of non-joinder, joinder could be excused if there were no other 'good reasons' to require joinder.[44] However, when proceedings are brought *at common law* in respect of a dispute over a legal chose in action, matters may be quite different.

So far as a court acting within its common law jurisdiction was concerned, if an action was brought against a contractual obligor ('B') concerning alleged breaches of its contractual obligations arising from a contract entered into with its obligee ('A'), A's equitable assignment of the benefits arising from that contract to an assignee ('C') would not strip A of its status as a contracting party. Nor would it make C any less a stranger to that contract. Therefore, absent a novation[45] or a statutory assignment[46] to C, *substantive* common law contract principles would require A to be party to the proceedings at law on such contract.

---

[43] It will be explained in Chapter 9 that *Brandt's* should be taken to have been a decision of the court in its equitable jurisdiction.

[44] For example, the ones mentioned by Viscount Cave in *Performing Right Society* (n. 41).

[45] The facts in Example 7.2 do not support novation. That would entail a fresh agreement being reached between A, B and C where, in consideration of A agreeing to release B from his obligations under the contract, B agreed to be obligated to C as regards the rewiring of the mansion.

[46] Pursuant to LPA1925, s. 136(1). This would require the assignment to be absolute and not by way of charge, in a writing signed by A, and B to be given written notice thereof.

Disputes over the performance of legal obligations may be heard by the court within its legal *or* equitable jurisdiction.[47] Since joinder of the assignor may be mandatory when the proceedings are within the court's common law jurisdiction due to substantive common law principles, but be merely required as a matter of 'procedural convenience' when equitable proceedings are brought instead, determination as to which joinder rule is applicable depends on whether the court's legal or equitable jurisdiction had been invoked.

Having discussed at length why joinder of the assignor of a legal chose is not absolutely necessary when proceedings in equity are brought by her assignee against the obligor, the following chapters will examine the question of joinder of the assignor when proceedings at common law are brought against the obligor by the assignee.

---

[47] The exceptions are legal choses arising from voluntary covenants executed under seal as 'the Court will not execute a voluntary contract; and … the principle of the Court to withhold its assistance from a volunteer applies equally, whether he seeks to have the benefit of a contract, a covenant, or a settlement': *Jefferys* v. *Jefferys* (1841) Cr & Ph 138, 141 (Lord Cottenham LC).

# 8

# Joinder of Assignor in Common Law Proceedings

This chapter will concentrate on the rules as to joinder of parties when proceedings are brought at *common law*. It will show how the rules as to parties to proceedings at common law and in equity are distinct from one another.

## A  Non-Enforcement of Equitable Assignment by Courts of Common Law

By 1808,[1] the courts of equity had come to accept that a chose in action was a presently existing thing over which a trust could be constituted, and so could be '*equitably* assigned'. But the courts of common law persisted in the view that a chose in action was a mere expectancy whose realization depended on the bringing of an action.[2]

Consequently, where a legal chose in action had been equitably assigned, and the assignee sought to bring proceedings against the obligor before a court of common law, those courts declined to take such assignee to have been authorized to bring such proceedings at law by reason of the assignment alone. So far as the assignee remained a stranger as a matter of common law to the obligation on which the proceedings were brought, the assignee would have no standing to commence common law proceedings at law, unless he had been duly authorized by the assignor to do so in a manner which was accepted by the common law courts. Thus, Willes J in the Common Pleas observed:[3]

> The rule [at common law] against assigning a chose in action stood in the way of an actual transfer of the debt, so as to enable the plaintiff to sue in

---

[1] See *Sloane* v. *Cadogan* (1808) in Sugden (1846), p. 1119, briefly discussed in Chapter 4, Section A(ii).

[2] As mentioned in *Sir Moyl Finche's Case* (1590) 4 Co Inst 85. This report should not be confused with the report of subsequent proceedings in *Sir Moyle Finch's Case* (1606) 6 Co Rep 63a.

[3] *Gerard* v. *Lewis* (1867) LR 2 CP 305, 309.

his own name; and therefore, it became necessary to give the power of attorney. But the intention of the parties in giving that power was to give the assignee the conduct and control of the litigation necessary for enforcing payment of the debts assigned.

Such authorization would have to be established by words or acts evidencing the requisite grant of authority to the assignee by the assignor over and beyond mere words of assignment. As Elphinstone observed in 1871:[4]

> Bearing in mind the importance, where a legal chose in action is assigned, of being able to sue the debtor at law in the name of the original creditor, a power of attorney is *always* inserted in the assignment of a legal chose in action, enabling the assignee 'to demand, sue for, recover, receive, and give effectual discharges for the debt, in the name of the assignor'.

It is not immediately obvious why the courts of common law declined to develop the common law in parallel with the developments in equity. Perhaps the traditional view was retained because the position adopted in equity appeared to serve the requirements of the time sufficiently well.[5] But whatever their reasons, until Judicature Act 1873, s. 25(6) came into force, the courts of common law continued to view choses in action to be mere expectancies which were incapable of being presently dealt with as a matter of common law. Indeed, had the common law developed in the same way as equity had done, it would not have been necessary to enact s. 25(6). As Scrutton LJ observed in 1919:[6]

---

[4] Elphinstone (1871), pp. 206–7. This practice appears still to be current: Beale, Gullifer & Paterson (2016), p. 223. For precedents of deeds of assignment incorporating a power of attorney of the sort mentioned by Elphinstone, see William Hughes, *Concise Precedents in Modern Conveyancing* (2nd edn, 2 vols., London: Law Times Office, 1855), vol. 1, pp. 282–95; Gilbert Horseman, *Precedents in Conveyancing* (3 vols., London: His Majesty's Law Printers, 1785), vol. 1, pp. 132–4: 'An assignment of a bond and judgment to a trustee for a purchaser to protect a purchase.' The provision for a power of attorney is set out at p. 133. Precedents of such deeds after the enactment of the Judicature Act 1873 tended to omit the power of attorney clause on the basis that such a clause would be unnecessary if the requirements for a statutory assignment set out in s. 25(6) of the 1873 Act had been satisfied: Thomas Key and H. W. Elphinstone, *A Compendium of Precedents in Conveyancing* (2 vols., London: William Maxwell and Son, 1878), vol. 1, p. 265. Those requirements may now be found in LPA1925, s. 136(1).

[5] Bailey (1932), pp. 549–50, suggested that the common law may have resisted going beyond recognition of the effects of an equitable assignment at common law to giving effect to the same by making common law remedies available because of the shadow cast by debtors' prisons. Reform of the system of imprisonment of debtors who had not paid their debts only began in 1869.

[6] *Ellis v. Torrington* [1920] 1 KB 399, 410–11.

It is elementary knowledge that for a long time Courts of common law and Courts of equity differed as to how far choses in action, and particularly causes of action, could be assigned. The common law treated debts as personal obligations and assignments of debts merely as assignments of the right to bring an action at law against the debtor and, except in a strictly limited number of cases, did not recognize any such assignments. Courts of equity always took a different view. They treated debts as property, and the necessity of an action at law to reduce the property into possession they regarded merely as an incident which followed on the assignment of the property.

Accordingly, in principle,[7] even today, in order for proceedings at law to be brought on a contractual chose in action that had been equitably assigned to an assignee, the assignee *must* have been authorized to bring the proceedings in a manner as would be recognized and given effect to *at common law*. The fact of equitable assignment, of itself, would not do.

Such authority may be granted by way of a formal document. Or the obligee might provide for such authority in express words within the equitable assignment documentation. Or, if no such provision had been made, the assignor might be called on by the assignee to grant such authority, before proceedings at law were brought; and if the assignor refused to provide such authority voluntarily without order, the assignee might initiate proceedings *in equity* against the assignor to compel her to furnish such authority, since the courts of equity had long recognized that in respect of assignments of contractual choses in action:[8]

[T]he form of assigning a chose in action is in the nature of a declaration of trust, *and an agreement* to permit the assignee to make use of the name of the assignor, in order to recover the possession. And therefore, when in common acceptation of a debt or bond is said to be assigned over, it must still be sued in the original creditor's name; the person, to whom it is transferred, being rather an attorney than an assignee.

---

[7] As will be discussed in Chapter 9, the difficult case of *William Brandt's Sons & Co. v. Dunlop Rubber Co.* [1905] AC 454 has been read to indicate otherwise. But as will be explained in Chapter 9, that is arguably a misreading of the decision.

[8] 2 Bl Comm 442 (emphasis added). See also Co Litt 232b, note (1); Story (1836), §1040. Anticipating Blackstone, much the same point was made in Thomas Wood, *An Institute of the Laws of England: or, the Laws of England in Their Natural Order, according to Common Use* (8th edn, London: Henry Lintot, 1754), 297: 'A Thing in *Action*, as a Statute, Bond, a Just Debt, is vulgarly said to be assignable over: But then One must Sue for the same in the Name of the Assignor. So that in Reality, it amounts to little more than a Letter of Attorney, to Sue in His Name.'

If the assignor refused to permit the assignee to make use of the assignor's name to bring proceedings at law as her duly appointed 'attorney', the assignee might bring proceedings in equity to so compel her to do so. Here, although equity will not assist a volunteer,[9] it is not quite true to say that:[10]

> At common law things in action were not assignable, and an assignee had to go to equity to enforce his claims. If the thing in action was a legal claim, he had to file a bill to compel the assignor to permit him to sue in the name of the assignor, and equity would help him only if he had given valuable consideration for the assignment.

As explained in Chapter 4, equity *would* aid volunteers such as trust beneficiaries, and also equitable assignees taking by way of gift.

## B  The *Vandepitte* Procedure

Prior to the administrative fusion effected by the Judicature Acts, the assignee of a contractual chose would need to bring two different proceedings before two different courts if he desired to bring an action at law against the obligor but the assignor was uncooperative. But after the Judicature Acts, these two proceedings could be brought by the assignee jointly in one proceeding before a single court by means of the 'procedural short-cut'[11] arising by means of the '*Vandepitte* procedure'[12] (which, strictly speaking, joins proceedings, not parties).[13]

In order to avoid circuity of action,[14] the *Vandepitte* procedure may be used to join two proceedings into one, as when a trustee holds the benefit of a contract on trust for trust beneficiaries and proceedings in equity are needed to compel the trustee to sue the contractual obligor at law. Should the contract be breached, the trustee is duty-bound in equity by reason of

---

[9] *Re D'Angibau* (1880) 15 Ch D 228, 246: '[V]olunteers have no right whatever to obtain specific performance of a mere covenant which has remained as a covenant and has never been performed.'

[10] *Holt* v. *Heatherfield Trust Ltd* [1942] 2 KB 1, 3.

[11] *Don King Productions Inc.* v. *Warren* [2000] Ch 291, 321D (Lightman J).

[12] Named after *Vandepitte* v. *Preferred Accident Insurance Corpn of New York* [1933] AC 70. It has been suggested that the procedure predates that decision: M. Smith, 'Locus Standi and the Enforcement of Legal Claims by Cestuis Que Trust and Assignees' (2008) 22 *Trust Law International* 140.

[13] *Harmer* v. *Armstrong* [1934] Ch 65, 83 (Lord Hanworth MR).

[14] Smith & Leslie (2018), para. 11.77.

his trust to bring proceedings at law against the defaulting obligor to seek damages to remedy any loss as may arise by reason of such breach. If the trustee declines to perform his equitable duty to bring such proceedings, his trust beneficiaries may bring proceedings in equity against him to compel him to bring such proceedings at law. The *Vandepitte* procedure therefore allows for two proceedings to be heard jointly within a single court with the beneficiaries as claimants, and the uncooperative trustee and the defaulting obligor as co-defendants. But conceptually, this is a joinder of two proceedings. It is not a joinder of additional parties to *a* proceeding.

When this procedure is applied to join the proceedings in equity against an uncooperative trustee for hearing together with the proceedings at law against the defaulting obligor, the beneficiary is not *joined* to the latter proceeding at law – the latter is still a proceeding at law between the trustee and the defaulting obligor, not a proceeding between the beneficiary and the defaulting obligor. And this is necessarily so, since the beneficiary remains a stranger to that contract.

The *Vandepitte* procedure may also be applied in the context of equitable assignments.[15] If the obligee to a contract equitably assigned the benefit of that contract to an assignee, the court in its equitable jurisdiction would recognize that such assignment entailed a trust of the benefit of the contract as well as an agreement to lend the assignee her name should it be necessary to bring proceedings at law. Thus, so far as the 'agreement' was supported by consideration, if the assignor refused to perform in accordance with the latter agreement, the assignee could bring proceedings in equity against the assignor to compel her to authorize the assignee to bring proceedings as her 'attorney', and then bring proceedings at law against the defaulting obligor.

But even if the agreement was *not* supported by consideration, and so was not enforceable in equity, since the assignment also entailed a trust, the assignee might bring proceedings against his assignor on the basis of the trustee–beneficiary relationship between them to compel the trustee to commence legal action against the defaulting obligor. So, again, if the assignor (looked on as trustee of the benefit of the chose assigned) refused to bring such proceedings at law against the obligor, the assignee (looked on as beneficiary of such trust) could bring proceedings in equity against the assignor to compel her to do so. Post-Judicature, then, instead

---

[15] *Barbados Trust Company Ltd* v. *Bank of Zambia* [2007] EWCA Civ 148; [2007] 1 Lloyd's Rep 495, [99] (Rix LJ).

of bringing two separate proceedings, one after the other, the assignee may join both proceedings in one, naming himself as the claimant, and the assignor and the defaulting obligor as co-defendants. But this is still not a case of *joinder* of the assignor to a proceeding brought by the assignee *at law* against the defaulting obligor: it is a joint hearing of two proceedings.

An equitable assignee of a contractual chose in action will, at law, remain a stranger to that contract. So an equitable assignee of such contractual chose has no standing at law by reason of such assignment. Similarly, so far as the common law will rarely (if ever) have defined duties arising in tort to be owed to equitable assignees by reason of such assignment alone, the fact of an equitable assignment will not give an assignee standing to bring proceedings at law in respect of any accrued cause of action arising from a breach of tort duties. So far as such tort duties were not owed to the assignee as assignee, an assignee will remain a 'stranger' to the cause of action.

Consequently, an equitable assignee of a legal chose in action may only bring proceedings at law against the obligor if he had already been authorized by the assignor to bring them, whether by reason of a grant of authority at the same time as the assignment, or, if none had been granted at that time, before proceedings were commenced against the obligor.[16]

If no such grant of authority had been made before commencement of proceedings, the *Vandepitte* procedure allowed the assignee to simultaneously bring proceedings in equity against the assignor, and at law against the obligor.[17] But even then, the assignor would still need to be made party to such proceedings at law. Consequently, the suggestion made by Smith and Leslie[18] that the *Vandepitte* procedure may explain why an assignor need not be joined to proceedings that have been brought by an assignee against a defaulting obligor is, with respect, not entirely convincing.

---

[16] And in such a case, the claimant-assignee would have to state clearly that he was bringing such proceedings at law in his representative capacity as the assignor's duly authorized agent.

[17] Or, if the assignment were voluntary, to compel the assignor to bring proceedings at law against the obligor because of her 'trustee-beneficiary' relationship with her assignee.

[18] Smith & Leslie (2018), paras 11.78–11.82, maintaining their position in Smith & Leslie (2013), paras. 11.43–11.47, a position which had been criticized in Meagher, Gummow & Lehane (2015), para. 6-520 for broadly similar reasons to the ones in the main text, above.

If the assignment was supported by consideration, then the assignee might join one proceeding in equity between the assignee and the assignor (by which the assignor might be ordered to grant the assignee the requisite authority to bring an action at law against the obligor); and a second at law between the assignee (as would be authorized by the assignor, if the first proceedings were successful) and the defaulting obligor. Alternatively, where the assignment was voluntary, then the assignee might join one proceeding in equity between the assignee and the assignor (by which the assignor might be ordered to bring proceedings at law against the defaulting obligor), and a second at law between the assignor and the obligor. But on either alternative, use of the *Vandepitte* procedure still requires the assignor to be joined as a party to the proceedings as a co-defendant.

Yet cases like *Brandt's*,[19] *Performing Right Society*,[20] *The Aiolos*,[21] *Weddell v. J. A. Pearce & Major*,[22] *Three Rivers District Council*,[23] *Bexhill UK Ltd v. Razzaq*[24] and *Raiffeisen Zentralbank Österreich AG*[25] each contain statements which may be taken to stand for the proposition that 'there is now a preponderance of authority supporting the proposition that when a legal chose is assigned, the need to join the assignor is procedural and not substantive',[26] leading to the supposition that the court may waive joinder of the assignor when proceedings *at law* are brought by the equitable assignee. However, for the reasons explained earlier, this is difficult.

As the editors of *Meagher, Gummow & Lehane* have pointed out: 'How a person not the legal owner can, the Judicature Act [1873] notwithstanding, prosecute what is, in effect, an action at common law for damages is not explained.'[27] And to argue, as Smith and Leslie do,[28] that the *Vandepitte* procedure allows the assignee to sue in her own name is beside the point, for the question is not how the assignee may sue in her

---

[19] *William Brandt's Sons & Co. v. Dunlop Rubber Co.* [1905] AC 454.
[20] [1924] AC 1.
[21] [1983] 2 Lloyd's Rep 25.
[22] [1988] Ch 26.
[23] [1996] QB 292.
[24] [2012] EWCA Civ 1376, [2001] QB 825.
[25] *Raiffeisen Zentralbank Österriech AG v. Five Star Trading LLC* [2001] EWCA Civ 68; [2001] QB 825.
[26] Smith & Leslie (2018), para. 11.54.
[27] Meagher, Gummow & Lehane (2015), para. 6-520.
[28] Above, n. 18.

own name, but how the assignee may sue without needing to join the assignor *at all*.

The solution to this conundrum may lie in challenging the unstated assumption that *Brandt's* was a case brought by assignees within the court's *common law* jurisdiction.

Though most judicial proceedings brought in respect of breaches of duties arising at law will be brought within the court's common law jurisdiction, that is not necessarily the case. Since the court has a concurrent *equitable* jurisdiction over many legal choses, an obligee (and hence her assignee) may, if need be, bring proceedings within the court's equitable jurisdiction.

Certainly, had proceedings been brought within the court's *common law* jurisdiction, the objection that the assignee *could not* bring such proceedings on grounds of his having been equitably assigned the benefit of that contract would be salient, so far as the court in its common law jurisdiction could not grant common law remedies to enforce such assignment at common law. But that is not so when the proceedings are brought within the court's *equitable* jurisdiction. And within that jurisdiction, the trust and agency effects which conceptually underpin the operation of equitable assignment may be not only recognized, but would also be fully enforced.

The following chapter will show how an equitable assignee of a legal chose in action may bring proceedings against the obligor within the court's *equitable* jurisdiction, even when the remedy sought may entail the payment of damages and/or entail the payment of a fixed sum of money. Consequently, a case like *Brandt's* (in which the court ordered the defendant-debtor to pay a fixed sum of money to the plaintiff-assignee) may well have been decided by the court in its equitable jurisdiction where there is only a rule of *practice* requiring joinder of the assignor,[29] instead of its common law jurisdiction, where, as a matter of substantive common law, no stranger to the obligation may commence any proceedings at law.

---

[29] As explained in Chapter 7.

# 9

# Non-joinder of Assignor of Legal Choses

Different rules apply to the question of joinder of parties, depending on whether the proceedings are brought within the court's equitable or common law jurisdiction. These complications do not arise so far as one is concerned with equitable choses, since by definition, these are matters as to which the courts of common law have no jurisdiction. But proceedings may be brought in the court's common law or concurrent equitable jurisdiction in respect of many legal choses in action.[1]

Pre-Judicature, one could easily tell whether proceedings had been brought within the court's common law or equitable jurisdiction: one merely had to see in which physical courtroom the dispute had been brought. But post-Judicature, it is no longer so obvious, since the High Court has both common law and equitable jurisdiction. Even the remedy that is ordered is only an uncertain guide, given that the equitable remedy of injunction is not restricted to obligations other than to pay a fixed sum of money,[2] and, since 1858, courts acting within their equitable jurisdiction have been empowered to award compensatory damages pursuant to Lord Cairns' Act. As will be explained in the sections that immediately follow, since 1858 it has been possible for damages to be awarded in conncection with breaches of common law obligations (such as those that arise from a contract) in equity. If so, it would follow that where proceedings for damages *are* brought within the court's equitable jurisdiction, the relevant rules on joinder of parties are not those applicable at common law, but are those applicable in equity, namely, those set out and described in Chapter 7.

The effect of Lord Cairns' Act is, however, limited to awards of damages. It does not extend to orders requiring the defendant to pay a fixed sum of money. Notwithstanding the limited effect of Lord Cairns'

---

[1] The exceptions are legal choses arising from covenants so far as they are unsupported by consideration, as 'equity will not aid a volunteer'.

[2] As will be shown below in Sections C and D.

Act, however, it is still possible for a court acting within its equitable jurisdiction to make an order compelling the payment of a fixed sum of money: such a remedy is *not* exclusively available to the court acting within its common law jurisdiction. Accordingly, the difficult case of *Brandt's*[3] can be re-characterized as a decision of the court acting within its equitable and not common law jurisdiction.

The difficulty with re-characterizing *Brandt's* as a decision of the court exercising its equitable jurisdiction is that the respondent debtor was ordered to pay a fixed sum of money in light of the unpaid price for goods sold under a contract of sale. It would not, therefore, be unreasonable to assume that such order had been made in a common law action of debt. If so, and since the remedy at law in debt would appear to be entirely adequate, the proposition that the claimant in *Brandt's* had brought proceedings within the court's equitable jurisdiction seems difficult. But this hides an error. If we remember that access to the court's equitable jurisdiction by reason of the common law's remedies being inadequate is not the only route to that jurisdiction, the proposition that *Brandt's* may have been a decision of the court acting within its equitable jurisdiction becomes less outlandish. This will be discussed in Sections C and D, below.

## A    The Equitable Remedy of Injunction or Specific Performance

Pre-Judicature, if an assignee wished to obtain equitable remedies against the obligor, he would have had to seek the assistance of the courts of equity, since by definition, the courts of common law would have had no power to grant equitable remedies (leaving aside the effects of the CLPA1854).[4]

Even today, an assignee of a contractual chose wishing to obtain an order of specific performance against the obligor to compel him to perform that which he had promised would seek this remedy within the court's equitable jurisdiction. And for an example of the circumstances where such proceedings might be brought by an equitable assignee within the court's concurrent equitable jurisdiction, reference may be made to the discussion of Example 7.2 in Chapter 7.

---

[3]  *William Brandt's & Co.* v. *Dunlop Rubber Co.* [1905] AC 454.
[4]  Pursuant to CLPA1854, ss. 79 and 82, the common law courts were given statutory powers to grant orders of injunction in certain circumstances.

## B   Equitable Damages Pursuant to Lord Cairns' Act

Suppose B's dilatory progress in Example 7.2 had caused C to sustain pecuniary losses as well: because of the delays, C had not been able to find tenants for the boarding house and, accordingly, had lost the rent he could have earned had the work been completed on time. Could C seek damages from B in his proceedings before a court of equity?

If the facts in Example 7.2 had occurred before 1858, the answer would have been 'no'. To recover damages, C would have had to bring further proceedings before a court of common law. But in that forum, if B challenged C's standing to sue him at law, a court of common law would hold that C, being a stranger to the contract, could not bring such proceedings. C would need to obtain the requisite authority from A first, by suit if A refused to honour the agreement arising implicitly from the equitable assignment to provide such authority.

The exclusivity of damages as a remedy of the common law courts was done away with by s. 2 of the Chancery Amendment Act 1858 (commonly known as Lord Cairns' Act): where a plaintiff could show a court of equity that he was entitled to relief by way of specific performance or injunction, and there were also grounds as would entitle him to damages were he to go to common law, s. 2 granted the court of equity power to award such damages, absolving the plaintiff from having to initiate separate proceedings at law.[5] And the effects of s. 2 were preserved by Judicature Act 1873, s. 24(7). Thus, so far as the jurisdiction of the Court of Chancery had been transferred to the High Court of Justice and the Court of Appeal, that equitable jurisdiction also encompassed a *statutory* power to award damages.

Had the events in Example 7.2 arisen in, say, 1880, if A also sustained pecuniary losses by reason of B's breach of contract, A could have brought proceedings against B in the High Court's equity jurisdiction to seek damages pursuant to Lord Cairns' Act, s. 2, so far as the dispute entailed a cause of action in equity for specific performance or an injunction. Consequently, C, as A's assignee, would be empowered by the agency effect to bring such proceedings in equity to seek an injunction against B, and Lord Cairns' Act damages, without needing to join A.

---

[5] *Ferguson* v. *Wilson* (1866) LR 2 Ch App 77, 88 (Turner LJ); *Jaggard* v. *Sawyer* [1995] 1 WLR 269, 284 (Millett LJ).

This position has been preserved, given the modern-day equivalent to the Judicature Act 1873, s. 24(7), now found in the Senior Courts Act 1981, s. 50.

It is not necessary to dwell on the 'broader' effect of Lord Cairns' Act beyond what is set out on its face.[6] It suffices to note that since 1858,[7] a court acting within its equitable jurisdiction has the power to award such damages as would be awarded by a court in its common law jurisdiction. On the facts of Example 7.2, so far as C *had* come within equity's jurisdiction, C could seek damages in addition to or in lieu of an order of specific performance against B, and such proceedings would *still* be entirely within the court's equitable jurisdiction in which the grant of authority to C to commence such proceeding in equity arising from A's equitable assignment to C, in and of itself, would be recognized. And as explained in Chapter 7, A would be bound in equity by such decision, notwithstanding her not having been joined. It would be advisable, however, as a matter of *practice*, to join A as a party to ensure that issue estoppel could be invoked against A should subsequent proceedings at law be brought by or against A. But there would be no substantive requirement such that non-joinder of A would render those proceedings flawed.

### C   Equitable Order Compelling Payment of Fixed Sums of Money where Common Law Remedies Are Inadequate

In Example 7.2, the obligation owed by B to A at common law was an obligation to perform an act other than to pay a fixed sum of money. Had proceedings been brought at law against B in respect of his breach of that obligation, the remedy at law would have been damages. But what if the obligation in question were an obligation to pay a fixed sum of money? Consider Example 9.1.

---

[6] Namely, the extent to which Lord Cairns' Act conferred the court with a power to award damages in respect of future breaches. 'In terms it gave power to substitute damages for an injunction. Such a substitution in the very nature of things involves that the damages are to deal with what would have been prevented by the injunction if granted': *Leeds Industrial Co-operative Society, Ltd* v. *Slack* [1924] AC 851, 857 (Viscount Finlay); *Jaggard* v. *Sawyer* (n. 5), 286–7. See also J. A. Jolowicz, 'Damages in Equity – A Study of Lord Cairns' Act' (1975) 34 CLJ 224, 227.

[7] The power to grant Lord Cairns' Act damages may have been 'accidentally' repealed in 1974, before being reinstated in the Senior Courts Act 1981: Jolowicz (n. 6). But cf. P. M. McDermott, 'Survival of Jurisdiction under the Chancery Amendment Act 1858 (Lord Cairns' Act)' (1987) 6 *Civil Justice Quarterly* 348.

---

### EXAMPLE 9.1

B has borrowed £10,000 from A. The terms of the loan contract specify that the loan is to be repaid in one year's time by tendering payment *to* C in ten equal instalments, at such times as C may demand. Even so, the contract stipulates that the provisions of the C3PA are not to apply to give C any third-party statutory rights.

Six months later, A equitably assigns the benefit of her legal chose against B under contract to C. Unfortunately, the issue as to C's authority to bring judicial proceedings against B as might be necessary to reduce the chose into possession is not discussed, as both parties assume that the words of equitable assignment are sufficient to have such effect in equity and at law.

As the twelve months following A's loan to B come to an end, C informs B that he would like B to pay him £1,000 for the first instalment on the anniversary date of the loan. C also informs B of A's equitable assignment to him.

B refuses to pay C anything at all.

---

B has plainly repudiated the terms of his contract with A. But C is not privy to the contract between A and B. Nor has C given any consideration at B's request thereunder. Thus, C would have had no standing in his own right to bring proceedings at law against B for B's repudiatory breach. Furthermore, since C has no entitlements arising under the C3PA, if C wished to bring proceedings against B in respect of this repudiatory breach, C may only do so as A's equitable assignee.

Suppose A had not effected any equitable assignment to C. In such circumstances, were A to bring proceedings at law against B for failing to tender payment to C once C had made a valid demand, the only remedy which A might obtain would be damages.[8] It would not be open to A to seek an order pursuant to the action for debt, because B's obligation was not a duty to pay a fixed sum of money to A.

But damages would likely be an inadequate remedy given that B's duty was not just to tender a single payment – it was an ongoing obligation to tender payments to C in ten equal instalments, on C's demand. A could, therefore, bring proceedings against B within the court's equitable (concurrent) jurisdiction, on grounds of the inadequacy of the remedy at common law, seeking an order of specific performance

---

[8] The statutory power granted to a court in its common law jurisdiction to issue an injunction under CLPA1854, s. 79, though preserved under the Judicature Act 1873, could not be invoked to order payment of sums not yet due.

to compel B to perform that which he had promised – i.e. tender payment to C on C's demand.[9]

If so, C, as A's assignee, would be taken by a court in its equitable jurisdiction to be authorized by reason of the 'agency effect' to bring such proceedings in equity as A's 'agent'. And, as explained in Chapter 7, it would not be necessary to join A to such proceedings since A would be bound in equity by the court's decision.

It would be entirely appropriate for the court, acting within its equitable jurisdiction, to grant the order sought by C, being an order of specific performance to compel B to perform that which he had contractually bound himself to do, namely, to pay a fixed sum of money (i.e. £1,000, being one-tenth of the £10,000 of the loan) to C, on demand. Notwithstanding that the remedy looks somewhat like a common law remedy, it is not – it is an *equitable* remedy.

Accordingly, non-joinder of A to such proceedings in the equitable jurisdiction of the court does *not* amount to a substantive defect as a matter of equitable principles. But again, to ensure that A would be subject to issue estoppel were proceedings at law brought subsequently by or against A, it would be advisable as a matter of practice to join A to such proceedings in the court's equitable jurisdiction.

### D   Equitable Order Compelling Payment of Fixed Sums of Money where Common Law Remedies Are *Not* Inadequate

Sections A to C above have shown that where the assignee of a legal chose in action brings proceedings against a defaulting obligor entirely within the court's equitable jurisdiction to obtain *equitable* remedies such as orders of specific performance, injunction and/or (equitable) damages pursuant to Lord Cairns' Act, since the court's common law jurisdiction is not engaged, there is no need to join the assignor to the proceedings. But it must be admitted that the analyses above hardly represent typical cases. Much more typical would be the situation described in Example 9.2.

---

[9] See e.g. *Beswick* v. *Beswick* [1968] AC 58. The possibility that an order of specific performance may issue in respect of a breach of a contractual obligation by B to pay a fixed sum of money to A on the application of C, to whom A had equitably assigned the benefit of the debt owed by B, was implicitly accepted in *Hammond* v. *Messenger* (1838) 9 Sim 327: see Section D, below, at text to n. 39.

---

**EXAMPLE 9.2**

Suppose A sells goods to B. B becomes duty-bound to pay the price for those goods to A: B becomes indebted to A. Should B fail to pay the price, notwithstanding his acceptance of the goods and title thereto having passed to B, A's sole remedy at law is an action in debt to compel B to pay the price for the goods.[10]

---

Should A equitably assign to C the benefit of B's indebtedness to her, it is clear that as a matter of substantive law, C has no *locus standi* to bring an action of debt against B: C is neither privy to the contract of sale between A and B, nor has C provided consideration at B's request in respect of that contract.

If the equitable assignment to C in Example 9.2 had been accompanied by suitable words authorizing C 'to demand, sue for, recover, receive, and give effectual discharges for the debt, in the name of the assignor',[11] C could bring an action of debt as A's 'attorney' against B. But absent such words, so far as a court in its common law jurisdiction was concerned, the fact of A's equitable assignment to C would not be recognized as a valid grant of authority at law. Although the court, when acting within its equitable jurisdiction, would recognize and give effect to an equitable assignee's authority to invoke the assignor's entitlements against the obligor as he pleased by virtue of that equitable assignment, including the assignee's power to bring proceedings in equity against the obligor,[12] that would be of little consequence when proceedings were brought at law, since a court acting within its common law jurisdiction would not do likewise.

Consequently, if A was unwilling to grant such authority to C, not-withstanding her being taken in equity to have agreed to do so, if the equitable assignment was supported by consideration from C, C could bring proceedings in equity to compel A to honour her agreement, and so be compelled to authorize C.

Alternatively, if the equitable assignment was gratuitous, so far as such equitable assignment entailed a trustee–beneficiary relationship between A and C by reason of the 'trust effect', C could bring proceedings in equity to compel A to bring proceedings at law against B as C's trustee.

---

[10] Damages are not generally available for non-payment of the principal sum. Damages are sometimes available in respect of consequential loss arising from late or non-payment, and/or interest for late payment. The issue is discussed in J. Edelman, *McGregor on Damages* (20th edn, London: Sweet & Maxwell/Thomson Reuters, 2018), paras. 30-001 to 30-011.

[11] As Elphinstone would have recommended: Elphinstone (1871), pp. 206–7.

[12] As explained in Section C.

Either way, proceedings at law could then be brought against B, either by C as A's duly authorized agent, or by A as trustee for C. And under the *Vandepitte* procedure, C might then bring both sets of proceedings for hearing together, naming A and B as co-defendants.[13]

This statement of the law is, however, incomplete.

In *Brandt's*, Lord Macnaghten observed as follows:[14]

> Strictly speaking, Kramrisch & Co. [the assignor], or their trustee in bankruptcy, should have been brought before the court. But no action is now dismissed for want of parties, and the trustee in bankruptcy had really no interest in the matter. At your Lordships' bar the [sic] Dunlops [the debtor] disclaimed any wish to have him present, and in both Courts below they claimed to retain for their own use any balance that might remain after satisfying Brandts [the assignee].

Relying on this and observations made in an assortment of other cases,[15] and in particular *The Aiolos*,[16] Peter Gibson LJ concluded that:[17]

> [t]hese authorities ... clearly establish that the equitable assignee can be regarded realistically as the person entitled to the assigned chose and is able to sue the debtor on that chose, but that save in special circumstances the court will require him to join the assignor as a procedural requirement so that the assignor might be bound and the debtor protected.

In so doing, Peter Gibson LJ (and Waite LJ, who was in agreement) followed the reasoning of the Court of Appeal in *Walter & Sullivan Ltd* v. *J. Murphy & Sons Ltd*. That was an unusual case where the assignor of a debt sought to

---

[13]  As explained in Chapter 7.

[14]  *Brandt's* (n. 3), 462. Earl Halsbury LC agreed with Lord Macnaghten. Lord James took a different view. Though he agreed with the majority that the assignor (Kramrisch & Co.) had only equitably (and not statutorily) assigned the debt owed them by the debtor (the Dunlop Rubber Company) to the assignee (William Brandt's Sons & Co.), he merely held that 'the defect in the parties to the suit can be remedied', so he did not agree that non-joinder of the assignors to the proceedings against the debtor could be entirely dispensed with by reason of the equitable assignment alone (at 464). Ultimately, Lord James held that on the facts, non-joinder was justified on the basis that there had, in effect, been a novation: '[F]or myself I go further, and think the plaintiffs [the assignees] are entitled to recover upon the ground that Dunlops [the debtors] *undertook* to pay them the amount in question. It seems to me that when the plaintiffs received the letter from the defendants of January 8, 1903, signed by Gooding, they were entitled to rely and act upon it' (emphasis added, at 464).

[15]  Namely, *Performing Right Society Ltd* v. *London Theatre of Varieties Ltd* [1924] AC 1; *Weddell* v. *J. A. Pearce & Major* [1988] Ch 26; *Deposit Protection Board* v. *Dalia* [1994] 2 AC 367, 387–8 (Sir Michael Fox).

[16]  [1983] 2 Lloyd's Rep 25.

[17]  *Three Rivers District Council* v. *Governor and Company of the Bank of England* [1996] QB 292, 313F–G.

bring proceedings in the court's common law jurisdiction against the debtor. Parker LJ (delivering the judgment of the court) said in *dicta*: 'Normally . . ., it is the assignee who . . . seeks to recover the debt, and in a case where, as here, section 136 of the Law of Property Act 1925 does not apply, he would have to join the assignor in order to bind him at law.'[18]

The question is how the court is able to ignore the need for joinder of the assignor as suggested by Lord Macnaghten in *Brandt's*.

Rejecting the proposition that an equitable assignment of a legal chose vests the assignee with an equitable chose in action, which 'prevails' over the common law chose in action,[19] some have suggested that application of the *Vandepitte* procedure explains why equitable assignors need not be joined.[20] But that cannot be, as the logic of the *Vandepitte* procedure as applied to a common law action *requires* joinder of the assignor.[21]

Alternatively, it has been suggested that the CLPA1854 may provide an explanation.[22] But this is also difficult, given the operative provisions in the CLPA1854 which, in this context, appear to be sections 79, 82, 83 and 85.[23]

Sections 79 and 82 empowered common law courts to grant injunctions restraining the repetition, continuance or committal of a breach of contract. However, a debtor who was being or under threat of being sued

---

[18] *Walter & Sullivan Ltd* v. *J. Murphy & Sons Ltd* [1955] 2 QB 584, 588 (Parker LJ).

[19] As Staughton LJ suggested in *Three Rivers District Council* v (n. 17), 393.

[20] M. Smith, 'Locus Standi and the Enforcement of Legal Claims by Cestuis Que Trust and Assignees' (2008) 22 *Trust Law International* 140; Smith & Leslie (2013), paras. 11.43–11.47.

[21] As explained in Chapter 8, Section B.

[22] A. Tettenborn, 'Assignments, Trusts, Property and Obligations' in R Bronaugh, J. W. Neyers and S. G. A. Pitel (eds.), *Exploring Contract Law* (Oxford: Hart, 2009), p. 273, fn. 17.

[23] The Statute Law Revision and Civil Procedure Act 1883, which repealed the Chancery Amendment Act 1858 (hereafter, 'Lord Cairns' Act'), also repealed ss. 79, 82, 83 and 85 of the 1854 Act. McDermott has suggested that the court of Chancery's jurisdiction to award 'Lord Cairns' Act damages' was preserved by the transfer of all its jurisdiction to the High Court by s. 16 of the Judicature Act 1873: P. M. McDermott, 'Survival of Jurisdiction under the Chancery Amendment Act 1858 (Lord Cairns' Act)' (1987) 6 *Civil Justice Quarterly* 348, 355. If so, the effects of ss. 79, 82, 83 and 85 of the CLPA1854 should have been similarly preserved by the transfer of the *common law* courts' jurisdiction to the High Court. For authority that ss. 79 and 82 have been preserved thus, see *Quartz Hill Consolidated Gold Mining Company* v. *Beall* (1882) 20 Ch D 501. The effect of s. 83 may also have been duplicated by s. 24(5), Judicature Act 1873, subsequently re-enacted *in pari materia* in s. 41, Supreme Court of Judicature (Consolidation) Act 1925, which is now implicitly encapsulated within s. 49, Senior Courts Act 1981 (as explained in Chapter 6, Section D). For discussion of the effects of s. 85, CLPA1854, and their preservation, see Chapter 12, Sections F to H.

at law, or who was suing another at law, was permitted by ss. 83 and 85 respectively to plead in that action such facts as would have justified the grant of a common injunction as a 'defence on equitable grounds' or a 'replication on equitable grounds'. Pre-Judicature, these provisions obviated the need to initiate parallel proceedings to obtain judicial orders that had hitherto been within Chancery's exclusive jurisdiction, but they did not address the question of joinder. The CLPA1854 does not, therefore, provide an explanation for the conundrum of *Brandt's*. A different explanation is thus called for.

It is suggested that the basis for such non-joinder may lie in recognizing that in cases like *Brandt's* the assignee is still seeking an equitable remedy by way of injunction within the court's auxiliary equitable jurisdiction.[24] That is, as with the examples mentioned in Sections A to C, above, the assignee is *not* bringing proceedings against the obligor in the court's common law jurisdiction at all.

Although the discussion thus far has focussed on the court's concurrent equitable jurisdiction, the court's equitable jurisdiction arises from other bases, as well. There is an exclusive jurisdiction over institutions such as the trust and equitable assignment, as well as an auxiliary jurisdiction:[25]

> Where relief was sought in the Court of Chancery by a plaintiff suing upon a legal title, and the relief did not come within any of the recognised heads of the concurrent jurisdiction, it was only granted, according to the principles of the court as laid down in the eighteenth century, either to prevent a multiplicity of suits or to prevent an irreparable injury. The cases in which relief was granted were said to come under the auxiliary jurisdiction, and, where the Court of Chancery was exercising its auxiliary jurisdiction, the court did not itself adjudicate upon the validity of the plaintiff's claim. That adjudication was made by the courts of common law; but the assistance of the Court of Chancery was asked either before the adjudication, to keep matters in *statu quo* until the rights of the parties could be determined at common law, or after the adjudication, to give a more complete remedy to the party in whose favour it had been made than he could obtain at common law.

---

[24] The court of Chancery also had a common law jurisdiction in certain narrowly defined areas: see W. S. Holdsworth, *A History of English Law*, vol. I (7th edn, revised, London: Methuen & Co, 1956), pp. 452–3. Although this common law jurisdiction was also transferred to the High Court pursuant to Judicature Act 1873, s. 16, it would have been of no relevance to the proceedings in *Brandt's*.

[25] Ashburner (1933), para. 5-6 (references omitted). *A History of English Law*, vol. I (7th edn, revised, London: Methuen & Co, 1956).

Perhaps the reluctance of the Chancery judges to adjudicate on issues at law was due to the different procedural mechanisms available to them on matters of evidence.[26] The common law courts had the jury, and could make findings as to contested facts. But though jury trial eventually became possible in Chancery,[27] recourse to it seems to have been rare.[28] Instead, the standard course was to rely on the documents pertaining to the dispute, and depositions taken on written interrogatories of the witnesses. Defects with this system were numerous:[29]

> The interrogatories were framed by counsel, who had no direct communication with the witness to be examined and often had no means of ascertaining what precise information he could give. Interrogatories for the cross-examination of adverse witnesses were of little use and rarely employed, as they were necessarily prepared without the least knowledge of what had been asked or said upon the examination-in-chief. The examiner in town never deviated from the interrogatories and never asked for any explanation. Commissioners in the country were sometimes instructed on the matters which were in issue between the parties, and they occasionally required further information. *At the hearing, if the evidence was conflicting or unsatisfactory to the court, as was frequently the case, the court directed issues to be sent to a court of common law,* and the evidence taken previously became altogether useless, as the finding of the jury on the issues, and not the original examination, determined the fact.

However, where the evidence before the court of equity was satisfactory and/or the key issues of fact were not disputed, the court might be persuaded not to send the matter to be heard at common law for a legal

---

[26] There were some pre-Judicature attempts to reduce the need to send parties to the courts of law. So s. 62, Chancery Procedure Act 1852, empowered the court of Chancery to decide on issues of legal title or rights without requiring the parties to go to law; and s. 1, Chancery Regulation Act 1862, required the court of Chancery to determine all questions of law or fact on which the parties' entitlement to relief depended.

[27] Lord Cairns' Act, s. 3.

[28] Patrick Polden, 'The Court of Chancery, 1820–1875' in Sir John Baker (ed.), *The Oxford History of the Laws of England* (vol. XI, Oxford: Oxford University Press), p. 690: 'Most of the judges, evidently with the support of the bar, ignored their new powers: only eight jury trials were held in 1859–60 and none at all in 1869–70' (references omitted).

[29] Ashburner (1933), p. 24. For more detailed accounts of some of the changes effected to the Chancery procedure in the mid-1800s with regard to taking of evidence, see M. Lobban, 'Preparing for Fusion: Reforming the Nineteenth-Century Court of Chancery, Part II' (2004) 22 *Law and History Review* 565, 588–9; A. Birrell, 'Changes in Equity, Procedure, and Principles' in *A Century of Law Reform* (London: Macmillan & Co., 1901), pp. 188–92.

remedy to be granted. Instead, on the principle set out in *Knight* v. *Knight*, that '[t]he court of equity in all cases delights to do complete justice, and not by halves',[30] the court could be prevailed upon to grant a final order in equity to settle the entire matter between the plaintiff and defendant and so avoid needlessly multiplying proceedings, notwithstanding the availability of an entirely adequate common law remedy. Thus, '[i]f the court was properly seised of one matter, which was closely connected with another matter not usually cognisable in equity, the acknowledged jurisdiction over the one drew to it a jurisdiction over the other, although that matter in itself could be properly dealt with in a court of law'.[31]

A number of authorities are cited as examples of this, but of these, the case of *Pearce* v. *Creswick*[32] is most pertinent in the present context.

### (i)   Pearce v. Creswick (1843)

Pearce was the administrator of one George Hurst, who had placed two deposits with the Sheffield and Rotheram Banking Company. In exchange for the deposits, Hurst had been given two receipts dated 18 August 1837, each stating that the Company had received of 'George Hurst the sum of one hundred pounds, to be accounted for'.[33] Holders of such receipts could give up the receipts within a year for cancellation by the Company in exchange for payment of the capital sum plus interest, or they could leave the sums in deposit for a further year on issue of further receipts in place of the earlier ones.

Hurst died on 21 January 1838, bequeathing the greater part of his property to the plaintiff, Pearce. However, the deceased's nephew, also named George Hurst, acquired possession of the two Company receipts in respect of Hurst's deposits, endorsed the receipts with his name, 'George Hurst', and presented them for payment at a branch of the Nottinghamshire Bank.

Ignorant of the nephew's forgery, the Nottinghamshire Bank cashed them, and then remitted the two fraudulently endorsed receipts to its London bankers on 3 February 1838, charging them the sum it had paid on encashment of these receipts. Two days later, the London bankers

[30]  (1734) 3 P Wms 331, 331 (Talbot LC).
[31]  Ashburner (1933), p. 42.
[32]  (1843) 2 Hare 286.
[33]  Ibid., 286.

were directed by the Company to credit the Nottinghamshire Bank for the amount paid, the two receipts having been delivered up to the Company for cancellation. But on 8 February 1838, news of Hurst's death reached the Company.

The plaintiff was granted letters of administration with the will annexed for Hurst's estate on 21 November 1839. Seeking discovery of the documents pertaining to the debt that had been owed to Hurst, the plaintiff filed a bill against the defendant, being the director and public officer of the Company. Inter alia, the plaintiff's bill also prayed that an account be taken of such sums as were due on the two receipts, and that the Company be decreed to pay the plaintiff (as Hurst's legal personal representative) such sums as would appear to be due from them on the taking of such an account.

Sir James Wigram V-C summarized the issues before him as follows:[34]

> The [deceased] was a creditor of the Sheffield and Rotheram Bank at the time of his death and the debt has not been paid to his executor, or to any person lawfully claiming under him. It cannot, therefore, be disputed that the Plaintiff will be wronged if he do [sic] not get relief in this or some other Court against some party. ... [T]he main question argued before me was this – whether the Court, in the case made by this bill, has jurisdiction both to give relief as well as discovery, or whether the bill ought not to have been confined to discovery only?

As to the question of jurisdiction, Wigram V-C ultimately held as follows:[35]

> The only remaining question is whether ... I ought to send the case to be tried in a Court of law ... It does not appear to me that there is in this case any need of sending the Plaintiff to a Court of law ... to try the question whether he is entitled to payment of the debt for which the receipts were given, in order to entitle him to delivery up of the receipts. There is, in truth, no answer set up to the Plaintiff's claim, so far as the debt is concerned, apart from the mode of recovering it. ... I cannot say that there is anything in such circumstances which has, in equity, absolved the Defendants from their original liability to pay the debt of which the receipts are evidence, or any reason why a Court of Equity should not exercise its jurisdiction to investigate a legal question with a view to equitable relief, or any reason why I should not myself decide that legal question. Having come to this conclusion with respect to the right of the Plaintiff to the money expressed in the receipts, and, as a necessary consequence, his right to the instruments, which are evidences of the debt,

---

[34] Ibid., at 292–3.
[35] Ibid., at 297–9 (emphasis added).

> so long as the debt is unpaid, I think the jurisdiction of this Court is not confined to relieving the Plaintiff from the mere difficulty which the absence of these instruments occasions, reserving further directions, and leaving him to try the same question in a Court of law, which, upon all the evidence that it is suggested the case affords, I have already decided in his favour; but that the Court may, at the hearing *decree payment to the Plaintiff of the principal debt and the interest and costs.*

Wigram V-C thus ordered the Company to pay the Plaintiff the principal debt of £200 and the interest, as well as costs.

*Pearce* v. *Creswick* demonstrates that a court of equity may issue an injunction compelling payment of a fixed sum, notwithstanding the availability of a perfectly adequate remedy at law via the action for debt. So long as some part of the dispute was properly within the equity jurisdiction (for example, to obtain discovery), and so long as he was persuaded that there was no good reason to send the matter for trial at law, a judge of the Chancery court could so order.[36] Since no key issues of fact were disputed in *Pearce*, and equity's jurisdiction had already been validly invoked, it was apposite for the Vice-Chancellor to make the order of injunction sought by the plaintiff, thereby avoiding needless multiplication of proceedings.

### (ii)   Legh v. Legh *(1799) and* Hammond v. Messenger *(1838)*

The possibility that a court in its equitable jurisdiction may grant an injunction to compel a debtor to tender payment of a fixed sum of money to an assignee so long as the assignee could bring himself within the court's equitable jurisdiction was recognized by Eyre CJ in *Legh* v. *Legh*, a decision of the court of Common Pleas. Hints as to when such an order may (or may not) be made can be also be found in Shadwell V-C's judgment in *Hammond* v. *Messenger*.

*Legh* v. *Legh* will be discussed at greater length in Chapter 10, but in brief, it concerned an action brought on a bond, the benefit of which had been equitably assigned to an assignee by way of security for a debt owed by the assignor to the assignee. The action was brought by the assignee in the name of the assignor seeking payment of the sums due on the bond. It is assumed, therefore, that the assignee had been authorized to bring such action through the grant of the power of attorney that

---

[36] This possibility was mentioned in passing in W. W. Cook, 'The Alienability of Choses in Action – Part II' (1917) 30 *Harvard Law Review* 449, 456 (text to nn. 23 and 24).

was typical of the time:[37] no objections had been raised by the defendant debtor as to this point.

Although notice of the assignment had been received by the debtor to the bond, he subsequently took a deed of release from the assignor. The principal question before the court of Common Pleas, then, was whether the order *nisi* obtained by the assignee cancelling the deed of release ought to be made absolute. In the course of concluding that insufficient cause had been shown by the debtor, for present purposes, Eyre CJ noted that:[38]

> I rather think the Court [of Common Pleas] ought not to allow the Defendant to avail himself of this plea [of release], *since a Court of Equity would order the Defendant* [the debtor] *to pay the Plaintiff* [the assignee] the amount of his lien on the bond, and probably all the costs of the application.

So as at 1799, it would appear that the Chancery saw no insuperable difficulty in ordering a debtor to pay a fixed sum of money on the application of an equitable assignee, and that such practice was so commonplace that judicial notice had been taken of it by common law judges.

*Legh* v. *Legh* does not provide clues, though, as to when such an order might be made in Chancery. For that, we may consider the Chancery case of *Hammond* v. *Messenger* where an equitable assignee of a debt sought a decree ordering the debtor to tender payment to him, but where Shadwell V-C declined to make the order.

Shadwell V-C began his judgment with the following observation: 'If this case were stripped of all special circumstances, it would be simply a bill filed by a plaintiff who *had obtained* from certain persons to whom a debt was due *a right to sue in their names for the debt.*'[39] By this, it would seem the plaintiff-assignee had *already* obtained 'a right to sue in their [the assignors'] names for the debt'. One would expect that that would have been the case since this appears to have been the standard commercial practice whenever legal choses were equitably assigned.[40] And if a power of attorney empowering the assignee to bring actions at law to bring the debt into possession had been granted,

---

[37]  See text to n. 4, in Chapter 8, above.
[38]  *Legh* v. *Legh* (1799) 1 Bos & Pul 447 (emphasis added).
[39]  *Hammond* v. *Messenger* (n. 9), 332 (emphasis added).
[40]  As one would expect of any prudent businessman of the time.

without more, such assignee could have no basis to bring himself within the Chancery jurisdiction.[41]

Accordingly, Shadwell V-C's decision to dismiss the bill is easily understood: if the assignee was *already* authorized at law to bring proceedings at law against the debtor, Messenger, for non-payment of the debt, there was no obvious basis to invoke the equity jurisdiction:[42]

> It [the Plaintiff's prayer for relief] then proceeds as follows: 'or that the Plaintiff may be at liberty to use the name of the Defendants, Wilks & Wooler, in an action at law to be brought by him against Messenger'. There is, however, no case stated which shews that Wilks & Wooler have at all interfered to prevent, or that they intend to prevent the Plaintiff from using their names at law.

Shadwell V-C did not hold that the proposition that a court of equity might issue an order of injunction to compel the debtor to pay a fixed sum of money was untenable. *Hammond* v. *Messenger* suggests that there could be cases where a court might issue an injunction within its equitable jurisdiction to compel performance of even a fixed sum of money.

What might those circumstances be?

Suppose, contrary to the usual commercial practice of the time, no power of attorney had been granted by the assignor in *Hammond* v. *Messenger*. Without such grant of authority for the purpose as would be recognized by a common law court, no proceedings at law could be brought by the assignee against the debtor. But, as previously explained,[43] by reason of equity's recognition that an equitable assignment of a legal chose in action amounted to a trust of the benefit of the contract and an agreement to lend the assignee the assignor's name should proceedings at law be required,[44] such assignee could bring proceedings in equity to compel performance of that agreement by injunction if the assignment was supported by consideration. Alternatively, if the assignment were gratuitous, since equity recognized that such assignment operated by means of a trust, the assignee could bring proceedings in equity to compel the assignor to bring proceedings at law against the obligor to the contract.

---

[41] Equity's reluctance to seize jurisdiction in such circumstances is, it seems, ancient. '[I]f he [the assignee] had an effective power of attorney he would be told to sue at common law': Bailey (1932), p. 555, relying on the authority of a decision in *Select Cases in Chancery*, Seldon Society 10, pl 95 (1408), pp. 88–90 at p. 90.

[42] *Hammond* v. *Messenger* (n. 9), 337.

[43] See Chapter 6, Section D.

[44] 2 Bl Comm 442.

Either way, an assignee of the benefit of a contract could seek the assistance of equity where the assignor was uncooperative. And once within that jurisdiction, to avoid needless multiplicity of proceedings, the court could grant an injunction, not just to compel the assignor to duly authorize the assignee so he could bring proceedings at law against the obligor, or to compel the assignor to bring those proceedings at law: the court could be persuaded to compel the obligor to pay the sums in question to the assignee on the principle in *Knight* v. *Knight*.[45]

There seems to be no reason why the reasoning employed in the later decision in *Pearce* v. *Creswick* on the basis of the principle in *Knight* v. *Knight* would not apply where the court's equitable jurisdiction had been validly invoked to seek an injunction to compel the grant of an authority, or to compel the bringing of an action at law. For, as Story observed:[46]

> Perhaps the most general, if not the most precise, description of a court of equity, is, that it has jurisdiction in cases of rights, recognized and protected by the municipal jurisprudence, where a plain, adequate and complete remedy cannot be had in the courts of common law. The remedy must be plain; for if it be doubtful and obscure at law, equity will assert a jurisdiction. It must be adequate; for, if at law it falls short of what the party is entitled to, that founds a jurisdiction in equity. *And it must be complete*; that is, it must attain the full end and justice of the case. *It must reach the whole mischief, and secure the whole right of the party in a perfect manner, at the present time, and in future; otherwise equity will interfere and give such relief and aid as the exigency of the particular case may require.* The jurisdiction of a court of equity is, therefore, sometimes concurrent with the jurisdiction of a court of law; it is sometimes exclusive of it; and it is sometimes auxiliary to it.

Consequently, had it been the case in *Hammond* v. *Messenger* that no authority which would have been recognized by a court in its common law jurisdiction had been granted to the assignee-plaintiff, or, having granted such authority, the assignor had revoked it, or was threatening to do so, it seems likely that Shadwell V-C would have decided the other way. In such circumstances, there *would* have been grounds to seek the assistance of equity to enforce the assignor's agreement to lend her name to the assignee by a mandatory injunction to compel the assignor to so authorize the assignee, if it had not previously been granted; or a prohibitory injunction

---

[45] (1734) 3 P Wms 331. For examples of such relief being granted in equity in connection with a trust of a legal chose in action, see *Tomlinson* v. *Gill* (1756) Amb 330, 27 ER 221; *Gregory* v. *Williams* (1817) 3 Mer 582, 36 ER 224.

[46] Story (1884), §33 (emphasis added, references omitted).

to compel the assignor to refrain from carrying out any threat to revoke such authority, if already made; or a mandatory injunction to compel the assignor to authorize the assignee anew, if he had already revoked such authority which had previously been granted. And once the assignee came within the jurisdiction of the court of equity, so far as it was possible for the court to completely dispose of the issues in dispute between the obligor and the assignee, it would make such orders to resolve those disputes, even if a court of common law could grant common law remedies as would have been adequate to the task.

### (iii)    William Brandt's v. Dunlops (1904)

The contested-for debt of £3,263 4s. 2d. in Brandt's arose and was equitably assigned[47] in 1903, well after the administrative fusion effected by the Judicature Acts. But the rules governing the invocation of the court's common law and equitable jurisdictions remained unchanged.[48] Consequently, the plaintiff-assignee (Brandt's) could not have brought an action against the defendant-debtor (Dunlops) within the court's common law jurisdiction without joinder of the assignor (Kramrisch) since Brandt's had neither provided consideration in support, nor was it privy to the contract of sale between Kramrisch and Dunlops.

The reports state that Kramrisch had authorized Brandt's to inform Dunlops that it was to tender payment for the goods purchased to Brandt's. But the reports do not reveal that Kramrisch had done anything to authorize Brandt's at law to bring a common law action in debt against Dunlops.[49]

If Brandt's had not been authorized at law to bring such common law proceedings, and had the proceedings been brought pre-Judicature, Brandt's would have had to first bring a suit in equity for an injunction

---

[47] The House of Lords held that there was a perfectly valid and effective equitable assignment on the facts, even if the requirements for a 'statutory' assignment pursuant to s. 25 (6) of the 1873 Act might not have been met: Brandt's (n. 3), 460–1 (Lord Macnaghten, with whom the Earl of Halsbury LC concurred) and 463–4 (Lord James).

[48] Given the limited effects of Judicature Act 1873, ss. 16 and 24.

[49] The words of the written assignment to Brandt's are reproduced at Brandt's (n. 3), 456–7. No mention is made of any grant of power of attorney to the assignee to bring actions at law on Kramrisch's behalf to recover the debt if unpaid. Nor do the reports of the first instance decision (reported as Brandts, Sons & Co. v. Dunlop Rubber Company Limited (1903) 8 Com Cas 174; (1903) 90 Law Times Rep 106) or the appeal to the Court of Appeal ([1904] 1 KB 387; (1903) 90 Law Times Rep 106) suggest otherwise.

to compel Kramrisch to grant it the requisite authority, or to compel Kramrisch to sue Dunlops at law. But post-Judicature, separate proceedings in Chancery were no longer required as both equity and common law jurisdictions were now united within a single judicial institution. Accordingly, when Brandt's began proceedings against Dunlops in 1903 before Warner J in the High Court, those proceedings may be conceived as having been brought within the High Court's *equitable* jurisdiction to obtain a suitable injunction to overcome the difficulty of not having been duly authorized at law to bring common law proceedings.

As recounted by Lord Macnaghten, with regard to the debt in question:[50]

> instead of remitting the sum of 3263*l*. 4*s*. 2*d*. to Brandts, as specially directed by Kramrisch & Co, the Dunlop Rubber Company, in compliance with a previous general order from Kramrisch & Co., paid the amount by cheque to Kleinwort & Co., who had not financed this particular transaction, and had nothing whatever to do with it. Ultimately Brandts wrote to the Dunlops pressing for the remittance, which was then overdue. They replied on February 9, 1903, that the amount had been paid, and added that they held Kramrisch & Co.'s receipt for it.

Given the above, Kramrisch would seem to have issued its receipt[51] with regard to a payment to 'the wrong people',[52] and the debt would still be outstanding.[53]

---

[50] *Brandt's* (n. 3), 457.

[51] But not, it seems, under seal. Unless set aside, receipts under seal are generally conclusive evidence of payment: *Rowntree* v. *Jacob* (1809) 2 Taunt 141.

[52] *Brandt's* (n. 3), 461. Receipts not under seal, as opposed to releases, are merely evidence acknowledging that money has been paid (*Skaife* v. *Jackson* (1824) 3 B & C 421, 422). And the evidential weight of erroneously issued receipts must surely be weak.

[53] There are faint hints that Dunlops may have tendered further payments to Kramrisch, over and beyond the mistaken payment to Kleinwort & Co.

Brandt's counsel throughout the proceedings was J. A. Hamilton KC, subsequently Lord Sumner. In *Performing Right Society Ltd* v. *London Theatre of Varieties Ltd* [1924] AC 1, 31, Lord Sumner suggested that 'Kramrisch ... had already been settled with and the Dunlop Company held his receipt', referring to counsel's submissions before the Court of Appeal ('[B]ut here Kramrisch & Co. have already been paid, and have given a receipt, and no claim could be set up by them': [1904] 1 KB 387, 391), and at first instance ('Here the defendants [Dunlops] have paid Kramrisch & Co., and are therefore in no danger of being sued by them and of being unable to plead payment': (1903) 8 Com Cas 174, 177).

Assuming Dunlops *had* tendered payment to Kramrisch, by invoking its power to accept conforming tenders of payment from Dunlops, Kramrisch would have enabled Dunlops to discharge its debt obligation at law by precise performance. However, by equitably assigning the debt to Brandt's, Kramrisch would have become equitably duty-bound to Brandt's to preserve the legal chose until directed by Brandt's to fully execute the bare trust underpinning such assignment. On the facts, if Dunlops had indeed

If so, in line with the principle in *Knight* v. *Knight*, the court could make a final order within its equitable jurisdiction to resolve the entire dispute between the parties subject to the 'rule of practice' requiring stay of such proceedings until the assignor be joined thereto as a precaution against the assignor re-litigating the issues at law. However, once 'the Dunlops disclaimed any wish to have him [Kramrisch or their trustee in bankruptcy] present',[54] thereby declining the protection provided by such 'rule of practice', there was no longer any reason for the House of Lords to stay proceedings within the court's equitable jurisdiction, Brandt's having come into that jurisdiction by reason (we may infer) of its not having previously been authorized by the assignor to bring such proceedings at law.

As *Pearce* v. *Creswick* shows, had the facts in *Brandt's* arisen pre-Judicature, when the courts of equity and common law were completely distinct administrative entities, the court of Chancery could have ordered Dunlops to pay the sums due on the contract for sale to Brandt's as assignees of the benefit of that contract. The same must hold, post-Judicature, when the separation between the High Court's equitable and common law jurisdictions had become entirely conceptual.

*Brandt's* is better read as a case where the court was acting within its equitable and not its common law jurisdiction, within which there is indeed a rule of practice requiring joinder of the assignor where circumstances merited it. Unlike *Hammond* v. *Messenger*, *Brandt's* was a case where part of the dispute between assignee and obligor sufficed to bring the assignee within the court's equitable jurisdiction. Once within that equitable jurisdiction, beyond seeking such remedy against the obligee-assignor as had been the initial basis for accessing that jurisdiction, the assignee might go further and obtain an injunction compelling the obligor/debtor to pay the sum owed on the contract of sale to the assignee. Since the entirety of such proceedings would have been brought

tendered payment to Kramrisch, it would have done so: (i) with actual knowledge of the assignment; and (ii) with deemed knowledge of its ramifications (since '*ignorantia juris non excusat*'); but (iii) without having made reasonable inquiries which, if made, would have revealed that the acceptance was unsanctioned and would be in breach of Kramrisch's equitable duty to Brandt's. Dunlops' tender would thus have *dishonestly assisted* in Kramrisch's breach of duty, for which Brandt's could seek equitable remedies. And as to such proceedings in equity, joinder of Kramrisch would also be unnecessary. The role played by the equitable wrong of dishonest assistance within the law of equitable assignment is explained more fully in Chapter 11, below.

[54] *Brandt's* (n. 3), 462.

within the court's equitable jurisdiction, the common law's substantive need for joinder of the assignor (by reason of the assignee neither being privy to the contract, nor having provided consideration in respect of it) would no longer be of concern. And although joinder of the assignor to such equitable proceedings might be required if circumstances merited it, such joinder was by no means absolutely necessary in every single case. As *Brandt's* shows, so far as joinder of the assignor might be advisable to bind it to the decisions handed down by the court within its equitable jurisdiction so as to preclude re-litigation of the same at common law, such joinder could be waived by the debtor for whose protection the rule had been devised.

## E   Conclusion

The preceding discussion allows us to respond to the criticism of *Brandt's* by the editors of *Meagher, Gummow and Lehane* that '[h]ow a person not the legal owner can, the Judicature Act notwithstanding, prosecute what is, in effect, an action at common law is not explained':[55] perhaps the assignee in *Brandt's* was not prosecuting an action at common law at all. If so, *Brandt's* is no authority for the proposition that equitable assignments of legal choses in action no longer entail a trustee–beneficiary relationship as between the assignor and her assignee. Indeed, once we recognize *Brandt's* to be a decision of the court in exercise of its *equitable* jurisdiction, it falls entirely in line with cases such as *Cator v. Croydon Canal*[56] or *Fulham v. McCarthy*.[57] Accordingly, reassessment is required of cases such as *Performing Right Society Ltd v. London Theatre of Varieties Ltd*,[58] *Central Insurance Co. Ltd v. Seacalf Shipping Co. (The Aiolos)*,[59] *Weddell v. J. A. Pearce & Major*,[60] *Three Rivers District Council v. Governor and Company of the Bank of England*,[61] *Bexhill UK Ltd v. Razzaq*[62] and *Raiffeisen Zentralbank Österreich AG v. Five Star Trading LLC*,[63] which have taken *Brandt's* as authority for the

---

[55] Meagher, Gummow & Lehane (2015), para. 6-520.
[56] (1843) 4 Y & C Ex 593.
[57] (1848) 1 HLC 708.
[58] [1924] AC 1.
[59] [1983] 2 Lloyd's Rep 25.
[60] [1988] Ch 26.
[61] [1996] QB 292.
[62] [2012] EWCA Civ 1376.
[63] [2001] EWCA Civ 68; [2001] 3 All ER 257.

proposition that 'when a legal chose is assigned, the need to join the assignor is procedural and not substantive',[64] leading to the supposition that the court may waive joinder of the assignor when proceedings *at law* are brought by the equitable assignee.

What appears to have passed unnoticed is that the rules of joinder of parties to proceedings brought within the court's equitable or common law jurisdiction are quite distinct from each other. Given their differences, when one is concerned with proceedings brought entirely within the court's equitable jurisdiction, joinder of the equitable assignor may quite rightly be termed a 'procedural' matter such that joinder of the assignor may be disregarded when there is no sufficiently good reason to require it, and the party for whose protection the rule was devised may even waive its operation. However, where the proceedings involve recourse to the court's *common law* jurisdiction, joinder of the assignor may well be required as a matter of substantive principle due to the substantive common law rules that may be applicable – for example, the rules of privity and consideration where a contractual chose has been assigned. If so, non-joinder of the assignor to such common law proceedings cannot be waived as a mere matter of procedure.

To support this proposition, one could look to the decision of the House of Lords in *Performing Right Society Ltd* v. *London Theatre of Varieties Ltd*:[65]

> In this action the society had claimed an injunction *and damages. [But t]he claim for damages was withdrawn,* as it was admitted that for this purpose the presence of the owner of the legal estate would be necessary to avoid the possibility that payment might be made to the wrong person. On the other hand, the right of the society to an interlocutory injunction for the protection of the property pendente lite was not questioned. But it was maintained by the defendants that it was impossible in the circumstances of the present case to grant a perpetual injunction at the instance of a plaintiff who was merely an equitable owner. Whether this contention of the defendants is right is the question on this appeal.

Quite so. Their Lordships ultimately concluded that non-joinder of the legal owners of the copyrights that had been equitably assigned to the appellants was fatal to their application for a final injunction in equity, for:[66]

---

[64] Smith & Leslie (2018), para. 11.54.
[65] [1924] AC 1.
[66] Ibid., 31 (Lord Sumner).

[i]n the absence of the publishers, the assignors, the respondents here have no means of excluding the possibility that some assignment, other than the assignment to the appellants might rank before it, and in such event they would have no answer to proceedings taken by such an assignee. If the publishers had been joined, they might have been interrogated on the subject. In the absence of the publishers the respondents are not even protected against proceedings by the publishers themselves brought on some future occasion.

Accordingly, there were good reasons to require joinder of the assignors even though the proceedings had plainly been brought within the court's equitable jurisdiction.

But *Performing Right Society* tells us that since the issue of a perpetual injunction is a matter solely within the court's equitable jurisdiction, joinder of the assignor *could* be excused in, 'special cases ... as in *William Brandt's Sons & Co. v. Dunlop Rubber Co.* where the defendant disclaimed any wish to have the legal owners made parties'.[67] As explained above, this is because the rule for joinder in such *equitable* suit is indeed a 'procedural' requirement stemming from concerns as to the operation of *res judicata* issue estoppel absent such joinder. But matters are quite different when an action at law is brought.

Recognition of this difference in treatment, coupled with a renewed appreciation of the breadth of the court's auxiliary equitable jurisdiction, means *Brandt's* need no longer be understood as a perplexing exception to the substantive rules requiring joinder at common law: *Brandt's* becomes a logical and coherent working out of equity's rules on joinder of assignors to proceedings brought within the court's equitable jurisdiction, given how issue estoppel rules are applied within that jurisdiction. Equity's recognition and enforcement of the trust (and agency) effect(s) underpinning equitable assignments generates sufficient privity of interest (and/or identity of persons) for *res judicata* purposes in connection with proceedings in equity, though not for proceedings within the court's common law jurisdiction. Far from being authority for the proposition that equitable assignments of legal choses in action has moved away from the trustee–beneficiary analysis, *Brandt's* may be read to be perfectly consistent with the proposition that an equitable assignment of a legal chose in action continues to rest on a trust effect.

[67] Ibid.,14 (Viscount Cave LC).

# PART IV

Notice

# 10

# Giving Notice of Equitable Assignments and Its Effect on Competing Assignees: The 'Rule' in *Dearle* v. *Hall*

## A Introduction

The preceding chapters have exposed the twin conceptual mechanisms which underpin the operation of equitable assignments. Whether the assignment be of a legal or of an equitable chose, in either case, the equitable assignment places the assignor and assignee in a relationship akin to that between a bare trustee and the beneficiary of such bare trust. However, an equitable assignment also entails the assignor delegating to the assignee such powers as the assignor may have against the obligor to the chose assigned, coupled with a release by which the assignee is permitted to invoke such delegated powers without regard for the assignor's interests. Importantly, the operation of these twin mechanisms of 'trust-plus-agency' does not depend on the obligor of the chose assigned having to be given notice of the assignment. Thus, an equitable assignment is 'complete' as between assignor and assignee without notice to the obligor. This is not to say, however, that notice of an equitable assignment has no significance at all.

Where the same legal or equitable chose in action has been equitably assigned multiple times, the competing claims between the equitable assignees will be accorded priority in accordance with the so-called 'rule' in *Dearle* v. *Hall* which accords priority by the order in which notice of assignment is given to the obligor, and not by the order in which the assignments were created. This chapter will explain the rationale and the limits of the operation of this 'rule'.

Once we have gained a clearer understanding of the 'rule' in *Dearle* v. *Hall*, it will become apparent that the very operation of such a rule refutes the proposition that notice of an equitable assignment will lead to the substitution of the assignee in place of the assignor as obligee, as some commentators appear to suggest may be the case. This will be explored in Section F, below.

## B   The 'Rule' in *Dearle* v. *Hall*

The 'rule' in *Dearle* v. *Hall*[1] is said to be an 'exception to the general principle that equitable interests take priority in the order in which they are created'.[2] Where an equitable[3] or legal[4] chose in action has been equitably assigned,[5] instead of applying the proposition that *qui prior est tempore potior est jure* to the order of the assignments, priority is determined by the order in which notice of the assignment is given by the assignee (or where the assignee has caused notice to be given by authorizing another to do so on his behalf)[6] and been received by the obligor[7] (or such entity as had been expressly or impliedly authorized to receive such notice on the obligor's behalf).[8] That is, the *qui prior est tempore potior est jure* rule appears to be applied by reference to the time when notice of assignment is given to the obligor.

In *Dearle* v. *Hall*, Brown was to be paid an annuity of £93 under the terms of a testamentary trust. In consideration for a sum of £204, he granted Dearle an annuity of £37, secured by a deed of covenant and a warrant of attorney to bring proceedings against the executors of that

---

[1]  (1828) 3 Russ 1; aff'd (1828) 3 Russ 48 (Lord Lyndhurst LC). It has been suggested that the 'rule' in *Dearle* v. *Hall* predates the decision: see Marshall (1950), p. 104, adopting a point made in George W. Keeton, *An Introduction to Equity* (1st edn, London: Sir Isaac Pitman & Sons, 1938), p. 147.

[2]  *E. Pfeiffer Weinkellerei-Weineinkauf GmbH & Co.* v. *Arbuthnot Factors Ltd* [1988] 1 WLR 150, 163 (Philips J).

[3]  E.g. the equitable chose in action of a beneficiary against her trustee arising under a trust. The rule in *Dearle* v. *Hall* was applied in that case, and in *Loveridge* v. *Cooper* (1827) 3 Russ 30, to determine the priorities between equitable assignees of equitable choses in action.

[4]  E.g. the common law chose in action of a creditor who has lent money to a debtor. It has also been applied to determine the priorities between equitable assignees of common law choses in action such as contract debts: see e.g. *Gorringe* v. *Irwell India Rubber and Gutta Percha Works* (1886) 34 Ch D 128; *Ward* v. *Duncombe* [1893] AC 369; *Marchant* v. *Morton, Down & Co.* [1901] 2 KB 829; *E. Pfeiffer Weinkellerei-Weineinkauf GmbH & Co.* v. *Arbuthnot Factors Ltd* (n. 2); *Compaq Computer Ltd* v. *Abercorn Group Ltd* [1991] BCC 484.

[5]  The operation of the 'rule' in *Dearle* v. *Hall* in connection with 'statutory' assignments under LPA1925, s. 136(1) is discussed in Chapter 15, Section B.

[6]  The 'rule' in *Dearle* v. *Hall* does not require notice to have been given personally by the assignee. So where the assignee had expressly or implicitly authorized another to give notice to the obligor on her behalf, such notice would satisfy the requirements of the rule. See e.g. *Re Russell's Policy Trusts* (1872) LR 15 Eq 26. Thus, notice can be effectively given by the assignor on behalf of the assignee if so authorized by the assignee: *James Talcott Ltd* v. *John Lewis Ltd & North American Dress Co. Ltd* [1940] 3 All ER 592.

[7]  Notice is only effective when received. Thus, if notice is given after office hours, it is treated as having only been received on the next business day: *Calisher* v. *Forbes* (1871) LR 7 Ch App 109.

[8]  See e.g. *Saffron Walden Second Benefit Building Society* v. *Rayner* (1880) 14 Ch D 406.

will. Subsequently, in consideration for a sum of £150, Brown granted Sherring an annuity of £27 on similar terms. In essence, Brown had equitably assigned his equitable interest in the testamentary trust to Dearle and Sherring by way of mortgage to secure his liability to each of them in respect of these two annuities.

Brown paid the annuities granted to Dearle and Sherring for a few years before defaulting in 1811. In 1812, Brown equitably assigned the whole of his interest in the annuity of £93 arising under the testamentary trust to Hall in consideration of a sum of about £711. Hall paid for the assignment, ignorant of Dearle's and Sherring's prior assignments, and notified the trustees of the fund of his equitable interest as Brown's assignee. The annuity payable under the testamentary trust being inadequate to satisfy the claims of Dearle and Sherring as mortgagees, on the one hand, and Hall, on the other, the issue arose as to which set of claims was to be preferred.

Drawing an analogy with a rule which had been established in connection with the bankruptcy legislation of the time, Sir Thomas Plumer MR held that in these circumstances, the later assignment would be given priority ahead of a prior assignment if the later assignee had given the obligor notice of assignment before the prior assignee had done the same:[9]

> It was not possible for Brown to transfer the legal interest [in the fund]: that could not but remain with the executors [of the will]; but wherever it is intended to complete the transfer of a chose in action, there is a mode of dealing with it which a court of equity considers tantamount to possession, namely, notice *given* to the legal depositary of the fund. ... To *give* notice is a matter of no difficulty: and whenever persons, treating for a chose in action, do not *give* notice to the trustee or executor, who is the legal holder of the fund, they do not perfect their title; they do not do all that is necessary in order to make the thing belong to them *in preference* to all other persons; and they become responsible, in some respects, for the easily foreseen consequences of their negligence.

Consequently, Hall had the better equity as against Dearle and Sherring, and his claim was to be satisfied in priority to the claims of the other two assignees, notwithstanding that Hall's assignment had arisen later in time.

This decision was upheld on appeal by Lord Lyndhurst LC.[10] The 'rule' in *Dearle* v. *Hall* was also approved by the House of Lords in

---

[9] *Dearle* v. *Hall* (1828) 3 Russ 1, 12–13 (emphasis added). The supposition is that the giving and receipt of notice are contemporaneous. But, if not, see n. 7, above. It would have been more precise to say that the 'rule' in *Dearle* v. *Hall* ranks the priority of competing claims in order of receipt of notice. But this is not how the rule is conventionally set out.

[10] Ibid., 57.

*Foster* v. *Cockerell*,[11] and though some doubts were expressed as to its merits, the 'rule' in *Dearle* v. *Hall* was again upheld by the House of Lords in *Ward* v. *Duncombe*.[12]

Over time, the 'rule' in *Dearle* v. *Hall* underwent further refinement.[13] First, although Plumer MR did not explicitly stipulate it, subsequent cases have confirmed that the 'rule' in *Dearle* v. *Hall* has no application in respect of a subsequent assignee who had not given value.[14] In addition, the case of *Lloyd* v. *Banks*[15] has been taken by some to set out how the 'rule' may be disapplied if the obligor should come to know of a prior assignment independently of notice by the prior assignee. Thus, *Guest on Assignment* sets out the 'rule' in *Dearle* v. *Hall* as follows:[16]

> In order to gain priority over an assignee under an earlier assignment an assignee under a later assignment must have:
>
> (1) given value for his assignment;
> (2) had no knowledge,[17] at the time when he gave value, of the existence of the earlier assignment;

---

[11] (1835) 3 Cl & F 456.

[12] [1893] AC 369, 375–8 (Lord Herschell), and 394 (Lord Macnaghten). *Ward* v. *Duncombe* was decided prior to the decision in *London Street Tramways Co. Ltd* v. *London County Council* [1898] AC 375. That decision is often taken to be the source of the doctrine by which the House of Lords was bound by its own decisions, a doctrine which was only put to rest by the *Practice Statement (HL: Judicial Precedent)* [1966] 1 WLR 1234. However, the proposition that the House of Lords was bound by its own decisions had come to be accepted for some time prior to *London Street Tramways Co. Ltd*. Most strikingly, in *New York Life Insurance Co.* v. *Styles* (1889) 14 App Cas 381, the House of Lords concluded that it was bound by its decision in *Last* v. *The London Assurance Corporation* (1885) 10 App Cas 438. Among the Law Lords in *New York Life Insurance Co.* were Lord Herschell and Lord Macnaghten. Given their views on *stare decisis* as applied to the House of Lords, it would only be consistent for them to have declined in *Ward* v. *Duncombe* to depart from the decision of the House of Lords in *Foster* v. *Cockerell*. For discussion of the evolving attitude of the House of Lords on the operation of *stare decisis* in the House of Lords, see David Pugsley, 'London Tramways (1898)' (1996) 17 *Journal of Legal History* 172, and Louis Blom-Cooper, '1966 and All That: The Story of the Practice Statement' in Louis Blom-Cooper, Brice Dickson and Gavin Drewry (eds.), *The Judicial House of Lords 1876–2009* (Oxford: Oxford University Press, 2009).

[13] Including statutory extension pursuant to LPA1925, s 137(1) to 'dealings with equitable interests in land, capital money, and securities representing capital money' effected after the LPA1925 came into force. But this development does not touch on the analysis below.

[14] *Re Wallis* [1902] 1 KB 719, 720, following *Justice* v. *Wynne* (1860) 12 Ir Ch Rep 289, 299 & 304 (Irish Court of Appeal in Chancery).

[15] (1868) LR 3 Ch App 488.

[16] Liew (2018), para. 6-21. See also Smith & Leslie (2018), para. 27.50; and, by the same authors, *Halsbury's Laws* (5th edn, 2017), Vol. 13, title 'Choses in Action', para. 47.

[17] Such knowledge may be actual, or it may be constructive: *Spencer* v. *Clarke* (1878) 9 Ch D 137; *Re Weniger's Policy* [1910] 2 Ch 291.

(3) given notice of his assignment to the debtor, trustee or other person (the 'fundholder') entitled to receive it;[18] and

(4) at the time that such notice is received, the fundholder must not have received notice of the earlier assignment.

The following discussion will examine each of these limbs. In doing so, it will be helpful to rely on the hypothetical set of facts in Example 10.1.

---

**EXAMPLE 10.1**

A lends B £10,000, and it is agreed that the loan will be repaid on 1 December 2020. On 1 January 2018, A equitably assigns to $C_1$ the benefit of this loan. On 2 January 2018, A equitably assigns the same to $C_2$ for value, such assignment being made for A's own interest without $C_1$'s approval.

On 11 January 2018, $C_2$ gives B notice of A's equitable assignment to her. And on 22 January 2018, $C_1$ gives B notice of A's equitable assignment to him.

On 1 December 2020, B is happy not to tender payment to A, but is unsure whether he should tender payment of £10,000 to $C_1$, or to $C_2$.

---

## C   Giving Notice First

The most striking aspect of the 'rule' in *Dearle* v. *Hall* is its seeming displacement of the 'usual' rule of priority, that *qui prior est tempore potior est jure* by reference to the order of creation; and that by way of exception, priority is instead determined by the order in which notice of assignment is given. However, the following will show that this part of the 'rule' in *Dearle* v. *Hall* is merely an application of the *qui prior est tempore* principle in its totality. By so doing, we expose the normative reason which underpins the importance of giving notice first.

The misapprehension begins with a failure to appreciate the full breadth of the 'usual rule'. This arises because the statement of the principle set out in *Phillips* v. *Phillips*[19] is incomplete. A fuller statement of the *qui prior est tempore* principle is set out in *Rice* v. *Rice*:[20]

> As between persons having only equitable interests, if their equities are in *all other respects equal*, priority of time gives the better equity; or *qui prior est tempore potior est jure*.

---

[18] The proposition in point (3) is often referred to as the 'first limb of the rule in *Dearle* v. *Hall*', in contradistinction to point (2): see e.g. Snell (2015), paras. 4-053 to 4-055.

[19] (1862) 4 De G F & J 208.

[20] (1853) 2 Drew 73, 78 See also *Abigail* v. *Lapin* [1934] AC 491, 502.

In Example 10.1, $C_2$ gave notice to B on 11 January, whereas $C_1$ gave notice to B on 22 January. Given $C_2$'s notice to B on 11 January, the equities between $C_1$ and $C_2$ would *not* be equal to each other. This is because of the operation of a rule of ethics which has commonly been termed 'the Golden Rule'.

One formulation of the Golden Rule which would probably not have been unfamiliar to judges presiding at the time of Sir Thomas Plumer MR would have taken the following form: 'And as ye would that men should do to you, do ye also to them likewise.'[21]

Although the Golden Rule is 'a rule sometimes claimed by Christianity as its own, [it is] found in some form in almost every ethical tradition, including that of Confucius'.[22]

By giving notice to B, $C_2$ will have acted in such a way as might potentially aid third and fourth parties considering whether to acquire interests in the subject matter that had been equitably assigned to $C_2$ on 2 January: such notice affords a modest level of publicity.

The level of publicity is modest because caselaw reveals that, although it would be expected of such third and fourth parties who might be considering entering into such dealings to make inquiries of the obligor, B is generally[23] under no duty to respond to such

---

[21] Luke 6:31 King James Version. Alternatively, see Matthew 7:12 King James Version. As to the legal effect of scripture, *Wingate's Maxims* assures us that, '[t]o such lawes as have warrant in holy Scripture, our Law giveth credence': Edmund Wingate and others, *Maximes of Reason: Or, The Reason of the Common Law of England* (London: R. & W. Leybourne, 1658), p. 6. Obviously, this is not the same 'golden rule' as is used in connection with the interpretation of statutes.

[22] Simon Blackburn, *Ethics: A Very Short Introduction* (Oxford: Oxford University Press, 2003), p. 101. For further discussion of the Golden Rule, see Harry J. Gensler, *Ethics and the Golden Rule* (New York: Routledge, 2013), and Jeffrey Wattles, *The Golden Rule* (Oxford: Oxford University Press, 1996).

[23] Unless the provisions of LPA1925, s. 137(3) apply. The editors of *Halsbury's Laws* (5th edn, 2017), Vol. 13 suggest in para. 61 that, '[i]t is the duty of the assignee to make inquiries, and the debtor or fundholder is not bound on receiving notice to volunteer information, unless the notice shows that the assignee has been deceived', relying on the authority of *Mangles v. Dixon* (1852) 3 HLC 702, 734. It is not clear, though, that such notice is to be equated with the reasonable inquiries posed by a third or fourth party planning to take an assignment, since one may not validly give notice of an assignment in anticipation: though no particular form of words is required for a notice to be validly given, the words used must nevertheless indicate that an assignment has already taken place: *William Brandt's Sons & Co.* v. *Dunlop Rubber Co.* [1905] AC 454, 462; *Denney Gasquet and Metcalfe* v. *Conklin* [1913] 3 KB 177, 180 (in connection with a written notice for the purposes of statutory assignment under Judicature Act 1873, s. 25(6)); *James Talcott Ltd* v. *John Lewis Ltd & North American Dress Co. Ltd* [1930] 3 All ER

inquiries.[24] But even so, where $C_2$ *had* given B notice of the 2 January assignment, *if* B were minded to respond to the reasonable inquiries of such third and fourth parties, B could inform them of $C_2$'s assignment, and leave it to the third and fourth parties to make up their minds whether to proceed any further. By contrast, on 11 January, following the notice given by $C_2$ to B, B would still have been ignorant of the 1 January assignment to $C_1$. Again, had reasonable inquiry been made of B by third and fourth parties, *even if* B had been minded to respond to them, B could not have provided any information about the 1 January assignment.

When we compare the relative merits of the behaviour of $C_1$ and $C_2$, as at 11 January, $C_2$ will have behaved in a better, more meritorious manner than $C_1$. This is because $C_2$ will have acted in such a way that would allow third and fourth parties *some* chance of discovering the encumbrance that had arisen in his favour on the chose in action in question, whereas $C_1$ had yet to do the same for the 1 January assignment.

Although neither $C_1$ nor $C_2$ could be said to owe any duty[25] to third and fourth parties deliberating whether or not to deal in the chose in action by giving notice ahead of $C_1$, $C_2$ will have acted over and beyond what he was duty-bound to other potentially interested parties to do. He would have done to others as he would have wished others might have done to him. By giving notice to B ahead of $C_1$, $C_2$ would have acted in accordance with the Golden Rule more expeditiously than $C_1$.[26]

---

592, 595. In short, one gives notice *of* an assignment; one does not give notice of one's *intentions* to take an assignment.

[24] *Low* v. *Bouverie* [1891] 3 Ch 82, 99–100 (*per* Lindley LJ, with whom Bowen LJ agreed). See also *Ward* v. *Duncombe* (n. 12), 393–4. This has, however, been modified by statute. Where an *equitable* interest arising *under a trust* of realty or personalty (i.e. an equitable chose in action) has been equitably assigned, only notices to the equitable obligor made in writing can have the effect of preserving priority: LPA1925, s. 137(3) read with s. 137(10). In such cases, where written notice has been received, the equitable obligor (i.e. the trustee) holding the personalty or realty on trust is obligated to produce such written notice if required to do so by anyone with an interest in the equitable interest arising from the trust: s. 137(8). Further, where the equitable interest that has been assigned arises in connection with realty, the liability of the equitable obligor holding the legal title to such realty to produce documents and furnish information shall, 'correspond to the liability of a trustee for sale': s. 137(9). For a discussion of the operation of s. 137, see L. C. B. Gower, 'The Present Position of the Rule in *Dearle* v. *Hall* – I' (1935) 20 *Conveyancer* 137 and L. C. B. Gower, 'The Present Position of the Rule in *Dearle* v. *Hall* – II' (1935) 20 *Conveyancer* 153.

[25] Given the explanation in Ernest C. C. Firth, 'The Rule in *Dearle* v. *Hall*' (1895) 11 LQR 337, 342, it is difficult to see how such duties could be owed to future, putative assignees.

[26] Of course, if $C_1$ had not given notice to B at all, the equities would be tipped even more strongly in favour of $C_2$.

Hence in comparing the relative merits of $C_1$ and $C_2$ against each other, in the spirit of the maxim that 'equity aids the vigilant and not the indolent',[27] $C_2$ will have the better equity as against $C_1$.

This being the case, the qualification to the *qui prior est tempore* principle will apply. Since the relative equities of $C_1$ and $C_2$ are *not* equal, $C_1$'s interest, though first in time to arise, shall not prevail over $C_2$'s interest. Rather, priority will be given to the interest of the party with the better equity by virtue of his having behaved more meritoriously.

## D   The Subsequent Assignee's Provision of Value and Lack of Knowledge of the Prior Assignment

### (i)   Provision of Value

It is relatively uncontroversial that the 'rule' in *Dearle* v. *Hall* may only be successfully invoked by subsequent assignees who have given value. Thus, in the Irish case of *Justice* v. *Wynne*, on appeal from a decision of the Lord Chancellor in Ireland,[28] Sir Francis Blackburne, Lord Justice of Appeal said:[29]

> [I]t would be a total perversion of the doctrine of this Court to allow want of notice of a prior title to be a ground of the defence of a puisne title or incumbrance acquired without consideration. That doctrine is founded on and limited to the purpose of protecting purchasers and never can be called in aid of the right of a party claiming under a voluntary instrument.

In this, Sir Francis was joined by the Lord Chancellor, who repudiated his position in the court below and explained:[30]

> [I]n favour of assignees for value, this distinction has been established, that the fact of giving notice to the debtor gives to the purchaser who adopts that precaution a better equity, if he takes without notice of a prior assignment; but, as it seems to me, that doctrine was introduced merely for the benefit of purchasers.

Similar views have been expressed in English courts. For example, in *United Bank of Kuwait* v. *Sahib*, Chadwick J noted as follows:[31]

---

[27] As to which, see Snell (2015), para. 5-011.
[28] *Justice* v. *Wynne* (1860) 10 Ir Ch Rep 489.
[29] *Justice* v. *Wynne* (1860) 12 Ir Ch Rep 289, 299.
[30] Ibid., 304.
[31] *United Bank of Kuwait Plc* v. *Sahib* [1997] Ch 107, 119–20 (emphasis added).

> The rule in *Dearle* v. *Hall* ... did not assist a subsequent assignee or chargee who was a volunteer. There could be no question of a volunteer being exposed to the risk of fraud when taking an assignment or charge for which he gave no value. *The volunteer could take no more than the assignor or chargor was able to give.*

This could be taken to suggest that part of the reason behind this aspect of the rule relies on drawing an analogy with the common law rule as to '*nemo dat quod non habet* (no one gives what he does not have)'.[32] However, the common law *nemo dat* rule has nothing to do with priority conflicts arising between equally valid, though competing, equitable assignees.

In Example 10.1, both equitable assignments to $C_1$ and to $C_2$ would have been valid. An equitable assignment will have been created so as to bind the assignor to her assignee once the 'three certainties' are manifested. As mentioned in Chapter 1, these are:

(1) certainty of the intention to assign;
(2) certainty as regards the chose that is the subject of the assignment; and
(3) certainty as regards the identity of the assignee.

Upon satisfaction of these requirements in respect of the equitable assignments to $C_1$ and $C_2$, A would be obligated thereafter to *both* $C_1$ and $C_2$ not to invoke her entitlements as against B for her own self-interest. Hence, reverting to the facts in Example 10.1, A would be duty-bound to $C_1$ to invoke her entitlements for $C_1$'s benefit and not her own. We may therefore speak of A 'losing' her beneficial interest in the chose assigned to $C_1$. But such language must be used carefully.

When we say A has lost her beneficial interest in the chose because it had been equitably assigned to $C_1$, this means that A will have become duty-bound in equity to $C_1$ to preserve the chose and to invoke her powers in connection with the chose for $C_1$'s benefit and not her own. This is because of the bare trust mechanism which underpins equitable assignment. To put it another way, A will no longer have a Hohfeldian privilege so far as $C_1$ is concerned to invoke those entitlements without

---

[32] W. Swadling, 'Property: General Principles', para. 4.06, in A. S. Burrows (ed.), *English Private Law* (3rd edn, Oxford: Oxford University Press, 2013). One consequence of the rule that no one may pass that which they do not have, is that 'where goods are sold by a person who is not their owner ... the buyer acquires no better title to the goods than the seller has': Sale of Goods Act 1979, s. 21.

regard for $C_1$'s interests: A will have become duty-bound to $C_1$ as though she were a bare trustee for $C_1$'s benefit. The loss of the privilege of not having to please $C_1$, because of her duty to $C_1$, is why we may speak of A no longer having a 'beneficial interest'.

However, the assignment to $C_1$ does not render A to be duty-bound in the same or analogous manner to any entity apart from $C_1$. Without more, A would still be under no duty to any 'non-$C_1$' as to how she may (or may not) exercise these entitlements. This is why the 'loss' of A's 'beneficial interest' in the chose does not preclude A from creating a perfectly valid assignment to $C_2$ at a later date.[33] Respectfully, therefore, suggestions that 'an assignor who assigns the same chose twice over is – by the time of the second assignment – seeking to transfer something '[s]he no longer has'[34] may be an oversimplification.

As explained previously, it is not the law that, where the beneficiary of a trust creates a bare sub-trust of her interest, such beneficiary 'drops out'.[35] On 1 January, A is duty-bound to $C_1$ to invoke those entitlements in a particular way. However, the assignment to $C_1$ does not subject A to any similar obligations to any entity *apart from $C_1$*. That is, despite the assignment to $C_1$, A is still under no duty to any entity other than $C_1$ to invoke those entitlements in any particular manner. Hence, as at 1 January, A would still be privileged as against any non-$C_1$ to invoke those entitlements as she pleased.

To put it another way, given the equitable assignment to $C_1$, A would no longer have the 'beneficial ownership' over her entitlements as B's creditor in light of her duties to $C_1$ as equitable assignor. But it does not follow that so far as $C_2$, a stranger to the assignment to $C_1$, was

---

[33] Consequently, it is best to avoid the confusion engendered in Viscount Kilmuir LC's speech in *BS Lyle* v. *Rosher* [1959] 1 WLR 8, 14 where his Lordship suggested that the 'rule' in *Dearle* v. *Hall* would only apply where there was 'a fundholder, someone who has, or has had, a beneficial interest, assignee No. 1 and assignee No. 2'. With respect, the assumption that an assignor might have *no beneficial interest at all* following an assignment is an oversimplification which mischaracterizes the nature of a beneficial interest. As explained in the main text, while it is true that the assignor would no longer be free vis-à-vis the first assignee to invoke her entitlements arising from the chose for her own benefit because of her duty to invoke those entitlements for the benefit of that assignee, the assignor would not be so duty-bound with regard to anyone else. She would still be privileged as to these others to invoke such entitlements without regard to *their* interests. For further criticism of *BS Lyle*, see Meagher, Gummow & Lehane (2015), paras. 8-185 to 8-210.

[34] Smith & Leslie (2018), para. 27.64.

[35] As explained in Chapter 5, Section B.

concerned, A would not be privileged to invoke those entitlements as against B without regard to $C_2$'s interests.

Despite the assignment to $C_1$, A would *still* be privileged as against $C_2$ to invoke her entitlements against B without regard to $C_2$'s interests. It would therefore be open to A to encumber herself in relation to $C_2$ (as a 'non-$C_1$'), to render herself duty-bound to $C_2$ to invoke her entitlements against B *for $C_2$'s benefit* by creating a perfectly valid assignment to $C_2$ on 2 January. And the creation of such additional duties vis-à-vis $C_2$ would not entail any manner of 'transferring' something that A did not have. Rather, A would be creating a new set of obligations (vis-à-vis $C_2$) which she was not previously under.

By effecting this second assignment to $C_2$, A would have created a situation where she would be subject to two masters, instead of just one: A would have exposed herself to the risk of having to breach her duties to one of her masters, should conflicting directions be given. Such conflict can only arise where both assignments are valid. And it is only in connection with *valid* assignments that the question may arise as to which of such valid assignments is to be given priority by being *preferred* over the other.

Where the common law principle of *nemo dat* is in play, the reasons for giving 'priority' to one claim over another are different. Suppose A contracts to sell her legal title in a book to $C_1$, and that under the terms of the contract, A is to deliver the book by hand to $C_1$ forthwith once payment is received. A does so when $C_1$ pays her the price. The result is that $C_1$ will have acquired legal title in the book,[36] as well as possession of the book. However, the following day, she persuades $C_1$ to lend her the book for a week, lying that she needs it to complete a research project. Having recovered possession, A then offers it for sale to $C_2$. $C_2$ accepts the offer and pays A the price in advance of delivery (which A promises will be done in a few days' time). However, having obtained payment from both $C_1$ and $C_2$ in advance of her obligation to deliver the book, A absconds from the jurisdiction, having given the book to V, a volunteer.

Suppose $C_1$ and $C_2$ discover that the book is now in V's possession. Each claims to be entitled to recover possession of the book from V on grounds of their respective contracts of sale with A. Though V has a possessory title to the book derived from A, that possessory title cannot

---

[36] Given s. 17(1) read with s. 18 Rule 1, Sale of Goods Act 1979, $C_1$ will have acquired legal title in the book upon the formation of the contract of sale.

prevail against either $C_1$ or $C_2$: A plainly had no legal title to the book to 'pass' to V given her prior dealings. So by reason of *nemo dat*, V has no legal title in the book, either. But as between $C_1$ and $C_2$, whose claim is stronger? Clearly, in the 'priority' conflict between $C_1$ and $C_2$ to obtain possession of the book, $C_1$ will prevail.[37] However, this result *also* rests on *nemo dat* reasoning.

$C_1$ will have a better claim than $C_2$ to recover possession of the book from V because $C_1$ has the legal title to that book (since at the time of the conveyance to $C_1$, A did have legal title in the book), whereas $C_2$ does not (since at the time of the conveyance to $C_2$, A no longer had *any* legal title in the book). $C_1$'s claim for possession will prevail because it is *valid* (being based on $C_1$'s legal title in the book) whereas $C_2$'s claim for possession will fail because it is *invalid* (being based on a non-existent title). *Nemo dat* reasoning is, therefore, helpful and relevant since you cannot give what you do not have. But *nemo dat* reasoning is unhelpful when we have, as in *Dearle* v. *Hall*-type situations, competition between valid claims.

Reinforcing the point that *nemo dat* reasoning is unhelpful in *Dearle* v. *Hall*-type situations, *nemo dat* reasoning cannot explain the role which value plays in the rule in *Dearle* v. *Hall*. In our example involving conveyance of the legal title to a tangible chattel such as a book by a contract of sale, it would not matter whether or not $C_2$ had given value. Even though $C_2$ had given value in exchange for A's *promise* to convey legal title in the book to $C_2$, that would merely make A's promise actionable by way of contract. But A would still have no legal title in the book to convey to $C_2$. So the transaction between A and $C_2$, so far as it was to effect a conveyance, would still be a nullity.

---

[37] On the facts in the example, the relationship between A and $C_1$ as vendor and purchaser would have come to an end once A physically delivered the book to $C_1$. Consequently, when A regained possession of the book by persuading $C_1$ to lend it back to her, A would not have been a 'vendor in possession' when she contracted to sell the book to $C_2$: A would have reacquired possession as a bailee, and not a vendor. Thus, neither Factors Act 1889, s. 8, nor Sale of Goods Act 1979, s. 24 would operate for $C_2$'s benefit: see *Pacific Motor Auctions Pty Ltd* v. *Motor Credits (Hire Finance) Ltd* [1965] AC 867 (PC), on appeal from the High Court of Australia, approving of the decision in *Mitchell* v. *Jones* (1905) 24 NZLR 932. Both *Pacific Motor* and *Mitchell* v. *Jones* were concerned with Antipodean provisions which were *in pari materia* with s. 24 of the Sale of Goods Act (which is itself derived from s. 8 of the Factors Act). The distinction set out in *Mitchell* v. *Jones* was also accepted to be correct in *Worcester Works Finance Ltd* v. *Cooden Engineering Co. Ltd* [1972] 1 QB 210, and *Union Transport Finance, Limited* v. *Ballardie* [1937] 1 KB 510.

So far, so interesting. But what, if any, is the substantive reason for requiring value to have been given by a subsequent assignee who wishes to take advantage of the 'rule' in *Dearle* v. *Hall*? The rationale for this lies in how knowledge is imputed, in equity, to volunteers.

In connection with conveyances of property which were held on trust, Lord Nottingham observed as follows: 'On conveyance without consideration notice of a trust is presumed and implied; or, which is all one, the party is as much bound as if he had had notice of the trust. But in conveyance for valuable consideration, there the purchaser is not charged with any former trust without notice.'[38]

In Example 10.1, had the equitable assignment to $C_2$ on 2 January been entirely voluntary, as a mere donee, $C_2$ would have been imputed with such knowledge as A would have had. Since A would have had actual knowledge of the prior assignment (and thus the underlying bare trust) to $C_1$, that knowledge would be imputed to $C_2$ if he had been a mere volunteer. The giving of *value* for the assignment, though, precludes $C_2$ from being imputed with A's knowledge of the same. Thus, in Example 10.1, the mere fact that A knew of the assignment to $C_1$ is no longer enough to burden $C_2$ with the same.

### (ii)   Lack of Knowledge of Prior Assignment

The second requirement for the rule in *Dearle* v. *Hall* to apply is that the subsequent assignee must not have had constructive or actual notice of the prior assignment when the subsequent assignment was effected. As explained in the preceding section, the reason for this is intertwined with the requirement that value must have been given by the subsequent assignee.

Some objections have been made against this aspect of the 'rule' in *Dearle* v. *Hall*. For example, de Lacy has pointed out that the requirement that the subsequent assignee must have had neither actual nor constructive notice of the prior assignment was not part of the actual decision in *Dearle* v. *Hall*.[39] He also suggests that the cases which support it are

---

[38] Lord Nottingham, *Lord Nottingham's 'Manual of Chancery Practice' and 'Prolegomena of Chancery and Equity'* (D. E. C. Yale, ed., Cambridge: Cambridge University Press, 1965), p. 253.

[39] John De Lacy, 'Reflections on the Ambit of the Rule in *Dearle* v. *Hall* and the Priority of Personal Property Assignments – Part 1' (1999) 28 *Anglo-American Law Review* 87, 113.

mistaken.[40] Consequently, it has been proposed that the 'rule' in *Dearle v. Hall* is not qualified in this way at all.[41]

Given Lord Nottingham's account of the law in his *Prolegomena*,[42] the requirement that the later assignee must have provided value flows from the difference in treatment between a mere voluntary assignee, and one who has given value: a voluntary assignee will be taken to have such knowledge as the assignor would have had, including knowledge of the prior assignment. Where the subsequent assignee had given value, however, such knowledge will not be imputed. But why is such knowledge important? It is important because it affects the true normative principle that lies at the heart of the so-called rule in *Dearle v. Hall*, which is that *if* the equities between the competing claimants are otherwise equal, *then* the 'first in time shall prevail'. Example 10.2 illustrates this point:

---

**EXAMPLE 10.2**

Same facts as in Example 10.1, except that when $C_2$ gave value for the equitable assignment on 2 January, $C_2$ knew of the prior assignment to $C_1$.

---

On the facts in Example 10.2, notwithstanding that $C_2$ had given notice to B ahead of $C_1$ on 11 January, the 'better equity' that $C_2$ would have acquired by his diligence is counteracted by $C_2$'s actual knowledge of the prior assignment. As at the time when $C_2$ acquired the benefit of the 2 January assignment when the required value in exchange was given, $C_2$ would have acted in a manner which was unconscionable since he knew of $C_1$'s prior equitable interest. In these circumstances, the qualification to the *qui prior est tempore* principle in *Rice v. Rice* would not be engaged, and thus $C_2$ would take subject to $C_1$'s prior equitable interest.

The discussion above shows that paragraphs (1), (2) and (3) of the formulation of the 'rule' in *Dearle v. Hall* in *Guest on Assignment* ought not have been described as forming part of an exception, departing from the *qui prior est tempore* principle. Instead, these three paragraphs demonstrate the application of the full statement of the *qui prior est*

---

[40]  Ibid., 114–27.

[41]  See also Duncan Sheehan, *The Principles of Personal Property Law* (2nd edn, Oxford: Hart, 2017), p. 105, in which different reasons are put forward to eliminate the restriction of the 'rule' in *Dearle v. Hall* to benefit only subsequent assignees for value. Professor Sheehan's analysis does not, however, address the points made in the main text.

[42]  See above, text to n. 38.

*tempore* principle set out in *Rice* v. *Rice* to a factual matrix involving multiple equitable assignments of the same intangible asset.

### E The Disapplication of the 'Rule' in Dearle v. Hall where the Obligor has Independently Acquired Knowledge of the Prior Assignment

The discussion thus far has considered instances where both assignees had given notice, albeit one after the other (in Example 10.1). But what of the situation in Example 10.3?

---

**EXAMPLE 10.3**

Same facts as in Example 10.1, except that $C_1$ did not give notice to B on 22 January or at all. However, on 3 January, the fact of A's assignment to $C_1$ on 1 January was reported in the newspaper, and B happened to read the news story. Consequently, when $C_2$ gave B notice of the 2 January assignment on 11 January, B already knew of the prior assignment to $C_1$, albeit by chance, and not through any act ascribable to $C_1$.

---

*Guest on Assignment* puts forward a limitation on the application of the 'rule' in *Dearle* v. *Hall* that, '[a]t the time that notice by the later assignee is received [by the fundholder/obligor], the fundholder [or obligor] must not have received notice of the earlier assignment'.[43] In this connection, '[k]nowledge acquired by the fundholder of the earlier assignment from any source will be enough'.[44]

Authority for this proposition is, it seems, drawn from *Lloyd* v. *Banks*,[45] as understood and applied in the first instance decision of Buller J in *Re Dallas*.[46] On this view of the law, $C_2$'s equitable interest in

---

[43] Liew (2018), para. 6-21.

[44] Ibid.

[45] (1868) LR 3 Ch App 488 (hereafter, *Lloyd* v. *Banks* (1868)). At fn. 91 to paragraph 6-21, Liew (2018) also mentions the bankruptcy cases of *Smith* v. *Smith* (1833) 2 C & M 231; *Re Tichener* (1854) 35 Beav 317; and *Ex parte Agra Bank; Re Worcester* (1868) LR 3 Ch App 555. However, each of these involved an assignment over certain choses *prior* to the assignor's bankruptcy, and were concerned with the distinct question as to whether such prior assignments had left the choses within the assignor's 'order and disposition' under the then applicable bankruptcy legislation. Their relevance to the problem at hand involving a prior assignment pursuant to insolvency legislation followed by an equitable assignment is, therefore, unclear.

[46] [1904] 2 Ch 385, 399. Although Buckley J's decision was affirmed on appeal, the Court of Appeal did not address this aspect of his reasoning. Nor has Buckley J's reading of *Lloyd* v. *Banks* on the point been considered by the Supreme Court.

Example 10.3 would be postponed to $C_1$'s because of the chance acquisition by B of knowledge of the assignment to $C_1$ and despite $C_1$ having done nothing to notify B of the 1 January assignment. This constraint derived from *Lloyd* v. *Banks* contradicts the proposition in this chapter that the 'rule' in *Dearle* v. *Hall* is derived from the principle in *Rice* v. *Rice* and so requires comparison of the diligence of rival assignees in giving notice of their respective assignments. If so, might it be the case that although the 'rule' in *Dearle* v. *Hall* might have originated as an application of the principle in *Rice* v. *Rice*, later developments like *Lloyd* v. *Banks* and *Re Dallas* have cut the rule off from its substantive roots by adding an unrelated qualification? It seems not, because, when read in context, we will find that the *Lloyd* v. *Banks* constraint does not impinge upon the 'rule' in *Dearle* v. *Hall*.

*Lloyd* v. *Banks* was not concerned with a problem of priority between two valid equitable assignments over the same chose in action. It was concerned with a 'priority' dispute between a valid and an *invalid* claim, for which the relevant rule to apply would be the *nemo dat* rule. Thus, Buller J's assumption in *Re Dallas* that *Lloyd* v. *Banks* engaged with the 'rule' in *Dearle* v. *Hall* was, with respect, mistaken.

### (i)  Lloyd *v.* Banks: *Some Context*

The facts in *Lloyd* v. *Banks* were as follows.[47] Banks, the defendant, was a solicitor. He was also the surviving trustee over certain funds which were held on trust under the terms of a marriage settlement created upon the marriage of Ann Cheese to Thomas Lloyd. Under the terms of the marriage settlement, Lloyd had an equitable remainder interest to the annuity, for his life, once Ann's prior life interest to the annual income from the trust funds came to an end. Lloyd's life interest in the annuity was, therefore, vested in interest, though not in possession: it was not a contingent interest.[48]

---

[47] The facts are more fully set out in the report of the decision of Lord Romilly MR in *Lloyd* v. *Banks* (1867) LR 4 Eq 222 (hereafter *Lloyd* v. *Banks* (1867)).

[48] As explained in Charles Harpum, Stuart Bridge and Martin Dixon, *Megarry & Wade: The Law of Real Property* (8th edn, London: Sweet & Maxwell, 2012), para. 9-002, in general, '[a] remainder is vested if two requirements are satisfied: (i) the person or persons entitled to it must be ascertained; and (ii) it must be ready to take effect in possession forthwith and be prevented from doing so only by the existence of some prior interest or interests' (references omitted). There is no mention in either *Lloyd* v. *Banks* (1867) or *Lloyd* v. *Banks* (1868) that Lloyd's life interest was contingent also on his surviving Ann.

Ann died in October 1861. The following month, Lloyd mortgaged his life interest in the funds to one Shephard. Notice of assignment was given to Banks in March 1862. However, Shephard did not know that on 19 January 1859, Lloyd had petitioned the Court for the Relief of Insolvent Debtors (hereafter, the Court for Relief), and that it had made the 'usual' vesting order.

Formal notice of these proceedings was not given to Banks until February 1864, but Banks admitted that he knew of them because, on 16 February 1859, he had read an advertisement in the *Hereford Journal* which stated that Lloyd had filed a petition which would be heard by the Court for Relief on 14 March 1859. Further, Banks testified that, in his capacity as solicitor for Lloyd's father-in-law, he had negotiated for the purchase of Lloyd's life interest under the settlement; and in those negotiations, Banks had dealt with Lloyd on the basis that he was an insolvent.[49] He also testified that he had declined to pay the annuities arising under the marriage settlement trusts to Lloyd, following Ann's death.[50]

Proceedings were eventually brought for the administration of the trusts of the settlement. In that suit, the Chief Clerk found that the assignee in insolvency was entitled to Lloyd's life interest in priority to Shephard. Dissatisfied with this, Shephard took out a summons to vary the certificate, and succeeded before Lord Romilly MR.[51] On appeal to Lord Cairns LC, however, the Chief Clerk's certificate was reinstated for the following reason: '[A]lthough I agree that the assignee in insolvency runs the risk of its being otherwise, but being so, it seems to me that the assignee in insolvency has a good title: he is the first incumbrancer in date; the trustee has notice of the insolvency, and nothing more is required.'[52] This is problematic, as the passage could be taken as suggesting that: (i) the interest of the assignee in insolvency was that of a mere incumbrancer; and (ii) that the reasons for the assignee having good title and, presumably, a better one than Shephard's title by reason of the

---

Alternatively, as Marshall explained: 'It is a familiar proposition that an interest in property may be either "vested in possession" or "vested in interest". An interest is said to be "vested in possession" if there is some person who is entitled to its present enjoyment; it is said to be "vested in interest" if there is some person who has a present fixed right to its future enjoyment': Marshall (1950), p. 199.

[49] *Lloyd v. Banks* (1867), 223 (headnote).
[50] *Lloyd v. Banks* (1868), 491.
[51] *Lloyd v. Banks* (1867), 225.
[52] *Lloyd v. Banks* (1868), 492.

equitable assignment of 1861 following Ann's death, were because the
assignee in insolvency's incumbrance was first in time *and* because
Banks, the trustee, had received notice of Lloyd's insolvency through
his chance reading of the advertisement in the *Hereford Journal* on
16 February 1859. This, however, would be an error.

First, we need to understand what happened when Lloyd filed his
petition in 1859. Prior to 1813, access to the Court of Bankruptcy was
limited to 'traders'.[53] Insolvent non-traders were thus liable to be
imprisoned with no recourse to the Court of Bankruptcy. However, the
Court for Relief was created in 1813.[54] It provided some relief for insolvent non-traders, principally by making orders to discharge insolvent
debtors whose persons had been taken in execution in respect of unpaid
debts from such custody or imprisonment.[55] And the statutes touching
on the operation of the Court for Relief were consolidated in 1838
pursuant to the Act of 1 & 2 Vict, c. 110 (hereafter the Insolvent Debtors
Relief Act 1838 or the 1838 Act).[56]

The Law Reports state that Lloyd 'took the benefit of the Insolvent
Debtors Act' in 1859,[57] and that he had 'presented his Petition to the Court

---

[53] As at 1867, the relevant bankruptcy legislation would have been found in the Bankrupt
Law Consolidation Act 1849 (12 & 13 Vict, c. 106), s. 55 of which listed those tradesmen
who would be deemed to be a 'trader' for the purposes of the Act.

[54] *Vide* the 1813 Act of 53 Geo III, c. 102 intituled 'An Act for the Relief of Insolvent
Debtors in England'. The operation of the 1813 Act was extended and amended by a
series of acts up to the early part of the Victorian period when *Lloyd* v. *Banks* was decided,
namely 54 Geo III, c. 23; 56 Geo III, c. 102; 1 Geo IV, c. 119; 3 Geo IV, c. 123; 5 Geo IV,
c. 61; 7 Geo IV, c. 57; 1 & 2 Vic, c. 110; and 10 & 11 Vic, c. 102. The Court for Relief was
ultimately wound up in 1869 when Parliament enacted the Bankruptcy Repeal and
Insolvent Court Act 1869 (32 & 33 Vict, c. 83) as part of the 1869 bankruptcy and
insolvency law reforms.

[55] For an account of the legislative history leading to the imprisonment of debtors in the
nineteenth century, see *Fourth Report of the Commissioners Appointed to Inquire into the
Practice and Proceedings of the Superior Courts of Common Law* (1831-2, No. 239),
pp. 5–8. The imprisonment of debtors was largely eliminated by the Debtors Act 1869 (32
& 33 Vict, c. 62), though execution against the person of the debtor would still be
permitted in certain limited situations.

[56] 1 & 2 Vict, c. 110, intituled 'An Act for abolishing Arrest on Mesne Process in Civil
Actions, except in certain Cases; for extending the Remedies of Creditors against the
Property of Debtors; and for amending the Laws for the Relief of Insolvent Debtors in
England'. This Act restated the law as had been consolidated in its predecessor statute in
the 1826 Act of 7 Geo IV, c. 56, intituled 'An Act to amend and consolidate the Laws for
the Relief of Insolvent Debtors in England' (hereafter, the '1826 Act').

[57] *Lloyd* v. *Banks* (1867), 222.

for the Relief of Insolvent Debtors' on 19 January 1859.[58] But in the *Law Journal* report of the Lord Chancellor's judgment, it is made clear that:[59]

> [o]n the 19th of January, 1859, Thomas Lloyd petitioned the late Court for Relief of Insolvent Debtors under the provisions of the 1 & 2 Vict, c. 110; and on the 22nd of the same month the usual vesting order was made, and an advertisement was published in a local newspaper commencing thus: 'Petition of insolvent debtor to be heard in the court of Francis Stack Murphy, Esq., Commissioner, at Court House, Portugal Street, Lincoln's Inn Fields, on the 14th day of March, 1859, at 10 o'clock in the morning . . .'

We may therefore conclude that Lloyd had filed his petition to the Court for Relief on 19 January 1859 under the Insolvent Debtors Relief Act 1838. Following filing of the petition, a vesting order was made in either January or June of the same year,[60] and an advertisement that Lloyd's petition would be heard on 14 March 1859 was published on 16 February 1859[61] in the *Hereford Journal*.[62] Since the vesting order was made and, further, an order of discharge from custody under the 1838 Act, was granted 'on the 22nd of April' in the following year,[63] we may deduce that Lloyd's petition to the Court for Relief was successful, and had not been dismissed for any reason.

### (ii)    Transfers under the Insolvent Debtors Relief Act 1838

Under the 1838 Act, insolvent debtors who were in actual custody for their unpaid debts,[64] could file petitions for relief to the Court for Relief – namely, they could petition for their assets to be transferred to

---

[58]  *Lloyd* v. *Banks* (1868), 488.

[59]  *Lloyd* v. *Banks* (1868) LJ 37 Chan Rep 881, 881. The same details are repeated by the Lord Chancellor in the *Law Journal* report of his judgment at 883.

[60]  The official Law Report of the decision of the Master of the Rolls states that the vesting order was made on 22 January after the filing of the petition. The same is reported in the *Law Journal* report of the Lord Chancellor's judgment. However, the official Law Report of the Lord Chancellor's judgment states that the vesting order was made on 22 June. This is probably not critical, but as the hearing of Lloyd's petition for discharge from custody was fixed for 14 March, it seems more likely that the vesting order would have been made before the hearing of the petition.

[61]  *Lloyd* v. *Banks* (1868), 488. Publications of such advertisement was provided for by s. 71, 1838 Act.

[62]  *Lloyd* v. *Banks* (1867), 223.

[63]  Ibid., 222.

[64]  1838 Act, s. 35.

the Provisional Assignee,[65] and to be to be discharged from custody thereafter.[66] As to such petitions for discharge, s. 37 of the 1838 Act provided as follows:[67]

> And be it enacted, [i] That upon the filing of such Petition by such Prisoner, . . . it shall be lawful for the said Court for the Relief of Insolvent Debtors, and such Court is hereby authorized and *required, to order that all the Real and Personal Estate and Effects of such Prisoner*, both within this Realm and abroad, except the Wearing Apparel, Bedding, and other such Necessaries of such Person and his Family, and the working Tools and Implements of such Prisoner, not exceeding in the whole the Value of Twenty Pounds, [ii] and all the future Estate, Right, Title, Interest, and Trust of such Prisoner in or to any Real and Personal Estate and Effects within this Realm or abroad which such Prisoner may purchase, or which may revert, descend, be devised or bequeathed, or come to him, before he shall become entitled to this final Discharge in pursuance of this Act, according to the Adjudication made in that Behalf . . . [iii] and all Debts due or growing due to such Prisoner, or to be due to him or her before such Discharge as aforesaid, *shall be vested in the Provisional Assignee for the Time being of the Estates and Effects of Insolvent Debtors in England*, and such Order shall be entered of Record in the same Court, and such Notice thereof shall be published as the said Court shall Direct; [iv] *and such Order when so made shall, without any Conveyance or Assignment, vest all the Real and Personal Estate and Effects of such Prisoner, and all such future Real and Personal Estate and Effects as aforesaid, of every Nature and Kind whatsoever, and all such Debts as aforesaid, in the said Provisional Assignee*: [v] Provided always, that in case the Petition of any such Prisoner shall be dismissed by the said Court, such vesting Order made in pursuance of such Petition shall from and after such Dismission by null and void to all Intents and Purposes: [vi] Provided also, that in case any such vesting Order as aforesaid shall become null and void by the Dismission of the Prisoner's Petition, all the Acts theretofore done by the said Provisional Assignee, or any Person or Persons acting under his Authority, according to the Provisions of this Act, shall be good and valid.

From [i] and [ii], above, we see that the Court for Relief was required to make a vesting order by which all realty and personality held by the petitioning insolvent, including any future estate, right, title, interest or

---

[65] The Provisional Assignee was an officer of the Court for Relief: 1838 Act, s. 24.

[66] Pursuant to s. 36 of the 1838 Act, any of the insolvent's creditors could also petition for the insolvent's assets to be transferred to the Provisional Assignee, and for the insolvent to be released from custody thereafter.

[67] For easier comprehension, references to petitions by the insolvent's creditors have been removed, and emphasis in italics as well as lower case roman numerals in square brackets in bold, have been added.

trust in any realty or personalty which he might purchase, or which might revert, descend, be devised to him, *prior to the time of his discharge from custody*, would be divested from him, and vested in the Provisional Assignee (being an officer of the Court for Relief), once the petition for discharge was filed

Next, **[iii]** and **[iv]** provided that such vesting of the insolvent's assets in the Provisional Assignee arose by reason of the Order without need for any further conveyance or assignment.[68] However, **[v]** stipulated that if the petition were dismissed, the vesting order would become null and void, though **[vi]** provided that such invalidity would have no retrospective effect with regard to any acts which the Provisional Assignee might have done.

It follows that assets of the insolvent debtor which were vested in the insolvent up to and including the time when he was discharged from custody would be transferred from the insolvent to the Provisional Assignee. But assets which vested in the insolvent *after* such discharge were treated differently. This after-acquired property would remain vested in the insolvent, although the Provisional Assignee (or such assignees in insolvency as might have been appointed in his place)[69] were granted certain powers for the realization of such property.[70]

In respect of an insolvent debtor's interests in realty or personalty as had vested in interest or in possession prior to his discharge from custody, ss. 87–9 would not apply. Instead, they would be transferred to the Provisional Assignee[71] by virtue of the vesting order under s. 37.[72] And although the legislation does not make it explicit, it appears that it was understood that the transfer had extinctive effects in that the Provisional Assignee would take the place of the insolvent debtor, such that

---

[68] This was a modification of the previous procedure under s. 11 of the 1826 Act which required the petitioner to execute a conveyance and assignment in favour of the Provisional Assignee in a form prescribed by the 1826 Act, together with his petition.

[69] Pursuant to s. 45 of the 1838 Act, which provided that whatever 'Estate, Effects, Rights, and Powers' of the petitioner as had been vested in the Provisional Assignee by operation of the Act would vest in such assignees as were appointed pursuant to s. 45, also 'without any Conveyance or Assignment ... in Trust for the Benefit of the Creditors of the Prisoner, in respect of or in proportion to their respective Debts'.

[70] See 1838 Act, ss. 87–9.

[71] And thereafter, to the assignees in insolvency pursuant to s. 45, 1838 Act.

[72] Section 37 of the 1838 Act replaced s. 11 of the 1826 Act. The two provisions were *in pari materia*, save that under s. 11 the transfer to the Provisional Assignee was effected by means of an assignment in a prescribed form which was to be filed together with the petition for relief.

the insolvent debtor would 'drop out'. Two cases, *Yorston v. Fether*,[73] and *Rochfort v. Battersby*[74] illustrate the point: we will examine them before concluding our analysis of *Lloyd v. Banks*.

In *Yorston v. Fether*, an action in debt was brought by the plaintiff. In his defence, the defendant pleaded that, prior to commencing the action, the plaintiff had petitioned the Court for Relief of Insolvent Debtors under the 1838 Act, and a vesting order had been made under that Act. The defendant contended that such vesting order, made prior to the commencement of the present action, divested the plaintiff of the causes of action in all debts which had been owed to the plaintiff, and revested them in the Provisional Assignee. Consequently, the defendant pleaded that the present proceedings had been wrongly brought by the plaintiff.

In reply, the plaintiff explained that the Court for Relief had dismissed his petition on 30 June 1845, after the present action had commenced.[75] The plaintiff therefore contended that the vesting order that had been made following the filing of his petition had been rendered null and void, given the first proviso to s. 37 of the 1838 Act.[76]

The Court of Exchequer held in favour of the defendant. Baron Parke explained the decision of the court as follows:[77]

> Independently of the proviso in the 37th section of this act, it is quite plain the plaintiff could have no right to maintain this action. Then, does that proviso give him the right? We must take it, that at the time the plaintiff commenced this suit he had no cause of action, and that in the interval between that time and the dismissal of the petition, the defendant had a good answer to the plaintiff's claim; and if the statute gives him a title to maintain the action now, he having had none when he sued out the writ, it does that which is unknown to the law in any other case. That, however, is not so; the words in the 37th section, 'in case the petition of any prisoner shall be dismissed, the vesting order made in pursuance of it shall, from and after such dismission, be null and void to all intents and purposes', can only mean that it shall be null and void *from the time it is declared so by the Insolvent Debtors Court*.

---

[73] (1845) 14 M & W 852. The decision is also reported as *Yorston v. Feather* (1845) LJ 15 Exch 31.

[74] (1849) 2 HLC 388 (HL, on appeal from the Irish Court of Chancery).

[75] The plaintiff's petition for discharge had been dismissed because his creditors had permitted his release from custody independently of his petition to the Court for Relief under the 1838 Act.

[76] Marked as [v] in the extract at text to n. 67, above.

[77] *Yorston v. Fether* (n. 73), 854. Alderson B came to the same conclusion, at 854–5. Rolfe B and Platt B concurred without providing any grounds.

This tells us that the effects of s. 37 could be undone if the insolvent debtor's petition was dismissed, but only prospectively. But if the petition was not dismissed, Baron Parke held that a s. 37 vesting order would, in connection with a common law debt, remove the petitioner's standing to bring an action at law on the debt, and revest it in the Provisional Assignee. Hence, the Provisional Assignee would take the place of the insolvent debtor, and the insolvent debtor would 'drop out'. In essence, the petitioner would become a stranger to the contract of debt, his place as creditor being taken by the Provisional Assignee.

A similar conclusion was reached by the House of Lords in *Rochfort* v. *Battersby*[78] in connection with an insolvent debtor's power to bring a suit in equity. In *Rochfort*, the House of Lords concluded that a petitioner who had been discharged from custody by the Court for Relief and whose realty and personalty had passed to the Provisional Assignee no longer had any interest in that property as would entitle him to be made a party to a suit in the Court of Chancery in Ireland.[79] Therefore, the insolvent debtor was not competent to appeal against the decision of that court.[80] The transfer would, accordingly, have rendered the insolvent debtor a stranger to the trust, overriding the intentions of the settlor or the express terms of the trust deed.

It may be noted, though, that the ramifications of the House of Lords' decision in *Rochfort* v. *Battersby* as to the extinction of an insolvent debtor's equitable interest were not drawn to the attention of Lord St Leonards in *Re Atkinson*,[81] the headnote of which suggests that, '[t]he title of an assignee for value of an equitable interest is not affected by a previous insolvency of the assignor, the [equitable] assignee having no notice of that insolvency'.[82]

---

[78] *Rochfort* v. *Battersby* (n. 74).

[79] The insolvent debtor in *Rochfort* v. *Battersby* had been discharged from custody in 1821, so it seems likely that he would have petitioned for relief pursuant to s. 4 of the 1820 Statute of 1 Geo IV, c. 119 intituled 'An Act for the Relief of Insolvent Debtors in England; to continue in force until the First Day of June One thousand eight hundred and twenty five'. Section 4 of the 1820 Act, which provided for the passing of the insolvent's property to the Provisional Assignee, was largely *in pari materia* with s. 11 of the 1826 Act. However, s. 4 of the 1820 Act did not provide for the transfer of 'future property' as might vest in the insolvent before his discharge from custody: that was only introduced with s. 11 of the 1826 Act, which was then carried into s. 37 of the 1838 Act.

[80] *Rochfort* v. *Battersby* (n. 74).

[81] (1852) 2 De G M & G 140.

[82] Ibid.

*Re Atkinson* concerned the competing claims to a capital sum which had been paid by the trustees of a testamentary trust into court pursuant to the provisions of the Trustees' Relief Act.[83] The competing claimants were the Provisional Assignee of an insolvent debtor who had been discharged from custody by order of the Court for Relief and who had been a beneficiary under the trust, and an assignee who had taken an assignment of the insolvent debtor's interest arising from that trust for value, after the insolvent's discharge from custody. Given that in *Re Atkinson* priority was given to the claim of the equitable assignee who had given notice of the equitable assignment to the testamentary trustees while they were entirely ignorant of the beneficiary's insolvency proceedings, one might take it as refuting the doubts expressed herein as to the relevance of *Lloyd* v. *Banks*. However, the authoritativeness of *Re Atkinson* is also doubtful.

First, *Re Atkinson* does not address the point made by the House of Lords in *Rochfort* v. *Battersby*. Second, the Lord Chancellor appears to have assumed that the claims of the equitable assignee, and the Provisional Assignee pursuant to the relevant insolvent debtor legislation,[84] were both valid claims. This, however, is suspect.

From the account of the facts in the report of the Vice-Chancellor's decision which led to the appeal to the Lord Chancellor, we find that the gift of a share in the fund to the insolvent debtor was contingent on him *surviving* his mother:[85]

> Agnes Atkinson (who died in the year 1821), by her will, made in 1814, gave a legacy of £700 to her three executors, upon trust to invest it, and to pay the income to Ann Argles, for her life; and on her death the testatrix directed the fund to be divided among all the children of Ann Argles *who should then be living*.

If this account of the wording of the will is accurate, it would be on all fours with the testamentary wording in *Batsford* v. *Kebbell* where Lord Loughbrough LC held that if distinct testamentary gifts had been made of the interest arising from a trust fund to a life tenant, with a gift of the capital by way of remainder, the remainder interest would not vest until the life tenant died.[86] Alternatively, given the testamentary wording, in order to come within the class of beneficiaries as to the capital, the

---

[83]  10 & 11 Vict, c. 96.
[84]  I.e. the 1826 Act.
[85]  *Re Atkinson's Trust Estate* (1851) 4 De G & Sm 548, 548 (emphasis added).
[86]  *Batsford* v. *Kebbell* (1797) 3 Ves Jun 363.

insolvent debtor would not only have had to be a child of the life tenant, he also had to have survived her death: if he pre-deceased the life tenant, his estate would take nothing.[87] Either way, the insolvent debtor's interest in the capital would not have vested until 1851 when he survived his mother, the life tenant.

If the legacy to the insolvent debtor had yet to vest in 1830 or in 1834, when the insolvent debtor was discharged from custody by order of the Court for Relief, and only vested in 1851, the insolvent debtor's interest would not have vested in time to it to be re-vested in the Provisional Assignee by virtue of the assignments which the insolvent debtor would have had to execute as part of his petition to be discharged under s 11 of the 1826 Act.[88] And if the interest in the capital *had* vested after the insolvent debtor's discharge from custody, the 1826 Act made no provision for the transfer or re-vesting of such 'after-acquired' interests to the Provisional Assignee. Indeed, the provisions in ss. 57, 58 and 59 of the 1826 Act which dealt with 'after-acquired' property could not operate unless the insolvent's entitlement in such 'after-acquired' property remained vested in him.[89]

Consequently, in *Re Atkinson*, when the insolvent debtor survived his mother in 1851, his interest in the legacy would have vested at that time. He then equitably assigned such vested interest to his assignee. But nothing in the 1826 Act would have divested such interest from the insolvent and re-vested it in the Provisional Assignee. The Provisional Assignee's claim was an invalid claim because he had been transferred nothing under the 1826 Act in respect of the insolvent debtor's 'after-acquired' property by way of his interest in the capital in 1830 or 1834, such interest only vesting in him in 1851. The Provisional Assignee's claim failed, therefore, because he had *no* interest, not because the equitable assignee had a *better* interest. The fact that notice had been given by the equitable assignee would, accordingly, have been irrelevant to the question of the Provisional Assignee's interest under the 1826 Act to that 'after-acquired' property in *Re Atkinson*.

---

[87] See *Sheffield* v. *Kennett* (1859) 27 Beav 207 (aff'd *Sheffield* v. *Kennett* (1859) 4 De G & J 593); followed in *Re Watson's Trusts* (1870) LR 10 Eq 36.

[88] As mentioned in n. 72, although s. 11 of the 1826 Act was *in pari materia* with s. 37 of the 1838 Act, it differed from s. 37 in that the assets would pass to the Provisional Assignee by means of an assignment in a prescribed form executed by the insolvent debtor, which had to be filed together with his petition for relief.

[89] Sections 57, 58 and 59 of the 1826 Act were *in pari materia* with ss. 87, 88 and 89, respectively, of the 1838 Act.

Returning to *Lloyd* v. *Banks*, we may recall that although Lloyd's reversionary life interest in the annuity arising from the trusts of his marriage settlement would have vested in interest by the time he filed his petition to the Court for Relief in 1859, it would not have vested in possession since Lloyd's wife, Ann, was still alive. But even so, Lloyd's reversionary life interest, which was vested in interest, would have been transferred from Lloyd to the Provisional Assignee when the 'usual vesting order' was made. That is, once the vesting order was made, Lloyd's place as beneficiary under such trusts would have been taken by the Provisional Assignee (and any assignees in insolvency subsequently appointed in his place),[90] and Lloyd would have become a stranger to those trusts.[91] Hence, when Lloyd purported to equitably assign 'his' interest under those trusts to Shephard in 1861, Lloyd had *no* such interest to assign to Shephard; and when Lloyd's wife died, the reversionary interest would vest in possession in the Provisional Assignee, and not in Lloyd. Shephard, as Lloyd's equitable assignee, could acquire no interest in that reversionary interest.

Since the vesting order extinguished Lloyd's remainder life interest in the annuity and re-vested it in the Provisional Assignee, Lloyd would have become a stranger to the trusts of the marriage settlement, with the Provisional Assignee taking his place, sometime in 1859. When other assignees in insolvency were appointed to replace the Provisional Assignee (as appears to have occurred), s. 45 would mean that Provisional Assignee would also have become a stranger to the trusts of the marriage settlement. But even so, as at 1861, Lloyd would have remained a stranger to the trusts of the marriage settlement, absent any further order of re-vesting.

As to such re-vesting, nothing in the reports suggests that the realty and personalty that had been transferred from Lloyd on the making of the vesting order were subsequently transferred back. Though the 1838 Act provided that applications could be made for the reassignment of any residual assets left in the hands of the assignee in insolvency after full repayment of the insolvent's debts,[92] none of the reports suggest that any such application had been made, or that Lloyd had ever repaid his creditors in full. Nor, given that Lloyd had been discharged

---

[90] Pursuant to s. 45 of the 1838 Act.
[91] Also see *Green* v. *Spicer* (1830) Tamlyn 396, and *Pym* v. *Lockyer* (1841) 12 Sim 394.
[92] Section 92, 1838 Act.

from custody by order of the Court of Relief, could the doctrine in *Grange* v. *Trickett* apply.[93]

Accordingly, when Ann died in 1861, the remainder life interest arising in connection with the trusts of the marriage settlement could not have vested in possession in Lloyd, being a stranger to those trusts. Rather, the life interest would have vested in possession in the assignee in insolvency who had succeeded the Provisional Assignee to whom Lloyd's life interest, while it was still vested in interest, had been transferred back in 1859. Consequently, Lloyd's equitable assignment of 1861 to Shephard would have been a purported equitable assignment of an interest that he no longer had.

The reason why the assignee in insolvency's claim to the annuity had 'priority' over Shephard's claim, therefore, was not because both had valid claims as against Banks, the trustee of the marriage settlement trusts. Rather, Shephard's claim against Banks was invalid because, as at 1861, Lloyd had no interest in the annuity to equitably assign to Shephard. *Lloyd* v. *Banks* was thus not a case where the *qui prior est tempore potior est jure* principle was relevant. Instead, it was a case where *nemo dat* reasoning applied: Lloyd had no interest to equitably assign to Shephard, given the operation of s. 37.

Having completed our detour into defunct insolvency law, it is now apposite to revisit that part of the Lord Chancellor's judgment in *Lloyd* v. *Banks* where he reasoned that: 'although I agree that the assignee in insolvency runs the risk of its being otherwise, but being so, it seems to me that the assignee in insolvency has a good title: he is the first

---

[93] (1851) 2 El & Bl 396. In this case, the court held that where an insolvent debtor who had filed a petition under the Insolvent Debtors Relief Act 1838 had been discharged from custody by consent of his detaining creditors without order from the Court of Relief, all assets transferred to the assignee in insolvency under the Act would be re-vested in the petitioner without need for further order of court. However, in *Re Manders* (1852), the Court for Relief rejected this proposition. In a judgment handed down on 2 January 1852, Mr Commissioner Law of the Court for Relief held that, '[t]he person of an insolvent debtor can be withdrawn from the jurisdiction of the court, but not his property, without an act of the court itself. The withdrawal of his person puts at once a stop to the operation of the vesting order on accruing property. So it prevents those further powers over future property . . . But the withdrawal of the person does not vacate the title to property already acquired and in hand.' (reported in David Cato Macrae and C. J. B. Hertslet, *Reports of Cases Relating to Insolvency; Vol. I (1847-1852)* (London: John Crockford, 1852), pp. 271–3. The controversy was finally resolved in *Kernot* v. *Pittis* (1853) 2 El & Bl 421 in an appeal to the Exchequer Chamber, where a court of seven judges unanimously overruled the decision in *Grange* v. *Trickett* on this point.

incumbrancer in date; the trustee has notice of the insolvency, and nothing more is required'.

Although the Bankruptcy Act 1861 had largely repealed the Insolvent Debtors Relief Act 1838[94] and, after eliminating the distinction between traders and non-traders,[95] had transferred the powers of the Court for Relief to the Court of Bankruptcy,[96] in *Lloyd* v. *Banks*, the Lord Chancellor was plainly conscious of the operation of the 1838 Act, given his aside that 'a solicitor reading an advertisement of that kind would know perfectly well that the law of this country required at that time that before an insolvent debtor could petition for his discharge the proper formalities must have been gone through, of his executing an assignment, or having a vesting order made'.[97] This suggests that the Lord Chancellor recognized that the assignee in insolvency would have had a good title by virtue of s. 37 of the 1838 Act. However, as previously noted, the assignee in insolvency could be ordered to reconvey such assets as had been vested in him if Lloyds's debts were fully repaid.[98] Hence, the Lord Chancellor's reference to the assignee in insolvency being an 'incumbrancer' reflected how the assignee in insolvency's position was roughly analogous to that of a mortgagee.

It follows that the Lord Chancellor's reference to notice would have had no relevance to the question as to whether Shephard's equitable assignment (which he had 'perfected' by giving notice to Banks) might be paid in preference to the Provisional Assignee: given the operation of s. 37, by the time of the purported assignment to Shephard, Lloyd had *no* interest. At best, he might have a residual interest analogous to the interest of a mortgagor's interest in any residue which might be left after satisfaction of the underlying debt. But because of *nemo dat* reasoning, Shephard's claim as equitable assignee would have to be postponed to that of the Provisional Assignee. The *qui prior est tempore potior est jure* principle would have had no part to play, and reference to the 'rule' in *Dearle* v. *Hall* would, accordingly, have been redundant. The reason, therefore, why the 'rule' in *Dearle* v. *Hall* did not apply to the benefit of

---

[94] Section 230, read with Schedule G, Bankruptcy Act 1861, by which the whole of the 1838 Act was repealed, save for ss. 1–22.

[95] 1838 Act, s. 69.

[96] Bankruptcy Act 1861, s. 1. By s. 10, the Commissioners of the Court for Relief were relieved of their posts, and by s. 21, the Provisional Assignee was made an Official Assignee of the Court of Bankruptcy.

[97] *Lloyd* v. *Banks* (1868), 491.

[98] See above, n. 92.

Shephard, who had given notice to Banks before 'formal notice' of the insolvency proceedings, had been given to Banks, was because the extinctive effect of the Insolvent Debtors Relief Act 1838 meant that that 'rule' was wholly inapplicable. The true significance of Banks's knowledge of Lloyd's status as an insolvent lies elsewhere.

### (iii)  Notice and Knowledge in Lloyd v. Banks

From the Lord Chancellor's judgment, it is clear that Banks not only knew that Lloyd had filed an insolvency petition: Banks knew that Lloyd *was* an insolvent debtor. And, knowing of Lloyd's insolvent status, Banks had refused to pay Lloyd the annuities that had accrued due under the marriage settlement trusts even though the prior life in interest had died. Importantly, Banks was *justified* in doing so, and would have been so justified even if he had had no knowledge of Lloyd's insolvency.

The chief significance of Banks's chance knowledge of Lloyd's insolvency was that it informed his decision not to pay Lloyd, which then led to the administration suit against him. But by withholding payment, Banks had avoided committing a breach of trust; for, given the operation of s. 37 of the 1838 Act, payment to Lloyd would have been a payment to a stranger to the trust. And payment to Shephard as equitable assignee of such a stranger could be no different. What is more, had Banks paid Lloyd or Shephard in the knowledge that Lloyd had become an insolvent, and so had become a stranger to the marriage settlement trusts, Banks would have committed a breach of trust in such a way as would have left him unable to defend himself.

In *Cothay v. Sydenham*, Lord Thurlow LC held as follows:[99]

> Now as to trustees, ... the Court expects from a trustee, that reasonable circumspection which a man, in conscience, ought to use on the occasion before him, and, to be sure, after knowing of the draught of this deed of appointment, he might reasonably have objected to paying the money without further enquiry. If he had refused, somebody must have filed a bill against him, and then the Court would have seen in some manner, whether any such deed had been executed in pursuance of that draught. ... The question must turn on the notice; the plaintiff's title is certainly efficient, unless the trustee can discharge himself by a *bona fide* payment of the money in his hands. This he clearly could do if he had no notice of any kind of any prior appointment. – If he had notice, he could not.

---

[99]  (1788) 2 Bro C C 391, 393–4.

Hence, relying on this, and on the authority of *Leslie* v. *Baillie*[100] and *Re Lord Southampton's Estate*,[101] it has been said that:[102]

> (1) The responsibility of handing the trust property to the persons entitled lies upon the trustee, so that if he acts beyond his powers his accounts are falsified and he is strictly liable for a substitutive performance of his obligations. . . .
>
> (2) if, however, the person who is really entitled to trust property is not the beneficiary who appears on the face of the settlement (but someone who claims through him), and the trustees have neither express nor constructive notice of such derivative title, they cannot be made to pay over again.

In *Lloyd* v. *Banks*, had Banks paid the annuity to either Lloyd after Lloyd had become a stranger to the trust, or to Shephard as equitable assignee of such stranger, Banks would have breached his duty to the Provisional Assignee who had taken Lloyd's place as beneficiary under the marriage settlement trusts by operation of statute. What is more, Banks could not have successfully defended himself against such liability since he had acquired knowledge of Lloyd's insolvency by his chance reading of the advertisement in the *Hereford Journal*. Even if such knowledge were taken to have been acquired independently of the Provisional Assignee, that did not matter, for the availability of the *Cothay* v. *Sydenham* defence did not depend on how such knowledge was acquired.

We may therefore see that *Lloyd* v. *Banks* was ultimately a decision where the court held that Banks had been justified in refusing to pay the annuity arising under the marriage settlement trusts to Lloyd. That was why the administration suit against Banks failed. That being the case, it was a misstep for Buckley J in *Re Dallas*[103] to have taken *Lloyd* v. *Banks* to have applied and/or developed the 'rule' in *Dearle* v. *Hall* so that the priority conferred by a later assignee by giving notice might be defeated if the obligor had somehow acquired knowledge of the prior assignment, even if the prior assignee had not given (or caused to be given) any notice. It follows, also, that the 'rule' in *Dearle* v. *Hall* is *not* disapplied in such circumstances, and suggestions in the secondary literature that it is should be reconsidered.

---

[100] (1843) 2 Y & C C C 91.
[101] (1880) 16 Ch D 178.
[102] Underhill & Hayton (2016), para. 50.1, p. 840. Alternatively, see Lewin (2015), para. 26-089. The trustee's liability to persons taking through 'the beneficiary who appears on the face of the settlement' may, possibly, share the same root as the equitable wrong of dishonest assistance. That wrong is discussed in Chapter 11.
[103] [1940] 2 Ch 385, 399.

## F  *Refuting the Notion that Notice of an Equitable Assignment Effects a Unilateral Change of the Obligor's Obligee*

In this section, the theory that notice of an equitable assignment causes a unilateral change to the obligation of the obligor by substituting the assignee in place of the assignor as the obligee to whom the obligation is owed will be further scrutinized. It will demonstrate that certain aspects and applications of the 'rule' in *Dearle v. Hall* are inconsistent with such an explanation of the effects of notice.

As has been explained in the preceding section, the 'rule' in *Dearle v. Hall* as restated and rehabilitated is not an unruly, unprincipled exception to the *qui prior est tempore potior est jure* principle. On the conteary, it is a normatively justified and entirely principled working out of the full *qui prior est tempore potior est jure* principle set out in *Rice v. Rice*.

As noted at the beginning of this chapter, several aspects of the operation of the 'rule' in *Dearle v. Hall* render the supposition that notice of an equitable assignment of a chose in action leads to the substitution of the assignee in place of the assignor as obligee to whom the equitable obligor is duty-bound to be untenable. This subsection will review three particular aspects of the operation of the 'rule' in *Dearle v. Hall*, to further show how its operation is incompatible with the proposition that notice has such substitutive effects. Admittedly, some of the cases which have discussed these effects have been cases of equitable assignments of equitable choses. However, since the 'rule' in *Dearle v. Hall* applies to both equitable assignments of equitable and legal choses in action alike, there would appear to be no principled reason to restrict these effects to cases of equitable assignments of equitable choses and not to equitable assignments of legal choses.

The 'rule' in *Dearle v. Hall* refutes the theory that notice of an equitable assignment has substitutive effects, whether the chose assigned be equitable or legal, for the following reasons. First, the limitation of the 'rule' in *Dearle v. Hall* to grant priority only to the claims of equitable assignees who had given value suggests that notice cannot have such substitutive effects. Second, the caselaw dealing with the effect of notice on one of a number of multiple obligors who are jointly duty-bound to the obligee/assignor also suggests that notice does not have the substitutive effects claimed for it. Third, if notice had the substitutive effects claimed for it, the cases could not have recognized that the 'rule' in *Dearle v. Hall* could give rise to a circularity problem. The fact that the cases have done so, and have had to propose solutions to such problem, suggests, therefore, that so far as the courts are concerned, notice does *not* have such substitutive effects. Each of these observations will be explored in the following subsections.

## (i)   Value

It is clear that the 'rule' in *Dearle* v. *Hall* only grants priority to the claim of a subsequent assignor who had given value. As Chadwick J said in *United Bank of Kuwait* v. *Sahib*:[104] 'The rule in *Dearle* v. *Hall* . . . did not assist a subsequent assignee . . . who was a volunteer. There could be no question of a volunteer being exposed to the risk of fraud when taking an assignment or charge for which he gave no value.'

As has been explained above,[105] the underlying reason for the rule in *Dearle* v. *Hall* is that by giving notice to the obligor to the chose assigned, the assignee will have acquired for himself a better equity than a competing assignee who had not done so at all, or who had done so more dilatorily. By giving notice, such assignee would have created conditions in which a subsequent assignee considering whether to give value in exchange for an assignment on the same chose some prospect of discovery of the prior interest. Accordingly, as between competing assignees who had both given value for their respective assignments, but where one assignee had given notice and the other had not (or had yet to do so), since their equities would *not*, in consequence, be equal, the usual rule of priority in equity, namely the *qui prior est tempore potior est jure* or 'first in time prevails', principle will not be applicable.

If, however, notice had substitutive effects such that upon receipt of such notice, the assignee whose assignment had been notified would be substituted in place of the obligee/assignor as the party to whom the obligor was duty-bound, and 'priority' over the claims of a prior assignee but who had yet to give notice, was gained on such substitutive grounds it is unclear why such effects should be limited only to a subsequent assignee who had given value. To put it another way, if notice of an equitable assignment did have substitutive effects, one would expect that 'priority' would be accorded to any assignee who had given notice, first, regardless as to whether or not such assignee had given value. The caselaw that limits the rule in *Dearle* v. *Hall* in this way therefore strongly suggests that notice cannot have such substitutive effects, for if it did, a

---

[104]   [1997] Ch 107, 119–20.
[105]   Above, Section C.

subsequent assignee of an equitable or legal chose who gave notice to the equitable obligor ahead of a prior assignee would be substituted in place of the obligee/assignor even if the subsequent assignment had been merely voluntary. It would not, accordingly, be possible to discriminate against such volunteer assignees, as the rule in *Dearle* v. *Hall* certainly does, and for the reasons explained above.

### (ii)    Notice to Multiple Joint Obligors

The application of the 'rule' in *Dearle* v. *Hall* where there are multiple joint obligors to the chose assigned also refutes the proposition that notice of assignment has the effect of substituting the assignee who had given such notice in place of the assignor as obligee to the chose assigned. To show this, we may consider Example 10.4.

---

**EXAMPLE 10.4**

Suppose $T_1$, $T_2$ and $T_3$ jointly (but not severally) hold the legal title to 10,000 BCL shares on trust for A. A equitably assigns the benefit of her interest in $T_1$'s, $T_2$'s and $T_3$'s jointly held legal title in the shares to $C_1$ for value. $C_1$ then gives $T_1$ notice of the assignment. $T_1$ plans to inform $T_2$ and $T_3$ of the assignment to $C_1$, but he dies before doing so. The legal title in the shares is thereafter held jointly by $T_2$ and $T_3$ as surviving trustees.

A then executes a deed of assignment, purporting to assign her equitable interest in the legal title in the shares now held by $T_2$ and $T_3$ to $C_2$ for value, after $C_2$ had made inquiries of $T_2$ and $T_3$ as to whether they knew of any prior assignments or encumbrances of the same. $T_2$ and $T_3$ had replied that they knew of no prior assignments or encumbrances, following which $C_2$ paid A £5,000 in exchange for the assignment to him. $C_2$ then gave notice to $T_2$ and $T_3$ of this assignment.

Much later, $C_1$ informs $T_2$ and $T_3$ of the prior assignment made by A.

---

If the notice given by $C_1$ to $T_1$ had the effect of unilaterally changing the obligation owed by $T_1$, one might think that $T_1$ would thereafter hold the legal title to the shares for $C_1$'s benefit, and not at all for A (A would have 'dropped out'). If so, since $T_1$ held such legal title in the shares *jointly* with $T_2$ and $T_3$, their *jointly owed* duty would also have been changed.

Accordingly, even though $T_1$ had died without informing $T_2$ or $T_3$ of the assignment to $C_1$, it would seem they would be bound to $C_1$ from the time of notice to $T_1$, even though they had remained ignorant of it until after notice of $C_2$'s assignment had been effected. Consequently, if notice of assignment had the effect of unilaterally changing the *joint* duty of $T_1$, $T_2$ and $T_3$, it would seem to follow that the assignment to $C_2$ would be a nullity, as $T_2$ and $T_3$ would not have owed any duty to A of which A might equitably assign to anyone.

But that is not the law. In *Meux* v. *Bell*, Wigram V-C held as follows:[106]

> In *Smith* v. *Smith* the Court of Exchequer decided that notice to one trustee was sufficient, at least so long as that trustee lived, and the circumstances of the case remained unaltered. The reason why notice to one was held sufficient was because nothing less than inquiry of all the trustees would satisfy a prudent inquirer. ... [I]n the altered circumstances which the death of the trustee, who alone had notice, would have introduced, inquiry of all the existing trustees would not have led the inquirer to a knowledge of the previous incumbrance, and the reasoning of the court in *Smith* v. *Smith* would no longer apply. *Timson* v. *Ramsbottom* supports this reasoning, and leaves *Smith* v. *Smith* untouched. Lord Langdale did not there decide that, if the trustee or executor, who in that case had notice, had been living at the time when the second incumbrancer gave notice of his incumbrance, the notice which that trustee or executor had would not, in such circumstances, have been sufficient. He decided only that there was no sufficient notice of the first incumbrance at the time when notice of the second incumbrance was given; and undoubtedly, at that time there was no sufficient notice of the prior incumbrance, for inquiry of all the then existing trustees would have been unavailing. ... In *Smith* v. *Smith* inquiry would, in the circumstances of that case, have led to a knowledge of the prior incumbrance, and the notice was therefore, properly held sufficient. In *Timson* v. *Ramsbottom* inquiry would not have led to a knowledge of the prior incumbrance, and the notice was properly held to be insufficient. I entirely concur in the principle of both those decisions.

The above analysis of *Smith* v. *Smith*[107] and *Timson* v. *Ramsbottom*[108] was then explicitly approved by Lord Herschell LC (with whom Lord Hannen agreed) in *Ward* v. *Duncombe*.[109]

Applying the principles set out in *Meux* v. *Bell* to the facts in Example 10.4, we have the following. Because the assignment to $C_2$ of A's equitable interest in the BCL shares was effected *after* $T_1$'s death, and $T_1$ had died before informing $T_2$ or $T_3$ of the assignment to $C_1$, assuming $T_2$ or $T_3$ had not been given notice of that earlier assignment by other means, it would not have been possible for $C_2$ to have discovered the

---

[106]  (1841) 1 Hare 73, 96–8.
[107]  (1833) 2 C & M 231.
[108]  (1837) 2 Keen 35. *Timson* was followed in *Re Phillips Trusts* [1903] 1 Ch 193.
[109]  [1893] AC 369, 381–2; although Lord Macnaghten expressed some doubt (at 394–5) as to the authoritativeness of *Timson* v. *Ramsbottom*.

prior assignment in favour of $C_1$ even if he had (as prudence would have required him) made inquiries of all extant trustees at the time of the assignment to him as to their knowledge of any prior assignments or incumbrances, assuming they had responded to his inquiries. Therefore, $C_2$ could not be treated as if he had taken A's assignment subject to the prior assignment to $C_1$ since there was no possibility of his discovering it, even if he had made inquiries of all the extant trustees at that point in time. Accordingly, not only would $C_2$'s claim as assignee be perfectly valid, it would be unencumbered by $C_1$'s prior claim and the rule in *Dearle* v. *Hall* would not apply for $C_2$'s benefit.

As explained above, the rationale for the rule in *Dearle* v. *Hall* rests, most probably, in this: by giving notice to the obligor, an assignee takes steps to publicize his interest so as to give others who might subsequently be interested in acquiring an interest in the same subject matter as had been assigned to the assignee some opportunity to discover such prior assignment, and so make an informed decision whether or not to proceed. Admittedly, this is an imperfect form of publicity, as the obligor is under no obligation to entertain or respond to any queries made of him by parties wondering whether to deal with the obligee by way of an assignment.[110] But there is at least a possibility that the obligor might cooperate: if the obligor had had no notice at all, there would be no such possibility. Hence, as Lord Lyndhurst LC held in *Foster* v. *Cockerell*, if the rule in *Dearle* v. *Hall* were otherwise:[111]

> it would enable a *cestui que trust* to commit a fraud, by enabling him to
> assign his interest, first to one, and then to a second incumbrancer, and
> perhaps, indeed to a great many more; and these later incumbrancers
> would have no opportunity of ascertaining, by any communication with

---

[110] $T_1$ would be privileged against $C_2$ to disclose the prior incumbrance had $C_2$ made inquiries before taking the assignment from A. In *Low* v. *Bouverie* [1891] 3 Ch 83, 99–100 Lindley LJ (with whom Bowen LJ substantially agreed) said: '[A] person who proposes to buy or lend money on [the beneficial interest of a *cestui que trust*] has no greater rights than the *cestui que trust* himself. There is no trust or other relation between a trustee and a stranger about to deal with a *cestui que trust*, and although probably such a person in making inquiries may be regarded as authorized by the *cestui que trust* to make them, this view of the stranger's position will not give him a right to information which the *cestui que trust* himself is not entitled to demand. The trustee, therefore, is ... under no obligation to answer such an inquiry. He can refer the person making it to the *cestui que trust* himself.' See also *Hallows* v. *Lloyd* (1888) 39 Ch D 686; *Ward* v. *Duncombe* (n. 12), 394 (Lord Macnaghten). However, trustees holding legal title to realty on trust are not so privileged: LPA1925, s. 137(9).

[111] (1835) 3 Cl & F 457, 475–6.

the trustees, whether or not there had been a prior assignment of the interest, on the security of which they were relying for provision of their claims.

Thus, where two assignees take assignments over the same chose in action without taking such steps to publicize their respective assignments, each is as bad as the other in their lack of concern for others who might subsequently deal with the assignor on the basis of preconceptions formed in ignorance of such assignments. And so, '[a]s between persons having only equitable interests, if their equities are in *all other respects* equal, priority of time gives the better equity; or *qui prior est tempore potior est jure*'.[112]

Even so, where one assignee has given notice (thus giving others who might apply to the obligor/debtor for information the possibility of making more informed decisions – if the obligor/debtor were to answer – as such assignee might himself have hoped to enjoy) whereas the other has not (or has yet to do so), the equities between these two assignees would *not* be equal. The assignee who had given notice will have acted over and beyond what he might have been duty-bound to do, and so would have acquired a better equity as compared with the other assignee. Consequently, in Example 10.4, notwithstanding that $T_2$ and $T_3$ would have had actual knowledge of $C_1$'s prior interest by 2 February 2016, payment of sums accruing due under the terms of the trust to $C_2$ thereafter in accordance with the rule in *Dearle* v. *Hall* would *not* be taken to be a wrongful act in equity.[113]

As explained in *Meux* v. *Bell* and *Ward* v. *Duncombe*, the cases of *Smith* v. *Smith* and *Timson* v. *Ramsbottom* tell us that the rule in *Dearle* v. *Hall* does not operate on the basis that notice of an equitable assignment of an equitable chose in action effects a unilateral change in the obligation owed by the obligor(s) to that equitable chose, such that they are no longer duty-bound to the original assignor-obligee, but are duty-bound, instead, to the assignee of whom they had received notice.[114]

---

[112] *Rice* v. *Rice* (1854) 2 Drew 73, 78.

[113] *Quaere* whether notice acquired by the obligor independently of the assignee ought to give rise to a similar equity. It was assumed in *Lloyd* v. *Banks* (1868) LR 3 Ch App 488 that it would. However, see discussion in Section E.

[114] The position in Scotland in respect of assignation is different. Intimation of assignation has the effect of extinguishing the entitlement of the assignor (or 'cedent', as the party making the assignation is often termed in Scots law): 'An assignation of a bond without intimation, is in like manner but one step to the transmission of a *jus crediti*, The cedent

But suppose all the extant trustees had been given notice in Example 10.4. Might each of their obligations have been unilaterally varied given such notice? Again, this is doubtful.

In *Re Wasdale*,[115] trustees of a trust fund were given notice of an assignment of a reversionary interest in that fund. They all subsequently retired, and new trustees were appointed in their place. Following the retirement of the original trustees, a subsequent assignment of the same reversionary interest was effected, and notice of the same was given to the new trustees. When the reversion fell in, both the first and second assignees applied for the reversion to be paid to them. In these circumstances, Stirling J held that the first in time rule would apply, and that the first assignees were to be paid the reversion in priority to the second assignees.

If the earlier notice to all of the original trustees had the effect of changing their duties, such that they were no longer duty-bound to the original beneficiaries under the terms of the trust, but were instead duty-bound to the first assignee, and this change was binding and effective in respect of the trustees who had knowledge of the assignment, it is difficult to explain why the *replacement* trustees might be so bound by a 'change' of which they had no knowledge at all. So the proposition that the change only affects such trustees who know about the assignment is also false. Indeed, if that were the rule, an unseemly and disorderly state of affairs would result. As Lord Mcnaghten observed in *Ward v. Duncombe*:[116] 'Certainly, I can imagine nothing more inconvenient than that it should be possible to have a scramble for priorities on the appointment of new trustees. Nothing, I think, would be less likely to conduce to the security of equitable titles.'

Although these were cases involving equitable assignments of equitable choses in action arising out of a trust, so far as they were resolved in reliance on the 'rule' in *Dearle* v. *Hall*, and so far as that 'rule' applies also to cases involving equitable assignments of legal choses in action, there

---

is not divested before intimation. The debt may be arrested by his creditor, and therefore not by the creditor of the assignee. After intimation, the debt is only arrestable by the creditor of the assignee': *Competing Creditors of Benjedward* (1753) (Court of Session) William Maxwell Morison, *The Decisions of the Court of Session . . . in the form of a dictionary*, Vol. I - II (Edinburgh: Archibald Constable and Company, 1811), 743, at 744; and intimation that an interest in funds held by a body of trustees is given to one of that number would be sufficient to have such effect: *Jameson v. Sharp* (1887) 14 R 643. But for doubts as to the breadth of *Jameson v. Sharp*, see Anderson (2008), para 6–45.

[115] [1899] 1 Ch 163.

[116] *Ward* v. *Duncombe* (n. 12), 395. Lord Herschell LC (with whom Lord Hannen agreed) came to much the same conclusion (at 382).

seems to be no reason why the same results would not follow had, in either *Meux* v. *Bell* or *Re Wasdale*, the chose in question had been legal rather than equitable. There is nothing in either case to suggest that the result would have been different had the chose been legal. If so, these cases suggest that the theory that notice of an equitable assignment has substitutive transfer effects cannot be true.

### (iii)   Circular Priority Problems

Caselaw has also recognized that the operation of the rule in *Dearle* v. *Hall* can lead to potential problems in terms of circularity of priority. In this subsection, it will be shown that the very existence of such circularity problems also demonstrates that notice of an equitable assignment cannot have the effect of substituting the assignee in place of the assignor as obligee to the chose assigned: if it did, such circularity problems would not arise.

Two English cases are often cited as illustrations of the circularity that may arise under the rule in *Dearle* v. *Hall*, namely *Re Wyatt*,[117] and *Re Weniger's Policy*.[118]

*Re Wyatt* was not, itself, a case involving a circularity problem. However, in the course of submissions, counsel put forward a hypothetical example which set up a circularity problem in an attempt to persuade the Court of Appeal to accept his arguments. As recounted by Lindley LJ in the Court of Appeal:[119]

> An ingenious puzzle was propounded by Mr Ford in the course of his able reply to induce us to depart from the principle which we have stated. Suppose, he said, there are two trustees of the fund, A and B. The first incumbrancer gives notice of his charge to A only; the second gives notice of his charge to A and B; then A dies, and a third incumbrance is created, of which notice is given to the surviving trustee B. Here, it is said, that the third incumbrance will stand after the second because B had notice of the second incumbrance; but he will also stand before the first, for B was unaffected by any notice of that incumbrance. The solution of the difficulty is probably to be found in the view that the third incumbrancer is subrogated to the rights of the first to the extent of his charge, and to that extent, and to that extent only, can take in priority of the second

---

[117] [1892] 1 Ch 188; aff'd sub nom *Ward* v. *Duncombe* (n. 12).
[118] [1910] 2 Ch 291.
[119] *Re Wyatt* (n. 117), 208–9. The judgment had been drawn up by Fry LJ, but was read out by Lindley LJ.

incumbrancer, by which the latter sustains no injury, but that as to any excess of the amount claimed by the third incumbrancer, he comes in after the second, so that the fund would be distributed as follows: First, to the third incubrancer, to the extent of the claim of the first. Secondly, to the second incumbrancer. Thirdly, to the third incumbrancer to the extent to which he might remain unpaid after the money he had received whilst standing in the shoes of the first incumbrancer.

The circularity problem in *Re Weniger's Policy* was, however, no mere speculation by counsel. In that case, Weniger had taken out an endowment policy with the Royal Insurance Company ('Royal'). He created a number of encumbrances on the policy (described in the report as 'charges' but referred to in the headnote as 'mortgages' – so it would seem that they may have been charges by way of mortgage, rather than charges by way of hypothecation) – as security for various advances he procured from a number of lenders. A circularity problem, however, arose in relation to three of lenders.

On 14 July 1905, Weniger mortgaged the benefit of his policy with Royal to Kapp. Next, on 27 November 1905, he mortgaged the benefit of his policy with Royal to the Indo-European Telegraph Company (IETC). Finally, on 25 May 1906, he mortgaged the benefit of his policy to Ramsay. Weniger then became financially embarassed, leading to his lenders rushing to give notice of their assignments. In particular, of these three lenders, Ramsay gave notice first on 29 August 1906; followed by Kapp, who gave notice on 31 August 1906; and lastly by IETC, which gave notice on 10 September 1906.

The circularity problem arose because when Ramsay gave notice to Royal of the assignment to him, although he was ignorant of the encumbrance in favour of Kapp, the facts were such that he was affixed with constructive knowledge of the encumbrance in favour of IETC when he took his assignment from Weniger. Therefore, although Ramsay could invoke the rule in *Dearle* v. *Hall* to assert priority over Kapp (Ramsay's notice being prior in time), Ramsay could *not* invoke that rule as against IETC. Kapp, however, could invoke the rule in *Dearle* v. *Hall* to assert priority over IETC, having neither actual nor constructive knowledge of the encumbrance in its favour when he took the assignment from Weniger. Hence Ramsay would have priority over Kapp; Kapp would have priority over IETC; but Ramsay could not have priority over IETC.

Parker J's solution to this circularity problem was similar to that which the Court of Appeal had surmised in *Re Wyatt*, holding that the claims were to be ranked in the order of Kapp, then IETC, then Ramsay, and then to subrogate Ramsay to Kapp's entitlements.[120]

It is unimportant for present purposes to examine whether these solutions to the circularity problem were correctly arrived at, though one might query why the courts resorted to ranking the competing claims by their order of creation first, before applying the subrogation principle.[121] What *is* significant is that in both these cases, the courts recognized that application of the rule in *Dearle* v. *Hall* would lead to a circularity problem. It follows that these decisions also refute the supposition that notice of an equitable assignment would lead to the substitution of the assignor in place of the assignee. For if that were the case, no priority circularity problem could have arisen.

For example, on the facts in *Re Weniger's Policy*, if the notice of the assignment to Ramsay had the effect of substituting Ramsay in place of Weniger as obligee to the policy to whom the sums owed under the policy were due, Kapp's notice to Royal would have been completely ineffectual so far as such notice would only go so far as to effect a substitution of Kapp in place of Weniger. And the same would be true of IETC's notice to Royal. Once Weniger was replaced by Ramsay as obligee to the chose assigned, Kapp's (or IETC's) entitlement to take Weniger's place would be rendered otiose. Accordingly, if this were indeed the effect of notice, the circularity problem would never arise as the *only* obligee to whom Royal was obligated would be Ramsay.

Crucially, for present purposes, we may note that although *Re Weniger's Policy* was concerned with the equitable assignment of legal choses in action arising from contracts of insurance, the hypothetical situation posited in *Re Wyatt* concerned the equitable assignment of *equitable* choses arising from a trust. So far as the circularity problem was recognized to arise in connection with the latter by reason of the operation of the 'rule' in *Dearle* v. *Hall*, it must follow, therefore, that such operation precludes the possibility that notice of an equitable

---

[120] *Re Weniger's Policy* [1910] 2 Ch 291, 296–7.

[121] As Gillooly noted, '[i]n neither case did the court explain why that ranking [in order of creation] should be used. Perhaps we may speculate that it was used as a last resort because the priority rule "cupboard" was otherwise bare. But of course the employment of that rule disregards the policy consideration that underlie the rule in *Dearle* v. *Hall* itself': Michael Gillooly, *Securities over Personalty* (Sydney: Federation Press, 1994), p. 111. An alternative solution is proposed in W. A. Lee, 'An Insoluble Problem of Mortgagees' Priorities' (1968) 32 *Conveyancer and Property Lawyer* 325, 329–36.

assignment of an equitable chose will substitute the assignee in place of the assignor/obligee.

To conclude, the three instances above derived from the caselaw on the application of the rule in *Dearle* v. *Hall* all refute the proposition that notice of an equitable assignment substitutes the assignee in place of the assignor. Suggestions that notice has such effect as a matter of English law cannot, therefore, be correct.

# 11

# Knowledge of Assignment: Substantive Effects in Equity between Obligor and Assignor

In addition to animating the 'rule' in *Dearle* v. *Hall*, the giving of notice introduces a new head of (potential) equitable liability as between the obligor and an equitable assignee.[1] That is to say, as a matter of substantive equitable principle, should an obligor to a legal or equitable chose in action act in such a way as would assist the assignor in breaching her equitable duties to her assignee arising by reason of the equitable assignment, despite having actual or constructive knowledge of those duties, the obligor would have committed the equitable wrong of what we now term 'dishonest assistance'.

This chapter will explain how an obligor may become so liable.

## A    Introduction

Where A lends B a sum of money, unless otherwise provided for, B would be duty-bound to A to do Φ, where 'Φ' means 'the act of repaying A the loan'. So far as C, a stranger to the loan, was concerned, B would not be duty-bound to C to do Φ. On the contrary: B would be privileged with regard to C to do Φ.

Now, if A equitably assigned the benefit of such loan contract to C, at common law, B would still be duty-bound to A to do Φ, notwithstanding such assignment and notice thereof. At the same time, at common law,

---

[1] Cf. *Deposit Protection Board* v. *Dalia* [1994] 2 AC 367, 386F (Russell LJ, with whom Sir Michael Fox agreed), rejecting Simon Brown LJ's careful analysis at 381B that, '[i]n the case of an equitable assignment [of a legal chose in action], the assignor remains the legal owner of the relevant chose (here the part of the debt assigned) whilst the assignee becomes entitled to the equitable interest in it – the "creditor in equity"'. The point was not addressed on appeal to the House of Lords. However, the majority's position in the Court of Appeal has been endorsed in Chitty (2015), para. 19-021, and at fn. 85, it is suggested that Simon Brown LJ's reasoning on the point was incorrect.

B would still be privileged as against C to do Φ, assignment and notice thereof notwithstanding. It was only a court of *equity* which might have a different view, recognizing and enforcing a (distinct) 'direct obligation' arising between the obligor and the assignee.[2]

Understanding this has, however, been obscured. To begin with, and despite contrary assertions,[3] when a chose in action such as a common law debt is equitably assigned, and the debtor comes to know of it, if the debtor performs to his obligee (i.e. his creditor) by tendering payment to his obligee, the acceptance of such tender by the obligee *does* discharge the debt at law. This was recognized by Turner LJ in *Stocks* v. *Dobson*, which was an appeal to the Court of Appeal in Chancery:[4]

> The debtor is liable, at law, to the assignor of the debt, and at law must pay the assignor if the assignor sues in respect of it. If so, it follows that he may pay without suit. The payment of the debtor to the assignor discharges the debt at law. The assignee has no legal right and can only sue in the assignor's name. How can he sue if the debt has been paid?
>
> If a Court of Equity laid down the rule that the debtor is a trustee for the assignee, without having any notice of the assignment, it would be impossible for a debtor safely to pay a debt to his creditor. The law of the Court [of Equity] has therefore required notice to be given to the debtor of the assignment, in order to perfect the title of the assignee.

Notice, once given, leads to the debtor acquiring knowledge of the fact of assignment as well as the constraints on the assignor's privilege to invoke her entitlements against the debtor: the debtor would be deemed to know that the assignor would now be duty-bound to the assignee not to invoke her entitlements without regard for the assignee's interests. And obviously, such notice may be given by the assignee, or any person whom the assignee expressly or implicitly authorizes to do so.[5]

That said, knowledge of the fact of assignment may be obtained through other sources, independent of the assignee.[6] But howsoever acquired, knowledge of the assignment allows a court (acting within its

---

[2] See also *Row* v. *Dawson* (1749) 1 Ves Sen 331, 333 (Lord Hardwicke LC).

[3] See references below at nn. 13–17.

[4] (1853) 4 De G M & G 11, 15–16.

[5] E.g. assignors expressly or implicitly authorized by assignees to give notice of assignment.

[6] As in *Lloyd* v. *Banks* (1868) LR 3 Ch App 488, where knowledge of prior insolvency proceedings against the assignor was acquired through the chance reading of a newspaper which carried an advertisement providing notification of the same.

equitable jurisdiction) to recognize and enforce a *further* equitable liability above and beyond the operation of the 'rule' in *Dearle* v. *Hall.*[7]

Professor Lionel Smith noted: 'It is wrong to get in the way of the performance of other people's obligations. Every system goes that far; they only differ on how generously to protect those who are owed obligations against interference by third parties.'[8] This general duty certainly arises at common law.[9] But an analogous wrong also exists in equity.

When the obligor to a chose in action acquires knowledge that the chose has been equitably assigned by the obligee/assignor, the obligor comes under an equitable duty to the assignee not to act with a dishonest state of mind so as to assist the obligee/assignor in breaching her equitable duties to the assignee. Breach of such duty by the obligee/assignor with the obligor's dishonest assistance would then render the obligor *personally* liable to the assignee for having committed the equitable wrong of what we now term 'dishonest assistance'.[10] And, although this form of equitable liability was formally made distinct from the equitable wrong of 'knowing receipt' in *Barnes* v. *Addy* in 1874,[11] the conception that it is wrong to interfere with the due performance of a trustee's duties by dishonestly assisting in their breach predates that case.[12]

---

[7] Which was discussed in Chapter 10.
[8] L. D. Smith, 'Philosophical Foundations of Proprietary Remedies' in Robert Chambers, Charles Mitchell and J. E. Penner (eds.), *Philosophical Foundations of the Law of Unjust Enrichment* (Oxford: Oxford University Press, 2009), p. 292.
[9] For example, in the form of the tort of inducement of breach of contract.
[10] Alternatively, there may be the wrong of 'inconsistent dealing with trust property': Charles Harpum, 'The Stranger as Constructive Trustee: Part 1' (1986) 102 LQR 114, 138–42.
[11] (1874) LR 9 Ch App 244. It may be noted that Lord Selborne LC did not, in his judgment in *Barnes* v. *Addy*, purport to set out any new principles of law.
[12] See e.g. *Andrews* v. *Bousfield* (1847) 10 Beav 511, where it was recognized that where a trustee (T) who holds trust funds for the benefit of trust beneficiaries (C) lends those funds in accordance with the terms of the trust to a borrower (B), if B repays the loan by tendering the appropriate sum of money to T in the knowledge that T was not, on the terms of the trust, empowered to accept payment, if T were to subsequently abscond with the sums received from B such that the trust fund is depleted by that amount, B will be held to be personally liable in equity to the trust beneficiaries to pay such sums to make good the depletion to the trust fund. For other examples, see *Attorney-General* v. *Corporation of Leicester* (1844) 7 Beav 176; *Pritchard* v. *Langher* (1690) 2 Vern 197; and *Penn* v. *Browne* (1697) 2 Freem 215.

Tolhurst,[13] Liew,[14] and works such as *Salinger on Factoring*,[15] *The Law of Security and Title-Based Financing*[16] and *Treitel on Contract*,[17] appear to suggest that payment to the creditor following notice of equitable assignment of the debt does not discharge the debt at common law.[18] But with respect, none of these views addresses the points made in this chapter and, more broadly, in this book. In particular, none of them addresses the question how an equitable doctrine like equitable assignment can change a common law obligation beyond merely asserting/assuming that it does. But perhaps that is not what is happening, at all?

In the case of a common law debt, the debtor who tenders payment to his creditor, despite knowing of the creditor's having equitably assigned the benefit of the debt to an assignee, does no wrong at common law to the creditor. Looked at in isolation, since this is precisely what the debtor had undertaken to the creditor that he would do, what he does is precisely *right* (in the sense of being correct, or justified). However, we cannot deny that the debtor will have contributed to the destruction of the equitable interest which the assignee has in the debt: his tender of payment, and its acceptance by the creditor-assignor, would have discharged (i.e. destroyed) the debt, the chose in action in which the assignee had an interest.

Suppose that, having accepting the tender of payment from the debtor, the creditor had spent the monies received on a luxury holiday for herself. If the creditor had been authorized by the terms of the assignment to accept such payment on behalf of the assignee, by virtue of the doctrine of overreaching,[19] the monies received by the assignee would have been subjected to the same bare trust as underpinned the equitable assignment of the chose in action. However, if the creditor had not been so authorized, then the monies received by the assignee (being the

---

[13] Tolhurst (2016), para. 8.06, 394; and also para. 4.20, 78; para. 4.24, 85. The point is repeated in Tolhurst & Carter (2014), p. 430.

[14] Liew (2018), para. 3-50.

[15] Salinger (2017), para. 8.21.

[16] H. G. Beale et al., *The Law of Security and Title-Based Financing* (3rd edn, Oxford: Oxford University Press, 2018), para. 7.99.

[17] Peel (2015), para. 15-022.

[18] See also, Chitty (2018), para. 19-021, especially text at fn. 86.

[19] On the doctrine of overreaching as applied in the main text, see David Fox, 'Overreaching' in Peter Birks and Arianna Pretto-Sakmann (eds.), *Breach of Trust* (Oxford: Hart, 2002), discussing the issue in the context of trusts. It is suggested that the same analysis applies, *mutatis mutandis*, in connection with equitable assignment given that part of its operation rests on the mechanism of a bare trust.

traceable substitute of the chose in action which had been assigned) would be subject to a bare constructive trust for the benefit of the assignee.[20] In neither case, however, would the creditor have been authorized to spend the monies received on a luxury holiday for herself: that would be a breach of either the bare trust over the funds by reason of overreaching (if the acceptance of payment was authorized) or the bare constructive trust as would be imposed over the monies (if the acceptance of payment was unauthorized).

In either case, *but for* such tender of payment, the opportunity for the assignee to expend the monies in question in a manner which amounted to a breach of her duties to her assignee would not have arisen. By so paying, the debtor would have *assisted* in the commission of that breach of duty. And if such assistance was accompanied by the requisite *knowledge* that the creditor was not authorized to accept such payment, then the debtor would have committed a breach of the equitable wrong of dishonest assistance.[21]

The analysis is not significantly different where the chose assigned is equitable rather than legal.

---

[20] It now seems relatively clear that as a matter of English law, sums tendered by a debtor to a creditor who had equitably assigned the benefit of the debt to an assignee will be held by the creditor-assignor as constructive trustee for the benefit of the assignee: *Barclays Bank Plc* v. *Willowbrook International Ltd and Anor* [1987] 1 FTLR 386, 391. For older authority, see *Bence* v. *Shearman* [1898] 2 Ch 582, 587 and 588 *per* Chitty LJ. See also the discussion of *Gorringe* v. *Irwell India Rubber and Gutta Percha Works* in Tham (2010), at text to fn. 199. That such a constructive trust will be imposed on the creditor over the sums received has also been accepted by other commentators: see e.g. Louise Gullifer, 'Should Clauses Prohibiting Assignment Be Overriden by Statute' (2015) 4 *Pennsylvania State Journal of Law and International Affairs* 47, 51; Turner (2018), p. 536, both of whom also rely on the authority of *Barclays Bank Plc* v. *Willowbrook International*.

[21] In consequence, where the creditor *had* been authorized by the assignee to accept payment on the assignee's behalf, and if the creditor had not expended the monies received in a manner which the overreached trust would not permit, the creditor would not have committed any breach of her duties to her assignee. In such a case, there would be no breach of duty for the debtor to assist. Hence, even if the debtor had merely known of the fact of assignment, but had not known that the assignee had authorized the creditor to accept payments on her behalf, no equitable wrong of dishonest assistance would have been committed by the debtor. As will be explained in this chapter, the degree of moral culpability required for a finding of 'dishonesty' is quite slight (see below, at Section E). Even so, where the debtor was aware that the creditor had been authorized by her assignee to accept payments on her behalf, but was ignorant of the creditor's plans to expend the monies received in a manner which would be in breach of her duties to her assignee, on the analysis in this chapter, such debtor would not have the requisite degree of knowledge as to render him liable to the assignee for dishonest assistance, even if the debtor had been negligent in failing to make further inquiries (see below, at Section F).

First, as explained in Chapter 3, in Sections F and G, notice cannot unilaterally change what an obligor (legal or equitable) is duty-bound to do in order to discharge his obligation. If that is so, then the mere acquisition of knowledge of such assignment, independently of notice by (or by the will of) the assignee, cannot have such effect either.

Second, as mentioned in Chapter 10, where a trustee of an express trust is obligated under the terms of that trust to pay an annuity out of the fund to a beneficiary, should the trustee pay the annuity to that beneficiary despite knowing that the beneficiary had equitably assigned her entitlement to an assignee, no term of the express trust will have been breached since it is precisely what the settlor had specified was to be done. But still, such tender to the beneficiary-assignor (and its acceptance by the beneficiary-assignor) would have extinguished the assignee's equitable interest in the chose that had been assigned. Such chose would be 'in action' no longer, as it would have been made a chose 'in possession' by reason of the tender of payment to, and acceptance by, the beneficiary-assignor. The trustee would, therefore, have assisted in the destruction of the assignee's interest in the chose in action.

Crucially, he would have assisted with knowledge of the assignee's equitable interest in the same. If so, it should have occurred to the trustee to make reasonable inquiries of the assignee whether the beneficiary-assignor was entitled to accept payments on behalf of her assignee. And had he inquired, he would have discovered that the beneficiary-assignor was *not* so authorized. Consequently, the equitable doctrine of constructive notice would apply, and the trustee would be treated as if he knew that the beneficiary-assignor had not been authorized to accept payments on behalf of the assignee, and so was acting in breach of her duties to her assignee to preserve the equitable chose in action until such time as the assignee instructed her to reduce that chose in action into possession.

This very point is illustrated in *Re Neil.*[22]

---

[22] (1890) 62 LT 649 (Chan Div). For another example, see *Re Pawson's Settlement* [1917] 1 Ch 541, where Sargant J alluded to the possibility that an express trustee might become *personally* liable to an assignee if he were to make payments to a trust beneficiary in accordance with the terms of the express trust if he had received notice that that beneficiary had assigned her equitable interest to an assignee (though, on the facts, Sargant J declined to hold that such liability was made out as the assignment had been by way of mortgage to secure a loan and the notice had not been accompanied by a request for the sums in question to be paid to the assignee-mortgagee instead of the assignor-mortgagor – see below, n. 87).

In this case an interest arising under a discretionary testamentary trust by which trustees had been granted an absolute and uncontrolled discretion to pay the whole or any part of the income or accumulations of income of the beneficiary's share of the settlor's estate was equitably assigned by the beneficiary. Notwithstanding notice of the assignment (which had been given to their solicitors), the trustees appointed and paid various sums of money to the assignor-beneficiary. Proceedings were then brought by the assignee (successfully) against the trustees, making them liable for these payments.

Holding for the assignee, Kekewich J rejected a contention by counsel for the trustees that the monies paid to the assignor-beneficiary were not beneficially his until they had actually been paid to him. Rather,

> it must be assumed that money paid by the trustees to [the assignor] or to any person in his behalf was his in their irrevocable determination immediately before the payment. [However, a]t that period they [the trustees] had notice or were affected with notice of the assignment. . . . [Consequently, t]he trustees are liable to pay to the plaintiff all moneys which have been paid by them to [the assignor], or to any person on his behalf, since the receipt by the trustees of the notice of the charge.[23]

The dispute in *Re Neil* concerned alleged breaches by the defendant-obligor's duties arising from a testamentary trust: it concerned breaches of equitable obligations. So the common law jurisdiction of the court would not have been engaged.[24] Consequently, Kekewich J's decision could not have involved the bars to pleading of defences which would have been available had the court's common law jurisdiction been in play.[25] It therefore seems likely that *Re Neil* was a case where a distinct *substantive* form of equitable liability was in issue.

Cotton LJ's suggestion in *Tramways Union Co.*[26] that notice 'perfects' the interest of an assignee of an equitable chose arising from a trust, and 'converts' the obligor thereto (being trustee for the assignor) into a trustee for the assignee, should not be read out of context, given the operation of the 'rule' in *Dearle* v. *Hall*.[27] As Lord Macnaghten pointed out in 1893 in *Ward* v. *Duncombe*:[28]

---

[23] *Re Neil* (ibid.), 651.

[24] In contrast with the dispute in *Legh* v. *Legh* (1799) B & P 447.

[25] As to which, see discussion in Chapter 12.

[26] *Société Générale de Paris* v. *Tramways Union Co.* (1884–5) 14 QBD 424; aff'd *Société Générale de Paris* v. *Walker* (1885) 11 App Cas 20 (HL).

[27] See Chapter 10, Section C.

[28] [1893] AC 369, 392 (emphasis added).

[I]t has been said that notice 'converts' the trustee of the fund into a trustee for the person who gives the notice. But that, again, is hardly accurate. The trustee of the fund is trustee for the persons entitled to the fund, whether he knows their names or not. The notice, no doubt, places him under a *direct responsibility to the person who gives the notice.*[29] If he disregards the notice, he does so at his peril. But before notice given he is just as much a trustee for the persons rightfully entitled as he is after he receives the notice, though of course, in the absence of notice, he would be safe in paying away the fund to those who appear by the instrument constituting the trust, or by title properly deduced from them, to be the true owners.

Notice of an equitable assignment of a chose cannot, in itself, lead to the obligor to that chose somehow becoming trustee for the benefit of the assignee on the terms of the express trust if the terms of that express trust did not provide for a suitable power in the assignee to such effect. For example, if the terms of the express trust were that the trust was for the benefit of the settlor's 'eldest son *or his assigns*', the words 'or his assigns' would vest the settlor's eldest son with a power to appoint another in his place. If the eldest son *did* appoint X 'as his assign', then X would become a beneficiary of the trust on the very terms of the express trust – and the relevance of the law on assignment would only be that compliance with its requirements would determine whether or not X was an 'assign' of the eldest son. Consequently, if X was such assign, X would not be a stranger to the trust. Rather, X would be a beneficiary of the trust on its express terms.

By accepting the office of trustee, subject to such power of appointment, the trustee to such express trust would have assented in advance to the possibility that the party to whom he was duty-bound and liable might be the settlor's 'eldest son or his assign'. Yet such substitution of the son's assign in place of the settlor's eldest son as beneficiary to the express trust would *not* be unilateral since the office of trustee may always be disclaimed,[30] and there was no duty on the putative trustee to accept the office as formulated by the settlor in this manner. So in these circumstances, the substitution of the eldest son's assign in place of the assign *would* have been assented to by the trustee in advance so far as he assumed office on these terms in the first place. However, as explained

---

[29] Here, Lord Macnaghten assumed that the notice of assignment would, as it often is, be given to the equitable obligor by the assignee. But notice need not be given by the assignee: it may be given by the assignor, and may even be derived from independent sources (e.g. *Lloyd* v. *Banks* (1868) LR 3 Ch App 488). The 'direct responsibility' generated by receipt of the notice, therefore, is not owed to the party giving the notice, but to the assignee who has been identified as such in the notice.

[30] *Robinson* v. *Pett* (1734) 3 P Wms 249, 251 (Lord Talbot LC).

in Chapter 10, where the terms of the express trust do *not* contain any provisions which, on their true construction, give rise to any such power, such substitutive effects cannot arise at all, and certainly do not arise by reason of the equitable assignment *simpliciter*.

Given the above, Lord Macnaghten's reference in *Ward* v. *Duncombe* to the trustee being placed under a 'direct responsibility' should not be understood as suggesting that the trustee of the fund had 'become' trustee for the assignee after having received notice of the equitable assignment to the assignee such that the assignor's place as trust beneficiary was taken by the assignee. If correct, the corollary would be that, after notice that the benefit of the express trust had been equitably assigned, the assignee would no longer be a stranger to the express trust, whereas the assignor would no longer be a beneficiary of the same. But this would violate the principle that the terms of a trust, once constituted, are also invariable unless powers otherwise had been reserved.

The better reading of Lord Macnaghten's words is this. In general, as Lord Nicholls pointed out in *Royal Brunei Airlines*:[31]

> [Trust b]eneficiaries are entitled to expect that those who become trustees will fulfil their obligations, *They are also entitled to expect, and this is only a short step further, that those who become trustees will be permitted to fulfil their obligations without deliberate intervention from third parties.* They are entitled to expect that third parties will refrain from intentionally intruding in the trustee–beneficiary relationship and thereby hindering a beneficiary from receiving his entitlement in accordance with the terms of the trust instrument.

The same analysis may be applied where a legal chose in action has been equitably assigned. If, say, the debtor to a contract debt received notice that his creditor had equitably assigned the benefit of that debt to an assignee, should the debtor tender payment to the creditor-assignor, that tender, if accepted by the creditor-assignor in cases where the assignee had not authorized such acceptance, could expose the debtor to a liability in equity for having destroyed the subject-matter of the assignee's equitable interest, and cases like *Roberts* v. *Lloyd*,[32] *Jones* v. *Farrell*[33] and *Applin* v. *Cates*[34] are good examples of such equitable liability.

---

[31] *Royal Brunei Airlines Sdn Bhd* v. *Philip Tan Kok Ming* [1995] 2 AC 378, 387B.
[32] (1840) 2 Beav 376.
[33] (1857) 1 De G & J 208.
[34] (1861) 30 LJ Chan 6.

As Professor Stone observed (in connection with equitable assignments of debts where the assignor had also granted the assignee with a
power of attorney to bring actions at law to reduce the debt into
possession, if need be):[35]

> [T]he double liability of the debtor [in *Roberts* v. *Lloyd* and *Jones*
> v. *Farrell*] cannot be predicated on any theory of property which came
> into his hands or legal right which remained with the assignor, but must
> rest on the fact that he, with knowledge of the assignee's right, has so
> acted as to interfere with the equitable protection which a court of equity
> throws about the power of attorney acquired by an assignee.

This chapter proposes that there is no principled reason to restrict
such accessory liability reasoning to cases where such power of attorney
had actually been executed. On the one hand, where an equitable chose in
action had been equitably assigned, as explained in Chapter 7, a court
acting in its equitable jurisdiction would recognize and give effect to the
'agency-effect' which underpins and is entailed by the equitable assignment. On the other, where a common law chose had been equitably
assigned, where no power of attorney had been granted contemporaneously, the assignee could compel the assignor to grant such power of
attorney *ex post facto* by injunction if the need were to arise. Whether the
chose assigned is equitable or legal, the significance of notice of assignment is not that it *changes* the associated equitable or legal obligations, by
substituting the assignee in place of the original obligee. Rather, such
notice is a necessary (though not sufficient) factor which exposes the

---

[35] H. F. Stone, 'The Nature of the Rights of the *Cestui Que Trust*' (1917) 17 *Columbia Law
Review* 467, 485. See also Tham (2010), p. 52, fn. 79; Trukhtanov (2010), p. 556, fn. 49. For
example, where B owes a debt of £10,000 to A, if B pays £10,000 in cash to A despite
knowing that A had previously equitably assigned the benefit of the debt to C, as explained
above (at text to n. 20), if A had not been authorized by C to accept such tender of
payment, A would be duty-bound to C to preserve the £10,000 received from B in cash
(being the traceable substitute for the chose in action – the debt) which A was duty-bound
to C to preserve by reason of the constructive trust which would arise. If A was to deplete
the £10,000 in breach of her duty to C to preserve and to account for it, C could falsify
such depletion of the account by A. A would then be subject to a personal liability to
reinstate the shortfall in the account. Since the shortfall could not have arisen but for B's
tender of payment to A, which enabled A to breach her duty to C to preserve the chose in
action, so far as B had *dishonestly assisted* A in breaching that duty to C, B would be liable
to C in the same extent as A. As to whether A (and therefore B, as a dishonest accessory)
might be held liable to compensate C for consequential losses sustained as a result of A's
breach of duty, such liability to make equitable compensation for consequential loss goes
beyond the scope of this book. That question has, however, been considered in J. Glister,
'Breach of trust and consequential loss' (2014) 8 *Journal of Equity* 235.

obligor(s) to the chose assigned to liability as an accessory in the equitable wrong of 'dishonest assistance'.[36]

Notice allows the debtor to be made *personally liable* as if he were a
trustee for the assignee: it allows for the imposition of a constructive trust
so as to expose the debtor to a personal liability to the assignee, looked at
as a form of 'beneficiary' given the bare trust mechanism which underpins the equitable assignment. In other words, notice 'perfects' the
assignee's equitable interest in that the debtor will treated as if he were
a constructive trustee (i.e. be 'liable as a constructive trustee')[37] were he to
act in ways which assisted the assignor in breaching her duties to her
assignee arising from the 'bare trust' aspect of the equitable assignment.[38]
Conversely, where the debtor had been ignorant of the equitable assignment (because he had received notice of it from neither the assignee nor
from any other independent source), although such debtor is still duty-
bound to the assignee not to dishonestly assist the assignor in breaching
her duties to the assignee, it becomes unlikely that the debtor could be
shown to have the requisite 'dishonest' state of mind (subject to the
doctrine of constructive notice) as to render him liable to the assignee.

In the following sections, it will be demonstrated how such dishonest
assistance liability in equity will arise in connection with two kinds of
assistive acts on the part of the obligor to the chose assigned, viewed as a
stranger to the equitable assignment: first, cases of precise performance to
the obligor (for example, by way of tender of payment as the obligor was
duty-bound to do); and second, cases where the obligor had colluded
with the obligee/assignor for the obligee/assignor to invoke certain of her
entitlements in a manner which would entail a breach of her duties to her
assignee (for example, where the obligor colluded with the obligee for
her to release the obligor from having to perform his obligations under

---

[36] It may also be a relevant factor to engage the 'equitable jurisdiction of the common law
courts'. This is discussed in Chapter 12.

[37] Thus, '[she] isn't [a trustee], but has to be treated as if [she] were' because '[p]rima facie,
the beneficiary of a trust cannot sue anyone except [her] trustee': Lionel D. Smith,
'Constructive Trusts and Constructive Trustees' (1999) 58 *Cambridge Law Journal*
294, 299.

[38] '[T]he double liability of the debtor [in *Roberts* v. *Lloyd* (1840) 2 Beav 378, and *Jones*
v. *Farrell* (11857) 1 De G & J 208] cannot be predicated on any theory of property which
came into his hands or legal right which remained with the assignor, but must rest on the
fact that he, with knowledge of the assignee's right, has so acted as to interfere with the
equitable protection which a court of equity throws about the power of attorney acquired
by an assignee': Harlan Stone, 'The Nature of the Rights of the *Cestui Que Trust*' (1917)
17 *Columbia Law Review* 467, 485.

the chose in question, even though such release would be contrary to the interests of the assignee and had not been sanctioned by him).

## B  Assistance through Tender of Performance to the Obligee/Assignor

As mentioned above, every stranger to an equitable assignment who, with a dishonest state of mind, induces *or assists* an equitable assignor to breach her duties to her equitable assignee by interfering with the assignee's equitable interest in the entitlements which had been equitably assigned, commits an equitable wrong which exposes such stranger to a form of equitable liability. This, it is suggested, is the equitable wrong which we now know by the name of 'dishonest assistance'.

Example 11.1 illustrates one way by which such liability may arise.

---

**EXAMPLE 11.1**

On 1 February 2018, B borrows £10,000 from A on terms that B is to repay £10,000 on 1 January 2019 to A.

On 1 September 2018, A equitably assigns the debt to C.

On 1 October 2018, C gives B notice of the assignment, and asks B to tender payment on 1 January 2019, to him instead of to A.

On 1 January 2019, despite C's notice of assignment and request of 1 October, B tenders £10,000 to A. A accepts the tender, even though C had not authorized her to do so. She then absconds from the country to parts unknown with the money received from B.

---

When B tenders payment of £10,000 to A, which tender A accepts, that acceptance is effective to discharge B's obligation to tender payment at common law. Consequently, if an action at law were brought against B in respect of A's loan of 1 February 2018, B could plead these facts to defend himself.[39] However, B's tender of payment and its acceptance by A would have led to the destruction of C's interest (as equitable assignee) in A's chose in action against B: that chose in action would have been reduced into possession through the combination of B's tender of payment and A's acceptance thereof.

---

[39] However, as will be explained in Chapter 12, B may be barred from pleading the facts which would support such a defence. If barred, the action at law might then proceed to judgment in lieu of defence.

Since the destruction of C's interest in A's chose in action in this manner could only have arisen with the assistance of B's tender of payment, that act of tendering payment would, of necessity, have assisted A in breaching her obligation to C to preserve the chose in action, until such time as she was called on (if at all) to reduce it into possession. Further, since B knew of C's interest in A's chose in action arising by reason of the equitable assignment to C, B would have rendered such assistance to A 'dishonestly'.[40] B would, accordingly, be liable to C in equity for having dishonestly assisted A in committing a breach of her obligations to C arising by reason of the equitable assignment. And the same liability would arise, even if the chose assigned had been an equitable one and not one arising at common law.

## C   Assistance through Collusion: Procuring the Grant of a Release

In *JD Wetherspoon plc* v. *Van de Berg & Co. Ltd*, Peter Smith J observed as follows:[41]

> Accessory liability does not [necessarily] involve a trust. It involves providing dishonest assistance to somebody else who is in a fiduciary capacity [and] who has committed a breach of his fiduciary duties.[42] . . . It must not be forgotten that in *most* cases the breach [of the fiduciary duties] can only occur as a result of the activities of the assistor.

It appears, therefore, that such a strong 'but for' causal link between the acts of the 'assistor' or accessory and the breach of duty by the obligor is true only in most, but not all, cases. In order for an act to assist an obligor to breach her duties to another, it is not necessary that act be a 'but for' cause of the breach: there must be some causal linkage,[43] which is of

---

[40] The details as to what is required for such 'dishonest' state of mind will be explained below, in Section E.

[41] [2009] EWHC 639 (Ch), [518] (emphasis added).

[42] The proposition that dishonest assistance liability may also arise in connection with assisting non-trustee fiduciaries was accepted by the High Court of Australia in *Consul Development Pty Ltd* v. *DPC Estates Pty Ltd* (1976) 132 CLR 373, 397; and the English Court of Appeal accepted that this was also the case in English law in *Novoship (UK) Ltd* v. *Mikhaylyuk* [2014] EWCA Civ 908; [2015] QB 499.

[43] *Brown* v. *Bennett* [1999] BCC 525, 533 (Morritt LJ). However, establishing a causal link between the supposed assistive acts of the accessory and the *loss* to the trust beneficiary arising from the trustee's breach of trust seems to be unnecessary: *Casio Computer Co. Ltd* v. *Sayo* [2001] EWCA Civ 661; [2001] ILPr 43, [15] (Tuckey LJ).

more than 'minimal importance'.[44] Consequently, proof that the obligor would probably have breached the duty in question even if the accessory had not acted as he had done would not preclude those acts from being acts of assistance.[45]

In addition, in *Royal Brunei Airlines* v. *Tan*, Lord Nicholls of Birkenhead summarized the 'accessory liability principle' as follows:[46]

> Drawing the threads together, their Lordships' overall conclusion is that dishonesty is a necessary ingredient of accessory liability. It is also a sufficient ingredient. A liability in equity to make good resulting loss attaches to a person who dishonestly *procures or assists* in a breach of trust or fiduciary obligation. It is not necessary that, in addition, the trustee or fiduciary was acting dishonestly, although this will usually be so where the third party who is assisting him is acting dishonestly.

This, coupled with the flexibility in the causation requirements for there to be 'assistance' means that '[t]he modern formulation of dishonest assistance covers conduct that would once have been analysed as the separate wrong of knowingly inducing or procuring a breach of trust'.[47]

As with the concept of assistance itself, the concept of 'inducement' or 'procurement' is also a broad one. So, for example, in *Eaves* v. *Hickson*,[48] where trustees had paid trust funds to the wrong person (and so had acted in breach of their duties under the trust) having been induced to do so by the production of a marriage certificate which had been forged by the father of the recipient, the father who had induced the trustees to act

---

[44] *Baden* v. *Société Générale pour Favoriser le Développement du Commerce et de l'Industrie en France SA* [1993] 1 WLR 509 (Ch D), 575 (Peter Gibson J): 'assistance must be an act which is part of the fraudulent and dishonest design and must not be of minimal importance'.

[45] *Balfron Trustee Ltd* v. *Peterson* [2001] IRLR 758 (Ch D), [21] (Laddie J).

[46] [1995] 2 AC 378, 392F–G (emphasis added). This is now accepted to be the law in England: *Ivey* v. *Genting Casinos (UK) Ltd (trading as Crockfords Club)* [2017] UKSC 67; [2018] AC 391, [74]. See also discussion below, in n. 81.

[47] Snell (2015), para. 30-076. However, in Australia, procurement or inducement of a breach of fiduciary duty has been kept distinct from other instances of assistance, following *Farah Constructions Pty Ltd* v. *Say-Dee Pty Ltd* (2007) 230 CLR 89; 236 ALR 209. See Jacob's Law of Trusts (2016), para. 13-35, and Meagher, Gummow & Lehane (2015), para. 5-430. In addition, in Australia, the 'dishonesty' in 'dishonest assistance' pertains to the principal breach by the trustee or fiduciary: and the principal breach of duty by the trustee or fiduciary must have been dishonest: *Farah Constructions Pty Ltd* v. *Say-Dee Pty Ltd*, [179]. The analysis in the main text may not, therefore, be applicable in quite the same way or to the same extent as a matter of Australian law. See discussion below at n. 81.

[48] (1861) 30 Beav 136.

in breach of their duties was made personally liable in equity to the beneficiaries who ought to have received the monies under the trust.

If dishonest assistance liability may arise for acts of inducement, that opens the door to such liability arising in instances where an obligor had induced his obligee to release him from his obligations, in breach of her own equitable obligations to another not to do so on her own account.

As Dean Ames noted:[49]

> [T]he common rules of property apply equally to ownership of things and ownership of obligations. For example, what may be called the passive rights of ownership are the same in both cases. The general duty resting upon all mankind not to destroy the property of another, is as cogent in favor of an obligee as it is in favor of the owner of a horse. And the violation of this duty is as pure a tort in the one case as in the other.

Ames went on to observe in a footnote that an illustration could be found in a release of obligations by an obligee:[50]

> From the nature of the case such a tort must be of rare occurrence. But instances may be put. [A], a *cestui que trust*, assigns his trust to [C], and afterwards, before the trustee is informed of the assignment, releases the trust to the trustee, as in *Newman* v. *Newman*[51] ... [C]'s right against the trustee is destroyed. [Then a]gain, suppose that [S], a stranger had maliciously incited [A] to make the release. [C]'s claim against [A] and [S] would be for compensation[52] for a purely equitable tort. Compare *Lumley* v. *Gye*[53] ...; *Bowen* v. *Hall*.[54]

In the above extract, Ames pointed out that where an equitable chose in action arising from a trust had been equitably assigned by a beneficiary of that trust ('A') to an assignee ('C'), and if A subsequently released the trustee of that trust ('T') from his duties under that trust, such release would have resulted in the destruction of A's entitlements against T in consequence (as was recognized to have occurred in *Newman* v. *Newman*). Such release would not, accordingly, be obviously in C's interest and would amount to a breach of A's equitable duties to C under

---

[49] 'Purchase for Value without Notice' (1887) 1 *Harvard Law Review* 1, at 10. This essay is reprinted in Ames (1913), and the equivalent passage is at p. 262.

[50] Ibid., 1 *Harvard Law Review* 10, fn. 1; Ames (1913), p. 262, fn. 1.

[51] (1885) 28 Ch D 674.

[52] Restitutionary liability as to gains or profits made by the accessory may also arise. See discussion in Chapter 15, Section G.

[53] (1853) 2 El & Bl 216.

[54] (1881) 6 QBD 333.

the equitable assignment (given the 'trust effect' identified in this book), unless C had sanctioned its release by A.[55]

In the extract, Ames went on to point out that where A had been incited by a stranger to the trust ('S') to effect such release, that incitement or inducement would amount to an 'equitable' tort, analogous to the common law tort of inducement (or procurement) of breach of contract as had arisen in *Lumley* v. *Gye* and *Bowen* v. *Hall.* Using Lord Nicholls's terminology in *Royal Brunei,* we could apply the label of dishonest assistance to such 'equitable tort' since that form of accessorial equitable liability encompasses also the dishonest *inducement* or *procurement* of a breach of an equitable obligor's equitable duties to her obligee. And if a stranger, S, may be liable in such a way for having dishonestly induced A to release T from T's duties to A under the trust, what if the dishonest inducement had come from T himself? There seems to be no reason why Ames's analysis would not be equally applicable.

To illustrate the above, it may be helpful to consider Example 11.2.

---

**EXAMPLE 11.2**

T holds assets on trust for A. A equitably assigns her entitlements to C, but A subsequently releases T from his duties under that trust, empowering T to deal with the trust assets in a manner contrary to the stipulations under the trust.

---

The release in Example 11.2, in a sense, 'destroys' C's entitlements vis-à-vis A as A's equitable assignee. This amounts to a wrongful interference with C's equitable entitlements by A for the reasons explained above since those entitlements of A's are now to be invoked by A for C's interest and not her own,[56] unless C had authorized A to so act in breach of her duties to him.

Next, suppose the situation described in Example 11.3.

---

**EXAMPLE 11.3**

Same facts as in Example 11.2, except that A was maliciously induced by S, a stranger to the assignment, to grant such a release.

---

[55] In effect, releasing A from her duty to invoke her entitlements against T (including her power to release T from his duties as trustee to her) for C's benefit.

[56] Those entitlements may, therefore, be viewed as a form of trust property held 'by' A on a bare trust for C's benefit (given the 'trust effect' which underpins the equitable assignment from A to C).

On the facts in Example 11.3, using Ames's terminology, by *maliciously* inducing A to release T from his trust obligations, S would be liable for A's wrongful interference. But how might such 'malice' arise? Could such malice with regard to C arise if S had had no inkling of A's duties to C *not* to act in this manner? It would seem not.

Now, let us suppose the facts in Example 11.4.

---

**EXAMPLE 11.4**

T holds assets on trust for A for her life. Under the terms of the trust, A is entitled to be paid an annuity by T out of the income from the trust assets. A equitably assigns her equitable life interest to C, and T is informed of the same.

Shortly afterwards, T becomes financially unstable. Desperate for funds, he speaks with A and persuades A to release T from his duties under the trust to pay the annuity for the coming year. Obviously, T does not make any further inquiries whether C, A's equitable assignee, was aware of A's actions, or if C was agreeable to his equitable interest as assignee being affected in this manner by A. T then proceeds to use the income that should have been paid in accordance with the terms of the trust to pay down on his own personal debt. But it is insufficient, and T is eventually made a bankrupt.

---

In Example 11.4, but for the release which A had granted T, T would be liable for having committed a breach of trust for diverting the annuity payment for the year for non-trust purposes. Given A's release, T may plead the facts of A's granting of the release as a defence if a suit were brought against him for the breach of duty. In a sense, A's entitlements against T would, therefore, be impaired to an extent, and so too would any person having derivative entitlements through A (for example, C, A's equitable assignee). However, having been notified of the assignment to C, in Example 11.4, T knew of C's equitable interest in A's annuity. Might T be liable in equity to C, given such knowledge?

We may note that in Example 11.4, T is just as much a stranger to the equitable assignment between A and C, as S had been in Example 11.3. If so, it is not obvious why T should not be treated as being liable to C in Example 11.4 in the same manner as S might be treated as liable to C in Example 11.3.

This leads us to Example 11.5.[57]

---

[57] The facts of this example are drawn from *Legh* v. *Legh* (1799) 1 Bos & Pul 447. That was a decision of the Court of Common Pleas, and the decision of the court ultimately rested on the so-called equitable jurisdiction of the courts of common law by which a court of common law could bar defendants before it from pleading the facts as would support certain kinds of defences if the court was satisfied that the plaintiff could obtain a common injunction from a

---

**EXAMPLE 11.5**

Same facts as Example 11.1, except that on 31 December 2018, despite C's notice of assignment and request of 1 October, B suggests to A that she might execute and deliver a deed of release so as to free B from having to tender any payment at all. After repeated entreaties from and discussion with B, A executes and delivers into B's possession a duly executed deed of release by which A grants B a release from having to pay anything for the loan made on 1 February 2018, and that the debt is forgiven, even though C had not directed A to execute such a deed of release.

Relying on this deed, on 1 January 2019 B fails to tender any payment to C. What is more, B ignores subsequent and repeated requests by C for B to tender payment to him as A's equitable assignee.

---

In Example 11.5, A's execution and delivery of the deed of release into B's hands would appear to have discharged B's debt obligation by reason of a unilateral release, and if an action at law were brought against B in respect of the loan, B could, in principle, plead the facts as to A's execution and delivery of the deed to defend himself.[58] However, so far as the collusion between A and B arising from B's entreaties of and discussions with A had caused A to execute and deliver the deed of release in Example 11.5 in breach of her duty to C, it would follow that B would be exposed to liability to C in dishonest assistance, even if it could be shown that A would have done the same thing without any suggestion or inducement from B. It would follow, therefore, that by colluding with A, B had induced A into committing her breach of duty with regard to C. Where B had so induced A with the requisite 'dishonest' mindset,[59] B would be liable to C in equity as an accessory for 'dishonest assistance'.[60]

---

court of Chancery to bar the defendant from making such plea on pain of being held in contempt of that court. This *procedural* response of a court acting within its common law jurisdiction to a substantive *equitable* wrong is explored further in Chapter 12).

[58] As will be explained in Chapter 12, the common law courts developed a procedural power to 'set aside' certain defences. In essence, this involved barring a defendant in these circumstances from pleading such facts pursuant to the so-called equitable jurisdiction of the common law courts. Although such power was replicated and extended by CLPA1954, s. 85, that did not abolish the power which had been acquired by the courts prior to its enactment: 'Wherever there is want of good faith in pleading a plea, we [i.e. the judges comprising the court of Kings' Bench, being a court of common law] have jurisdiction to set it aside independently of the Common Law Procedure Act, 1854': *Bartlett* v. *Wells* (1862) 1 B & S 836, 840 *per* Crompton J (in argument).

[59] This will be discussed in Section E.

[60] As will be explained in Chapter 12, B could also be enjoined from pleading the facts as would otherwise shield B from liability were an action at law brought against B for

## D   Assistance by Omission?

The discussion above has concentrated on cases where the 'accessory' (i.e. B in Examples 11.1 and 11.5) had performed some positive act prior to A's breach of duty which had assisted their breach. Such 'assistance' could arise though pre-breach acts which *causally* enabled A to commit her breach where, but for the commission of those 'assistive' acts, A's breach could or would not have occurred. That said, 'but-for' causation may not be strictly necessary: 'assistance' may also arise through acts of collusion. Where A had breached her duties to C following 'inducement' through encouragement by B, if the encouragement had more than 'minimal importance', assistance by inducement may still be made out.

In Example 11.1, B's act of assistance lay in B's positive act of tendering payment to A. In contrast, in Example 11.5, B's act of assistance lay in B's collusive encouragement of A which led to A's execution of the deed of release. But may assistance only be effected through positive acts? Might it be possible to perform some form of assistive act by inaction or omission? For example, what of a situation as in Example 11.6?

---

EXAMPLE 11.6

Same facts as Example 11.5, but there was no collusion between A and B prior to A's execution of the deed of release. However, A had confided in B a couple of days before executing the deed of release that she had fallen out with C and wished to harm C's interests by executing the deed of release.

B, despite knowing of A's stated (and malicious) intentions towards C, and despite believing that A would follow through on her threat, did not alert C as to what he had learned from A. And, following A's execution and delivery of the deed of release a few days later, B declined to tender any payment to A or to C, safe in the knowledge that if an action at law was brought against him on the unpaid debt, he could rely on the deed of release as a defence.

---

non-payment. Such equitable injunctive relief was then replicated by the common law courts which developed for themselves an analogous jurisdiction, sometimes termed the 'equitable jurisdiction of the common law courts' by which a common law court might bar a defendant before it from pleading certain common law defences in circumstances where it was clear an equitable injunction might have been obtained to bar such pleading. So barred by the common law court, the plaintiff's action might then proceed to judgment in lieu of defence: see *Legh* v. *Legh* (1799) 1 Bos & Pul 447. This power was then given a statutory basis under s. 85, Common Law Procedure Act 1854, before being transferred to the High Court of the Supreme Court of Judicature pursuant to the Judicature Act 1873.

The facts of Example 11.6 could be taken to illustrate a situation where A had, yet again, breached her duty to C to preserve the chose in action that had been equitably assigned to C until C might direct A to fully execute the bare trust which underpinned the assignment. However, unlike the situation in Example 11.5, in Example 11.6, B would appear to have had no prior or contemporaneous involvement with A's wrongful invocation of her power (as creditor to B) to grant B a release effective at law, save that by failing to alert C of what he had learned of A's intentions, B made it more likely that A would follow through on her threat. Had B warned C, C might have had some opportunity to act by, say, obtaining an injunction to bar A from carrying out her threat. However, if the analysis in this chapter were accepted, it would be difficult to see on what basis B might be said to have committed any equitable wrong vis-à-vis B in failing to take steps to notify C of A's threatened breach of her obligations with regard to B in time for C to have done something to try to prevent it from occurring since this would appear to be an instance of complete inaction by B prior to A's eventual breach.[61]

It is sometimes suggested that dishonest assistance may only arise from positive actions by the 'accessory': assistance through inaction or omission is denied even as a possibility. Some support for this may be found in Lord Nicholls's opinion in *Royal Brunei Airlines* v. *Tan* where, in clarifying the modern law on dishonest assistance, the wrong of dishonest assistance was described in terms which presupposed positive acts:[62]

> Beneficiaries are entitled to expect that those who become trustees will fulfil their obligations. They are also entitled to expect, and this is only a short step further, that those who become trustees will be permitted to fulfil their obligations without deliberate *intervention* from third parties. They are entitled to expect that third parties will refrain from intentionally *intruding* in the trustee–beneficiary relationship and thereby hindering a beneficiary from receiving his entitlement in accordance with the terms of the trust instrument.

---

[61] One could, alternatively, focus on B's post-breach actions in failing to tender payment, and in actively pleading the facts as would support a defence of release were an action at law brought for non-payment. But such omissions/acts would have arisen post-breach. This is because it is difficult, if not impossible, to see how an act/omission which arises *after* the occurrence of a breach can ever be said to have assisted in its occurrence: the chronology simply precludes this, unless A and B had previously colluded so as to come up with some common scheme which involved A breaching her obligations vis-à-vis C.

[62] *Royal Brunei Airlines* v. *Tan* (n. 31), 387A–C.

Relying on these observations, Tomlinson J opined in *Fitzalan-Howard* v. *Hibbert* that, 'as Lord Nicholls emphasised in his speech at page 387, dishonest assistance normally involves positive assistance – "dishonest intervention", "intentional intru[sion]" or "interfere[nce] with the due performance by the trustee".'[63] This has led some commentators to suggest that 'there is no such thing as dishonest assistance of a breach of trust by omission'.[64]

One might also take note of Lord Selborne LC's language in his famous exposition of the law on the point in *Barnes* v. *Addy*:[65]

> [I]n this case we have to deal with certain persons who are [express] trustees, and with certain other persons who are not [express] trustees. . . . Those who create a[n express] trust clothe the [express] trustee with a legal power and control over the trust property, imposing on him a corresponding responsibility [or duty to the trust beneficiary]. That responsibility may no doubt be extended to others who are not properly [express] trustees, if they are found either making themselves trustees *de son tort*, or *actually participating* in any fraudulent conduct of the trustee to the injury of the *cestui que trust*. But, on the other hand, strangers are not to be made constructive trustees merely because they act as the agents of trustees in transactions within their legal powers, transactions perhaps of which a Court of Equity may disapprove, unless those agents receive and become chargeable with some part of the trust property, or unless they assist with knowledge in a dishonest and fraudulent design on the part of the trustees.

In an unreported decision, Carnwarth J took this passage to show that 'for a third party to become liable as a "knowing assistant" he must be an active participant in the breach of trust'.[66] However, that is not the only way to read Lord Selborne's speech.

Though there appears not to be much English authority directly on the point, it is suggested that the positions adopted by Tomlinson and Carnwarth JJ in reliance on Lord Nicholls's opinion in *Royal Brunei*, and Lord Selborne's speech judgment in *Barnes* v. *Addy*, respectively, may go too far. First, it is not completely clear that either Lord Nicholls or Lord Selborne was aiming to set out exhaustive statements as to what might amount to assistance: the tenor of each passage would appear to

---

[63] [2009] EWHC 2855; [2010] PNLR 11.

[64] Kelvin Low, 'Nonfeasance in Equity' (2012) 128 LQR 63, 64.

[65] (1874) LR 9 Ch App 244, 251–2 (emphasis added).

[66] *Nightingale Finance Ltd* v. *Scott* (Ch D; unreported decision of Carnwath J, 18 November 1997; [1997] Lexis Citation 4477).

suggest otherwise. Second, relying on the authority of *Fitzalan-Howard v. Hibbert*,[67] the editors of *Underhill and Hayton* have noted: 'A failure to act should be capable of amounting to assistance, albeit that a claimant will usually find assistance easier to prove where the defendant has taken some positive step.'[68] That said, it was acknowledged in a footnote that, '"mere passive acquiescence" in a breach is generally unlikely to suffice'.[69] The difficulty, therefore, lies in proving how an omission or inaction occurring *prior* to the relevant breach can have any assistive effect. Since the question whether any particular act (positive or, perhaps, otherwise) has the effect of assisting in the commission of a breach of duty is a question of fact, and not of law,[70] suggesting that omissions can never amount to acts of assistance which might generate dishonest assistance liability probably go too far. Indeed, as Dietrich has noted, 'if there were no liability for "omissions", then this would raise difficult probative issues and necessitate that fine conceptual distinctions between "active" and "passive" be drawn'.[71] Drawing such fine distinctions in connection with an equitable doctrine could run counter to equity's concern with substance and not with form.

It would follow that some kinds of omissions or inaction on the part of the stranger to the trust may still amount to 'assistance' for present purposes. Speculation as to what such circumstances might require would go beyond the scope of the present work.[72] But perhaps this is a situation where one should never say never, at least until the cases provide clearer authority on the point.

That having been said, as will be explained in the following chapter, the obligor's acquisition of knowledge that his obligee had equitably

---

[67] [2009] EWHC 2855; [2010] PNLR 11, [47]–[48].

[68] Underhill & Hayton (2016), para. 98.53.

[69] Underhill & Hayton (2016), para. 98.53, fn. 1, given the observations of Dodds-Streeton J in *Re-Engine Pty (in liq.) v. Fergusson* [2007] VSC 57; (2007) 209 FLR 1, [210] that: '[i]t seems self-evident that assistance should "make a difference" and forward or advance the primary breach or misconduct in some way. Mere passive acquiescence in the breach would not, in the ordinary case, suffice to establish liability on the ground of assistance Further, it appears that assistance must take the form of some activity or conduct over and above mere knowledge of the fiduciary's breaches.'

[70] *Baden v. Société Générale pour Favoriser le Développement du Commerce et de l'Industrie en France SA* [1995] 1 WLR 509, [246] (Peter Gibson J): 'As to the third element it seems to me to be a simple question of fact, whether or not there has been assistance.'

[71] Joachim Dietrich, 'The Liability of Accessories under Statute, in Equity, and in Criminal Law: Some Common Problems and (Perhaps) Common Solutions' (2010) 34 *Melbourne University Law Review* 106.

[72] For some suggestions, see Dietrich & Ridge (2015).

assigned the chose in action to which his obligation pertained can have other *procedural* effects, even independently of any question of substantive liability for dishonest assistance. That is, even if it were the case that dishonest assistance required some form of active assistance or collusion which induced the assignor to breach her equitable duties to her assignee, omissions falling short of these could still be sufficient to bar the obligor from pleading certain defences.

### E    Dishonestly Assisting in the Breach of Another's Obligations

As has been made clear in *Royal Brunei Airlines* v. *Tan*,[73] *Twinsectra* v. *Yardley*[74] and *Barlow Clowes International* v. *Eurotrust International*,[75] liability for dishonest assistance requires two things:

**I**  a breach of duty[76] by the primary wrongdoer (A); and
**II** knowledge: the assistant (B), must know or be taken to have known of such breach of duty to such an extent that his assistance may be said to have been rendered 'dishonestly'.

In Example 11.1, where B has received notice of an assignment by A to C of A's legal chose in action against B in respect of the loan, B may be found to have had actual or constructive knowledge that his actions would assist A's breach of her duties to C (namely, a breach by A of her duties to C not to accept a conforming tender of payment without C's authority to do so) to make B liable to C as an accessory to such breach.[77]

The law on dishonest assistance was restated by Lord Nicholls as follows:[78]

---

[73]  see n. 31.
[74]  [2002] UKHL 12; [2002] 2 AC 164.
[75]  [2005] UKPC 37; [2006] 1 WLR 1476.
[76]  For reasons of brevity, the discussion in this chapter will focus on a breach of a common law obligation arising from contract. However, the principles involved apply equally to common law obligations arising by way of covenant, as well as to equitable obligations arising by way of trust.
[77]  It should not be open to B to argue that, as a layperson, he was unaware of the legal significance of an assignment – that by such assignment, A would have 'lost' her privilege to invoke each and every one of her entitlements associated with the chose in action as she pleased and would, instead, have become duty-bound in equity to C to invoke those entitlements in accordance with C's directions, given that 'ignorance of the law is no excuse'.
[78]  *Royal Brunei Airlines* v. *Tan* (n. 31), 392–3 (emphasis added). As mentioned previously, this is now the position as a matter of English law: *Ivey* v. *Genting Casinos (UK) Ltd (trading as Crockfords Club)*, above, n. 46. However, for the reasons explained in n. 81, given the rejection of *Royal Brunei* by the High Court of Australia in *Farah Constructions*

Drawing the threads together, their Lordships' overall conclusion is that dishonesty is a necessary ingredient of accessory liability. It is also a sufficient ingredient. A liability in equity to make good resulting loss attaches to a person who dishonestly procures or assists in a breach of trust or fiduciary obligation. It is not necessary that, in addition, the trustee or fiduciary was acting dishonestly, though this will usually be so where the third party who is assisting him is acting dishonestly. . . .

From this statement of the principle it follows that this appeal succeeds. The money paid to B.L.T. [Borneo Leisure Travel Sdn Bhd] on the sale of tickets for the [claimant] airline was held by B.L.T. upon trust for the airline. *This trust, on its face, conferred no power on B.L.T. to use the money in the conduct of its business. The trust gave no authority to B.L.T. to relieve its cash flow problems by utilising for this purpose the rolling 30-day credit afforded by the airline.* Thus B.L.T. committed a breach of trust by using the money instead of simply deducting its commission and holding the money intact until it paid the airline. The defendant [Tan] accepted that he knowingly assisted in that breach of trust. *In other words, he caused or permitted his company to apply the money in a way he knew was not authorised by the trust of which the company was trustee.* Set out in these bald terms, the defendant's conduct was dishonest. By the same token, and for good measure, B.L.T. also acted dishonestly. The defendant was the company, and his state of mind is to be imputed to the company.

It is unnecessary to enter into the debate[79] whether the question of 'dishonesty' for present purposes necessitates application of a subjective[80] or an objective[81] test. Accepting the proposition adopted in *Barlow*

---

*Pty Ltd* v. *Say-Dee Pty Ltd* (n. 47), the discussion in the main text may not be applicable as a matter of Australia in precisely the same way.

[79] Given the Supreme Court's approbation of *Royal Brunei* in *Ivey* v. *Genting Casinos (UK) Ltd (trading as Crockfords Club)*; and see also n. 81, below.

[80] See *Twinsectra Ltd* v. *Yardley* (n. 74), [27]–[35] (Lord Hutton); [19]–[20] (Lord Hoffmann); and with both of whom Lord Steyn agreed. The majority, therefore, rejected Lord Millett's contrary view (at [114]–[144]).

[81] As the Privy Council took to be the case in *Barlow Clowes (PC)* (n. 75), [15] and [18]. The English Court of Appeal has repeatedly adopted the analysis set out in *Barlow Clowes* as to the effect of *Twinsectra* on the 'objective' test set out in *Royal Brunei Airlines* (n. 31): see *Abou-Rahmah* v. *Abacha* [2006] EWCA Civ 1492; [2007] 1 All ER (Comm) 827, and *Starglade Properties Ltd* v. *Nash* [2010] EWCA Civ 1314. For a possible explanation why Lord Hoffmann took the position in *Barlow Clowes* that *Twinsectra* had not departed from the Privy Council in *Royal Brunei Airlines*, see Davies (2015), p. 118. For earlier discussion of the controversy, see T. M. Yeo, 'Dishonest Assistance: Restatement from the Privy Council' (2006) 122 LQR 171; and Sir Anthony Clarke MR, 'Claims against Professionals: Negligence, Dishonesty and Fraud' [2006] *Professional Negligence* 70. It has been suggested that the subjective/objective dichotomy may well be a red herring: T. M. Yeo and H. Tjio, 'Knowing What is Dishonesty' (2002) 118 LQR 502. See also *Attorney General of Zambia* v. *Meer Care & Desai* [2007] EWHC 952 (Ch), [333]–[334], where Peter Smith J suggested that the distinction is an 'over-elaboration'. That said,

*Clowes* that the House of Lords in *Twinsectra* had not set out a statement of the English law on dishonest assistance which departed from Lord Nicholls's statement of the law of Brunei on the matter in *Royal Brunei*,[82] we may simply observe what Lord Nicholls held to be 'dishonesty' on the facts before the Privy Council in *Royal Brunei Airlines*.

Tan, the respondent, had conceded that he actually knew that B.L.T., the company of which he was the directing mind, had no authority from Royal Brunei Airlines to deal with the monies it had received on trust for Royal Brunei Airlines in the manner it did. In Hohfeldian terms, B.L.T. was not *privileged* against Royal Brunei Airlines to deal with the money in question as it had done without the Airlines' prior consent.

Given such knowledge of his company's lack of authority, Tan 'caused or permitted his company' to use the money in a manner which was not authorized and which it was not privileged to so use. In so doing, Tan's conduct was 'dishonest'.

Lord Nicholls's closing words in *Royal Brunei Airlines* reveals that the degree of turpitude associated with the label of 'dishonesty' in the context of dishonest assistance is relatively slight:[83] acts done in the knowledge

given the observations of the Supreme Court in *Ivey* v. *Genting Casinos (UK) Ltd (trading as Crockfords Club)*, [62] and [64], it would seem that there can no longer be any doubt that *Royal Brunei* is an accurate statement of English law on the point.

The position in Australia may, however, be different, given that in *Farah Constructions Pty Ltd* v. *Say-Dee Pty Ltd* (n. 47), the High Court of Australia declined (at [163]) to adopt the analysis in *Royal Brunei Airlines*, choosing instead to frame an accessory's liability in these contexts in terms of *knowing* (as opposed to dishonest) assistance. Consequently, it appears that in Australia, the accessory liability of a stranger to a trust (or other fiduciary relation) does not take a dishonest mindset on the part of the accessory to be sufficient. Instead, 'there must also be a dishonest and fraudulent design by the fiduciary': Jacob's Law of Trusts (2016), pp. [13–39]. For a discussion contrasting the English and Australian positions on the question of 'dishonesty' and as to whom is to have such mindset, see Dietrich & Ridge (2015), pp. 239–40. Still, even under the Australian position, the liability of the accessory requires demonstration of the requisite knowledge of the obligor's dishonesty on the part of the accessory. The discussion in the main text, therefore, should still be applicable, *mutatis mutandis*, if the primary obligor's breach can also be shown to have been fraudulent.

[82] Which appears to have been presumed to be the same as that in England: no Bruneian case authority was cited in Privy Council's opinion.

[83] This is unsurprising, given the usage of 'fraud' in equity's exclusive jurisdiction. As Lord Haldane LC said in *Nocton* v. *Lord Ashburton* [1914] AC 932, 954: 'But when fraud is referred to in the wider sense in which the books are full of the expression, used in Chancery in describing cases which were within its exclusive jurisdiction, it is a mistake to suppose that an actual intention to cheat must always be proved.'

that the trustee or fiduciary had no authority (i.e. was not privileged) to act as the trustee/fiduciary had done may be enough to render those acts dishonest. Carelessness or inadvertence would not, therefore be enough: 'conscious impropriety' is required for one to act dishonestly or 'with a lack of probity'.[84]

Thus, a court is at liberty to find such dishonesty given the defendant's *knowledge* that the acts of the primary wrongdoer had been unauthorized – which is to say that the primary wrongdoer had not been *privileged* to do as she had done.[85] Or, to put it yet another way, 'the dishonest assistant must know that the person he is assisting is *not entitled* to do what he is doing'.[86] Where the assignment to the assignee was absolute and not by way of security, the normal inference would be that such an assignor would not be so entitled. However, where the assignment to the assignee had been by way of mortgage to secure a loan, it would appear that such inference would not be drawn, particularly where notice of the assignment had not been accompanied by any request for payments to be made to the mortgagee-assignee instead of the mortgagor-assignor.[87]

## F   'Good and Compelling Reasons'

The finding that the assistant had acted 'dishonestly' arises from a process of inference. As Lord Nicholls put it: 'Honest people do not intentionally deceive others to their detriment. Honest people do not knowingly take others' property. Unless there is a very good and

---

[84] *Royal Brunei Airlines* v. *Tan* (n. 31), 389C–E.

[85] All of which is entirely consistent with Lord Hoffmann's explanation in *Barlow Clowes* (n. 75), [15].

[86] *Ultraframe (UK) Ltd* v. *Fielding* [2005] EWHC 1638 (Ch) [1504] (Lewison J, emphasis added).

[87] *Re Pawson's Settlement* [1917] 1 Ch 541, where an equitable life interest in the income of certain stocks and other personalty vested in trustees of a settlement had been equitably assigned by the life tenant by way of mortgage as security for a loan. At 544, Sargant J held that: 'In the case of a mortgage of real estate, whether held in fee or for life, the mortgagor, in the absence of notice by the mortgagee to the tenants to pay the rents to him, is undoubtedly entitled to remain in possession of the rents and profits, and that is the ordinary understanding as to the income of personal property which has been mortgaged. I am not prepared to say, without definite authority – which has not been shown to me – that the mere giving of notice of the existence of a mortgage of personal property to the trustees holding that property has any further effect in depriving the mortgagor of the receipt of income than it would have in the case of a mortgage of real estate. Accordingly, I hold that the plaintiff is not entitled to recover from the trustees *personally* the income paid by them to the tenant for life' (emphasis added).

compelling reason,[88] an honest person does not participate in a transaction if he knows it involves a misapplication of trust assets to the detriment of the beneficiaries.'[89] Where a person participates in a transaction, knowing it involves a misapplication of trust assets to the detriment of the beneficiaries, the court should infer that such participation which assisted in the misapplication was dishonest, unless there were good and compelling reasons to explain why that person assisted in the misapplication.

'Dishonesty' depends on the state of knowledge of the assistant. Reverting to the facts of Example 11.1, so far as B took no further steps to displace what he is deemed to know (having been notified of the assignment), that A would not, thereafter, be privileged to invoke her powers arising in connection with the debt without C's authorization, B's payment to A on 1 January 2019 will have been performed *knowing* that she was not entitled or authorized to do so, and may therefore be taken to have been performed 'dishonestly'. But what if B had been misled?

Suppose A had forwarded B forged warrants of authority purportedly executed by C which authorized A to accept payment on 1 January 2019. Or A had forwarded forged deeds indicating that C had reassigned the benefit of the debt back to A. In such circumstances, if it were found that B had been genuinely misled by these assurances, and B had honestly believed that A had been entitled to act as she did, notwithstanding the prior assignment to C, it must surely be open to the court to conclude that B had not, after all, acted dishonestly.

This appears to be so, even if B's honest mistake had resulted from his carelessness in failing to make further checks, perhaps by making direct contact with the assignee, C, to verify A's authority to accept a conforming tender. After all, as Lord Nicholls explained, '[H]onesty and its counterpart dishonesty are mostly concerned with advertent conduct, not inadvertent conduct. Carelessness is not dishonesty.'[90] And:[91]

> There may be cases where, in the light of the particular facts, a third party [dealing with trustees] will owe a duty of care to the beneficiaries [to check that a trustee is not misbehaving]. As a general proposition,

---

[88] Such as, for example, the need to salvage another's property from imminent destruction by fire.

[89] *Royal Brunei Airlines* v. *Tan* (n. 31), 389.

[90] *Royal Brunei Airlines* v. *Tan* (n. 31), 389.

[91] Ibid., 392.

however, beneficiaries cannot reasonably expect that all the world dealing with their trustees should owe them a duty to take care lest the trustees are behaving dishonestly.

Ordinarily, therefore, where the assistant had grounds to be reassured about the primary obligor's entitlement to act as she did, notwithstanding indications otherwise by reason of the prior assignment to the assignee, mere carelessness on the assistant's part in not taking any further verificatory steps may well be non-actionable. Even a careless assistant may have acted honestly, and so would not be liable for having dishonestly assisted the primary obligor in breaching her equitable duties to her obligee.

There may also be situations where the assistant had given assistance under duress[92] and/or undue influence. If a negligent assistant may be taken to have made an honest mistake as to the primary obligor's entitlement to act as she did, the same may also be true where the assistance had been rendered under duress and/or undue influence. In such circumstances, it may inappropriate to infer that the assistance in question had been rendered dishonestly. Such instances of assistance ought therefore be excused. Alternatively, perhaps, to the extent the remedies in question are equitable and therefore discretionary, there could be some grounds for the court to withhold them on such facts.

---

[92] At the risk of anachronism, *Applin* v. *Cates* (1861) 30 LJ Chan 6 may well be an instance where *economic* duress was applied by an assignor-creditor on the debtor to tender payment to him, instead of the assignee, despite the debtor having received notice of the assignment. In this case, the assignee of the licence fees which were payable periodically under a contractual licence brought proceedings in equity against the licensee who had been given notice of the equitable assignment. The assignee sought, inter alia, an injunction compelling the licensee to pay the fees that had accrued since 9 August 1859, even though the licensee had tendered payment of such fees to the licensor-assignor, and an injunction to restrain the licensee from tendering any further payments to the licensor-assignor. Wood V-C granted the latter injunction, but not the former. In his opinion, the debtor 'was not in default at all. Having notice that [the licensor] disputed the validity of the assignment, he could not with safety pay the instalments to the plaintiff [the assignee], nor, having regard to the clause in the letter of licence enabling [the licensor] to determine it on default in punctual payment, could he take the course of withholding payment until it was settled which party was entitled; for if he had done so, and it had been ultimately determined that the assignment to the plaintiff was invalid, he would have been at the mercy of [the licensor], who could in the mean time have determined the letter of licence and negotiated the bills. Under such circumstances, [the licensee] was justified in continuing to pay [the licensor] until the plaintiff obtained an injunction': at 30 LJ Chan 8.

## G   The Dishonesty of the Accessory's Agents or Employees

Dishonest assistance liability does not necessarily stop with the obligor who has dishonestly assisted the assignor-obligee's breach of duty as regards her assignee. As Lord Langdale MR said in *Attorney-General v. Corporation of Leicester*:[93]

> [I]t cannot be disputed that the agent of a trustee, whether a corporate body or not, knowing that a breach of trust is being committed, interferes and assists in that breach of trust, he is personally answerable, although he may be employed as the agent of the person who directs him to commit that breach of trust.

And there is Lord Nicholls's own advice that, '[d]rawing the threads together, their Lordships' overall conclusion is that dishonesty is a necessary ingredient of accessory liability. It is also a *sufficient* ingredient'.[94]

The possibility arises, therefore, that an agent or an employee of an obligor who has been directed to act in such a way as assists the defaulting obligee/assignor in breaching her duties to her assignee may be liable for dishonest assistance. Yet such liability rests on the requisite dishonest state of mind being made out: such agent or employee would only be liable for *dishonest* assistance if they actually knew of the assignment, or had such knowledge imputed to them by reason of the doctrine of constructive notice.

If B instructs his bank to debit his account and to credit the amount to A, and the bank does so, even though the bank's actions as B's agent have enabled (and so assisted) A to breach her duties to C, it is unlikely that the bank may be said to have had any actual knowledge of the assignment to C; nor is there anything to put the bank on notice. So the bank may not be held to have breached its duty to C not to dishonestly assist A in breaching her equitable duties to C.

Similarly, if T (who holds 10,000 BCL shares on bare trust for A) instructs the BCL company secretary to make changes to the company share register by reregistering T's holdings in the name of X, and the company secretary does so, notwithstanding that T may have dishonestly assisted A to breach her duties to C (to whom A had equitably assigned her equitable interest in the shares held on trust by T) in doing so, given that T had been given notice of such assignment, the company secretary

---

[93] (1844) 7 Beav 176, 179; cited with approval in *Royal Brunei Airlines* v. *Tan* (n. 31), 385.
[94] *Royal Brunei Airlines* v. *Tan* (n. 31), 392 (emphasis added).

will not be so liable if the company secretary had neither actual knowledge of the assignment, nor were there any grounds as to put him on
notice. And this may be illustrated by cases like *Abou-Rahmah*
v. *Abacha*,[95] where the entire focus of the decision was simply whether
the defendant bank had sufficient knowledge of the fraudulent breach of
trust perpetrated on the claimants by the defendant's customer who
maintained a deposit account with the bank.

## H    The Defences of 'Necessity' and/or 'Justification'

This leads us to the final point to be addressed in this chapter: whether
there may be a defence of 'justification' if dishonest assistance liability has
been established. Cases like *Abou-Rahmah* suggest not, as in that case no
attempt was made to suggest that the defendant bank's act of allowing its
customer to draw down on the deposit account (which was an act that
the defendant bank was contractually duty-bound to allow, so far as the
account was in credit) would have excused the defendant, if that act
might have been found to have been an act of dishonest assistance. And
the same again may be said of *Barlow Clowes*[96] itself – no heed was taken
of the fact that one of the 'dishonest assistants' in that case was contractually obligated to the defaulting obligor in that case to act as it had done.
This suggests that there is no such defence of 'justification'.[97]

It is admitted that the proposition that one may act dishonestly, and so
commit an equitable wrong, even whilst discharging one's legal duty,
seems odd. But such an outcome is not unknown even at common law.

For example, a tortfeasor who has trespassed on land is hardly ever
permitted to excuse his trespass because it was committed in the course
of his fulfilling a contractual duty to another. And even if such act could
be justified by some conception of necessity,[98] and even if such defence of
necessity could possibly be applied to the commission of an equitable

---

[95]  *Abou-Rahmah* v. *Abacha* (n. 81).

[96]  *Barlow Clowes (PC)* (n. 75).

[97]  That said, if the duty which had to be discharged by the defendant assistant was of a
'higher' order than a 'mere' contractual duty, more might be said of the 'justificatory'
effect of the assistant's carrying out of that duty (for example, perhaps, a duty pertaining
to protection of fundamental human rights). That, however, remains speculation at this
point in time as thus far there appears to be no case on point.

[98]  For a brief account of the defence of necessity in tort, see Clerk & Lindsell (2018), paras.
3-145 to 3-154.

wrong,[99] it is difficult to see how B's act of tendering payment to A could be justified by any conception of necessity when B could equally well have safeguarded his position (in most cases)[100] by initiating interpleader proceedings and paying the sum in question into court.[101]

Of greater concern in the present context is the nascent conception of 'justification' as a defence. This has been extensively discussed in Davies's *Accessory Liability*.[102]

This defence appears to qualify the liability of a third party to a contract who would otherwise be determined to have committed the tort of inducement of breach of that contract. The question is whether such defence applies to qualify the equitable liability of a dishonest assistant.

Perhaps the clearest statement of this defence within the context of the tort of inducement of breach of contract is to be found in Darling J's judgment[103] in *Read* v. *Friendly Society of Operative Stonemasons of England, Ireland and Wales*:[104]

> I think the plaintiff has a cause of action against the defendants, unless the Court is satisfied that, when they interfered with the contractual rights of [the] plaintiff, the defendants had a sufficient justification for their interference – to use Lord Macnaghten's words.[105] This sufficient justification they may have had, and they may prove it . . . I think their sufficient justification for interference with [the] plaintiff's right must be an equal[106] or superior

---

[99] Which has been denied, given the different historical origins of tort as compared with equitable wrongs: see James Goudkamp, *Tort Law Defences* (Oxford: Hart, 2013), pp. 21–3. However, cf. James Edelman, 'Equitable Torts' (2002) 10 *Torts Law Journal* 64.

[100] *Applin* v. *Cates* (n. 92) illustrates a situation where an application for interpleader would not have completely safeguarded the obligor.

[101] As the Lord Chancellor highlighted in *Jones* v. *Farrell* (1857) 1 De G & J 208, 218–19.

[102] Davies (2015), chapter 7, section 2. For a briefer account, see Goudkamp, *Tort Law Defences*, pp. 119–21. Dr Goudkamp ultimately agrees that it should be regarded as a defence to the tort.

[103] With whom Channell J agreed. Lord Alverstone CJ did not comment on the question of justification.

[104] [1902] 2 KB 88, 96, holding the Friendly Society to be liable to Read for having induced his employers to breach their contract of employment with him. The court's decision was affirmed on appeal on different grounds: *Read* v. *The Friendly Society of Operative Stonemasons of England, Ireland and Wales* [1902] 2 KB 732.

[105] Here, Darling J was referring to a passage from *Quinn* v. *Leathem* [1901] AC 495, where, at 510, Lord Macnaghten said: 'A violation of legal right committed knowingly is a cause of action, and . . . it is a violation of legal right to interfere with contractual relations recognized at law if there be no sufficient justification for the interference.'

[106] The Australian position appears to be narrower, recognizing a defence of justification only so far as the defendant had been purporting to be justified by a *superior* right to the contractual right of the plaintiff which he had interfered with. See e.g. *Independent Oil*

right in themselves, and that no one can legally excuse himself to a man, of whose contract he has procured the breach, on the ground that he acted on a wrong understanding of his own rights, or without malice, or bona fide, or in the best interests of himself, nor even that he acted as an altruist, seeking only the good of another and careless of his own advantage.

As with the defence of necessity, it is arguable whether a defendant-debtor who has paid his creditor may claim to have been acting in a manner that is *justified* in equity so far as that act of payment was in fulfilment of his common law duty, despite his having received notice of his creditor's assignment of the benefit of the debt to an assignee. This is difficult, because the defendant-debtor's position would have been equally well safeguarded (in most cases)[107] had he initiated interpleader proceedings and paid the sum in question into court.

But even without going into the rationale underpinning justification as a defence, Davies recognizes that a different approach is applied where the defendant has interfered with equitable *fiduciary* obligations:[108] 'The situation is different where the claimant's contract creates a fiduciary relationship with the primary wrongdoer. In such circumstances, the beneficiary's equitable interest does trump the defendant's contractual rights and the defence of justification will not be available.'

Though no authority is cited in support for the proposition, and despite Davies's dissatisfaction with it, so far as the *common law* may recognize a defence of justification which would excuse a defendant from being held liable at common law for having wrongfully (tortiously) interfered with a common law contractual right, it is a different question altogether whether equity would recognize the same or similar defence when the defendant has wrongfully (dishonestly) interfered with an *equitable* right. Given the historical ordering of equitable and contractual rights,[109] there is no obvious reason to suppose that a *common law*

---

*Industries Ltd* v. *Shell Co. of Australia Ltd* (1937) 37 SR (NSW) 394, 416; cited with approval in *Zhu* v. *Treasurer of New South Wales* [2004] HCA 56; (2004) 218 CLR 530, [139]. Davies argues that the broader English approach is preferable: Davies (2015), pp. 232–3.

[107] *Applin* v. *Cates* (n. 92) provides a counterexample: see discussion in Chapter 9.

[108] Davies (2015), p. 233.

[109] As enshrined in the maxim, 'where the rules of Equity and the common law diverge, Equity shall prevail'. The effect of this is best summarized in the notes to the extract of *The Earl of Oxford's Case* (1615) 1 Chan Rep 1 in F. T. White and O. D. Tudor, *White & Tudor's Leading Cases in Equity: With Notes* (E. P. Hewitt and J. B. Richardson, eds., 9th edn, London: Sweet & Maxwell, 1928), p. 622. This position is preserved under Senior Courts Act 1981, s. 49.

defence, based on the defendant's fulfilment of his *common law* duty, would necessarily immunize him from proceedings brought against him in *equity*.

Certainly, there appears to be no authority to the contrary.

The editors of *Lewin on Trusts* refer to only three defences (apart from the defence of limitation) which may be generally available to a defendant found to have committed dishonest assistance, namely concurrence, acquiescence and release.[110] The editors of *Lewin* also go on to suggest that the cases show how, in certain limited circumstances, the defences of contributory negligence, *ex turpi causa* and contribution under the Civil Liability (Contribution) Act 1978[111] might be available.[112] But there is no mention of any cases of 'justification'[113] by reason of the assistant's fulfilment of a duty he was already subject to as a defence.[114]

This is only to be expected. Though the defendant may well have been discharging some *other* duty when he acted as he did, the discharge of such duty does *not* preclude his liability to a claimant when the defendant *knows* that acting as he had done would have the effect of *assisting* the breach of equitable duties owed to the claimant by an obligor, such knowledge therefore rendering the acts of assistance to be dishonest.

Admittedly, the defendant who has knowledge of facts which would lead a reasonable man to infer that certain acts on his part would aid the equitable obligor to breach her equitable duties to her equitable obligee is placed in a difficult position: he may have become subject to conflicting duties in equity and at law. But that is precisely the situation for interpleader or payment into court to be resorted to;[115] and in addition, express trustees who have actual or constructive knowledge of such wrongdoing may apply to court for directions, or seek relief under s. 61, Trustee Act 1925. Last of all, since the remedy against the defendant lies within equity, the defendant could, potentially, be relieved by reason of the weak discretion afforded the court in respect of equitable remedies.

---

[110] Lewin (2015), para. 40-058.
[111] Civil Liability (Contribution) Act 1978.
[112] Lewin (2015), paras. 40-058 to 40-061.
[113] Or, for that matter, necessity.
[114] Snell (2015) similarly makes no mention of either 'justification' (in the sense used in the main text) or 'necessity' as a defence to dishonest assistance.
[115] Lewin (2015), para. 3-011.

# I Conclusion

Starting from the proposition that every equitable assignee is owed certain duties by his assignor, as mentioned at the beginning of this chapter, such assignee is entitled to demand that third-party strangers to the assignment are not to knowingly interfere with the discharge of those duties. That is to say, every stranger to an equitable assignment is duty-bound to the assignee not to dishonestly assist the assignor in breaching her duties to her assignee. Given such duty not to commit dishonest assistance, the significance of notice or, more precisely, the acquisition of knowledge of the assignment by the obligor, becomes clearer: such knowledge, howsoever it might have been come by, is part of the requirements by which the duty not to commit dishonest assistance may be breached. Once such knowledge is gained by the obligor, acts such as payment or performance to the assignor leading to a discharge of the obligation can potentially lead to a breach of that duty, thereby exposing the obligor to liability in equity for dishonest assistance.[116]

Crucially, the analysis in this chapter explains why, for example, a trustee (T) who is duty-bound under the terms of an express trust to pay an annual income to a trust beneficiary (A) out of the funds held on trust who pays such sums to A despite having knowledge of A's having equitably assigned the benefit of her equitable interest in the annuity to an assignee (C) may be held to be liable to C in respect of such sums. The liability arises not because T had failed to discharge his duty as specified in the express trust in favour of A. On the analysis put forward in this book, T would have discharged such duty (which remains unchanged, notwithstanding T's knowledge of the equitable assignment and A's obligations thereunder). However, having done so despite such

---

[116] The analysis in this chapter might not apply if the assignment by the obligee-assignor to the assignee had 'become' a statutory one under LPA1925, s. 136(1). This is sketched out in Chapter 15, Section F where the case of *Liquidation Estates Purchase Company, Limited* v. *Willoughby* [1898] AC 321 is discussed. That discussion suggests that *Liquidation Estates Purchase Company* may be authority for the proposition that LPA1925, s. 136(1)(c) has the effect of divesting a creditor-assignor's power to give a good discharge by accepting a conforming tender of payment from the debtor (the obligor). If that be the true effect of s. 136(1)(c), the basis for an obligor to have to pay again would be different in cases where the assignment had become statutory. No dishonest assistance liability would lie in such cases, as the obligee-assignor's acts of acceptance would not reduce into her possession the chose in action as had been assigned to the assignee.

knowledge, T would be liable to C for having dishonestly assisted A in breaching her duties to C.

What is more, as explained in this chapter, a similar form of liability in equity may arise in the analogous case where a common law debt has ben equitably assigned. This, however, does not exhaust the impact of notice (and knowledge) of an equitable assignment on the obligor to the chose assigned as a matter of English law. In addition to generating a new equitable cause of action by way of dishonest assistance liability set out in this chapter, the obligor's acquisition of knowledge of the equitable assignment of the chose to which his obligation pertains can constrain the obligor's ability to plead certain defences if he were to be sued in legal or equitable proceedings.

As has been mentioned in this chapter, in connection with the facts in Example 11.1, the facts that B had tendered payment to A, and that A had accepted such tender, would support a defence by B of 'payment' or, more generally, 'discharge by precise performance' if an action were brought at law against B in respect of the £10,000 loan which A had extended to B. However, where, as in Example 11.1, the facts supporting such a defence had arisen *after* B had acquired knowledge of the equitable assignment to C, B could be barred from pleading the facts as would support such a defence to the action at law. So barred, unless other defences were available and pleaded, the action at law against B would proceed to judgment in default, and a judgment debt at law would arise as between the successful plaintiff to those proceedings and B. Therefore, in a case like this, an alternative 'procedural' route to rendering B liable by barring B from making certain pleadings could also arise. The routes by which such pleadings may be barred will now be explored in the following chapter.

# 12

# Knowledge of Assignment: Procedural Avoidance in Equity and by Statute of 'Equities' or 'Defences'

## A  Introduction

Chapter 11 has shown that an obligor who tenders performance to his obligee in purported discharge of his obligations arising under a chose in action between them, despite knowing that the obligee had previously equitably assigned the benefit of the chose to an assignee, may have breached an equitable duty to the assignee not to do so. When the trustee of a fund is given notice by an assignee to whom the beneficiary of the trust fund had equitably assigned her interest, Lord McNaghten observed that '[t]he notice, no doubt, places him [the trustee of the fund] under a direct responsibility to the person who gives the notice'.[1] This 'direct responsibility', to use more modern-day terminology, refers to the equitable duty not to commit acts which would dishonestly assist the trustee of the fund in breaching his duties to the trust beneficiaries. Breach of such duty would then expose the dishonest accessory to substantive liability arising under the equitable wrong of dishonest assistance.[2]

Receipt of notice of assignment alerts the obligee to the equitable duties as are owed by the assignor to her assignee. That said, knowledge of the equitable assignment has further *procedural* effects as between an obligor and the assignee: it may cause the obligor to be barred from pleading certain defences which would otherwise be available on substantive grounds should the obligor be sued, and it is this procedural effect which animates the rule that equities (or defences) arising as between an obligor and an obligee-assignor 'run' as against the assignee, until such time as notice of assignment is received by the obligor.

---

[1] *Ward v. Duncombe* [1893] AC 369, 392.
[2] See also *Re Neil* (1890) 62 LT 649 and *Re Pawson's Settlement* [1917] 1 Ch 541, discussed in Chapter 11, nn. 18 and 86, respectively.

This procedural aspect of an obligor's knowledge of equitable assignment forms the subject matter of this chapter.

## B    An Equitable Assignee Takes 'Subject to Equities'

As Lord Cottenham observed in *Mangles* v. *Dixon*: 'If there is one rule more perfectly established in a court of equity than another, it is, that whoever takes an [equitable] assignment of a chose in action . . . takes it subject to all the equities of the person who made the assignment.'[3] Hence, an equitable assignee of a legal[4] or equitable[5] chose in action will take the assignment 'subject to equities' as against the obligor to the chose, unless some other agreement had been reached between the obligee/assignor and obligor.[6]

This is the case, even if the assignment is bona fide and for value. As Romilly MR explained in *Cockell* v. *Taylor*:[7]

> The rule relative to the equities which attach on a chose in action has been established in many cases. It has not been disputed, nor can it be doubted, that the purchaser of a chose in action does not stand in the situation of a purchaser of real estate for valuable consideration without notice of any prior title, but that the purchaser of a chose in action takes the thing bought subject to all the prior claims upon it.

And, as *Guest on Assignment* points out, '[t]his means (inter alia) that [the assignee] will in principle be exposed to any defence, right of set-off or right of retainer which would have been available to the debtor or obligor against the assignor'.[8]

---

[3]  (1852) 3 HLC 702, 731.

[4]  E.g. in *Turton* v. *Benson* (1718) 2 Vern 764, where the assignees of a bond which had been executed in fraud of a marriage settlement were held to be 'attended with the same equity, as if remaining with the same obligee' (at 2 Vern 765); and in *Graham* v. *Johnson* (1869) LR 8 Eq 36, 43 (Romilly MR).

[5]  E.g. *Phipps* v. *Lovegrove* (1873) LR 16 Eq 80, 88 (James LJ); *Stephens* v. *Venables (No. 1)* (1862) 30 Beav 625. The basis for this rule, as applied to equitable assignments of equitable choses is not quite the same as the basis for its application to equitable assignments of legal choses, as the following will demonstrate.

[6]  Any doubt that the obligor and obligee/assignor might not have the power to dispense with the operation of this rule as between themselves in connection with the operation of the Statutes of Set-off was dispelled by the Court of Appeal in *Halesowen Presswork & Assemblies Ltd.* v. *National Westminster Bank Ltd.* [1971] 1 QB 1 (reversed on other grounds [1972] AC 785); *Gilbert-Ash (Northern) Ltd* v. *Modern Engineering (Bristol) Ltd* [1974] AC 689, 722–3 (Lord Salmon). For further discussion of the point, see Liew (2018), para. 7-25, and the authorities cited therein.

[7]  (1852) 15 Beav 103, 118.

[8]  Liew (2018), para. 7-01.

Such 'running' of 'equities' as against the assignee comes to an end, however, when the obligor acquires knowledge of the assignment, say, when the obligor receives such notice from the assignee,[9] the assignor, or even through his own reasonable inquiries.[10] As James LJ noted in *Phipps* v. *Lovegrove*, where an equitable interest arising under an express trust had been equitably assigned:[11]

> Down to the date at which the notice of assignment was given to the trustees, the trustees were at liberty to deal with the fund, and to have equities created in their favour by the *cestuis que trust*, until they received notice that some other person had come in and displaced those equities. An insurance office might lend money upon a policy of insurance to a person who had insured his life [with the insurance office], notwithstanding any previous assignment by him of the policy, of which no notice had been given to them. Trustees who have got a legal estate, or an estate of any kind, either money or land, may lend money to the *cestui que trust*, and get a beneficial interest in the trust property if they have no notice that there have been any prior incumbrancers. They have got the legal estate and they have got the legal right; they have therefore got, in respect of the charge created in their favour, before they have got any notice of anything else, a right to retain that which the law has given them.

For example, if a bond which was liable to being vitiated by the debtor on grounds of misrepresentation by the creditor[12] had been equitably assigned to an assignee, the 'equity' arising from such misrepresentation would also 'run' against the assignee, regardless of when notice had been given since the debtor's power to rescind the debt would have accrued upon the execution of the bond. Alternatively, if a testamentary gift of an interest under a codicil to a will was invalid for non-compliance with testamentary formalities, the fact that it had been equitably assigned by the purported beneficiary under such (invalid) codicil would have no effect on the ability of the executors of the will to plead such invalidity as part of their defence, if proceedings were brought against them on the codicil. Or, where a related cross-claim had arisen as between the obligee and the obligor, and whose

---

[9] As occurred in *Phipps* v. *Lovegrove* (1873) LR 16 Eq 80.

[10] As Sir William Page Wood LJ explained in *Ex parte Agra Bank; Re Worcester* (1868) LR 3 Ch App 555, the key issue lay in whether the 'person owing the debt or duty' was fixed, 'with the consequences of acting contrary to the *knowledge* he [had] acquired of the equitable interest of the parties' (at 559) (emphasis added), recognizing that such knowledge could result from notice of assignment from the assignor, or from the obligor's own reasonable inquiries.

[11] *Phipps* v. *Lovegrove* (1873) LR 16 Eq 80, 88.

[12] See e.g. *Graham* v. *Johnson* (1869) LR 8 Eq 36.

due performance by the obligee to the obligor was so entangled with the chose in action which had been equitably assigned that its non-performance would 'impugn' the obligor's obligations under the chose which had been assigned, the obligor would be entitled to plead a defence by way of substantive equitable set-off were he to be sued at law on the chose assigned.[13] In all three instances, the facts grounding the respective defences would have accrued prior to the assignment to the assignee. Each 'equity' or defence would have arisen prior to any notice of the assignment. As a result, each equity of this sort may be pleaded by way of defence against any action or suit brought against the respective obligor.[14] The obligor's consciousness of the subsequent equitable assignment would not, therefore, bar the obligor from pleading such defences in any proceedings on the chose.

Other equities or defences may arise post-assignment. For example, following the constitution of a common law chose in action in debt, the obligor might take a deed of release from the obligee,[15] tender payment to the obligee,[16] or enter into further (and separate) dealings with the obligee as would generate a liquidated cross-claim.[17] Plainly, the facts supporting these defences may arise prior to, or after the equitable assignment. This, however, is not significant for present purposes. What *is* significant is whether the facts constituting such defences had arisen before or after the obligor became aware of the assignment to the assignee.

Thus, where a bond had been equitably assigned to an assignee, if the obligor to that chose was given a release by his obligee, and then received

---

[13] *Business Computers Ltd* v. *Anglo-African Leasing Ltd* [1977] 1 WLR 578 (Chan Div).

[14] See e.g. *Redman* v. *Permanent Trustee Company of New South Wales Ltd* (1916) 22 CLR 84. That case was concerned with an equitable assignment of an equitable interest which had purportedly been appointed to the assignor under the terms of a testamentary trust. The High Court of Australia held that the appointment to the assignor was void, and Griffith CH and Barton J held that such invalidity affected the assignee no less than the assignor, since '[t]he assignee of an equitable interest, even for valuable consideration, takes subject to all the equities and infirmities of his assignor's title. It is one of the infirmities of the title of the assignor of an equitable interest that his right to it may be disputed and defeated by litigation in a competent Court between competent parties' (at 91).

[15] Giving rise to a defence of release.

[16] Giving rise to a defence of payment.

[17] Giving rise to a defence of statutory set-off pursuant to the Statutes of Set-off (if both the claim and the cross-claims arose from common law choses in action), or a defence of equitable set-off by analogy with the Statutes of Set-off (if both the claim and cross-claim were liquidated, but the Statutes of Set-off would not have applied because one of the liquidated sums had arisen out of an equitable chose in action, or if the requirement of mutuality of parties as required by the Statutes of Set-off can only be satisfied by taking into account equitable titles).

notice of the assignment, the obligor is not barred from pleading such release by way of defence.[18] Similarly, where the obligor had tendered payment to his obligee in discharge of his indebtedness under a bond before receiving notice that the benefit of the debt had been equitably assigned to another, such obligor may not be barred from pleading such tender of payment to and its acceptance by the obligee as a defence to any proceedings on the chose against him for non-performance.[19] Finally, where the obligor to a debt had entered into cross-dealings with his creditor which would entitle him to raise a defence of statutory set-off pursuant to the Statutes of Set-off were he to be sued on the debt, the obligor may assert such statutory set-off defence in respect of cross-dealings entered with the creditor obligee prior to his receiving notice that the debt had been equitably assigned to an assignee, should proceedings on the debt be brought against him.[20] However, matters are otherwise if the release, tender of payment or cross-dealings had arisen *after* receipt of notice.[21]

Given the above, two questions arise. First, why do 'equities' run, even those that have arisen post-assignment? And second, why do they *stop* running, following receipt of notice by the obligor?

Though the proposition that an assignee takes subject to equities, including equities which might have arisen post-assignment but prior to the obligor's receipt of notice of assignment, is of long standing, the conceptual basis for the proposition is opaque. *Guest on Assignment* suggests that '[t]he debtor or obligor is not to be prejudiced as a result of the assignment',[22] relying on the observation of Lord Millett in *Mulkerrins* v. *PricewaterhouseCoopers* that:[23]

---

[18]  *Graham* v. *Johnson* (1869) LR 8 Eq 36, 43.

[19]  *Williams* v. *Sorrell* (1799) 4 Ves Jun 389.

[20]  *Norrish* v. *Marshall* (1821) 5 Madd 475.

[21]  See e.g. *Legh* v. *Legh* (1799) 1 Bos & Pul 447 (release and/or payment of bond after receipt of notice of assignment); *De Pothonier* v. *De Mattos* (1858) El Bl & El 461 (release of freight payable under a charter party after notice of assignment); *Aspinall* v. *London & North-Western Railway Co.* (1853) 11 Hare 325; *Brice* v. *Bannister* (1878) 3 QBD 569, 578 (Cotton LJ); *Liquidation Estates Purchase Company, Limited* v. *Willoughby* [1898] AC 321; and *Yates* v. *Terry* [1902] 1 KB 527 (payment of a contract debt after notice of assignment); *Stephens* v. *Venables (No. 1)* (1862) 30 Beav 625 (set-off by trustee arising by way of cross-claims with trust beneficiary permitted for cross-claims arising prior to notice of assignment, but not permitted for those arising after notice).

[22]  Liew (2018), para. 7-01.

[23]  *Mulkerrins* v. *PricewaterhouseCoopers (a firm)* [2003] UKHL 41; [2003] 1 WLR 1937, [15].

> The reason that the debtor's consent is not required to [sic] an assignment
> of a debt is that the assignment cannot prejudice him. The assignment is
> subject to equities, which means that any set-off which the debtor may
> have against the assignor can be asserted against the assignee.

Smith and Leslie appear to do much the same, though they rely instead
on a passage in Westbury LC's judgment in *Phillips* v. *Phillips*,[24] and
suggest that the rationale for the rule rests on the proposition that 'the
assignee of a chose in action cannot acquire a better right than the
assignor had, and the assignee must take the chose in action subject to
all the equities affecting it in the hands of the assignor which are in
existence before notice is received by the debtor.'[25]

With respect, these 'justifications' merely beg the question. The result
of the rule that an equitable assignee takes subject to equities, including
any equities arising between the assignor and obligor prior to the obligor's receipt of notice of the assignment, is that an assignee's position as
against the obligor will be no better than the assignor's position as against
the obligor, had there been no assignment. However, to use the *result* of
the rule to explain its *operation* appears circular.

Is a more convincing rationale available? As will be shown in Section C,
the 'substitutive transfer' model of equitable assignment is a poor fit for
explaining the rule as to the running of equities because it answers neither
the first nor the second of the two questions set out above. The composite
'trust-plus-agency' model, however, makes for a better fit, as it does
answer the first question. However, as the following will show, it, too,
does not answer the second. In the case of an equitable assignment of an
equitable chose in action, equities will stop running as against the assignee
following notice of the assignment where it would be unconscionable for
the obligor to assert the facts pertaining to such post-notice equity by way
of defence as against the assignee's proceedings in equity on the equitable
chose.[26] In the case of an equitable assignment of a legal chose, however,
the basis for the operation of the rule is more complex. For that, we need
to appreciate how the courts of Chancery, and later, the courts of
common law, exercised procedural control over the pleading of defences
at law.[27]

---

[24] (1861) 4 De G F & J 208, 215–16.
[25] Smith & Leslie (2018), para. 26.45 (emphasis added).
[26] This will be explained in Section D.
[27] This is explored from Section E onwards.

## C Explaining the Rule that 'Equities Run until Notice of Assignment': Two Models

### (i) Substitutive Transfer Model of Assignment: A Poor Fit

It is not possible to explain the operation of the rule that 'equities run until notice' if equitable assignment operated by means of substitutive transfer as this rule is simply inconsistent with such conception. If equitable assignment operated by way of substitutive transfer, the rule would be that equities would run until the time of assignment, and not until such time as when notice was received.

The rule developed through the cases provides that an equitable assignee takes the benefit of the chose assigned, subject to any 'equities' as might have arisen between the obligee-assignor and the obligor, prior to the obligor's receipt of notice of such assignment. This includes post-assignment equities arising between the time of assignment and the time when notice was received. This phenomenon cannot be explained using the 'substitutive transfer' conception of equitable assignment.

On the substitutive transfer conception, the assignor would have become a stranger to the chose in action which, post-assignment, would have become a chose in action as between the obligor and the assignee. How any dealings between the obligor and the assignor, if seen as a stranger to the chose in action between the obligor and assignee, can have any legal effect on the discharge of the obligations arising under such chose is not obvious. The same is true of an equitable chose which has been equitably assigned as Example 12.1 shows:

---

**EXAMPLE 12.1**

T holds certain funds on an express trust for $A_L$ for her life, and $A_R$ as remainder-man. Under the terms of the trust, T is to pay a sum of £1,000 out of the trust funds to $A_L$ every year on her birthday, for so long as she lives.

On 1 January 2018 (two months before her birthday), $A_L$ equitably assigns her life interest in the express trust to C in a suitably signed writing, and for value. However, neither $A_L$ nor C notify T of the assignment.

On 12 March 2018 (which is $A_L$'s birthday), ignorant of the assignment to C, T pays £1,000 out of the trust funds to $A_L$, which $A_L$ accepts. However, instead of transferring the sum received to C as $A_L$ ought to do, given her equitable assignment of her life interest to C, $A_L$ absconds with the monies, leaving no substantial assets behind. On 15 March 2018, C makes inquiries of T, not having received anything from $A_L$. It is only then that T becomes aware of the equitable assignment to C.

---

On the above facts, if C brought proceedings in equity against T for failure to perform his duties under the terms of the trust in relation to the £1,000 which was due to be paid to $A_L$ on 1 March 2018, T would be entitled to plead the facts pertaining to his having paid $A_L$ that day *whilst ignorant of the equitable assignment to C* by way of defence against such a suit.[28] If C were to seek to falsify T's payment of the £1,000 to $A_L$ on 1 March 2018 on grounds that the payment was contrary to the terms of the express trust, T would be entitled to be absolved by pleading not only the fact of his payment to $A_L$, but also that the payment had been made whilst he was ignorant of the assignment to C.[29]

Some have insisted that, by virtue of the equitable assignment of her equitable life interest to C, $A_L$'s place as beneficiary to the express trust had been taken by C. But if this were the law, $A_L$ would have become a stranger to the express trust as at 1 January 2018, her place having been taken by C. Consequently, when T extracted £1,000 from the trust funds and forwarded that sum to $A_L$ on 1 March 2018, that would have been a payment to a stranger to the trust and would, accordingly, have been in breach of the trust's express terms (on the supposition that its terms had been modifed by the equitable assignment).

The caselaw is clear that where a trustee makes payment to a non-beneficiary in the honest (but mistaken) belief that that stranger was entitled under the terms of the trust, such honest but mistaken belief does not exculpate the trustee. As the Supreme Court acknowledged in *Ivey* v. *Genting Casinos (UK) Ltd (trading as Crockfords Club)*,[30] the liability of an express trustee who has failed to perform his duties under the terms of such trust is strict. And, as Millett LJ (as he then was) pointed out in *Armitage* v. *Nurse*: 'A breach of trust may be deliberate or inadvertent',[31] before going on to recognize that a breach of trust could be committed fraudulently, or non-fraudulently (such as where the trustees deliberately act in breach of trust by acting beyond their powers under the terms of

---

[28] As explained in Chapter 11, C may have an alternative claim in equity against T for the commission of the equitable wrong of dishonest assistance by which a distinct *constructive* trust might be imposed so as to render T liable to C as a *constructive* trustee. As to such accessory liability as a constructive trustee, T might also plead the fact of his ignorance of the assignment to C as part of his defence to such accessory liability.

[29] Payment to $A_L$, being in precise conformity with the duty which the settlor of the express trust had set out, would plainly entitle T to be discharged in respect of his duty to tender payment for that calendar year. As for T's non-liability to C where he had no notice (actual or constructive) of C's derivative entitlement through $A_L$, see Chapter 11.

[30] [2017] UKSC 67; [2018] 1 WLR 391, [62].

[31] [1998] Ch 241, 251.

the express trust but 'in good faith and in the honest belief that they are acting in the interests of the beneficiaries'.[32]

There are also authorities setting out the proposition that a trustee who pays the wrong person due to an honest, reasonable, but mistaken interpretation of an obscurely worded instrument will also have committed a breach of trust.[33] Indeed, a trustee may be held to have acted in breach of trust for having paid sums out of the trust fund in reliance on a forged document.[34] Yet in none of these cases was the defaulting trustee permitted any exculpatory defence; meaning to say, not only was the duty strict, the courts declined to develop any defences as might give trustees some protection. Thus, the courts held that there was no defence even if the defaulting trustee had acted in reliance on advice which turned out to be bad or erroneous.[35]

Given the above, the 'substitutive transfer' conception of equitable assignment cannot explain the 'equities run until notice' rule and, indeed, is contradicted by the cases which have set it out.

---

[32] It is also possible for a breach of trust to be committed unknowingly, for example, where the trustee had acted in the mistaken, but honest, belief that he was entitled on the terms of the trust to act as hehad done, but where he actually was not: *National Trustees Company of Australasia* v. *General Finance Company of Australia* [1905] AC 373. In the analogous context of breaches of fiduciary duties of a company director, see *Bishopsgate Investment Management Limited (in liquidation)* v. *Maxwell (No. 2)* [1994] 1 All ER 261, 265 (Hoffmann LJ) and 269c (Ralph Gibson LJ).

[33] *Palmer* v. *Wakefield* (1840) 3 Beav 227; *Hilliard* v. *Fulford* (1876) 4 ChD 389.

[34] *Eaves* v. *Hickson* (1861) 30 Beav 136, where the trustees paid sums to illegitimate children in breach of trust after being deceived by a forged marriage certificate.

[35] *Doyle* v. *Blake* (1804) 2 Schoales & Lefroy 230 (High Court of Chancery, Ireland), 243 (Lord Redesdale LC): 'If, under the best advice he [the executor of a will] could procure, he acts wrong, it is his misfortune; but public policy requires that he should be the person to suffer'; foll'd in *Re Knight's Trusts* (1859) 27 Beav 49; and also *Peers* v. *Ceeley* (1852) 15 Beav 209, 211 (Sir John Romilly MR): 'The Court can never sanction the proposition, that a party, having acted in a manner which the Court has decided to be improper, can protect himself by shewing that he had received bad advice, however eminent the person may be who gave it.'

The position was only ameliorated somewhat by the Judicial Trustees Act 1896, s. 3, which has since been re-enacted as Trustee Act 1925, s. 61. For further discussion of the s. 61 'statutory excuse' for breach of trust, see John Lowry and Rod Edmunds, 'Excuses' in Peter Birks and Arianna Pretto-Sakmann (eds.), *Breach of Trust* (Oxford: Hart, 2002). In Australia, equivalent provision may be found in the Trustee Act 1925 (ACT), s. 85; Trustee Act 1925 (NSW), s. 85; Trustee Act (NT), s. 49A; Trusts Act 1973 (Qld), s. 76; Trustee Act 1936 (SA), s. 56; Trustee Act 1898 (Tas), s. 50; Trustee Act 1958 (Vic), s. 67; Trustees Act 1962 (WA), s. 75.

### (ii)  'Trust-Plus-Agency' Model: A Better Fit

As the following will show, the 'trust-plus-agency' model of equitable assignment is a much better fit with the rule that equities run until notice, at least so far as it accommodates post-assignment equities.

Since an equitable assignee is enabled to invoke the assignor's entitlements against the obligor to the chose assigned by reason of the assignor's having delegated her powers to the assignee, it must follow that so far as the assignor's invocation of those entitlements was qualified by any prerequisites or constraints, these would also apply to the assignee when acting as the assignor's delegatee. And, when an assignee directs her assignor to bring judicial proceedings against the obligor, it must follow that the obligor may rely on the same prerequisites or constraints to bar their successful prosecution.

Though the proceedings might well have been initiated or brought by the assignee, the assignee is, after all, suing 'in right of' the assignor. This is most obvious where the proceedings are at law in respect of a common law chose in action, given the substantive need for joinder of the assignor. But it is also the case where the proceedings are in the court's equitable jurisdiction in respect of an equitable chose in action. In Chapter 7, it was explained that the lack of need for joinder in the latter situation stems purely from the necessarily different treatment of a court when acting within its equitable jurisdiction in connection with its recognition and enforcement of distinctly equitable institutions such as equitable assignment. Therefore, that joinder is not absolutely necessary in that context does not denote a substitution of the assignee in place of the assignor so as to extinguish the assignor's entitlements. Hence, so far as the substantive law provides for substantive defences which may be pleaded by the obligor in proceedings brought against him on the chose assigned, even if such defences rested on post-assignment dealings between the obligor and the assignor, those defences would still be available to the obligor despite the assignment.

On the trust-plus-agency conception of equitable assignment, since the assignee does not 'replace' the assignor, the assignor does not become a 'stranger' to the obligations arising under the chose in action. Consequently, if the substantive law would have afforded the obligor a defence to judicial proceedings on the chose in action had it not been assigned by the obligee to the assignee, that defence could continue to be raised even if the proceedings had ultimately been brought for the benefit of the assignee, given his beneficial interest as equitable assignee of the chose. This would follow because such proceedings would *still* be brought against the obligor 'in right of' the obligee/assignor. This would be the case given that the equitable assignment, alone and without more,[36] generates no independent duty–obligation jural relation between the assignee and the obligor.

That said, the trust-plus-agency conception of equitable assignment does not explain why equities 'run' until notice of assignment is received. The following sections will attempt to provide explanations as to why the 'rule' that equities run as against the assignee is qualified in this way.

## D Notice and the Running of Equities in Equitable Assignments of Equitable Choses

In *Stephens* v. *Venables*, Sir John Romilly MR held as follows:[37]

> When a trustee or executor *receives* notice that a legatee has charged his legacy in favour of a stranger, the trustee is bound to withhold all further payments to that legatee, unless made with the consent of the mortgagee of the legacy. All rights of set-off and adjustment of equities between the legatee and the executor already existing at the date of the notice have *priority* over the charge, and may properly be deducted from the amount coming to the mortgagee; but the trustees can create no new charge or right of set-off after that time. A debt due to the trustees before the notice of charge received by him may be set off against the share of the legatee, but no debt which accrued due subsequently to that period can be allowed to work any deduction from the share charged to the mortgagee. *Were it otherwise*, the charge made by the legatee, whether residuary or pecuniary, would be worth nothing, *the trustees might, after the receipt of notice of the charge, embark in a speculation with the legatee, and if, in the course of it, a balance accrued due to the trustee from the legatee, he might set it off against the legacy, and leave the mortgagee with nothing.*

The practical reason for the 'rule' that equities run *until* notice is received is therefore a simple one: if it were otherwise, the entire institution of equitable assignment would be made practically pointless: there would be a lacuna which an obligor might find all too easy to exploit.

---

[36] As explained in Chapter 10, the fact of equitable assignment coupled with the requisite knowledge as well as acts which would assist in the commission of breaches of equitable duties by the assignor arising from the 'trust' mechanism which underpins equitable assignment can generate an independent and substantive obligation between the assignee and the obligor by which the obligor is duty-bound to the assignee not to dishonestly assist the assignor in committing breaches of her duties to the assignee.

[37] *Stephens* v. *Venables* (1862) 30 Beav 625, 627–8; 54 ER 1032, 1033–4 (emphasis added).

An equitable obligor who enters into further cross-dealings with his obligee despite having received notice that the equitable chose had been equitably assigned to an assignee can hardly claim to have entered into those cross-dealings in ignorance of the assignee's beneficial interest. That knowledge carries with it certain equitable obligations: for one, the obligor is duty-bound to the assignee not to dishonestly assist the obligee-assignor in breaching her duties to her assignee. But the assignee's derivative equitable interest could be adversely impacted by means other than through assisting in breaches of the obligee-assignor's duties.

The trust-plus-agency effects of equitable assignment necessarily entails that equities arising between the obligor and the equitable obligee-assignor, even post-assignment ones, will bind and be exigible against the assignee. After all, the assignee is still claiming through the obligee-assignor by reason of the agency effect. Left unqualified, the institution of equitable assignment would allow the obligor to adversely affect the assignee's interest in the assigned chose by creating such equities as would diminish or even eliminate any recovery by the assignee should the chose in action be subsequently reduced into possession through the bringing of proceedings in equity. Since these cross-dealings with the obligee-assignor would not necessarily involve any breach of duty by the obligee-assignor, if the rule was not qualified in some way, it would be all too easy for an obligor to whittle down the assignee's equitable interest to nothing: hence the need for a qualification to the 'rule' as to the running of equities as would bind the assignee, were he to bring proceedings in equity to reduce the equitable chose into possession.

As to why the qualification should have been developed by reference to notice, once notice is received, the obligor can scarcely claim to have been caught by surprise by the curtailment of his entitlement to successfully invoke equities by way of defence. But even so, the qualification to the 'rule' does not deny the substantive merits of the obligor's post-notice 'equity': the qualification merely denies that the obligor may successfully invoke it by way of defence to the suit on the equitable chose which had been assigned. Consequently, it would be open to the obligor to raise it as a defence to any other proceeding which the obligee might bring against him.

### E    Barring the Pleading of Defences by Way of Injunction and the 'Equitable Jurisdiction of the Courts of Common Law'

The explanation above as to why the 'rule' as to running of equities is qualified by notice does not, however, quite explain how, and why, the same qualification is applied where a common law chose had been equitably assigned, and where proceedings at law are brought. To more fully understand how the qualification to the 'equities run until notice' rule came to be in this context, we need to go back to the time before the Judicature Act reforms.

### (i)   Injunctive Relief from the Court of Chancery

Prior to the mid-1800s, it was not uncommon for bills to be filed before the court of Chancery to seek common injunctions[38] to enjoin the respondent to the bill from commencing or continuing[39] with proceedings in other courts (such as a court of law).[40] In the first edition of his treatise on the law of injunctions,[41] Kerr set out the intricacies of such

[38]  Drewry (1841), p. v: 'In practice, injunctions are of two kinds. An injunction of the first kind is grantable as an order *of* course, without reference to merits, upon the defendant's making default in appearing, or in pleading, answering, or demurring within the time prescribed by the practice of the Court. An injunction of the second kind is, on the contrary, always granted upon merits, and may, under circumstances, be granted at any stage of the suit . . . An injunction of the first kind is properly called a *common injunction*, and is that which is most generally obtained in suits where the object of the injunction is to stay proceedings at law.'

[39]  The power to enjoin the continuation of proceedings which had already been commenced in a common law court was removed by Judicature Act 1873, s. 24(5), with the command that the effect which would otherwise be achieved by such injunction should henceforth be achieved by way of a defence. The power to enjoin the commencement of proceedings, however, was not legislatively removed and it remains the basis on which anti-suit injunctions may be brought within the practice of private international law.

[40]  Such injunctions were issued by the court of Chancery to restrain not just proceedings before the common law courts, but also proceedings before the Ecclesiastical Courts, the Admiralty Court, other courts of equity (such as the Court of Exchequer, which had equity jurisdiction until 1841), and even other proceedings before the court of Chancery itself, as well as proceedings in foreign courts: see Drewry (1841), pp. 96–108, and the cases cited therein.

[41]  Kerr (1867). The technicalities of the grant of common injunctions to enjoin the commencement or to stay proceedings in other courts was also extensively discussed in a revised edition of Drewry (1841) in Charles Stewart Drewry, *The Law and Practice of Injunctions: With a Supplement Containing Cases Decided since 1841* (London: S. Sweet, 1849). In the second edition of *Kerr on Injunctions*, published in 1878 after the Judicature Act 1873 reforms had come into force, the chapters on the filing of bills for common injunctions to enjoin or stay proceedings in other courts in the previous edition were excised because, given Judicature Act 1873, s. 24(5), no action before the courts of the Supreme Court of Judicature could be enjoined by common injunction. For an illustration of the effect of s. 24(5), see *Garbutt v. Fawcus* (1875) LR 1 Ch D 155.

injunctions to restrain proceedings in courts of law[42] in detail over five chapters (out of twenty-nine). Plainly, such injunctions formed a substantial part of Chancery practice at the time.

As to the basis on which such relief might be granted, reference may be made to the Lord Chancellor's observations in *Hill* v. *Turner*: 'For an injunction, when awarded, does not deny, but admits the jurisdiction of the court of common law; and the ground upon which it issues is that they [i.e. the plaintiff at law] are making use of their jurisdiction [i.e. the jurisdiction of the court of common law] contrary to equity and conscience.'[43] Given this, Kerr took the basis for granting such injunctions to be to 'prevent the judgment of the Courts of law from being made an instrument of injustice'.[44] These views were not novel, and similar sentiments had been expressed in 1787 by Mitford:[45]

> Sometimes a party, by fraud, or accident, or otherwise, has an advantage in proceeding in a court of ordinary jurisdiction which must necessarily make that court an instrument of injustice; and it is therefore against conscience that he [i.e. the plaintiff at law] should use the advantage. In such cases, to prevent a manifest wrong, courts of equity have interposed, by restraining the party whose conscience is thus bound from using the advantage he has improperly gained; and upon these principles bills to restrain proceedings in courts of ordinary jurisdiction are still frequent, though the courts of common law have been enabled, by the assistance of the legislature, as well as by a more liberal exertion of their inherent powers,[46] to render applications of this nature to a court of equity unnecessary in many cases where formerly no other remedy was provided.

In more contemporary idiom, such relief reflected the second-order operation of the courts of Chancery to combat opportunistic applications

---

[42] Such injunctions could and were granted to stay proceedings not only in other courts of law, but also against other courts of equity (such as the court of Exchequer prior to 1841 before its equity jurisdiction was merged with that of the court of Chancery pursuant to the 1841 statute of 5 Vict, c. 5 (or the 'Judicial Administration Act 1841'). For an account of such injunctions, see Drewry (1841), pp. 103–5.

[43] *Hill* v. *Turner* (1737) 1 Atk 515.

[44] Kerr (1867), p. 14, relying on the authority of *Hill* v. *Turner*.

[45] Mitford (1787), p. 116. The first edition of this book (published in 1780) did not address this point. Mitford was appointed Solicitor-General for England in 1793, before becoming Attorney-General a few years later. He was then granted a peerage and made Baron Redesdale, and was appointed Lord Chancellor of Ireland from 1802 to 1806. Unsurprisingly, this treatise became a very influential work which ran for many editions.

[46] It would appear that by this, Mitford was referring to the so-called equitable jurisdiction of the courts of common law. That jurisdiction will be discussed below.

of first-order rules, such as those as might be applied by the common law courts.[47]

But the bill for a common injunction could equally be issued to bar the respondent in equity from pleading *defences* were he to be sued in a court of law. This, also, was not uncommon, and again Mitford's work on equity pleadings from 1787 is instructive: 'The courts of equity will interfere upon the same grounds to relieve against instruments which destroy as well as against instruments which create rights; and therefore will prevent a release which has been fraudulently[48] or improperly obtained from being made a defence in an action at law.'[49]

Reports of proceedings in equity where bills seeking injunctive relief to bar defendants to a parallel action at law from pleading certain defences which had been obtained 'fraudulently or improperly' may be found even in the years leading up to reforms brought about by the Judicature

---

[47] See e.g. Henry E. Smith, 'Equitable Defences as Meta-Law' in Paul S. Davies, Simon Douglas and James Goudkamp (eds.), *Defences in Equity* (Oxford: Hart, 2018).

[48] In this context, no very strict conception of 'fraud' would have been applied. As Lord Ellesmere noted in *The Earl of Oxford's Case* (1615) 1 Ch Rep 1, 6: 'The Cause why there is a Chancery is, for that Mens Actions are so divers and infinite, That it is impossible to make any general Law which may aptly meet with every particular Act, and nor fail in some Circumstances.' Or, more to the point, in Lord Hardwicke LC's words in *Lawley* v. *Hooper* (1745) 3 Atk 278, 279: 'The court very wisely hath never laid down any general rule beyond which it will not go, lest other means of avoiding the equity of the court should be found out; Therefore they always determine upon the particular circumstances of each case; and wherever they have found the least tincture of fraud in any of these oppressive bargains, relief hath always been given.' Similar sentiments were repeated in correspondence between Lord Hardwicke and Lord Kames in connection with the publication of the latter's *Treatise on the Principles of Equity* in 1760 in a letter from 1759. The letter has been reproduced in full in Alexander Fraser Tytler (Lord Woodhouselee), *Memoirs of the Life and Writings of the Honourable Henry Home of Kames* (vol. I, 2nd edn, Edinburgh: T. Cadell amd W. Davies, 1814), pp. 329–45; and the relevant portion (at p. 341) reads: 'But as to relief against frauds, no invariable rules can be established. Fraud is infinite, and were a court of equity once to lay down rules, how far they would go, and no farther, in extending their relief against it, or to define strictly the species or evidence of it, the jurisdiction would be cramped, and perpetually eluded by new schemes, which the fertility of man's invention would contrive.' Lord Redesdale, Lord Chancellor of Ireland, set out much the same view in in *Webb* v. *Rorke* (1806) 2 Schoales & Lefroy 661, 666: 'Cases cannot always be found to serve as direct authority for subsequent cases; but if a case arises of fraud, or presumption of fraud, to which even no principle already established can be applied, a new principle must be established to meet the fraud, as the principles on which former cases have been decided, have been from time to time established, as fraud contrived new devices; for the possibility will always exist, that human ingenuity, in contriving fraud, will go beyond any cases which have before occurred.'

[49] Mitford (1787), p. 118.

Acts 1873 and 1875. Examples of such bills may be found in *Stewart* v. *The Great Western Railway Company and Saunders*,[50] and *Lee* v. *Lancashire and Yorkshire Railway Company*,[51] both of which involved pleas of payment; *Aspinall* v. *London and North-Western Railway Co.*,[52] which involved a plea of release; and *Re Northern Assam Tea Company*,[53] which involved a plea of statutory set-off pursuant to the Statutes of Set-off.

If granted, the defendant to the bill in equity would be faced with contempt proceedings if he were to ignore the injunction by proceeding to plead the defence in question in the action at law. Conversely, if the defendant complied with the injunction, no defence would be filed in the action – and unless the action at law was met with some other defence which was not also barred by injunction, judgment on the action would follow in lieu of any defence. But enjoining a defendant at law from pleading common law defences in this way entailed parallel proceedings in equity. To address the attendant problems of multiplicity of proceedings, a partial solution was developed by the courts of common law which developed a so-called 'equitable jurisdiction' of its own.[54]

### (ii)    The 'Equitable Jurisdiction of the Common Law Courts'

Equitable relief by way of a bill seeking an injunction to bar the pleading of a defence at law had been a regular feature of Chancery practice, and probably had been so for a considerable period of time, given Mitford's account. Confirmation of this may be seen in the following extract from Lord Abinger CB's decision in *Phillips* v. *Clagett* in the Court of Exchequer which was handed down in 1843:[55]

---

[50] (1865) 3 De G J & S 319, where the Lord Westbury LC affirmed the decision of Sir R. T. Kindersley VC in the court below: (1865) 2 Dr & Sm 438. As a result, the defendants were enjoined from pleading in the action at law that the plaintiff had been paid a liquidated sum in full and final settlement as compensation for the injuries he had sustained as a passenger on a train operated by the defendants which had collided with another train owing to the negligence of the defendants' servants or agents.

[51] (1871) LR 6 Ch 527, where the bill seeking to enjoin the defendant railway company from pleading payment of a liquidated sum in full and final settlement of the plaintiff's action at law was dismissed on grounds that the plaintiff had not pleaded any particulars pertaining to fraud on the part of the defendant.

[52] (1853) 11 Hare 325.

[53] (1870) LR 10 Eq 458, 464.

[54] As to which, see below.

[55] (1843) 11 M & W 84, 91 (Lord Abinger CB). Although the Court of Exchequer had both equitable and common law jurisdiction, its equity jurisdiction was taken away by statute in 1841 pursuant to the Administration of Justice Act 1841. In any event, no issue of

It has been the practice of Courts of law (especially in modern times), where they see that justice demands the interference of a Court of equity, and that a Court of equity would interfere – in every such case to save parties the expense of proceeding to a Court of equity, by giving them the aid of the equitable jurisdiction of a Court of common law, to enable them to effect the same purpose.

But this passage reveals that judges of the common law courts did not merely take note of the practice of granting injunctive relief to restrain common law proceedings which their brethren in the court of Chancery had entertained. As Lord Abinger CB noted, the common law courts seized a peculiar jurisdiction of their own:[56]

From that principle has arisen where they [the courts of common law] have prevented a plea of release, or any other matter of the same sort, from being pleaded; and where they have seen clearly and distinctly that a Court of equity would declare the release to be void, they set the release aside, in order to save the parties the necessity of having recourse to a tedious, and certainly sometimes an expensive, litigation.

The development of the 'equitable jurisdiction of the common law courts' did not extinguish the court of Chancery's jurisdiction to grant injunctions to enjoin the bringing or continuation of proceedings in other courts.[57] So the two 'equitable jurisdictions', one in Chancery and its shadow in the courts of common law, continued to operate in parallel.

As to the manner by which such defences would be 'set aside' or barred by a common law court acting within its so-called equitable jurisdiction, Lord Abinger explained as follows:[58]

In the cases cited, where the release has been given by one party in fraud of another and in collusion, or whether by a mere nominal plaintiff having no interest whatever in the subject-matter of the action, or under other circumstances of the same character, which perhaps may be found in other cases, the ruling principle which has governed the Courts has been, that it has appeared manifest that Court of equity could do nothing else but set the release aside.

---

equity jurisdiction arose in *Phillips* v. *Clagett* as the proceedings had been brought by way of an action on the case.

[56] *Phillips* v. *Clagett* (ibid.).

[57] See e.g. *Codd* v. *Wooden* (1790) 3 Bro C C 72; *Evans* v. *Bicknell* (1801) 6 Ves Jun 174, 182. To extinguish such jurisdiction, once it had been asserted by the court, statutory language to that effect would be necessary: *Slim* v. *Croucher* (1860) 1 De G F & J 518, 528.

[58] *Phillips* v. *Clagett* (n. 55), at 11 M & W 81.

These words tell us a number of things. First, they confirm that, in certain circumstances, a plaintiff bringing proceedings at law against a defendant on a common law debt could bring proceedings in equity against that defendant to restrain that defendant from pleading certain defences which might otherwise be effective to absolve him from liability in the common law action.[59]

Second, that being the case, such plaintiff could have alternative recourse to seek the 'aid of the equitable jurisdiction of a Court of common law'.[60] Without need to commence separate proceedings by way of a suit in equity, the plaintiff in the action at law could apply directly to the court of law to set aside or bar the defendant from pleading defences which would otherwise be enjoined by the court of Chancery, thereby saving the time and expense of bringing such parallel proceedings.

Third, this state of affairs had been the law for quite some time, and a notable example from 1799 may be found in the case of *Legh* v. *Legh*.[61] The case concerned an action on a bond brought by an assignee in the name of the creditor on the bond against the debtor. In his defence, the debtor first pleaded that he had been given a release by the creditor, whom he alleged he had paid. However, it was conceded that he had, by such time of payment and release, received notice of the assignment in favour of the assignee. On these facts, Eyre CJ held:[62]

[59]  Although there are a number of cases (such as *Mountstephen* v. *Brooke* (1819) 1 Chitty's King's Bench Practice Reports 390; *Johnson* v. *Holdsworth* (1835) 4 Dowling's Practice Cases 63) where the deed of release itself was ordered to be set aside and cancelled, the basis for such power is unclear. In his judgment in *Phillips* v. *Clagett* (n. 55), Parke B concurred with Lord Abinger in declining to exercise the equitable jurisdiction of the common law courts. However, Parke B doubted whether the courts of law might not have gone too far in setting aside the release itself (at 11 M & W 93). Similar doubts were expressed by Sir W. Page Wood VC in *Aspinall* v. *London & North-Western Railway Co.*, at 11 Hare 335.

[60]  See also authorities cited in William Tidd, *The Practice of the Courts of King's Bench and Common Pleas in Personal Actions and Ejectment* (2 vols., 9th edn, London: Joseph Butterworth and Son, 1828), vol. I, pp. 677–8.

[61]  (1791) 1 Bos & Pul 447. An even earlier example may be found in the decision of the court of King's Bench in *Payne* v. *Rogers* (1780) 1 Doug 407. In *Barker* v. *Richardson* (1827) 1 Y & J 362, 365, Hullock B observed that, '[t]he Courts have exercised the jurisdiction sought to be enforced in this case [i.e. the equitable jurisdiction of the common law courts], on several occasions, since the case of *Payne* v. *Rogers*'. In Marshall (1950), p. 74, it is suggested that the equitable jurisdiction of the common law courts may be traced even further back, to the case of *Carrington* v. *Harway* (1676) 1 Keb 803.

[62]  *Legh* v. *Legh*, at 1 Bos & Pul 447 (emphasis added). As explained in Chapter 9, a court of Chancery may make an order of specific performance to compel a defendant to a bill to

The conduct of the Defendant has been against good faith, and the only question is, whether the Plaintiff must not seek relief in a Court of Equity? The Defendant ought either to have paid the person to whom the bond was assigned, or have waited until an action was commenced against him, and then have applied to the Court. Most clearly it was in breach of good faith to pay the money to the assignor of the bond and take a release, and *I rather think the Court ought not to allow the Defendant to avail himself of this plea, since a Court of Equity would order the Defendant to pay the Plaintiff the amount of his lien on the bond, and probably all the costs of the application.*

Buller J arrived at a similar conclusion:[63]

There are many cases in which the Court has set aside a release given to prejudice the real Plaintiff. All these cases depend on circumstances. If the release be fraudulent, the Court will attend to the application.

In consequence, the defendant's plea of release was barred, and the court recommended that the parties go before the prothonotary to ascertain what sum was due to the plaintiff on the bond. But counsel for the plaintiff then sought leave to plead a further defence, this time, of payment of the bond. As to this, Eyre CJ held:[64]

The Court has in many cases refused to allow a party to take his legal advantage, where it has appeared to be against good faith. Thus we prevent a man from signing judgment who has a right by law to do so, if it would be in breach of his own agreement. In order to defeat the real Plaintiff, this Defendant has colluded with the nominal Plaintiff to obtain a release; and I think therefore the plea of release may be set aside consistently with the general rules of the Court. *And if so, the Defendant cannot be permitted to plead payment of the bond, as that would amount to the same thing.*[65]

Significantly, the court in *Legh* v. *Legh* made no substantive findings on the merits of the two pleas of release or of payment. Instead, the court barred the defendant from pleading these defences, because the 'fraudulent circum-stances' under which such release and payment had been effected meant

---

pay a fixed sum of money due on a bond if the dispute is otherwise appropriately brought within its jurisdiction.

[63] Ibid., at 1 Bos & Pul 447.

[64] Ibid., at 1 Bos & Pul 447, 447–8 (emphasis added).

[65] Buller J's response to counsel's contention for leave to plead the defence of payment was more cryptic, holding that '[t]he Court proceeds on the ground, that the Defendant has in effect agreed not to plead payment against the nominal obligee': 1 Bos & Pul 448.

that it would be contrary to 'good faith' to so plead. But what might these 'fraudulent' circumstances which led to mala fide pleas be?

These lay in the fact that the debtor had received notice of the equitable assignment of the benefit of the bond to the assignee, before the debtor's receipt of the release from, and the making of payment to, the creditor(-assignor) of the bond. Given such knowledge, the obligor would have known of the equitable beneficial interest of the assignee in the debt arising from the bond. But Eyre CJ also found that the defendant had *colluded* with the creditor-assignor to obtain the release. It followed, then, that this was an appropriate case for the court to exercise the 'equitable jurisdiction of the courts of common law' to bar the mala fide pleas which would result from these 'fraudulent' acts on the part of the defendant.[66] Without making any decision as to the substantive merits of the defendant's defence of release and/or payment, the court in *Legh* v. *Legh* imposed a *procedural* bar, precluding the defendant from pleading these defences in the action which had been brought before the

---

[66] For other instances of the barring or setting aside of pleas of common law defences by a court of common law, see *Jones* v. *Herbert* (1817) 1 Taunt 421; and *Innell* v. *Newman* (1821) 4 B & Ald 419. In *Jones* v. *Herbert*, the court of Common Pleas recognized that it had the power to set aside a plea of release 'upon the ground of fraud', but declined to exercise it on the basis that the plaintiff making the application had to make out 'a very strong case of fraud' which the plaintiff had failed to do: at 1 Taunt 422. In *Innell* v. *Newman*, in an action brought on a promissory note before the court of King's Bench, the defendant was not permitted to plead a release on the basis of a deed of release which had been executed by one of the co-plaintiffs, who were husband and wife. It transpired that although the action had been brought in the names of the two spouses, it was really the action of the wife who was acting in her representative capacity as the executrix of a will. Importantly, she was separated from her husband, and in their deed of separation, the husband had covenanted that he would allow her to enjoy as her distinct and separate estate and property all effects she might acquire subsequent to their separation. Of the four presiding judges, Holroyd J was of the view that the release 'ought not to be allowed to be available to the defendants, being given under such circumstances, and in the progress of the cause. ... I think that this release is clearly in fraud of the deed of separation ... and he [the husband] ought not to be allowed to release the debt; for to do so would be a fraud upon the persons having an interest under the will of the testator': at 4 B & Ald 422. Though the other three presiding judges in *Innell* v. *Newman* did not avert to such 'fraud', they agreed that the plea of release ought to be barred, and also that the deed ought to be given up and cancelled. However, as noted above at n. 59, doubt has been expressed as to whether the common law court's powers extended quite so far as to allow it to set aside a deed of release (as opposed to setting aside a *plea* of release) by ordering it to be delivered up to be cancelled: see *Phillips* v. *Clagett* (n. 55), and also *Aspinall* v. *London & North-Western Railway Co.* (n. 52).

court.[67] The consequence, therefore, was that if the matter were to proceed to final judgment, once the prothonotary had made his findings as to the sums which were due, a judgment debt *at law* would have arisen as between the defendant debtor and the plaintiff creditor, in whose name the assignee had brought the action. The end result, therefore, would be that the obligor would have to 'pay again'.[68]

As to what the requirements were for the so-called equitable jurisdiction of the common law courts to bar the pleading of defences which might otherwise have been available on the merits, reference was made above to Abinger CJ's observations in *Phillips* v. *Clagett*.[69] But the judgments handed down by the other two judges in that case also cast useful light on this issue. First, Parke B noted as follows:[70]

> If such a release is a fraud in point of law upon one of the parties to it, the Court would not interfere; that is the proper subject for a replication; they can only interfere when it is a fraud on third persons, *and when a Court of equity would clearly set aside the release, not merely as between the parties one of whom releases, but where they would set it aside as against the defendant.* In order to call upon the Court to exercise its equitable jurisdiction, it must be made out manifestly and clearly that there has been a fraud by some person upon the plaintiff seeking to enforce the demand, and that the defendant was a party to that fraud. Unless that can be made out manifestly and clearly, this Court ought not to interfere.

## Supplementing this, Alderson B observed:[71]

> Where the party is an interested party, and where by the law all persons having a joint interest have a right to release and to dispose of the debt, how is his acting on that right which the law gives him as arising out of his interest, a fraud? Then what other ground exists in this case except that? It seems to me that there is none, and that even if there were, – if fraud were made out, – it is not traced to the defendant. *It is not only necessary that it should be a fraud on the party injured, but it also should be shewn that the defendant is cognizant of it, so as not to be in the situation of an innocent party.*

---

[67] For further examples, see *Hickey* v. *Burt* (1816) 7 Taunt 48; *Mountstephen* v. *Brooke* (n. 59); *Manning* v. *Cox* (1823) 7 Moore CP 617; *Barker* v. *Richardson* (n. 61).

[68] The facts in *Legh* v. *Legh* might have disclosed the type of dishonest assistance liability arising in equity which was discussed in Chapter 11. However, as *Legh* v. *Legh* was a case decided by the court of Common Pleas which had no equitable jurisdiction, dishonest assistance liability cannot form the basis of the decision in that case.

[69] At text to n. 58.

[70] At 11 M & W 93.

[71] *Phillips* v. *Clagett*, at 11 M & W 96. The remaining judge, Gurney B, concurred with Alderson B.

Hence, to invoke this jurisdiction (which remained a jurisdiction of the *common law* courts, notwithstanding its 'equitable' colour), it was not enough to show that a 'fraud' of some kind had been perpetrated on the party in whose interest the action was being brought. It was also necessary to show that the defendant to the action *actually* knew[72] of such 'fraud': the equitable doctrine of constructive notice would not have been available to a plaintiff seeking to invoke the equitable jurisdiction of the common law courts.

To illustrate, we may consider a case like *Barker* v. *Richardson*,[73] a decision in the Exchequer of Pleas from 1827. In this case, proceedings within the common law jurisdiction of the court of Exchequer had been brought jointly by two partners, Barker and Owen, on a debt owed by the defendant. In his defence, Richardson, pleaded a release which had been granted by Owen. Barker successfully applied to have this pleading set aside on the basis that on the terms of the deed which provided for the dissolution of their partnership, Owen had agreed that Barker was to collect the partnership debts, discharge the partnership's debts from such proceeds, and then to pay Owen his share of the surplus, if any. Explaining his reasons for setting aside the defendant's plea of release, Baron Hullock held:[74]

> Now in this case, Barker, who is the real plaintiff, by the terms of the dissolution, was to collect the debts due to, and satisfy the claims upon, the partnership; and the other plaintiff, Owen, had by the agreement relinquished all interest in the debt, of which the defendant was fully aware. . . .

---

[72] So far as the common law courts were concerned, knowledge of such 'fraud' had to be 'imputed by direct evidence': *Furnival* v. *Weston* (1822) CP 7 Moore 356, 357. And in *Arton and Dowson* v. *Booth* (1820) CP 4 Moore 192, where a debtor paid one of two partners before receiving a release, while ignorant that arrangements had been made between the partners in their deed of dissolution that the other partner was to receive payment, the court of Common Pleas declined to set aside the debtor's plea of release on grounds that 'fraud' had to be clearly established, 'and such fraud cannot be inferred, but must be manifestly apparent': CP 4 Moore 195 (*per* Park J). That said, it appears the courts of common law would set aside a plea of release if the affidavits in support showed that the release had been granted without consideration having been given in exchange: see e.g. *Mountstephen* v. *Brooke* (n. 59); and also *Johnson* v. *Holdsworth* (1835) 4 Dowling's Practice Cases 63.

[73] See above, n. 61.

[74] *Barker* v. *Richardson* (n. 61), 365–6. Garrow B and Vaughan B also agreed that the affidavits disclosed a sufficient extent of fraud to set aside the plea of release. It may be noted that in this case, the deed of release was also ordered to be delivered up and cancelled. The case having been decided by the Exchequer of Pleas in 1827, prior to the loss of its equitable jurisdiction in 1841, this aspect of the court's decision may be explicable as an exercise of its powers when acting within its equitable jurisdiction.

> [I]n this case no one can doubt that the defendant was privy to the fraud [by Owen on Barker]. He knew of the dissolution of partnership, and the terms upon which it was dissolved; and when the payment of this debt was demanded, made no claim of set off, but subsequently, with a full knowledge of the facts, took a release from Owen. The whole case is so pregnant with fraud, that we should not do justice between the parties were we not to interfere and set aside the plea in this stage of the proceedings.

Where the plaintiff was not in a position to swear that the defendant had actual knowledge of the 'fraud' that had been perpetrated on the plaintiff, but where it was possible to show that such defendant ought to be deemed to have the requisite knowledge by virtue of the equitable doctrine of constructive notice, the plaintiff might still seek the assistance of the court of Chancery to obtain an injunction to enjoin the defendant from pleading defences in the plaintiff's action at law. The two 'equitable' jurisdictions operated differently because of the non-applicability of the doctrine of constructive notice in courts of common law. Consequently, as Crompton J observed in the court of King's Bench in *Bartlett* v. *Wells*: 'There have been cases in which a Court of equity has acted in the exercise of its peculiar jurisdiction as to fraud, *which is different from that in our Courts*, but we are not to act as a Court of equity in enforcing mere equitable rights.'[75]

## F   Legislative Supplementation of the Powers of the Courts of Chancery and of Common Law to Bar Pleadings

The ability of the court of Chancery to issue injunctions to enjoin the pleadings at law, and the parallel 'equitable jurisdiction of the courts of common law' which the courts of Common Pleas, King's Bench and Exchequer seized for themselves was, in 1854, supplemented by Parliament. In that year, Parliament enacted the Common Law Procedure Act 1854, s. 85 of which provided as follows: '**LXXXV.** The Plaintiff may reply, in answer to any Plea of the Defendant, Facts which avoid such Plea upon equitable Grounds; provided that such Replication shall begin with the Words "For Replication on equitable Grounds," or Words to the like Effect.'

By this provision, Parliament granted the courts of common law a discretionary power[76] to allow a plaintiff at law to respond to the

---

[75] *Bartlett* v. *Wells* (1862) 1 B & S 836, 842–3 (emphasis added).

[76] *Hunter* v. *Gibbons* (1856) 1 H & N 459, 466 (Bramwell B): 'The statute [CLPA1854] does not give to the plaintiff an absolute right to reply equitably. The Court must see that there

defendant's defences by way of a 'replication on equitable grounds'. The purpose of s. 85 was explained in *Vorley* v. *Barrett* as follows: 'The very object of the Common Law Procedure Act in these clauses [providing for replications on equitable grounds] was, to enable courts of law to administer equitable relief, without driving the parties to the useless and vexatious expense of proceedings in a court of equity.'[77]

The chief point of distinction of this statutory grant of power to the common law courts from the so-called equitable jurisdiction of the common law courts which had been seized by the common law courts independently of Parliament was this: by legislative fiat, Parliament had authorised the judges of the common law courts to grant relief (albeit by way of a pleading 'on equitable grounds') as a court of Chancery would have done by way of injunction. The requirement of proof of actual fraud before the common law courts would exercise their so-called equitable jurisdiction was, therefore, inapplicable so far as these statutory replications were concerned. However, this did not entirely remove the need for recourse to a court of Chancery.

As the caselaw developed, the judges of the common law courts took the view that the plea of a 'defence on equitable grounds' as had been envisaged in CLPA1854, s. 83 was only permitted where equitable relief in a court of Chancery would have been granted unconditionally.[78] That being the case, and given the similarity in wording between ss. 83 and 85, it was accepted that the same restriction would also apply to pleas of a 'replication on

---

[77] is some chance that the facts sought to be replied would avoid the plea [i.e. the defendant's defence] on equitable grounds.'

[77] (1856) 1 CB (NS) 225, 240 (Crowder J). Creswell J made similar observations at 1 CB (NS) 240. In this case, a defence of release was met by the plaintiff's 'replication on equitable grounds' pursuant to CLPA1854, s. 85 on the equitable ground that the release had only included a reference to the claim on which the present action was brought by reason of mistake.

[78] *Mines Royal Societies* v. *Magnay* (1854) 10 Exch 489, where a 'defence on equitable grounds' was not permitted because the Court of Exchequer concluded that had injunctive relief in Chancery been sought, such relief would only have been granted on terms. This result duly led to the commencement of proceedings in Chancery, in which further prosecution of the action at law in was indeed enjoined, but on terms: *Magnay* v. *Mines Royal Company* (1855) 3 Drew 130. Lord Campbell CJ explained the rationale for this constraint in *Wodehouse* v. *Farebrother* (1855) 5 El & Bl 277, 289–90. Consequently, such equitable plea would be struck out, as provided for in CLPA1854, s. 86: 'Provided always, that in case it shall appear to the Court, or any Judge thereof, that any such equitable Plea or equitable Replication cannot be dealt with by a Court of Law so as to do Justice between the Parties, it shall be lawful for such Court or Judge to order the same to be struck out on such Terms as to Costs and otherwise as to such Court of Judge may seem reasonable.'

equitable grounds'.[79] Hence, where the assessment was that an injunction might only have been granted on terms, the statutory 'defence on equitable grounds' or 'replication on equitable grounds' would fail.[80]

At this point, to further illustrate the operation of s. 85, it will be helpful to consider three cases: *De Pothonier v. De Mattos*, *Watson v. Mid-Wales Railway* and *Wilson v. Gabriel*.

### (i)   De Pothonier v. De Mattos (1858)[81]

In this case, the plaintiff, a shipowner, had entered into a charterparty with the defendant under which the plaintiff's ship, the *Bella Donna* was to load coals at Birkenhead for discharge at Constantinople in exchange for an agreed freight to be paid by the defendant. After the charterparty had been agreed, but before the freight had been earned, the plaintiff sold the *Bella Donna* to Salveson, and also equitably assigned to him the defendant's charterparty. Subsequently, Salveson brought proceedings in the plaintiff's name at common law in the court of Queen's Bench against the defendant for non-payment of the freight that was due.

The defendant made three pleas by way of defence:[82]

---

[79] Both counsel in *Vorley* v. *Barrett* (n. 77) accepted that the constraint as was applied to CLPA1854, s. 83, also applied to s. 85: 1 CB (NS) 235 and 236. It may be noted that Campbell CJ's explanation of the rationale for the restriction as applied to s. 83 in *Wodehouse* v. *Farebrother* (n. 78) would apply equally well to an equitable plea by way of a replication on equitable grounds. Also, in *Hunter* v. *Gibbons* (n. 76), having held that the replication on equitable grounds in that case in answer to a defence of limitation to an action for trespass on the plaintiff's land to excavate coal ought not to be allowed, Bramwell B pointed out (at 1 H & N 466) that, '[i]n equity, the plaintiff would be entitled to the value of the coal, less the cost of getting it; at law he would be entitled to its value at the mouth of the pit, without deduction. If then this replication was allowed, it would alter the rights of the parties.' That is, since equitable relief to enjoin the plea of limitation would only have been granted on terms, it was not open to the court to exercise such power as it had been granted under CLPA1854, s. 85 to allow the replication on equitable grounds to stand against the defendant's plea of limitation.

[80] It may be noted that the Common Law Commissioners had recommended that courts of law be permitted to receive pleas on equitable grounds, even in circumstances where an injunction might only have been granted in a court of Chancery on terms: 1852-3 [1626] *Royal Commission to inquire into Process, Practice and System of Pleading in Superior Courts of Common Law, Second Report.* However, the common law courts took Parliament to have rejected this recommendation, given the enactment of CLPA1854, s. 86.

[81] *De Pothonier* v. *De Mattos* (n. 21).

[82] Ibid., El Bl & Bl 462-3.

Plea **I**: that before the goods had been loaded onboard the plaintiff's ship, the plaintiff had discharged the defendant from performance of the agreement for good and sufficient consideration. Alternatively,

Plea **II**: that the defendant had, before the bringing of the action, discharged the plaintiff's claim by payment. And further in the alternative,

Plea **III**: that after the accruing of the said causes of action, the plaintiff had released and discharged the defendant from the said causes of action and all damages in respect thereof, albeit not by deed under seal, but for good and sufficient consideration.

In his replication on equitable grounds as provided for by CLPA1854, s. 85, the plaintiff set out the assignment to Salveson. The plaintiff also pointed out that the plaintiff's discharge in Plea **I**, the acceptance of payment by the plaintiff in Plea **II**, and the release granted by the plaintiff in Plea **III**, had all been carried out without Salveson's authorization. Most crucially of all, the plaintiff also set out that the defendant had had notice of the equitable assignment to Salveson before the plaintiff's discharge, acceptance or release in each of these pleas.

The court[83] held that these replications on equitable grounds were good. Consequently, judgment was entered in favour of the plaintiff and, presumably, the defendant charterer would have become indebted by reason of the judgment debt that would have arisen in consequence.

Lord Campbell CJ explained the reasons for holding in favour of the plaintiff as follows:[84]

> I am of opinion that these equitable replications are good. The object of sect. 85 of The Common Law Procedure Act, 1854, was to allow an equitable replication to a plea which sets out facts that can be answered upon equitable grounds: such a plea, in fact, as the Court [of King's Bench] would, before the statute, have set aside in the exercise of what was called its equitable jurisdiction. Ever since *Winch* v. *Keeley* (1 TR 619), Courts of law have allowed the assignee to sue in the name of an assignor, and where any defence to the assignees' claim is founded on fraud by the nominal plaintiff, will set such defence aside.[85] By the statute [i.e. the Common Law Procedure Act 1854] it was intended that the

---

[83] Comprising Lord Campbell CJ, Coleridge, Erle and Crompton JJ. Crompton J was, however, absent and did not hand down any judgment.

[84] *De Pothonier* v. *De Mattos* (n. 21), El Bl & Bl 466–8.

[85] This appears to be a reference to the 'equitable jurisdiction of the common law courts'.

assignee should be allowed to put his own answer to such a defence upon the record [i.e. on the pleadings], instead of bringing it forward, as he was obliged to do so before, by affidavit. ... Here the replications [of the nominal plaintiff] are clearly within the statute: they deny that the nominal plaintiff had any right[86] to release, inasmuch as, at that time, he had no [beneficial] interest, and is, in consequence, not the real plaintiff when the action was brought. The replications, therefore, 'avoid' the 'plea on equitable grounds'.

Coleridge J agreed with the Chief Justice:[87]

> Before the statute [i.e. the Common Law Procedure Act 1854], a cestui que trust could sue in the name of the trustee; and in certain cases, as here, the assignee in the name of the assignor. The declaration here is met by an inequitable plea. That plea we could, in the exercise of our equitable jurisdiction, have set aside before the statute; and the object of sect. 85 was to give to the plaintiff the power of answering such a plea himself, and making such answer a part of the record, when it avoids the plea upon the equitable grounds. The replications do so here; and the plaintiff is therefore entitled to judgment.

Erle J agreed:[88]

> The replications here are clearly such as the Legislature intended, under sect. 85, to enable a plaintiff to put upon the record, instead of going into a Court of equity for relief, or availing himself, by a circuitous process, of the equitable jurisdiction of the Courts of law. Here the party really interested is suing in the name of the nominal plaintiff. The plea[s I, II and III of the defendant are] ... a legal answer to the nominal plaintiff, but not an equitable answer to the real plaintiff, the assignee; the replications avoid that plea upon equitable grounds, and are clearly within the provisions of the statute.

Under s. 85 of the 1854 Act, litigants were empowered to raise points in answer to defences which might formerly have been barred through a parallel application to a court of equity for an injunction. Now, instead of having to file a separate bill, such litigants could plead a 'replication on

---

[86] In the context, so far as the nominal plaintiff had become duty-bound to the assignee, Salveson, to invoke his entitlements under the charterparty against the defendant for the assignee's interest, and thus was duty-bound not to invoke his powers of discharge, acceptance or release without the assignee's assent or authorization, the nominal plaintiff would have lost his Hohfeldian *privilege* to invoke these entitlements without regard to Salveson's interests.

[87] *De Pothonier v. De Mattos* (n. 21), 467–8.

[88] Ibid., 466–8.

equitable grounds' in response to the defence in the same action at law. Apart from saving the litigants the cost and complications of mounting parallel proceedings in equity, the statutory 'replication on equitable grounds' under s. 85 was also broader than the so-called equitable jurisdiction of the common law courts since the additional requirement of proof of actual knowledge of the 'fraud' to make the defendant 'party' to it did not apply to the statutory procedure.

As this book has explained, an equitable assignment of a legal chose in action entails a trust over the benefit of the chose in action. Given such trust, the plaintiff in *De Pothonier* v. *De Mattos* would have been duty-bound (as assignor) to Salveson (as assignee). Specifically, the plaintiff would have been duty-bound to preserve the common law debt which had been equitably assigned: i.e. he would be duty-bound *not* to reduce it into possession without Salveson's prior approval (as Lord Campbell CJ recognized in the extract above).

Having received notice of the assignment, the defendant would have had actual knowledge of it, and would also be deemed to know of its implications as to the plaintiff's obligations in respect of Salveson. Then, the defendant would be expected to make reasonable inquiries of Salveson in light of such knowledge when dealing with that debt in the manner particularized in the defendant's three pleas. *Inter alia*, had reasonable inquiries been made, the defendant would have discovered that the plaintiff had not been authorized by Salveson to act as he had done. The defendant would thus have realized that the defendant's actions were in breach of his duties as assignor.

Had the requisite bill been filed in a court of equity, an injunction would have been issued, given such constructive knowledge. If so, a s. 85 'replication on equitable grounds' would arise in the proceedings at law which had been brought by Salveson in the plaintiff's name. (By way of contrast, the court would not have invoked the 'equitable jurisdiction of the common law courts' without satisfactory proof of actual fraud on the defendant's part.)

The 'equitable jurisdiction of the common law courts' was supplemented, not abolished, by the enactment of s. 85.[89] Even so, like the 'equitable jurisdiction of the common law courts', the statutory 'replication on equitable grounds' did not operate as a substantive rule of law:

---

[89] *Bartlett* v. *Wells* (n. 75), 840 (Crompton J, in argument): 'Wherever there is want of good faith in pleading a plea, we have jurisdiction to set it aside independently of the Common Law Procedure Act, 1854.'

given its purpose (to duplicate the injunctive relief which would otherwise have required a duplicate bill to be filed in the court of Chancery), its operation remained entirely within the procedural realm.[90]

### (ii)   Watson v. Mid-Wales Railway Company (1867)[91]

Another illustration of the operation of s. 85 to procedurally bar or neutralize a defence of statutory set-off in line with the Statutes of Set-off may be found in *Watson* v. *Mid-Wales Railway Company* (in which the application also succeeded).

In that case, choses in action arising from four Lloyd's bonds[92] issued by the Mid-Wales Railway Company ('Mid-Wales') to Watson had been equitably assigned by Watson to the Joint Stock Discount Company, Limited ('JSDC'). When sums due on the bonds were not paid, JSDC brought an action against Mid-Wales in Watson's name.

In its defence, Mid-Wales pleaded that it was entitled to set-off arrears of certain rents payable quarterly, such rents having arisen from a lease of certain property for twenty-one years which had been entered into between it and Watson on 22 March 1865 (four days after the issue of the Lloyd's bonds).

By his replication on equitable grounds, Watson, the nominal plaintiff, set out certain facts relating to his assignment to JSDC. Most significantly, the replication asserted that Mid-Wales had been given notice of the assignment before the particular rental arrears which it was now seeking to set off had accrued. This was met by a rejoinder from Mid-Wales, in which it pointed out that the lease had arisen between it and Watson prior to the assignment of the Lloyd's bonds to JSDC (and thus had arisen before notice of the assignment had been given to it).

In the Court of Common Pleas, Bovill CJ, Willes J and Montague Smith J declined to give effect to Mid-Wales' set-off defence. First, so far as the defendant had pleaded facts which would support an equitable set-

---

[90]   The importance of this will be made explicit in Section I, below.

[91]   (1867) LR 2 CP 593.

[92]   The nature of a 'Lloyd's bond' was explained in William Richard Fisher, *The Law of Mortgage and Other Securities upon Property* (2 vols., 3rd edn, London: Butterworths, 1876), vol. I, fn. (e) to §386, pp. 262–3. Alternatively, see Henry Jaffard Tarrant, *Lloyd's Bonds: Their Nature and Use* (London: Stevens and Haynes, 1867).

off based on implied agreement,[93] or a substantive equitable set-off,[94] the court of Common Pleas held that the requirements for such defences were not satisfied.[95] In particular, as to substantive equitable set-off, Bovill CJ noted as follows:[96]

> No case has been cited to us where equity has allowed against the assignee of an equitable chose in action[97] a set-off of a debt arising between the original parties subsequently to the notice of assignment, out of matters not connected with the debt claimed, nor in any way referring to it. The plaintiff has a clear legal right. At the time when the bond was given the lease did not exist; the lease when granted did not refer to the bond; it did not make the rent payable under it a charge on the money secured by the bond; the two instruments were entirely collateral, and had no reference to one another.

---

[93] As to equitable set-off on the basis of agreement between the parties, the court found that no such intention was present, no reference having been made in the one transaction to the other. *Watson* v. *Mid-Wales Railway Company* (n. 91), 598 (Bovill CJ), 600 (Willes J), and 601 (Montague Smith J). This variety of equitable set-off is briefly discussed in Derham (2010), para. 3.03.

[94] As explained in Derham (2010), para. 4.03 (references omitted):

> The traditional basis of this form of equitable set-off [i.e. substantive equitable set-off] is that the plaintiff's title to his or her demand is impeached. The concept of impeachment has not been precisely defined. In general terms, what it requires, in the absence of some other equitable ground for being protected such as fraud, is that there be a sufficiently close connection between the demands. . . . The closeness of the connection that courts of equity traditionally required has been expressed in various terms, for example that the cross-demand must go to the very root of the plaintiff's claim, or that it must call in question, impugn, disparage or impede the title to the claim, or that there must be some equitable ground for protection such as inseparability, or, as the New Zealand Court of Appeal expressed it, that the link between the demands must be such that the two are interdependent.

[95] As a court of common law, unless statute provided otherwise, the court of Common Pleas would not have had the jurisdiction to give effect to any form of *equitable* set-off. However, in *Watson*, the court of Common Pleas could do so because of the CLPA1854, s. 83, by which a defendant before a court of common law was empowered to plead a 'Defence on equitable grounds'. For discussion of s. 83, see Chapter 6.

[96] *Watson* v. *Mid-Wales Railway Company* (n. 91), 598; and also 600 (Willes J), and 601 (Montague Smith J).

[97] So far as substantive equitable set-off had been developed and applied in the court of Chancery (which would, in the main, be concerned with equitable choses), Bovill CJ recognized that such set-off was not available unless there was a sufficient degree of interconnectedness between the claim and cross-claim. He was not suggesting that the Lloyd's bonds before him were equitable choses in action.

That said, even if the lease and the Lloyd's bonds were taken to be independent of each other so as to preclude substantive equitable set-off, they remained liquidated claims at law which had arisen between the same parties (so far as a court of common law was concerned) in the action at law: i.e. there was sufficient mutuality of parties.

As explained in Chapter 8, a court of common law would recognize the beneficial equitable interest of an assignee. But enforcement of such equitable institutions arising with the exclusive jurisdiction of the Chancery courts remained beyond the common law courts. Thus, for the purposes of the action before the court of Common Pleas in *Watson* v. *Mid-Wales Railway*, Watson, the nominal plaintiff, *was* the plaintiff, and against whom Mid-Wales Railway had a cross-claim. There was, accordingly, sufficient mutuality of parties.[98] Consequently, the question would arise as to whether the facts as pleaded by Mid-Wales entitled them to raise the defence of a procedural *statutory* set-off by reference to the Statutes of Set-off.

The court concluded that the grounds for such a defence *were* satisfied. However, the plaintiff's replication on equitable grounds had set out sufficient grounds for denying effect to such defence (or, to use the language of Lord Campbell CJ in *De Pothonier* v. *De Mattos*, to 'avoid' the defence). Willes J held as follows:[99]

> [This] is the bare case of A. owing B. and B. owing A. debts contracted at different times, and payable at different dates. Judging from the character of the transaction, is there any reason why we should not treat the debts as what they appear to be, distinct and independent debts? If this is so, and the set-off is no parcel of the contract, but only a matter of procedure, there is no reason for binding one debt to the other, so as to prevent the plaintiff from recovering his debt by reason of the defendants being owed something by a third person.

---

[98] That is to say, the claim and cross-claim must be 'mutual' in that they should arise between the same parties and in the same right or interest, so far as a court acting within its common law jurisdiction was concerned. In this connection, it does not matter that the plaintiff might no longer have the equitable beneficial interest in the chose in action on which the action is brought (say, because the plaintiff had assigned the chose, or had constituted himself trustee of the same). This is the position in Derham (2010), para. 17.03. Judicial authority for the point may also be found in *Isberg* v. *Bowden* (1853) 8 Exch 852; and *Tucker* v. *Tucker* (1833) 4 B & Ad 745, 751 (Littledale J): '[U]nder the Statutes of Set-Off the Court can only notice an interest at law.'

[99] *Watson* v. *Mid-Wales Railway Company* (n. 91), 601 (Willes J, with whom Montague Smith J agreed).

As to why there was 'no reason' to 'bind one debt to the other', the key fact appears to have been that notice of the assignment to JSDC had been given to Mid-Wales *before* the quarterly rents in question had accrued due. As Bovill CJ held, having already concluded that there were no grounds for any equitable set-off: 'Under these circumstances, the bond having been assigned and notice given of the assignment, the question arises, how far rent *subsequently accruing due* under the lease can be set off against the money due upon the bond.'[100]

The significance of notice having been received by Mid-Wales before the quarterly rents in issue had accrued due was also highlighted by Montague Smith J:[101]

> From the cases on the subject the principle may be deduced that the equitable interests remain after the transfer, subject to all the rights which attach upon them until notice. And it is entirely in concurrence with this principle that contracts which are independent of one another should not remain after notice, subject to any new liability.

From the above, we may infer that Bovill CJ and Montague Smith J had deduced that, as the quarterly rents in issue had accrued due only after notice of the assignment to JSDC had been received, a court of Chancery would have issued an injunction to bar a plea of statutory set-off in reliance on such cross-claims to an action at law on the Lloyd's Bonds. Consequently, a replication on equitable grounds based on such facts would preclude such plea without need to mount parallel proceedings in Chancery to obtain such an injunction. Indeed, in *Jeffryes* v. *Agra and Masterman's Bank*,[102] a decision which had been cited in argument[103] in support of the replication on equitable grounds, Sir Page Wood VC had made precisely the same point:[104]

---

[100] Ibid., 598.

[101] Ibid., 601.

[102] (1866) LR 2 Eq 674.

[103] *Watson* v. *Mid-Wales Railway Company* (n. 91), 594.

[104] *Jeffryes* v. *Agra and Masterman's Bank* (n. 102), 680. That was a case where the benefit of a debt had been equitably assigned, and notice of the same had been given to the debtors. The question then arose as to whether the debtor could assert a statutory set-off in respect of cross-claims which accrued before, as well as after, receipt of such notice of assignment. It was held that it did not matter that the cross-claims, having accrued due prior to receipt of notice, were only payable *after* that point in time, as explained by Clauson J in *Re Pinto Leite and Nephews* [1929] 1 Ch 221, 235–6. Thus (at 236): 'The proposition to be deduced from [*Jeffreyes* v. *Agra and Masterman's Bank*] seems accordingly to be that, when the debt is at the date of the assignment payable in future, the debtor can set off against the assignee a debt which becomes payable by the assignor to the debtor after notice of assignment, but before the assigned debt becomes payable, if,

How, then, is the case affected by the notice they [the debtors] received of the assignment of this debt on the part of Speltz [the creditor-assignor]? I apprehend that they cannot be in any worse position as to liabilities actually accrued before they had notice of the assignment, not matured when they had notice of the assignment, but matured when the debt became payable. They would have a right to say:– 'We held all these various securities, we knew all our rights of set-off, we knew that when these became due there would be other debts due at the same time, and that we should set the one off against the other, and our right cannot be interfered with by any dealing of yours with strangers until we have notice of such dealing.' The moment they have notice they cannot claim a set-off in respect of any debts not actually due at the time they received notice of the payment of the bills, for the notice would make them liable at once to be sued in respect of the several sums they had retained.

What is critical, though, is the time when the cross-claims in question fall due.

*Watson* v. *Mid-Wales Railway Company* leads us to the following conclusions. First, there was no merit to any defence resting on the *equitable* defence of substantive equitable set-off. Second, the Mid-Wales Railway Company had satisfied the substantive criteria by which the procedural defence of set-off pursuant to the Statutes of Set-off, and so could set-off its liquidated cross-claim arising by reason of the lease with Watson against Watson's claim against it on the Lloyd's bonds by way of defence. However, since the cross-claim only accrued due *after* notice of the assignment had been given to it, this was a case where Watson could have obtained an injunction from the court of Chancery to enjoin Mid-Wales Railway Company from pleading such defence at law in the common law action. Third, that being the case, it was open to Watson to plead these facts by way of a replication on equitable grounds, pursuant to CLPA1854, s. 85, leading to such defence being set aside. The result, therefore, was that, having received notice of the assignment, the obligor to the chose assigned could no longer raise the defence of statutory set-off by reference to a liquidated cross-claim which accrued due between it and the assignor after such notice in the action at law which had been brought in the assignor's name by the assignee.

The corollary to this would be that if the debt had accrued *before* notice of assignment was received by the obligor, the procedural bar to pleading such defence of statutory set-off would no longer apply: and this was precisely the conclusion of the Court of King's Bench in *Wilson* v. *Gabriel*.

but only if, the debt so to be set off was debitum in praesenti [i.e. accrued due, though not payable yet] at the date of notice of assignment.'

## *(iii)* Wilson *v.* Gabriel *(1863)*[105]

In this case, the freight payable upon the completion of a contract of carriage of goods was equitably assigned by the carrier to assignees for value. However, the cargo-owners had lent certain sums to the carrier at some point in time before notice of the assignment was received by them. When the assignees brought an action against the cargo-owners in the name of the assignor, the cargo-owners pleaded the debt which the assignor owed them by way of defence, seeking to set-off such debt against the claim for unpaid freight. The defence was permitted to stand, notwithstanding the pleading of a replication on equitable grounds setting out the facts of the assignment to the assignees, and the fact of notice. The reasons for this were set out by Blackburn J as follows:[106]

> The plaintiff here sues for a debt, and the defendants plead a set-off. There was a debt due when the action commenced, and therefore at law the defendants have a perfect right to set off against it a debt due to them. Messrs Early & Smith [the assignees], the real plaintiffs in the cause, call on us to do what they otherwise would have called on a Court of equity to do, namely, grant an injunction to prevent this; for that is what this replication amounts to. It is not, as [counsel for the defendants] contends, that we are to see affirmatively that this is an equitable set-off; but we are to see whether the plaintiff has a right to ask a Court of equity to prevent the defendants setting up their legal right of set-off [under the Statutes of Set-off]. *Equity will never do that when equities are equal.* . . . Here, Messrs Early & Smith allowed the plaintiff [the assignor] to appear to be the true owner of this freight, and upon that what was the right between them and the other party, either by natural equity or this artificial thing we call by the name of equity? So early as *George* v. *Clagett* (7 TR 359) the ground of which is correctly stated in the well considered judgment of the Exchequer in *Isberg* v. *Bowden* (8 Exch 852, 859), it was held that where a factor sells goods as his own, and the buyer knows nothing of any principal, the buyer may set off any demand he may have on the factor against a demand to request of those goods made by the principal.

*George* v. *Clagett*[107] was a case where a factor had sold goods belonging to his principal, the plaintiff, to the defendant. When the principal brought an action at law against the defendant for the price of the goods,

---

the defendant was permitted to rely on cross-claims which he had created with the factor on the basis that when he bought the goods, he had done so on the impression that the factor was dealing as principal in his own right. In *Isberg* v. *Bowden*, Baron Martin explained that *George* v. *Clagett*, as well a number of other cases, was decided on the following principle:[108]

> where a principal permits an agent to sell as apparent principal, and afterwards intervenes, the buyer is entitled to be placed in the same situation at the time of the disclosure of the real principal, as if the agent had been the real contracting party, and is entitled to the same defence, whether it be by common law or by statute, payment or set-off, as he was entitled to at that time against the agent, the apparent principal.

Plainly, *George* v. *Clagett* was no direct authority for the dispute before the court in *Wilson* v. *Gabriel*, since that concerned an action brought by an undisclosed principal, whereas in *Wilson* v. *Gabriel*, no issue relating to undisclosed principals arose. However, Blackburn J was seeking to draw an analogy with that case.

In the case of undisclosed principals, where the undisclosed principal had *enabled* the agent to pass himself off as if he were a principal in his own right, parties who contracted with the agent on such basis, ignorant of the true state of affairs as between the agent and undisclosed principal, would not be disadvantaged by the fact that the counterparty to the contract was, as a matter of agency law, the undisclosed principal, although this would cease once the agent–principal relationship was known. In *Wilson* v. *Gabriel*, an analogous situation had arisen. As set out in the extract from his judgment which has been reproduced above, Blackburn J had noted in *Wilson* v. *Gabriel* that 'Messrs Early & Smith [the assignees] allowed the plaintiff to appear to be the true owner of this freight, and upon that what was the right between them and the other party, either by natural equity or the artificial thing we call by the name of equity?' That is, just as the undisclosed principal had 'led' the defendant in that case to treat and deal with the agent in that case as if he were a principal in his own right, by failing to give notice to the defendant of the assignment, the assignees in *Wilson* v. *Gabriel* had similarly 'led' the defendant to treat and deal with the assignor in that case as if the beneficial interest in the freight had not been divested from him. The equities as between the assignees and the defendant were not, therefore,

---

[108] *Isberg* v. *Bowden* (n. 98), 859, following *Tucker* v. *Tucker* (n. 98). This appears to be a substantive rule of common law as applied to undisclosed principals.

'equal': they were tipped against the assignee. So there was no call for equity to intervene so as to enjoin the defendant from pleading the defence of statutory set-off; and there would equally be no call for a court of common law to give effect to the plaintiff's replication on equitable grounds in response to the defendant's defence based on statutory set-off.

Where the assignee's failure to give notice of assignment had led the obligor to deal with the obligee-assignor in the mistaken belief that no other interests would be affected by such dealings, and where those dealings with the obligee-assignor had not been entered into 'fraudulently' in the knowledge that other interests would be affected, the pleading of a statutory set-off defence arising by reason of such cross-dealings could not be other than bona fide. This explains, therefore, *why* a court of equity might enjoin the pleading of a defence of statutory set-off, and hence why a replication on equitable grounds might lead to the 'avoidance' of a defence of statutory set-off. Leaving aside a case of collusion between the obligor and the assignor, an assignee who had not given notice of the assignment might have created the very circumstances which enabled the assignor to obscure the fact that she was no longer beneficially entitled to the chose in question. In such circumstances, having created the situation by which the debtor/obligor could be misled, it could not be open to the assignee to claim to have any better equity than the debtor/obligor who had been 'misled', as a result.

## G   Reform under the Judicature Acts 1873 and 1875

The three 'procedural' techniques discussed above in Sections D and E by which a defendant might be barred from pleading certain defences in proceedings at law were preserved by the Judicature Act 1873. First, in addition to providing for the establishment of the High Court of Justice ('the High Court') to be a 'Superior Court of Record', the Judicature Act 1873, s. 16 also provided that:

> there shall be transferred to and vested in the said High Court of Justice the jurisdiction which, at the commencement of this Act, was vested in, or capable of being exercised by, all or any of the Courts following: [that is to say,]

> (1) The High Court of Chancery, as a Common Law Court[109] as well as a Court of Equity . . .

---

[109] For an account of the limited common law jurisdiction of the court of Chancery, see 3 Bl Comm 47–9. It was 'never a very important part of its jurisdiction': W. Holdsworth,

(2) The Court of Queen's Bench;

(3) The Court of Common Pleas at Westminster;

(4) The Court of Exchequer, as a Court of Revenue, as well as Common Law Court[.]

The jurisdiction by this Act transferred to the High Court of Justice shall include (subject to the exceptions herein-after contained) the jurisdiction which, at the commencement of this Act, was vested in, or capable of being exercised by, all or any one or more of the Judges of the said Courts, respectively, sitting in Court or Chambers, or elsewhere, when acting as Judges or a Judge, in pursuance of any statute, law, or custom, and all powers given to any such Court, or to any such Judges or Judge, by any statute, and also all ministerial powers, duties, and authorities, incident to any and every part of the jurisdiction so transferred.

Consequently, the equity jurisdiction of the court of Chancery was transferred to and vested in the High Court. That is, its power to adjudicate matters pursuant to *equitable* principles, and to grant *equitable* remedies in light of its conclusions in connection with such principles, would be vested in the High Court.

The jurisdictions (i.e. powers) of the courts of Queen's Bench, Common Pleas and Exchequer were likewise transferred. Hence, so far as the court of Queen's Bench had the power to adjudicate matters in accordance with the principles as had been developed by and were applied within the common law courts (i.e. 'common law' principles), and to grant common law remedies in light of its conclusions in connection with such principles, that power would also be vested in the High Court.

Second, the Judicature Act 1873, s. 24(1) provided:

**24.** In every civil cause or matter commenced in the High Court of Justice law and equity shall be administered by the High Court of Justice and the Court of Appeal respectively according to the Rules following:

(1.) If any plaintiff ... claims to be entitled ... to relief upon any equitable ground ... against any right, title, or claim whatsoever asserted by any defendant or respondent in such cause or matter ... which heretofore could only have been given by a Court of Equity, the said Courts respectively, and every Judge thereof, shall give to such plaintiff or petitioner such and the same relief as ought to have been given by the Court of Chancery in a suit or proceeding

*A History of English Law*, vol. I (7th edn, revised 1956, London: Methuen & Co., 1956), p. 452.

for the same or the like purpose properly instituted before the
passing of this Act.

Were a defendant to an action at law brought before the High Court to
assert 'any right, title, or claim whatsoever' by way of defence, if the
plaintiff could have claimed relief 'upon any equitable ground ... which
heretofore could only have been given by a Court of Equity' against such
'right, title or claim whatsoever' of the defendant, s. 24(1) empowered the
High Court to 'give to such plaintiff or petitioner such and the same
relief ... [had] a suit or proceeding for the same or the like purpose
[been] properly instituted before the passing of [the Judicature Act
1873]'. Thus, if an injunction could have been obtained in a court of
equity to enjoin a defendant from pleading a defence in an action at
common law prior to the administrative fusion effected by the 1873 Act,
such relief would continue to be available to the plaintiff in any proceeding commenced in the High Court. What is more, it seems such relief
could be given without the need to commence separate proceedings by
filing further originating process for such 'equitable relief'.[110]

Third, the Judicature Act 1873, s. 24(6) provided as follows:

> (6) Subject to the aforesaid provisions for giving effect to equitable rights
> and other matters of equity in manner aforesaid, and to the other express
> provisions of this Act, the said Courts respectively, and every Judge
> thereof, shall recognize and give effect to all legal claims and demands,
> and all estates, titles, rights, duties, obligations, and liabilities existing by
> the Common Law or by any custom, or created by any Statute, in the
> same manner as the same would have been recognized and given effect to,
> if this Act had not passed, by any of the Courts whose jurisdiction is
> hereby transferred to the said High Court of Justice.

As explained in Section E(ii), the courts of common law had 'followed'
equity by developing for themselves the so-called equitable jurisdiction of
the common law courts. And, as explained in Section F, this development
was supplemented by CLPA1854, s. 85, by which plaintiffs in an action at
law were granted the right to plead a 'replication on equitable grounds' in a
court of common law so as to avoid pleas of defence before those courts.

---

[110] In *Eyre* v. *Hughes* (1876) 2 Ch D 148, Bacon VC held that pursuant to Judicature Act
1873, s 24(2), the court had the power to give effect to an equitable defence relied on by a
defendant to a foreclosure suit without the need for a cross bill or counter-claim to be
filed. By parity of reasoning, it would seem that the same should be true for a plaintiff
relying on an equitable entitlement pursuant to s. 24(1).

Reading ss. 16 and 24(6) of the 1873 Act together, having been transferred the common law courts' jurisdiction, the High Court would then 'recognize and give effect to ... all ... rights, duties, obligations, and liabilities existing by the Common Law or ... by any Statute, *in the same manner as the same would have been recognized and given effect to, if [the 1873 Act] had not passed*' by any of the courts whose jurisdiction had been transferred to the High Court. Hence, the High Court would also be empowered to give effect to the entitlements of plaintiffs as would formerly have arisen within the 'equitable jurisdiction of the common law courts', as well as the slightly more widely available entitlements arising from CLPA1854, s. 85, when acting within such common law jurisdiction as had been transferred to it.

Fourth, s. 24(7) empowered the High Court to exercise the powers which had been transferred from its predecessor courts so as to avoid multiplicity of legal proceedings:

> (7) The High Court of Justice and the Court of Appeal respectively, in the exercise of the jurisdiction vested in them by this Act in every cause or matter pending before them respectively, shall have power to grant, and shall grant, either absolutely or on such reasonable terms and conditions as to them shall seem just, all such remedies whatsoever as any of the parties thereto may appear to be entitled to in respect of any and every legal or equitable claim properly brought forward by them respectively in such cause or matter; so that, as far as possible, all matters so in controversy between the said parties respectively may be completely and finally determined, and all multiplicity of legal proceedings concerning any of such matters avoided.

The effect, therefore, was that the High Court was empowered to grant common law and equitable remedies in respect of causes of action over which the Chancery courts would previously have had concurrent jurisdiction, and no separate proceedings or originating process would need to be filed.

To illustrate, we may look at the 1893 case of *Christie* v. *Taunton, Delmard, Lane and Company*.[111]

In this case, certain debentures were issued by Taunton, Delmard, Lane and Company, Limited ('the Company'), to one Richard Taunton. These debentures were equitably assigned by Richard Taunton to the Birmingham and Midland Bank, Limited ('the Bank'). The Company was subsequently wound up, and the question arose as to whether it was entitled to set-off against the debentures which had been assigned to the

---

[111] [1893] 2 Ch 175.

Bank sums due from Richard Taunton for unpaid calls on shares which the Company had previously issued to him. Pertinently, the calls were made prior to the date the Bank received notice of the assignment, but they were to be paid later.

To decide the question before him, Stirling J began by analysing what the position as between the Bank and the Company would have been had it not been wound up. On this supposition:[112]

> I think that if the [Company] were sued by the [Bank], it would be entitled to be placed in the same position as it [the Bank] occupied relatively to [Richard] Taunton on the 5th of November, 1890, on which day Taunton was indebted to the company for calls payable on the 20th of November, while the company was indebted to Taunton on the debentures, which did not become payable until a later date. If, then, no winding-up had intervened, and Taunton, or the bank in Taunton's name, had sued on the debentures, the question would be whether the company could set off the debt which accrued due on the 3rd of November (the date of the call), but did not actually become payable until the 20th of November. ... If it be inquired whether a Court of Equity would, in an action at law brought before the Judicature Acts, have interfered by way of injunction to prevent the company from setting up the legal right of set-off, I think the answer must be in the negative. The [Bank] not only neglected to take advantage of the conditions of the debentures by obtaining a transfer capable of registration, *but did not even perfect the equitable title by giving notice until after the debt had accrued due and, what is still stronger, until after the bank had notice that it had so accrued.*

As had been observed by Blackburn J in *Wilson* v. *Gabriel*, a court of equity would *not* issue an injunction on the application of a party interested in an action at law to bar the defendant to that action at law from pleading certain defences, 'when equities are equal'.[113] The inference, therefore, is that such injunction would only issue if the equities were *not* equal, but were found to tip in favour of the assignee. The further inference is that the equities as between the defendant obligor and assignee would tip *against* the assignee if she were to delay giving notice to the obligor. And the equities would tip because an assignee who had delayed in giving such notice to the obligor would have given the obligor the false impression that the obligee to whom the obligor was duty-bound was herself not duty-bound to any other entity in any manner as to her entitlements as obligee when the reality was otherwise.

---

[112] Ibid., 183–4 (emphasis added).
[113] *Wilson* v. *Gabriel* (n. 105), 248.

## H The Position in England and Wales Today

The position which had been reached in the period immediately following the enactment of the Judicature Acts continues to be the case even today.

In the decades which followed, ss. 16, 24(1), 24(6) and 24(7) of the 1873 Act were re-enacted, *in pari materia*, in the Supreme Court of Judicature (Consolidation) Act 1925 as ss. 18, 37, 42 and 43, respectively. When the 1925 Act was repealed by the Senior Courts Act 1981,[114] s. 18 was re-enacted, *in pari materia*, as s. 19, of the 1981 Act. As for ss. 37, 42 and 43, these were re-enacted in a more compressed form in s. 49(2) of the 1981 Act. There is, accordingly, a continuous legislative chain linking a judge of the High Court today with the judges of the court of Chancery, and of the common law courts, prior to the administrative fusion effected by the Judicature Acts. In consequence, we may indeed say that, *in a loose sense*, payment of a debt to a creditor-assignor despite having had notice of the debt does not 'discharge' the debt at law *so far as the assignee is concerned* even though the wrongful payment by the debtor *does* discharge the debt at common law *so far as concerns the creditor-assignor*. That discharge is part of the basis for equity to intervene in the first place: if there were no such discharge at law, there would be no basis for equity to intervene. But given the jurisdictions as had been transferred to the High Court from the court of Chancery and the courts of common law, payment in circumstances that would have supported the issue of a common injunction permanently and unconditionally enjoining pleading of said payment would no longer be an effective defence against an assignee who brought a claim for non-payment at law within the court's common law jurisdiction.

The reason why this is so, however, does not rest on any unilateral change to the chose in action that had been assigned. The reason for this outcome rests on the procedural devices which were first developed by the court of Chancery, which were then adopted by the courts of common law, and which were then further extended by Parliament pursuant to the Common Law Procedure Act 1854. Each of these developments fed into the proposition that 'equities' such as tender of payment, the grant of a release or the assertion of cross-claims with the obligee could also be asserted as against an assignee, whether bringing proceedings in her own name in equity, or in the name of the assignor

---

[114] Senior Courts Act 1981, s. 152(4) read with Schedule 7.

at common law, so long as the equities had accrued prior to receipt of notice of the assignment. But the mechanism in play is essentially a procedural one, where a defendant is barred from pleading a defence which is otherwise completely made out in terms of its substantive requirements.

Crucially, we must note that since such procedural interference rests on the availability of facts as would have justified the issue of a common injunction had the plaintiff bringing the action at law sought relief in equity, these mechanisms are *personal* to the plaintiff. As such, these devices continue to respect the overriding principle that a unilateral change of the identity of the obligor is not generally permitted. It follows, therefore, that it is not correct to say, as some have done,[115] that payments to the creditor-assignor do *not* effect a discharge at law. As explained above, *Legh* v. *Legh* is no authority for such a proposition.

## I  Conclusion

We now see the answers to the two questions as to why equities run as against an assignee, even equities which had arisen after notice. This is the logical and necessary result of the operation of the trust-plus-agency mechanisms of equitable assignment. As to why, following notice, equities *cease* to run in cases where a common law chose in action had

---

[115] See e.g. Joshua Williams, T. Cyprian Williams and W. J. Byrne, *Principles of the Law of Personal Property, Intended for the Use of Students in Conveyancing* (18th edn, London: Sweet & Maxwell, 1926), p. 38: '[I]f the claim were for payment of money and the person liable, notwithstanding that he had had notice of an assignment, persisted in paying the assignor, he was not discharged from his duty, but remained liable to pay over again to the assignee', relying on the authority of *Legh* v. *Legh* (1799) 1 Bos & Pul 447, *Jones* v. *Farrell* (1857) 1 De G & J 208, *Flower* v. *Lyme Regis Corpn* [1921] 1 KB 488, 489 and 491; Peel (2015), pp. 725–6, fn. 95; N. Ruddy, S. Mills and N. Davidson, *Salinger on Factoring* (5th edn, London: Sweet & Maxwell, 2017), para. 8.21; H. Beale, M. Bridge, L. Gullifer and E. Lomnicka, *The Law of Security and Title-Based Financing* (3rd edn, Oxford: Oxford University Press, 2018), para. 7.81, citing the authority of *Brice* v. *Bannister* (1878) 3 QBD 569; and *James Talcott Ltd* v. *John Lewis & Co. Ltd* [1940] 3 All ER 592. For Australian commentary, see Tolhurst (2016), para. 8.06 (at p. 394), citing the authority of *Legh* v. *Legh*, *Brice* v. *Bannister*, *Liquidation Estates Purchase Co. Limited* v. *Willoughby* (n. 21), *Brandt's* [1905] AC 454, *Swan and Cleland's Graving Dock and Slipway Company* v. *Maritime Insurance Co.* [1907] 1 KB 116; *James Talcott Ltd* v. *John Lewis Ltd* [1940] 3 All ER 592; *Pettit & Johnson* v. *Foster Wheeler Ltd* (1950) 2 DLR 42 (aff'd (1950) 3 DLR 320). Tolhurst suggests, however, that 'an assignee would have to give credit to the obligor if the obligor had paid the assignor by cheque which was still outstanding at the time of notice: see *Bence* v. *Shearman* [1898] 2 Ch 582; *Felix Hadley & Co.* v. *Hadley* [1898] 2 Ch 680', at p. 394.

been equitably assigned, this is because of the procedural bars against the *mala fide* pleading of certain kinds of defences in certain 'fraudulent' contexts – contexts which some might characterize as revealing 'opportunistic' (ab)uses of entitlements which the law otherwise would accord to their holders:[116] and such a qualification had to be developed in order to prevent the institution of equitable assignment from being all-too-easily subverted.

But does any of this matter? Besides a more precise appreciation of its manner of operation, the 'procedural' account of the rule that equities run until notice be received has significant practical effects. If the rule that equities run until notice is procedural, then the effects which the barred defences might otherwise have *outside of litigation* between those parties would still occur.

For example, suppose that B, having borrowed £10,000 from A, then borrows a further £20,000 from A. Suppose that B then sells A £2,000-worth of goods on credit. Next, suppose A equitably assigns the debt of £10,000 to $C_1$, and the debt of £20,000 to $C_2$; and $C_1$, but not $C_2$, gives notice of assignment to B before the £2,000 cross-claim arose.

When B fails to repay the debts, proceedings are brought by $C_1$ and $C_2$ at law in A's name against B. But at this point in time, A is still indebted to B in the £2,000, which has by now become due and payable.

On these facts, in respect of $C_1$'s claim as A's assignee of the £10,000 debt, B will be procedurally barred from pleading the £2,000 which A owes B by reason of the cross-claim. That, however, does not deny B the possibility of pleading that cross-claim by way of defence to the action on the debt of £20,000 that had been assigned to $C_2$, the procedural bar having no effect beyond the barring of the defence in a particular action.

---

[116] Smith, 'Equitable Defences as Meta-Law' (n. 47).

# PART V

Statutes

# 13

# 'Statutory' Assignments under Law of Property Act 1925, Section 136(1)

## A  Introduction

The law on so-called statutory assignments made in accordance with the provisions of what is now s. 136(1) of the Law of Property Act 1925[1] is almost as poorly understood as equitable assignment. When a chose in action has been assigned in a manner recognized at common law or in equity, *and* the requirements in s. 136(1)[2] are satisfied, the specific entitlements spelt out in ss. 136(1)(a), (b) and (c) shall pass from the assignor and are transferred to the assignee. Thus, where an equitable assignment of a chose in action has 'become' a 'statutory' assignment, *those* entitlements (but no others) are transferred to the assignee and lost to the assignor. Thus, as to those entitlements, the trust and agency effects underpinning such equitable assignment are overridden. This is apparent on the face of the provision:

> 136 Legal assignments of things in action
>
> (1) Any absolute assignment by writing under the hand of the assignor (not purporting to be by way of charge only) of any debt or other legal thing in action, of which express notice in writing has been given to the debtor, trustee or other person from whom the assignor would have been entitled to claim such debt or thing in action, is effectual in law (subject to equities having priority over the right of the assignee) to pass and transfer from the date of such notice –
>
> (a) the legal right to such debt or thing in action;
> (b) all legal and other remedies for the same; and
> (c) the power to give a good discharge for the same without the concurrence of the assignor:
>
> Provided that, if the debtor, trustee or other person liable in respect of such debt or thing in action has notice –

---

[1] Or 'LPA1925'.

[2] In this and the following chapter, references to s. 136 and s. 136(1). refer to LPA1925, s. 136 and LPA1925, s. 136(1), respectively, unless otherwise indicated.

> (a) that the assignment is disputed by the assignor or any person claiming under him; or
>
> (b) of any other opposing or conflicting claim to such debt or thing in action;
>
> > he may, if he thinks fit, either call upon the persons making claim thereto to interplead concerning the same, or pay the debt or other thing in action into court under the provisions of the Trustee Act 1925.

The first, and perhaps the most important thing we should note about this piece of legislation is that the subject matter which is 'passed' and 'transferred' by it is *not* the 'debt or thing in action' which had been assigned. That is to say, no part of s. 136(1) passes or transfers the debt or thing in action itself: the provision plainly provides that the matters which are 'passed' and 'transferred' are the three sets of entitlements which are mentioned in the paragraphs which follow on from the words 'of such notice'. Statements like those in *Dry Bulk Handy Holding* v. *Fayette International* that, '[i]n the case of statutory assignments under s. 136 of the Law of Property Act 1925, the debt or other chose in action is transferred only if notice in writing of the assignment has been given to the debtor or other obligee'[3] are, therefore, misleading and unhelpful: they misrepresent the operation of the statute and are belied by its plain wording.

Second, the statute does not define what an 'assignment' entails. It merely asserts that an assignment will be accompanied by the effects spelt out in ss. 136(1)(a), (b) and (c), so long as the assignment be absolute and the formal requirements of a signed writing and written notice are satisfied. Consequently, entitlements extraneous to these subsections are not 'transferred'. Hence any extraneous entitlement arising in connection with a chose in action that had been equitably assigned will not be transferred to the assignee, and the trust and agency effects underpinning the equitable assignment will still apply to such entitlement.

'Statutory' assignments are, accordingly, 'additive': they build on the effects which would otherwise arise by reason of such assignment[4] as had

---

[3] [2012] EWHC 2107 (Comm), [2013] 1 All ER (Comm) 177, [56].

[4] As will be explained below, outside of LPA1925, s. 136(1), choses in action may be equitably assigned; but there are also some instances where choses in action may be assigned at law (by the Crown), and also other instances where certain limited types of choses in action may be assigned at law. Since the only form of assignment which is generally available is equitable assignment, this chapter will discuss how statutory assignment pursuant to LPA1925, s. 136(1) builds on the effects of equitable assignment.

already been effected,[5] but only so far as the particular entitlements specified in ss. 136(1)(a), (b) and (c) are concerned. As will be explained in this chapter, the list of entitlements in ss. 136(1)(a), (b) and (c) is not exhaustive: other entitlements falling beyond those words exist. Therefore, so far as choses in action may be regarded as a form of intangible property, statements suggesting that '[i]ntangible property can be transferred *absolutely* pursuant to s. 136 of the Law of Property Act 1925'[6] cannot be correct. Taken literally, such statements would seem to suggest that *all* entitlements associated with the chose in question are transferred from the assignor to her assignee. But that is *not* what the statute says, and it is not what the statute does.

So far as the entitlements set out in ss. 136(1)(a), (b) and (c) have passed from a statutory assignor and been transferred to the assignee, the statutory assignor will have lost her power to invoke them, leaving the assignee as the only entity with the power to do so. The significance of the statute is, therefore, not that it allows the assignee to invoke these entitlements, but that it removes the assignor's ability to do so.

The rest of this chapter will examine the operation of s. 136(1). However, before proceeding further, the short account which follows as to the legislative history behind the enactment of Judicature Act 1873, s. 25(6), on which s. 136(1) is based, may provide some helpful context.

## B    Legislative History and Purpose

Section 136(1) of the Law of Property Act 1925 was a re-enactment of what had been the Judicature Act 1873, s. 25(6). Save for the substitution of 'thing in action' for the law French 'chose in action', and formatting changes by setting out various clauses as subsections, the two provisions are *in pari materia*. There is certainly no caselaw that suggests that these minor alterations resulted in substantive changes to the pre-1925 law. Therefore, in this and the remaining chapters, 'thing in action' and 'chose in action' will be used interchangeably.

---

[5]  Cf. A. M. Tettenborn, *An Introduction to the Law of Obligations* (London: Butterworths, 1984), p. 203: 'The effect of equitable assignment, whatever form it takes, is the same as that of statutory assignment; that is, the benefit of the obligation becomes vested in the assignee.' This is so because a statutory assignment *is* an equitable assignment, albeit with certain additional effects mandated by the statute.

[6]  M. Smith, 'Assignments of Intangibles as Security: Some Unlitigated Pitfalls' (2015) 9 *Butterworths Journal of International Banking and Financial Law* 558, 558 (emphasis added).

The enactment of the Judicature Act 1873 represented the culmination of decades of legal reform.[7] It was the result of an extensive review of legal procedure but was not, in the main, conceived to have significant substantive effects:[8]

> [T]he orthodox view remains that expressed by Ashburner in a metaphor which retains its currency more because it is memorable than apposite – indeed it is singularly unpicturable: 'the two streams of jurisdiction, though they run in the same channel, run side by side and do not mingle their waters'.

Presented to both Houses of Parliament in 1869, the First Report of the Judicature Commission[9] set out the following introductory observations:[10]

> In commencing the inquiry which we were directed by Your Majesty to make, the first subject that naturally presented itself for consideration was the ancient division of the Courts, into the Courts of Common Law, and the Court of Chancery, founded on the well known distinction in our law between Common Law and Equity.
>
> This distinction led to the establishment of two systems of Judicature, organized in different ways, and administering justice on different and sometimes opposite principles, using different methods of procedure, and applying different remedies. Large classes of rights, altogether ignored by the Courts of Common Law, were protected and enforced by the Court of Chancery, and recourse was had to the same Court for the purpose of obtaining a more adequate protection against the violation of Common Law rights than the Courts of Common Law were competent to afford. The Common Law Courts were confined by their system of procedure in

---

[7] M. Lobban, 'Preparing for Fusion: Reforming the Nineteenth-Century Court of Chancery, Part I' (2006) 22 *Law and History Review* 389; M. Lobban, 'Preparing for Fusion: Reforming the Nineteenth-Century Court of Chancery, Part II' (2006) 22 *Law and History Review* 565. Alternatively, and more briefly, see 'The Judicature Acts 1873–1875: Vision and Reality' in Sir J. I. H. Jacob, *The Reform of Civil Procedural Law and Other Essays in Civil Procedure* (London: Sweet & Maxwell, 1982), pp. 301–21.

[8] P. Polden, 'Mingling the Waters: Personalities, Politics and the Making of the Supreme Court of Judicature' (2002) 61 CLJ 575, 575–6, citing a passage from W. Ashburner, *Ashburner's Principles of Equity* (D. Browne, ed., 2nd edn, London: Butterworth & Co., 1933), p. 18.

[9] One of the members of the Commission was Sir Roundel Palmer, who as Lord Selborne, was Lord Chancellor between 1872 and 1874. Lord Selborne was instrumental in shepherding the passage of what became the Judicature Act 1873 through Parliament.

[10] Great Britain, Judicature Commission, *First to Fifth Reports of the Commissioners on the Judicature: With Minutes of Evidence and Appendices, 1868–74*, vol. 13 (Shannon: Irish University Press, 1970), pp. 13–14, reproducing pp. 5–6 of the First Report of the Judicature Commissioners 1868–69 [4130] Vol. XXV (hereafter, 'First Report').

most actions – not brought for recovering the possession of land – to giving judgment for debt or damages, a remedy which has been found to be totally insufficient for the adjustment of the complicated disputes of modern society. . . .

The evils of this double system of Judicature, and the confusion and conflict of jurisdiction to which it has led, have been long known and acknowledged.

The cure prescribed by the Judicature Commission went beyond a mere blending or transfer of the respective jurisdictions of the Courts of Common Law and Chancery. That had been attempted in the earlier part of the century[11] and had been found somewhat wanting.[12] A different approach was needed:[13]

We are of the opinion that the defects above adverted to cannot be completely remedied by any mere transfer or blending of jurisdiction between the Courts as at present constituted; and that the first step towards meeting and surmounting the evils complained of will be the consolidation of all the Superior Courts of Law and Equity, together with the Courts of Probate, Divorce, and Admiralty, into one Court, to be called 'Her Majesty's Supreme Court', in which Court shall be vested all the jurisdiction which is now exercisable by each and all the Courts so consolidated.

This consolidation would at once put an end to all conflicts of jurisdiction. No suitor could be defeated because he commenced his suit in the wrong Court, and sending the suitor from equity to law or from law to equity, to begin his suit over against in order to obtain redress, will no longer be possible.

But consolidation of the administration of the courts would serve little purpose without adoption of a consolidated procedure. This formed the second major recommendation of the Commission.[14]

The recommendations of the Judicature Commission eventually led to the introduction of the Supreme Court of Judicature Bill. The chief

---

[11] Via e.g. the Common Law Procedure Act 1852, the Common Law Procedure Act 1854 and the Common Law Procedure Act 1860. Common law courts had also been legislatively conferred powers that had otherwise only been exercised by courts of Equity in earlier periods of time, e.g. 8 & 9 Will. III, c. 11; 4 Anne, c. 16; 7 Geo. II, c. 20 and 4 Geo II, c. 28.

[12] Great Britain, Judicature Commission, *First to Fifth Reports* (n. 10), pp. 14–15, reproducing pp. 6–7 of the First Report.

[13] Ibid., p. 17, reproducing p. 9 of the First Report.

[14] Ibid., pp. 18–19, reproducing pp. 10–11 of the First Report.

architect of the bill was, probably, Lord Selborne LC.[15] This Bill followed the scheme of reform suggested by the Commission, setting out a consolidated Supreme Court uniting the jurisdictions of the Court of Chancery, the Courts of Common Law, of the Probate and Divorce Court, of the Admiralty, of the London or Central Court of Bankruptcy and the Courts of Pleas of the Counties Palatine of Lancaster and Durham, and of the Courts created by Commissions of Assize. That step having been taken, the Bill then set out directions as to how these jurisdictions were to be exercised in the High Court within which all these disparate courts were 'fused'.

In his speech on the Second Reading of this Bill in the House of Lords,[16] Lord Selborne LC said of the Bill:[17]

> [These] directions are given under seven heads.[18] First, the Court in all its branches will give effect to the equitable rights and remedies of plaintiffs; secondly, it will do the same with respect to equitable defences by defendants; thirdly, it will give effect to counter claims of defendants; fourthly, it will take notice of all equitable rights and liabilities of any persons, appearing incidentally in the course of any proceedings; fifthly, it will stay proceedings, when necessary, by the authority of the Judges before whom an action is pending, and not by injunctions to be obtained, from other Judges; sixthly, it will give effect, subject to all equities, to legal rights and remedies; and lastly, it will deal, as far as possible, with all questions in controversy in one and the same suit, so as to do complete justice between the parties, and prevent a multiplicity of proceedings.

The primary goal was *not* to create a fusion of the substantive rules as applied hitherto in the various courts. Lord Selborne explained:[19]

> It may be asked ... why not abolish at once all distinction between law and equity? I can best answer that by asking another question – Do you

---

[15] In his memoirs, Lord Selborne said, 'It [the Judicature Act 1873] was the work of my own hand, without any assistance beyond what I derived from the labours of my predecessors; and it passed, substantially, in the form in which I proposed it': R. Palmer, Earl of Selborne, *Memorials Part II: Personal and Political 1865–1895* (Lady S. M. Palmer, ed., 2 vols., London: Macmillan & Co., 1898), vol. 1, p. 298.

[16] When the bill was presented before the House of Commons, the Attorney-General made broadly similar points to those made by Lord Selborne (at Hansard, HC, vol. 216, cols. 644–5, 9 June 1873).

[17] Hansard, HL, vol. 214, cols. 338–9, 13 February 1873.

[18] These seven heads were eventually enacted as Judicature Act 1873, s. 24.

[19] Hansard, HL, vol. 214, col. 339, 13 February 1873. When the Bill went to the House of Commons, the Attorney-General made broadly similar points: Hansard, HC, vol. 216, cols. 644–5, 9 June 1873.

wish to abolish trusts? If trusts are to continue, there must be a distinction between what we call a legal estate and an equitable estate. The legal estate is in the person who holds the property for another; the equitable estate is in the person beneficially interested. The distinction, within certain limits, between law and equity is real and natural and it would be a mistake to suppose that what is real and natural is to be disregarded, although under our present system it is often pushed beyond those limits. I content myself with saying that those rights and remedies which belong to the system of law and jurisprudence under which we actually live, and which are consistent with each other should be equally recognized and effect given to them, in all branches of the Court.

The Lord Chancellor recognized, however, that there could be some areas where points of conflict in the substantive rules as applied in the various courts had arisen. As to these, Lord Selborne explained:[20]

There are some points ... in which, from this division of jurisdiction, unnecessary discrepancies have been introduced by reason of arbitrary rules established in different Courts. They are not very numerous. It is possible that some may have been overlooked: and on the suggestion of a high authority, I have added in the Bill general words to provide that where there is any variance between the rules of law and those of equity, and the matter is not expressly dealt with, the rules of equity shall prevail. But there are cases in which I think it desirable at once to legislate – in some respects to declare the law, and in some respects to improve it, by abolishing distinctions which might lead to confusion.

What were these discrepant points? In his speech, Lord Selborne mentioned nine:[21]

The first alteration is a rather important one. It is proposed that in the administration of insolvent estates by the Court after the death of the debtor, substantially the rules applicable to bankruptcy shall be adopted. There seems to be no good reason why the estate of an insolvent debtor should be administered in one way while he is living and in another way when he is dead.[22] The next is in respect of limitation as to trusts, that the statutes of limitation shall not apply between express trustees and *cestui que trusts*:[23] then the distinction between legal and equitable waste is done

---

[20] Hansard, HL, vol. 214, cols. 339–40, 13 February 1873.

[21] Ibid., col. 340, 13 February 1873.

[22] See Judicature Act 1873, s. 25(1); but this provision was repealed without it ever coming into operation, and was substituted by Judicature Act 1875, s. 10, which provided for the extension of the bankruptcy rules to apply also to instances of winding up of insolvent companies.

[23] See Judicature Act 1873, s. 25(2). But now see Limitation Act 1980, s. 21.

away with.[24] Again, merger by law is not to take place where an equitable interest continues.[25] Mortgagors in possession are to be allowed to sue in their own names.[26] It is proposed to adopt the equitable and not the common law rule as to stipulations in contracts which are in equity deemed to be not of the essence of the contract;[27] to adopt the equitable rule as to liability for misrepresentation;[28] and also to remove certain technical impediments, now existing in equity, in the way of applications for injunction and the appointment of receivers in certain cases.[29] In respect of collisions at sea it is proposed to adopt, instead of a rule which now holds good in the Court of Admiralty, the rule of common law as to contributory fault or contributory negligence.[30] . . . Then, as to the custody of infants[31] and other matters of conflict, not enumerated, the rules of equity are to prevail.[32]

---

[24] See Judicature Act 1873, s. 25(3). Now see LPA1925, s. 135.

[25] See Judicature Act 1873, s. 25(4). Now see LPA1925, s. 185.

[26] See Judicature Act 1873, s. 25(5). Now see LPA1925, s. 98.

[27] See Judicature Act 1873, s. 25(7). Now see LPA1925, s. 41.

[28] Clause 26(8) of the Supreme Court of Judicature HL Bill (14) initially provided as follows: 'In any suit or proceeding for damages or other relief on the ground of any untrue representation of fact, by reason of which any loss is alleged to have been sustained, it shall not be necessary to prove knowledge of the untruth of such representation by the person who made the same, if such person knew that information was being sought thereon by the person to whom the representation was made in any matter concerning his interest.' This clause was left out of the Judicature Act 1873, as enacted, following amendments proposed by the Lord Chancellor leading up to the re-commitment of the Bill before the Select Committee: see p. 1 of the *Amendments to be Moved in Committee (on Re-commitment) by the Lord Chancellor (45a), Sessional Papers 1873, Vol. VII.*

[29] See Judicature Act 1873, s. 25(8), which also provides for the making of orders of mandamus, an addition proposed when the Bill went before committee – see page 16 of the Supreme Court of Judicature [HL] Bill (as amended by the Select Committee) (73.), Sessional Papers 1873, Vol. VII. In this context, 'mandamus' denotes the power of enforcing by mandamus the specific performance of legal duties granted to common law courts pursuant to Common Law Procedure Act 1854, s. 68, modifying the prior position at common law wherein mandamus would lie only in respect of duties or rights of a public nature.

[30] Following debate in the House of Commons (Hansard, HC, vol. 216, col. 671, 9 June 1873), to maintain continued consistency with the practice of admiralty courts in continental Europe and the United States of America, Judicature Act 1873, s. 25(9), as enacted, stipulated that the Admiralty rule was to prevail: that where both parties were to blame, the loss would be shared equally (see page 4 of the *Supreme Court of Judicature Bill [HL] – Commons Amendments (234),* Sessional Papers 1873, Vol. VII).

[31] See Judicature Act 1873, s. 25(10). In the Judicature Act 1925, this was re-enacted in s. 44.

[32] See Judicature Act 1873, s. 25(11). Now, see Senior Courts Act 1981, s. 49(1). The source of inspiration for this provision may have been a suggestion of Sir Alexander Cockburn, Chief Justice of the Court of King's Bench. In a letter of 7 February 1873 to the Lord Chancellor, he wrote: 'I could have wished to have seen all distinction between Law and Equity removed for ever . . . by equity being converted into law . . . being sought in the

The principal legislative purpose of the Act was to effect an administrative fusion – to transpose the jurisdictions that had hitherto been
exercised in several courts of Common Law, Equity, Admiralty and so
forth, to a new Supreme Court.[33] That done, the Act also provided rules
as to how these multiple jurisdictions were to be exercised by the
judicial officers of the fused court via s. 24 of the Judicature Act 1873.
And last, where the exercise of that jurisdiction might produce
instances where the substantive rules of one jurisdiction might conflict
with those of another, one would consult s. 25 of the Judicature Act
1873.[34]

But, interestingly, Lord Selborne made no reference to the question
of 'statutory' assignment under the Bill. The Attorney-General was
similarly reticent,[35] even though provision for it had been made from
the outset:[36]

> (6) Any absolute assignment, by writing under the hand of the assignor
> (not purporting to be by way of charge or security[37] only), of any debt or
> other legal chose in action, of which express notice in writing shall
> have been given to the debtor, trustee, or other person from whom the
> assignor would have been entitled to receive or claim such debt or chose
> in action, shall be, and be deemed to have been effectual in law (subject to

---

fusion not of the substantive law, but of jurisdiction . . . I cannot but suggest that a clause
should be added to your Bill, to enact that whenever law and equity are in conflict, equity
should supersede the law': Selborne Papers, Lambeth Palace Library Manuscripts, 1865,
f. 130, cited and extracted in E. Heward, *A Victorian Law Reformer: A Life of Lord
Selborne* (Chichester: Barry Rose Law Publishers, 1997), pp. 139–40.

[33] *Ind, Coope & Co.* v. *Emmerson* (1887) 12 App Cas 300, 308 (Lord Watson, with whom
Lord Fitzgerald agreed). See also, J. A. Strahan, *Strahan's Digest of Equity* (R.
A. Eastwood, ed., 6th edn, London: Butterworth & Co., 1939), pp. 14–15.

[34] Sir W. S. Holdsworth, *A History of English Law* (2nd edn, 12 vols., London: Methuen &
Co. Ltd, 1937), vol. XII, p. 603; *Walsh* v. *Lonsdale* (1882) 21 Ch D 9, 14, Jessel MR said:
'There is only one Court, and the equity rules prevail in it.' These comments may,
however, go slightly too far given that the Judicature Act 1873, ss. 25(1)–(10) did not
*uniformly* give precedence to the rules of equity, and the Judicature Act 1873, s. 25(11)
only applies insofar as no specific provision had been made otherwise in s. 25. Perhaps
the most accurate summary of the effect of the Judicature Act 1873, s. 25, is to be found in
*Torkington* v. *Magee* [1902] 2 KB 427, 430.

[35] Hansard, HC, vol. 216, cols. 644–5, 9 June 1873.

[36] Clause 26(6) of the *Supreme Court of Judicature HL Bill (14)*. Other than as indicated in
the text, this clause remained largely unchanged as the bill made its progress through
both Houses and the Select Committee.

[37] The underlined words 'or security' were deleted from Clause 26(6) of the *Supreme Court
of Judicature HL Bill (14)* after its Second Reading on 11 March 1873: see p. 15, *Supreme
Court of Judicature HL Bill [as amended on report] (45)*.

all equities affecting the same) to pass and transfer the [legal][38] right to such debt or chose in action from the date of such notice, and all legal and other remedies for the same, and the power to give a good discharge for the same, without the concurrence of the assignor: Provided always, that if the debtor, trustee, or other person liable in respect of such debt or chose in action shall have had notice that such assignment is disputed by the assignor or anyone claiming under him, or of any other opposing or conflicting claims to such debt or chose in action, he shall be entitled, if he think fit, to pay the same into the High Court of Justice under and in conformity with the provisions of the Acts for the relief of trustees.

As is plain from the first paragraph of s. 25, as enacted in the 1873 Act, that section was intended to modify substantive rules extant at common law, in admiralty and in equity, insofar as they might each be applicable in common and give rise to divergent results. So, as one commentator observed of s. 25:[39]

The present section undertakes to render uniform the rules of law administered in the several divisions of the Court in the points as to which they were in conflict. The method which has been adopted is to deal in the first ten subsections with specific cases in which conflicting rules have hitherto existed, and to provide what rule is to prevail for the future. The rule adopted is in general that of the Court of Chancery. But in sub-s. 1, as altered by s. 10 of the [Judicature] Act of 1874, the Bankruptcy Rule, and in sub-s. 9 the Admiralty Rule, are adopted; and in sub-s. 8, a rule is adopted different in some respects from any hitherto in force. By sub-s 11, it is enacted generally, that in cases not specifically provided for the equity rule is to prevail.[40]

In such a case, s. 25 was to provide a code of priorities – in the main, favouring rules of equity.[41]

As Jessel MR stated in *Salt* v. *Cooper*:[42]

---

[38] The word 'legal' was added to Clause 26(6) of the *Supreme Court of Judicature HL Bill (14)* after its Second Reading on 11 March 1873: see p. 15, *Supreme Court of Judicature HL Bill [as amended on report] (45)*.

[39] A. Wilson, *Wilson's Supreme Court of Judicature Acts, Rules, and Forms* (M. M. Mackenzie and C. A. White, eds., 5th edn, London: Stevens & Sons, 1886), p. 27.

[40] For accounts as to the limited effect of Judicature Act 1873, s. 25(11), see F. W. Maitland, *Equity Also, The Forms of Action at Common Law: Two Courses of Lectures* (A. H. Chaytor and W. J. Whittaker, eds., 1st edn, Cambridge: University Press, 1909), pp. 16–22, 156–70; and Sir W. S. Holdsworth, 'Equity' (1935) 51 LQR 142, 134–49.

[41] See main text to n. 21, above. See also 'The Supreme Court of Judicature Act – Part II. Jurisdiction and Law' (1873) 55 *The Law Times* 372; G. W. Keeton and L. A. Sheridan, *Equity* (2nd edn, Abingdon: Professional Books, 1976), pp. 57–60.

[42] (1880) 16 Ch D 544, 549. The decision of Jessel MR was upheld on appeal to the Court of Appeal, although it did not refer to his analysis of the effect of the Judicature Act 1873. See also *Joseph* v. *Lyons* (1884) 15 QBD 280, 287.

It is stated very plainly that the main object of the Act was to assimilate the transaction of Equity business and Common Law business by different Courts of Judicature. It has been sometimes inaccurately called 'the fusion of Law and Equity'; but it was not any fusion, or anything of the kind; it was the vesting in one tribunal the administration of Law and Equity in every cause, action, or dispute which should come before that tribunal. That was the meaning of the Act. [But t]hen, as to that very small number of cases in which there is an actual conflict, it was decided that in all cases where the rules of Equity and Law were in conflict, the rules of Equity should prevail.[43] That was to be the mode of administering the combined jurisdiction, and that was the meaning of the Act. To carry that out, the Legislature did not create a new jurisdiction, but simply transferred the old jurisdictions of the Courts of Law and Equity to the new tribunal, and then gave directions to the new tribunal as to the mode in which it should administer the combined jurisdictions.[44]

The operation of what eventually became s. 25(6), however, was not quite the same as the other subsections. As mentioned above, although the Lord Chancellor took pains to explain the changes to the substantive law that would result to each and every other limb of clause 26 of the Bill (which would later be enacted as s. 25 of the Judicature Act 1873), and even briefly explained the effect of what would become s. 25(11), the Lord Chancellor made no mention of the provision relating to assignments. Given the pains taken to explain the substantive changes to be effected in the other parts of clause 26 of the Bill, why was no similar effort made in respect of the wording pertaining to assignments?

One possible answer is that it would not have made sense to discuss these words alongside a discussion of the *substantive* changes effected by the rest of clause 26. As many later cases have explained, the legislative purpose behind what was eventually enacted as the Judicature Act 1873, s. 25(6) was to overcome a *procedural* concern over the need for joinder of the assignor if the assignee desired proceedings to be brought against the obligor on the chose assigned at common law, as well as some consequential and associated complications.

For example, as Day J explained in *Burlinson* v. *Hall* where an action had been brought by an assignee of a debt in circumstances where the

---

[43] Subject to the qualifications in relation to Judicature Act 1873, ss. 25(1) and 25(9), above at n. 29.

[44] Similar sentiments may be found in *Walker* v. *The Bradford Old Bank, Limited* (1884) 12 QBD 511.

assignment had been effected in writing and written notice had been given in accordance with the requirements of s. 25(6):[45]

> Prior to the Judicature Act [1873] he [i.e. the assignee] must have brought two actions– one in his own name, the other in the name of Tucker [the assignor]. The Judicature Act was intended to simplify procedure, and diminish the costs of it. It was intended – not in any way to limit but – rather to extend the right of suitors, and it provides that where a person is entitled to debts assigned to him he may sue in his own name instead of – as before the Judicature Act – suing in the name of the assignor and giving him an indemnity.

Nor was he alone in this view. In *Marchant* v. *Morton, Down & Co.*, Channell J described s. 25(6) as having the following effect: 'I think ... that that sub-section is merely machinery. It enables an action to be brought by the assignee in his own name in cases where previously he could have sued in the assignee's name, but only where he could so sue.'[46]

And this was also the view of Lord Lindley in *Tolhurst* v. *Associated Portland Cement*: 'The Judicature Act, 1873, s. 25, clause 6, has not made contracts assignable which were not assignable in equity before, but it has enabled assigns of assignable contracts to sue upon them in their own names without joining the assignor.'[47]

But s. 25(6) was also aimed at resolving other problems beyond complications pertaining to joinder of assignors, some of which were highlighted in Chitty LJ's judgment in *Durham Brothers* v. *Robertson*:[48]

> In his suit in equity[49] the assignee of a debt, even where the assignment was absolute on the face of it, had to make his assignor, the original creditor, party in order primarily to bind him and prevent his suing at law, and also to allow him to dispute the assignment if he thought fit. This

---

[45]  (1884) 12 QBD 347, 349.

[46]  [1901] 2 KB 829, 852. Channell J repeated these views in *Torkington* v. *Magee* [1902] 2 KB 829 (reversed on other grounds: [1903] 1 KB 644).

[47]  *Tolhurst* v. *Associated Portland Cement Manufacturers (1900) Limited.* [1903] AC 414, 424, reiterating the position adopted in the Court of Appeal: [1902] 2 KB 660, 676 'Now this section [i.e. s. 25(6)] relates to procedure only. It does not enlarge the class of choses in action, the assignability of which was previously recognised either at law or in equity. It is designed to avoid the necessity of going first to a Court of equity and then to a Court of law' (Cozen-Hardy LJ).

[48]  [1898] 1 QB 765, 769–70.

[49]  Though the problem of joinder was particularly acute where proceedings were brought at law on a legal chose in action which had been equitably assigned, where proceedings were brought *in equity* on such legal chose in action, joinder of the assignor would still be desirable (see Chapter 9).

was a fortiori the case where the assignment was by way of security, or by way of charge only, because the assignor had a right to redeem. Further, the assignee could not give a valid discharge for the debt to the original debtor unless expressly empowered to do so. The original debtor, whether he admitted the debt or not, was not concerned with the state of the accounts between the assignor and the assignee where the debt was assigned by security; and the rule was that where he did not dispute the debt he should have his costs of suit out of the debt: he was regarded in the light of a stakeholder. . . .

Now it was in order to afford some remedy for this state of the law that sub-s. 6 was passed.

So, although s. 25(6) was aimed at resolving the problem of joinder of the assignor to an action at law or a suit in equity, that was not its only legislative purpose. It was also aimed, inter alia, at resolving the problems pertaining to an assignee's power to give an effective discharge to the original debtor at law: absent express authority to do so, a debtor's tender of payment to an equitable assignee would, at law, be regarded as being little different from tender of payment to a stranger, and such equitable assignee if not expressly authorized by the assignor to give a good discharge as the assignor's duly authorized agent could not 'give' a good discharge.

As explained in Chapter 9, this would mean that the debtor could, in principle, be sued at law on the debt, the debt being, at law, unpaid. Though this invidious result could be remedied by seeking an injunction to bar the bringing of proceedings at law on such 'unpaid' debt, or, eschewing the bringing of proceedings in Chancery, by pleading a 'defence on equitable grounds' pursuant to CLPA1854, s. 83 before the court of common law before which the action in debt had been brought, the former would require the bringing of parallel proceeding before a court of Chancery, whereas the latter would only be available where the court of common law was satisfied that equitable injunctive relief would have been granted unconditionally and not on terms. There was, accordingly, a lacuna, in that parallel proceedings would be required in cases where it was doubtful whether unconditional injunctive relief would have been granted. However, as Chitty LJ explained, this lacuna was filled in by Parliament through the enactment of s. 25(6).

## C Misnomer

Although debts or things in action are often said to have been 'statutorily assigned', as mentioned above, the statute does not set out an independent mode of statutorily assigning a 'debt or thing in action'. It merely mandates certain additional effects when a debt or other legal[50] thing in action is 'absolutely assigned',[51] otherwise than by way of charge;[52] in a signed writing;[53] and when written notice[54] of such assignment is given[55] and been received by[56] the obligor. These effects would *not* be present independently of the statute: they are additional effects by Parliamentary will. What is more, these additional effects will apply even where the debt or thing in action had been equitably assigned for no consideration: the statute does not require it.[57] As will be explained below, when we pay

[50] 'Legal', in this context, has been construed to refer to both legal *and* equitable choses in action: *Western Wagon and Property Company* v. *West* [1892] 1 Ch 271; *Torkington* v. *Magee* [1902] 2 KB 427, 430; *Re Pain* [1919] 1 Ch 38, 44; *Harding* v. *Harding* (1886) 17 QBD 442, 445; and *Compania Colombiana de Seguros* v. *Pacific Steam Navigation Co.* [1965] 1 QB 101. Some commentators have suggested, however, that such a construction is in error. This will be discussed further, in Section G, below.

[51] An assignment that is contingent on the fulfilment of a condition precedent is not an 'absolute' assignment within the ambit of the Judicature Act 1873, s. 25(6): *Re Williams* [1917] 1 Ch 1, 5 (Astbury J) (aff'd: [1917] 1 Ch 1, 6–9 on other grounds).

[52] Assignments by way of charge fall beyond LPA1925, s. 136(1): *Jones* v. *Humphreys* [1902] 1 KB 10, but an assignment by way of mortgage does not: *Raiffeisen Zentralbank Österreich AG* v. *Five Star Trading LLC* [2001] EWCA Civ 68; [2001] QB 825, [74].

[53] It is unclear whether a writing signed by a duly authorized agent of the assignor on the assignor's behalf or in her name would satisfy the requirements of s. 136(1). This may be contrasted with LPA1925, s, 53(1)(c), which expressly provides for it. In *Wilson* v. *Wallani* (1880) 5 Ex D 155 (Exch), a reference in Bankruptcy Act 1869, s. 23 to a disclaimer by the trustee 'by writing under his hand' was construed narrowly, such that a disclaimer signed by the trustees' solicitor was held to fall outside the ambit of the provision.

[54] Written notice under Judicature Act 1873, s. 25(6) is mandatory, even where the obligor is illiterate, and known by the assignor and assignee to be so: *Hockley* v. *Goldstein* (1920) 90 LJ KB 111, 112 (Bailhache J). Presumably, the same is true of LPA1925, s. 136(1).

[55] Notice may be given by the assignor, the assignee, or an authorized representative: e.g. *Bateman* v. *Hunt* [1904] 2 KB 530; *Ramsey* v. *Hartley* [1977] 1 WLR 686. Further, no time frame is legislatively stipulated. Thus, notice may be given even after the death of the assignor: *Walker* v. *The Bradford Old Bank, Limited* (1884) 12 QBD 511, so long as it has been given before proceedings are commenced: *Re Westerton* [1919] 2 Ch 104; *Compania Colombiana de Seguros* v. *Pacific Steam Navigation Co* [1965] 1 QB 101. However, in *Williams* v. *Atlantic Assurance Co. Ltd* [1933] 1 KB 81, Scrutton LJ was prepared to accept that sufficient written notice might have been given so as to effect a statutory assignment through service of a pleading in which reference was made to the assignment (although Slesser LJ in the same case thought otherwise); and in *Weddell* v. *J. A. Pearce & Major* [1988] Ch 26, Scott J appeared to accept that written notice given after proceedings had commenced was effective so as to create an effective statutory assignment.

[56] The notice is effective 'from the date of such notice', meaning the assignment takes effect as a statutory assignment from the date the notice is received by the obligor. Actual, physical receipt by the obligor is not necessary, and the notice is effective upon receipt at the obligor's place of business: *Holt* v. *Heatherfield Trust Ltd* [1942] 2 KB 1, 6.

[57] *Harding* v. *Harding* (1886) 17 QBD 442; *Re Westerton* [1919] 2 Ch 104; *Holt* v. *Heatherfield Trust Ltd* [1942] 2 KB 1.

attention to the words of the Judicature Act 1873, s. 25(6), and of its modern-day equivalent in LPA1925, s. 136(1), we will see that it merely supplements the existing law.[58]

Neither the Judicature Act 1873, s. 25(6), nor LPA1925, s. 136(1), provides a definition as to what would amount to an 'assignment' for their purposes.[59] It follows that an 'assignment' for their purposes must be any form of assignment of a debt or thing in action which might otherwise be recognized and given effect to at law or in equity. As was held in *Curran v. Newpark Cinemas*: '[S]ection 136(1) . . . does not provide that a document which would not, independently of the sub-section or its predecessor . . ., have operated as an absolute assignment at law or in equity is to have the force of an absolute assignment for the purposes of the sub-section.'[60] Given this, in *Curran v. Newpark Cinemas* the Court of Appeal concluded that where a debt or thing in action has not been effectively equitably assigned in the first place, and where none of the mechanisms permitting its assignment at law apart from s. 136(1) has been validly invoked, s. 136(1) could not be invoked since there has been no 'assignment' for it to be applied to.

Most debts and things in action will be assigned *inter vivos* in equity and not at law. Although things in action may be assigned at law by or to the Crown, and assignments at law are possible in respect of certain specified types of things in action (for example, certain types of intellectual property right) by reason of statute,[61] because there is no generally applicable doctrine allowing for *inter vivos* assignments at law, it is probable that when one assigns a debt or thing in action, one would do so in equity. Consequently, most instances of 'statutory' assignment will be cases where the statutory effects mandated by s. 136(1) will have been overlaid upon an equitable assignment of a debt or other thing in action. Rather than being a distinct form of assignment, leaving aside cases where there had been a true *inter vivos* assignment at law, in most cases, statutory assignments are better understood as a subtype or subclass of equitable assignment. That said, the language of 'statutory assignment of a debt' or 'statutory assignment of a thing in action' is endemic. But we should still take care to understand what it properly means.

---

[58] It is arguable that a failure to appreciate this has led to a divergent approach being taken in Australia. This is discussed in greater detail in Chapter 15, Section C.

[59] No definition is provided for 'assignment' in the Judicature Act 1873. As for LPA1925, s. 205 is also silent as to what amounts to an 'assignment' for the purposes of the Act.

[60] [1951] 1 All ER 295, 299H.

[61] See Chapter 14, Section B.

By enacting s. 25(6), Judicature Act 1873, and retaining its operation in s. 136(1), Parliament did not, 'forbid or destroy equitable assignments or impair their efficacy in the slightest degree'.[62] Rather, 'section 136 of the Law of Property Act 1925 does not create a statutory right of assignment in itself as so much regulates the effects of assignments which have taken place'.[63]

The operation of s. 136(1) may thus be compared with what happens when a registrable charge is registered pursuant to Part 25 of the Companies Act 2006: a registrable charge under Part 25 of the Companies Act 2006 remains a charge, albeit one whose effects may be supplemented by the statute (e.g. by s. 874 which supplements the effects of a registrable but unregistered charge as against certain categories of persons). Similarly, an equitable assignment which may be 'converted' into a statutory assignment remains an equitable assignment, albeit one whose effects have been supplemented by the statute.

Just as the provisions of Companies Act 2006, Part 25 do not create some novel form of charge, the provisions within s. 136(1) do not create any novel form of 'legal' assignment in contradistinction to pre-existing forms of assignment which had previously been developed in the general law. Therefore, unlike cases like *Walsh* v. *Lonsdale*[64] or *Milroy* v. *Lord*,[65] where the court declined to recharacterize an attempt to effect a mode of dealing at law as a different form of dealing in equity which had plainly not been intended, where the debt or thing in action had been equitably assigned to begin with, where an equitable assignment has been made absolutely, in a suitably signed writing, and written notice been given to the obligor, the equitable relationship is always present by way of foundation, and the material question is whether it has legal (i.e. statutory) effects superimposed upon it.

## D   The Statutory Effects

Where a debt or thing in action has been equitably assigned, if that equitable assignment was: (i) absolute (meaning it was not conditional, nor was it by way of charge); (ii) in a written document signed by the assignor; and (iii) written notice of such assignment was given to the obligor, such equitable assignment exhibiting '[t]he sacred triangle of

---

[62] *William Brandt's Sons & Co.* v. *Dunlop Rubber Co. Ltd.* [1905] AC 454, 462.
[63] *Hockin* v. *The Royal Bank of Scotland* [2016] EWHC 925 (Ch), [44] (Asplin J).
[64] (1882) 21 Ch D 9.
[65] (1862) 4 De G F & J 264.

"writing, absolute, and notice"[66] no longer takes effect *merely* as a bare trust plus agency so far as the entitlements specified in s. 136(1) are concerned.

The most significant impact of compliance with the requirement set out in s. 136(1) has already been mentioned above: the particular entitlements spelt out in ss. 136(1)(a), (b) and (c) are transferred *from* the assignor *to* the assignee. They are no longer the assignor's to assert or invoke. The significance of compliance with s. 136(1) is not, therefore, that the 'statutory' assignee may invoke the entitlements of the assignor. That would already have been the case given the equitable assignment, albeit with possible joinder complications. The major change generated by s. 136(1) is that so far as the matters set out in ss. 136(1)(a), (b) and (c) are concerned, the statutory assignor may no longer invoke them. Nor would the statutory assignor's authorization of another to invoke such entitlements be effectual since a principal may only empower an agent to invoke such entitlements which the principal still retains.

Though the statutory requirements in s. 136(1) may have been met, extraneous entitlements falling beyond the section are not transferred to the assignee. As to these, the trust and agency effects that underpin the equitable assignment of the debt or thing in action will still apply.

One example of such an extraneous entitlement would be the option to extend the validity of the recording contract encountered in *Warner Bros. v. Rollgreen*.[67] That power was certainly an entitlement which arose from the contractual thing in action that had been equitably assigned (to begin with). However, it is difficult to characterize such a power to be 'the legal right to such debt or thing in action', one of the 'legal and other remedies', or 'the power to give a good discharge for the same without the concurrence of the assignor', as would have been transferred under ss. 136(1)(a), (b), or (c), respectively.[68] And the same may be said of other kinds of options, for example, options for a lease of premises.[69] But

---

[66] Marshall (1950), p. 177.

[67] [1976] 1 QB 430.

[68] More detailed discussion of the construction of these phrases in LPA1925, s. 136(1) follows, in Section E, below.

[69] In *County Hotel and Wine Co. Ltd* v. *London & North Western Railway Co.* [1918] 2 KB 251 (aff'd: [1919] 2 KB 29 and [1921] AC 85 (HL), McCardie J held that the benefit of an option to grant a lease of premises had been validly assigned in 1916. The first instance report records (at [1918] 2 KB 255) that the assignment was in writing, and that written notice had been given. It therefore seems probable that the requirements for 'statutory' assignment pursuant to the Judicature Act 1873, s. 25(6), were likely to have been

apart from options, it is suggested that other examples of entitlements which are potentially extraneous to the entitlements listed in ss. 136(1) (a), (b) and (c) may include the entitlements arising from: (i) an 'acceleration of payment' clause; (ii) an 'entire agreement' clause; (iii) a 'no-reliance' clause; (iv) a pre-emptive purchase clause; an anti-assignment clause prohibiting assignment without obtaining the prior consent of the obligor to such assignment; (v) a choice of jurisdiction clause; or (vi) a choice of law clause.

It is also suggested that there are other entitlements which are not associated with any particular contractual clause, but yet are associated with a chose in action. For example, there are the entitlements arising from: (i) the power to suspend strict adherence to the express requirements under a contract; (ii) the power to affirm the contract despite an anticipatory repudiatory breach having been committed, thereby bringing the attendant power to discharge the contract for such breach to an end; (iii) the power to affirm the contract despite an actual breach of a condition, or of an innominate term with the requisite degree of harm, so as to bring the attendant power to discharge the contract for such breach to an end; (iv) the power to affirm the contract despite it being liable to be rescinded in light of a vitiating factor, thereby extinguishing the power to rescind such contract; and (v) the statutory power granted to a third party to a contract pursuant to the Contracts (Rights of Third Parties Act) 1999, s. 2, to permit the contracting parties to vary or rescind the terms of their contract in such a way as would impact on the third party's vested entitlements.

These lists of entitlements, above, plainly do not exhaust the class of entitlements arising out of or in connection with a chose in action. There

---

satisfied. By this option, the holder would have had the Hohfeldian power to require the counterparty to grant a lease to the assignee, and if the holder declined to do so, the holder would be in breach of its duty to do so, where no duty would have existed prior to and but for the exercise of the option. The question as to whether this Hohfeldian power had 'passed from' the assignor and been 'transferred to' the assignee did not, however, arise in argument. That the benefit of an option to grant a lease was assignable was also accepted by the Court of Appeal in *Griffith* v. *Pelton* [1958] Ch 205, where, arguably, the requirements for a statutory assignment had also been satisfied. But yet again, the question as to whether the benefit of such an option would be divested from the assignor to the assignee did not arise. Such options may, however, be 'personal' in that their grant had been on the basis that their exercise was to be personal to the grantee: *Re Cousins* (1880) 30 Ch D 203, in which it was held that options granted on such terms may not be transmitted to the executors of the grantee following his death. If so, it would seem to follow that *inter vivos* assignment would also be barred.

must be others. But these few examples provide some food for thought as to the breadth and diversity of entitlements which cannot, and do not, fall within the language of ss. 136(1)(a), (b) or (c).

Though the point is often missed,[70] the three classes of entitlements specified in s. 136(1) are not exhaustive of the universe of entitlements as may arise from or are associated with each and every chose in action that may possibly be made the subject of an assignment. Thus, it is not the case that a statutory assignee steps into the shoes of the statutory assignor and takes her place as against the obligor in every possible respect. So statements like '[s 136] transfers the obligation lock, stock and barrel to the assignee, [so] he – and he alone – can sue on it, *and erases the assignor from the picture*'[71] may overstate its effect. The obligor is 'erased', but surely only in respect of the entitlements to which ss. 136(1)(a), (b) and (c) apply.

As will be explained below, s. 136(1)(a) has the effect of allowing the statutory assignee *alone* to sue. But that is not to say that the 'debt or legal thing in action' which had been assigned has been transferred to the assignee. That cannot be, since the burdens of an obligation may not pass by any form of assignment,[72] nor is it what s. 136(1) purports to do. Again, it bears repeating that s. 136(1) merely transfers the specific entitlements set out in ss. 136(1)(a), (b) and (c). Those entitlements plainly exclude the assignor's 'burdens'. Nor do they encompass *all* conceivable 'benefits' which may arise in connection with the particular chose which had been assigned. If so, the assignor cannot 'drop out', and the statutory assignee cannot take the obligee-assignor's place as a party to the contract so as to be brought into privity with the contractual counterparty.[73]

In this context, it is helpful to look closely at the Court of Appeal's decision in *Re Milan Tramways*.[74] Although that decision accepts that

---

[70] See e.g. Tolhurst (2016), para. 5.09; Snell (2015), para. 3-010.

[71] A. Tettenborn, 'Equitable Assignment and Procedural Quibbles' (1995) 54 CLJ 499, 501 (emphasis added).

[72] In general, 'burdens' arising in connection with an obligation may not be effectively transferred to another by assignment. For exceptions and discussion as to how burdens may, in effect, be transmitted though not assigned, see Smith & Leslie (2018), chapter 21.

[73] For example, where the benefit of debts owed to a vendor by its customers is statutorily assigned to a factor, the factor is not brought into privity with the customers. See e.g. *Bibby Factors Northwest Limited* v. *HFD Limited* [2016] EWCA Civ 1908, [50].

[74] *Re Milan Tramways Company* (1884) 25 Ch D 587, on appeal from the decision of Kay J in *Re Milan Tramways Company* (1882) 22 Ch D 122 (Chan Div).

equities as would have arisen between the original assignor would run against the original assignee, and all sub-assignees taking through him, it rejects the proposition that equities as might arise between the obligor and the original assignee would also run against all sub-assignees taking subsequently through him, even where the first assignment had been statutory. *Re Milan Tramways* demonstrates that a conception of statutory assignment which entails the substitution of the statutory assignee in place of the assignor such that the assignor 'drops out' is untenable. Statutory assignment cannot operate by substituting the statutory assignee in place of the assignor, wholesale, such that the obligations arising under the chose assigned would thereafter be owed by the obligor to the statutory assignee for, if that were so, equities arising as between the obligor and the statutory assignee *would* run against subsequent sub-assignees taking through the statutory assignee – contrary to the holding of the Court of Appeal in *Re Milan Tramways*.

In this case, the Milan Tramways Co. ('B') was ordered to be wound up on 12 January 1877. Six creditors of the company ('A1–6') proved the debts owed them in the insolvency. They then assigned their entitlements to be paid dividends out of the assets of the company to Hutter ('$C_1$') by deeds dated variously between October and December 1879. Written notice appears to have been given to the official liquidator, making the assignments to $C_1$ statutory assignments.[75]

$C_1$ had been a director of B. On 23 January 1880, the official liquidator took out a summons against $C_1$ on the basis that he had been guilty of misfeasance vis-à-vis the company in having wrongfully accepted eighty-five shares in the company from the promoter, the nominal value of the shares being £2,000.

On 25 February 1880, $C_1$ assigned for value to Theys ('$C_2$') the entitlements which A1–6 had assigned to him. Notice of this sub-assignment was given to the liquidator the following day.[76] Though the sub-assignment to $C_2$ was plainly 'absolute and not by way of charge', none of the reports disclose whether *written* notice had been given to B's liquidator; nor do they disclose if the sub-assignment had been effected in a duly signed writing. If either one of these requirements had been left unsatisfied, the sub-assignment to $C_2$ could only have been an equitable one. However, this seems highly improbable, since the proceedings in *Re Milan Tramways* had been brought by $C_2$ in his own name, without

---

[75] See counsel's submissions at *Re Milan Tramways* (1884) 25 Ch D 587, 590.
[76] Ibid., 588–9.

joining $C_1$ as co-plaintiff. This is easily explicable if the sub-assignment by $C_1$ to $C_2$ had been a statutory one, where the requirements of 'absolute, writing and notice' had all been satisfied, but not otherwise.

On 31 May 1880, $C_2$ took out a summons in his sole name, praying, inter alia, that his name be entered on the list of creditors in respect of the proofs which had been submitted by A1–6. As to this summons, no order was made, directions being given merely that the liquidator should retain any dividends coming to $C_1$ until further order.

On 28 July 1880, judgment was given for the official liquidator in respect of his summons against $C_1$ for misfeasance in office, and $C_1$ was ordered to pay a sum of £2,000 being the assessed value of the shares which $C_1$ had received in breach of his fiduciary duties as a director of B. This sum was not paid.

On 4 August 1881, an order was made giving the official liquidator liberty to declare a dividend of 11s in the pound on the proved debts. In consequence, in respect of the proofs which had been submitted by A1–6, a dividend totalling £1,267 19s 1d was to be paid.

On 27 October 1881, $C_2$ took out another summons, again in his sole name, asking that the £1,267 19s 1d be paid out to him. But the official liquidator opposed this, claiming that they were entitled to a 'set-off' by reason of the order of 27 July 1880 against $C_1$ in the sum of £2,000.

Kay J allowed $C_2$'s claim in full, denying that the official liquidator was permitted to set off the £2,000 against $C_2$'s claim. On appeal, the Court of Appeal upheld his decision.

Before the Court of Appeal, counsel for the liquidator made two submissions. First, that a set-off would have been available as against $C_1$ (Hutter) in light of the 27 July order against him for £2,000, and that 'his assignee [could not] be in a better position [since] the assignee of a debt takes it subject to *its* [the assignor's] *equities*'. [77]

Second, and in the alternative:[78]

> [i]f there [was] not a right to set off the debts there [was] a right to retain the dividends.[79] When Hutter became transferee of these debts the company acquired a right to retain the dividends on them against his debt. By sect. 25, sub-sec. 6, of the Judicature Act, 1873, Hutter [$C_1$] became

---

[77] Ibid., 590 (emphasis added).
[78] Ibid.
[79] Though the submissions do not make it clear, it has been suggested that the alleged power to retain the dividends would have arisen by reason of the rule in *Cherry* v. *Boultbee* (1839) 4 My & Cr 442: see Derham (2010), para. 17.60.

entitled to sue for these debts in his own name, but only subject to the equities attaching on them, *and he could only transfer subject to this equity, which was an equity affecting the dividends.*

Both propositions were doubted by the Court of Appeal. As to the first point, Fry LJ pointed out that the necessary implication of counsel's submission would be that there would be a cumulation of equities: 'each successive assignee [would be] in a worse position than his predecessors'.[80] More substantively, Fry LJ (with whom the Lord Chancellor agreed on this point) was not convinced that this was a case where any legal or equitable set-off could be asserted against $C_1$.

As to the second submission, Fry LJ held as follows:[81]

> [A]s to the claim to retain the dividends, the Appellant forgets that the dividend was not declared till after the order for payment of the £2000, and that the order for that payment was not made till after the assignment of the debts to Theys. We cannot hold that the fact of Hutter having once been the owner of these debts created an inchoate equity to set off whatever might be found due from him against the dividends to become payable in respect of those debts. No right to retain the dividends could arise unless at the time when they were declared they belonged to a person who was indebted to the company.

The conclusion reached by Kay J at first instance, which was affirmed by the Court of Appeal, is inexplicable if statutory assignment had the effect of substituting the statutory assignee in place of the assignor *in toto*, to the extent of leaving the obligor of the chose assigned to be obligated to the statutory assignee instead of the assignor. To illustrate this, let us suppose, for the sake of argument, that statutory assignments did have such substitutive effect.

On this hypothesis, when A1–6 statutorily assigned the benefit of their entitlements as creditors who had proved in B's liquidation to $C_1$, $C_1$ would have taken the place of A1–6 as the obligee(s) to whom B's liquidator was obligated to distribute a dividend, were it eventually ascertained that B's assets outweighed its liabilities. By operation of statute, if the statute operated in this substitutive manner, were $C_1$ to bring proceedings against B's liquidator in respect of the proofs of debt in question, those proofs of debts would be treated as if they had been submitted *by $C_1$*. But $C_1$ was then adjudged to be liable to B for breach of his duties as a director. So if $C_1$ sued B's liquidator in respect of the

---

[80] *Re Milan Tramways* (1884) 25 Ch D 587, 590 (in argument).

[81] Ibid., 594. Having rejected the first submission, it was not strictly necessary for the court to address the second, since the the second submission would only be significant if the first submission had been accepted to be valid.

dividends arising from the proofs of debt in question, B's liquidator would have been perfectly justified to raise $C_1$'s cross-liability to withhold payment of the dividend (invoking the rule in *Cherry* v. *Boultbee*[82]) even if the cross-liability for breach of $C_1$'s director's duties had arisen independently from the entitlement to be paid a dividend in B's liquidation.

When $C_1$ statutorily assigned *his* entitlement to be paid a dividend to $C_2$, by operation of the statute, on the same supposition that statutory assignments effect a substitutive transfer, although $C_2$ would indeed take $C_1$'s place as the obligee to whom B's liquidator would be obligated to pay the dividend, the statute would also qualify $C_2$'s entitlement in that $C_2$ would have to take subject to all equities which B's liquidator might have as against $C_1$. The result, therefore, would be that there would be an accumulation of equities.

Had B's liquidator been entitled to assert any cross-claim against A1–6, B's liquidator would have been able to assert that against $C_1$. When B's liquidator was entitled to assert an equity (such as that arising by reason of the rule in *Cherry* v. *Boultbee*), had proceedings been brought on the dividend by $C_1$, B's liquidator would have been entitled to take advantage of the prior cross-claim against A1–6 (had there been one) *and* the *Cherry* v. *Boultbee* equity against $C_1$'s claim, if statutory assignment operated by way of substituting $C_1$ in place of A1–6. If so, following the statutory assignment to $C_2$, when $C_2$ brought the proceedings for the dividend against B's liquidator, B's liquidator would have been able to assert both sets of equities as had accumulated previously against $C_2$. Yet this is precisely the result that was rejected in *Re Milan Tramways*.

If statutory assignment truly substituted $C_1$ in place of A1–6 as the party to whom the liquidator was obligated to pay dividends upon the conclusion of the liquidation proceedings, then, when $C_1$ statutorily assigned '*his*' entitlement to be paid dividends to $C_2$, all equities as might have arisen as between $C_1$ on the one hand, and B on the other, would 'run' against $C_2$, as well. If $C_1$ had 'replaced' A1–6, were $C_1$ to sue in respect of the liquidation, $C_1$ would have brought such proceedings in his own right (it would have been *his* right to be paid dividends) and not in right of A1–6. And had this been the case, the liquidator's equity against $C_1$ to withhold payment given the rule in *Cherry* v. *Boultbee* would be an equity exercisable against $C_1$ in respect of $C_1$'s 'own' claim against B arising from the liquidation. $C_2$'s entitlements against B arising from

---

[82] (1839) 4 My & Cr 442.

$C_1$'s statutory assignment to $C_2$ would, on a substitutive understanding of statutory assignment, be subject to the equities as between $C_1$ and B. In short, it would not have been open to Fry LJ to observe that 'at no time were the cross-demands between the same parties',[83] for if $C_1$ had replaced A1–6, then B's cross-claim for $C_1$'s misfeasance would be a cross-demand between the same parties, even if $C_1$ had previously equitably assigned 'his' claim in the liquidation to $C_2$, since $C_2$ would still be claiming in right of $C_1$.

*Re Milan Tramways* tells us that when $C_2$ assigned to $C_1$, though $C_1$ would also be subject to equities, the pertinent equities would be those which might have arisen as between the obligor (in the person of B's liquidator), on the one hand, and A1–6, on the other. The fact that there might have been equities as could have been invoked against $C_1$ would not matter: equities which arose between the obligor and an intermediate statutory assignee would not run against subsequent statutory assignees. Thus, as Cotton LJ observed, 'Theys [$C_2$] is not coming here to enforce any right of Hutter [$C_1$], but the rights of the creditors who proved [A1–6]'.[84] Nor, in Cotton LJ's opinion, did the assignment to $C_1$ being compliant with s. 25(6) make any difference: 'No doubt that enactment makes the assignment of a chose in action carry the right for the assignee to sue in his own name subject to equities. But there is nothing to prevent the ultimate assignee from suing in the name of the original creditors, free from any equities which only attach on the intermediate assignee.'[85] It follows that only the equities as would have arisen between the original statutory assignors and the obligor would run against an immediate statutory assignee, and any statutory assignees taking from him.

In light of the above, one must doubt whether statements that the effect of statutory assignment is to substitute the assignee in place of the assignor might not be overstating matters.

## E   Construction

As mentioned above, s. 136(1) re-enacts Judicature Act 1873, s. 25(6). They are *in pari materia*, save for the substitution of 'thing in action' in the 1925 Act for 'chose in action' in the 1873 Act. Presumably for ease of reading, the unbroken text of s. 25(6) was also broken up into subclauses

---

[83] Ibid., 593.
[84] Ibid.
[85] Ibid.

and subparagraphs, but these formatting changes do not appear to have effected any substantive changes.

Although the *travaux préparatoires* leading to the passing of the Judicature Acts are voluminous,[86] and there is a substantial body of secondary material commenting on the process of law reform leading to their enactment,[87] neither set of resources provides any reliable indication of Parliament's intentions when it enacted s. 25(6).[88] That provision appears to have attracted little comment as it proceeded through the Houses of Parliament: no substantial changes were made to Clause 26(6), Supreme Court of Judicature HL Bill (14)[89] (which ultimately became s. 25(6) of the 1873 Act) as it progressed through Parliament. Parliament's intentions remaining obscure, close reading of the words in the statute will be necessary to ascertain its intentions in enacting them.

Though Parliament did not provide any definition as to what a 'debt or thing in action' might encompass, Parliament distinguished between such 'debt' or 'thing in action' and the three varieties of entitlements which are now set out as ss. 136(1)(a), (b) and (c). Given the distinction, it must follow as a matter of statutory interpretation that these three entitlements are aspects of the 'debt or thing in action' which had been assigned. But each category of entitlement cannot be taken to be equivalent to the 'debt' or 'thing in action'. If that were the case, then the prepositions 'to' or 'for' in each of ss. 136(1)(a), (b) and (c) would do no work.

For example, one cannot sensibly speak of a legal right to a 'debt' or 'thing in action' if the 'legal right' and the 'debt' or 'thing in action' are one and the same. Nor can one sensibly speak of any legal and other remedies 'for' such debt or thing in action, if 'legal and other remedies', on the one hand, and 'debt' or 'thing in action', on the other, were

---

[86] See e.g. Great Britain, Judicature Commission, *First to Fifth Reports* (n. 10), pp. 13–14, reproducing pp. 5–6 of the First Report.

[87] See references cited in Meagher, Gummow & Lehane (2015), chapter 2.

[88] Hansard, HL, vol. 214, cols. 331–65, 13 February 1873 (First Reading of the Supreme Court of Judicature Bill), See, in particular, cols. 339–40 (Lord Selborne LC). However, no mention is made of that any matters pertaining to the Judicature Act 1873, s. 25(6). The Attorney-General's speech to the House of Commons (Hansard, HC, vol. 216, cols. 644–5, 9 June 1873) is similarly silent.

[89] Ibid. There appear to have been two amendments to the Bill after its Second Reading on 11 March 1873 before it was enacted as the Judicature Act 1873. First, the words 'or security', after the phrase 'by way of charge', were deleted from the Bill. Second, the word 'legal', in the phrase 'to pass and transfer the legal right to such debt or chose in action' in the Judicature Act 1837, s. 25(6) as enacted, did not appear in the original Bill. See Supreme Court of Judicature HL Bill [as amended on report] (45), p. 15.

equivalents. Lastly, it is impossible to speak sensibly of the power to give a good discharge 'for' such 'debt' or 'thing in action' if the concept of a 'power to give a good discharge', on the one hand, and 'debt' or 'thing in action', on the other, refer to the same thing. These prepositions tell us that 'the legal right', 'all legal and other remedies', and 'the power to give a good discharge' are *aspects* of and are related to, such 'debt' or 'thing in action' as may have been assigned.

Furthermore, since the entitlements listed in ss. 136(1)(a), (b) and (c) do not exhaust the entire universe of entitlements as may possibly arise in connection with a chose in action, it would still be incorrect to take them to be the equivalent of the debt or thing in action which had been assigned even if these three sets of entitlements were summed together. And this construction of the statute is reinforced when proper account is taken of the Court of Appeal's reasoning and decision in *Read v. Brown*,[90] as the following will show.

### (i)    Section 136(1)(a): 'the Legal Right to Such Debt or Thing in Action'

Section 136(1)(a) provides for certain effects to be superimposed on an 'absolute assignment' of 'any debt or other legal thing in action'. If, say, a debt or thing in action was equitably assigned, once the 'triangle' of 'writing, absolute, and notice' has been fulfilled, s. 136(1)(a) provides that '*the* legal right to such debt or thing in action' will 'pass' from the assignor and 'transfer' to the assignee.

To understand what this 'legal right' that would have passed from the assignor and been transferred to her assignee entails, it is helpful to recall that, as originally drafted, at its First Reading in the House of Lords, clause 26 of the Supreme Court of Judicature Bill, which was eventually enacted as s. 25 of the Supreme Court of Judicature Act 1873, merely provided that the right to such debt or chose in action would pass from the assignor and transfer to the assignee. The word 'legal', qualifying the 'right to such debt or . . . chose in action' was only introduced at some point before the Second Reading on 11 March 1873. Why, one might ask? It is suggested that this qualifier was added to make it more obvious that the particular entitlement associated with the 'debt or . . . chose in action' which had been assigned and which was to be passed and

---

[90]  (1888) 22 QBD 128.

transferred was the assignor's power to commence *legal proceedings* as against the obligor to the chose assigned. That is to say, this part of the Bill was aimed at resolving the problem of the need for joinder of assignors to proceedings at law when a common law chose in action had been assigned.

In *Read* v. *Brown*, the assignee of a debt arising from a sale contracted in Surrey sued the purchaser in the Mayor's Court in the City of London on grounds that the assignee's cause of action had arisen 'wholly or partly' in the City[91] because the assignment had been executed there.[92]

Manisty J and Pollock B held that the Mayor's Court had jurisdiction.[93] Their decision was upheld by the Court of Appeal.

Lord Esher MR observed that 'In construing s. 25, sub-s. 6, we must adopt the ordinary rule as to the construction of Acts of Parliament, that of giving, if possible, a meaning to each word.'[94] In consequence, Lord Esher rejected the defendant's contention that 'the legal right' to a debt was the same thing as the 'legal and other remedies' for the debt since, if that were correct, 'the provision that the assignment shall transfer "the legal right to the debt" [would be] mere tautology'.[95] That, Lord Esher held, would be:[96]

> a wrong rule of construction; the words mean what they say; they transfer the legal right to the debt as well as the legal remedies for its recovery. The debt is transferred to the assignee and becomes *as though* it had been his from the beginning; *it is no longer to be the debt of the assignor at all, who cannot sue for it, the right to sue being taken from him*; the assignee becomes the assignee of a legal debt and is not merely an assignee in equity, and the debt being his, he can sue for it, and sue for it in his own name. We must give that meaning to the language of the subsection.

It is possible to read too much into this passage, for example by taking Lord Esher to have held s. 25(6) as having transferred *the debt itself* from

---

[91] Mayor's Court of London Procedure Act 1857, s. 12.

[92] Written notice of the assignment had also been given, so this was a 'statutory' assignment under s. 25(6), Judicature Act 1873.

[93] *Read* v. *Brown* (1888) 22 QBD 128, 130.

[94] Ibid., 132 (Lord Esher, with whom Fry LJ agreed; emphasis added). At 133, Lopes LJ also agreed with Lord Esher's construction of the section that the subject matter of the first and second limbs of the Judicature Act 1873, s. 25(6) were distinct from each other: '[statutory] assignment passes to the assignee, not only the legal remedies for the debt, but the legal right to the debt itself'.

[95] Ibid., 132.

[96] Ibid.

the assignor to the assignee, such that the assignor was no longer the creditor in respect of the debt, with the assignee taking her place as creditor. But, as mentioned above, that is not what Parliament enacted in s. 25(6). The choice of words enacted by Parliament pointedly did *not* 'pass' or 'transfer' the 'debt or chose in action'. What *was* passed and transferred by those words was, inter alia, the 'legal right' to such debt or chose in action: which, as Lord Esher pointed out, was distinct from the 'legal and other remedies' for the same.

Paying close attention to Lord Esher's language, we see that he was conscious of the distinction. He did not simply hold that the debt was transferred to the assignee: he said that following the assignment in compliance with the requirements of the statute, it was *as though* the debt had been the assignee's from the outset. Importantly, Lord Esher went on to hold that the debt was no longer that of the assignor, 'who cannot sue for it, the right to sue being taken from him'. Here, it is easy to confuse cause and effect, for if the debt had indeed been transferred, the effect of such transfer would also be to render the assignor to be a stranger to the debtor–creditor relationship and, as such, would take away the assignor's power to bring legal proceedings against the debtor in respect of disputes arising from that debtor–creditor relationship. But we may note that Esher MR could equally be taken to have held that it was *because* the assignor could no longer sue (i.e. commence legal proceedings) for the debt, that the assignor could be treated *as though* the debt were the assignee's from the beginning and was no longer the debt of the assignor.

Between these two possibilities, it is suggested that the latter is more satisfactory given Lord Esher's approach to statutory interpretation. If Lord Esher had concluded that the right to bring proceedings had been removed from the assignor *because* the debt was no longer the assignor's, there would have been no need to legislate for the transfer of 'the legal right' to the debt, all the 'legal and other remedies' for the same, as well as the 'power to give a good discharge' for the same. Reference to the passing and transfer of these specific entitlements would have been otiose. So, unless Lord Esher was ignoring his own advice, the latter interpretation must surely be more consistent with his reasoning. That is to say, the 'legal right to the debt or thing in action' which is passed from the assignor and transferred to the assignee by operation of what is now s. 136(1)(a) denotes the assignor's *power* to bring legal proceedings against the obligor to the debt or legal thing in action which had been equitably assigned from the assignor to her assignee, such power being distinct from the 'legal or other remedies' which would be passed and transferred by operation of s. 136(1)(b).

### (ii)   Section 136(1)(b): 'All Legal and Other Remedies for the Same'

If s. 136(1)(a) provides for the transfer of the assignor's power against the obligor to the debt or thing in action assigned to bring legal proceedings against the obligor in the assignor's own name to the exclusion of the assignee, what does it mean for a statutory assignment to 'transfer and pass' the 'legal or other *remedies*' set out in s. 136(1)(b)?

The word 'remedy' is ambiguous, as Dr Zakrzewski has pointed out.[97] One extremely broad functional definition of remedy within the legal context is that it is 'some means provided by the law for redressing a grievance',[98] and '[A]nything that makes a bad situation better can be called a remedy.'[99] But within that very broad definition, Zakrzewski identifies five narrower usages of 'remedy', each of which entails judicial involvement, namely:

(1)   an action or cause of action;[100]
(2)   a substantive right that exists prior to the commencement of legal proceedings and the making of an order or pronouncement of a court in those proceedings;[101]
(3)   a court order as a remedy;[102]
(4)   the means of enforcing a court order as a remedy;[103] or
(5)   the final outcome as a remedy, meaning 'the actual act, thing, or occurrence that effects or amounts to the redress or relief that the claimant obtains'.[104]

---

[97]   See also P. Birks, 'Rights, Wrongs and Remedies' (2000) 10 OJLS 1, 9–17.
[98]   Zakrzewski (2005), p. 11; and also p. 45: '[A]nything that makes a bad situation better can be called a remedy.'
[99]   Ibid., p. 43.
[100]  Ibid., p. 11. Zakrzewski suggests that this usage originates from the forms of action (p. 12), and that it is 'a hangover [sic] from the time when forms of action were thought to be remedies in themselves' (p. 50).
[101]  Ibid., p. 13.
[102]  Ibid., p. 17.
[103]  Ibid., p. 18.
[104]  Ibid., p. 21.

In addition, Zakrzewski also notes a sixth usage, namely, the 'self-help' remedy:[105] 'What is usually referred to as a self-help remedy is a privilege or immunity which permits the aggrieved person to act in a particular way. A self-help "remedy" enables the claimant to realize his or her rights through his or her own acts.' The proposition in this Section is that these six types of 'remedy' are precisely the types of 'legal and other remedies' which are passed and transferred from the assignor to her assignee by operation of s. 136(1)(b). This will be demonstrated in the subsections which follow, beginning with a discussion of the ambit of the phrase, 'other remedies'.

(a)   'Other Remedies': Self-Help 'Remedies'

The law provides for and recognizes both legal remedies in the form of judicial orders and self-help 'remedies'. The former arise by reason of court order, following the successful prosecution of a claim. Key examples of these would be the equitable remedy of specific perform-ance and the common law remedy of damages. The law also recognizes that a wronged party may, in some cases, 'help himself' to make good the wrong suffered without need for prior judicial sanction (though acting upon a supposed self-help remedy where the grounds upon which such remedy are absent may itself be a wrongful act). An example of a self-help remedy (in the present context) would be the contractual promisee's power to discharge a contract by 'accepting' the promisor's anticipatory repudiatory breach, or the promisor's actual breach of a condition or of an innominate term which has the effect of depriving the promisee of substantially the whole of the benefit of the contract.[106] It is also suggested that the phrase 'other remedies' in

---

[105] Ibid., p. 47.

[106] See e.g. *Pacific Brands Sport & Leisure Pty Ltd* v. *Underworks Pty Ltd* [2006] FCAFC 40; [2007] 230 ALR 56 (Federal Court of Australia (Full Court)), [55], in which a majority of the Full Court suggested that had the Conveyancing Act 1919 (NSW), s. 12 (which is *in pari materia* with LPA1925, s. 136(1)) been applied to an assignment of an 'entire chose' arising from a contract, it would place, 'the assignees in the same position in relation to repudiatory conduct as [the assignors] would have been had it retained the chose. Accordingly, we consider the assignees would have had available to them by way of remedy (*inter alia*) the right to claim damages for non-performance of [the obligors'] primary obligation and the power to elect to put an end to all primary obligations of both parties that remained unperformed.'

s. 136(1)(b) would also include the power of a promisee to rescind a contract which was liable to be vitiated at law, as when a contract is vitiated by fraud,[107] or duress.[108]

It is suggested that the language in s. 136(1)(b) as to the transfer of 'other remedies' is straightforward. By these words, the statute 'transfers' from obligee-assignor to the assignee such remedial entitlements as the obligee/assignor may invoke or assert against the obligor in connection with the chose in action assigned by way of self-help, *without* judicial order. So, by reason of s. 136(1)(b), it is open to a statutory assignee (but not the assignor) to invoke or assert those self-help 'remedies' so far as the statute would have transferred them to the assignee.

(b)    'Legal Remedies': Remedies Arising otherwise than by
       Way of Self-Help

If the 'other remedies' mentioned in s. 136(1)(b) refer to the assignor's self-help remedies, it would seem to follow that the 'legal remedies' mentioned therein must refer to remedies arising by way of judicial order, or, in other words, *judicial* remedies. It is suggested that, for the purposes of s. 136(1)(b), 'legal remedies' includes 'any means provided by the law for redressing a grievance entailing a judicial order'. That is, 'legal remedies' in s. 136(1)(b) may be broadly construed to encompass any of the five more discrete usages identified by Zakrzewski. Therefore, the 'legal remedies' referred to in s. 136(1)(b) denote all *remedial* entitlements of the assignor which would arise on judicial order.

This would include remedies at common law such as an order for damages, or equitable remedies such as an order of specific performance, an injunction, or an account. It would also include equitable remedies

---

[107] *Load* v. *Green* (1846) 15 M & W 216, 219: 'the transaction is not void except at the option of the seller'. See also *Clarke* v. *Dickson* (1858) El Bl & El 148; *Clough* v. *London and North Western Railway Co.* (1871) LR 7 Ex 26; *HIH Casualty and General Insurance Ltd* v. *Chase Manhattan Bank* [2003] UKHL 6, [2003] 1 All ER 349, [98] (Lord Hobhouse).

[108] *Whelpdale's Case* (1604) 5 Co Rep 119a; *Enimont Overseas AG* v. *RO Jugotanker Zadar (The Olib)* [1991] 2 Lloyd's Rep 108; *Dimskal Shipping Co. SA* v. *International Transport Workers Federation (The Evia Luck)* [1992] 2 AC 152; *Halpern* v. *Halpern (No. 2)* [2006] EWHC 1728 (Comm), [2007] 1 QB 88 (reversed on appeal in *Halpern* v. *Halpern (No. 2)* [2007] EWCA Civ 291, [2007] 3 All ER 478, but not on this point). For other instances where the power to rescind is available at common law, see O'Sullivan, Elliott & Zakrzewski (2014), para. 10.23.

such as rectification, as well as rescission[109] for unilateral mistake as to terms, non-fraudulent misrepresentation, actual and presumed undue influence.[110] These 'legal remedies' would also include the tertiary remedies for enforcement of judgments.[111]

But, as Zakrzewski noted, these 'legal remedies' would also include the assignor's 'causes of action'. And as to these, Lopes LJ pointed out in *Read* v. *Brown* as follows:[112] 'I agree with the definition given by the Master of the Rolls of a cause of action, and that it includes every fact which it would be necessary to prove, if traversed, in order to enable a plaintiff to sustain his action.' Section 136(1)(a) passes and transfers the assignor's power to bring legal proceedings against the obligor to the chose assigned to her statutory assignee. But that in itself might not necessarily mean that the assignee would be entitled to plead the facts which would have comprised the *assignor's* cause of action against the obligor. Fortunately, by transferring 'all legal . . . remedies for the same', s. 136(1)(b) would also transfer the assignor's 'cause of action' to her assignee. Thus, there could be no doubt that a statutory assignee would indeed be entitled to plead such facts as part of *his* cause of action against the obligor, and may do so to the exclusion of the assignor.[113]

---

[109] In this connection, we should keep in mind that the entitlement to seek such judicial order for rescission is not, in and of itself, a chose or thing in action, and so may not be assigned in isolation: As Lord Hoffmann reminded us in *Investors Compensation Scheme Ltd* v. *West Bromwich Building Society* [1998] 1 WLR 896, 916, in connection with rescission of a mortgage: '[I]t is important to notice that a claim to rescission is a right of action but can in no way be described as a chose in action or part of a chose in action.'

[110] For a more exhaustive list of the vitiating factors for which an order for rescission in equity may be sought, see O'Sullivan, Elliott & Zakrzewski (2014), para. 10.25.

[111] *Goodman* v. *Robinson* (1886) 18 QBD 332, 335. That said, it is still necessary for the statutory assignee to comply with such formalities as may be prescribed by the Rules of Court (now, the Civil Procedure Rules) for such tertiary enforcement remedies: *East End Benefit Building Society* v. *Slack* (1891) 60 LJQB 359.

[112] *Read* v. *Brown* (1888) 22 QBD 128, 133. At 131, Lord Esher MR had held that: 'What is the real meaning of the phrase "a cause of action arising in the City?" It has been defined in *Cooke* v. *Gill* to be this: every fact which it would be necessary for the plaintiff to prove, if traversed, in order to support his right to the judgment of the Court.' In *Cooke* v. *Gill* (1873) LR 8 CP 107, prior to his appointment as Master of the Rolls, Brett J (as he then was) had held that, '"Cause of action" has been held from the earliest time to mean every fact which is material to be proved to entitle the plaintiff to succeed, – every fact which the defendant would have a right to traverse' (at 116).

[113] Civil proceedings before a court of law are brought by parties with the standing to do so. And such parties with standing may plead the facts as make up their cause of action against the defendant to those proceedings. But the question of standing is distinct from the question as to whether there is a cause of action. This is evident from the rules of

*(iii)   Section 136(1)(c): 'the Power to Give a Good Discharge'*

Section 136(1)(c) says what it does, and does what it says. Insofar as the assignor had (prior to the assignment) *the* power to 'give' a good discharge, post-assignment, that power would be transferred to the assignee.

As explained above, s. 136(1)(b) transfers to the assignor the assignee's remedial entitlements. Some remedial entitlements entail Hohfeldian powers (e.g. the self-help power of an obligee to accept a repudiatory breach of contract and so discharge the contract). So all *remedial* powers would be 'transferred' by reason of s. 136(1)(b).

However, not all powers held by an obligee against an obligor are 'remedial'. In practically all instances of voluntarily undertaken obligations, the obligee has the power to 'give' a good discharge by waiving precise performance by the obligor to the debt or thing in action assigned. Such power of discharge is seldom, if ever, viewed to be 'remedial'.

For example, precise performance as would discharge contracts for sale and delivery of goods or contracts for a loan of money often entails cooperation by the party to whom delivery or tender is to be made. Where goods are to be delivered, such delivery must be accepted before the contract is fully performed. And the same is true of the duty to repay money borrowed by way of a loan. So, if tender or delivery is to be made to the obligee, the obligee will have the power to effect discharge by *accepting* the tendered goods or money. Such power of acceptance is hardly 'remedial': it is simply a power to *effect* discharge. Then, in an employment contract, there is invariably provision for a contractual termination clause by which the contract may be terminated by giving notice. Such power is, again, no 'remedy', though it does lead to discharge.

court which distinguish between applications to order that any legal person who had been improperly or unnecessarily made a party to legal proceedings should cease to be a party (CPR rule 19.2(3) read with Practice Direction 19A, and formerly, Rules of Supreme Court, Order 15, rule 6(2)(a)); and applications to dismiss proceedings on grounds that the claimant's claim disclosed no reasonable cause of action (CPR rule 16.2 read with Practice Direction 16, and formerly, Rules of Supreme Court, Order 18, rule 19 (1)(a)). The division of labour between ss. 136(1)(a) and (b) as discussed in the main text, in that the former addresses the transfer of the assignor's power to bring proceedings against the obligor (i.e. her standing to commence proceedings), and the latter addresses the transfer of the assignor's cause of action (conceived of as a 'legal remedy'), reflects this.

One could read the verb 'to give' to mean a unilateral act of grant without any requirement for a quid pro quo in exchange: i.e. one could construe s. 136(1)(c) as transferring the power to *give* a good discharge by waiving precise performance by the obligor to the debt or thing in action that had been assigned: that is, the power to *release* the obligor from his duty.[114] Alternatively, if one were to read the verb 'to give' more generously, one might take it to refer to the power to *give effect to* a discharge of a debt by accepting a conforming tender of payment, and the analogous power to *give effect to* a discharge of a thing in action such as a contract for sale and delivery of goods by accepting a conforming delivery of those goods.

Although there is some basis for thinking that the latter may be the better construction,[115] even without taking a definitive position on the matter, we may note that s. 136(1)(c) only provides for the transfer of a single power. Parliament provided in s. 136(1)(c) that 'the' power to grant a discharge be transferred, not that 'all' powers to grant discharges be transferred (as may be contrasted with the wording in s. 136(1)(b)). Consequently, if the particular thing in action assigned entails more than one (non-remedial) power which has the effect of discharging the obligor, since s. 136(1)(c) only provides for the transfer of *one* such power, any other non-remedial powers having the effect of discharging the obligation cannot be 'transferred to the assignee by that subsection.

If this narrow construction of s. 136(1)(c) be the true one, it would further substantiate the proposition made above: the list of entitlements in ss. 136(1)(a), (b) and (c) which is transferred by operation of statute does not exhaust the universe of all possible entitlements as may arise between an obligor and an obligee to a chose or thing in action. But even if s. 136(1)(c) were read more broadly to encompass any and all powers of the obligor as would result in the discharge of the chose or thing in action, that still leaves aside entitlements such as those arising from options, arbitration clauses, and the like (as had been mentioned in Section D, above). The words used in s. 136(1) are inapt to capture all entitlements, and if what was intended was for *all* the entitlements arising from a debt or thing in action to be transferred to the assignee by operation of s. 136(1), the words used in s. 136(1) seem to fall short.

---

[114] If executed by deed, such release is immediately effective: LPA1925, s. 155.

[115] It is arguable that s. 136(1)(c) could encompass the power of a creditor to discharge a debt by accepting a tender of payment: see discussion of *Liquidation Estates Purchase Company, Limited* v. *Willoughby* [1898] AC 321 in Chapter 15, Section F.

## F   Confirmation, Corroboration and Consequences

Confirmation that the analysis of s. 136(1) above is correct may be found in the reasoning and conclusions reached in a number of 'black hole' cases. If statutory assignment did not operate in the manner set out above, statutory assignments would be yet another way to prevent 'black hole' problems from arising. However, that is not the case, as the following will show.

### (i)   Transfer of Legal Remedy: Contract

It may be thought that the transfer of legal remedies such as the common law remedy of damages is of particular significance, as it provides a partial solution to the thorny 'black hole' problem in contract law.

As explained in Chapter 6, where a common law chose in action has been equitably assigned, should the equitable assignee wish to bring an action at law against the obligor on that chose, complications may arise if the facts show that the assignor has sustained 'no loss'. This is because the equitable assignee will necessarily be bringing the action 'in right of' the assignor. That being so, the court would assess the assignor's losses when determining the appropriate quantum of damages to be awarded, rather than loss which might have been sustained by the assignee. That could, therefore, lead to a 'black hole' problem.[116]

On some views of the operation of statutory assignment, such 'black hole' problems might be obviated if the assignment was statutory. Indeed, Lord Browne-Wilkinson appears to have assumed that the 'black hole' problems which seemed to have plagued both appeals before the House of Lords in *Linden Gardens Trust Ltd* v. *Lenesta Sludge Ltd*[117] would have disappeared had the statutory assignments in both appeals not been made ineffective by the anti-assignment provisions in the contracts which were in issue. However, the facts and decision in *Darlington Borough Council* v. *Wiltshier Northern Ltd*[118] reveal that this belief may be misguided.

In this case, the Darlington Borough Council (DBC) entered into a contract with Morgan Grenfell (Local Authority Services) Ltd (MG)

---

[116] Cf. G. J. Tolhurst, 'The Nature of an Assignee's Right to Damages for Breaches of Contract That Occur Prior to Assignment' (2008) 24 *Journal of Contract Law* 77, suggesting that cases which have recognized such a problem may have fallen into error.

[117] [1994] 1 AC 85.

[118] [1995] 1 WLR 68.

under which MG would arrange for construction to be carried out on land owned by DBC. Under the terms of this contract, MG was contractually bound to effect an assignment of the benefit of any construction contracts it might make with builders. But the contract also provided that MG was not to be liable in any way to DBC if there should be any shortcomings in the work done by the builders.[119]

Pursuant to this contract, MG entered into multiple building contracts with Wiltshier Northern Ltd ('Wiltshier') to do the requisite work on DBC's land. The work was done poorly, in breach of the standard required under the terms of the building contracts with MG, and substantial expense was eventually incurred by DBC to rectify the problems caused by Wiltshier's contractually defective work.

DBC subsequently brought an action against Wiltshier for breach of the contractual obligations which had arisen in its building contracts with MG. This action was brought by DBC in its own name, without joining MG, as MG had statutorily assigned[120] to DBC the benefit of its building contract with Wiltshier, as well as all accrued causes of action against Wiltshier arising thereunder. Unlike the two appeals which were heard in *Linden Gardens Trust Ltd* v. *Lenesta Sludge Ltd*, the building contracts between MG and Wiltshier did not contain any anti-assignment provisions.

Wiltshier sought to defend itself on grounds that since MG had no proprietary interest in the land on which the work was to be done, nor any proprietary interest in the buildings which were constructed by Wiltshier, and since MG had no liability to DBC in respect of shortfalls in Wiltshier's work, MG had suffered no loss from Wiltshier's defective work. Had the action been brought by MG against Wiltshier, it would seem that MG would have sustained no loss for which damages might be ordered. Consequently, Wiltshier argued that as statutory assignee, DBC could recover no substantial damages either. Fortunately for the DBC, the Court of Appeal held that it could recover substantial damages. For present purposes, the basis on which these substantial damages were awarded is particularly telling.

---

[119] It seems these arrangements were entered into to circumvent restrictions on local authority borrowing.

[120] See *Darlington Borough Council* v. *Wiltsier Northern Ltd* (1993) 37 Con LR 29, 42, where Judge Newey QC noted that not only had MG effected an absolute assignment to DBC of the benefit of the various building contracts it had entered into with Wiltshier by way of deed, '[o]n 10 September [1991] [DBC] gave Wiltshier written notice of the assignment in accordance with s. 136 of the Law of Property Act 1925.'

The Court of Appeal held for DBC as statutory assignee on two alternative grounds. First, it held that, even accepting that MG had suffered 'no loss' of its own, *as an exception* to the rule that damages may only be recovered for one's 'own loss' arising from a contractual promisor's breach of contract, and not the loss of a third party to the contract, the 'narrow ground' exception identified by Lord Browne-Wilkinson in *Linden Gardens Trust Ltd* v. *Lenesta Sludge Ltd*[121] was applicable on the facts before the court. Consequently, even if MG had suffered 'no loss' of its own, it could recover substantial damages by reference to the loss of DBC as a third party to the contract by reason of the 'narrow ground'.[122] Then, since DBC was a statutory assignee, it would have acquired MG's entitlement to sue for and recover such damages. Hence, substantial damages quantified by reference to DBC's losses were recoverable by DBC as statutory assignee of MG – notwithstanding that on this ground of analysis, MG had suffered no loss of its own.[123]

In the alternative, a minority in the Court of Appeal was prepared to accept that the so-called 'broad ground' posited by Lord Griffiths in *Linden Gardens Trust Ltd* v. *Lenesta Sludge Ltd*[124] was, in principle, good law, albeit with some slight qualifications;[125] and that it could be successfully invoked by MG. That is to say, Wiltshier's breaches of contract would cause a 'loss' to MG by reference to the injury to MG in not having received the bargain for which it had contracted – what has been termed in much of the secondary literature on the point as the contractual promisee's 'performance interest'.[126] Consequently, it would be inaccurate to consider MG to have suffered 'no loss' at all – rather, on this view

---

[121]  Above, n. 117, 114–15.

[122]  Above, n. 118, 74–5 (Dillon LJ) and 80 (Steyn LJ). Waite LJ agreed with Dillon and Steyn LJJ on this point.

[123]  Ibid.

[124]  Above, n. 117, 97.

[125]  Above, n. 118, 80 (Steyn LJ): 'Subject to one qualification, it will be clear from what I said earlier that I am in respectful agreement with the wider principle [set out by Lord Griffiths]. It seems to me that Lord Griffiths based his principle on classic contractual theory.' Departing from Lord Griffiths's view, Steyn LJ was of the view that in awarding damages on the 'broad ground', the court might impose a precondition by requiring the claimant to provide an undertaking that the damages, when awarded, would be used to cure the defects caused by the promisor's defective performance (at 80–1). Dillon LJ did not think it was necessary to consider Lord Griffith's wider principle (at 75). Waite LJ did not indicate that he agreed with Steyn LJ on the point (at 81).

[126]  See e.g. B. Coote, 'The Performance Interest, *Panatown*, and the Problem of Loss' (2001) 117 LQR 81.

of the law, MG would have suffered substantial loss by reference to the injury to its performance interest, and substantial damages could be awarded in respect of such loss. When MG statutorily assigned to DBC the benefit of its accrued causes of action against Wiltshier, DBC would have acquired MG's entitlements against Wiltshier in respect of such causes of action which would have allowed MG to recover substantial damages. On this alternative ground, then, DBC would also be permitted to recover substantial damages.

It is unnecessary for present purposes to conclusively determine which of these alternative approaches is the right one. What is significant is that in *Darlington Borough Council* v. *Wiltshier Northern Ltd*, the Court of Appeal accepted that DBC's action would not have been allowed to succeed *simply* by dint of the statutory assignment by MG to DBC of its accrued causes of action against Wiltshier for breach of contract. If not for the application of the narrow and/or broad grounds posited by Lord Browne-Wilkinson and Lord Griffith in *Linden Gardens Trust Ltd*, the Council's action would have failed. The decision and reasoning in *Darlington Borough Council* is therefore on all fours with the analysis of LPA1925, s. 136(1) put forward above.

The obvious consequence of the above analysis is that a statutory assignee cannot recover any *more* than what the assignor could have recovered. This is necessarily the case given that a statutory assignee is still recovering in right of the assignor. To illustrate this limit on recovery, it is helpful to consider the case of *Offer-Hoar* v. *Larkstore*.[127]

In that case, Starglade Ltd (A) owned a parcel of land. It engaged Technotrade Ltd (B) to prepare a soil inspection report for the said parcel to obtain planning permission to develop it. This contract did not contain an anti-assignment clause. The soil inspection report indicated no substantial risk of subsidence, and planning permission was granted. Starglade then sold the parcel of land to Larkstore (C) with the benefit of full planning and building control permissions. Larkstore subsequently also obtained possession of the Technotrade report and relied on it for various purposes without seeking Technotrade's consent.

A landslip occurred in the course of developing the parcel of land, causing damage to the claimants' adjoining land. Inter alia, they sued Larkstore for negligence and nuisance.

---

[127] [2006] EWCA Civ 1079, [2006] 1 WLR 2926.

It appeared that the soil inspection report might not have been pre-pared with the requisite degree of care. So on 23 February 2004, more than five years after acquisition of the land from Starglade, in consider-ation of £1 and its promise to share any sums recovered from Techno-trade, Larkstore procured an assignment from Starglade of the benefit of Starglade's contract with Technotrade on the following terms: 'Star-glade with full title guarantee assigns to Larkstore the report together with all the benefit and interest and rights of Starglade in or under the report and the right to enforce the same TO HOLD [sic] to Larkstore absolutely.'[128] The assignment further granted Technotrade the 'right to sue in respect of breaches of Technotrade of its duties and obligations and to bring all such claims against Technotrade as are available at law.'[129] Written notice of the assignment was given to Technotrade,[130] making it a 'statutory' s. 136(1) assignment.[131]

The preliminary point on appeal was whether Larkstore was entitled to recover substantial damages from Technotrade as Starglade's 'statutory' assignee for the losses accruing to it as owner of the land following its reliance on Technotrade's report, even though Starglade (the assignor) had not suffered any loss at the time of the assignment: having sold the land to Larkstore before such subsidence, and being under no contractual duty to indemnify or to compensate Larkstore for the same, it appeared that Starglade had suffered no relevant loss despite Techno-trade's breach of contract. The Court of Appeal held that substantial damages could be awarded.

Mummery LJ held that substantial damages were available despite Starglade suffering no substantial loss at the time of the assignment: 'What was assigned by Starglade [A] to Larkstore [C] was a cause of action for breach of contract against Technotrade [B] and the legal remedies for it. It was not an assignment of "a loss" ... The assignment included the remedy in damages for the cause of action.'[132]

The reference to Starglade having assigned a 'cause of action' is helpful. It reinforces the point made above, that s. 136(1)(b) transfers all legal

---

[128] Ibid., [15].
[129] Ibid.
[130] Ibid., [17].
[131] No appeal had been lodged against the finding in the court below that Starglade's assignment to Larkstore was not champertous as Larkstore had a genuine commercial interest in enforcement of what had been Starglade's claim against Technotrade: *Offer-Hoar* v. *Larkstore Ltd* [2005] EWHC 2742 (TCC), [35].
[132] Above, n. 127, [41], with whom Rix and Peter Smith LJJ agreed.

remedies from the statutory assignor to her assignee, including the assignor's cause of action, meaning that set of facts which must be pleaded and which is capable of being traversed by the defendant. It was therefore open to Larkstore to plead the facts which would have comprised Starglade's cause of action against Technotrade for breach of its contractual duties arising in connection with its preparation of the soil investigation report, had there been no assignment of the benefit of the contract to Larkstore. That is, the operation of s. 136(1) was not to transfer Starglade's 'loss', but Starglade's 'cause of action'.

This was not all. As Mummery LJ's judgment made clear, s. 136(1) transferred 'the remedy in damages for the cause of action'. As explained above, s. 136(1)(b) would pass from Starglade not only its cause of action against Technotrade for breach of contract but also its entitlement to the legal remedy of contract damages arising from such cause of action. However, that did not mean that the statutory assignment allowed Larkstore to recover substantial damages in respect of its *own* loss. As statutory assignee, it was still recovering in respect of Starglade's loss – a point which *Darlington Borough Council* v. *Wiltshier Northern Ltd* makes plain. The question is therefore whether Starglade could be said to have sustained no relevant loss from Technotrade's breach of contract, given that it had sold the subject land to Larkstore many years prior for full value, in ignorance of the fact of breach by Technotrade.

In this connection, care needs to be taken. Mummery and Rix LJJ recognized that as the obligor ought not to be exposed to any greater duty or liability by reason of such assignment, a ceiling should be set as to the damages awarded to the statutory assignee. They therefore agreed[133] with Staughton LJ's analysis in *Linden Gardens Trust Ltd* v. *Lenesta Sludge Disposals Ltd* that:[134]

> [I]t is said that in such a case [where a cause of action for damages has been assigned] the assignee can recover no more as damages than the assignor could have recovered.
>
> That proposition seems to me well founded. It stems from the principle already discussed, that the debtor is not to be put in any worse position by reason of the assignment. ... But in a case such as the present one must elucidate the proposition slightly: the assignee can recover no more

---

[133] Above, n. 127, [51]–[54] and [74]–[77], respectively.

[134] (1992) 30 Con LR 1, 16–17 (emphasis in original). Nourse LJ and Sir Michael Kerr agreed with Staughton LJ on this point. The House of Lords did not address this part of the Court of Appeal's reasoning when the case came before it.

damages than the assignor could have recovered if there had been no assignment, *and if the building had not been transferred to the assignee.*

The reason for this 'ceiling' lies in the formulation of the counterfactual construct to ascertain causation for loss.

As has been noted in Chapter 6, damages are usually assessed at the time when the cause of action accrues. This is because 'losses' accruing to the claimant prior to this point in time cannot be said to have been 'caused' by the defendant. And to ascertain whether a particular loss has been 'caused' by a particular breach of duty by the respondent, we conduct a thought experiment: we consider whether, as at the point in time when the cause of action accrued, matters would have turned out differently had the respondent not breached the duty in question.

If B contracts with A to build A a house on A's land, but does the building work in a defective manner, leading A to have to incur additional costs to remedy such defective work, to ascertain whether B's defective work *caused* A's loss in the form of these additional expenses, we imagine a counterfactual world in which B did not perform defectively, and trace the consequences from such non-defective performance. If, in that counterfactual world, we see that there would have been no need for A to incur such additional expense, then A's incurring of such expense would have been caused by B's defective work, since 'but for' such defective work, A would not have needed to incur these costs.

What may pass unnoticed, however, is that the exercise is conducted with regard to the state of the world as it stood, at the point when the purported cause of action accrued. So in the example above, we set up the counterfactual world as at the point in time B performed defectively (since that is when the contractual cause of action would have accrued). We then hypothesize what would have happened had there been no defective performance at that point in time. All other events are, however, ignored. For example, it would not matter that, in actuality, following B's defective performance, the contract was discharged by frustration because a fire which had started from a neighbouring property had spread to A's property, and had burned the property down to the ground.

This event, occurring after the accrual of A's cause of action against B, is ignored when we construct the counterfactual world for purposes of ascertaining whether B's breach of duty had indeed caused A to sustain the loss which is now in issue. This is so even though the subsequent event of the fire, if taken to be a frustrating event, would excuse any need for *further* performance of the contract by B, and so would preclude any claims for loss pertaining to B's non-performance of any outstanding obligations beyond that point in time. (However, the fire could have limited impact on B's secondary obligations arising by reason of A's cause of action against B for B's defective works).

Supposing A had taken out fire insurance, and was fully indemnified by reason of such policy such that she could use such funds to rebuild the building, now without any defects: it would not follow that A would have suffered 'no loss' by reason of B's defective building works. The incidence of the fire, the destruction of the building, A's recovery because of her foresight in taking out fire insurance cover, and A's making of such a claim on her fire policy with her insurers would all be irrelevant to the question of ascertainment of A's loss occasioned by B's breach of duty because they are all events occurring *after* that point in time when A's cause of action had accrued. Nor could account be taken of them by reason of doctrines such as mitigation of loss: plainly, though the effect of A's indemnification by the insurance company would be to enable A to have the means to have the building constructed anew, A had taken out the policy prior to B's breach, and A's claim on the policy would have had nothing to do with B's breach: these steps cannot, therefore, be taken to be mitigatory steps. They are *res inter alios acta* which have no bearing on A's cause of action against B.

Obviously, when A took out the fire insurance policy, A could not have known of breaches of a contract which had not even been formed. Since it is normally the case that one is only expected to 'mitigate' *after* one is aware that there is a breach,[135] acts done in ignorance of a breach of duty, but which coincidentally have the effect of reducing one's losses resulting from that breach, cannot be acts which are in mitigation of that loss, as a matter of legal principle (whatever their practical effect).

Further, and more generally, as Viscount Haldane LC stated in *British Westinghouse Co.* v. *Underground Electric Railways*: 'When in the course of his business he [the claimant] has taken action *arising out of the transaction*, which action has diminished his loss, the effect in actual

---

[135] *Youell* v. *Bland Welch & Co. Ltd (The Superhulls Cover Case) (No. 2)* [1990] 2 Lloyd's Rep 431, 461 (on mitigation in contract), citing with approval *Eley* v. *Bedford* [1972] 1 QB 155, 158 (on mitigation in tort).

diminution of the loss he has suffered may be taken into account even though there was no duty on him to act.'[136] If so, acts which are performed by a claimant independently of the transaction of which the contract which had been breached was a part, but which coincidentally would have the effect of reducing the losses sustained as a result of that breach, are also not mitigatory acts.

In our example involving A and B, although A's acts of taking out of the fire insurance and her act of claiming upon it and recovering the indemnity from the insurers certainly led to A's loss being reduced in fact, as a matter of the law of mitigation, they would have to be ignored. These acts are not mitigatory acts within the meaning of that legal concept, and do not result in B being able to say that A's loss having been successfully mitigated, A should not recover anything in respect of such successfully mitigated loss. Rather, these acts and recoveries having nothing to do with any mitigatory duty on A's part, they are to be disregarded for mitigation purposes.

It would follow, therefore, that on the facts in *Offer-Hoar* v. *Larkstore*, Starglade's sale of the subject land to Larkstore would have been a matter which was *res inter alios acta* so far as Technotrade's contractual duties to Starglade were concerned. When the land was sold to Larkstore, Technotrade had *already* breached its contractual duty to Starglade: the contractual cause of action as between Starglade and Technotrade arising from the breach had already accrued and Starglade's subsequent sale of the land to Larkstore changed nothing. As explained above, it could not be said that such sale (for full value) would have the effect of eliminating the loss to Starglade arising from Technotrade's breach of duty since the counterfactual world constructed to establish 'but for' causation would be built on the basis of matters as they stood at the point in time when the cause of action accrued – i.e. before the subject land was sold to Starglade.

Next, it could not be said that the sale of the land for full value to Starglade would operate as a form of mitigation so as to reduce Starglade's recoverable loss arising in connection with such cause of action. Although the monies received from such sale would certainly reduce Starglade's loss, they could not reduce recoverable loss since such sums did not arise by way of any mitigatory act on the part of Starglade. On the facts of *Offer-Hoar* v. *Larkstore*, it could not be said that Starglade had

---

[136] [1912] AC 673, 689 (emphasis added).

sold the land to Larkstore *in order to* mitigate its losses arising from Technotrade's breach of its contractual duty to prepare the soil subsidence report with due care. Though the sale to Larkstore for full value put Starglade in funds, like the example above where A had recovered an indemnity from her insurer in light of the fire which had razed her land and the defectively constructed building on it, the sale transaction had nothing to do with mitigating Larkstore's loss arising in connection with its cause of action against Tehnotrade. Thus, it was *not* a mitigatory step at all, and it would not have any effect in reducing Larkstore's *recoverable* loss from Technotrade.

The Court of Appeal was therefore right to observe that the sale of the land to Starglade was to be ignored when assessing the damages which were to be awarded to Starglade, as statutory assignee of Larkstore's accrued cause of action against Technotrade for its breach of contract. In the counterfactual world where Technotrade *had* prepared the report with due care, and ignoring all subsequent events (such as the sale of the subject land to Starglade), Larkstore would have sustained losses of the type which were in issue before the court, being losses pertaining to the expense of making good the subsidence caused by development works which relied on the prognosis set out by Technotrade in its soil investigation report. This type of loss would have been suffered 'by' Larkstore, once the breach occurred – even though it would not reveal itself until much later (i.e. when the subsidence occurred after the development works had been carried out). Since the fact of the sale of the land to Larkstore would be ignored for the purposes of establishing causation of loss, and such sale to Larkstore would also *not* amount to a step in mitigation of Larkstore's loss, the sums realized by such sale would be ignored, and Larkstore *would* sustain a substantial loss in terms of the expenses of making good the subsidence caused by the development works. And when Larkstore statutorily assigned the cause of action to Starglade, it enabled Starglade to recover in right of Larkstore: Starglade could recover, as Larkstore's assignee, all that *Larkstore* could have recovered as against Technotrade. The reason for the 'ceiling' on Starglade's recovery was, therefore, simply because that was precisely what Starglade was empowered to recover as Larkstore's statutory assignee. Since Starglade was recovering in right of Larkstore, it necessarily followed that Starglade could not recover anything more than what Larkstore could have recovered.

The upshot is that a 'statutory' assignment of a contractual chose in action does *not* effect any form of substitutive 'transfer' which would cause the assignee to replace the assignor as obligee to whom the obligor would be obligated. Instead, such statutory assignment is, in essence, an equitable assignment, though with certain additional statutorily mandated effects which override certain aspects of the equitable assignment (such as the continued ability of the assignor to invoke the various entitlements specified in ss. 136(1)(a), (b) and (c)). This view is further corroborated when we turn to examine the position when a cause of action sounding in tort is statutorily assigned.

### (ii)   Transfer of Legal Remedy: Tort

*Offer-Hoar* v. *Larkstore* is an example of an equitable assignment of an accrued cause of action to recover damages for breach of contract which was then embellished with the additional statutory effects of s. 136(1). 'Causes of action' in the sense of an obligee's entitlement to commence legal proceedings against an obligor in respect of an accrued entitlement to damages *and* the obligee's entitlement to plead the facts which make up such cause of action, are choses or things in action which may be equitably assigned.[137]

Since causes of action, even those which arise in tort, are also choses in action,[138] it would appear that save for equitable assignments which 'savour' of maintenance or champerty, it ought also be possible to equitably assign an accrued cause of action in tort. Thus, notwithstanding suggestions to the contrary,[139] '[t]he better view ... is that even a right of action in tort can be assigned if it is incidental or ancillary to the transfer of a property right or interest to the assignee or if the assignee has a genuine commercial interest in taking the assignment for his own benefit'.[140] If so, how does the analysis put forward above as to

---

[137] Although the validity of such assignments may be impugned if they be tainted by maintenance or champerty: *Prosser* v. *Edmonds* (1835) 1 Y & C Ex 481; *Trendtex Trading Corp.* v. *Credit Suisse* [1982] AC 679. However, if the assignee is shown to have a genuine and legitimate interest in taking the assignment, these concerns as to maintenance or champerty would be overridden, and would not bar the efficacy of the assignment: *Trendtex Trading Corp.*, ibid.; *Mulkerrins* v. *PricewaterhouseCoopers (a firm)* [2003] UKHL 41, [2003] 1 WLR 1937. For criticism of the uncertainties created by this decision, see A. Tettenborn, 'Assignment of Rights to Compensation' (2007) LMCLQ 392.

[138] *Curtis* v. *Wilcox* [1948] 2 KB 474; *Ord* v. *Upton* [2000] Ch 352; *Simpson* v. *Norfolk and Norwich University Hospital NHS Trust* [2011] EWCA Civ 1149;[2012] QB 640, [12].

[139] E.g. *May* v. *Lane* (1894) 64 LJQB 236, 238; *Defries* v. *Milne* [1913] 1 Ch 98, 109.

[140] Liew (2018), para. 1-18, references omitted.

the operation of s. 136(1)(b) apply to an equitable assignment of an accrued cause of action in tort?

Tort duties entail a primary claim-right/duty jural relation that the duty-bearing party not commit acts prohibited by the law of the tort. The primary duty in such tort is then owed to the parties defined by the said tort.

When the primary duty is breached, the tortfeasor will be subjected by operation of law to an additional secondary duty to pay the victim of the tort damages assessed by a court of competent jurisdiction.[141] But this secondary duty does not override and displace the original primary duty: where B is duty-bound to A not to act negligently, but has breached that duty on a certain day, that breach does not mean that B is no longer duty-bound to A not to act negligently. The primary duty continues to bind A and B – just that as at a particular point in time, B had breached it, thereby generating a secondary duty to pay damages to be assessed in respect of *that* breach of duty at *that* point in time.

Given this secondary duty which is imposed by operation of law, the tortfeasor will be duty-bound to the victim of the tort to pay damages. But since the damages are to be awarded following quantification and assessment of the victim's loss by a court, the torteasor's duty to pay damages also entails a *liability* in that the victim will have a power to bring the tortfeasor before a court for an adjudication and assessment.

As Hohfeld noted in connection with the breach of the primary duties arising from a contract between A and X, if X breached his primary duties to A under that contract without valid excuse:[142]

> [A] new legal relation – a secondary, or remedial, obligation – arises between A and X. The latter, as a consequence of the breach of his primary duty, is now under a remedial duty to make *non-specific* reparation, that is a duty to pay to A damages . . . and correspondingly, A has a remedial right. . . .
>
> If X fails to act under his remedial duty, A has *ab initio* the power, by action in the courts, to institute a process of compulsion against X. At this point, we reach, as the correlative of the power of A, the liability of X.

And the same may said in respect of breaches of primary duties arising in tort.

---

[141] 'The wrong generates a new right exigible only against the wrongdoer': Stevens (2007), p. 59.

[142] Hohfeld (1923), pp. 202–3, reprinting Hohfeld, 'Nature of Stockholders' Individual Liability for Corporation Debts' (1909) 9 *Columbia Law Review* 285.

To the above, one clarification should be added. The secondary duty of the party-in-breach that has breached the primary duty (whether arising in contract or in tort), is inchoate: it is a duty to make 'non-specific' reparation. At common law, this takes the form of damages as assessed by the court. Consequently, this secondary duty cannot be discharged by performance *until* the assessment has been made.

This does not mean that there is no such duty before assessment. It only means that discharge of such duty is possible only *after* such assessment.[143] Thus, such secondary duty cannot be breached until the assessment is made.[144] Consequently, 'prepayments' to the victim who has sustained the breach of the primary duty cannot count as performance of the secondary duty[145] (though credit must be given).

The subject matter of an accrued cause of action where primary tort duties have been breached is distinct from the subject matter which comprises those primary tort duties. A primary tort duty entails a claim-right/duty jural relation *not* to commit the acts defined by the tort. The secondary duty, however, entails a claim-right/duty jural relation to pay such damages as the court may assess. Thus, when one equitably assigns an accrued cause of action in tort, the objects of such assignment are not the jural relations associated with the primary obligation, but the jural relations associated with the secondary obligation, which are distinct.

What, then, transpires when the requirements of 'absolute, writing and notice' are satisfied in connection with the equitable assignment of a tortious cause of action? If the requirements of LPA1925, s. 136(1) are met, the effect is to transfer to the assignee the assignor's 'legal right' to the thing in action assigned (i.e. her power or standing to sue in her own name), as well as the 'legal ... remedies for the same', meaning, in particular, the assignor's cause of action (i.e. those facts which would

---

[143] Cf. S. A. Smith, 'Why Courts Make Orders (And What This Tells Us About Damages)' (2011) 64 *Current Legal Problems* 51, 71–85.

[144] The nature of this secondary duty is not dissimilar from the nature of a primary contractual duty in a building contract where the client is to pay *such* sum as the Quantity Surveyor jointly appointed by the parties assesses to be due. There is no duty to pay anything *until* the Quantity Surveyor makes the assessment, and so no breach of such duty until the assessment is made.

[145] And thus, prepayment of 'damages' ahead of the court's assessment does not discharge this secondary duty, rendering the party-in-breach to be liable to pay interest under Senior Courts Act 1981, s. 35A(1): *Edmunds* v. *Lloyds Italico & l'Ancora Compagnia di Assicurazione e Riassicurazione SpA* [1986] 1 WLR 492, 495–6; cited with approval in *Fast Ferries One SA* v. *Ferries Australia Pty Ltd* [2000] 1 Lloyd's Rep 534.

have had to be pleaded to support the action) and the assignor's entitlement to an order or award of damages arising from those facts. But these
damages must still be assessed by reference to the assignor's losses, and
not the assignee's losses.

Confirmation that the above analysis is correct may be found in the
(occasional) practice of insurers to take statutory assignments from their
assured of their causes of action against tortfeasors, rather than relying
simply on their right of subrogation.[146] Where an indemnity has been
paid out on a policy of indemnity insurance by the insurer to the assured,
the insurer may bring proceedings against the tortfeasor in the name of
the assured[147] by reason of its right of subrogation.[148] These being the
proceedings of the assured, the court will be concerned to assess the
assured's loss as had been caused by the tortfeasor's tortious act, and not
the insurer's loss (which would be the quantum of the indemnity paid out
to the assured, plus interest).

If the subrogated action is successful, and if, say, 'there is a favourable
movement in currency rates or some other windfall'[149] damages are
awarded in excess of the indemnity (plus interest) which had been
paid out to the assured, then the insurer must account for the excess to
the assured.[150] However, if the assured were to execute a statutory

---

[146] It has been suggested that insurers prefer not to take such statutory assignments from
their assureds, 'as they dislike the unfavourable publicity which flows from their names
appearing on the record as parties to litigation': C. Mitchell, S. Watterson, A. Fenton and
H. Legge, *Subrogation: Law and Practice* (Oxford: Oxford University Press, 2008),
para. 10.180. However: '[Subrogation] cannot be exercised until payment. It will be lost
if the assured is a company which is ordered to be dissolved. The amount which the
insurers may retain is limited to the precise sum that they have paid. If the insurance
proceeds are paid in sterling but the subrogated action is brought in another currency,
for example, adverse movements in the exchange rate could mean that insurers might
suffer a shortfall': R. Merkin and J. Steele, *Insurance and the Law of Obligations* (Oxford:
Oxford University Press, 2013), p. 117.

[147] *London Assurance Company* v. *Sainsbury* (1783) 3 Dougl 245, 250 (Buller J) and 253
(Lord Mansfield).

[148] If suing by reason of its subrogation right, the insurer's name should not appear on the
record as a party to the action: *Simpson & Co.* v. *Thomson* (1877) 3 App Cas 279, 286
(Lord Cairns LC) and 293 (Lord Blackburn); *Esso Petroleum Ltd* v. *Hull Russell & Co.
Ltd (The Esso Bernicia)* [1989] AC 643, 663 (Lord Goff).

[149] R. Merkin, J. P. Summer and L. Hodgson, *Colinvaux's Law of Insurance* (11th edn,
London: Sweet & Maxwell/Thomson Reuters, 2016), para. 12-007.

[150] *Yorkshire Insurance Co. Ltd* v. *Nisbet Shipping Co. Ltd* [1962] 2 QB 330. See also *Glen
Line Ltd* v. *A-G* (1930) 36 Com Cas 1 (HL), 14 (Lord Atkin). It appears that a trust is
impressed on the excess for the benefit of the assured: *Lonrho Exports Ltd* v. *Export
Credit Guarantee Dept* [1999] Ch 158, 181–2 (Lightman J). Conversely, if the assured,

assignment of her cause of action against her tortfeasor to the insurer, the insurer's position would be different.

If an action were brought by the insurer as statutory assignee, damages would still be assessed by reference to the assured's loss arising from the tortfeasor's tortious breach.[151] But given the statutory assignment to the insurer, not only might the insurer sue in its own name,[152] the insurer would be permitted to retain the whole of the damages recovered. As Roskill J explained: '[I]t is well established that upon abandonment an underwriter can recover more than 100 per cent if the abandoned property realises more than the amount paid by way of loss. ... I see no reason in principle why a different result should follow from the enforcement of rights under a valid legal [i.e. statutory] assignment.'[153]

Given *Read* v. *Brown*, *Offer-Hoar* v. *Larkstore*, and the indemnity insurance cases, it becomes clear that the effect of s. 136(1) is not as expansive as might initially be thought. In particular, notwithstanding the assignor's 'legal and other remedies' having been transferred to the assignee by reason of s. 136(1)(b), where the requirements of s. 136(1) are met following the assignment of a debt or other thing in action, the statutory assignee is entitled to the 'legal ... remedies for the same'. Consequently, post-assignment, *only* the assignee may invoke or assert these 'legal remedies' by reason of s. 136(1)(b) so far as the statute would have transferred such 'judicially ordered' remedial entitlements of the assignor to the assignee. Such legal remedies would no longer be available to the assignor, for she would no longer even 'have' any cause of action as against the obligor, such cause of action having also been passed from her and been transferred to her assignee. However, the 'transfer' effected by

---

after having been indemnified by her insurer, were to receive a payment in diminution of her loss arising from the tortfeasor's breach of contract via legal action or otherwise, the assured must account to her insurer for such receipt to the extent that it leaves her more than fully indemnified for her loss: *Lord Napier and Ettrick* v. *Hunter* [1993] AC 713.

[151] See e.g. *King* v. *Victoria Insurance Company Ltd* [1896] AC 250, where the Privy Council upheld the decision of the Supreme Court of Queensland ((1895) 6 QLJ 202) in which it had allowed the claim of an insurer who had taken a statutory assignment under the Queensland equivalent to what is now LPA1925, s. 136(1) of its assured's cause of action against the defendant tortfeasor to sue and recover damages quantified by reference to the assured's loss, and not its own loss (which would be in the amount of the sums it had paid to the assured by way of indemnity).

[152] If an insurer sued in its own name relying merely on its right of subrogation, the action would be struck out: *Central Insurance Co. Ltd* v. *Seacalf Shipping Corp. (The Aiolos)* [1983] 2 Lloyd's Rep 25.

[153] *Compania Colombiana de Seguros* v. *Pacific Steam Navigation Co.* [1965] 1 QB 101, 121. The point does not appear to have been questioned or doubted in subsequent cases.

s. 136(1)(b) still does not go so far as to permit the statutory assignee to recover for his own losses. Although the 'statutory' assignee may certainly bring proceedings at law in his own name without need to join the assignor, such proceedings by the 'statutory' assignee are still proceedings in right of the assignor, and in respect of the assignor's losses.

## G   'Debt or Other *Legal* Thing in Action'

The discussion thus far has concentrated on the question of the entitlements which are passed from a statutory assignor to her assignee. The question arises, however, as to whether these effects are applicable to assignments of things in action arising at common law, as well as those arising in equity, because s. 136(1) appears to only apply to instances where a 'debt or other *legal* thing in action' had been assigned.

In *Harding* v. *Harding*,[154] it was assumed that an assignment of a subsisting equitable interest could fall within the Judicature Act 1873, s. 25(6). Further, cases such as *Manchester Brewery Company* v. *Coombs*[155] and *Re Pain*[156] adopted the conclusion arrived at by the Supreme Court of Queensland in *King* v. *Victoria Insurance Co. Ltd* from which an appeal had been made to the Privy Council.[157]

In that case, the Queensland Supreme Court held that the term 'legal chose in action' in the Queensland Judicature Act,[158] s. 5(6) denoted all rights which a court of law or equity would, before the passage of the act, have considered to be lawful.[159] When the matter went on appeal, the Privy Council upheld the decision below, but on a different ground.

---

[154] (1886) 17 QBD 442. This case concerned a voluntary assignment of a testamentary gift of a sum of money under a will. The question arose as to whether such an assignment, being voluntary and unsupported by consideration, was effective. In answer, the court pointed out that so far as the assignment satisfied the requirements under Judicature Act 1873, s. 25(6), such statutory assignment would be effective without consideration. The court, accordingly, was prepared to assume that equitable choses in action could be subjected to the statutory regime set out in the Judicature Act 1873, s. 25(6).

[155] [1901] 2 Ch 608, 619.

[156] [1919] 1 Ch 38, 44 (Younger J).

[157] *King* v. *Victoria Insurance Co. Ltd* [1896] AC 250.

[158] Judicature Act (40 Vict, c. 84) (Queensland, Australia). Section 5(6) of this Queensland statute was *in pari materia* with Judicature Act 1873, s. 25(6).

[159] *King* v. *Victoria Insurance Co. Ltd* (1895) 6 QLJ 202 (Supreme Court of Queensland), 204: '[T]he test to be applied for determining the validity of an assignment of a "chose in action" which is in accordance with … [the Act], is whether the subject matter of the assignment and the circumstances under which it is made are such that before the Act a court of law or equity would have considered the assignment a lawful one, and would

However, as to the ambit of the phrase 'legal chose in action' observed as follows:[160]

> [t]heir Lordships do not express any dissent from the views taken in the Court below of the construction of the Judicature Act with reference to the term 'legal chose in action'. They prefer to avoid discussing a question not free from difficulty, and to express no opinion what limitation, if any, should be placed on the literal meaning of that term.

In addition, there is Channell J's well-known statement in *Torkington* v. *Magee*: 'I think the words "debt or other legal chose in action" mean "debt or right" which the common law looks on as not assignable by reason of its being a chose in action, but which a court of equity deals with as being assignable.'[161] Considerable academic commentary[162] supports Channell J's statement of the law.

In this connection, it is helpful to recall that '[u]ses, trusts, and other equitable interests in property, though regarded by equity as conferring proprietary rights analogous to the rights recognized by law in hereditaments or in chattels, were regarded by the common law as being merely choses in action'.[163] And, 'At the beginning of the eighteenth century, it was quite settled that equity would recognize the validity of the assignment both of debts and of other things *recognized by the common law as choses in action*.'[164]

As always, it is imperative that the wording of the statute be kept firmly in focus. Here, we should note its provision that:

> Any absolute assignment ... of any debt or other *legal* thing in action, of which express notice shall have to be given to the debtor, trustee, or other person from whom the assignor would have been entitled *to receive or*

---

have given in respect of it such relief as, according to the practice of the court, was appropriate' (Griffith CJ).

[160] Above, n. 157, at 256.

[161] *Torkington* v. *Magee* [1902] 2 KB 427, 430-1.

[162] See e.g. Liew (2018), para. 2-09; Bridge (2018), para. 21-058; J Crossley Vaines, *Crossley Vaines' Personal Property* (E. L. G. Tyler and N. E. Palmer, eds., 5th edn, Oxford: Butterworths, 1973) 265; E. P. Wolstenholme and Sir B. L. Cherry, *Wolstenholme and Cherry's Conveyancing Statutes*, Vol. 1 (J. T. Farrand, ed., 13th edn, London: Oyez, 1972), p. 245; W. R. Warren, *The Law Relating to Choses in Action* (London: Sweet & Maxwell, 1899), p. 162.

[163] Holdsworth (1925), p. 516.

[164] Ibid., p. 536. This construction was accepted (albeit in *dicta*) in *Federal Commissioner of Taxation* v. *Everett* (1980) 143 CLR 440, 447 (*per* Barwick CJ, and Stephen, Mason and Wilson JJ). See also Marshall (1950), pp. 166-8; Tudsbery (1912), pp. 10-12.

*claim such debt or thing in action*, shall . . . pass and transfer the legal right
to such debt or thing in action.

The reference to how notice is to be given to such entity from whom the
assignor would otherwise have been entitled to recover the said debt or
thing in action, i.e. to *reduce* that debt or thing in action *into possession*, is
telling, for it tells us the true ambit of the qualification that only 'legal'
things in action are to be affected by the statute: these are that subclass of
things in action which may be reduced into possession.[165] As Rigby LJ
reminded us in *May v. Lane*:[166]

> We have been referred to section 25, sub-section 6 of the Judicature Act,
> 1873, which speaks of the assignment of any debt, or other legal *chose in
> action*; and it has been said that this, which at the most could only be a
> *chose in action*, is a legal *chose in action* within the meaning of that sub-
> section. I do not agree with that contention. A legal *chose in action* is
> something which is not in possession, but which must be sued for in order
> to recover possession of it.

The phrase 'debt or other *legal* chose in action' should, therefore, be
construed to denote not legal (as opposed to equitable) choses in action,
but those choses in action which were recognized as such at common
law, that is to say, choses enforceable by action at common law, as well as
choses enforceable by suit in equity.[167] If so, it would follow that it is
possible to effect a 'statutory' assignment of an equitable chose in action.
Since a 'statutory assignment' is *not* a distinct type of assignment, but
merely supplements *such* assignments as may be recognized at law or in
equity, so far as an equitable assignment may be effected of an equitable
chose, the effects of s. 136(1) may be applied in respect of a validly
assigned equitable chose. There is, accordingly, no reason why one might
not 'statutorily' assign either legal *or* equitable choses in action.

But doubts have been expressed as to these views. For example, the
commentary in *Smith & Leslie* suggests that statutory assignment may

---

[165] The observation in Charles Sweet, 'Choses in Action' (1895) 11 LQR 238, 240 that '[t]he
draftsman of the Bankruptcy Act, 1869, probably never heard that any question had
arisen as to stocks, shares, copyrights and patents being choses in action, and the
question was obviously not present to the mind of the draftsman of the Judicature
Act, 1873' may therefore have been an unjustified criticism of the efforts of Lord
Selborne, LC, by whose hand the Judicature Act was drawn up.

[166] (1894) 64 LJ QB (NS) 236, 238.

[167] Holdsworth does recognize, however, the awkwardness of such a construction: 'the
phrase "legal chose in action" is not a very happy one to express "a thing regarded by
the common law as a chose in action"': Holdsworth (1925), p. 536, fn. 3.

only be applied to assignments of legal choses in action, and not at all for equitable choses.[168]

Smith and Leslie make three points in support of their limited and (admittedly) plainer reading of s. 136(1). First, they reject the formulation of the Queensland Supreme Court in *Victoria Insurance Co. Ltd* because the '"Courts of Law" did not in fact consider assignments of choses in action to be valid at all'.[169] Second, they suggest that the '"mischief" that s. 136 was intended to cure was the need to join the assignor in those cases where the assignor's presence was otiose', but there would have been no need to join the assignor of an equitable chose in action were proceedings to be brought on such equitable chose by an assignee since the assignee of such a chose would be entitled to bring proceedings in equity in his own name in any event. Hence, there would be 'no mischief for s. 136 to cure, so far as equitable choses in action are concerned'.[170] Finally, Smith and Leslie suggest that as 's. 136 transfers "the legal right" to the interest to the subject of the assignment[, i]t is hard to understand how legal title to an equitable interest can be transferred from assignor to assignee, when the assignor never held that legal title'.[171]

It is suggested that the position set out in cases like *Re Pain* is precisely correct, and the force of these criticisms can be deflected.

As to the first point of criticism, it arguably goes too far to say that the courts of common law did not consider assignments of choses in action to be valid *at all*. As has been explained in Chapter 8, even before the enactment of the Judicature Act 1873, s. 25(6), the courts of common law were already prepared to recognize the equitable beneficial interest of an equitable assignee in a chose in action that had been equitably assigned by an assignor-obligee. Although the *enforcement* of such equitable entitlements by means of the grant of common law remedies by courts of common law was certainly problematic, it was not the case that courts of common law would not have anything to do with the beneficial entitlements of an equitable assignee at all.

---

[168]  Smith & Leslie (2018), para. 16.16. Roughly the same conclusion is arrived at in Tolhurst (2016), paras. 5.07–5.15, although Dr. Tolhurst suggests that there may be 'one exception where there is a chain of assignments and where the first assignment involves an equitable assignment of a legal interest' (at para. 5.07). Similar scepticism may be found in G. W. Keeton and L. A. Sheridan, *Equity* (3rd edn, London: Kluwer Law Publishers, 1987), p. 249; Marshall (1950), p. 166.
[169]  Smith & Leslie (2018), para. 16.14, text to fn. 26.
[170]  Ibid., para. 16.15.
[171]  Ibid., para. 16.16.

Smith's and Leslie's second point is more substantial. They say:[172]

> [T]he 'mischief' that s. 136 was intended to cure was the need to join the
> assignor in those cases where the assignor's presence was otiose. Yet . . . it
> has never been necessary, on substantive grounds,[173] to join the assignor
> where there is an equitable assignment of an equitable chose. There is,
> thus, no mischief for s. 136 to cure, so far as equitable choses in action are
> concerned.[174]

If it were true that equitable assignments of equitable choses operate
substantively by effecting a substitutive transfer of the assignee in place of
the assignor as obligee to the equitable chose which had been assigned (as
Smith and Leslie assert is the case), it would indeed follow that application of s. 136(1) to such assignments would be otiose as there would be
no work for the statute to do. However, as explained this book, that
misunderstands how equitable assignments of equitable choses operate.

As explained in Chapter 4, whether the chose assigned be one arising
at law, or in equity, the equitable assignment of either type of chose
cannot entail any form of substitutive transfer. Rather, in both cases, the
'trust-plus-agency' mechanisms operate to simulate the appearance of a
substitutive transfer.

Equitable assignments of legal or equitable choses alike entail a trust
coupled with an agency. Hence, whether the chose assigned is equitable
or legal, an equitable assignor must necessarily retain all her entitlements
against the obligor so she may be duty-bound to her assignee in her
invocation of those entitlements. Further, if the equitable assignor lost
those entitlements, she would no longer be in a position to delegate
invocation of such entitlements to her assignee. So both the trust and
agency effects conceived in this book to underpin equitable assignment
*require* the assignor's entitlements against her obligor to remain wholly
and completely intact.

This means, however, that where the equitable assignment *remains* a
'mere' equitable assignment, absent the 'transfer' effects mandated by s
136(1), an equitable assignor can still change her obligor's jural relations
by invoking her powers against her obligor: they remain *her* powers, and
she may invoke them, whether in compliance with her duties to her

---

[172] Smith & Leslie (2018), para. 16.15.
[173] As explained in Chapter 7, the reason why it was not usually necessary for an assignor of
an equitable chose to be joined to proceedings brought by her assignee against the
equitable obligor is procedural, and not substantive, as Smith and Leslie contend.
[174] The same point is made in Tolhurst (2016), para. 5.14.

assignee, or not. Though she could be enjoined from invoking them, invocation of such powers in breach of her duties to her assignee does not render such invocation a nullity.

Conceived as a composite of trust *plus* agency, equitable assignments do not strip assignors of their powers against their obligors. As Dean Ames observed:[175]

> The assignee of an equitable chose in action, eg, a trust, of course sues in his own name without the aid of a statute. But here, too, there is no novation. If the Hibernicism may be pardoned, the assignee of a trust, like an attorney, stands in the place of his assignor, but does not displace him. A release from the assignor to the innocent trustee frees the latter's legal title from the equitable incumbrance. *Newman* v. *Newman*.[176] So, if a *cestui que trust* should assign his trust first to A. and then to B., and B. should, in good faith,[177] obtain a conveyance of the legal title from the trustee, he could hold it against A.

However, when the statutory requirements in s. 136(1) are satisfied, the powers and claim-rights set out in ss. 136(1)(a), (b) and (c) are transferred to the assignee. So following such transfer, the statutory assignor is barred from invoking them. Accordingly, the assignee would be entitled to assert or invoke entitlements *to the exclusion of the assignor*: the assignor will no longer have these entitlements following the 'statutory' assignment to the assignee.[178]

The relevance of s 136(1) to an assignee of an equitable chose is, therefore, that it precludes the assignor from invoking the entitlements which had been transferred by the statute. Invocation by the assignor of such powers as had been transferred by the statute would simply be ineffectual, and the assignee would be absolved from the need to seek equitable relief to enjoin such acts to protect his interests. Therefore, statutory assignment of an equitable chose is far from being an unnecessary exercise in redundancy as some appear to suggest.

---

[175] Ames (1909), 585–6, fn. 3.

[176] (1885) 28 Ch D 674 (Ch).

[177] As shown in Chapter 11, the significance of this requirement lies in the equitable wrong that would arise if the equitable obligor were to act in such a way as would assist in the commission of a breach of trust or fiduciary duty arising between his equitable obligee (in her capacity as assignor) and her assignee. Further, as shown in Chapter 12, such knowledge may also allow the assignee to bar the debtor from making certain kinds of defences.

[178] See discussion in Section D.

That leaves Smith and Leslie's third criticism. As to this, much the same point may be made in response. Though it would not make sense to speak of a 'transfer' of legal title to an *equitable* chose in action, that only addresses the operation of the first limb of statutory assignment. Statutory assignments also address the transfer of the assignor's legal and other remedies in connection with the chose in action that had been assigned, as well as the assignor's power to give a good discharge. It is by no means clear that the divestment of *these* entitlements from the assignor to the assignee have no bearing where chose assigned is equitable, rather than legal.

Given the above, there is, perhaps, some utility in extending the operation of statutory assignments to assignments of equitable, as well as legal, choses in action. Equitable choses in action (or, more properly, 'choses in equity', being those choses which were enforceable by bringing a suit in equity) also exist, and these would fall within this language, precisely as the cases tell us. What may well fall *outside* the ambit of such 'legal choses in action', perhaps, would be those choses in action which are not open to being reduced into possession through the bringing of legal proceedings, for example, choses in action in the manner of intellectual property entitlements.[179]

It will be explained in Chapter 14 that intellectual property entitlements may *not* be 'transferred' by the mechanism set out in LPA1925, s. 136(1): when what is to be transferred is the intellectual property entitlement itself (as opposed to any right of action arising from infringement of such entitlement, or the right of action to challenge the existence of such intellectual property entitlement, or contractual licences permitting limited exploitation of intellectual property entitlements), s. 136(1) is simply not applicable since its operation is limited to legal things in action, being, as has been suggested, only such things in action which can be reduced into possession by the bringing of an action.

An intellectual property entitlement such as copyright is *not* a matter which is capable of being reduced into possession through the bringing of

---

[179] H. W. Elphinstone, 'What is a Chose in Action?' (1893) 9 LQR 311, 314, making the point that until there is a breach of intellectual property entitlements such as those arising from a patent, a trade mark or a copyright, there is no cause of action; and since these entitlements are negative, there is nothing that can be reduced into possession through the bringing of an action until the negative entitlement is breached.

an action. If A holds the copyright to a literary work, and R breaches that copyright, A 'acquires' a cause of action for breach of copyright. A also acquires associated entitlements such as standing to bring proceedings for such breach, as well as entitlements to plead the facts making up the cause of action, and also the entitlement that damages be assessed in compensation of her losses arising as a result. *Such* secondary entitlements in the manner of remedies such as damages *are* capable of being reduced into possession, and so would fall within the ambit of s. 136(1). However, A's copyright per se is not since, absent any breach, the negative obligation imposed on every non-holder of that copyright not to infringe it is simply not capable of being 'reduced into possession': there is *nothing* that can be reduced into A's possession.[180] And the same may be said of other intellectual property entitlements which operate by means of analogous negative obligations.[181]

It is suggested that the hostility to the applicability of s. 136(1) to assignments of equitable choses in action demonstrated in some quarters misses the mark. Although it may well not be as critical for an assignee of an equitable chose in action to be empowered to bring proceedings against an equitable obligor in his own name, since that is already permitted independently of the statute, as pointed out above, the statute has other effects, the most significant of which is how it *precludes* the assignor from invoking the entitlements set out in ss. 136 (1)(a), (b) and (c). Thus, although an assignee of an equitable thing in action may certainly bring proceedings in equity against the obligor, the effect of ss. 136(1)(a), (b) and (c) would be to bar the assignor of an equitable debt or thing in action from being able to bring such proceedings, to strip away from the assignor access to all 'legal and other remedies for the same', as well as the 'power to give a good discharge for the same'.

---

[180] This may be why Patents Act 1977, s. 30(1), provides that a patent is *not* a thing in action.

[181] Smith & Leslie (2018) posit another reason for the inapplicability of s. 136(1) to 'assignments' of intellectual property entitlements: para. 20.11 (in respect of patents); para. 20.42 (in respect of copyright); para. 20.74 (in respect of unregistered design rights); and para. 20.88 (in respect of registered trade marks). Essentially, it is suggested that because of the 'multilateral' nature of these obligations where an indeterminately large number of obligors will be duty-bound to the holders of such intellectual property entitlements, it would be impossible to give the written notice as is required to trigger the operation of s. 136(1).

## H   Comparison: Indian Transfer of Property Act 1882

An interesting comparison may be had with the different approach taken by the Parliamentary draftsman when analogous provisions for the transfer of debts and other 'actionable claims' were legislated for application in India in the Indian Transfer of Property Act 1882.

First, after providing that 'a mere right to sue cannot be transferred',[182] and that '[p]roperty of any kind may be transferred, except as otherwise provided by this Act or by any other law for the time being in force',[183] s. 8. of the 1882 Indian Act provides that:

> Unless a different intention is expressed or necessarily implied, a transfer of property passes forthwith to the transferee *all* the interest which the transferor is then capable of passing in the property and in the legal incidents thereof.
>
> Such incidents include, when the property is land, the easements annexed thereto, the rents and profits thereof accruing after the transfer, and all things attached to the earth;
>
> ... and, where the property is a debt or other actionable claim, the securities therefor (except where they are also for other debts or claims not transferred to the transferee), but not arrears of interest accrued before the transfer;
>
> and, where the property is money or other property yielding income, the interest or income thereof accruing after the transfer takes effect.[184]

As to how property in respect of 'actionable claims' is to be transferred, s. 130 says:

> (1) The transfer of an actionable claim whether with or without consideration shall be effected only by the execution of an instrument in writing signed by the transferor or his duly authorized agent, shall be complete and effectual upon the execution of such instruments, and thereupon all the rights and remedies of the transferor, whether by way of damages or otherwise, shall vest in the transferee, whether such notice of the transfer as is hereinafter provided be given or not:
>
> PROVIDED that every dealing with the debtor other actionable claim by the debtor or other person from or against whom the transferor would, but for such instrument of transfer as aforesaid, have been entitled to

---

[182]  Transfer of Property Act 1882 (India), s. 6(e).

[183]  Ibid., s. 6.

[184]  H. S. Gour, *The Law of Transfer in British India* (4th edn, Calcutta: Thacker, Spink and Co., 1916) states that Transfer of Property Act 1882 (India), s. 8 was drawn from Conveyancing and Law of Property Act 1881, ss. 6 and 63.

recover or enforce such debt or other actionable claim, shall (save where the debtor or other person is a party to the transfer or has received express notice thereof as hereinafter provided) be valid as against such transfer.

(2) The transferee of an actionable claim may, upon the execution of such instrument of transfer as aforesaid, sue or institute proceedings for the same in his own name without obtaining the transferor's consent to such suit or proceeding and without making him a party thereto.

Section 131 then provides that a notice of transfer of an actionable claim shall be in a writing signed by the transferor or his duly authorized agent, and s. 132 stipulates that the transferee of an actionable claim shall take it subject to all the liabilities and equities to which the transferor was subject at the date of the transfer.[185]

Sections 130–32 of the Indian Act of 1882 do the work, and more, of s. 25(6) of the 1873 Act. When read with s. 8 of the 1882 Act, we see that the Act passes *all* the interest of the transferor in the property in question, and *all* the legal incidents arising in connection with that property, to the transferee. This may be contrasted with the considerably more elaborate (and restrained) language now found in s. 136(1).

The Indian Transfer of Property Act 1882 came into force on 1 July 1882,[186] seven years after the Judicature Act 1873. The difference between the effects of the two Acts is striking, given that the 1873 Act has no equivalent to s. 8. And although s. 8 of the 1882 Act appears to have been drawn from s. 63 of the Conveyancing and Law of Property Act 1881, and that section was re-enacted as s. 63, LPA1925, both iterations of s. 63 have only been applied to conveyances of estates in land, even though their wording, on their face, admit of a broader application.[187]

---

[185] The burdens owed by the transferor to the obligor are, accordingly, capable of being transferred under the Indian Transfer of Property Act 1882.

[186] Transfer of Property Act 1882, s. 1.

[187] The Conveyancing and Law of Property Act 1881 was repealed by LPA1925, s. 207 read with the 7th Schedule. Conveyancing and Law of Property Act 1881, s. 63 was re-enacted as LPA1925, s. 63. Although 'property' in both the Conveyancing and Law of Property Act 1881 and LPA1925 was defined to include real and personal property, and also any chose/thing in action (Conveyancing and Law of Property Act 1881, s. 2(i); LPA1925, s. 205(1)(xx)), the context within which Conveyancing and Law of Property Act 1881, s. 63 and LPA1925, s. 63 are to be read are dissimilar. It seems relatively clear that LPA1925, s. 63 is to be read merely as dealing with conveyances of estates in land, given that practically all of the sections before and after it are concerned with such convey-ances, and not conveyances of personalty such as things in action. No such limiting contextual clues are present with regard to the Conveyancing and Law of Property Act 1881, s. 63 of the 1881 Act. But even so, LPA1925, s. 63 is usually taken to be a mere restatement of the Conveyancing and Law of Property Act 1881, s. 63. If so, the latter

Given the above, rather than contorting the plain meaning of the words in s. 136(1), we should recognize their inherent limitations. Although we may say that the 'statutory' assignment provided by s. 136 (1) entails an extinction and a re-grant, only those entitlements specified in ss. 136(1)(a), (b) and (c) are affected, and the statute does not transfer any extraneous entitlements to the assignee.

The statutory modifications now found in s. 136(1) may therefore have a 'procedural' cast, since they 'merely' affect the assignor's power to bring a claim, all her legal and other remedies associated with the debt or thing in action assigned, and her power to give a good discharge in respect of such debt or thing in action assigned. Yet as with the Statutes of Set-off, these 'procedural' modifications effected substantive changes,[188] as they almost inevitably tend to do.[189] Therefore, although s. 136(1) is 'mere machinery',[190] it is procedural machinery that has substantive effects.

The above has suggested that statutory assignments are necessarily entwined with equitable assignments, so far as the debt or thing in question had been equitably assigned in the first place. Properly understood, s. 136(1) does not create an independent mode of assignment. Rather, assignments are effected in such manner as common law or equity may otherwise permit, supplemented by the effects in s. 136(1), where applicable. Hence, if the debt or thing in action had been equitably assigned, and if the requirements in s. 136(1) are satisfied, the entitlements set out in s. 136(1) are transferred to the assignee; no more, no less.

As will be explained in greater detail in Chapter 15, this affects how we conceive of the role of the rule in *Dearle* v. *Hall.* In brief, this means that

provision might never have been understood to have any operation with respect to assurances of things in action. See *Halsbury's Laws* (5th edn, 2012), vol. 32, para. 441, fn. 3.

[188] And consequently, the concern as to whether statutory assignments entail merely procedural or substantive effects is, arguably, misplaced: statutory assignments arising where the LPA1925, s. 136(1) requirements are met entail both, so far as the *procedural* changes effected by that section have *substantive* effects. Cf. Tolhurst (2016), chapter 5.

[189] 'The law of procedure exists only for the sake of giving efficacy ("execution and effect") to substantive law. But in doing so it tends to impose *conditions* on the execution of substantive law. It follows that adjective [i.e. procedural] law is both a necessary instrument of, and a potential obstacle to, the execution of substantive law': G. J. Postema, *Bentham and the Common Law Tradition* (Oxford: Clarendon Press, 1986), p. 342.

[190] *Marchant* v. *Morton, Down & Co.* [1901] 2 KB 829, 832 (Channell J); and *Torkington* v. *Magee Torkington* v. *Magee* [1902] 2 KB 427, 435.

the rule in *Dearle* v. *Hall* may be disapplied where disputes arise as to the priority in which the entitlements caught within ss. 136(1)(a), (b) or (c) are to be exercised in light of multiple and inconsistent assignments, some of which may be statutory. However, where the priority disputes pertain to entitlements falling beyond those enumerated in s. 136(1), then the rule in *Dearle* v. *Hall* will continue to be applicable. It also affects the validity of gifts of legal choses in action. But before moving on to Chapter 15, in which the impact of the analyses of equitable and statutory assignment set out in this book will be examined, the following chapter will compare and contrast the operation of an assignment under s. 136 (1), with other modes of assignment prescribed by statute.

# 14

# Statutory Dealings in Specific Classes of Intangible Assets

## A   Introduction

The preceding chapter has shown how LPA1925, s. 136(1), works. It has shown that Parliament did not create a mode of assignment which was substantively distinct from equitable assignment.

Section 136(1) does not transfer a debt or thing in action. It merely provides that, when there has been an assignment of a debt or thing in action, *certain* entitlements shall pass from the assignor and be transferred to the assignee. As the wording in s. 136(1) shows, Parliament simply intended to supplement the operation of what would otherwise be an equitable assignment *simpliciter*.

Section 136(1) may be applied, in general, to assignments of any debt or 'legal thing in action'. However, specific legislation providing for dealings in particular types or classes of choses in action have been enacted, for example, in connection with the transfer, transmission or vesting of various kinds of intellectual property entitlements, or with the assignment of certain kinds of policies of assurance. This chapter will examine a small selection of these statutory modes of dealing, applying the lessons learned from the analysis of s. 136(1) in Chapter 13, and also seeing how Parliament has used different techniques and different language to allow for different manners of dealing.

## B   Comparison: Patents, Copyright and Registered Trade Marks

In this section, comparisons will be drawn with the ways in which Parliament has legislated for the transfer, transmission or vesting of certain types of intellectual property, namely patents, copyright and trademarks. The aim in this section is not to provide an exhaustive account of the operation of these provisions. Rather, it is merely aimed at highlighting significant differences between these modes of dealing, and their relationship with equitable and statutory assignment pursuant to LPA1925, s. 136(1).

## (i) Patents

The first thing that should be noted is that patents have, from the outset, been 'assignable' at law. That is to say, the common law courts have long recognized and accepted that the benefit of a patent can be *conveyed* inter vivos from the grantee of a patent, to such person as he/she pleases, much in the way the legal title to realty or tangible personalty may be conveyed. The most important consequence of this is that, following an assignment of a patent, the former proprietor may no longer assert any of the entitlements associated with being a proprietor of a patent: the new proprietor becomes the *sole* entity with such entitlements. Thus, given cases like *Franklin Hocking & Co. Ltd* v. *Franklin Hocking*,[1] the editors of *Terrell on the Law of Patents* report that, '[w]hen a patent has been assigned, the new proprietor is entitled, in the absence of any provision in the assignment to the contrary, to prevent the assignor from manufacturing the patented article'.[2]

Following the assignment, the former proprietor is no longer proprietor of the patent at all: the 'new' proprietor is the entity to whom the patent had been assigned. Therefore, unless the former proprietor was licensed to do so, his continued manufacture of the patented article, post-assignment, would be an infringement of the monopoly granted by the patent. It would also follow that, following the assignment of the patent,[3] only the new proprietor may bring proceedings against an infringing party in respect of its infringement; only the new proprietor may validly grant licences to third parties to exploit the patent; and only the new proprietor may validly effect a further assignment of the patent.

Formerly, the power of a patent proprietor to effect an assignment with the above effect was explicitly set out in the terms of the grant of the letters patent by the Crown. As Littledale J observed in the King's Bench in 1830: 'All monopolies are illegal unless allowed by a patent, which cannot be assigned at all unless power[4] to that effect is given by the

---

[1] (1887) RPC 255, 259.

[2] Terrell (2016), para. 16-63.

[3] Assuming such assignment to have been validly effected in accordance with the formality requirements now set out in Patents Act 1977, s. 30(6).

[4] See also Patent Law Amendment Act 1852 (15 & 16 Vict, c. 83), s. 35.

Crown.'[5] Consequently, unlike other forms of intellectual property
(for example, copyright or registered trade marks), patents were capable
of being *legally* assigned so long as these words of assignability were
provided for in the grant of the patent (though any assignment[6] might
be subject to any restrictions imposed by the Crown when making the
grant).[7] As a result, there was no need for the court of Chancery to
provide assistance in the present 'transfer' of entitlements arising out of
a patent: there was, therefore, no room for a patent to be 'equitably
assigned'.[8]

Even though patents are now granted without such express words
permitting their assignment,[9] it would appear the old understanding is

---

[5] *Duvergier* v. *Fellows* (1830) 10 B & C 826, 829 (aff'd on appeal: *Duvergier* v. *Fellowes*
(1832) 1 Cl & F 39).

[6] Though the position has been relaxed in subsequent legislation (as to which, now see
Patents Act 1977, s. 30(6)), formerly, a patent could only be 'legally assigned' by the due
execution of a deed of assignment because, 'a patent which is created by deed can only be
assigned by deed': *Re Casey's Patents* [1892] 1 Ch 104, 113 (Lindley LJ).

[7] A patent could also be granted on terms that if it were assigned otherwise than in
accordance with its provisions, the patent would be invalidated. For example, in *Duvergier*
v. *Fellows* (1830) 10 B & C 826, the court was concerned with a patent which provided that
if it were assigned to or held in trust for more than five persons, the patent would be
rendered void. Presumably, this meant that the patent would be void if it were assigned to
more than five persons jointly by way of a tenancy in common or joint tenancy.

[8] Save, perhaps, in connection with cases where there was a specifically enforceable
*agreement* to 'assign' a patent: see text to n. 14, below.

[9] The standard preamble to form of grant of a patent by the Crown as set out in the
Schedule of the Patents Rules 1968 (SI 1968/1389) provided as follows:

> KNOW YE, THEREFORE, that We, of our especial grace, certain know-
> ledge, and mere motion do by these presents, for Us, our heirs and
> successors, give and *grant unto the person(s) above named and any succes-*
> *sor(s), executor(s), administrator(s) and assign(s) (each and any of whom*
> *are hereinafter referred to as the patentee)* our especial licence, full power,
> sole privilege, and authority, that the patentee or any agent or licensee of
> the patentee and no others, may subject to the conditions and provisions
> prescribed by any statute or order for the time being in force at all times
> hereafter during the term of years herein mentioned, make, use, exercise
> and vend the said invention within our United Kingdom of Great Britain
> and Northern Ireland, and the Isle of Man, and that the patentee shall have
> and enjoy the whole profit and advantage from time to time accruing by
> reason of the said invention during the term of sixteen years from the date
> hereunder written of these presents: . . . [emphasis added]

The 1968 Rules came into force from 1 November 1968, but were revoked following
the enactment of the Patents Act 1977 by SI 1978/216.

not lost, merely reformulated.[10] Arguably, the old understanding is retained (though perhaps somewhat obtusely) by the wording of Patents Act 1977, s. 30: '(1) Any patent or application for a patent is personal property [(without being a thing in action)], and any patent or an such application and rights in or under it may be [transferred, created or granted] in accordance with subsections (2) to (7) below.'

Two points may be noted in respect of this provision. First, by making it clear that patents are personal property, but not things in action, patents cannot be made the subject matter of a present equitable assignment. This also means that the statutory effects arising from LPA1925 s. 136(1) may not be applied to such dealings in a patent.[11]

Second, s. 30(1), the principal operative section, does not use the verb 'to assign'. Instead, it refers to a patent (or an application for a patent) being 'transferred . . . or granted'. These words reflect the historical position, that patents have always been capable of being legally *transferred* (that is, conveyed), in the manner mentioned above.

There are certain formal requirements in order for a patent to be presently transferred. Section 30 goes on to set out how a patent may be transferred:

(2) Subject to section 36(3) below, any patent or any such application, or any right in it, may be assigned or mortgaged. . . .

(5) Subsections (2) to (4) above shall have effect subject to the following provisions of this Act.

(6) Any of the following transactions, that is to say –

(a) any assignment or mortgage of a patent or any such application, or any right in a patent or any such application;

(b) any assent relating to any patent or any such application or right;

shall be void unless it is in writing and is signed by or on behalf of the parties[12] to the transaction (or, in the case of an assent or other

---

[10]  The conception that a patent was granted to the inventor and his assigns is preserved, to an extent, in the Patents Act 1977, s. 7(2). The assignees of an inventor of an invention are entitled to be granted a patent pursuant to s. 7(2)(c): Terrell (2016), paras. 4–20; as are the (sub-)assignees of such assignees: Roughton, Johnson & Cook (2014), para. 9.15.

[11]  It is suggested in Roughton, Johnson & Cook (2016), para. 10.3 that, in *Letter F: Juridical Nature of Patents and Patent Applications and Registration of Interests therein* (Parliamentary Counsel Papers, Patents Bill 1977), the Parliamentary Draftsman confirmed that LPA1925, s. 136(1) is not applicable to assignments of patents.

[12]  The formality requirement that the assignment be in a writing signed by both parties to the assignment was amended by reg. 10 of the Regulatory Reform (Patents) Order 2004 (SI 2004/2357) such that assignments after 1 January 2005 need only be made in a writing signed by or on behalf of the assignor alone.

transaction by a personal representative, by or on behalf of the personal representative) or in the case of a body corporate is so signed or is under the seal of that body.

Consequently, a *transfer* by assignment of a patent which does not conform with the formalities mandated by s. 30(6) is void.[13]

That said, notwithstanding the invalidity of a purported transfer for non-compliance with s. 30(6), it may be that the facts of the case permit a finding that the parties had entered into an *agreement* to transfer the patent. If the facts were such as to permit the equitable doctrine of conversion to apply, such agreement to transfer the patent could be given effect in equity, as Jacob J suggested in *Baxter International Inc.* v. *Nederlands Produktielaboratorium vood Bloedtransfusiapparatuur BV.*[14]

In that case, a patent was assigned in writing by the original proprietors to an intermediate assignee, but the writing was not signed by the intermediate assignee. The intermediate assignee then made a further assignment to the first plaintiff, but again, the first plaintiff did not sign the further assignment. The formality requirements of s. 30(6) were thus not fulfilled in respect of either the first or the further assignment. However, both assignments contained covenants of further assurance in which the respective assignors covenanted that they would execute all documents necessary to vest title in the said patents in the respective assignees.

When the first plaintiff sued the defendant for patent infringement, the defendant contended that, as the requirements of s. 30(6) had not been satisfied, the first assignment was void, and so the intermediate assignee had nothing to assign to the first plaintiff. The defendant therefore contended that the first plaintiff should be struck out as they had not been assigned the patent in question. Jacob J rejected the contention on the basis that although the assignments were void so far as one was concerned with their assignment in accordance with the provisions of the 1977 Act, he was prepared to hold that the documents which had been signed by the original proprietors and the intermediate assignee amounted to agreements to assign. Then, by reason of the equitable doctrine of conversion, such agreement to assign would be given effect

---

[13] A transfer of a patent pursuant to Patents Act 1977, s. 30(6) is a registrable transaction: s. 33(3); and registration of a registrable transaction confers certain effects, notably those set out in s. 33(1). However, registration is not required for the transfer to be valid.

[14] [1998] RPC 250.

as an equitable assignment, equity deeming as done that which ought to be done.[15]

If correctly decided, this case suggests that although a patent may not be presently transferred in any manner other than in accordance with the formal requirements set out in s. 30(6), where the facts show that there was, in essence, an agreement to transfer a patent, it appears that the promisee to such *agreement* to transfer, if supported by valuable consideration, could be regarded in equity as the 'proprietor' of the patent, at least as against the promisor to such agreement, and any volunteers claiming the benefit of the patent through such assignor, or any purchasers claiming the benefit of the patent through such assignor, but who had taken with notice of the promisee's equitable interest. However, it seems unlikely that such promisee, relying on his equitable interest arising from the agreement to assign, may invoke the powers of a proprietor of a patent to apply to the comptroller to allow the specification of the patent to be amended,[16] to seek the restoration of a patent following a failure to pay fees for its renewal,[17] to surrender the patent,[18] or, as Jacob J was prepared to accept, to bring proceedings in their sole name against patent infringers to obtain final judgment.[19] Though the promisee could certainly obtain equitable injunctive relief to compel the promisor to do any of these acts, the promisee would not be entitled to act in its own right, no such right having been effectively assigned to the promisee.

---

[15] Ibid., 253. That said, the report does not make it clear whether the assignments had been made for valuable and executed consideration. If the assignments had been purely voluntary, the equitable rule on which Jacob J relied would not have been available. Assuming executed consideration had been given, the equitable doctrine of conversion would apply (see the judgments of Baron Gilbert and Baron Price in *The Earl of Coventry's Case* (1724), as reported in an Appendix to R. Francis, *Maxims of Equity* (3rd edn, London: Henry Lintot, 1746). Although this case is also reported in 10 Mod 463, that report does not reproduce the judgments of Baron Gilbert or Baron Price). See also Ashburner (1933), p. 258. Consequently, the remedy of injunction would be available to the promisee to compel the promisor to execute the requisite legal formalities to transfer the patent by reason of the promisee's equitable beneficial interest arising by reason of this doctrine. If no executed consideration had been furnished (not even in part), but executory consideration had been given in support of the promise to transfer the patent, an equitable beneficial interest might be vested in the promisee so far as the remedy of specific performance might be available to him, by analogy with the doctrine in *Walsh* v. *Lonsdale* (1882) 21 Ch D 9, 14.

[16] Patents Act 1977, s. 27(1).

[17] Ibid., s. 28(2).

[18] Ibid., s. 29(1).

[19] [1998] RPC 250, 253–4.

Finally, it may be noted that it was formerly possible for a patent to be dealt with under the Patents Act 1949 in respect of a *part* of the United Kingdom:

> **21.** – (1) A patent sealed with the seal of the Office shall have the same effect as if it were sealed with the Great Seal of the United Kingdom, and shall have effect throughout the United Kingdom and the Isle of Man:
>
> Provided that a patent may be assigned for any place in or part of the United Kingdom or Isle of Man as effectually as if it were granted so as to extend to that place or part only.

Although the grant of a patent in the United Kingdom under the 1949 Act would have been a grant of a singular entitlement, this provision would have had the effect of allowing such singular unitary grant to be treated as if multiple grants had been made in respect of the various territorial and geographical regions which make up the United Kingdom: what had been a grant of a singular patent monopoly is deemed to have been granted fragmentarily. Thus, if A, the holder of a patent X, desired to assign a 'part' of that patent to C so far as the patent might be applied within the City of London, the grant would be treated as if two grants had been made to A, one to A in respect of the City of London, and another in respect of the United Kingdom *excluding* the City of London. It would then be possible for A to effect a conveyance of one of these two grants (the one pertaining to the City of London) to C.

No equivalent provision may be found, however, in the Patents Act 1977.[20] It is no longer possible for *this* kind of 'partial' dealing in a fragment of patent to be effected as a matter of English law. However, the language used in s. 21(1) of the 1949 Act puts forward an interesting contrast to the legislative position in respect of partial assignments of copyright under the Copyright, Designs and Patents Act 1988, and the Trade Marks Act 1994, as the following will show.

---

[20] Today, if A wished to confer C the entitlement to exploit the patent within a particular geographical region within the United Kingdom today, A could grant C an exclusive licence to that effect. And if A also wished for C to be empowered to bring proceedings in right of A for patent infringements within that region, there is nothing to preclude A from granting C the requisite authority to do so. These would not, however, insulate C from the effects of A's insolvency or bankruptcy. Insulation of C from such insolvency risks could, nevertheless, still be achieved if A were to equitably assign such 'parts' of A's patent to C as C might be interested to acquire.

## (ii)   Copyright

Under the Copyright, Designs and Patents Act 1988, certain statutory provisions may be found relating to dealings in copyright by the holder thereof. Copyright is a right arising at common law, and so, may be said to be a common law chose in action.[21] The 1988 Act provides:

> **90.** – (1) Copyright is transmissible by assignment, by testamentary disposition or by operation of law, as personal or moveable property.
>
> (2) An assignment or other transmission of copyright may be partial, that is, limited so as to apply –
>
> (a) to one or more, but not all, of the things the copyright owner has the exclusive right to do;
>
> (b) to part, but not the whole, of the period for which the copyright is to subsist.
>
> (3) An assignment of copyright is not effective unless it is in writing signed by or on behalf of the assignor.

Analogous wording may be found in respect of unregistered[22] design rights,[23] and also a performer's property rights.[24] These provisions have

---

[21] It had been a matter of debate if copyright amounted to a chose in action at all: see the debate in H. W. Elphinstone, 'What Is a Chose in Action?' (1893) 9 LQR 311; S. Brodhurst, 'Is Copyright a Chose in Action?' (1895) 11 LQR 64; T. Cyprian Williams, 'Property, Things in Action and Copyright' (1895) 11 LQR 223; Charles Sweet, 'Choses in Action' (1895) 11 LQR 238. The proposition in this book is that it is, for the purposes of the law of equitable assignment, even though a copyright (like most intellectual property rights) cannot, strictly speaking, be reduced into possession through the bringing of an action. Given the statutory language, it would appear Parliament had accepted this to be so, given its conception that copyright was to be 'transmissible' by 'assignment': See below.

[22] Registered designs are dealt with under the Registered Designs Act 1949, as amended by the Copyright, Designs and Patents Act 1988 and the EC Designs Directive (Directive 98/71/EC). Section 19 of the 1949 Act provides that, 'when a person becomes entitled by assignment, transmission or operation of law to a registered design ... he shall apply ... for the registration of his title as proprietor'. There is no provision setting out what an 'assignment' for the purposes of the 1949 Act may be. Consequently, it seems that s. 19 may have co-opted the institution of equitable assignment, adopting the same legislative technique as was used for LPA1925, s. 136(1). The effect of such an assignment has, however, been clarified with certain amendments introduced by the Intellectual Property (Enforcement, etc). Regulations SI 2006/1028). First, reg. 15A provides that a registered design right is personal property. Second reg, 15B(1) provides that, '[a] registered design ... is *transmissible* by assignment, testamentary disposition or operation of law in the same way as other personal or moveable property' (emphasis added). Given s. 15B(1), the analysis in the main text as to how copyright may be transmitted would also apply to registered designs.

[23] Copyright, Designs and Patents Act 1988, s. 222.

[24] Ibid., s. 191B.

also been extended to apply to the transmission of the publication right,[25] and the database right.[26] The discussion below, however, will concentrate on the transmission of copyright.

First of all, we should note that s. 90(1) does not merely provide for the assignability of copyright: it provides that copyright is transmissible by, inter alia, assignment. The concepts of 'transmission' and 'assignment' must therefore be distinct.[27]

Second, like the provision in LPA1925, s. 136(1), s. 90 does not answer the question '*what* is an "assignment" of a copyright?' Section 90(3) simply states that, in order for an 'assignment' of a copyright to be validly made, such 'assignment' must be in writing signed by the 'assignor'.[28] This tells us *how* a valid assignment is to be made. But as to *what* such an 'assignment of a copyright' *is*, we are left none the wiser. Like LPA1925, s. 136(1), s. 90 sets out no substantively distinct conception of 'assignment' on its own terms. As will be argued below, s. 90 merely co-opts or builds upon pre-existing conceptions of assignment without creating any novel statutory variant, and this has been the position since the Copyright Act 1911.

Section 90 re-enacts s. 36, Copyright Act 1956, and the two provisions are *in pari materia*. In both, we find legislative reference to how copyright may be transmitted in a number of ways, one being assignment. This may be contrasted with s. 5 of the Copyright Act 1911, which merely provided that a copyright could be assigned as a whole,[29] or even partially.[30] Even so, each of these provisions simply states that copyright

---

[25] SI 1996/2967, reg. 17.

[26] SI 1997/3032, reg. 23. The following rights arising under the Copyright, Designs and Patents Act 1988 are, however, not assignable *inter vivos*: Moral rights arising under Ch. IV (s. 94); and the performer's non-property rights (s. 192A(1)).

[27] Keeping in mind the exhortation in *Read* v. *Brown* (1888) 22 QBD 128 that every word in a statute should be given effect to.

[28] 1988 Act, s. 90(3). For unregistered design rights, see s. 222(3).

[29] Copyright Act 1911, s. 5(1).

[30] Ibid., s. 5(2). Under the 1988 Act, copyright is vested in the 'owner' of the copyright (s. 16), and the author of a work is the 'first owner' of the copyright arising from that work (s. 11(1)). This elaborates on the position under Copyright Act 1956, s. 4, which simply provided that the copyright in works arising under the 1956 Act vested in the author of such work. Given the wording of Copyright Act 1911, s. 2(1), one may infer that copyright in a work arising under that Act would be in the 'owner' of the copyright, and by s. 5(1), the author would be the 'first owner' of that copyright.

This may be contrasted with the position under earlier legislation. Under the first Copyright Act of 1709 (the Statute of Anne, 8 Anne c. 19), the Crown granted copyright to the author of books then printed for a term of twenty-one years, and to books not then printed the sole right to have them printed for a term of fourteen years, and the grant was

may be assigned, and also stipulates *how* a valid copyright 'assignment' may be made. But they do not set out *what* amounts to an assignment of such copyright. As with LPA1925, s. 136(1), these provisions exhibit a strikingly similar unconcern over this question.

Given the language of s. 90 of the 1988 Act, we see that it does not appear to rest on a conception of 'legal' *assignment* as would involve a *transfer* of a copyright 'at law'. It relies, instead, on the concept of *transmission* of copyright, of which 'assignment' is merely one mode of 'transmission'.[31] Though the language is different from that used in connection with the 'transfer' of patents under the Patents Act 1977, it is submitted that the result is the same. Just as a transfer of a patent substitutes the transferee for the transferor as proprietor of the patent, where there has been a transmission of copyright by means of an assignment, the 'transmittee'/assignee is substituted for the 'transmittor'/assignor as holder of the copyright. However, that is not to say that the statute mandates any particular mode of *assignment* which is distinct from equitable assignment.

As explained in Chapter 13, the unconcern in LPA1925, s. 136(1) with identifying what an assignment of a 'debt or legal thing in action' might be shows that Parliament's strategy was to build on the existing institution of equitable assignment: there was no need to build a new engine from the ground up because the old one would do. By parity of reasoning with the analysis in Chapter 13, it would seem to follow that an 'assignment' of a 1988 Act copyright operates by way of an *equitable* assignment. However, the operation of s. 90(3) of the 1988 Act is analogous to the operation of LPA1925, s. 53(1)(c).

---

expressly made to the author, and also to the author's assigns. The grant of a copyright under the 1709 Act was therefore akin to the grant of a patent by the Crown prior to 1977 (although protection for the grantee of a copyright was only allowed for books whose titles had been registered with the Company of Stationers). The need for registration was only abolished under the Copyright Act 1842 (5 & 6 Vict, c. 45), though under the 1842 Act, the grant of copyright in a work was still made to the author and his assigns (see s. 3, 'assigns' being defined in s. 2 to 'mean and include every person in whom the interest of an author in copyright shall be vested, whether derived from such author before or after the publication of any book, and whether acquired by sale, gift, bequest, or by operation of law or otherwise'). As noted above, however, the manner by which copyright was vested under the 1911, 1956 and 1988 Acts was/is different, since such copyright is *not* vested in 'assigns' by reason of the grant.

[31] The provisions for transmission of copyright under the Copyright, Designs and Patents Act 1988 are also applied to the publication right (SI 1996/2967, reg. 17) and the database right (SI 1997/3032, reg. 23).

Just as compliance with the formalities imposed by that section is mandatory for an equitable assignment of a subsisting equitable chose or thing in action to be valid, compliance with the formalities of s. 90(3) of the 1988 Act is mandatory for an equitable assignment of a copyright to be valid. But if s. 90(3) was complied with, the equitable assignment of that copyright *would* have been validly made: such formally valid equitable assignment would then, by statute, *transmit* the copyright from the assignor to her assignee.[32] As to what such 'transmission' entails, the 1988 Act does not tell us, though we can make an educated guess.

It has never been doubted that, following the transmission of a copyright pursuant to a validly executed assignment, the assignee may bring proceedings against a defendant for copyright infringement in the assignee's own name: joinder of the assignor in such contexts has never been an issue.[33] It would seem to follow, then, that when there has been a transmission of copyright by a valid assignment, there would have been a substitutive transfer of the assignor (who had initiated such transmission by executing a formally valid assignment of the copyright in the form of a signed writing, as required by s. 90(3)), by her assignee (to whom the copyright would have been transmitted by that very assignment).[34]

The proposition above, that 'assignment' in s. 90 pertains to and builds on the institution of equitable assignment, rests on the explicit provision in s. 90(2) that it is possible to effect a *partial* assignment of a copyright. Section 90(2) tells us that the holder of a copyright may effect an assignment *or* some other mode of 'transmission'[35] of something less than the entire suite of entitlements making up the copyright,[36] or for a

---

[32] Compliance with s 90(3) would also trigger the operation of LPA1925, s. 136(1). However, the entitlements 'transferred' by the latter would be overshadowed by the transmission effected by s 90(1) under the 1988 Act. On the other hand, non-compliance with s 90(3) would render an equitable assignment of a copyright to be wholly ineffective and void. There would then be nothing for LPA1925, s. 136(1) to 'transfer'; nor would there be anything for s 90(1) to 'transmit'.

[33] Copinger (2016), para. 5-77: the point appears to be so self-evident and well accepted that no authorities are cited.

[34] The same analysis would apply, *mutatis mutandis*, in respect of transmission of unregistered design rights under the 1988 Act, s. 222(1).

[35] In the context, since s. 90(1) of the 1988 Act provides that copyright is transmissible by assignment, by testamentary disposition or by operation of law, it would seem to follow that the 'other transmissions' referred to in s. 90(2) must refer to the ways by which copyright is transmissible, other than by assignment.

[36] 1988 Act, s. 90(2)(a).

lesser period than the whole of the remaining period for which those entitlements are to persist pending expiry.[37]

It would be an error to take s. 90(2) as having provided that one may effect a transmission of a *part* of one's copyright, in the same ways as s. 90(1) allows for the transmission of the whole of it. Section 90(1) provides that copyright is transmissible by assignment, by testamentary disposition or by operation of law. It is arguable, therefore, that the 'other transmissions' referred to in s. 90(2) refer to the *other* ways by which copyright is transmissible, apart from assignment. That is to say, s. 90(2) sets out the proposition that it is possible to equitably assign a copyright in part, to make a grant by way of testamentary disposition of a copyright in part, or to apply such other rule as permits 'transmission by operation of law' *apart from* assignments or testamentary dispositions, of a part of the copyright. Leaving those matters aside, though, s. 90(2) simply tells us what an assignment may do: we are told that we may assign *parts* of a copyright; and that although parts of a copyright may well be *transmitted* by operation of law apart from assignment or testamentary disposition, that would be a matter for the rules in those other branches of the law.

A copyright comprises of a diverse range of entitlements.[38] But the holder thereof is conceived of as holding *a* copyright.[39] A whole is made up of the sum of its parts, yet not one of the parts can be said to be the whole. So, too, is a copyright made up of the various entitlements spelt out in the 1988 Act: none of the individual entitlements may be said to be *that* copyright, or *a* copyright in its own right. Given this, the provision in s. 90(2) as to how the holder of a copyright may assign parts of her entitlements arising from that copyright is a clear indicator of the equitable nature of the assignment.

The parallel, here, is with assignments of debts. When A lends B £10,000, thereby creating a debt of £10,000, B is obligated to A in a *single* debt of £10,000: A is owed a single debt of £10,000, and not 10,000 debts of £1 each. Since a debt comprises a single chose (albeit one which entails a multitude of entitlements),[40] and since the common law does not allow for such entitlements to be broken up and dealt with in

---

[37] Ibid., s. 90(2)(b). For expiry of copyright, see Copyright, Designs and Patents Act 1988, ss. 12–15. For expiry of unregistered design rights, see Copyright, Designs and Patents Act 1988, s. 216(1).

[38] Namely those set out in the 1988 Act, ss. 16–21.

[39] 1988 Act, s. 1(1): 'Copyright is *a* property right' (emphasis added).

[40] For example, A has the power to give a good discharge by executing a deed of release; the power to make an offer of variation; the power to permit B to discharge the debt by accepting a conforming tender of payment, to name a few.

disparate units, it is not possible for the statutorily mandated effects set out in LPA1925, ss. 136(1)(a), (b) or (c) to be passed from A to C if all that A had assigned was, say, £2,000 out of the £10,000 which was owed by B. It is for this reason that it is not possible for *parts* of a debt to be made the subject of a statutory assignment pursuant to LPA1925, s. 136 (1): assignments of parts of a debt (conceived of as a singular thing in action) can only be effected using the conceptual device of an *equitable* assignment.[41] If so, that must be the kind of 'assignment' which is in play, too, in s. 90(2) of the 1988 Act so far as it recognizes that it is possible to 'assign' a copyright 'partially'.[42]

There is also another aspect of the legislative wording which is striking, for the 1988 Act provides that it is possible for copyright in works which have yet to come in existence to be assigned. Thus, it is possible to *vest* a 'future' copyright by way of a signed agreement to assign such 'future' copyright:[43]

> **91.** – (1) Where by an agreement made in relation to future copyright, and signed by or on behalf of the prospective owner of the copyright, the prospective owner purports to assign the future copyright (wholly or partially) to another person, then if, on the copyright coming into existence, the assignee or another person claiming under him would be entitled as against all other persons to require the copyright to be vested

---

[41] See *Re Steel Wing Company, Ltd* [1921] 1 Ch 349.

[42] Given the discussion in the main text, it may be necessary to reconsider certain *dicta* in Lord Uthwatt's speech in *Withers (H.M. Inspector of Taxes)* v. *Neversole* [1948] 1 All ER 400 in connection with 'partial assignments' under the Copyright Act 1911 (at p. 404): 'A partial assignment can only mean an assignment of some of the rights included in the copyright. The effect of a partial assignment of copyright for a period less than the whole term is not to create any new right, but only to divide the existing right. In the result, there are two separate owners, each with a distinct property. Neither holds under the other. Nothing new, except a position which may give rise to friction, has been created.' This observation was not strictly necessary to the holding of the House of Lords, which was that the partial assignment effected a sale of part of the assignor's capital assets, and so the monies raised were not taxable as income. It may also be noted that the wording under the 1911 Act was significantly different, so far as it provided in s. 5(3) that, '[w]here, under any partial assignment of copyright, the assignee becomes entitled to any right comprised in copyright, the assignee as respects the right so assigned, and the assignor as respects the rights not assigned, shall be treated for the purposes of this Act as the owner of the copyright, and the provisions of this Act shall have effect accordingly.' Given the distinction in the 1988 Act between transmission of copyright, of which assignment of copyright is but one way to effect such transmission, it is arguable that Lord Uthwatt's reasoning may no longer be valid, given the changed wording of the legislation. On the problems created by 'partial assignment' of copyright, see discussion below in connection with the facts in Example 14.1.

[43] The analogous provision with regard to unregistered design rights is found in the 1988 Act, s. 223.

in him, the copyright shall vest in the assignee or his successor in title by virtue of this subsection.

(2) In this Part –

'future copyright' means copyright which will or may come into existence in respect of a future work or class of works or on the occurrence of a future event; and

'prospective owner' shall be construed accordingly, and includes a person who is prospectively entitled to copyright by virtue of such an agreement as is mentioned in subsection (1).

In this connection, the consensus appears to be that, given the requirement that such 'assignments' are to be by way of *agreement*, whereas otherwise there need only be a written document signed by the assignor, these assignments of 'future' copyrights are only possible where a contract supported by consideration to effect an assignment has been made.[44]

Again, one could compare this kind of 'assignment' with the law on equitable assignment on future choses in action, i.e. choses in action which have yet to arise at the time of the supposed assignment. Indeed, reference may be made to the decision of the House of Lords in *Performing Right Society Ltd* v. *London Theatre of Varieties Ltd* in which the assignment of copyrights in works yet to be written at the time of their purported assignment were in issue. In that case, which concerned assignments of copyrights pursuant to the Copyright Act 1911 (in which there was no equivalent provision to what is now s. 91 in the 1988 Act), Viscount Cave LC held as follows:[45]

Sect. 5, sub-s. 2, of the [1911] Act provides that the author of a work may assign the copyright either wholly or partially and may grant any interest in the right by licence, but that 'no such assignment or grant shall be valid unless it is in writing signed by the owner of the right in respect of which the assignment or grant is made or by his duly authorised agent.' ... There was on the respective dates of the instruments under which the appellants claim no existing copyright in the songs in question, and therefore no owner of any such right; and this being so, neither of those instruments can be held to have been an assignment 'signed by the owner of the right' within the meaning of the section.[46] No doubt when a person executes a document purporting to assign property to be afterwards acquired by him, that property on its acquisition passes in equity to the assignee: *Holroyd* v. *Marshall*;[47] *Tailby* v. *Official Receiver*;[48] but how such

---

[44] See e.g. Copinger (2016), para. 5-112(e).
[45] [1924] AC 1 (HL), 13.
[46] See also ibid., 23–4 (Lord Atkinson).
[47] (1862) 10 HL Cas 191.
[48] (1888) 13 App Cas 523.

a subsequent acquisition can be held to relate back, so as to cause an instrument which on its date was not an assignment under the Act to become such an assignment, I am unable to understand. The appellants have a right in equity to have the performing rights assigned to them and in that sense are equitable owners of those rights; but they are not assignees of the rights within the meaning of the statute.

As a matter of the general law, it is plainly possible to effect an 'equitable assignment' of future choses in action, so long as the facts support a finding that there was, in fact, an agreement to assign such chose in action, as and when it arose, and which was supported by valuable consideration. But, being an equitable assignment, the usual problems of joinder would surface. As the House of Lords held in *Performing Right Society*, no final injunctive relief would be ordered unless and until the assignor was joined,[49] and thus the Court of Appeal below had rightly dismissed the Society's suit for such perpetual injunction as it had refused to join the assignors.[50] It would seem[51] that this led to the introduction of s. 37 of the Copyright Act 1956:

> **37.** – (1) Where by an agreement made in relation to any future copyright, and signed by or on behalf of the prospective owner of the copyright, the prospective owner purports to assign the future copyright (wholly or partially) to another person (in this subsection referred to as 'the assignee'), then if, on the coming into existence of the copyright, the assignee or a person claiming under him would, apart from this subsection, be entitled as against all other persons to require the copyright to be vested in him (wholly or partially, as the case may be), the copyright shall, on its coming into existence, vest in the assignee or his successor in title accordingly by virtue of this subsection and without further assurance.

This wording has been substantially adopted in s. 91 of the 1988 Act, albeit in slightly simpler form.[52] But what is important here is to note that the *object* of s. 91, is not the 'agreement to assign': the object of s. 91

---

[49] As explained in Chapter 7, this would ensure that the assignors, when joined, would be bound by the decision of the court by reason of *res judicata*. For judicial support, see Lord Sumner's speech in *Performing Right Society* (n. 45), 31.

[50] *Performing Right Society* (n. 45), 15 (Viscount Cave LC); 18, 20 (Viscount Finlay); 31–2 (Lord Sumner).

[51] *B4U Network (Europe) Limited* v. *Performing Right Society Limited* [2013] EWCA Civ 1236; [2014] Bus LR 207, [11].

[52] It also forms the basis of the equivalent provision, s. 223(1), for 'future' unregistered design rights.

is the vesting of such 'future copyright' as had been the subject of the 'agreement to assign' upon its coming into existence. Where, say, the agreement to assign pertained to 'future copyright' in a literary work yet to be created, once that work was written, the author of that work would be the 'first owner' of the copyright pursuant to ss. 9 and 11 (in most cases), but then, s. 91(1) would vest the copyright arising at that point in the promisee to the agreement to assign.[53] Given such statutorily mandated vesting, there would then not be any need to join the promisor who had promised to assign that 'future' copyright.

Close reading of ss. 90 and 91 reveal that although these sections create distinctive conceptual statutory constructs (respectively, those of *transmission* of copyright, and the *vesting* of 'future copyright'), they do not create distinct modes of assignment. On the contrary: these provisions rest upon pre-existing notions of assignment, in particular, equitable assignment. But does this matter?

In one respect, it most certainly does. As mentioned above, all that s. 90(2) does is recognize that it is possible to assign a 'part' of a copyright by reference either to time periods or to particular types of entitlement within the copyright. On the analysis above, such assignment is necessarily equitable: that is, s. 90(2) does not provide for a deemed fragmentation of the copyright, as s. 21 of the Patents Act 1949 would formerly have done in respect of 'partial' assignments of a patent. This has advantageous consequences, as Example 14.1 shows.

---

**EXAMPLE 14.1**

A, the author of a literary work which was published in 2010, has assigned the benefit of her copyright in that work to C for a period of two years commencing from the beginning of 2020, in accordance with s. 90(2)(a) of the 1988 Act.

It is now 2021, and piracy of the work in breach of the copyright in it has become rampant. But instead of commencing proceedings against the copyright infringers, C is content to sit back and to let the infringers do their worst.

---

Obviously, continued production of illicit copies of the work would adversely affect the residual value of the copyright to A, when the two-year period of copyright which had been assigned to C lapsed.

---

[53] See *Performing Right Society Limited* v. *B4U Network (Europe) Limited* [2012] EWHC 3010 (Ch), [54]–[55].

If assignment of copyright under the 1988 Act operated by way of a substitutive transfer of C in place of A so that C replaced A as holder of the copyright for the period of the assignment, then it would follow that A could have *no* entitlement as copyright-holder during that period since she would *not* be the holder of the copyright for those two years. So, unless C had covenanted with A that C would bring such proceedings on A's direction, A would be powerless.

That, however, would not be the case on the model of assignment set out in this section of the book: since the assignment of the copyright for those two years would still be an equitable one, A would *not* 'drop out' and be replaced by C as holder of the copyright for that period. Rather, all that would have happened would be that A had enabled C to invoke A's entitlements as holder of the copyright, such that both C *and* A might invoke them for the two years commencing in 2020. Accordingly, not having 'lost' her entitlements for the duration of the two-year period, it would still be open to A to mount enforcement proceedings against the copyright-infringing pirates, if C were to take no steps to defend his (and A's) entitlements arising from the copyright. A ought, therefore, to be entitled to obtain an injunction to enjoin the pirates from continuing with their acts of infringement, without having to wait for the two-year period to run out.[54]

Had Parliament intended for it to be possible for copyright to be transmissible in parts, it would have been simple enough for it to have used language in s. 90(2) which mirrored the language in s. 90 (1). But that was not the language enacted by Parliament. If read carefully, we can see that Parliament's intention in s. 90(2) was not to allow for the partial transmission of copyright, but to recognize that it was possible for parts of a copyright, namely, by reference to one or more of the copyright-holder's exclusive entitlements by reason of such holding, or by reference to parts of the period for which the copyright was to subsist, to be assigned. There is, accordingly, no transmission of parts of a copyright: and assignments of such parts of a copyright must operate independently of the statute, the statute

---

[54] The details of assessment of loss (whose loss?) and quantification of damages will have to be examined elsewhere. But the principle, at least, seems relatively clear: it should be possible for A to not only obtain an injunction to compel the pirates to cease and desist – if the infringers' actions can be shown to impact on A's future loss after the two-year period ended, then it should still be possible for A to recover substantial damages for such future loss from the infringing parties.

merely recognising that a copyright could indeed continue to be *equitably* assigned, in part.

### (iii)  Registered Trade Marks

Statutory provision has also been made with respect to assignments of registered trade marks. The Trade Marks Act 1994 provides as follows:

> **24.** – (1) A registered trade mark is transmissible by assignment, testamentary disposition or operation of law in the same way as other personal or moveable property.
>
> It is so transmissible either in connection with the goodwill of a business or independently.
>
> (2) An assignment or other transmission of a registered trade mark may be partial, that is, limited so as to apply –
>
> (a) in relation to some but not all of the goods or services for which the trade mark is registered, or
> (b) in relation to use of the trade mark in a particular manner or a particular locality.
>
> (3) An assignment of a registered trade mark, or an assent relating to a registered trade mark, is not effective unless it is in writing signed by or on behalf of the assignor or, as the case may be, a personal representative.
>
> Except in Scotland, this requirement may be satisfied in a case where the assignor or personal representative is a body corporate by the affixing of its seal.

The wording in this provision is strikingly similar to the provisions in s. 90 of the Copyright, Designs and Patents Act 1988: the provisions are, in essence, identical, leaving aside differences in wording necessitated by the nature of a registered trade mark. Given the similarity of wording, the observations which were made above in connection with the transmission of copyright under the 1988 Act would apply, *mutatis mutandis,* to the transmission of registered trade marks under the Trade Marks Act 1994. For the same reasons, we may conclude that s. 24 of the Trade Marks Act 1994 merely co-opts equitable assignment as one of the means by which a registered trade mark may be 'transmitted', though it prescribes that such assignments would be ineffective if made other than in a writing signed by the assignor:[55] it does not create any distinct mode of assignment on its own terms.

---

[55] An invalidating function which is similar to that provided by LPA1925, s. 53(1)(c), in connection with equitable assignments of subsisting equitable things in action.

## C   Comparison: Policies of Assurance Act 1867 and Marine Insurance Act 1906

To round off the comparative exercise, in this section, comparisons will be made with the legislative provisions dealing with the assignment by the insureds under two forms of insurance contract: policies of life assurance under the Policies of Assurance Act 1867, and policies of marine insurance under the Marine Insurance Act 1906. An attempt will also be made to highlight some of the differences which may arise, depending on whether these matters are assigned pursuant to either of these statutes or pursuant to LPA1925, s. 136(1).[56]

### (i)   Policies of Assurance Act 1867

As Smith and Leslie have pointed out, where a policy of life assurance has been taken out by an insured on her own life, it is not possible to assign the *policy* itself: 'An assignment of a life policy itself would amount to the creation of a fresh insurance on a different life. In other words, this would not be a case of transfer but a case of creating new rights. Accordingly, any such assignment will be ineffective.'[57] The subject matter which may be validly assigned by the insured may therefore only be in respect of *claims* against the insurer on the life policy.

   As to claims on a life policy, it is possible to distinguish between assignments of presently enforceable claims (i.e. claims where the contingency upon which the insurance money is payable has already occurred), and assignments of future or potential claims (i.e. claims where the contingency upon which the insurance money is payable has yet to occur). However, all claims on a life policy, whether presently enforceable or not, are capable of assignment.

---

[56] Unlike the case with assignments of copyright, unregistered design rights or registered trade marks, the requirements for the effects of LPA1925, s. 136(1) to be triggered *can* be satisfied in connection with assignments of claims arising under life policies, or marine policies since these are not multital obligations involving an inchoate multitude of obligors.

[57] Smith & Leslie (2018), para. 17.68 (references omitted).

So far as specific legislation on such assignments is concerned, reference may be made to the Policies of Assurance Act 1867:

> **1.** Any person or corporation now being or hereafter becoming entitled, by assignment or other derivative title, to a policy of life assurance, and possessing at the time of action brought the right in equity to receive and the right to give an effectual discharge of the assurance company liable under such policy for monies thereby assured or secured, shall be at liberty to sue at law in the name of such person or corporation to recover such monies.

Again, in common with LPA1925, s. 136(1), as well as the statutory provisions dealing with the transmission of copyright and registered trade marks, this section does not tell us what an assignment of a life assurance policy *is*, although it tells us what the effect of a valid assignment of such policy will be. If valid, the assignment would put the assignee 'at liberty to sue at law in the name of [his assignor]'. That is to say, the assignee would have the power to bring an action at law against the insurer, but in the name of the assignor. However, there is a prerequisite before such power may be exercised as against the insurer:

> **3.** No assignment made after the passing of this Act of a policy of the assurance shall confer on the assignee therein named, his executors, administrators, or assigns, any right to sue for the amount of such policy, or the monies assured or secured thereby, until a written notice of the date and purport of such assignment shall have been given to the assurance company liable under such policy at their principal place of business for the time being, or in case they have two or more principal places of business then at some one of such principal places of business, either in England or Scotland or Ireland, and the date on which such notice shall be received shall regulate the priority of all claims under any assignment, and a payment bona fide made in respect of any policy by any assurance company before the date in which such notice shall have been received shall be as valid against the assignee giving such notice as if this Act had not been passed.

Unlike LPA1925, s. 136(1), or the provisions dealing with the transmission of copyright or registered trade marks, although the power which is granted to an assignee pursuant to s. 1 of the Policies of Assurance Act 1867 rests on the operation of equitable assignment, no *mandatory* formal requirements are imposed as prerequisites. Instead, we find the following permissive provision: '**5.** Any such assignment *may* be made either by endorsement on the policy or by a separate instrument in the words or to the effect set forth in the schedule[58] hereto, such endorsement or separate instrument being duly stamped [emphasis added].'

Next, if we compare ss. 1, 3 and 5 to the provisions set out in LPA1925, s. 136(1), we may note that the provisions here are much less elaborate. Interestingly, there is no provision for *any* entitlements to pass and transfer. Instead, s. 1 of the 1867 Act is a *permissive* enactment: it *permits* the assignee to an assignment (which has also fulfilled the (formal) requirements in s. 5) to bring legal proceedings against the insurer, although the assignee must still sue in the name of the assignor. Similarly, s. 5 of the 1867 Act *permits* such assignments to be made by means of either an endorsement on the policy or by way of a separate instrument: yet there is no mandatory requirement that the assignment be in either form. Then, unlike LPA1925, s. 136(1), no provision is made to transfer from the assignor to the assignee 'all legal and other remedies' in relation to the chose assigned, or 'the power to give a good discharge'. Instead, we find that for s. 1 of the 1867 Act to apply, the assignee thereunder must already be entitled *in equity* to receive the insurance monies, and to give an effectual discharge for the same. Last, s. 3 of the 1867 Act serves to provide the insurer with an immunity: until the written notice specified therein is served on the insurer in the manner specified, no action may be brought against the insurer by an assignee at all.

Even more plainly than with LPA1925, s. 136(1), s. 1 of the Policies of Assurance Act 1867 provides for a statutory superstructure resting on a foundation based on equitable assignment.[59] Section 3 clarifies that an assignment of claims arising under a life policy may be equitably assigned even by way of a simple endorsement or the execution of an instrument worded along the lines of the form set out in the Schedule, but also creates an immunity for the insurer so long as written notice of the assignment is not given in the manner specified in s. 5. But it is also

---

[58] The form set out in the Schedule reads as follows:

> I *AB* of *&c*, in consideration of, *&c*, do hereby assign unto *CD*, of, &c, his executors, administrators, and assigns, the [within] policy of assurance granted, *&c [here describe the policy]*.
> In witness, *&c*.

[59] The operation of the 1867 Act is not exclusive: it is still possible to equitably assign the benefit of claims arising under a life policy, and if the requirements of LPA1925, s. 136(1) are satisfied as well, those statutory effects would be applicable. See e.g. *Re Williams* [1917] 1 Ch 1, 4 where Astbury J took the view that it was possible to assign such claims either under the 1867 Act, or in accordance with Judicature Act 1873, s. 25(6).

broader in operation than LPA1925, s. 136(1) since it also applies the same statutory superstructure to instances where other forms of derivative title have been acquired. Thus, where a trust *simpliciter* had been constituted over the benefit of a claim arising under a life policy in favour of a trust beneficiary, the beneficiary would be able to sue the insurer in her own name pursuant to s. 1.[60] There is, accordingly, nothing in the 1867 Act that supports the proposition that it creates an assignment by way of 'substitutive transfer'. Indeed, it does not even empower the assignee to sue in his own name.

### (ii)    Marine Insurance Act 1906

Finally, we come to assignments of marine policies pursuant to the Marine Insurance Act 1906:

> **50.** – (1) A marine policy is assignable unless it contains terms expressly prohibiting assignment. It may be assigned either before or after loss.
>
> (2) Where a marine policy has been assigned so as to pass the beneficial interest in such policy, the assignee of the policy is entitled to sue thereon in his own name; and the defendant is entitled to make any defence arising out of the contract which he would have been entitled to make if the action had been brought in the name of the person by or on behalf of whom the policy was effected.
>
> (3) A marine policy may be assigned by indorsement thereon or in other customary manner.

We may note, yet again, that there is no explicit provision for any substantive requirements for an assignment under this section. The 'assignment' which is to be effected in this section is, accordingly, an *equitable* assignment, a point which is emphasized by the reference in s. 50(2) to how, 'where a marine policy has been assigned so as to pass the *beneficial* interest in such policy', the assignee would be entitled to sue the insurer in his own name.[61]

---

[60] In respect of such trust, it would appear that the formality requirements in s. 2 of the 1867 Act would not apply as they are explicitly required only of an 'assignment'.

[61] In contrast to the position under the Policies of Assurance Act 1867, s. 1. Unlike the position in the 1867 Act, the Marine Insurance Act 1906 also does not provide for any immunity to the insurer pending receipt of any form of written notice, so an assignee may sue in his own name pursuant to s. 50 even if no notice of assignment had been given to the assignor prior to the bringing of such action.

We may also note that, as with the Policies of Assurance Act 1867, the 1906 Act does not 'pass or transfer' any entitlements from the assignor to the assignee, although it does permit the assignee to sue in his own name, doing this without taking anything away from the assignor, unlike LPA1925, s. 136(1).[62] It therefore follows that, where s. 50 has been triggered, but where the requirements of LPA1925, s. 136(1) have not been met, the assignor may still bring proceedings against the insurer. Control of such risks would therefore rely on the availability of injunctive relief to the assignee to restrain the assignor from bringing such proceedings if that was not desired by the assignee.

## D    Conclusion

The brief and non-exhaustive survey of these variously worded forms of 'statutory' assignment reveals a number of interesting points. First, it reveals that the *transfer* by way of an assignment of patents under the Patents Act 1977 operates in a quite different register: this statutory transfer effects what is, in essence, a conveyance of 'legal title' in the patent because patents have always been assignable at law – first, by deed, and now, by means of a writing signed by the assignor and the assignee.

Second, leaving aside the case of patents, the foregoing reveals a consistent pattern of co-option of equitable assignment reasoning as the bedrock on which the *transmission* by assignment of copyright and registered trade marks, on the one hand, and the *assignments* of life and marine policies, on the other, rest. These statutory provisions do not set out any form of assignment by way of 'substitutive transfer' distinct from the institution of equitable assignment which has been set out in this book. At most, these various kinds of statutorily prescribed ways of 'dealing' in the intangible personalty in issue just provide for different statutory elaborations which supplement the effects of equitable assignment. If 'transfer' is to be applied to these assignments, it may only be used in the loosest sense, and we would do well to rid ourselves of the supposition that Parliament intended something that it plainly did not.

---

[62] The operation of s. 50 of the 1906 Act is not exclusive: it is still possible to equitably assign the benefit of a marine policy, and if the requirements of LPA1925, s. 136(1) are satisfied as well, those statutory effects would be applicable. See e.g. *Raiffeisen Zentralbank Österreich AG* v. *Five Star Trading LLC* [2001] QB 825 (CA).

# PART VI

## Consequences

# 15

## Why It Matters

The proposition addressed and examined in this book is that equitable assignment is a *sui generis* institution comprising two mechanisms. First, a mechanism akin to that which operates when an express bare trust is constituted. Second, a mechanism akin to that which operates pursuant to an atypical principal–agent relationship, where the agent is released from having to invoke such powers as the principal had delegated, subject to the default fiduciary constraints which apply in most principal–agent relationships.

It is also suggested that 'statutory' assignment under LPA1925, s. 136(1) is an augmentative doctrine which does not create a distinct mode of assignment. Instead, it merely mandates certain effects spelt out in ss. 136(1)(a), (b) and (c) when the requirements of 'absolute, writing and notice' are satisfied with regard to a chose that had *otherwise* been validly assigned at law or in equity. Therefore, where a chose in action had been equitably assigned in circumstances where the requirements in s. 136(1) were also met, the trust and agency effects which would otherwise apply would be overridden so far as concerns the entitlements set out in ss. 136(1)(a), (b) and (c).

The practical significance of constructing theoretical models of equitable and statutory assignments on these bases is substantial, many aspects of which have already been discussed in the course of this book. The following will set out eight further matters of practical importance.

## A  Anti-Assignment Clauses

In *Linden Gardens Trust Ltd*, Lord Browne-Wilkinson held as follows:[1]

> [T]he existing authorities establish that an attempted assignment of contractual rights in breach of a contractual prohibition is ineffective to

[1] *Linden Gardens Trust Ltd* v. *Lenesta Sludge Disposals Ltd* [1994] 1 AC 85, 108F–G. The effectiveness of anti-assignment clauses in some contracts formed on or after 31 December 2018 is now subject to the Business Contract Terms (Assignment of Receivables) Regulations 2018. See main text following n. 32, below.

> transfer such contractual rights. . . . If the law were otherwise, it would defeat the legitimate commercial reason for inserting the contractual prohibition, viz., to ensure that the original parties to the contract are not brought into direct contractual relations with third parties.

Since then, it has been accepted that an assignment in breach of an anti-assignment clause can be denied effect. However, controversy remains. In particular, Professor Goode asked, inter alia, whether these clauses 'prohibit equitable as well as statutory assignments'.[2] Answering his own question, Professor Goode pointed out that the first issue would be one of construction: whether the wording of the anti-assignment clause would encompass both equitable and statutory assignments. But even if it did, he was of the view that, '[since] the prohibition [was] solely for the benefit of the debtor[, it] should not affect the transfer of property as between assignor and assignee'.[3] In other words, Professor Goode was not convinced that there were sound reasons to allow the contractual aspect of a promise or undertaking not to effect an assignment in contravention of an anti-assignment clause to have third-party effects on an assignee.

Despite having some judicial support,[4] Professor Goode's view is still not universally shared. For example, Dr Tolhurst and Professor Carter take a 'property view' of anti-assignment clauses (as opposed to the 'contract view' which they take Professor Goode to have adopted), and they suggest that the 'property view' is preferable.[5] In essence, they appear to suggest that an assignment in breach of an anti-assignment clause is completely ineffective, and is not merely a breach of the (contractual) promise not to effect an assignment in contravention of the anti-assignment clause.[6]

The analysis in this book suggests that an intermediate position is possible. On the one hand, as *Linden Gardens Trust Ltd* provides, where the assignment has become statutory, the anti-assignment clause can

---

[2] Goode (2009), p. 310.

[3] Ibid.

[4] See e.g. *Barbados Trust Company Ltd* v. *Bank of Zambia* [2007] EWCA Civ 148; [2007] 1 Lloyd's Rep 495.

[5] Tolhurst & Carter (2014), where at pp. 408-12, the primary arguments in favour of their 'property view' of anti-assignment clauses based on their reading of Lord Browne-Wilkinson's speech in *Linden Gardens Trust Ltd* are set out.

[6] One gathers that this may be the import of the 'property' view proposed by Tolhurst and Carter given their drawing of an analogy with a case where custody, but not possessory title, to a tangible chattel had been given (at Tolhurst & Carter (2014), p. 407).

preclude the statutorily mandated 'transfer' effects from arising, since these are effects which impinge on the relationship between obligor and statutory assignee.

On the other hand, however, where we are only concerned with an equitable assignment *simpliciter*, an anti-assignment clause might only bar the efficacy of such assignment so far as it affects relations between the obligor and the assignee, but leaving relations between the obligee-assignor and her assignee largely intact. Given the 'trust-plus-agency' model of equitable assignment set out in this book, we may see how this could arise.

In particular, so far as an equitable assignment entails an agency effect by which the assignee is delegated the obligee-assignor's powers arising from the chose assigned, such delegation may be neutralized if the anti-assignment clause is construed to have the effect of precluding the delegation of any powers by the obligee to another. When a non-delegable power granted to a donee is purportedly exercised by a delegatee of that donee, the delegatee's exercise of the power is a nullity. There is simply no such power to be exercised by the delegatee because that power could only be exercised by the original donee: that is what it *means* for the power to be 'non-delegable'. If so, the same would be true of an assignee who purports to invoke a power purportedly delegated to her by reason of an equitable assignment, in breach of an anti-assignment clause, *if*, on its true construction, it precluded delegation by the obligee of her powers arising under the contract.

That does not mean, though, that the equitable assignment is wholly nullified by the presence of the anti-assignment clause: there is still its 'bare trust' aspect. As to that, the anti-assignment clause has no bearing, and rightly so, for that relationship is solely concerned with the relations between the assignor and the assignee (unless, on its true construction, the anti-assignment clause also barred the constitution of a trust).

With this in mind, it is apposite to look more closely at the *locus classicus* on the effect of anti-assignment clauses.

### (i)  *Rereading* Linden Gardens Trust Ltd *v.* Lenesta Sludge Ltd

As noted above, Lord Browne-Wilkinson accepted in *Linden Gardens Trust Ltd* that an attempted assignment of contractual rights in breach of an anti-assignment clause was 'ineffective to transfer such contractual rights', and that this has to be so in order not to frustrate the 'legitimate commercial reason for inserting the contractual prohibition ... to ensure that the original parties were not brought into direct contractual relations with third parties'.[7] Lord Browne-Wilkinson was careful, however, to stipulate the limited extent to which non-compliant assignments in breach of an anti-assignment clause might be rendered ineffective by such non-compliance:[8]

> [A] prohibition on assignment normally only invalidates the assignment as against the other party to the contract so as to prevent a transfer of the chose in action: in the absence of the clearest words it cannot operate to invalidate the contract as between the assignor and the assignee and even then it may be ineffective on the grounds of public policy.

Lord Browne-Wilkinson was concerned only with the invalidation of the effects of a 'statutory assignment'. This is because both appeals involved statutory, and not equitable assignments[9] – a fact which is sometimes missed.[10] Hence, so far as English authority on the effect of

---

[7] *Linden Gardens Trust Ltd* v. *Lenesta Sludge Disposals Ltd* (n. 1), 108F–G.

[8] Ibid., 108C–D.

[9] The two conjoined appeals in *Linden Gardens Trust Ltd* (n. 1) were: (1) *Linden Gardens Trust Ltd* v. *Lenesta Sludge Disposals Ltd and Others* (1990) 25 Con LR 28; and (2) *St Martin's Property Corporation Ltd* v. *Sir Robert McAlpine & Sons Ltd* (1991) 25 Con LR 51. In both cases, the assignments were absolute and not by way of charge. Both assignments had also been executed by way of deed, and so would have been in the form of a signed writing. Written notice had been given in the *St Martin's* case: (1991) 25 Con LR 51, 58; and also [1994] 1 AC 85, 101. Thus, the assignment in the *St Martin's* case was a statutory assignment. Unfortunately, the position is less clear in the *Linden Gardens* case. Notice was certainly given, since 'nothing turned on notice': (1992) 30 Con LR 1, 11 (Staughton LJ). However, such notice must have been written such that the LPA1925, s. 136(1) requirements were satisfied since the proceedings were brought by the assignee in its own name. The litigation in the *Linden Gardens* case had initially been brought by the assignor, Stock Conversion Ltd. However, following the assignment in favour of the assignee, Linden Gardens Trust Ltd, 'Linden Gardens Trust were substituted for Stock Conversion as plaintiffs ... Stock Conversion were at one time plaintiffs in the action, but [were so] no longer': (1992) 30 Con LR 1, 6 (Staughton LJ). Since the *Linden Gardens* case had been brought within the court's common law jurisdiction, given that common law damages for breach of contract were sought, the non-joinder of the assignor and its replacement by the assignee denotes that the assignment must have become statutory.

[10] See e.g. Turner (2018), p. 534, criticizing the regret expressed by Gloster LJ in *Abu Dhabi Bank PJSC (formerly National Bank of Abu Dhabi)* v. *BP Oil International Ltd* [2018] EWCA Cov 14, [29]–[30], that parties in that case had assumed without argument that Lord Browne-Wilkinson's speech in *Linden Gardens Trust Ltd* v. *Lenesta Sludge Disposals Ltd* (n. 1), 108 was authority for the proposition that non-compliance with an anti-assignment provision would also lead to invalidation of the equitable assignments which were before the court. The proposition that an anti-assignment clause might cause an equitable assignment to be invalidated even as between the assignor and assignee was also adverted to by the Court of Appeal in *Reed Publishing Holdings Ltd* v. *Kings Reach Investments Ltd* (CA, unreported, 25 May 1983), relying on the reasoning of

assignments which are in breach of an anti-assignment clause is concerned, such case law as there is in favour of the proposition that such assignments are ineffective involve statutory assignments,[11] and not equitable assignments, *simpliciter*.[12]

The fact that both assignments before the court were statutory is significant. In the course of his speech, Lord Browne-Wilkinson considered the case of *Tom Shaw and Co. v. Moss Empires*,[13] in which Darling J had held that the prohibition on assignment in that case could 'no more operate to invalidate the assignment than it could to interfere with the laws of gravitation'.[14] As to this, Lord Browne-Wilkinson held that:[15]

> [i]f this is the right view of the case, it is unexceptionable: a prohibition on assignment normally only invalidates the assignment as against the other party to the contract so as to prevent a *transfer* of the chose in action: in

Croom-Johnston J in *Helstan Securities Ltd* v. *Hertfordshire County Council* [1978] 3 All ER 262, but without noticing that that was a case involving a statutory assignment.

[11] Both conjoined appeals in *Linden Gardens Trust Ltd* v. *Lenesta Sludge Disposals Ltd* involved statutory assignments (see n. 9, above) The other significant English decisions on point are *Helstan Securities Ltd* v. *Hertfordshire County Council* [1978] 3 All ER 262 (which involved a statutory assigment under LPA1925, s. 136(1)), and *Re Turcan* (1888) 40 Ch D 5 (which involved an assignment pursuant to the statutory provisions in the Policies of Assurance Act 1867 which, as was explained in Chapter 14, operates in a similar manner to statutory assignment under LPA1925, s. 136(1)). Unfortunately, Croom-Johnston J's analysis was purportedly followed in *Reed Publishing Holdings Ltd* v. *Kings Reach Investments Ltd* (n. 10, above) even though it involved an equitable assignment *simpliciter* of the benefit of a contract.

[12] Leaving aside *Abu Dhabi Bank PJSC (formerly National Bank of Abu Dhabi)* v. *BP Oil International Ltd* (n. 10), where, as previously mentioned, the parties assumed that Lord Browne-Wilkinson's views on the effect of anti-assignment clauses applied also to equitable assignments.

[13] (1908) 25 TLR 190.

[14] Ibid., 191. The assignment in that case was an equitable assignment *simpliciter* because, even though it was absolute, in writing, and notice in writing may well have been given, the subject matter of the assignment was in respect of a part of the fees which the assignor, Bastow, would earn under a contract of engagement with Moss Empires, Ltd. The engagement had been secured with the assistance of the plaintiff-assignee, Bastow's theatrical agents. Since the equitable assignment to the plaintiff was effective, notwithstanding the anti-assignment provision in the contract of engagement between Bastow and Moss Empires, Ltd, the plaintiff's claim against Moss Empires, Ltd (alongside which Bastow had been joined as co-defendant) seeking an order compelling it to pay to the plaintiff that portion (10 per cent) of Bastow's engagement fees was allowed. The impermissibility of effecting a statutory assignment of a future chose in action is discussed in greater detail in Section E below.

[15] Above, n. 1, 108D.

the absence of the clearest words it cannot operate to invalidate the
contract as between the assignor and the assignee and even then it may
be ineffective on the grounds of public policy.

By this, Lord Browne-Wilkinson explicitly approved of Darling J's conclusion as to the effect of an anti-assignment clause on the validity
and effectiveness of an equitable assignment. He then briefly reviewed
*Helstan Securities Ltd* v. *Hertfordshire County Council*,[16] *Re Turcan*,[17]
and *Reed Publishing Holdings Ltd* v. *Kings Reach Investments Ltd*,[18]
before noting that:[19]

> the existing authorities establish that an attempted assignment of con-
> tractual rights in breach of a contractual prohibition is ineffective to
> *transfer* such contractual rights. I regard the law as being satisfactorily
> settled in that sense. If the law were otherwise, it would defeat the
> legitimate commercial reason for inserting the contractual prohibition,
> viz., to ensure that the original parties to the contract are not brought into
> direct contractual relations with third parties.

In addition, Lord Browne-Wilkinson observed that the historical development of the law on assignment of leases was diametrically different to
that of assignment of other kinds of contractual rights, rendering the law
applicable to former to be of little relevance to the law applicable to the
latter;[20] all of which led him to conclude that 'an assignment of contractual rights in breach of a prohibition against such assignment is ineffective
to *vest* the contractual rights in the assignee'.[21]

On the analysis in this book, an equitable assignment *simpliciter* never
entails any transfer of any entitlements, contractual or otherwise, from
an assignor to her assignee. Unless supplemented by statute, all that
transpires when an assignor effects an equitable assignment of her
entitlements arising under a chose in action is that the assignor becomes
duty-bound to her assignee in the manner of a bare trustee (by virtue of
the 'trust effect'), whilst also delegating to her assignee such powers as the
assignor might have as against the obligor to the chose assigned, but freed
from the fiduciary obligations which would usually accompany most
typical delegations of power to an agent (by virtue of the atypical 'agency

---

[16] [1978] 3 All ER 262.
[17] (1888) 40 Ch D 5.
[18] CA, unreported, 25 May 1983.
[19] Above, n. 1, 108F–G (emphasis added).
[20] Ibid., 108G–109C.
[21] Ibid., 109C–D (emphasis added).

effect'). Yet, although the assignee is, by such delegation, empowered to act as if he were the assignor and is freed from any duty to invoke such delegated powers for the benefit of the assignor, it would remain the case that such assignor would not 'drop out'. And by neither of these mechanisms are the obligee-assignor's contractual rights taken from her so as to be *vested* in her assignee.

For both the 'trust' and 'agency' effects to operate, the assignor would have to remain firmly in the picture. There could, therefore, be no transfer of any entitlements to the assignee *from* the assignor in the sense that the assignor might thereafter no longer have such entitlements at all. To achieve that, recourse to statute is necessary – for example, where the requirements of statutory assignment under LPA1925, s. 136(1) have also been satisfied: though even in that context, the operation of the statute is much less extensive than one might initially assume. The conclusion, therefore, is that *Linden Gardens Trust Ltd* only deals with statutory assignments falling within LPA1925, s. 136(1). The policy concerns expressed by Lord Browne-Wilkinson having no application to what happens when an equitable assignment is effected, *Linden Gardens Trust Ltd* ought not to be taken to bar the efficacy of equitable assignments, at least in respect of their 'trust' aspect.

That said, it may be that if an anti-assignment clause were construed so as to preclude delegation by the obligee of powers that had been conferred on her, a provision for 'non-delegation' may well prevent an equitable assignment from having full effect, as the following will show.

### (ii)   Anti-Delegation and Anti-Assignment: Operation of Equitable and Statutory Assignments Contrasted

When a statutory assignment of a contractual chose in action compliant with the requirements of 'absolute, writing and notice' in LPA1925, s. 136 (1) has been made, *certain* contractual entitlements pass from the assignor and are transferred to the assignee. *These* entitlements (but no others) would be divested from the assignor.[22] Consequently, as to these entitlements, the contractual obligor would be compelled to deal with, and only with, the assignee, the assignor having 'dropped out of the picture'.

---

[22] See Chapter 13.

The analysis in this book reveals that the mechanisms which underpin the operation of equitable assignment do not entail any form of substitutive transfer such that the equitable assignee is substituted in place of *and to the exclusion of* the assignor. The policy reasons which Lord Browne-Wilkinson highlighted to justify the invalidating effects of an anti-assignment clause would not apply to an equitable assignment, given that its effects largely concern the assignor and assignee.

An anti-assignment clause could, however, affect the operation of an equitable assignment substantially, if construed in a particular way. This will be shown through Examples 15.1–15.3.

---

### EXAMPLE 15.1

B contracted with A to paint A's house commencing in sixty days' time for a fee of £1,000 to be paid in advance of the commencement of work. The contract provided A with a power to terminate the contract by giving notice so long as B had yet to commence work, with a countervailing contractual duty on B to make a refund of 50 per cent of the sums paid in advance, and that the contract contained a clause under which the parties agreed that the contractual power of termination granted to A was non-delegable, and could only be exercised by A.

One week before B was to start work, A equitably assigned the benefit of the contract to C. C then orally notified B of the assignment,[23] and purported to invoke the power that had been granted to A to terminate the contract.

---

On the facts in Example 15.1, given the 'agency' effect underpinning the equitable assignment from A to C, in the usual case C would be empowered to invoke A's power to terminate the contract *in right of A*. However, A's power to terminate was created on the basis that it was non-delegable. It would therefore not be in A's remit to delegate to another a power which was vested in her on the basis that it could not be delegated for another to exercise: the purported delegation would be a nullity.[24] Consequently, given the no-delegation clause, it must be right

---

[23] Since the notice was not in writing, this would remain an equitable assignment *simpliciter*.

[24] See e.g. *Green v. Whitehead* [1930] 1 Ch 38, in which a trustee purported to delegate certain of his powers as trustee to another by means of a power of attorney, even though the powers were to have been exercised in light of the trustee's own judgment and discretion. The power of attorney was held to be ineffective, the powers being non-delegable, and the attornies could not exercise these powers of the trustee: at 45 (Eve J). The decision was upheld on appeal but on a different ground.

to say that B may ignore C's invocation of A's power to terminate the contract: there is simply *no power for C to invoke*, the termination power being one that was solely for A, and no one else. That being so, would the analysis be different if there had been an anti-assignment clause instead?

---

### EXAMPLE 15.2

Same facts as in Example 15.1, except that instead of the no-delegation clause, the contract contained an anti-assignment clause under which A covenanted that she would not effect any assignment of the benefit of the contract at all.

---

It is arguable, at least, that an anti-assignment clause *may* be construed as having a similar operation as a no-delegation clause. *If* so construed, the results in Examples 15.1 and 15.2 would be the same: in both, B would be entitled to ignore the purported exercise by C of A's power to terminate the contract, and for the same reason. In both, the power to terminate was A's, and only A's, to invoke. What A purported to delegate to C to invoke would, accordingly, have been a non-existent power.

But even if the anti-assignment clause in Example 15.2, were construed to have the same 'anti-delegation' effect as the no-delegation clause in Example 15.1, the validity of the equitable assignment in both examples so far as their respective 'trust' aspects were concerned would be left untouched. This would mean that, notwithstanding the effects of the equitable assignment and the negation of its 'agency' aspect in either Example 15.1 or 15.2, C's position would not be any different even if A were to be rendered insolvent following the assignment.[25] In particular, given the 'trust effect' which underpins every equitable assignment, C would have acquired an equitable beneficial interest in the contract with B in Example 15.2 which would take it out of A's pool of available assets for distribution to her creditors. Finally, given the limited operation of an equitable assignment, so far as it largely only addresses the jural relations between assignor and assignee *inter se*, the policy reasons highlighted by Lord Browne-Wilkinson in *Linden Gardens Trust Ltd* would not be engaged in relation to this aspect of the equitable assignment in Example 15.2.[26]

---

[25] Subject to any statutory powers granted to A's trustee-in-bankruptcy to avoid onerous transactions or transactions in fraud of A's creditors.

[26] An equitable assignment in 'breach' of an anti-assignment clause could, of course, vest B with the power to discharge the contract with A by reason of breach. This would be an

What, then, if the equitable assignment to C had become a statutory assignment?

---

**EXAMPLE 15.3**

Same facts as in Example 15.2, except that A equitably assigned the benefit of the contract with B to C in a duly signed writing, and written notice of the same was given to B. A's equitable assignment to C had, therefore, become a statutory assignment.

---

As has been explained in Chapter 13, every statutory assignment is, in essence, an equitable assignment *plus* certain statutory effects: namely, that the specific entitlements set out in ss. 136(1)(a), (b) and (c) shall be divested from and be vested in the (now statutory) assignee. The contractual power to terminate the contract in Example 15.3 is not, however, a power which falls within any of these provisions. The effect of the anti-assignment clause in Example 15.3 would, therefore, be the same as it was in Example 15.2: C could not terminate the contract pursuant to any contractual termination provision because no such provision had been made, the only provision being one allowing for A, and only A, to terminate the contract. That said, for the policy reasons set out by Lord Browne-Wilkinson in *Linden Gardens Trust Ltd* (which have been discussed in the preceding subsection), the statutory effects mandated by LPA1925, s. 136(1) would be negated.

Given the above, it follows that anti-assignment clauses have a limited operation. In the first place, given the policy reasons identified by Lord Browne-Wilkinson, they apply to bar 'substitutive transfer'-type effects which arise when statutory mechanisms like those in LPA1925, s. 136(1) are engaged. However, since all statutory assignments are, in essence, equitable assignments but with statutory embellishments, that would

---

interpretive issue to begin with, as a contractual promise 'not to assign' could be construed to bar the making of an equitable assignment *simpliciter*, or one which also complied with the requirements of LPA1925, s. 136(1), thereby creating a so-called statutory assignment. As to the power to discharge for breach of such a contractual term, that would depend on whether the anti-assignment clause amounted to a condition, a warranty, or an innominate term whose breach led to B being deprived of substantially the whole of the benefit of the contract with A. Such breach, however, is predicated on the efficacy of the assignment: if the anti-assignment clause had the effect of negating the assignment, rendering it to be ineffective, there would be no breach – one cannot breach a promise to do an act if that act is nugatory.

strip away the statutory overlay and expose the equitable assignment beneath.

Second, if, on their true construction, an anti-assignment clause is taken to encapsulate the contracting parties' intention that the powers arising from the contract are to be non-delegable, and are to be invoked solely and exclusively by the obligee, the agency aspect of equitable assignment would no longer be fully effective. This is because an assignee may only invoke such *delegable* entitlements as her assignor has.

Third, even so, this would not render the equitable assignment to be wholly ineffective. Even if the anti-assignment clause were construed to have the effect of precluding delegation of powers by the assignor, that would not affect the trust aspect of the equitable assignment: so far as the assignor and assignee were concerned, notwithstanding the breach of the anti-assignment clause, their relationship as assignor and assignee would remain intact.[27] Thus, as Lord Browne-Wilkinson had noted: 'it cannot operate to invalidate the contract as between the assignor and the assignee'.[28] Statements by the Court of Appeal in cases like *R v. Chester and North Wales Legal Aid Area Office (No. 12), Ex p. Floods of Queensferry Ltd*[29] to the contrary should, therefore, be treated with some reservation.

### (iii)   Commercial Significance

The distinction between the invalidation of the effects mandated by, say, LPA1925, s. 136(1), and the continued validity (at least in part) of the equitable assignment which underpins such 'statutory assignment' is commercially important. As Professor Goode noted:[30]

---

[27] The discussion in the main text leaves aside the question as to whether contracting parties may provide for a clause precluding trusts from being constituted over the benefit of such contract. In *dicta*, it was assumed in *Don King Productions Inc. v. Warren* [2000] Ch 291, 321; *Barbados Trust Co. Ltd v. Bank of Zambia* [2007] 1 Lloyd's Rep 495, [43], [88]; and *First Abu Dhabi Bank PJSC v. BP Oil International Ltd* [2018] EWCA Civ 14, [28], that such 'anti-trust constitution' clauses may be created by party agreement, and will have such effect. This has, however, been doubted: see Turner (2018), p. 537.

[28] *Linden Gardens Trust Ltd v. Lenesta Sludge Ltd* (n. 1), 108C. Statements to similar effect as to the limited effectiveness of an anti-assignment clause as affecting the relations between the assignor and her assignee may be found in *Hendry v. Chartsearch Ltd* [1998] CLC 1382, 1394D–E.

[29] [1998] 1 WLR 1496, 1501 (Millett LJ) and 1504 (Hobhouse LJ).

[30] Goode (2009), p. 300.

The common law has always attached great importance to the concept of alienability of property, regarding it as contrary to the public interest for assets to be tied up indefinitely. So there are long-established rules striking down excessive restrictions on alienation, either as being repugnant to the grant made to the intending transferor or as being contrary to public policy. These rules have traditionally been directed to physical assets in general and land in particular; but in modern commerce, transactions involving physical assets are dwarfed in value by dealings in pure intangibles, particularly debts, intermediated securities and derivatives. It is thus important that legal rules based on freedom of contract do not impair the free flow of intangibles in the stream of trade.

Given the importance of these concerns to protect freedom of commerce in trade and other dealings with intangible assets, as Goode has pointed out, many jurisdictions have severely restricted the efficacy of anti-assignment provisions through legislative enactment.[31] Indeed, in England and Wales, Parliament has enacted the Small Business, Enterprise and Employment Act 2015,[32] sections 1 and 2 of which provide that the Secretary of State may make regulations to render contractual provisions preventing the assignment of receivables to have no effect in connection with many kinds of contracts.

The requisite regulations were duly made on 23 November 2018 by way of the Business Contract Terms (Assignment of Receivables) Regulations 2018, SI No. 1254 (the '2018 Regulations'). Regulation 1(2), read with regulation 2(1) of the 2018 Regulations, provides that a term in a contract formed on or after 31 December 2018 that prohibits or imposes a condition, or other restriction, on the assignment of a receivable arising under that contract or any other contract between those parties, shall have no effect, although Regulation 3(1) goes on to provide that this prohibition shall not apply where the supplier of the goods, services or intangible assets giving rise to the receivable was a 'large enterprise or a special purpose vehicle' as defined in Regulation 3(2) and (3).

The 2018 Regulation represents a significant legislative inroad on the ability of contractual obligors to bar effective assignments. But it is patently not designed to bar the effectiveness of all anti-assignment clauses. Consequently, the analysis set out in Section A, above, will remain pertinent to cases arising prior to the date when the

---

[31] Ibid., pp. 316–18, making reference to Uniform Commercial Code, §9–406(d); UNIDROIT Convention on International Factoring, Art. 6(1); and 2001 UN Convention on the Assignment of Receivables in International Trade, Art 9(1).

[32] Small Business, Enterprise and Employment Act 2015 (c. 26).

2018 Regulation is to have effect, as well as to cases falling within the exception provided by Regulation 3.

## B   The 'Rule' in *Dearle* v. *Hall*

The 'rule' in *Dearle* v. *Hall* was extensively re-examined in Chapter 10. Careful rereading of the case within its historical context reveals that it is a misnomer to speak of a 'rule in *Dearle* v. *Hall*'. In truth, this so-called rule is a careful working-out of a much broader set of principles. In particular, it is the result of the application of the Golden Rule of ethical behaviour, in conjunction with the overarching equitable rule of priority that 'where the equities are equal, the first in time shall prevail'. Realization that this is the case has important consequences in the application of the 'rule'. First, it means that there is no reason why the 'rule' in *Dearle* v. *Hall* should be confined to resolving priority conflicts arising only between equitable assignees. Second, the discussion of the limited effect of the statutory provisions in LPA1925, s. 136(1) also casts light upon when such 'rule' may be displaced.

### (i)   The 'Rule' in Dearle v. Hall *as Applied to Equitable Charges by Way of Hypothecation*

There is a view that the rule in *Dearle* v. *Hall* may apply to instances of priority conflicts between the holders of fixed or floating charges over the same chose in action, and also to priority conflicts between equitable assignees of a chose in action and holders of fixed or floating charges over the same chose in action. In an appeal from the New Zealand Court of Appeal, Lord Hoffmann observed as follows:[33]

> If the policy is effected in the name of the mortgagee, he is entitled in law to payment of the proceeds. But his interest remains by way of *charge* to secure the mortgage debt and he will be accountable to subsequent mortgagees or the mortgagor for any surplus. If the policy is effected in the name of the mortgagor, the mortgagee still has an interest by way of *charge* in the proceeds. How as a matter of legal analysis does this interest take effect? Necessarily by way of assignment. A *charge* on a fund belonging at law to someone else operates as a partial equitable assignment (see *Durham Brothers* v. *Robertson* [1898] 1 QB 765 at p. 769). It is

---

[33] *Colonial Mutual General Insurance Co. Ltd* v. *ANZ Banking Group (New Zealand) Ltd* [1995] 1 WLR 1142 (PC) 1144.

subject to the rule in *Dearle* v. *Hall* (1828) 3 Russ 1 as to notice to the debtor in the same way as any other equitable assignment.

The passage above has been taken as authority by some for the proposition that the rule in *Dearle* v. *Hall* 'applies to competing assignments by way of charge and not only to outright assignments'.[34] Furthermore:[35]

> (3) If the floating charge crystallises automatically on the attempted creation of a subsequent specific equitable charge, the floating chargee takes priority in equity on grounds of time. . . .
> (5) Priority under proposition (3) could be reversed in the case of book or other debts, including credit bank accounts, if the subsequent specific chargee or absolute purchaser gives first notice to the debtor under the rule in *Dearle* v. *Hall*.

These views have also been applied in Hong Kong.[36]

An equitable assignment entails the creation of a 'trust-plus-agency' relationship between assignor and assignee; but an equitable charge by way of hypothecation does no such thing. As Millett J (as he then was) observed in *Re Charge Card Services Ltd*:[37]

> [The essence of an equitable charge [i.e. a charge by way of hypothecation] is that, without any conveyance or assignment to the chargee, specific property of the chargor is expressly or constructively appropriated to or made answerable for payment of a debt, and the chargee is given the right to resort to the property for the purpose of having it realised and applied in or towards payment of the debt. The availability of equitable

---

[34] *Palmer's Company Law* (Geoffrey Morse (Principal editor), ed., 25th edn, London: Sweet & Maxwell 1992), fn. 7 to para. 13.151 (Palmer R.123: November 2009). This is assumed to be the case in Oditah (2009), p. 351.

[35] William James Gough, *Company Charges* (2nd edn, London: Butterworths, 1996), pp. 254 and 276.

[36] *ABN AMRO Bank NV* v. *Chiyu Banking Corp. Ltd* [2000] HKCFI 373; [2001] 2 HKLRD 175, [60].

[37] [1987] 1 Ch 150 (Ch) 176. Controversially, Millett J also observed that, 'the benefit of a debt can no more be appropriated or made to the debtor than it can be conveyed or assigned to him . . . [because] once any assignment or appropriation to the debtor becomes unconditional, the debt is wholly or partially released': *Re Charge Card Services Ltd* [1987] 1 Ch 150 (Ch) 176. This dicta was ultimately disapproved by the House of Lords in *Re Bank of Credit and Commerce International SA (No. 8)* [1998] AC 214 (HL) 225–8 (Lord Hoffmann). But that does not affect the analysis in the main text.

remedies has the effect of giving the chargee a proprietary interest by way
of security in the property charged.[38]

If so, how is it legitimate for a 'rule' pertaining to competing equitable
assignments to be applied to competing equitable charges, given their
fundamental structural differences?

As explained in Chapter 10, the 'rule' in *Dearle* v. *Hall* is not a rule
'about' equitable assignments. The decision in *Dearle* v. *Hall*, and the
cases which follow and apply it, are actually all applications of the
generally applicable rule of priority in equity that, when the equities are
equal, the first in time shall prevail. Since the 'rule' in *Dearle* v. *Hall* is not
a special rule of priority developed in connection with equitable assignment, there is no problem with applying 'it' to other contexts where there
are competing equitable interests. In truth, there is no such 'rule', and we
confuse ourselves by treating it as if there was one.

There is, therefore, no conceptual difficulty with applying the 'rule' in
*Dearle* v. *Hall* to priority conflicts between equitable assignees and
chargees, or, for that matter, between equitable chargees where no
equitable assignees feature at all. This is not because the creation of a
charge amounts to a 'partial' equitable assignment. Even though there are
certainly cases which sometimes describe equitable charges in that
manner,[39] as explained above, equitable charges are structurally different
from equitable assignments. But since the 'rule' in *Dearle* v. *Hall* is an
application of the general rule of priority that when the equities are equal,
the first in time shall prevail, so far as an equitable charge is as much a
species of equitable interest as an equitable assignment, the same rule of
priority is applicable to both.

### (ii) The 'Rule' in Dearle v. Hall *as Applied to Equitable Assignments that Have become 'Statutory'*

The analysis in Chapter 13 suggests an additional complication to the
question whether the rule in *Dearle* v. *Hall* applies where two equitable
assignments have been effected over the same chose in action, but the
later equitable assignment satisfies the requirements under s. 136(1)
whereas the prior one did not, or only did so at a later date.

---

[38] See also P. G. Turner, 'Assignments by Way of Charge' (2004) 24 *Australian Bar Review*
280, 290.
[39] See e.g. *Durham Brothers* v. *Robertson* [1898] 1 QB 765, 769.

Section 136(1) does not create some manner of assignment which is completely distinct from equitable assignment. Therefore, a 'statutory assignment' pursuant to the 1925 Act does not substitute the assignee for the assignor as obligee to the chose assigned. Nor does the Act pass every single conceivable entitlement of the assignor arising from the chose assigned to the assignee: that is not what the statutory language does. If so, some care needs to be taken over the application of the 'rule' in *Dearle v. Hall* when the same chose has been both equitably and statutorily assigned pursuant to LPA1925, s. 136(1). Based on the analysis in Chapter 13, it would appear that in *some* contexts, the 'rule' in *Dearle v. Hall* would have no application, but in others it would, and this would depend on whether the entitlements which might have been affected by s. 136(1)(a), (b) or (c) were in issue.

This gloss appears not to have been appreciated in the debate on the issue thus far. On the one hand, Dr Oditah has suggested that a statutory assignee should have priority as against an equitable assignee, regardless of the sequence by which notice had been given, and without any qualification as to the limited subject matter to which s. 136(1) pertains.[40]

But, according to Smith and Leslie: 'Despite some powerful arguments to the contrary,[41] it is now clear that the rule [of *Dearle* v. *Hall*] applies to legal (i.e. s. 136) assignments as much as it does to equitable assignments.'[42] Relying on the authority of Phillips J's judgment in *E. Pfeiffer Weinkellerei-Weineinkauf GmbH & Co. v. Arbuthnot Factors Ltd*,[43] Smith and Leslie take a contrary position to Oditah's as to the applicability of the *Dearle* v. *Hall* 'rule' to statutory assignments. However, like Oditah, Smith and Leslie also pay no heed to the limited effect of LPA1925, s. 136(1), and to whether the particular priority conflict in question relates to competing invocations of the entitlements set out in s. 136(1)(a), (b) or (c).

In the *Arbuthnot Factors* case, the plaintiff sold wine to Springfield Wine Importers Ltd ('Springfield'). The sale agreement incorporated a retention of title clause. Springfield resold the wine on credit terms to

---

[40] Oditah (1989), pp. 527–32; Oditah (1991), para. 6.18. See also Oditah (2009), pp. 351–3.

[41] Namely, that put forward in Oditah (1989). Smith & Leslie (2018) acknowledge that, '[T]he position was, for a long time, unclear' (para. 27.95, fn. 94), and in opposition to Dr Oditah's views, they refer to the views set out in Goode (1976), p. 555, and McLauchlan (1980), 93–4.

[42] Smith & Leslie (2018), para. 27.95. The same position is adopted in Salinger (2017), paras 8-16 to 8-18; and in Liew (2018), paras 6-26 to 6-30.

[43] [1988] 1 WLR 150.

various customers. Springfield then entered into a factoring agreement by which it agreed to assign to the defendant absolutely debts owed to it by its customers, whilst warranting that 'no reservation of title by any third party' applied to all or any part of the wine that had been sold. Assignments to the defendant company were made in accordance with the agreement, and written notice given to the sub-purchasers. Given such notice, Springfield's customers paid the sums owing on the wine purchased from Springfield to the defendant.

The 'triangle' of 'absolute, writing and notice' required by s. 136(1) having been complied with, the defendant factors were statutory assignees. Springfield failed, however, to pay what was due to the plaintiff for the wine it had supplied. Relying on its retention of title clause, the plaintiff brought proceedings, claiming to be the beneficial owner of the proceeds of each sub-sale which had been paid to and received by the defendant, and that the defendant's entitlement to such proceeds as assignee was subject to the plaintiff's prior equitable claim.

Phillips J held that the title-retention clause in the sale agreement:[44]

> constitute[d] an agreement by Springfield to assign to the plaintiff future choses in action, namely future debts owed by sub-purchasers to Springfield up to the amount of any outstanding indebtedness on the part of Springfield to the plaintiff. ... The agreement was plainly by way of security, and the assignments under it were capable of being redeemed by payment by Springfield of the outstanding indebtedness.

Although the defendant conceded that the plaintiff might have an equitable interest in the debts owed to Springfield by the sub-purchasers of the wine, and that that interest had arisen prior to the defendant's interest in those debts by way of the statutory assignment to the defendant, it contended that its interest had priority over that of the plaintiff because, inter alia, if the defendant was to be treated for priority purposes as though the assignment had been equitable and not statutory, then the rule in *Dearle* v. *Hall* ought to be applied. And if so, priority would be determined by the order by which notice of the assignments had been received by the respective debtors. On the facts, since the defendant had given notice first, it thus had priority over the plaintiff.[45]

---

[44] Ibid., 161.
[45] Ibid.

Phillips J agreed.[46] However, his attention had not been drawn to Goff J's *obiter* observations in *Ellerman Lines Ltd* v. *Lancaster Maritime Co. Ltd ('The Lancaster')*, which suggested the opposite: that a statutory assignee would *always* be accorded priority over an equitable assignee,[47] observations which Dr Oditah has taken to support the proposition that the rule in *Dearle* v. *Hall* has no application *at all* to priority conflicts involving a statutory assignment.[48]

The conflict between the two positions was considered by Mummery J in *Compaq Computers Ltd* v. *Abercorn Group Ltd*,[49] where he appeared to agree with Phillips J's observations in *E. Pfeiffer* that, 'even if there is a legal assignment for value without notice of a prior equity, priorities fall to be determined as if the assignment had been effected in equity'.[50] In particular, Mummery J noted as follows:[51]

> Section 136(1) provides that the assignment is 'subject to equities having priority over the right of the assignee'. The effect of those words is to create, in the case of a statutory assignment of a chose in action, an exception to the general rule that an equity will not prevail against a bona fide purchaser of a legal estate for value without notice of the prior equity.

Mummery J's reasoning echoes that put forward by Professor McLauchlan, who had suggested that 'there appears to be no reason why the term "equities" [in s. 136(1)] should not bear its common meaning as a compendious phrase for equitable remedies and rights, personal and proprietary, and thus include equitable interests held by third parties. On this interpretation an assignment complying with section 136 becomes equitable for priority purposes'.[52]

Unfortunately, as Oditah has pointed out, such analysis resting on the provision pertaining to 'equities':[53]

> involves a massive *petitio principii*. . . . A legal assignee takes only *subject to equities having priority over the right of the assignee*. What these equities are, the subsection does not say. Even if one were to assume . . .

---

[46] Ibid., 163.
[47] *Ellerman Lines Ltd* v. *Lancaster Maritime Co. Ltd (The 'Lancaster')* [1980] 2 Lloyd's Rep 497 (Comm) 503.
[48] Oditah (1989), p. 530.
[49] *Compaq Computer Ltd* v. *Abercorn Group Ltd* [1991] BCC 484.
[50] *E. Pfeiffer Weinkellerei-Weineinkauf GmbH & Co.* v. *Arbuthnot Factors Ltd* (n. 44), 162F.
[51] *Compaq Computer Ltd* v. *Abercorn Group Ltd* (n. 49), 502.
[52] McLauchlan (1980), p. 92.
[53] Oditah (1989), pp. 516–17 (emphasis in italics in original, emphasis in bold italics added). The point is repeated in Oditah (1991), para. 6.15.

that 'equities' includes 'equitable assignments', yet, it is only those equitable assignments which, independently of section 136(1), prevail over a legal assignment, that will be preserved. These will not necessarily cover all equitable assignments of which notice is given to the debtor before notice of the legal assignment is received. In short, it is impermissible to use *Dearle* v. *Hall* to subordinate a subsequent legal assignment to a prior equitable assignment for that is to assume that independently of section 136(1) equitable assignments prevail over a subsequent legal assignment if the equitable assignees give first notice to the debtor. Put in another way, section 136(1) subordinates a legal assignment only to those equities having priority over it, not necessarily to all equities. Since the subsection is silent on the equities it contemplates, recourse must be had to the general law. It is settled law that every assignment must now take effect subject to the debtor's right of set off.[54] *But it is not law that a prior equitable assignment prevails over a later legal assignment by reason only that notice of it was given to the debtor before he received notice of the legal assignment.*

There does not appear to have been any judicial consideration of the precise point made by Oditah. Clarification of the point will certainly be welcome. But whichever way the point may ultimately be clarified, it is suggested that neither Oditah's position, nor the 'orthodox' position set out by Smith and Leslie, presents a complete picture of the problem.

If we focus on what s. 136(1) does and does not say, the proposition that it effects some sort of 'transfer' of the '*legal title* in a chose in action' must fall away. Section 136(1) does *not* have that effect. It simply provides that where there has been an assignment of a debt or other legal chose in action, certain statutorily mandated effects are to arise when the triangle of 'absolute, writing and notice' is satisfied in that certain entitlements (but not any others) are 'transferred' as a result of s. 136(1)(a), (b) or (c).

We cannot say that such an assignment has the effect of passing the 'legal title' to such chose,[55] if this means that it passes and transfers to the assignee the *entirety* of the assignor's common law entitlements associated with the chose, because that is not what ss. 136(1)(a), (b) and (c) say.

---

[54] It is also settled that an assignee takes subject to 'equities' such as any powers of rescission as the obligor may have against the assignee in respect of the obligation between them, or any other 'defences' that may impeach the existence or enforceability of the obligation to which the chose in action assigned pertains. For a discussion of the 'equities' to which an assignee is subject, see e.g. Guest & Liew (2015), chapter 7.

[55] See also Richard Calnan, *Taking Security* (4th edn, London: LexisNexis, 2018), paras 4.45–4.46.

While those three subsections may well deal in most cases with all, or practically all, of the assignor's entitlements arising out of most forms of chose in action, they are not exhaustive and, as has already been pointed out,[56] one good example of an entitlement which falls beyond the ambit of s. 136(1) is the power arising out of a contractual option.[57]

It is not, therefore, possible to ignore the operation of the rule in *Dearle* v. *Hall* just because at least one of two competing equitable assignments has fulfilled the requirements in s. 136(1) and may have triggered the effects in s. 136(1)(a), (b) or (c). We should also consider whether that which had been statutorily transferred is relevant to the dispute, and if not, the rule in *Dearle* v. *Hall* may still be significant.

To illustrate a situation where the rule in *Dearle* v. *Hall* may be applicable notwithstanding satisfaction of s. 136(1), it is helpful to consider Example 15.4.

---

### EXAMPLE 15.4

B makes and sells widgets.

A has been buying B's widgets for some time. As B's prices fluctuate depending on the price of his raw materials, A would like to 'lock in' B's prices. To that end, A enters into a 'promotional contract' with B in which B agrees that, in consideration for a fee of £1,000, for the following year, in respect of orders placed by A: (i) B will charge £1 per widget in respect of the first 1,000 widgets ordered; and (ii) in respect of any orders beyond that, B will charge £1.50 per widget.

The contract contains no anti-assignment clause.

The following week, in a signed writing, A equitably assigns the benefit of her promotional contract with B to $C_1$. Oral notice of this assignment to $C_1$ is given to B.

A few days later, A equitably assigns the benefit of her contract with B a second time in a signed writing to $C_2$. Written notice of this second assignment is given by $C_2$ to B. Section 136(1) would, accordingly, be triggered in respect of the later assignment to $C_2$.

Six months pass and no orders have yet been placed under the promotional contract.

At this time, $C_1$ writes a letter to place an order for 1,000 widgets. He leaves the letter with B's receptionist at B's business premises.

Coincidentally, $C_2$ is meeting with B at the same time. At the meeting, $C_2$ informs B that he wishes to place an order for 2,000 widgets.

B has the capacity to perform both sets of orders. But who is to be charged, and how much?

---

[56]  In Chapter 13, Section D.
[57]  Other examples are also suggested in Chapter 13, Section D.

If priority was given to $C_1$'s order, B would be entitled to charge $C_1$ £1 per widget for the whole of $C_1$'s order (i.e. £1,000), and $C_2$ £1.50 per widget for the whole of $C_2$'s order (i.e. £3,000).

But if priority were given to $C_2$'s order, B would be entitled to charge $C_2$ £1 per widget for the first 1,000 widgets of his order (i.e. £1,000) plus a further £1.50 per widget for the remaining 1,000 widgets (i.e. £1,500), and to charge $C_1$ £1.50 per widget for all 1,000 widgets ordered by $C_1$ (i.e. £1,500).

Though the total amount B would be entitled to charge would be the same (£4,000), the amount payable by $C_1$ and $C_2$ would be different, depending on whether priority was given to $C_1$'s order or $C_2$'s order, given the terms of the promotional contract. So on these facts, whose order has priority?

On the analysis in this book, s. 136(1) has no application in respect of $C_1$'s and $C_2$'s invocation of the power contained in the promotional contract to place orders for B's widgets. This power is, in essence, a power arising from a 'sell' option: B had bound himself to 'sell' widgets at a price of £1 per widget for the first 1,000 widgets ordered under the promotional contract, and thereafter at a price of £1.50 per widget, for a period of a year.

This power arising from the option is not (i) *the* legal right to the debt or thing in action that had been equitably assigned; (ii) any legal or other *remedy* for the same; nor (iii) *the* power to give a good discharge without concurrence of the assignor. This power is extraneous to s. 136(1). So the statutory transfers mandated by s. 136(1) would not apply.

Accordingly, in lieu of anything else, it is suggested that the rule in *Dearle v. Hall* would continue to be salient. Applying that rule, $C_1$, having given notice to B first (albeit orally), would have priority over $C_2$.[58] Therefore, B is entitled to charge $C_1$ £1,000 for $C_1$'s order of 1,000 widgets, and $C_2$ £3,000 for $C_2$'s order of 2,000 widgets, under the terms of the promotional contract he had entered into with A. On these facts, it would be going beyond the provisions of the statute to hold that priority ought to be given to $C_2$'s order simply because $C_2$'s assignment had become 'statutory' whereas $C_1$'s remained purely equitable.

---

[58] Had the notices of assignment been received on the same day, they would be regarded as having been received simultaneously: *Calisher v. Forbes* (1871) LR 7 Ch App 109. In such circumstances, priority would be determined by the order in which the assignments had been created: *Re de Groot* [2001] 2 Qd R 359.

The point in this section, therefore, does not resolve the dispute as to whether the rule in *Dearle* v. *Hall* is rendered otiose when there is 'competition' between equitable assignments, one of which has 'become' a 'statutory' assignment ahead of the other. That question remains open, given the circularity of the reasoning employed in *Compaq Computers*. But even if Oditah's analysis were accepted, it would follow that where the particular entitlements in dispute are extraneous to s. 136(1), then so far as its 'transfer' effects would not have been engaged, the rule in *Dearle* v. *Hall* would continue to be relevant.

## C   Present Gifts of Legal Choses in Action by Parol

As explained in this book, an equitable assignment operates by means of the dual mechanisms of a bare trust, coupled with an unusual form of agency. Since neither of these conceptual devices requires consideration or value to have been given to operate, an equitable assignment of a chose in action may also be effected without need for consideration, so long as it is in present existence and is not a 'future' chose. That is, it is possible to effect an equitable assignment of a chose in action by way of gift.

This conclusion is no surprise, for the cases have long accepted that one may equitably assign equitable[59] or legal[60] choses in action by way of gift. The question arises, however, whether the enactment of s. 25(6) of the Judicature Act 1873 changed matters, at least in connection with the assignment of legal choses in action.

Some doubts may arise as to whether the pre-Judicature Act position continues to be the case, given the analysis of the High Court of Australia in *Olsson* v. *Dyson*.[61] That case was concerned with a debt which had been assigned in the State of Victoria by way of absolute gift (and not by way of charge) through oral words alone. Notice of the assignment was also given orally.

The High Court of Australia held that the gift failed for non-compliance with the requirements for a 'statutory' assignment set out

---

[59] *Sloane* v. *Cadogan* (1808). This case is discussed at length in Chapter 4, Section A(ii). Other cases which have recognized that it is possible to equitably assign equitable choses by way of gift include *Kekewich* v. *Manning* (1851) 1 De G M & G 176, 201–2.

[60] *Richardson* v. *Richardson* (1867) LR 3 Eq 686. For other authorities, see *Fortescue* v. *Barnett* (1834) 3 My & K 36; *Blakely* v. *Brady* (1839) 2 Drury & Walsh 311; *Re Patrick* [1891] 1 Ch 82, in which the assignment had been effected by a deed of settlement before Judicature Act 1873, s. 25(6) came into operation.

[61] (1969) 120 CLR 365.

in the South Australian equivalent[62] to what is now LPA1925, s. 136(1). It took the view that since those provisions enabled legal choses in action to be assigned at law, it was no longer possible to effect an assignment, save in compliance with the terms of the statute. Applying the principle that equity does not aid volunteers, this would mean that, unless the transaction had been for value (and not by way of gift), and unless the facts supported a finding that there had been an enforceable *agreement* to effect an assignment, gifts of a legal chose in action (such as a debt) would be invalid if they did not comply with the statutory requirements.[63]

Following *Olsson* v. *Dyson*, and given the approach taken by the High Court of Australia in *Corin* v. *Patton*,[64] the position in Australia seems to be that, where an assignor had failed to execute an assignment in the form of a writing under her hand (i.e. where she had not executed a duly signed written assignment), the assignor would have failed to perform acts which she, *and only she*, could perform in order to satisfy the requirements of the Australian equivalents to LPA1925, s. 136(1) or Judicature Act 1873, s. 25(6). It would seem, therefore, that such gift would therefore fail for want of writing.[65]

The analysis in Chapter 13 reveals why this position seems never to have been followed as a matter of English law. The pre-1873 law is still good law in England and Wales, just as Lord Macnaghten had noted in 1904: 'Why that which would have been a good equitable assignment before the statute should now be invalid and inoperative because it fails to come up to the requirements of the statute, I confess I do not understand. The statute does not forbid or destroy equitable assignments or impair their efficacy in the slightest degree.'[66]

---

[62] Law of Property Act 1936 (SA), s. 15. Similar legislation has been enacted in each of the Australian states and territories: Civil Law (Property) Act 2006 (ACT), s. 205; Conveyancing Act 1919 (NSW), s. 12; Law of Property Act 2000 (NT), s. 182; Property Law Act 1974 (Qld), s. 199(1) and (2); Conveyancing and Law of Property Act 1884 (Tas), s. 85; Property Law Act 1958 (Vic), s. 134; and Property Law Act 1969 (WA), s. 20.

[63] *Olsson* v. *Dyson* (n. 61), at 368 (Barwick CJ), 375–6 (Kitto LJ, with whom Menzies and Owen JJ agreed), and 387 (Windeyer J). Windeyer J had made similar observations in *Norman* v. *Federal Commissioner of Taxaion* (1963) 109 CLR 9, [9] of his judgment.

[64] (1990) 169 CLR 540.

[65] It is not as critical that the assignor might not have given written notice of the assignment, since the statute does not prescribe that such notice must be given by the assignor (see e.g. *Bateman* v. *Hunt* [1904] 2 KB 530, 535, construing Judicature Act 1873, s. 25(6)). So long as someone (e.g. the assignee) gives such written notice, the doctrine that the assignor must perform all that she, and she alone, could do, would be satisfied.

[66] *William Brandt's Sons* v. *Dunlop Rubber Co. Ltd* [1905] AC 454, 461.

As explained in Chapter 13, neither LPA1925, s. 136(1) nor Judicature Act 1873, s. 25(6), which it replaced, were enacted to create any distinctive mode of assignment which might supplant, or even provide an alternative to equitable assignment. A 'statutory' assignment *is* an equitable assignment, albeit with certain statutorily mandated embellishments.

Although Windeyer J observed in *Olsson* v. *Dyson* that an assignor 'must' comply with the requirements as to a signed writing 'because the statute so requires', else the effects mandated by the statute would not otherwise arise, he (and the other members of the High Court) seem to have taken the view that s. 15 of the South Australian Law of Property Act 1936 (which is *in pari materia* with what is now LPA1925, s. 136(1)) did something more than transfer the *particular* entitlements which were specified within it. On the analysis in this book, that position may be doubted. Rather, the rationalization that s. 136(1) 'statutory' assignments are augmented equitable assignments (i.e. they are equitable assignments *plus*) is consistent with the English view that s. 136(1) does not invalidate equitable assignments of choses in action falling within its ambit which fail to comply with those requirements of s. 136(1) which only the assignor could complete (i.e. in connection with the need for a signed writing).[67] Therefore, as a matter of principle and authority, it remains possible for an assignor to make a present gift of a legal chose in action (such as a debt) orally without the need for a signed writing as a matter of English law.

## D   Assignment of *Parts* of a Chose in Action

This book suggests that where a chose in action may be seen to be made up of discrete claim-right/duty and power/liability jural relations between the obligee and obligor to the chose, the 'assignment' of such a chose by the obligee to an assignee entails modifying the privilege/no-right and

---

[67] In *Holt* v. *Heatherfield Trust Ltd* [1942] 2 KB 1, Atkinson J recognized that a gift of a legal chose could be validly made even if no written notice had been given as, under LPA1925, s. 136(1), such notice could be given by the assignee. Atkinson J did not mention, however, if the assignment had also been merely parol. Smith and Leslie take Atkinson J's reticence on the point to be suggestive that the outcome might have been different had the assignment been parol: Smith & Leslie (2018), para. 11.178. As explained in the main text, this would misunderstand the operation and effect of both Judicature Act 1873, s. 25 (6), and LPA1925, s. 136(1).

immunity/disability jural relations between obligee-assignor and assignee in respect of the claim-right/duty and power/liability jural relations between the obligee-assignor and the obligor. By conceptualizing equitable assignments to operate by means of a trust as well as an agency effect, this book has shown that the same mechanisms underpin equitable assignments of legal and equitable choses in action alike.

This, in turn, entails rejection of the 'substitutive transfer' model, which is important, because the substitutive transfer model cannot explain how or why *parts* of a debt may be effectively equitably assigned.

As was recognized in *Re Steel Wing Company, Ltd*,[68] it is not possible to invoke s. 136(1) when a fraction of a debt is supposed to have been assigned. This is because such assignment of part of a debt is not 'absolute' for the purposes of s. 136(1).[69] But, even so: 'The assignment of part of a debt however operates in equity to transfer the part assigned, and consequently in my judgment constitutes the assignee a creditor in equity of the company in respect of that part.'[70]

Though, as will have been made clear, the language of 'transfer' is not entirely apt, the sense of what P. O. Lawrence J was implying is tolerably clear. As was held in *Hunter* v. *Moss*,[71] an express trust may be validly constituted over fifty out of 950 shares registered in the name of the settlor. Though the specific shares have not been identified, such a trust does not fail for want of certainty of subject matter. As Briggs J explained: 'A trust of part of a fungible mass without the appropriation of any specific part of it for the beneficiary does not fail for uncertainty of subject matter, provided that the mass itself is sufficiently identified and provided also that the beneficiary's proportionate share of it is not itself uncertain.'[72] And for Briggs J, though he acknowledges that there remains some uncertainty as to the operation of such a trust, the most persuasive analysis of such a trust was that it operated 'by creating a beneficial co-ownership share in the identified fund, rather than in the

---

[68] [1921] 1 Ch 349.

[69] See e.g. *Durham Brothers* v. *Robertson* [1898] 1 QB 765, 774 (Chitty LJ); *Forster* v. *Baker* [1910] 2 KB 636, 640-1 (Bray J, aff'd on appeal to the Court of Appeal: [1910] 2 KB 641-2); *Raiffeisen Zentralbank Österriech AG* v. *Five Star Trading LLC* [2001] EWCA Civ 68, [2001] QB 825, [75].

[70] *Re Steel Wing Company, Ltd* (n. 68) (Ch), 355.

[71] [1994] 1 WLR 452 (CA; leave to appeal refused).

[72] *Re Lehman Brothers International (Europe)* [2010] EWHC 2914 (Ch) [225] (Briggs J); aff'd *Re Lehman Brothers International (Europe) (in administration) (No. 4)* [2011] EWCA Civ 1544; [2012] 2 BCLC 151 [73]-[77].

conceptually much more difficult notion of seeking to identify a particular part of that fund which the beneficiary owns outright'.[73]

Once we recognize that an equitable assignment entails the constitution of a trust over the chose assigned, when one is assigning a fraction of a debt owed (say, 25 per cent of the debt), such assignment entails equitable co-ownership.[74] That is, the trust which underpins such assignment may be conceived to be a trust for the benefit of the assignee *and* the assignor over the entirety of the debt as tenants-in-common in undivided shares in the ratio of 25/75.

Given this, if the debt was unpaid, the assignor would be duty-bound to the assignee by reason of such trust, above, to bring an action at law against the debtor in respect of the unpaid debt. If the assignor performed such duty, the sums realized by such action would then be overreached and be held by the assignor on the *same* trust as arose by reason of the equitable assignment; that is, she would hold the sums received on trust for her assignee and herself in the ratio of 25/75, and so far as the sums received might *then* be apportioned, the assignee could require the assignor to pay over her fractional share.[75]

The 'trust-plus-agency' model of equitable assignment can, therefore, explain how parts of a debt may be assigned, and it is equally straightforward to apply it to assignments of other legal or equitable choses. For example, given the 'trust' aspect of equitable assignment, there is no difficulty with 'partial' assignments of an equitable chose which is entire and indivisible (as, for example, an equitable interest in a single company share).

By way of contrast, the 'partial' trust model of equitable assignment put forward by some others which assumes that an equitable assignor of

---

[73] *Re Lehman Brothers International (Europe)* (n. 72), [232] (Briggs J), citing with approval the analysis in Goode (2003). A similar approach was adopted in a decision by Campbell J sitting in the Equity Division of the Supreme Court of New South Wales in *White v. Shortall* [2006] NSWSC 1379, 60 ACSR 654, [210]–[212]. In so doing, Briggs J implicitly rejected the academic criticisms of *Hunter v. Moss* [1994] 1 WLR 452 in Eva Micheler, *Property in Securities: A Comparative Study* (Cambridge: Cambridge University Press 2007), p. 130; and Erica Johansson, *Property Rights in Investment Securities and the Doctrine of Specificity* (London: Springer, 2009), pp. 94–9, 167–71.

[74] See e.g. Goode (2003), p. 385.

[75] 'There is no good reason why it should be impossible for a settlor to declare himself a trustee of 50 out of 950 of his indistinguishable shares, when he could clearly declare himself a trustee of all of them, or as to an unappropriated 900 for himself and as to an unappropriated 50 for another beneficiary, who could clearly insist on a distribution of 50 – it would not matter which': Lewin (2015), para. 3-007.

an equitable chose in action 'drops out'[76] would appear to deny that an equitable assignment of an equitable chose entails the constitution of a trust over such chose. To that extent, they appear to accept that such assignments operate by means of a 'substitutive transfer'. But since such substitutive transfer cannot explain the validity of equitable assignments of fractional parts of legal choses in action which are entire and indivisible, it also cannot explain how equitable choses in action which are similarly entire and indivisible may be assigned 'in part'.

If the substitutive transfer model of equitable assignment of equitable choses were true, it would not be possible to equitably assign part of an equitable chose. The marketability of parts of such choses would, accordingly, be reduced. Fortunately, as this book has sought to show, that is not the law.

## E   'Statutory' Assignments of Future Choses in Action and the Need for Consideration

Section 136(1) 'statutory' assignments *are* equitable assignments, but with a limited statutory overlay in respect of certain entitlements. This has certain consequences. First, as has already been explained in Chapter 13, it means that there is no reason why we may not 'statutorily' assign an equitable chose in action. Second, it means that so far as one may only 'equitably assign' a future chose in action where the facts support a finding that there had been a specifically enforceable *agreement* to assign such future chose, the same must be true of a 'statutory' assignment: that is, notwithstanding that one may effect a 'statutory' assignment without need for consideration, it does not follow that one may effect a 'statutory' assignment of a future chose in action without consideration.

If a statutory assignment operated entirely distinctly from an equitable assignment, one might be prepared to accept that, so far as a statutory assignment may take effect without the need for consideration, it might be possible to statutorily assign a *future* chose in action without consideration. The analysis in Chapter 13 tells us, however, that that view cannot be correct.

First, a future chose in action may be validly assigned in equity if the assignment is supported by consideration.[77] Thus, so far as the

---

[76] See e.g. Snell (2015), para. 3-022; Liew (2018), para. 3-05; Smith & Leslie (2018), paras 11.06–11.09. This view is discussed in Chapter 4, Section A(ii).

[77] *Meek* v. *Kettlewell* (1842) 1 Hare 464; *Re Tilt* (1896) 74 LT 163, 543 (Chitty J); *Re Ellenborough* [1903] 1 Ch 697 (Ch).

statutory effects mandated by s. 136(1) may be applied to a valid equitable assignment, where the chose assigned is a future chose, those statutory effects would only arise so far as the future chose had been validly assigned in equity, meaning an assignment that was supported by consideration. Without such consideration, there could be no effective equitable assignment of such future chose, and nothing for s. 136(1) to act on.

Secondly, an equitable assignment 'becomes' a statutory assignment only when the 'triangle' of 'absolute, writing *and notice*' is fulfilled. Consequently, it is impossible for there to be a state of affairs where the effects mandated by s. 136(1) are applied in relation to an equitable assignment of future choses in action when those future choses have yet to arise.

Where an attempt is made to 'statutorily assign', say, future book debts, each trade debtor must be given written notice of the same. Yet such notice may only be given at or after the point in time when the debtor–creditor relationship is created, and not before. This follows from the express wording of s. 136(1) itself,[78] stipulating that written notice is to be given to 'the debtor, trustee or other person from whom the assignor would have been entitled to claim such debt or thing in action'.

One only becomes a 'debtor', 'trustee' or relevant 'other person' when the debt, trust or other relevant chose in action has arisen, and not before. So it would seem that to effect a valid *statutory* assignment of a future chose in action such as a future book debt, written notice must be given *after* the book debt had arisen.[79] But by then, the book debt would be 'future' no more – it would have become a *present* book debt. And if written notice is given *then*, it would not be written notice pertaining to a *future* book debt. Thus,[80]

---

[78] The same point appears to have been made in Salinger (2017), para. 8-20.

[79] An analogy may also be drawn with cases which have shown how the rule in *Dearle* v. *Hall* may be applied to cases of multiple assignments of the same future chose in action where notices were given by the assignees before and after the said chose in action came into being: notices given whilst the chose in action had yet to come into being are simply ineffective. See *Buller* v. *Plunkett* (1860) 1 J & H 441; *Webster* v. *Webster* (1862) 31 Beav 393; *Somerset* v. *Cox* (1865) 33 Beav 634; *Boss* v. *Hopkinson* (1870) 18 WR 725; *Calisher* v. *Forbes* (n. 58); *Addison* v. *Cox* (1872) LR 8 Ch App 76; *Johnstone* v. *Cox* (1880) 16 Ch D 571 (aff'd: (1881) 19 Ch D 17); *Re Dallas* [1904] 2 Ch 385.

[80] Oditah (2009), pp. 352–3.

[E]ffective notice cannot be given until there is both a receivable and a debtor by whom it is owed and to whom notice can be given.

Accordingly, the required notice cannot be anticipated or carried out prospectively.

This echoes the position set out in *Goode on Legal Problems of Credit and Security* which states that only a presently existing debt can be assigned pursuant to LPA1925, s. 136.[81]

In opposition to these views, there is some (admittedly scant, and regrettable) judicial support for the contrary position. These will now be briefly examined.

In *Jones* v. *Humphreys*, Lord Alverstone CJ thought that 'there is no doubt that an absolute assignment of future debts may be a good assignment for the purposes of the section [i.e. s. 25(6), Judicature Act 1873, which is *in pari materia* with s 136(1)]'.[82] This was, however, *obiter*, as Lord Alverstone held that the 'assignment' had been effected by way of charge. Thus, it would have fallen out of the statute for that reason, in any event.[83] Further, although Darling and Channell JJ agreed with Lord Alverstone on his holding, neither expressed any view on his observations by way of *dicta*.

Further indirect support for the proposition that one may effect a valid statutory assignment of a future chose in action may be found in Fletcher Moulton LJ's judgment in *Glegg* v. *Bromley*, where the Court of Appeal considered whether the 'fruits of an action' *before* final judgment in the action had been handed down[84] had been effectively assigned. Fletcher Moulton LJ's judgment contains the following, rather cryptic, passage:[85]

[Counsel] claim that this was an assignment of future property. In olden times before the Judicature Act [1873] such an assignment would not be recognized in law. The parties would have had to go to equity to get it enforced, and equity would not enforce such an assignment if it was voluntary. Therefore prior to the Judicature Act you must have shewn that there was some good consideration for it before it would have had

---

[81] Goode (2017), para. 3-11. See also Roy Goode, 'Some Aspects of Factoring Law – I: The Acquisition of Rights in the Receivables' [1982] *Journal of Business Law* 240, 242: 'An assignment of future receivables takes effect only in equity'. No authority was provided for this proposition either.

[82] [1902] 1 KB 10, 13.

[83] Ibid., 13–14.

[84] The assignment of the fruits of an action *after* final judgment would be a straightforward present assignment of the judgment debt.

[85] [1912] 3 KB 474, 486 (emphasis added).

> any practical operation, and they claim that the same effect must be given
> to it now. I am not disposed to disagree with them in their view of the law.
> I think that an assignment of future property does require to be some-
> thing more than a mere voluntary assignment, a gift, *in order that it may
> have legal operation*.

This passage suggests that Fletcher Moulton LJ considered that there was
something in the proposition that a statutory assignment of a future
chose in action or expectancy could be validly made, such that one could
assign future property as to enable that assignment to have 'legal operation'. However, in the end, Fletcher Moulton LJ inclined towards thinking otherwise: there had to be more than a 'mere voluntary assignment',
notwithstanding the wording of the statute.

Perhaps the clearest authority for the proposition that statutory assignment of future choses in action is possible without any need for consideration, contradicting the position suggested in *Goode on Legal Problems of
Credit and Security*, is to be found in the decision of the High Court in
*Walker v. The Bradford Old Bank*.[86]

In this case, Reynolds purported to assign to Walker the credit balance
outstanding in a deposit account he maintained with the defendant bank
as at the time of his death.[87] At the time of the assignment, Reynolds had a
credit balance of £48 with the defendant bank. When he died, the account
with the defendant bank had a credit balance of about £217. After Reynolds' death, Walker gave the defendant bank notice of the assignment and
demanded to be paid such sums as stood to Reynolds' credit. When the
defendant bank declined to do so, Walker successfully sued the defendant
bank. The High Court accepted that the assignment was a statutory
assignment pursuant to s. 25(6), Judicature Act 1873,[88] and ordered the
sum in the account in credit be paid to Walker on his receipt alone.

This decision is interesting because the subject matter of Reynolds'
assignment to Walker was, necessarily, a *future* chose in action since at
no point was Reynolds barred from drawing down on the account, or

---

[86] (1884) 12 QBD 511.

[87] The assignment was in furtherance of a voluntary settlement: Walker was to hold the
subject matter of the assignment on various trusts for the benefit of Reynolds and
Reynolds' two daughters.

[88] As to whether the assignment to Walker was an effective equitable assignment of a future
chose, notwithstanding the lack of consideration in support, Smith J (with whom
Williams J agreed) held that it was not open to the defendant bank 'to attempt to
impeach the settlement' on this ground: *Walker v. The Bradford Old Bank, Limited*
(1884) 12 QBD 511, 516.

adding to it, while he lived: it was an assignment of *such* sum as stood in credit in the account at a future in point in time.[89]

Although there was, on the assignment to Walker, a present debt of £48 owed by the bank to Reynolds, which was repayable on demand, that debt was extinguished with every intervening deposit into and withdrawal from the account.[90] So when the account balance came up to £217 on Reynolds' death, that was, in essence, a *different* debt from the one which existed at the time of the assignment: it was a chose in action which did not exist at the time of that assignment. Hence, at the time of the assignment to Walker, it was still a *future* chose in action. This was, therefore, a case where a future chose in action had been assigned.[91]

This was recognized in *Skipper & Tucker* v. *Holloway and Howard*, leading Darling J to observe as follows:[92]

> A future debt does not exist at the time of the assignment, and therefore it is not necessary that there shall be a present debt of an exact amount in order that it may be validly assigned. *Walker* v. *[The]Bradford Old Bank* is an authority for the proposition that there can be a legal [i.e. statutory] assignment of a future debt.

And in the third edition of *Halsbury's*,[93] it was said that one may statutorily assign '[a] specified future debt ... as, for example, [1] the

---

[89] Specifically, the assignment provided that 'all moneys now *or hereafter* to be standing to the credit of the said Robert Vincent Reynolds in the books of or at the said bank' were 'hereby assigned, together with power to the said William Walker ... to sue and give receipts for all sums of money now due': ibid., 512.

[90] The facts suggest that 'dividend warrants, cheques, and moneys were from time to time paid in the usual way, and upon which cheques were drawn. [But a]fter the 2nd of November, 1882, no moneys were paid into the defendants' bank to the credit of the account': ibid., 513.

[91] Without addressing the point in the main text, Liew (2018), para. 2-08, adopts Smith J's characterization of the transaction before the court (at 12 QBD 516-17) to have been a case of an *accruing* debt arising out of an *existing* contract, and so was an assignment of a present chose. There are two problems with this. First, although there was an existing banker–customer contract between the Bradford Old Bank and Reynolds at the time of the purported assignment to Walker, the wording of Reynolds's assignment is inapt to reflect that Reynolds had intended to assign the benefit of such banker–customer contract to Walker (see above, n. 89). Second, even if it had been Reynolds's intention to presently assign to Walker the benefit of his banker–customer contract with the Bradford Old Bank, it seems likely that the entitlements arising under such banker–customer contract would have been personal to Reynolds. If so, no assignment of the same could have been effected.

[92] [1910] 2 KB 630, 634.

[93] *Halsbury's Laws* (3rd edn, 1953), vol. 4, para. 1003; cited with approval by McCarthy J in *Mcleay* v. *Commissioner of Inland Revenue* [1963] NZLR 711 (Supreme Court of New

balance standing at any time after the date of the assignment to the credit of the assignor at a bank, [2] or future rents, or [3] a retention fund under a building contract'. Significantly, the first of these three examples was drawn from the judgment in *Walker* v. *The Bradford Old Bank*.

It is submitted that *Walker* provides only very weak support for the proposition that a statutory assignment of a future chose in action is possible. It did not fully consider the two constraints noted above, namely: (i) that s. 136(1) sets out no independent conception of assignment, but is parasitic on the notions of assignment as are already recognized at law or in equity; and (ii) that statutory assignment only takes effect upon receipt of the notice of assignment by the relevant obligor, and such notice may not be effectively given ahead of time before the obligation had arisen. Indeed, the second constraint was not considered because in *Walker* v. *The Bradford Old Bank*, no notice of the assignment had been given while the assignor was alive: 'express' notice[94] was only given to the bank after the assignor's death, by which time the 'future' chose was future no longer: it had become a present debt.

Given the points noted above, taking *Walker* v. *The Bradford Old* to stand for the proposition that it is possible to statutorily assign (without need for consideration) a future chose in action so long as the assignment is absolute, in writing, and written notice is given *before* the future chose had come into being, is difficult. Commentators who have taken the decision in *Walker* to have gone as far as that may be reading too much into it. The more conservative position, it is suggested, is that consideration is always required in order for an 'equitable assignment' of a future chose in action to arise by reason of the doctrine of conversion, and that if the requirements of LPA1925, s. 136(1) are also met, then the additional statutory effects prescribed in ss. 136(1)(a), (b) and (c) will apply. However, should commercial necessity require future choses to be made capable of being assigned without need for consideration, it will need plainer words that those in s. 136(1) to achieve such ends.

---

Zealand), 718; and by Menzies J in *Norman* v. *Federal Commissioner of Taxation* (1963) 109 CLR 9, 21.

[94] Which, we presume, was in writing.

## F Discharge by Acceptance of Performance: Limitation and Remedies

As explained in Chapters 11 and 12, when we realize that an equitable assignee never 'drops out' but retains her entitlements as obligee to the legal or equitable chose as had been equitably assigned, it follows that it is possible for the obligor to validly discharge his obligation by tendering performance to the obligee-assignor, despite having received notice of the assignment. Though this may give rise in some cases to the possibility of a form of secondary accessory liability so far as such tender of performance with knowledge of the assignment might mean that the obligor would have committed the equitable wrong of dishonest assistance,[95] and although the obligor might be barred in some circumstances from pleading the facts as would support a defence of discharge by precise performance,[96] in principle, such performance *would* discharge the obligor's duty to his obligee which had arisen under the chose in action which had been assigned.

Applied to the assignment of a common law debt, this analysis challenges the proposition that a debtor, B, who tenders payment to his creditor, A, despite having received notice that A had equitably assigned the benefit of the debt to an assignee, C, has to pay again, this time to C *because* the tender to A did not discharge the debt at common law. Instead, it suggests that the payment discharges the debt at common law[97] (unless otherwise provided by statute),[98] but such discharge then generates a secondary, accessorial, liability to the assignee in equity.[99]

This has immediate consequences for the equitable assignee C, so far as questions of limitation are concerned. In addition, if this analysis is correct, assignees like C will have to consider the impact of equitable bars to relief.

If a debtor like B is liable to the assignee in equity for dishonest assistance, the limitation defence set out in s. 5 read with s. 6 or s. 8 of the Limitation Act 1980[100] will be irrelevant. Those provisions apply to

---

[95] See Chapter 11.

[96] See Chapter 12.

[97] See also Tham (2010), p. 360.

[98] E.g. s. 141(1), LPA1925, which provides that the rent and benefit of a lessee's covenants arising under a lease of land arising prior to 1 January 1996 shall be 'annexed and incident to and shall go with the reversionary estate'. See also Megarry & Wade (2012), para. 20-068.

[99] See Chapter 11.

[100] Consequently, 'there is no room for the equitable doctrine of laches': *Re Pauling's Settlement Trusts* [1962] 1 WLR 86, 115; aff'd on this point, *Re Pauling's Settlement Trusts* [1964] 1 Ch 303, 353.

causes of action based on simple contract or specialty, respectively. But as to the *equitable* liability of B arising from his dishonest assistance, one looks to s. 21(3) of the 1980 Act, as the House of Lords explained in *Williams* v. *Central Bank of Nigeria*.[101]

Further, if B's liability derives from the equitable wrong of dishonest assistance, B may also be liable to make restitution for any gains which his assistance might have generated.[102] Therefore, two distinct heads of equitable liability are open to the assignee in these cases.

Then there is the other alternative, for C might bring an action at law against B in A's name as A's equitable assignee. As explained in Chapter 12, a debtor like B may be barred from pleading the facts which would otherwise support a defence of payment if he were to be sued by C (as equitable assignee) in A's name if B had tendered payment to A with the knowledge of the assignment to C. However, this entitlement of C to bar B from pleading such facts is rooted in the so-called 'equitable juris-diction of the common law courts' or the statutory power first granted to the common law courts by CLPA1854, s. 85, both of which were drawn from the availability of injunctive relief. So drawn, the availability of this form of procedural relief to C would necessarily also be subject to equitable bars such as laches. Whether C might successfully bring an action at law in A's name against B would therefore not simply rest on a question of limitation of actions at law: the success of the action against B would also depend on whether C's entitlement to bar such pleas of payment by B might itself be barred by equitable defences such as laches.[103]

The discussion above must, however, be qualified as a different result would arise if the equitable assignment to B had 'become' a 'statutory' assignment.

In Chapter 13, it was suggested that s. 136(1)(c) may be construed as transferring the power to accept a conforming tender of performance. This construction finds some support in *Liquidation Estates Purchase Company* v. *Willoughby*.[104] In that case, Walker contracted to purchase a partnership business, hoping to resell it at a profit. Together with two co-investors,[105] Kennedy placed £6,000 with Walker to finance the

---

[101] [2014] UKSC 10; [2014] AC 1189, discussed in Stephen Watterson, 'Limitation of Actions, Dishonest Assistance and Knowing Receipt' (2014) 73 CLJ 253.

[102] See discussion in Chapter 11, n. 52.

[103] For completeness, other equitable concerns such as 'clean hands' would also be a concern.

[104] [1898] AC 321.

[105] Namely Willoughby and Lord Paulet, who placed £9,000 and £10,000, respectively, on similar terms: each would be repaid £18,000 and £20,000, respectively, out of the proceeds of resale, that being double what each had placed.

purchase, on Walker's promise to repay £12,000 out of the proceeds of resale (being double Kennedy's investment), such sum being secured by a charge over the resale proceeds.

Kennedy then mortgaged his interest arising under his agreement with Walker to Norton to secure a loan of £6,200.[106] Despite receiving written notice of the mortgage dated 24 October 1888 from Norton's solicitors, in July 1889 Walker paid Kennedy £5,122 out of the proceeds of resale of the business; and in June 1890 Walker caused property worth £5,000 to be conveyed to Kennedy in part-satisfaction of the debt owed.

Meanwhile, Kennedy mortgaged his equity of redemption in his interest to Lord Windsor. Walker was also informed of this in 1891.

In 1893, Norton's and Lord Windsor's respective interests in Kennedy's interests against Walker were assigned to the Liquidation Estates Purchase Company. In 1889, not having been paid anything, Willoughby, one of the co-investors, brought proceedings against Walker, naming Lord Paulet and Kennedy as co-defendants. In those proceedings, a considerable sum consisting of the proceeds of resale charged by Walker was paid into court, and it was ordered that it should be applied to satisfy Lord Paulet's and Willoughby's claims before anything should be paid in respect of Kennedy's share, on the assumption that Kennedy had already received part payment in advance of Lord Paulet and Willoughby by reason of Walker's actions in 1889 and 1890.

The Liquidation Estates Purchase Company, being assignee of both Norton's and Lord Windsor's respective interests in Kennedy's interests against Walker, brought the present proceedings against Willoughby, Kennedy, Lord Paulet's trustee in bankruptcy and some others claiming derivative beneficial interests in Lord Paulet's interest, Walker, and the purchasers of the partnership business.[107]

The plaintiff claimed an account of what was due to them under Kennedy's mortgage to Norton, and 'as transferees of Lord Windsor's interest ... to have the fund in court ... applied towards payment of

---

[106] Though the judgments in the House of Lords often referred to Kennedy having 'charged' his interest to Norton, Norton's security interest was not a charge by way of hypothecation. As Lord Herschell noted (at [1898] AC 331, emphasis added): 'The notion that Norton's rights could be affected because a payment was wrongfully made to his *mortgagor* [i.e. Kennedy] does not appear to me to rest on any sound foundation.' In addition, the facts in the report of the Court of Appeal's decision referred to the security arrangement between Kennedy and Norton to be a mortgage: [1896] 1 Ch 726, 726; as did Kay LJ in his dissenting judgment: [1896] 1 Ch 726, 736.

[107] *Liquidation Estates Purchase Company* v. *Willoughby* [1896] 1 Ch 726, 728.

what should be found due to the [plaintiff], and other relief'.[108] The issue, therefore, was whether Walker's actions in 1889 and 1890 had reduced the sums due to Kennedy, as had been assumed in the earlier proceedings. On appeal, the House of Lords concluded that:[109] 'Payment to Kennedy after that notice [from Norton's solicitors] was a payment which Norton, so long as he had an interest in the fund, was not bound to recognise. . . . [I]t was no payment at all.'

Consequently, it held that the sum paid into court should be applied to Willoughby, Lord Paulet and the plaintiff without regard to Walker's actions in 1889 and 1890.

Though none of the judgments nor any of the arguments refers to it, it seems reasonably clear that the benefit of the contract (and of the charge) between Walker and Kennedy had been 'statutorily' assigned to Norton on 24 October 1888, when Walker received written notice of the same.[110] Nowhere is it suggested that the assignment by way of mortgage to Norton was parol, and given the very substantial sums involved, it is inconceivable that Norton would have taken security other than by a written agreement in Kennedy's hand. Since an equitable assignment by way of mortgage *is* an absolute assignment for the purposes of 'statutory' assignment,[111] and written notice of the assignment had been given, this was an equitable assignment by way of mortgage which had 'become' a 'statutory' assignment.[112]

Although Kennedy *was* joined to the proceedings, the plaintiff appears to have brought the proceedings in its own right. There is no indication of the plaintiff seeking any order compelling Kennedy to permit it to bring the present proceedings against Kennedy's co-defendants as one would expect if the assignment had been merely equitable. Absent such

---

[108]    Ibid.

[109]    Ibid., 336 (Lord Macnaghten). Lord Herschell was of similar opinion (at 331): 'Kennedy having assigned his interest to Norton, and Norton having given notice of this assignment to Walker, any payment subsequently made by him to Kennedy could, as it seems to me, have no more effect as against Norton than if it had been made to a stranger.' And similarly, the Lord Chancellor held: 'Can it make any difference that Walker, in defiance of his duty, thought proper to divert a certain sum of money from the gross fund in favour of Kennedy at a time when to his knowledge Kennedy had no right to receive it?' (at 328).

[110]    [1898] AC 321, 322.

[111]    See Chapter 13, n. 52.

[112]    The view in the main text, that *Liquidation Estates* was a case of a statutory assignment, appears to be shared in Liew (2018), para. 2-18, fn. 177. However, *Liquidation Estates* was assumed in *Halsbury's Laws* (5th edn, 2009), vol. 13, para. 70, fn. 3, to be a case of a mere equitable assignment.

order, if Kennedy had effected statutory assignments in favour of Norton and Lord Walton, and they had also effected statutory assignments in favour of the plaintiff,[113] since such statutory assignments would have transferred Kennedy's standing and cause of action against Walker to, ultimately, the plaintiffs,[114] it would have been unremarkable for the plaintiffs to have brought the proceedings in their own name.

But more importantly, it is arguable that, by operation of the wording which may now be found in LPA1925, s. 136(1)(c), Kennedy's power as against Walker to grant a discharge would also have been transferred from Kennedy to Norton. Consequently, it would follow that any payments or conveyances of other property by Walker to Kennedy would be ineffective, thus leading to Lord Macnaghten's conclusion that payment to Kennedy was one which Norton (so far as he had an interest in the fund) was entitled to ignore: 'it was no payment at all'.

Given the analysis of equitable assignment, and the effect of s. 136(1)(c) when such equitable assignment 'becomes' a 'statutory' assignment, we need to distinguish between 'statutory' and non-statutory assignments of debts because a debtor who tenders payment to his creditor following notice of a 'statutory' assignment of the debt cannot claim to have discharged his debt obligation at common law.

Such payment is, in essence, a payment to a stranger to the debt contract because the assignor no longer has the power to give a discharge. Consequently, the debt remains unpaid. Further, no equitable liability for dishonest assistance may arise, for on this view of s. 136(1)(c), the assignor could owe her assignee no duties as to her exercise of a non-existent power.

## G   Debtor's Liability to Account and Irrecoverability of Payments Tendered to the Assignor of a Debt Following Notice

Where the benefit of a debt owed by B to A has been equitably assigned to C, and notice of such assignment has been received by B, if B tenders payment to A in purported discharge of the debt and A accepts such tender, that would lead to the debt being discharged by performance.[115]

---

[113] Norton was not made party to the plaintiff's proceedings, so his assignment to the plaintiff must have been statutory.

[114] See Chapter 13, Sections E(i) and (ii).

[115] See Chapters 11 and 12.

At common law, no issue of any continuing obligation on the part of B to repay the debt would arise, the debt having been extinguished at law. However, where A dissipates or absconds with the monies so received in breach of her equitable duties to preserve the traceable substitute of the debt, so far as B had knowledge of the assignment (having received notice of the same), B could be held to be liable to C in *equity* for having committed the wrong of dishonestly assisting A to commit a breach of her equitable duties to C.[116] Alternatively, where such knowledge is present, B may be barred from pleading the facts as would support his defence of discharge by performance. So barred, judgment might then be handed down in respect of an action at law in respect of that debt, leading B to have to 'pay again'.

The discussion in Section F, above, has outlined the impact of this analysis on the equitable assignee, C. However, this analysis will also affect the debtor, B.

Firstly, quite apart from being liable to have to 'pay again', if it is correct to say that B's tender of payment to A would have amounted to an act of dishonest assistance, B could be made liable to account to C for any gains B might have made from having assisted in A's breach of her duties to C. Restitutionary liability in respect of any gains or profits made by reason of B's acts of assistance appears also to be possible, so far as B, as dishonest assister, is held to be liable as a constructive *trustee*: C could insist that B account for any gains made from having assisted in A's breach of duty.

In England, the possibility for such a remedy was recognized in *Fyffes Group Ltd* v. *Templeman;*[117] *Ultraframe (UK) Ltd* v. *Fielding;*[118] and in *Novoship (UK) Ltd* v. *Mikhaylyuk.*[119] In addition, in *Akita Holdings* v. *Attorney-General of the Turks and Caicos,*[120] delivering the opinion of the Privy Council, Lord Carnwath JSC, quoted Longmore LJ's judgment in *Novoship* on the availability of these remedies for the equitable wrong of dishonest assistance without any suggestion that granting similar remedies to the two types of equitable wrongs was questionable

---

[116] See Chapter 11.

[117] [2000] 2 Lloyd's Rep 643 (Comm), 672.

[118] [2005] EWHC 1638 (Ch), [1538].

[119] [2014] EWCA Civ 908, [2015] QB 499, [93] (permission to appeal to the Supreme Court refused on 10 November 2014). In *Fyffes* and in *Novoship*, no restitutionary award was granted at least partially on grounds that the gains made by the accessories and their wrongdoing were insufficiently causally linked.

[120] *Islands* [2017] UKPC 7; [2017] AC 590, [15].

in any way (at [15]). Further afield, such a remedy was granted against a dishonest assister in *Nanus Asia Co. Inc.* v. *Standard Chartered Bank*;[121] and the availability of restitutionary accounting remedies as to gains made by an accessory's acts of dishonest assistance recognized in *Novoship* was also adopted in a decision of the Singapore High Court in *Von Roll Asia Pte Ltd* v. *Goh Boon Gay*.[122]

Secondly, B can have no restitutionary recourse against A to recover the sums that had been tendered to A. Since the basis for such payment was to effect a discharge of the debt *at law*, and that was indeed the result upon acceptance of such payment by A, B could not seek recovery of the sum from A on account of A's unjust enrichment. There would not, in such circumstances, be any unjust factor by reference to failure of consideration or basis.

This of course leaves open the possibility of recovery on other grounds. For example, if B had been wrongly assured by A that C had authorized A to accept a conforming tender of payment, even though C had done no such thing, B's payment to A on the basis of such a fraudulent misrepresentation could well be actionable under the tort of deceit. But restitutionary recovery on grounds of unjust enrichment would not, it seems, be readily available.

## H   Deconstructed Assignments

As analysed in this book, equitable assignments of a chose in action are made up of (i.e. 'constructed' from) two components: a bare trust as between the 'assignor' and her 'assignee' in which the 'assignor' constitutes herself to hold the benefit of the chose in action for the benefit of her assignee, coupled with an unusual form of agency by which the assignee is authorized to invoke the assignor's entitlements as against the obligor to the chose assigned without regard for the assignor's interests. Further, as has been explained in Chapter 6, Section A, the conjunction of the proprietary effects of the trust with the delegation of powers by the agency results in the agency becoming irrevocable. An equitable assignment is, therefore, constructed of a trust plus an agency that is irrevocable because of the presence of the proprietary interests arising from the trust. It follows that an 'equitable assignment' of a chose

---

[121] [1990] 1 HKLR 396.
[122] [2017] SGHC 82; [2018] 4 SLR 1053.

in action would arise, so long as the requisite bare trust and agency relationships are established. Even if the word 'assignment' was never used, as equity regards the substance and not the form, so long as the requisite *functions* effected by the bare trust and agency have arisen and are coincident, the end result will be taken to be an equitable assignment. But if an equitable assignment may be 'constructed' in this manner, what happens when it is 'deconstructed'?[123]

Suppose, in our familiar example of A, B and C where B had borrowed a sum of money from A, A had first authorized C to act in A's place with regard to B, and had only constituted herself bare trustee of the benefit of the chose in action arising from the debt owed by B at a much later period in time ('Scenario I'). Conversely, suppose A had constituted the bare trust first, and then authorized C to act in her place much later ('Scenario II'). Should such 'deconstructed' arrangements where the two aspects of trust and agency are separated by substantial amounts of time also be viewed as equitable assignments, at least at the point when both relations have been constituted and have become coincident? It does not appear that there has been any decided caselaw on point. One may, however, reason as follows.

In relation to Scenario I, it is improbable that the agency relationship will be taken to be irrevocable, given that it was not created to further or promote any proprietary interest of the delegatee at the time of its creation[124] (there being none at that point in time). Therefore, on the analysis in this book, it would seem that a deconstructed arrangement such as that in Scenario I would not amount to an equitable assignment because the element of 'irrevocability' might not have been made out.

In relation to Scenario II, the result may be less clear. If the court is satisfied that it had been agreed that the agency be irrevocable, and that 'the authority [had been] given to secure an interest of the agent' (such as C's equitable proprietary interest by reason of the prior constitution of the bare trust in Scenario II),[125] it may be possible for such agency that is created later to be taken to be irrevocable. If so, by that point in time, though no earlier, an equitable assignment may well have been created.

The possibility of a 'deconstructed' equitable assignment arising by means of a bare trust, followed by the requisite delegation of authority to

---

[123] I am indebted to Dr F. Wilmot-Smith for putting the question to me.

[124] See discussion in Chapter 6, Section A.

[125] *Angove's Pty Ltd* v. *Bailey* [2016] UKSC 47; [2016] 1 WLR 3179, [7]. At [8], it was recognized that the 'agreement that the agency be irrevocable' need not be express, and may be inferred from the context.

the beneficiary of said trust (as in Scenario II), raises some difficult questions where the chose in question is equitable, rather than legal. This is due to the formalities imposed by LPA1925, s. 53(1)(c).

Section 53(1)(c) provides that a disposition of a subsisting equitable interest (for example, an equitable chose in action) may only be made by a writing under the hand of the disponor (or his duly authorized agent), or by way of a will. It is undoubted that an equitable assignment constitutes a 'disposition' for the purposes of s. 53(1)(c): so an equitable assignment of a subsisting equitable chose in action must be made in the form of a suitably signed writing, or in the form of a will. An equitable assignment of a subsisting equitable chose by parol is a nullity.

If the chose in Scenario II, above, were an equitable chose (arising, say, out of a testamentary trust over assets held by T, as testamentary trustee, in favour of A, as sole beneficiary under a will), so far as there might be said to have been an 'equitable assignment' at the later point in time when C was authorized to use A's entitlements against T, the obligor to the equitable chose in question, it would seem that A would have to conform with the formalities required by s. 53(1)(c) for such acts as would result in the 'disposition' of A's interests to be validly performed. That is to say, if A were to authorize C other than in the requisite signed writing, that delegation of authority as would lead to the creation of a 'deconstructed' equitable assignment 'disposing' of A's interest in the equitable chose would be invalid. Yet even so, it may be that the beneficial interest conferred on C by reason of the bare trust which A had previously constituted would continue: there seems to be no obvious reason why A's prior intention to constitute such a trust should be frustrated by the statute.

It must be admitted, though, that the suggestions above are just that. The questions raised in this section never having been asked of the courts, their definitive answer still lies in the future.

## I   Concluding Remarks: 'Everything Should Be as Simple as It Can Be, but Not Simpler'[126]

If the purpose of law reform is to reduce incoherence in the law, the analysis in this book suggests that the need to reform the law of

---

[126] 'I remember a remark of Albert Einstein, which certainly applies to music. He said, in effect, that everything should be as simple as it can be, but not simpler . . .': R. Sessions, 'How a "Difficult Composer" Gets That Way', *New York Times*, 8 January 1950,

assignment is less pressing than initial appearances would suggest. The law on equitable assignment is admittedly complex; and it can be confusing if we fail to pay close attention to the historical interaction between the courts at common law and in equity. But the law on equitable assignment is not incoherent.

What needs reform, arguably, is not the law as it stands, but our understanding of it. And if targeted law reform to simplify the law on assignment is thought desirable, it is necessary to be clear about what one is simplifying.

The robustness[127] of the English law of assignment, both in its equitable and statutory guises, is striking. Without much significant theorizing, practitioners of law and equity worked out a pragmatic, practical and generally effective means of allowing intangible assets in the form of choses in action to be treated *like* property, whilst respecting the liberties afforded to a legal person to determine what obligations he would be bound to do, and to whom he would be bound. But perhaps because it works so well, comparatively little effort has been expended to explain *how* equitable and statutory assignment do what they do.

Professor Birks observed: 'The role of the academic branch of the profession has been transformed. One of its main tasks is to make explicit the principles on which the courts are operating, and thus to safeguard the formal rationality of the law, something Gaius took for granted as his duty.'[128] In keeping with that view, this book attempts to add to the work of the community of judges, practitioners and scholars who have dispelled the cobwebs shrouding the judicial pronouncements and practice of several centuries. Certainly, none of the work in this book would have been possible but for the paths that have been previously trodden.

Finally, as Einstein said: 'It can scarcely be denied that the supreme goal of all theory is to make the irreducible basic elements as simple and as few as possible without having to surrender the adequate representation of a

---

reprinted in *Roger Sessions on Music: Collected Essays* (E. T. Cone, ed., New Jersey: Princeton University Press, 1979), at p. 169. It is possible that Sessions was referring to Einstein's remarks in his Herbert Spencer Lecture of 1933 - see text at n. 129, below.

[127] In the sense of it being 'anti-fragile'.

[128] Peter Birks, 'Fictions, Ancient and Modern' in Neil MacCormick and Peter Birks (eds.), *The Legal Mind: Essays for Tony Honoré* (Oxford: Clarendon Press, 1986), p. 101.

# SHOULD CHRI
# ABANDON THE DOCTRINE
# OF THE TRINITY?

# Michael A. Barber

Universal Publishers
Boca Raton, Florida

*Should Christianity Abandon the Doctrine of the Trinity?*

Universal Publishers
Boca Raton, Florida
USA•2006

ISBN: 1-58112- 940-8

www.universal-publishers.com

# Table of Contents

# 1 Introduction

In view of the great quantity of books available in support of the doctrine of the Trinity, it may seem unusual to find that this book denies it. Fortunately the author should fare better than the individuals referred to in the book's opening paragraphs in view of the available freedom of speech. But it may be viewed as heretical nonetheless. The central doctrine of Christian churches, accepted by far and away the majority as a divinely authored teaching, the Trinity seems entrenched beyond question of doubt.

This book endeavours to provide a comprehensive answer to the question of the Trinity dogma. Although theologians and Christian writers have provided abundant material to define and explain the teaching of the Trinity, it is the contention of this book that the doctrine is nowhere taught — nor even alluded to — in the Holy Scriptures, and that it should be formally denied.

## Support Sought From Bible Manuscripts

Bible students rely on Bible translations when studying God's Word, in contrast with the Hebrew, Aramaic, and Greek manuscripts. This book reveals that scriptures which support the teaching of the Trinity in some Bible versions are incorrectly translated. The student can be forgiven for readily accepting the Trinity when his or her own Bible clearly teaches it! Such is the power of the Bible (see Hebrews 4:12), that *translations* have taken on the status that the original *manuscripts* by the Bible writers held. However, no translation today can claim to be "inspired by God" (2 Timothy 3:16). Consequently, throughout this book, appeal is made to Bible manuscripts to verify the true sense of a passage of text.

Thus, extensive use is made of the most basic resource available to Bible students — the Hebrew and Greek texts from which all Bible translations are drawn. This method is considered to be more accurate than relying on a translation because (a) translations can be coloured by doctrinal or partisan beliefs, or at least open to the suspicion of such, and (b) the meaning is extracted "from the horse's mouth" as it were. To illustrate: If you were to undertake a deep study, say of history, would you not appreciate the value of studying (as far as is possible) the actual texts of famous historians of ancient times, such as Herodotus or Josephus, rather than relying on an interpretative view of a modern-day historian? Granted, a modern-day teacher would provide you with a lucid and encapsulated knowledge of such works. But if you sought the unadulterated truth of history, without allowing yourself to be side-tracked by possibly erroneous interpretation or even propaganda, then nothing but the *original* would suffice. This is what an examination of the Hebrew and Greek Bible manuscripts provides.

For this reason, frequent use is made of highly respected Hebrew and Greek grammars and dictionaries. As there may be readers who are not acquainted with these languages, assistance is given by depicting all such words in bold, fully-capitalised text. For example, the Hebrew word for God is written thus: **E.LO.HIM'**. The syllables are separated by dots, and the accent (the syllable which takes the stress) is indicated by a single quotation mark following the syllable. This convention applies even when quotations are made from works which contain actual Hebrew and Greek characters; in which case the transliterated words are placed in square brackets, thus: θεος **[THE.OS'**: *God*].

## Every Known Key Scripture ...

Exponents of the Trinity use many "support texts" in defence of the doctrine; that is, scriptures that they believe prove the Trinity. When countering these arguments, it is insufficient to disprove one scripture. It is the belief of Trinitarians that, though a scripture they may select for support may prove difficult to defend on its own, other scriptures add weight to it. And herein lies the purpose of this book. It purports to cover *every known key scripture* used by Trinitarians in support of the doctrine, and to refute each one using God's Word the Holy Bible. A comprehensive index at the back contains all the scriptural references used. This presupposes the most common way the book is expected to be used. If background information on a given scripture is required, the index will no doubt be the first port of call.

It will become apparent to the reader that a moderate amount of repetition takes place within this volume. This is quite intentional. It fulfils a two-fold purpose, (a) as a teaching aid ("repetition is the mother of retention"), and (b) in the supposition that the volume will be used more as a reference aid than as a book to be read in chapter sequence like a novel. It is thus with a view to thoroughness that ideas relevant to two or more chapters may be found in each place rather than the reader being sent from place to place within the book.

## Conventions Used in the Book

Where squares brackets [such as these] are used, they indicate interpolations into quoted documents. For example, books often refer to Hebrew and Greek words and expressions without providing a translation. The translation is often supplied, but is placed in square brackets to indicate that it is not in the original work.

## Abbreviations Used

**LXX**: The Greek Septuagint. A translation from the Hebrew into the Greek produced during the third and second centuries before Christ during the ascendancy of the Greek empire under Alexander the Great.

**MS**: Manuscript. A document, usually made from papyrus or animal skin, on which a copy of a Bible book was made.

**MSS**: Manuscripts.

**MT**: Masoretic Text. The Hebrew text from which modern-day translations of the Old Testament are made. This usually makes reference to the text contained in the authoritative *Biblia Hebraica*, a master Hebrew Text by Rudolf Kittel first produced in 1906.

# PART ONE:

# ROOTS AND CONTROVERSIES

# 2 One Branch, Many Roots

Joan Bocher was burned to death in England in 1550 AD. Her crime? The *Encyclopædia Britannica* (1964) says: "She was condemned for open blasphemy in denying the Trinity, the one offence which all the church had regarded as unforgivable ever since the struggle with Arianism."

On October 27th, 1553 AD, Michael Servetus, a medical practitioner, was burned at the stake at Geneva, Switzerland, for denying the doctrine of the Trinity.

In 1693 AD a pamphlet attacking the Trinity was burned by order of the House of Lords, and the following year its printer and author were prosecuted.

In 1697 AD Thomas Aikenhead, an 18 year old student, was charged with denying the Trinity and hanged at Edinburgh, Scotland.

In 1711 AD Sir Isaac Newton's friend, William Whiston (translator of the works of Jewish historian Josephus), lost his professorship at Cambridge for denying the Trinity.

*An Historical Account of Two Notable Corruptions of Scripture,* detailing Sir Isaac Newton's condemnation of the Trinity teaching, was first published in 1754, twenty-seven years after Newton's death, due to the controversies surrounding the doctrine.

What is it about the doctrine of the Trinity that has created such extreme examples of religious intolerance? Moreover, what was it that the above people, and others like them, saw in this teaching that impelled them to deny it at such great cost?

Merely a superficial study of its origin will reveal how deeply rooted in paganism the doctrine is. Advocates of the Trinity are as well aware of these facts as are its opponents. The difference lies in the attitude toward these roots; whether they are palatable or acceptable to the Christian conscience.

How far, then, do these roots extend, and where do they originate?

"We worship one God in Trinity, and Trinity in Unity; neither confounding the persons, nor dividing the substance. For there is one person of the Father, another of the Son, and another of the Holy Ghost. But the Godhead of the Father, of the Son, and of the Holy Ghost is all one: the glory equal, the majesty coeternal. Such as the Father is, such is the Son, and such is the Holy Ghost. ... The Father eternal, the Son eternal, and the Holy Ghost eternal. ... So likewise the Father is almighty, the Son almighty, and the Holy Ghost almighty. ... So the Father is God, the Son is God, and the Holy Ghost is God. And yet there are not three Gods, but one God. ... The Father is made of none, neither created nor begotten. The Son is of the Father alone; not made, nor created, but begotten. The Holy Ghost is of the Father and of the Son; neither made, nor created, nor begotten, but proceeding. ... And in this Trinity none is afore or after other; none is greater or less than another. But the whole three persons are coeternal together, and coequal. So that in all things, as is aforesaid, the Unity in Trinity and the Trinity in Unity is to be worshipped. He therefore that will be saved must thus think of the Trinity."

These are the words of the *Athanasian Creed* (as quoted from *M'Clintock & Strong's Cyclopoedia*) formulated in the 4th century AD. The Creed was a result of a controversy which raged from the 2nd to the 4th centuries (and beyond).

The earliest record of the use of the word Trinity is in the writings — in the Greek language — of Theophilus of Antioch, 181 AD. The Latin word from which our English term is derived, **TRINITAS**, is first found in the writings of Tertullian (200 AD), who also first used the formula **UNA SUBSTANTIA, TRES PERSONAE**, "one substance, three persons." The doctrine owes something to the work of the so-called ante-Nicene Fathers, the most outstanding of which were Ignatius, Irenaeus, Tertullian, and Origen.

Sabellius, of the 3rd century, taught that the thinking of none of the three persons of the Trinity was subordinate to the others. The teachings of Apollinarius and Athanasius, among others, paved the way for the Nicene Creed of 325 AD. Here the doctrine was formally adopted by the Church and given a clear-cut, definitive formula.

Interestingly, though, at the time of the Nicene Creed, the doctrine was not so "clear-cut" as many suppose. For example, it says nothing about the Holy Spirit being a person. Even the nature of the Father and the Son, as defined later, was not so "clear-cut." Note what *The New Catholic Encyclopedia* states:

> "Whether the Council intended to affirm the numerical identity of the substance of Father and Son is doubtful."

The so-called Cappadocian Fathers, Basil, Gregory of Nyssa, and Gregory Nazianzus helped to further crystallise the teaching. It was given formal statements in a synodical letter of a council held in Constantinople in 382 AD. A document, called the Tome of Damasus, written by Damasus, Bishop of Rome, contained the following statements:

> "If anyone denies that the Father is eternal, that the Son is eternal, and that the Holy Spirit is eternal: he is a heretic.

> "If anyone denies that the Son of God is true God, just as the Father is true God, having all power, knowing all things, and equal to the Father: he is a heretic.

> "If anyone denies that the Holy Spirit ... is true God ... has all power and knows all things, ... he is a heretic.

> "If anyone denies that the three persons, the Father, the Son, and the Holy Spirit, are true persons, equal,

eternal, containing all things visible and invisible, that they are omnipotent, ... he is a heretic.

"If anyone says that [the Son who was] made flesh was not in heaven with the Father while he was on earth: he is a heretic.

"If anyone, while saying that the Father is God and the Son is God and the Holy Spirit is God, ... does not say that they are one God, ... he is a heretic."

Therefore this book itself (the book you are holding) constitutes a very great heresy. But a heresy from what? From a teaching which, through many agonies, was "adopted" by the church several centuries after the death of our Lord.

However, can you think of any of the teachings of the apostles which had to be "adopted" by the church? Surely the body of truth laid down between the covers of the Bible, completed toward the end of the 1st century, did not contain any teachings that required adoption by Jesus' followers. And, following Paul's "rule", the church should surely "keep to what is written." — 1 Corinthians 4:6, *Jerusalem Bible.*

It is here that the teaching of the Trinity lies in direct contrast with the contents of the Holy Scriptures. It is the Scriptures themselves which deny the truth of the doctrine.

# 3 The Role of Constantine the Great

The one who organised and orchestrated the Nicene Council of 325 AD was a non-Christian, Constantine the Great. Constantine was emperor of Rome during many of the debates which raged over the Trinity. He saw in these controversies the potential to tear his empire apart and so wanted to use the pagan beliefs so close to his heart in order to weld the fractions together. Cardinal Newman, in his book *The Development of Christian Doctrine*, says concerning this:

> "Constantine, in order to recommend the new religion to the heathen, transferred into it the outward ornaments to which they had been accustomed in their own."

The *Encyclopædia Britannica* says:

> "Constantine himself presided, actively guiding the discussions, and personally proposed ... the crucial formula expressing the relation of Christ to God in the creed issued by the council, 'of one substance with the Father' ... Overawed by the emperor, the bishops, with two exceptions only, signed the creed, many of them much against their inclination."

History informs us that Constantine was incriminated in the murder of seven of his close friends and family. Moreover, he was a sun-worshipper. And as far as his spiritual and intellectual credentials go, was he qualified to propose the teaching of the Trinity? *A Short History of Christian Doctrine* states:

> "Constantine had basically no understanding whatsoever of the questions that were being asked in Greek theology."

In proof of this is the fact that Trinitarians did not really come to the fore until the 4th century. At the beginning of the 3rd century the majority of Church Fathers believed in Unitarianism — that the Father is one God, and Jesus is the Son of God. The aforementioned Theophilus' Trinity was actually a far cry from the 4th century controversy — it consisted of "God, and His Word, and His wisdom." The Trinity of Tertullian was inconsistent. He believed that "there was a time when there was no Son."

Another who believed that there was a time when the Son was not was Arius, presbyter of the Church at Alexandria, Egypt. Arius was in the thick of the Trinity controversy, opposing the views of Alexander, his bishop, and Athanasius, who believed the three persons of the Godhead were of the same substance (Greek: **HU.PO'STA.SIS**), being not three but one God. Arius publicly opposed Alexander in 318 AD on the eternal pre-existence of the Son, after which Alexander excommunicated him from the Church. But Arius found many allies and "in a short time the whole East Church became a metaphysical battlefield." This resulted in the Council of Nicea, organised by emperor Constantine in 325 AD, where Arius' views were condemned. He was banished to Illynia by Constantine's order.

Toward the end of his life, however, Constantine favoured Arius' views — this with the support of Eusebius of Nicomedia — and, after five years, Arius was recalled from exile. Many Trinitarian bishops were banished, and even Athanasius himself was banished to Gaul (France).

After Constantine's death, though, the Trinitarians once again came to the fore. In 381 AD the ecumenical Council of Constantinople reaffirmed the Council of Nicea with a few alterations. This is regarded today as the definitive theological statement on the doctrine — that God, though three persons, is to be worshipped as one God. It is subscribed to by the Roman Catholic

Church, the Eastern Orthodox Church, and most Protestant churches.

Hence, after considerable dispute and confusion, and many Church Council's and synodical letters, the Church finally adopted the teaching of the Trinity. As is summed up by *The Encyclopedia Americana* (Vol. XXVII, p. 294L):

> "Christianity derived from Judaism and Judaism was strictly Unitarian [believing that God is one person]. The road which led from Jerusalem to Nicea was scarcely a straight one. Fourth century Trinitarianism did not reflect accurately early Christian teaching regarding the nature of God; it was, on the contrary, a deviation from this teaching."

Thus the Trinity is a "deviation," in direct contrast to Paul's counsel in Galatians 1:8 to reject any teaching that is not part of the "version of the Good News" (*Jerusalem Bible*) laid down by the Bible writers.

# 4 Ancient and Pagan Trinities

Today the doctrine is found throughout the entire realm of Christendom. However, non-Christian religions also have their Triads and Trinities of gods. The Buddhist Triads are plentiful: Manjusri, Sakyamuni, and Samanta-bhada, the Three Holy Ones of the Hua-yen School; Mahasthama, the embodiment of Wisdom, and Amitabha, and Avalokitesvara, the embodiment of Compassion; Bhaishajvaguru, Sakyamuni, and Amitabha to name a few. Then there is the Taoist Triad of Yuan-shih T'ien-chun, Tao Chun, and Lao Tzu. The Hindu Trinity consists of Brahma the Creator, Vishnu the Supreme God, and Shiva the Destroyer. There are also the Norse gods of Odin, Thor, and Freyr, and the Zoroastrian gods of Sraosha, Mithra, and Rashnu.

In almost every religion of the world a Triad of gods of one form or another is worshipped by the religion's adherents. And herein lie clues to the common roots of the belief. For, though the details differ, the essential elements of each belief remain the same. This formula is borne out by tracing the doctrine to the remote past. It goes beyond the time of Plato and Aristotle — the Greek philosophers who had a strong influence on the Church's decision to adopt the Trinity. It is seen in the religion of the ancient Persians (Zoroastrians) and in the gods of the Assyrian empire (virtual mirrors of the gods of ancient Babylon). Of greater antiquity is the Egyptian Triad of Osiris, Isis (Osiris' wife), and Horus (his son).

However, the earliest records of all, pre-dating Christianity by some twenty-three centuries, lead to the plains of Shinar, and to the founder of Babylon, Nimrod. Evidence to this effect is found in Alexander

Hislop's book *The Two Babylons*, which compares the practices and beliefs of the Roman Catholic Church with those of ancient Babylon. On pages 12, 16, 17, Hislop says:

"If the Egyptians and Greeks derived their arithmetic and astronomy from Chaldea, seeing these in Chaldea were sacred sciences, and monopolised by the priests, that is sufficient evidence that they must have derived their religion from the same quarter. Both Bunsen and Layard in their researches have come to substantially the same result. The statement of Bunsen is to the effect that the religious system of Egypt was derived from Asia, and "the primitive empire in Babel." ... So utterly idolatrous was the Babylonian recognition of the Divine unity, that Jehovah, the Living God, severely condemned His own people for giving any countenance to it: 'They that sanctify themselves, and purify themselves in the gardens, after the rites of the ONLY ONE, eating swine's flesh, and the abomination, and the mouse, shall be consumed together' (Isaiah lxvi. 17). In the unity of that one Only God of the Babylonians, there were three persons, and to symbolise that doctrine of the Trinity, they employed, as the discoveries of Layard prove, the equilateral triangle, just as it is well known the Romish Church does at this day. In both cases such a comparison is most degrading to the King Eternal, and is fitted utterly to pervert the minds of those who contemplate it, as if there was or could be any similitude between such a figure and Him who hath said, 'To whom will ye liken God, and what likeness will ye compare unto Him?'"

Hislop goes on to describe the Babylonian, Assyrian, Indian, and Buddhist Trinities. His intention, in harmony with the sub-title of his book *The Papal Worship Proved to be the Worship of Nimrod and His Wife* — is to prove the pagan origins of Mary worship. However, due to his characteristic thoroughness of research, he actually succeeds in doing more (though his book is, as a result, in some discord). For, while criticising the Catholic worship of

Mary and child on the one hand, he tries to defend the 'Scripturalness' of the Trinity on the other. Surely if the worship of Mary-and-child is "proved to be the worship of Nimrod and his wife" — Nimrod being in opposition to the will of God — then this conclusion cannot be divorced from the fact that the Trinity too (the worship of Father-Mother-Son as one) is also from the same pagan roots.

# 5 Pagan Philosophies, or Biblical Truth?

In order to maintain the former opinion (that Christ is the "origin" or, "ruler" of God's creation) support is sought from Greek philosophy, from Christian writers such as Origen, and from Jewish wisdom literature. It is generally admitted amongst Bible commentators that the Trinity is not taught in the Bible, but some claim that the *idea* must have been in the minds of the Bible writers (even if it did not flow from their pens). And support is sought amongst Scriptural statements, which they feel harmonise with their views. For one example, the book, *The Trinity in the New Testament*, by Arthur W. Wainwright, places great store by the "I am" statements made by Jesus in the book of John (as do so many others, saying that this is a claim to the divine title). But then, on page 91, makes this comment:

> "The 'I AM' sayings, however, in the fourth gospel do not directly imply that Jesus is linked with Yahweh. It is rather a case of undefined suggestion."

Can a book that contains *"undefined suggestion"* prove itself a reliable guide for "setting things straight"? And does it make sense to assert that the Trinity was on the minds of the Bible writers when the concepts of the doctrine are not included in their writings? — 2 Timothy 3:16, 17; compare 2 Timothy 1:13 and Acts 20:27.

Regarding the development of the Trinity doctrine and its ascendancy to the first place amongst Christendom's teachings, note the following references:

> "The trinity of persons within the unity of nature is defined in terms of 'person' and 'nature' which are

G[ree]k philosophical terms; actually the terms do not appear in the Bible. The trinitarian definitions arose as the result of long controversies in which these terms and others such as 'essence' and 'substance' were erroneously applied to God by some theologians." — *Dictionary of the Bible*, by John L. McKenzie, p. 899.

"Neither the word Trinity, nor the explicit doctrine as such, appears in the New Testament, nor did Jesus and his followers intend to contradict the Shema in the Old Testament: 'Hear, 0 Israel: The Lord our God is one Lord' (Deut. 6:4). The doctrine developed gradually over several centuries and through many controversies. By the end of the 4th century the doctrine of the Trinity took substantially the form it has maintained ever since." — *The New Encyclopaedia Britannica*, Micropaedia, Vol. X, p. 126.

"The formulation 'one God in three Persons' was not solidly established, certainly not fully assimilated into Christian life and its profession of faith, prior to the end of the 4th century. But it is precisely this formulation that has first claim to the title THE TRINITARIAN DOGMA. Among the Apostolic Fathers, there had been nothing even remotely approaching such a mentality or perspective." — *The New Catholic Encyclopedia*, Vol. XIV, p. 299.

"The Platonic trinity, itself merely a rearrangement of older trinities dating back to earlier peoples, appears to be the rational philosophic trinity of attributes that gave birth to the three hypostases or divine persons taught by the Christian churches. This Greek philosopher's [Plato, fourth century BCE] conception of the divine trinity ... can be found in all the ancient [pagan] religions." — *The Nouveau Dictionnaire Universel*, edited by M. Lachatre, Vol. 2, p. 1467.

*The Encyclopedia of Religion* states:

"Exegetes and theologians today are in agreement that the Hebrew Bible does not contain a doctrine of the Trinity ... Although the Hebrew Bible depicts God as the father of Israel and employs personifications of God such as Word (*davar*), Spirit (*ruah*), Wisdom (*hokhmah*), and Presence (*shekhinah*), it would go beyond the intention and spirit of the Old Testament to correlate these notions with later trinitarian doctrine.

"Further, exegetes and theologians agree that the New Testament also does not contain an explicit doctrine of the Trinity. God the Father is source of all that is (Pantokrator) and also the father of Jesus Christ; 'Father' is not a title for the first person of the Trinity but a synonym for God. ... In the New Testament there is no reflective consciousness of the metaphysical nature of God ('immanent trinity'), nor does the New Testament contain the technical language of later doctrine (*hupostasis, ousia, substantia, subsistentia, pros'opon, persona*). ... It is incontestable that the doctrine cannot be established on scriptural evidence alone."

The *New Catholic Encyclopedia* concurs, saying:

"There is the recognition on the part of exegetes and Biblical theologians, including a constantly growing number of Roman Catholics, that one should not speak of Trinitarianism in the New Testament without serious qualification. There is also the closely parallel recognition on the part of historians of dogma and systematic theologians that when one does speak of an unqualified Trinitarianism, one has moved from the period of Christian origins to, say, the last quadrant of the 4th century. It was only then that what might be called the definitive Trinitarian dogma 'one God in three Persons' became thoroughly assimilated into Christian life and thought. ... The formula itself does not reflect the immediate consciousness of the period of origins; it was the product of 3 centuries of doctrinal development." — 1967, Volume XIV, page 295.

Can it really be heretical, then, to assert that the Trinity is not taught in the Holy Scriptures? The teaching was the "product of 3 centuries of doctrinal development." Moreover, *The New Encyclopædia Britannica* says:

> "The trinitarian creed of Christianity ... sets it apart from the two other classical monotheistic religions [Judaism and Islam]."

Judaism, of course, is the direct descendant of the religion of the Jews of the Old Testament. The Jews had not the remotest concept of a Trinity. Nor did they regard God as anything other than a concrete single God, and Christ as the promised Messiah, deliverer of Israel.

Thus, the Trinity was developed by the early church even though ...

> "... the Bible of Christians includes no assertions about God that are specifically trinitarian." — *The New Encyclopædia Britannica.*

The *New Catholic Encyclopedia* also says:

> "The doctrine of the Holy Trinity is not taught in the O[ld] T[estament]."

So where did the teaching come from if not from the writings of the Greek philosophers?

Similarly, in his book *The Triune God,* Jesuit Edmund Fortman admits:

> "The Old Testament ... tells us nothing explicitly or by necessary implication of a Triune God who is Father, Son and Holy Spirit. ... *There is no evidence that any sacred writer even suspected the existence of a [Trinity] within the Godhead.* ... Even to see in [the Old Testament] suggestions or foreshadowings or 'veiled signs' of the trinity of persons, is to go beyond the words and intent of the sacred writers."

Most Trinitarians are happy to admit the lack of references to the Trinity in the Old Testament, but what of the New Testament? It is natural to assume that the understanding of the nature of God and Christ would be crystallised in the New Testament. However, *The Encyclopedia of Religion* says:

"Theologians agree that the New Testament also does not contain an explicit doctrine of the Trinity."

And Jesuit Edmund Fortman states:

"The New Testament writers ... give us no formal or formulated doctrine of the Trinity, no explicit teaching that in one God there are three co-equal divine persons. ... Nowhere do we find any trinitarian doctrine of three distinct subjects of divine life and activity in the same Godhead."

Yale University professor E. Washburn Hopkins stated:

"To Jesus and Paul the doctrine of the trinity was apparently unknown; ... they say nothing about it."

Historian Arthur Weigall agreed, when he said, in *The Paganism in Our Christianity*:

"Jesus Christ never mentioned such a phenomenon, and nowhere in the New Testament does the word 'Trinity' appear. The idea was only adopted by the Church three hundred years after the death of our Lord."

Roman Catholic Cardinal Hosius is quoted as having said:

"We believe the doctrine of a triune God, because we have received it by tradition, though not mentioned at all in Scripture."

And finally, *The New International Dictionary of New Testament Theology* asserted:

"Primitive Christianity did not have an explicit doctrine of the Trinity such as was subsequently elaborated in the creeds."

## The Teaching of the Twelve Apostles

A document written at about the turn of the 1st century (perhaps shortly after the completion of the Bible) is known as the *Teaching of the Twelve Apostles*. It is also known as *The Didache*, from the Greek meaning "teaching." Although it was not considered to be part of the Bible "canon," it contained the basics of Christian teaching, and was one of the earliest statements against the Trinity. It contains the following prayer:

> "We thank you, Holy Father, for your holy Name which you have made to dwell in our hearts; and for the knowledge and faith and immortality which you have made known to us through Jesus your Servant. Glory to you forever! You, Almighty Master, created everything for your Name's sake ... And to us you have graciously given spiritual food and drink, and life eternal through Jesus your Servant."

This document does not teach the Trinity. In *The Influence of Greek Ideas on Christianity,* Edwin Hatch quotes the above and then says:

> "In the original sphere of Christianity there does not appear to have been any great advance upon these simple conceptions. The doctrine upon which stress was laid was, that God is, that He is one, that He is almighty and everlasting, that He made the world, that His mercy is over all His works. There was no taste for metaphysical discussion."

Clement of Rome, one of the early church fathers, makes no mention of a Trinity, either directly or indirectly, in his writings. In the *First Epistle of Clement to the Corinthians,* he states:

> "The apostles have preached the Gospel to us from the Lord Jesus Christ; Jesus Christ has done so from God. Christ therefore was sent forth by God, and the apostles by Christ.

> "May God, who seeth all things, and who is the Ruler of all spirits and the Lord of all flesh—who chose our Lord Jesus Christ and us through Him to be a peculiar people—grant to every soul that calleth upon His glorious and holy Name, faith, fear, peace, patience, long-suffering."

Polycarp of Smyrna, who lived during the latter part of the first century and into the second is said to have had contact with the apostle John. He is regarded as being the writer of the *Epistle of Polycarp to the Philippians*. In this work he wrote:

> "May the God and Father of our Lord Jesus Christ, and Jesus Christ Himself, who is the Son of God, ... build you up in faith and truth."

Not only is there a clear distinction between the Father and the Son, but the Almighty is called "the God and Father of our Lord Jesus Christ," just as occurs not a few times in the Bible.

Following the writings of the Apostolic Fathers, there came the Apologists, who sought to defend Christian teachings against the insurgence of Roman and Greek mythologies. Even here, there was no Trinitarian controversy. *The Formation of Christian Dogma*, pp. 122 & 125 said:

> "In the Primitive Christian era there was no sign of any kind of Trinitarian problem or controversy, such as later produced violent conflicts in the Church. The reason for this undoubtedly lay in the fact that, for Primitive Christianity, Christ was ... a being of the high celestial angel-world, who was created and chosen by God for the task of bringing in, at the end of the ages, ... the Kingdom of God."

The Apologist Justyn says in his *Dialogue With Trypho:*

> "There is ... another God and Lord subject to the Maker of all things; who is also called an Angel, because He [the Son] announces to men whatsoever the Maker of all things — above whom there is no other God — wishes to announce to them. ... [The Son] is distinct from Him who made all things, — numerically, I mean, not in will."

Not only does Justyn *not* teach the doctrine of the Trinity, he makes a clear distinction between the Son and the Father. Regarding Justin, the book *Church of the First Three Centuries* says:

> "Justin regarded the Son as distinct from God, and inferior to him: distinct, not, in the modern sense, as

forming one of three hypostases, or persons, ... but distinct in essence and nature; having a real, substantial, individual subsistence, separate from God, from whom he derived all his powers and titles; being constituted under him, and subject in all things to his will. The Father is supreme; the Son is subordinate: the Father is the source of power; the Son the recipient: the Father originates; the Son, as his minister or instrument, executes. They are two in number, but agree, or are one, in will; the Father's will always prevailing with the Son."

The distinction between God and Christ is made as clear as the facets of a diamond. They are "distinct in essence and nature." They have a separate existence as two distinct beings. Moreover, the Father is "supreme," and the Son is "subordinate."

Although Tertullian was the first to use the term "one substance, three persons," in *Against Hermogenes*, he wrote:

"We should not suppose that there is any other being than God alone who is unbegotten and uncreated. ... How can it be that anything, except the Father, should be older, and on this account indeed nobler, than the Son of God, the only-begotten and first-begotten Word? ... That [God] which did not require a Maker to give it existence, will be much more elevated in rank than that [the Son] which had an author to bring it into being."

Thus, the Son is a created being and hence subordinate to the Father. In his work *Against Praxeas*, Tertullian further distinguishes the Son from Almighty God, saying:

"The Father is the entire substance, but the Son is a derivation and portion of the whole, as He Himself acknowledges: 'My Father is greater than I.' ... Thus the Father is distinct from the Son, being greater than the Son, inasmuch as He who begets is one, and He who is begotten is another; He, too, who sends is one, and He who is sent is another; and He, again, who makes is one, and He through whom the thing is made is another."

So even at the very early time of the Apologists (2nd century), there was no clear doctrine of the Trinity, only the "makings" of some of its ideas. It took another century of "development" to finally adopt the pagan philosophies of the non-Christian Greek writings. As *The Church of the First Three Centuries* says:

"The modern popular doctrine of the Trinity ... derives no support from the language of Justin: and this observation may be extended to all the ante-Nicene Fathers; that is, to all Christian writers for three centuries after the birth of Christ. It is true, they speak of the Father, Son, and prophetic or holy Spirit, but not as co-equal, not as one numerical essence, not as Three in One, in any sense now admitted by Trinitarians. The very reverse is the fact. The doctrine of the Trinity, as explained by these Fathers, was essentially different from the modern doctrine. This we state as a fact as susceptible of proof as any fact in the history of human opinions.

"We challenge any one to produce a single writer of any note, during the first three ages, who held this [Trinity] doctrine in the modern sense."

## Pagan Philosophies in Light of Biblical Context?

The harmony of the Scriptures clearly provides no room for the extra-biblical doctrine of the Trinity. In order to include the teaching in their Bible versions, individuals turn for support to the very pagan philosophies that the Bible condemns. (1 Corinthians 1:20, 21; 2 Corinthians 6:14) However, such a resort comes under the biblical curse:

"If anyone makes an addition to these things, God will add to him the plagues that are written in this scroll [of Revelation]; and if anyone takes anything away from the words of the scroll of this prophecy, God will take his portion away from the trees of life and out of the holy city, things which are written about in this scroll." — Revelation 22:18, 19.

"Even if we or an angel out of heaven were to declare to you as good news something beyond what we declared to you as good news, let him be accursed [or, be a thing devoted to destruction]." — Galatians 1:8.

Though it is sometimes argued that "the Church" has accepted the Trinity as a divinely inspired teaching and has thus "sanctioned" the belief, the above scriptures preclude any teaching which is contrary to biblical truth. The burden of proof, then, which rests upon Trinitarians, is heavy.

PART TWO:

ONE GOD, THE FATHER

# 6 "The Lord Our God Is One Lord"

So begins the Shema, the Jewish confession of faith. The above words are actually those of Moses, writing in his "Second Law," the book of Deuteronomy, or, as the Jewish rabbis call it, **MISH.NAH' HAT-TO.RAH'** meaning "Repetition (or Duplicate) of the Law." — Deuteronomy 6:4.

The Jewish belief in one God was passed on to Christianity and the Islamic faith. According to Dr. J. H. Hertz, a rabbi:

> "This sublime pronouncement of absolute monotheism was a declaration of war against all *polytheism* ... In the same way, the Shema excludes *the trinity* of the Christian creed as a violation of the Unity of God."

According to the Trinitarian view, this "One Lord" included the Father, the Son, and the Holy Spirit — the three divine "persons." In taking this position they introduce into Scripture enormous complexities which require the philosophies of worldly intellectuals to unravel. (Note Matthew 11:25.) But in fact these difficulties have never been unravelled. They may be likened to a man caught in quicksand who struggles in an effort to free himself, only to find that such struggling sinks him deeper!

The dogma of the Trinity was set out garrulously by the church fathers in the 4th century, as discussed in the opening chapters of this book. Since then church writers have sought to justify that position by seeking support from the Scriptures. However, this amounts to what the dictionary terms *eisegesis*, the opposite of *exegesis*. When a Bible student employs *exegesis*, he/she allows the Bible text to provide its own interpretation, that is, reading *out from* the words. The Greek word **EX** means "out of," *gesis* comes from **HEGE'ESTHAI** meaning "to guide." Thus the investigator "guides out" of the reading the interpretation the writer intended. By contrast, the student who employs *eisegesis* reads meaning *into* the text. **EI'SE** is the Greek word for "into." To justify interpretations based on eisegesis, the student is required to seek confirmation from sources other than the Bible.

Returning to the scripture under discussion, the 'Lord' of Deuteronomy 6:4 translates the divine name — **YHWH** by transliteration from Hebrew. Thus, Moses identifies the God of Israel with the person of Yahweh, or Jehovah. The **YHWH** is a proper name applied exclusively to God. Some Bible versions indicate the divine name by printing LORD in all capitals (see the preface to the *Revised Standard Version*, for example, and its footnote to Exodus 3:15).

There are two striking examples of the distinction between the LORD (God) and the Lord (Jesus Christ), one in the Old Testament and another in the New Testament. Note what the Psalmist says:

"The LORD says to my lord: 'Sit at my right hand, till I make your enemies your footstool.'" — Psalm 110:1; *Revised Standard Version*.

This underscores the Trinitarians' dilemma. If, within the *one God*, there are three divine personalities, why does the Psalmist here refer to that *one God*, **YHWH**, and then proceed to an entirely distinct reference to the Son? — Compare Luke 20:41-43.

Did the apostle Paul consider the "one God" to be composed of these three divine persons?:

"There is for us only one God, the Father, who is the Creator of all things and for whom we live; and there is only one Lord, Jesus Christ, through whom all things were created and through whom we live." — 1 Corinthians 8:6; *Good News Bible.*

The apostle does not make the confusing equation: $1/3 + 1/3 + 1/3 = 1$, as if each person of the Trinity were equated to a third part of something. Nor the even more incredible $1 + 1 + 1 = 1$; a person being *added* to another person, then *added* to still another person, and the result being, not a person, but *one* of something which is not a person but a God! The apostle Paul refers to the *one God*, that is the whole God, **YHWH**, as one, the Father. He then proceeds to a separate and distinct reference to the *one Lord*, Jesus Christ.

There are some who have even proffered the incredible equation: $1 \times 1 \times 1 = 1$ in an effort to solve the difficulty. But this is surely philosophical gibberish! It makes sense neither to the rational philosophic nor to the irrational devotionist. How can a person be *multiplied* by another person and in turn by another, and the result of the equation be "one" of something which is said *not to be* a person?

If an exponent of the Trinity heard the expression "one God," no doubt the three personages would come to his mind. *One* of those persons is said to be the Father. He thus composes a part, namely one third, of that *one God*. Thus, what would we expect to see in the Scriptures each time this "one God" was mentioned? Would not logic expect to see at least an allusion to the divine persons within this God? Then why is it that we consistently find the contrary?

"One God and Father of us all, who is above all and through all and in all." — Ephesians 4:6; *Revised Standard Version.*

It is perhaps ironic that Trinitarians use the above scripture (along with verses 4 & 5) in support of their doctrine, simply because the spirit, the Lord Jesus Christ, and God are mentioned in close proximity. But notice the individual who is identified as the "one God." It is not the Father, Son, and Holy Spirit, but just "the Father"? Then who is the "one Lord" previously mentioned? Surely this is Jesus Christ. (Compare also Galatians 3:20.) This distinction is underscored by *The Divinity of Jesus Christ* by John Martin Creed:

> "When the writers of the New Testament speak of God they mean the God and Father of our Lord Jesus Christ. When they speak of Jesus Christ, they do not speak of him, nor do they think of him as God. He is God's Christ, God's Son, God's Wisdom, God's Word. Even the Prologue to St. John, which comes nearest to the Nicene Doctrine, must be read in the light of the pronounced subordinationism of the Gospel as a whole; and the Prologue is less explicit in Greek with the anarthrous θεος [**THE.OS'**, *God*] than it appears to be in English."

Furthermore, does the mere proximity of the names in the same scripture prove the Trinity?

## The Three "Persons" at Jesus' Baptism

The idea of the "proximity of the names" (God, the Son, and the Holy Spirit) in the same passage of scripture is often used at Matthew 3:16, 17. Here, at the baptism of Jesus, the Holy Spirit descends upon him in the form of a dove, followed by the declaration of the Father:

> "This is my son, my beloved, on whom my favour rests." — Matthew 3:17; *New English Bible.*

However, John the Baptist was also present in the same immediate proximity. Are we to conclude that he too was a member of the Trinity? This is clearly an absurd suggestion. Yet, why should the mere fact that the three names occur together prove the Trinity? It is only a Trinitarian that can see a reference to the Trinity here. As has been said before, take the teaching of the Trinity out of the textbooks of

Christendom, and scriptures such as the above are unable to teach such a complicated doctrine. If there were no Trinity, would the presence of the names here have any significance?

Likewise with Paul's words to the Ephesian Christians, where he makes reference to Christ, saying:

> "In union with him you too are being built together with all the others into a place where God lives through his Spirit." — Ephesians 2:22; *Good News Bible.*

The mere proximity of references to God, Christ, and the Holy Spirit, can only have meaning to one who already believes the Trinity. It cannot *teach* the Trinity. — See also 2 Corinthians 13:14.

And at the oft-quoted Genesis 1:26, it is merely God talking to his heavenly son. His statement, "Let *us* make man," agrees with the statement in the book of John, namely:

> "Without him [Jesus] was not anything made that was made." — John 1:3; *Revised Standard Version.*

It is also in harmony with the Proverbs:

> "I was by his side, a master craftsman, delighting him day after day." — Proverbs 8:30; *Jerusalem Bible.*

Therefore, the statement by God at Genesis 1:26 is merely God's invitation to his son to share in the creation of all other things. — Compare Colossians 1:16.

Returning to Deuteronomy 6:4, the same argument applies. The reference to "one Lord" has a simple meaning to the unbiased Bible student. Far from supporting the complex and highly philosophical doctrine of the Trinity, this scripture actually refutes it.

This reference to the "one God" is seen throughout the Old Testament. Isaiah the prophet contrasts the God of Israel with the useless idols of the nations. (Isaiah 43:10, 11; 44:6; 46:9, 10) Very often these references are accompanied by the divine name, Yahweh, thus identifying the personal name and hence the personality of this "one God," the Father. — Compare John 17:6.

Christian writer Ignatius, in *The Ante-Nicene Fathers,* Volume I, page 52, refers to God as "the only true God, the unbegotten and unapproachable, the Lord of all, the Father and Begetter of the only-begotten Son," clearly distinguishing between God, the Father, and His Son. On p. 58 he speaks of "God the Father, and the Lord Jesus Christ." And he asserted: "There is one God, the Almighty, who has manifested Himself by Jesus Christ His Son."

In the same work, he also said:

"There is one God of the universe, the Father of Christ, 'of whom are all things;' and one Lord Jesus Christ, our Lord, 'by whom are all things.'"

Although Ignatius refers to Christ as "God the Word," this does not mean he was identifying Jesus as *the* Almighty God. There are several scriptures (discussed in later chapters) that refer to Jesus as "God." (Isaiah:9:6; John 1:1, 18; John 20:17) However, this refers, not to *who* Jesus is, but *what* he is, as the later discussions show.

# 7 "This Is the True God"

The title "the true God" (Greek: **HO A.LE'THI.NOS THE.OS'**) is applied exclusively to the Father. (John 17:3) This indicates that the Father is greater than both the Son and the Holy Spirit. It uniquely identifies the Bearer of the title. For this reason some have sought to apply this term to the Son, and will even offer inadequate translations and far-fetched interpretations to support this view.

One scripture some use is 1 John 5:20. Note how this reads from the *Living Bible*:

> "And we know that Christ, God's Son, has come to help us understand and find the true God. And now we are in God because we are in Jesus Christ his Son, who is the only true God; and he is eternal life."

Admittedly, the *Living Bible* is more of a paraphrase of the Scriptures than a translation. But it reflects the interpretation some place on the verse even though they use an accurate rendering. Note the *Revised Standard Version*:

> "And we are in him who is true, in his Son Jesus Christ. This is the true God and eternal life." — 1 John 5:20.

Note that the word "this" (Greek: **HOU'TOS**) stands nearest to the noun "Jesus Christ." Which is why some believe the apostle John had Jesus in mind when he made his reference to "the true God". However, *Moulton's Grammar of New Testament Greek*, by Dr. N. Turner (Vol. 3 dealing with Syntax), says that **HOU'TOS** refers, not necessarily ...

> "... to the noun which is nearest, but to the noun which is most vividly in the writer's mind (deictic). Mt 3:17 **HOU.TOS' ESTIN HO HUI.OS' MOU.** Ac 4:11 **HOU'TOS** Jesus (although *God* is the nearest

noun), 8:26 **HAU'TE ES.TIN' E'REMOS** the road (not Gaza, though Gaza is the nearer noun), Mt 3:3 **HOU'TOS** (refers right back to 1), 1 Jo 5:20 (God, not Christ, is the true God)."

It is Jesus Christ who has given us knowledge of "the true one." It is thus God, the Father, not Christ, who is the true God.

In treating 1 John 5:20, note what Dr. G. B. Winer's *Grammar of New Testament Greek* (translated and enlarged by W. F. Moulton) has to say on this (page 195):

"The pronoun **HOU'TOS** sometimes refers, not to the noun which stands nearest to it, but to one more remote, which is to be regarded as the principal subject, and which therefore was to the writer the nearest *psychologically*, than any other: A. iv. 11, **HOU.TOS'** [this] (**IE.SOUS' KHRI.STOS'** [Jesus Christ] in ver. 10, though **HO THE.OS'** [the God] is the nearest noun) **ESTIN HO LI'THOS** [is the stone]. So in 1 Jo v. 20, **HOU.TOS' ESTIN HO ALETHI.NOS' THE.OS'** this is the true God], the pronoun refers to **HO THE.OS'** [the God] — not **KHRI.STOS'** [Christ] (which immediately precedes), as the older theologians maintained on dogmatic grounds; for, in the first place, **ALETHI.NOS' THE.OS'** [true God] is a constant and exclusive epithet of the Father; and, secondly, there follows a warning against idolatry, and **ALE.THI.NOS' THE.OS'** is always contrasted with **EI'DO.LA** [an idol]."

The context of Holy Scripture offers the best proof against the Trinitarian view of 1 John 5:20, for we find the expression "true God" at John 17:3, where another clear distinction is made between the *only true God* and Jesus Christ:

"Now this is eternal life: that they may know you, the only true God, *and* Jesus Christ, whom you have sent." — John 17:3; *New International Version.*

Concerning this scripture, Clement of Alexandria, an Apologist of the 2nd century AD, said:

> "To know the eternal God, the giver of what is eternal, and by knowledge and comprehension to possess God, who is first, and highest, and one, and good. ... He then who would live the true life is enjoined first to know Him 'whom no one knows, except the Son reveal (Him).' (Matt. 11:27) Next is to be learned the greatness of the Saviour after Him." — *Who Is the Rich Man That Shall Be Saved?* VII, VIII.

God, the eternal Father, is clearly seen as distinct from the Son.

# 8 Was God Manifest In The Flesh?

At 1 Timothy 3:16 the *King James* version tells us that "God was manifest in the flesh." It is today, though, universally acknowledged that the correct reading (that is, of the Greek manuscripts) is "He" or "Who," giving: "Who was manifest in the flesh."

It has already been mentioned that the teaching is not found in the Holy Scriptures. And this fact, along with an examination of the "God"-versions of 1 Timothy 3:16, provides an insight into the desire of Trinitarians *to see the teaching in* God's Word.

The translators of the *King James* version of 1611 used the *Textus Receptus*, the Received Text, for their translation. At that time this Greek text was so highly regarded that many considered it to be inspired of God. Its text read "God was manifest in the flesh." However, the value of the *Textus Receptus* has since been discredited by scholars and superseded by the three major manuscripts (among others), all of them of great antiquity, and therefore nearer to the original writings of the inspired penmen: The Vatican manuscript No. 1209 of the 4th century, the Sinaitic manuscript also of the 4th century (discovered by Tischendorf at a monastery at the foot of Mount Sinai in 1844), and the Alexandrine manuscript of the early 5th century.

The Alexandrine manuscript has the most revealing text, for it shows an alteration by a much later hand.

The very old manuscripts used abbreviations for commonly used words such as **THE.OS'**, "God," and **KU'RI.OS**, "Lord," etc. The abbreviation for **THE.OS'** was θC̄. However, were it not for those two horizontal lines, this is identical to the word OC, meaning "who."

The Alexandrine manuscript was found to have *originally* read OC, *who*, but this 'much later hand' added those two small lines, changing the reading to θC̱, **THE.OS'**, "God." It was only examination by a microscope which revealed this!

The Sinaitic manuscript and the Vatican Manuscript No. 1209 read OC, "who," giving the most accurate reading:

"Who was manifest in the flesh." — 1 Timothy 3:16.

## The Three Witness Bearers

A more blatant example of textual corruption occurs at 1 John 5:7. Here the *King James* Bible adds the words: "in heaven, the Father, the Word, and the Holy Ghost: and these three are one." Not only does the Sinaitic manuscript not include these words, neither does any Greek manuscript prior to the 16th century. It is believed that a manuscript now at Trinity College was purposely written about 1520 AD in order to accommodate these words! They found their way into the Greek text of Erasmus, a scholar of the 16th century, and later became part of the *Textus Receptus*. Regarding this, note what Bruce M. Metzger says in his book *The Text of the New Testament* (p. 101):

> "Among the criticisms levelled at Erasmus one of the most serious appeared to be the charge of Stunica, one of the editors of Ximenes' Complutensian Polyglot, that his text lacked part of the final chapter of I John, namely, the Trinitarian statement concerning "the Father, the Word, and the Holy Ghost: and these three are one. And there are three that bear witness in earth" (I John v. 7-8, King James version). Erasmus replied that he had not found any Greek manuscript containing these words, though he had in the meanwhile examined several others besides those on which he relied when first preparing his text. In an unguarded moment Erasmus promised that he would insert the *Comma*

*Johanneum,* as it is called, in future editions if a single Greek manuscript could be found that contained the passage. At length such a copy was found — or was made to order! As it now appears, the Greek manuscript had probably been written in Oxford about 1520 by a Franciscan friar named Froy (or Roy), who took the disputed words from the Latin Vulgate. Erasmus stood by his promise and inserted the passage in his edition (1522), but he indicates in a lengthy footnote his suspicion that the manuscript had been prepared expressly in order to confute him."

These two examples of textual corruption are discussed in a book written by no less a scholar than Sir Isaac Newton, entitled: *An Historical Account of Two Notable Corruptions of Scripture.* It was published in 1754, some twenty-seven years after Newton's death, for reasons the opening paragraph of this book (the book you are holding) reveals.

## The Father and I Are One

The "oneness" of the Father and the Son is referred to in John's gospel:

"The Father and I are one." — John 10:30; *Good News Bible.*

Many speculations arise as to the meaning of these words. In what sense are Father and Son "one"? There are two guides that help answer that question: Greek grammar, and scriptural context.

## John 10:30 and Greek Grammar

In the Greek language there are three words that are all translated by the English word "one." These are **HEN** ['εν], **HEIS** ['εις], and **MI'A** [μια]. These are in the neuter, masculine, and feminine genders respectively. The feminine **MI'A** is used at Matthew 19:5 in Jesus' words "the two will become *one* flesh." Both the feminine and the masculine are used in Jesus' statement about the "other sheep":

"So there shall be *one* [**MI'A**] flock, *one* [**HEIS**] shepherd." — John 10:16.

The masculine **HEIS** is used at 1 Corinthians 8:6 where Paul spoke of "one God, the Father."

But the gender at John 10:30 is neither masculine nor feminine. The neuter **HEN** is used here.

The apostle John uses the Greek word **HEN** (*one*, neuter) 16 times (twice at John 20:12). A comparison of each of these occurrences proves most constructive:

without him there came to be not one [**HEN**] thing
1:3
there had been only one [**HEN**] boat there
6:22
"I did one [**HEN**] deed, and you all marvel at it."
7:21
"We have one [**HEN**] Father, God."
8:41
"One [**HEN**] thing I know, that though I was blind, now I see."
9:25
"I and the Father are one [**HEN**]."
10:30
to gather into one [**HEN**] the children of God who are scattered
11:52
"that they may be one [**HEN**], even as we are one"
17:11
"that they may all be one [**HEN**]"
17:21
"that they may be one even as we are one [**HEN**]"
17:22
"that they may become perfectly one [**HEN**]"
17:23
it was necessary that one [**HEN**] man should die for the people
18:14
"a custom that I should release one [**HEN**] at the Passover"

18:39

apart from the bandages rolled up into one [**HEN**] place
20:7

one [**HEN**] at the head and one [**HEN**] at the feet
20:12

were every one [**HEN**] of them to be written
21:25

The majority of the above occurrences could be translated "one thing" — one boat, one deed, one place. The expression at John 8:41 "one Father," regards not the *person* of the Father, but the *position* or *state* of being the Father. At John 18:14 it is an individual who is released, regardless of gender.

Contrast some of the occurrences of the masculine **HEIS** ("one"):

First this one [**HEIS**] found his own brother Simon
1:41

one [**HEIS**] of his disciples, Andrew the brother of Simon Peter
6:8

one [**HEIS**] of you is a devil
6:70

one [**HEIS**] of them, Caiaphas
11:49

Judas Iscariot, one [**HEIS**] of his disciples
12:4

one [**HEIS**] of you will betray me
13:21

one [**HEIS**] of the officers standing by struck Jesus
18:22

Other examples are plentiful. Thus, Jesus, in saying "I and my Father are *one*," is not referring to some*one* but some*thing*. The oneness shared by Father and Son is a *thing* not a personality. They share a oneness of thought and purpose.

By contrast, Paul's statement at Romans 3:20 that "God is one" uses the masculine **HEIS** to express this thought. Indeed, whenever the expression "one God" occurs, the masculine **HEIS** is used:

one [**HEIS**] God, the Father
　1 Corinthians 8:6
one [**HEIS**] God, the Father
　Ephesians 4:6
For there is one [**HEIS**] God, and one [**HEIS**] mediator
　1 Timothy 2:5
You believe there is one [**HEIS**] God, do you?
　James 2:19

Novatian, a Christian writer of the third century AD, commented:

> "Since He said *'one' thing*, let the heretics understand that He did not say 'one' *person*. For *one* placed in the neuter, intimates the social concord, not the personal unity ... Moreover, that He says *one*, has reference to the agreement, and to the identity of judgment, and to the loving association itself, as reasonably the Father and Son are one in agreement, in love, and in affection."—*Treatise Concerning the Trinity*, chapter 27.

In the Old Testament, Malachi uses the Hebrew **E.CHADH'** (*one*) when speaking of "one Father" and "one God." Even the Qur'an concurs with this when it says:

> "Your God is One God; there is no God save Him, the Beneficent, the Merciful." — Surah 2:163.

This also has legal implications. If this "one God" consists of both Father and Son, then how is it that Paul reasons on the following?

> "The Law was promulgated by angels, assisted by an intermediary. Now there can only be an intermediary between two parties, yet God is one." — Galatians 3:20; *Jerusalem Bible*.

The two parties are (1) God, and (2) the congregation. And the intermediary is Christ. How can Christ be both party to the covenant and at the same time the intermediary to it?

## John 10:30 and the Context

Jesus later spoke about the oneness of the Father and Son and explained its meaning. He said:

> "The glory which thou hast given me I have given to them, that they may be one even as we are one." — John 17:22; *Revised Standard Version.*

This bears out that the oneness of the Father and the Son is a oneness of purpose or endeavour. They share a commonality of goals, beliefs, and objectives. They are of one mind. Jesus prayed that his followers could share this oneness.

Irenaeus, a Christian writer of the 2nd century AD, said:

> "And thus one God the Father is declared, who is above all, and through all, and in all. The Father is indeed above all, and He is the Head of Christ." — *Against Heresies,* Book V, chapter 18.2.

\*          \*          \*          \*

The original manuscripts by the Bible writers were inspired of God, but no copy (unless by the same writer) was inspired. Tampering with the sacred text is a serious matter, and one doing so could well find himself under a biblical curse! — Revelation 22:18, 19.

# 9 E.LO.HIM' —
## Many Persons In *One* God?

The Hebrew word **E.LO.HIM'** ("God") is a plural noun — sometimes it is used in the sense of simple plurality, "gods," as at Jeremiah 25:6. It is the plural nature of the word that has caused many to apply it to the Trinity doctrine. Its first occurrence in the Bible is at Genesis 1:1.

> "In the beginning God [**E.LO.HIM'**] created the heavens and the earth."

There are several effective arguments against this view, for one thing the plurality of **E.LO.HIM'** does not actually help the Trinitarian position! For example, recall the insistence on 'three persons in one God.' At the very best, a reasonable examination of this word (supposing the harmony of Scripture supported the view) would be the teaching of three *Gods* within this "Godhead." However, Trinitarians insist that there are three *persons* in one God.

This plurality is considered to have support in texts such as Genesis 1:26, 3:22 and 11:7, where God uses plural pronouns like "Let us." However, note what *The New Schaff-Herzog Encyclopedia of Religious Knowledge* (1957, Vol. 12, p. 18) says:

> "Only an inaccurate exegesis which overlooks the more immediate grounds of interpretation can see references to the Trinity in the plural form of the divine name Elohim, the use of the plural in Gen. i. 26, or such liturgical phrases of three members as the Aaronic blessing of Num. vi. 24-26 and the Trisagion of Isa. vi. 3."

To this list may be added the blessing of Jacob upon Joseph's sons Ephraim and Manasseh, in which he invoked God twice, and "the angel" once. — Genesis 48:15, 16.

The Hebrew language, indeed Semitic languages as a whole, use the plural of words in a way which is alien to Western thinking. The plural is used for *intensification* of an idea, or a *heightening* to be conveyed to the reader's mind. For example, Joseph is referred to as **A.DHO.NEH'**, "lord," that is, Most Excellent Lord. — Genesis 42:30.

The late Professor Benjamin Davidson, referred to as the "first Hebraist," and author of the highly respected *Hebrew Grammar*, has much to say on the plural **E.LO.HIM'** in his book *The Theology of the Old Testament*, published by T. & T. Clark (Edinburgh). Note what he says on pp. 99, 100:

> "The plural form of the word *Elohim* might be supposed to have some bearing on the question of unity. And, indeed, by many it has been supposed to bear testimony to the plurality of gods originally worshipped among the Shemitic peoples; and by others, who seem to consider the name Elohim part of God's revelation of Himself, to the plurality of persons in the Godhead. The real force of the plural termination, as we have already said, is not easy, indeed, to discover. But a few facts may lead us near it. In Ethiopic the name of God is *Amlák*, a plural form also of a root allied to *melek* — a *king*. All Shemitic languages use the plural as a means of heightening the idea of the singular; the precise kind of heightening has to be inferred from the word. Thus *water —* **[MA'YIM]** — is plural, from the fluidity and multiplicity of its parts; the *heavens —* **[SHA.MA'YIM]** — from their extension. Of a different kind is the plural of *adon —* *lord*, in Hebrew, which takes plural suffixes except in the first person singular. Of this kind, too, is the plural of *Baal*, even in the sense of *owner*, as when Isaiah uses the phrase **[E.BHUS' BE.A.LOW']** *[the manger of his owner]* (i. 3). Of the same kind also is the plural *teraphim, penates*, consisting of a simple *image*. And

of this kind probably is the plural *Elohim* — a plural not numerical, but simply enhancive of the idea of *might*. Thus among the Israelites the *might* who was God was not an ordinary might, but one peculiar, lofty, unique. Though the word be plural, in the earliest written Hebrew its predicate is almost universally singular. Only when used of the gods of the nations is it construed with a plural verb; or, sometimes, when the reference is to the general idea of the Godhead. This use with a singular predicate or epithet seems to show that the plural form is not a reminiscence of a former Polytheism. The plural expressed a *plenitude of might*. And as there seems no trace of a Polytheism in the name, neither can it with any probability be supposed to express a plurality of persons in the Godhead. For it cannot be shown that the word is itself part of God's revelation; it is a word of natural growth adopted into revelation, like other words of the Hebrew language. And the usage in the words *baal, adon, rab,* and such like, similar to it in meaning, leads us to suppose that the plural is not numerical, as if *mights*, but merely intensifying the idea of might. Nor can it be shown to be probable that the doctrine of a plurality of persons should have been taught early in the history of revelation. What the proneness of mankind to idolatry rendered imperative above all and first of all, was strenuous teaching of the Divine Unity."

Thus, in summary, the Hebrew word **E.LO.HIM'**, "God," cannot "with any probability be supposed to express a plurality of persons in the Godhead."

## The Plural of Excellence or Majesty

The philosophical attachments to the title **E.LO.HIM'** — 'three persons in one God' — are far too complex for the simple faith of the Israelites. From the foregoing it can be seen why the plural was used and what it meant to the ancient Israelites; namely, the *pluralis excellentiae* or *maiestatis* the plural of excellence or majesty. This device was known to and understood by the Hebrews. Note what Gesenius' *Hebrew Grammar* says on this (pp. 398, 399):

"The *pluralis excellentiae* or *maiestatis*, as has been remarked above, is properly a variety of the abstract plural, since it sums up the several characteristics belonging to the idea, besides possessing the secondary sense of an *intensification* of the original idea. It is thus closely related to the plurals of amplification, treated under e, which are mostly found in poetry. So especially **E.LO.HIM'** *Godhead, God* (to be distinguished from the numerical plural *gods*, Ex 12:12, &c.). The supposition that **E.LO.HIM'** is to be regarded as merely a remnant of earlier polytheistic views (i.e. as originally only a numerical plural) is at least highly improbable, and, moreover, would not explain the analogous plurals (see below). That the language has entirely rejected the idea of numerical plurality in **E.LO.HIM'** (whenever it denotes *one* God), is proved especially by its being almost invariably joined with a singular attribute (cf. para. 132*h*), e.g. **E.LO.HIM' TSAD.DIQ'** [God is righteous] Ps. 7:10, &c. Hence **E.LO.HIM'** may have been used originally not only as a numerical but also as an abstract plural (corresponding to the Latin *numen*, and our *Godhead*), and, like other abstracts of the same kind, have been transferred to a concrete single god (even of the heathen)."

Thus, Hebrew has "entirely rejected the idea of numerical plurality in **E.LO.HIM'**." The inspired Bible writers many times refer to the 'concrete *single* gods' as **E.LO.HIM'**, despite their being false gods, inasmuch as their devotees regarded them with grandeur and awe. Compare these references which each use a plural form of "god":

Israel made Baal-berith their *god* (**E.LO.HIM'**)
        Judges 8:33
they went into the house of their *god* (**E.LO.HIM'**)
        Judges 9:27

Is it whom Chemosh your *god* (**E.LO.HE'KHA**) ...
Judges 11:24

sacrifice to Dagon *their god* (**E.LO.HE.HEM'**)
Judges 16:23

'*our god* (**E.LO.HE'NU**) has given us Samson'
Judges 16:23

gave way to praising *their god* (**E.LOHE.HEM'**)
Judges 16:24

his hand is against Dagon *our god* (**E.LO.HE'NU**)
1 Samuel 5:7

Ashtoreth the *goddess* (**E.LO.HE'**) of the Sidonians
1 Kings 11:5, 33

Call for Baal, for he is *a god* (**E.LO.HIM'**)
1 Kings 18:27

Baal-zebub the *god* (**E.LO.HE'**) of Ekron
2 Kings 1: 2, 3, 6, 16

the house of Nisroch *his god* (**E.LO.HOW'**)
2 Kings 19:37

the house of Nebuchadnezzar's *god* (**E.LO.HIM'**)
Daniel 1:2

the star of *your god* (**E.LOHE.KHEM'**)
Amos 5:26

As *your god* (**E.LO.HE'KHA**) is alive
Amos 8:14

sailors called each one to *his god* (**E.LO.HOW'**)
Jonah 1:5

each one in the name of his *god* (**E.LO.HOW'**)
Micah 4:5

Those who worshipped these false gods referred to them as **E.LO.HIM'** attributing to them might, majesty, and excellence. It is for this reason that the plural **E.LO.HIM'** is used rather than the singular **E.LO'AH**. But they were not Triads or Trinities. Observe what *The International Standard Bible Encyclopaedia* (Vol. II, p. 1265) says:

"It is characteristic of Heb. that extension, magnitude and dignity, as well as actual multiplicity, are expressed by the pl[ural]. It is not reasonable, therefore, to assume that plurality of form indicates primitive Sem[itic] polytheism. On the contrary, historic Heb. is unquestionably and uniformly monotheistic."

Additionally, even the arch-enemy, Satan, is referred to as **E.LO.HE'**, *God* (plural) at 2 Corinthians 4:4 in Hebrew versions of the New Testament.

A further argument against the Trinitarian view, as was mentioned in the above quotations from Davidson and Gesenius, is the fact that a *singular* attribute accompanies **E.LO.HIM'** (and its related forms) on the vast majority of occurrences in application to a 'concrete, single god.' For example, the expression quoted by Gesenius at Psalm 7:10 (v. 9 in our Bibles), **E.LO.HIM' TSAD.DIQ'**, "God is righteous," where the word righteous is in the *singular*. If **E.LO.HIM'** meant a numerical plurality, we would here find in Hebrew the plural for "righteous," namely, **TSA.DIQ.QIM'**. But, in fact, the *singular* **TSA.DIQ'** occurs. Similarly with the oft quoted Genesis 1:1, in the expression **BA.RA' E.LO.HIM'**, "God created," the verb **BA.RA'** is a *singular* verb. This demonstrates that **E.LO.HIM'** is the plural of majesty or excellence and not a numerical plural. This is what *The American Journal of Semitic Languages and Literature* (Vol. XXI, p. 208) says:

"That the language of the O[ld] T[estament] has entirely given up the idea of plurality in **E.LO.HIM'** (as applied to the God of Israel) is especially shown by the fact that it is almost invariably construed with a singular verbal predicate, and takes a singular adjectival attribute. ... **E.LO.HIM'** must rather be explained as an *intensive plural,* denoting *greatness,* and *majesty,* being equal to The Great God. It ranks with the plurals **A.DHO.NIM'** and **BE.A.LIM'**, employed with reference to human beings."

Even the Greek Septuagint, with its philosophical overtones, does not take the **E.LO.HIM'** as a numerical plural. The Greek translators of the Septuagint used

the *singular* **THE.OS'** ("God") to translate the *plural*
**E.LO.HIM'**.

At Isaiah 6:3, and the so-called Trisagion, the
Septuagint uses the singular **KU'RI.OS** in the
sentence: **HA'GIOS, HA'GIOS, HA'GIOS KU'RI.OS
SABA.OTH'**, "Holy, holy, holy is the Lord of hosts." It
then uses the singular pronoun **AU.TOU'** (from
**AU.TOS'**, "him") in the next statement:

| **PLE'RES** | **PA'SA HE** | **GE** | **TES** |
|---|---|---|---|
| fullness | of all the | earth | the |

| **DO'XES** | **AU.TOU'** |
|---|---|
| glory | of him |

The Septuagint's use of **KU'RI.OS** here without the
article ("the") indicates the presence of the divine
name, **YHWH**. And this is what we find in the Hebrew
Masoretic Text. It is thus an address made by the
seraphs to the *person* of Yahweh. Additionally, the
three-fold repetition of **QA.DHOSH'** "holy," far from it
being an indication of the 'three persons of the
Godhead,' is a further way that the Hebrew language
implies emphasis. Observe what *The Pentateuch and
Haftorahs* says on this:

> "holy, holy, holy. Threefold repetition in Heb. poetry
> indicates the superlative degree: God is the highest
> Holiness. 'Holy — in the highest Heaven, the place of
> His Divine abode; holy — upon earth, the work of His
> might; holy — for ever and ever unto all eternity"'
> (*Targum Jonathon*).

*Gesenius' Hebrew Grammar* in section 133 under
the heading "The Comparison of Adjectives.
(Periphrastic Expression of the Comparative and
Superlative)" says, p. 431:

> "The intensification of attributes by means of
> repetition belongs rather to rhetoric than to syntax,
> e.g. Ec 7:24 **'A.MOQ' 'A.MOQ'** exceeding deep; 1 S
> 2:3, Pr 20:14; the adjective is even used three times
> in Is 6:3. — Cf. the repetition of adverbs for the same
> purpose in Gn 7:19, Nu 14:7 (**ME.ODH' ME.ODH'**

*exceedingly*, also **BIM.E'ODH ME.ODH'** Ex 1:7, &c); Ez 42:15.

Also, *The Teacher's Commentary*, edited by G. Henton Davies (revised edition), says:

> "Holy, holy, holy. The threefold repetition is for emphasis; there is no reference to the doctrine of the Trinity."

It is not that advocates of the Trinity doctrine are necessarily unaware of the above facts, it is rather an example of *eisegesis* (the opposite of *exegesis*), reading *into* the text rather than out *from* it.

The contention is made by exponents of the Trinity that, though the Bible writers understood not the concept of the Trinity, the Holy Spirit guided their pen to leave *allusions* to the doctrine in what they wrote. Thus, they may not have understood references to the Trinity in the plural of **E.LO.HIM'**, but the "idea is there anyway". However, we have seen *why* the Hebrew language used the plural — as a heightening or intensification of an idea. But where is the *scriptural* basis for reading more into the text? If the idea was not on the pen of the writers, how is it on the mind of their readers?

The plurality of the Hebrew word for God, **E.LO.HIM'**, then, is for the purpose of emphasis or majesty, or to intensify the idea of the word, and cannot be used to support the teaching of the Trinity.

# 10   Three Divine Persons, or Three Angels?

Support is also sought for the doctrine of the Trinity in Genesis 19:24 in the account regarding the three angels who came to Abraham to announce that he and Sarah would have a son and to foretell the overthrow of Sodom and Gomorrah. Genesis 19:24 says:

> "Then Jehovah rained upon Sodom and upon Gomorrah brimstone and fire from Jehovah out of heaven." — *American Standard Version.*

However, Bible versions favoured by Trinitarians read, "the LORD rained down burning sulphur on Sodom and Gomorrah — from the LORD" — *New International Version.* It is thus asserted that the Lord (Jesus) sent down sulphur and fire from the Lord (God, the Father). However, notice that LORD is capitalised in both cases, indicating the presence of the divine name, **YHWH** (see the preface to the *New International Version* regarding the divine name) in the original Hebrew Masoretic Text.

Additionally, this phraseology is common in Hebrew. Note the following examples from the *Revised Standard Version*:

> the LORD said 'Moses shall come near to the LORD'
> Exodus 24:1 ,2
> *Solomon* assembled the people before *Solomon*
> 1 Kings 8:1
> the LORD said 'I will deliver them by the LORD'
> Hosea 1:6,7
> 'I will make them strong in the LORD' says the LORD
> Zechariah 10:12

Again this is not the kind of usage we see in English. We would not say: "Susan sent Jane a letter from Susan." That would be needless repetition. But in Hebrew it is not quite the same. Use of repetition is a common thing, especially when the writer or speaker wishes to make his/her meaning abundantly clear without possibility of ambiguity.

Another point, of course, that compounds the problem here, as mentioned above, is the rendering of the divine name, **YHWH**, as "LORD." It is a common practise, followed by most modern Bible versions, but tends to cloud the meaning in scriptures such as Genesis 19:24. In saying "the LORD rained upon Sodom and upon Gomorrah brimstone and fire from the LORD," the reader could be forgiven for assigning two distinct identities to each "LORD" until the original Hebrew is consulted. Each occurrence of LORD (as the full capitalisation in many versions indicates) reveals the presence of the divine name, **YHWH**, or Yahweh. This is reminiscent of the Psalmist's words:

"The LORD said to my Lord ..." — Psalm 110:1

Here, though, the second "Lord" is **A.DHO.NAI'** in Hebrew, which *does* mean Lord, clearly distinguishing the two personages. This agrees with the Proverbs:

"Who has ascended to heaven and come down? Who has gathered the wind in his fists? Who has wrapped up the waters in a garment? Who has established all the ends of the earth? What is his name, and what is his son's name? Surely you know!" — Proverbs 30:4; *Revised Standard Version.*

God (Yahweh) is referred to in the Old Testament as the 'God of Abraham the God of Isaac and the God of Jacob.' Jesus was not that God. Notice what the apostle Peter said:

"The God of Abraham, Isaac, and Jacob, the God of our fathers, has given the highest honour to his *servant Jesus.*" — Acts 3:13; *New English Bible.*

Jesus is defined as the servant of God, not as God himself. And here we see a tie-in with the Old

Testament expression ("God of Abraham, Isaac, and Jacob") with the New Testament discussion of Jesus' role. For example, during the apostles' prayer at Acts 4:24-30, they twice used the expression "your servant Jesus." Exponents of the Trinity speak of the "humanity of God," explaining that Jesus assumed the position and stature of a servant when on earth. However, the above prayer was uttered some time after Jesus' ascension to heaven, and yet he is still the 'servant of God' and therefore in subjection to Him.

Returning to the Genesis account, a comparison of Genesis 18:22 with 19:1, proves that they were, in fact, merely angels:

> the *men* turned from there, and went toward Sodom
>> Genesis 18:22
>
> The two *angels* came to Sodom
>> Genesis 19:1

Angels often spoke the *very words* that God himself would have spoken had he been personally present. For example, the angel who visited Abraham spoke as if he were God himself at Genesis 18:1, 13, 17, 20, 22, 26, 33. However, in the same chapter the angels — including the one acting as chief spokesman — are referred to as "men": verses 2, 10, 16, 22.

In v. 22 it is said that the "men" went to Sodom, but the "LORD" remained. Inasmuch as there were three "men" originally (18:2), two went to Sodom (19:1), and one acted as spokesman before Abraham (18:10 says "man" rather than "men"), logically this latter angel was the chief spokesman, the chief representative before God.

Similarly, at Genesis 16:7, it is an "angel of the LORD" who visits Hagar. But after the visitation Hagar said: "Have I indeed *seen God* and still live?" — v. 13; *New English Bible*.

Other angels, though representatives of God, spoke as if they were God, or were *viewed* as if they were

God: Genesis 32:30; Exodus 3:2, 4, 6; 4:24; Numbers 22:32; Joshua 5:14 (compare 6:2); Judges 2:1; 6:11, 15, 22; 13:3, 8, 20; 1 Kings 19:5, 7, 11, 15; Acts 7:30-32; 12:7, 17.

The Trinitarian view of this passage (Genesis 18 & 19) tends to overstep the bounds of absurdity. Why should the fact that God sent three angels, as opposed to two, or one, have anything to do with the mystical divine persons of the Godhead? Where is the *Scriptural* evidence for this connection? Hebrew scholar Delitzsch observed that:

> "The idea that the Trinity is represented in the three is in every point of view untenable."

A further three-fold repetition occurs at Revelation 4:8 which says: "Holy, holy, holy, is the Lord God Almighty" (*Revised Standard Version*). This bears a strong resemblance to the vision of Isaiah (6:3) previously discussed. Interestingly, the Sinaitic Manuscript's *original* reading here has holy, not three, but *eight* times. The additional statement "who was and who is and who is coming," **HO EN KAl HO ON KAI HO ER.KHO'MENOS**, a Greek equivalent of the Hebrew expression at Exodus 3:14, is dealt with later in this book.

# 11   Titles Exclusive to the Father

The following paragraphs list the titles and names attributed to the Father. The fact that these are given to no other person, not even to Jesus, serves to distinguish the Father and the Son as entirely distinct individuals.

To no-one else but the Father is the title of Creator (Hebrew **BO.RE'**) applied: Ecclesiastes 12:1; Isaiah 40:28; 42:5; 43:1, 15; 45:18; Amos 4:13; 1 Peter 4:19 (compare Proverbs 8:22).

**EL SHAD.DAI'**, *God Almighty*, is applied to the Father in seven places: Genesis 17:1; 28:3; 35:11; 43:14; 48:3; Exodus 6:3; Ezekiel 10:5.

The corresponding Greek term **PAN.TO.KRA'TOR** (*supreme over all*; from **PAS**, *all*, and **KRA'TOS**, *power, dominion*) occurs ten times: 2 Corinthians 6:18; Revelation 1:8; 4:8; 11:17; 15:3; 16:7, 14; 19:6, 15; 21:22. Both words are used exclusively of the Father. The title **SHAD.DAI'** on its own occurs 41 times, again always with reference to the Father. Only God, the Creator, can rightly be called almighty, he having supreme power and authority over all, absolute dominion. There are no half measures here. The expression carries the connotation of the ultimate, with indications of an infinity beyond human comprehension. The power is not just considerable, but is boundless, it has no limitations. As Job was compelled to say:

> "I have come to know that you are able to do all things, And there is no idea that is unattainable for you." — Job 42:2.

Only one person can rightly and authentically bear the title of Almighty. Furthermore, the Bearer of such a title could, of necessity, never be given a subordinate position or title. One who is infinite in glory, majesty, power, and authority, could have neither an equal nor a superior. Yet Jesus is frequently referred to by such expressions as "son," "slave," "only-begotten," "apostle," (meaning: *one sent forth*). Never are such titles applied to God.

The Rock (Hebrew **HATS-TSUR'**), a title applied to the Father only, describes his qualities of perfect justice, unwavering faithfulness, uprightness, strength, a secure height and refuge, and a source of salvation. As a name it occurs 20 times: Deuteronomy 32:4, 15, 18, 30, 31; 2 Samuel 22:47; 23:3; Psalm 18:46; 19:14; 28:1; 78:35; 89:26; 92:15; 95:1; 144:1; Isaiah 17:10; 26:4; 30:29; 44:8; Habakkuk 1:12.

God is known by many other 'names,' such as *Ancient of Days* (Daniel 7:9, 13, 22), *Father* (Isaiah 64:8), *Holy Father* (John 17:11), *Holy God* (Joshua 24:19), *Grand Instructor* (Isaiah 30:20), *King of Eternity* (1 Timothy 1:17), *Majestic One* (Hebrew **AD.DIR'** — Isaiah 33:21), *Most High* (Hebrew **EL.YON'** — Deuteronomy 32:8; Psalm 9:2; 83:18). However, these are not proper names as such, they are actually titles. The personal and distinctive name of God, designated by the Hebrew tetragrammaton (four letters), **YHWH** by transliteration, often rendered Yahweh, is by far the most common designation applied to the Father. Regarding this name, Professor Davidson, in his *Theology of the Old Testament* (pp. 36, 37), says:

> "In so far as God reveals himself He acquires a name. Men call that which they know by a name. God, in revealing Himself, proclaimed His own name — Jehovah, Jehovah merciful and gracious."

This personal name of God occurs 6,828 times in the Masoretic Text. It distinguishes the personality of the Father, the Most High God (Hebrew **EL-EL.YON'** — Psalm 83:18). However, the ancient Jewish scribes introduced the practise of pronouncing **E.LO.HIM'** ("God") or **A.DHO.NAI'** ("Lord") instead of **YAH.WEH'**.

This has added to the confusion between the Lord *Yahweh* and the Lord *Jesus*. However, the distinction is nonetheless maintained even in the New Testament. — Note the expression 'our Lord *and* his Christ' at Revelation 11:15.

The presence of the divine name in the Old Testament also helps to resolve such texts as Romans 10:13. Here most translations read: 'Everyone who calls on the name of the Lord will be saved.' The 'Lord' is not capitalised as the Greek text simply has **KU'RI.OS**, *Lord*, here. However, the apostle Paul quotes from the book of Joel where the divine name *does* occur in the Hebrew Masoretic Text.

"Everyone who calls on the name of the LORD will be saved." — Joel 2:32; *New International Version.*

These considerations serve to underscore the distinction between the Father and the Son, and their entirely separate existence (compare 1 Corinthians 8:5, 6 where the "one God" is referred to as "the Father").

# PART THREE:

## JESUS CHRIST — CREATOR, OR CREATED?

# 12   The Deity of Christ

This chapter deals with the deity, or divinity, of Christ. This is perhaps the most difficult area of the subject in terms of clarifying the true nature of Christ. The Bible clearly states that Jesus is divine. But it is obviously the interpretation of "divine" that differs between adherents of the Trinity and its opponents.

This section demonstrates that humans, angels, pagan gods, even Satan himself, are referred to as "divine." In biblical terms this has a broad meaning, and does not necessarily assert that the one referred to as divine is God himself.

## The Subordination of Christ

Moreover, the Scriptures repeatedly make reference to the subordination of the Son to the Father. This occurs both in the Old and the New Testaments. On this point, Martin Werner, Professor in the University of Bern, said:

> "Wherever in the New Testament the relationship of Jesus to God, the Father, is brought into consideration, whether with reference to his appearance as a man or to his Messianic status, it is conceived of and represented categorically as subordination."

Examples of Jesus' subordination to God are given by Theology Professor Boobyer: Jesus ...

> "... confesses or denies men before God (Matt. x. 32f.; Luke xii. 8); he intercedes with God on our behalf and as heavenly paraclete ["helper"] pleads our cause with the Father (Rom. viii. 34; Heb. vii. 25; ix. 24; 1 John ii. 1); he is the mediator between men and God (1 Tim. ii. 5) ... St. Paul is quite explicit about it ... to quote from the relevant passage in the

New English Bible translation '... when all things are thus subject to him, then the Son himself will also be made subordinate to God ... and thus God will be all in all' (1 Cor. xv. 28)."

Here again the Apostolic Fathers offer no support for exponents of the Trinity. For example, J. N. D. Kelly, in his *Early Christian Doctrines,* writes regarding the view of Hermas, who wrote *Shepherd,* in the first part of the 2nd century, saying that the "Son of God is older than all his creation." He says (on pp. 94-95):

"In a number of passages we read of an angel who is superior to the six angels forming God's inner council, and who is regularly described as 'most venerable', 'holy', and 'glorious'. This angel is given the name of Michael, and the conclusion is difficult to escape that Hermas saw in him the Son of God and equated him with the archangel Michael.

"There is evidence also ... of attempts to interpret Christ as a sort of supreme angel ... Of a doctrine of the Trinity in the strict sense there is of course no sign."

It is interesting that Jesus should here be associated with the archangel Michael. This name comes from three Hebrew words: **MI** meaning "who?" **CHI** meaning "like," and **EL** meaning "God," giving the full meaning of Michael as: "Who is like God?" A rhetorical question denoting the uniqueness of God.

Also, Hermas' referring to Christ as "older than all his creation" agrees with other scriptures in which Jesus is described as a "creature," that is, one who is a created being. The three principle scriptures on this discussion are Proverbs 8:22, Colossians 1:15, and Revelation 3:14.

Dr. H. R. Boer, in his book *A Short History of the Early Church,* writes about the Apologists, the church writers who succeeded the Apostolic Fathers, saying:

"Justin and the other Apologists therefore taught that the Son is a creature. He is a high creature, a creature powerful enough to create the world but, nevertheless, a creature. In theology this relationship of the Son to the Father is called *subordinationism*. The Son is subordinate, that is, secondary to, dependent upon, and caused by the Father. The Apologists were subordinationists."

In the book *The Formation of Christian Dogma,* Dr. Martin Werner says concerning the earliest understanding of the relationship of the Son to God:

"That relationship was understood unequivocally as being one of 'subordination', *i.e.* in the sense of the subordination of Christ to God. Wherever in the New Testament the relationship of Jesus to God, the Father, is brought into consideration, . . . it is conceived of and represented categorically as subordination. And the most decisive Subordinationist of the New Testament, according to the Synoptic record, was Jesus himself . . . This original position, firm and manifest as it was, was able to maintain itself for a long time. 'All the great pre-Nicene theologians represented the subordination of the Logos to God.'"

Similarly, R. P. C. Hanson, in *The Search for the Christian Doctrine of God,* states:

"There is no theologian in the Eastern or the Western Church before the outbreak of the Arian Controversy [in the fourth century], who does not in some sense regard the Son as subordinate to the Father."

And Dr. Alvan Lamson, in *The Church of the First Three Centuries,* says regarding church writers before the Council of Nicaea (in 325 AD):

"The inferiority of the Son was generally, if not uniformly, asserted by the ante-Nicene Fathers ... That they viewed the Son as distinct from the Father is evident from the circumstance that they plainly assert his inferiority. ... They considered him distinct and subordinate."

Anglican bishop John Robinson said, concerning the deity of Christ, in his best-selling book *Honest to God*:

> "In practice popular preaching and teaching presents a supranaturalistic view of Christ which cannot be substantiated from the New Testament. It says simply that Jesus *was* God, in such a way that the terms 'Christ' and 'God' are interchangeable. But nowhere in Biblical usage is this so. The New Testament says that Jesus was the Word of God, it says that God was in Christ, it says that Jesus is the Son of God; but it does not say that Jesus was God, simply like that."

There are a number of texts that Trinitarians point to that they claim exalt Jesus to the position of Almighty God. It is these scriptures that are dealt with in this section.

# 13   The Fullness Of Divine Nature

"For the full content of divine nature lives in Christ."
So says Paul at Colossians 2:9 (*Good News Bible*).
Other translations read similarly:

"For in him the whole fullness of deity dwells bodily."
(*Revised Standard Version*).
"Because in him dwells All the FULLNESS of the DEITY
bodily."
(*Emphatic Diaglott*).
"It is in Christ that the entire Fulness of deity has
settled bodily."
(*Moffatt*).
"For in Christ all the fulness of the Deity lives in bodily
form."
(*New International Version*).

The Greek word generally rendered "deity" at this
place is **THE.O'TES**, a word taken from **THE.OS'**,
"God." The Trinitarian view of this passage is seen in
the writings of Greek scholar Trench (as quoted in
Vine's *Expository Dictionary of New Testament Words*,
Vol. 1, pp. 328, 329):

"Paul is declaring that in the Son there dwells all the
fulness of absolute Godhead; they were no mere rays
of Divine glory which gilded Him, lighting up His
Person for a season and with a splendour not His
own; but He was, and is, absolute and perfect God;
and the Apostle uses *theotes* to express this essential
and personal Godhead of the Son."

Trench declared that Jesus "was, and is, absolute
and perfect God." But is that the idea the apostle Paul
intended to convey?

Some claim a subtle distinction between
**THE.O'TES** of Colossians 2:9 and the slightly
differently spelled **THEI.O'TES** of Romans 1:20 —
saying that the former is closer to 'essence' or 'being,'

while the latter is closer to 'divine nature.' This accounts for renderings such as the *New English Bible*:

> "For it is in Christ that the complete *being* of the Godhead dwells embodied." — Colossians 2:9.

Notice the context of this scripture. In verse 8, Paul warns against the "philosophy and empty deceit" (*Revised Standard Version*) of the world, comparing this with the Christ. (See v. 3) And yet the teaching of the Trinity was adopted by the Church "more on the basis of Greek philosophical ideas than on Old Testament motifs." (*Encyclopaedia Britannica*, Micropaedia, Vol. VI, p. 302) Paul was clearly aware of the Platonic Trinity. He must also have known of Aristotle's views. Says *The Paganism in Our Christianity*, by Arthur Weigall (p. 198):

> "In the Fourth Century B.C. Aristotle wrote: 'All things are three, and thrice is all: and let us use this number in the worship of the gods; for, as the Pythagoreans say, everything and all things are bound by threes, for the end, the middle, and the beginning have this number in everything, and these compose the number of the Trinity.'"

Yet what did Paul say concerning his teachings and the Old Testament?:

> "I teach nothing except what the prophets and Moses said." — Acts 26:22; *Living Bible*.

Concerning Greek philosophy, Paul said:

> "For Jews demand signs and Greeks seek wisdom, but we preach Christ crucified, a stumbling block to Jews and folly to Gentiles, but to those who are called, both Jews and Greeks, Christ the power of God and the wisdom of God." — 1 Corinthians 1:22-24; *Revised Standard Version*.

Could Paul, in his statement at Colossians 2:9, have been contradicting his opinion of the worldly-wise Greeks and introducing philosophy into the simple faith of the Christians? He was warning them *away* from philosophy, not leading them to it! (Note Paul's discussion with the philosophical Stoics and Epicureans at Acts 17:18-34 and the simplicity of his explanation of God.) Moreover, his teaching was not merely *centred* on the Old Testament, but it *derived from it*. And, if the Trinity doctrine is not found in the New Testament, neither is it found in the Old Testament. Paul's attitude (at 1 Corinthians 11:1) mirrored that of Jesus Christ. — Matthew 5:17; Luke:4:4, 8, 12.

## Christ Possesses the Personality of His Father

What, then, did Paul mean by the fullness of the **THE.O'TES** dwelling bodily in Christ? The lexicon of *Liddell and Scott* (25th edition, abridged) gives as the meaning of **THE.O'TES**: "divinity, divine nature." *A Greek Lexicon of the New Testament and Other Early Christian Literature*, by Bauer-Arndt-Gingrich gives: "deity, divinity." This refers to the position or state of being divine, godhood.

Although quoting Trench's views on Colossians 2:9, Vine says in his book (*Expository Dictionary of New Testament Words*) under the heading "Divinity":

> "*Theotes* indicates the Divine essence of Godhood, the Personality of God; theiotes, the attributes of God, His Divine nature and properties."

The "Personality of God," the "Godhood," is different from saying that the very "being" of God dwells in Christ. Christ may well possess the qualities of God, but this does not make him God! This agrees with the view of **THEI.O'TES** presented in Vincent's *Word Studies in the New Testament* (Vol. III, p. 16) which says:

> "**THEI.O'TES** is god*hood*, not god*head*. It signifies the sum-total of the divine attributes."

Robinson's *Greek and English Lexicon of the New Testament* (p. 334) gives as one meaning of **THE.O'TES**: "the divine nature and perfections."

Paul said that the "fullness" of the divine nature dwells in Christ. This translates the Greek word **PLE'ROMA**. According to *Bagster's* Lexicon (1977 edition, edited by H. K. Moulton), **PLE'ROMA** means *that which fills up, full measure, entire contents, full extent, full number, that which fills up a deficiency, full development, plenitude.*

A comparison of the word's seventeen occurrences in the New Testament will further clarify its meaning:

its *full strength* would pull from the garment
    Matthew 9:16
its *full strength* pulls from it
    Mark 2:21
they took up fragments, 12 baskets *full*
    Mark 6:43
baskets *full* of fragments
    Mark 8:20
we all received of his *fullness*
    John 1:16
the *full number* of them
    Romans 11:12
the *full number* of people of the nations
    Romans 11:25
love is the *fulfilment* of the Law
    Romans 13:10
a *full measure* of blessing from Christ
    Romans 15:29
the earth and *that which fills* it
    1 Corinthians 10:26
when the *fullness* of the time arrived
    Galatians 4:4
the *full limit* of the times
    Ephesians 1:10
the *fullness* of him who fills up all things
    Ephesians 1:23
filled with all the *fullness* that God gives
    Ephesians 3:19

the stature of the *fullness* of the Christ
    Ephesians 4:13
God saw good for all *fullness* to dwell in Christ
    Colossians 1:19
in him all the *fullness* of divine nature lives
    Colossians 2:9

At John 1:16, the apostle says that we have all received out of Christ's "fullness, even grace upon grace." Out of the fullness of Jesus' superlative qualities we have received God's "indescribable free gift" of grace, or merciful kindness, undeserved kindness. Accordingly, this has come to be "*through Jesus Christ.*" — 2 Corinthians 9:15; John 1:17.

Paul spoke of his yearning to see the Roman Christians in order that he may impart a "spiritual gift" to them, that they may thereby be strengthened spiritually. He thus explained:

"I know that when I come to you I shall come with a full measure [**PLE'ROMA**] of blessing from Christ." — Romans 15:29.

Therefore, his spiritual gifts to them would be in a complete, or full measure; Paul being the one *through whom* this blessing would be imparted. — Romans 1:11.

That **PLE'ROMA** is synonymous with **TE'LEI.OS** ("complete, fully developed, perfect, fully realised") can be seen from a comparison of the use of **PLE'ROMA** at Ephesians 4:13 with the use of **TE'LEI.OS** in the same verse and at Colossians 1:28. Paul spoke, at Ephesians 4:13, of "mature manhood" (lit, a *perfect* man)" attaining to the measure of the stature of the fullness of Christ" (*Revised Standard Version*). At Colossians 1:28 Paul desires to "present every man mature in Christ," attaining this by teaching them "all wisdom."

Thus, the fullness of the Christ in Ephesians 1:23, Colossians 1:19 and 2:9 refers to his qualities and attributes which are in *full measure* as those of God.

The fullness, or the **PLE'ROMA**, of Christ's love is highlighted at Ephesians 3:19 where Paul describes the "love of Christ which surpasses knowledge, that you may be filled with all the fullness [**PLE'ROMA**] of God."

## The Divine Nature Dwells "Bodily" in Christ

Paul further says that the divine nature dwells "bodily" in Christ. This translates the Greek word **SOMATI.KOS'**, from **SO'MA** "body." An investigation of its use at Colossians 2:17 will demonstrate its use here (2:9) where **SO'MA** ("body") is placed in contrast with **SKI.A'** ("shadow"). At Hebrews 10:1, Paul says that the "law contains but a shadow [**SKI.AN'**], and no *true image*, of the good things which were to come" (*New English Bible*) (compare Hebrews 8:5).

So the Law of Moses is compared to that which is shadowy, unreal; whereas the "true image," the *true substance*, belongs to the Christ:

"All such things are only a shadow [**SKI.A'**] of things in the future; the reality [**SO'MA**] is Christ." — Colossians 2:17; *Good News Bible*.

Thus the very qualities, attributes, characteristics, the nature of God are not merely *symbolically* represented in Christ, but they are present "bodily," in *reality*, in *substance*. It is not that God himself somehow dwells in Christ, as if the *body* (Greek: **SO'MA**) or the *being*, the *life-force*, of God is in Christ. This is clearly not what Paul meant. He said that the divine nature dwelt "bodily" in Christ. There is nothing unreal or ethereal about the qualities that Jesus possesses. He has the Father's superlative qualities in full measure and in perfect balance.

A comparison of Colossians 1:19 with 2:9 will serve to strengthen the rendering of "divine nature" for **THE.O'TES**. Note the following rendering:

"For it was by God's own decision that the Son has in himself the full nature of God." — Colossians 1:19; *Good News Bible* .

If Jesus "was, and is, absolute and perfect God," then why should there be a need on God's part to *give to his* Son the fullness of divine nature? Did he not always possess this nature?

*Nature* translates the Greek word **PHU'SIS**. This comes from the root **PHU'O** meaning *to bring forth*, to *produce*, to *bring to birth*. **PHU'SIS** applies to the "natural powers or constitution of a person or thing" (Vine). The *Greek-English Lexicon of the New Testament*, by Grimm-Thayer (p. 661) says on this:

> "*the sum of innate properties and powers by which one person differs from others*, distinctive native peculiarities, natural characteristics. ... **HE PHU'SIS HE ANTHRO.PI'NE** ["the nature belonging to man"] (the ability, art, skill, of men, the qualities which are proper to their nature and necessarily emanate from it), Jas. iii. 7 ... **THEI'AS KOINO.NOI' PHU'SEOS** ["sharers of divine nature"], (the holiness distinctive of the divine nature is specially referred to), 2 Pet. i. 4.

## Those Born Again Also Share Divine Nature

A comparison of 2 Peter 1:4 with Colossians 2:9 proves beyond any doubt that the latter scripture provides no support for the doctrine of the Trinity. Just as Jesus has become a partaker of divine nature, so too can those to whom Peter addresses his letter! He says:

> "God's divine power has given us everything we need to live a truly religious life through our knowledge of the one who called us *to share in* his own *glory* and goodness. In this way he has given us the very great and precious gifts he promised, so that by means of these gifts you may escape from the destructive lust that is in the world, and may come to *share the divine nature*." — 2 Peter 1:3, 4; *Good News Bible*.

This emphasises the fallacy of the Trinity argument. For if Christ is a sharer, not of the nature, attributes and qualities of God, but of the *very being* of God, then Jesus' followers also partake of the *very being* of God. The *New English Bible*, having committed itself to the rendering "complete being" at Colossians 2:9, has here:

> "Through this might and splendour he has given us his promises, great beyond all price, and through them you may ... come to share in the *very being* of God." — 2 Peter 1:4.

Either the number of divine persons within the "Godhead" needs expanding, or Colossians 2:9 does not support the teaching of the Trinity!

# 14 'Your Throne, O God,'
## or 'Your Throne Is God,' Which?

| Trinitarian Renderings of Hebrews 1:8 | |
|---|---|
| Thy THRONE, O God | Benjamin Wilson |
| Thy throne, O God | *King James Version* |
| Your Kingdom, O God | *Living Bible* |
| Thy throne, O God | *New English Bible* |
| Thy throne, O God | *American Standard Version* |
| Your Kingdom, O God | *Good News Bible* |
| Thy throne, O God | *Douay* |
| Your throne, O God | *New International Version* |
| **Non-Trinitarian Renderings of Hebrews 1:8** | |
| Thy throne, given of God | Isaac Leeser |
| God is your throne | *An American Translation* |
| God is thy throne | Archbishop Newcome (improved vers. 1808) |
| God is thy throne | Moffatt |
| Thy throne is God | *American Standard Version* footnote |
| God is your kingdom | *Good News Bible* footnote |
| God is thy throne | *New English Bible* footnote |
| Your divine throne | *Revised Standard Version* |
| God is your throne | Steven Byington |

Many view the above reference as an indication of the teaching of the Trinity. The Psalm is an address (prophetically) to Jesus Christ. And many of the above versions address him as "O God." Is this correct?

In Paul's quotation of Psalm 45:6, the critical question is this: How does the translator deal with the three principal words that occur in this text, namely: "God ... Throne ... Forever"? Is the word "God" (Greek:

**THE.OS'**; Hebrew: **ELO.HIM'**) to be regarded as being in the vocative of address (i.e. "O God") as Trinitarians maintain, or in the nominative case (i.e. "Your throne *is God"*), or even in the genitive case (i.e. "Your throne is *of God"*)? Rules of grammar only help a little in resolving the question, but biblical context makes the point very clear.

## A Psalm "with Reference to the Son"

The forty-fifth Psalm is a Messianic prophecy addressed to the Christ. As the apostle Paul put it, it is "with reference to the Son." (Hebrews 1:8) In verse two of the Psalm it reads: "God has blessed you to time indefinite." And verse seven reads: "God, your God [compare John 20:17], has anointed you." The Psalmist then goes on to describe the marriage of the king, which parallels Revelation 19:7, 8 and the "marriage of the Lamb."

The "God" of verses two and seven (of Psalm 45) who blesses and anoints the Christ is the same "God" of verse six. Hence this God (**ELO.HIM'** in Hebrew) could properly be considered in the nominative case; that is, he is not addressing the Messiah "O God," but is saying that God (**ELO.HIM'**, as in verses two and seven) *is* the throne, or the Possessor of the kingly authority.

In the Hebrew text this clause does not contain a single verb. The presence of a verb would make it easy to put-one's-finger so to speak on the case-inflection of the noun **ELO.HIM'**. Hence, there is the further possibility that **ELO.HIM'** is the genitive of possession; that is, "Your throne is *of god"* (compare Isaac Leeser's version above). This has a similar meaning to the above consideration with the sense that the kingly authority, or the seat of ruling authority, *belongs to* God. The Messiah is thus granted the authority to rule by God, to whom the ultimate power and right belong.

# Psalms — Book II, the "Elohistic" Book

Book II of the Psalms (containing Psalms 42-72) is referred to as "Elohistic" because **ELO.HIM'** ("God") occurs more times than does the divine name (**YHWH** in Hebrew characters), which is not consistent with the rest of the Scriptures. Interestingly, a suggestion advanced by many Bible commentators is that the original reading of Psalm 45:6 was:

"Your throne *will be* (Hebrew: **YIH.YEH'**) to time indefinite."

And the scribe, when copying, mistook this Hebrew word **YIH.YEH'** for the very similar divine name **YHWH**. In ancient Hebrew manuscripts, there were no vowels, so that **YIH.YEH'** ("will be") was written **YHYH** (using Hebrew characters: יהיה) and the divine name was written **YHWH** (using Hebrew characters: יהוה). Note the great similarity between the two.

There was a common practise at this time to substitute the divine name, **YHWH**, for **ELO.HIM'** ("God"), or for **A.DHO.NAI'** (Hebrew: "Lord"; as for instance, at Psalm 44:2 and 54:4). Some scholars believe that this scribe mistook the Hebrew **YHYH** ("will be") for the divine name **YHWH**, and then substituted **ELO.HIM'** according to this common practise when making his own copy of the text. Thereafter other scribes, in making copies of this text, continued to write "God" instead of the correct Hebrew word **YIH.YEH'** ("will be"). The inclusion of this word gives the sentence its only verb; and, as any student of grammar knows, the verb is often said to be the chief word in a sentence.

Regarding this view, *The Polychrome Bible* by J. Wellhausen says in a note to Psalm 45:6:

"Heb. **YHWH** (**YIH.YEH'**), which a subsequent editor mistook for **YHVH**, i.e. **JHVH** (Heb.**YAH.VEH'**)

Also, in its 1930 edition, Weymouth's *New Testament in Modem Speech* in a footnote on Hebrews 1:8, and regarding the expression "O God," says:

"Ps. 45 is a Royal Marriage Song, and this translation ["O God"] involves the direct address of an earthly king by the title 'God.' The obvious difficulty has led to various conjectures: (1) 'Thy throne is the THRONE OF God' (so Revised Version margin in the Psalm). (2) 'Thy throne is God for ever and ever.' (3) A corrupt Hebrew text, Yahweh (God) being a mistake for the almost identical Hebrew word meaning 'shall be' ... 'Thy throne shall be for ever and ever. This conjecture is widely adopted."

In a footnote to Psalm 45:7, Rotherham's *Studies in the Psalms* calls attention to another likely Elohistic alteration, and concerning the expression "God, thy God," it says:

"Doubtless for an original 'Yahweh thy God'."

Hebrew scholar Delitzsch maintains the same view, as does the above mentioned Bible by J. Wellhausen.

In support of the above is the frequent use in the Psalms of such expressions as "Yahweh your God" and "Yahweh our God" as an examination of the following texts will show: Psalm 7:1, 3; 13:3; 20:7; 30:2, 12; 35:24; 38:15, 21; 40:5; 76:11; 86:12; 90:17; 94:23; 99:5, 8, 9; 104:1; 105:7; 106:47; 109:26; 118:5; 122:9; 123:2. At Psalm 10:12 the similar expression "O Yahweh, O God" occurs, whilst at 50:1: "The Divine One, God, Yahweh," similar to the expression at Joshua 22:22 (compare Psalm 118:27). The repetition of "God" in expressions similar to that of Psalm 45:6 is lacking elsewhere in the Psalms; in fact, it is only found on seven occasions, 43:4; 48:14; 50:7; 63:1; 67:6; 68:8 and 77:13. Notice that all but one of these occur in the "Elohistic" Book II. Further, the first occurrence (43:4) is contested both in the Targums and in the Vatican manuscript no. 1209, which reads: "O Yahweh, my God," rather than "O God, my God."

The fifty-third Psalm contains at least five scribal alterations from an original "Yahweh" **(YHWH)** to "God" **(ELO.HIM')**. These five (at verses 1, 2, 4, 5 & 6) are alterations for which there exists strong evidence. In verse five the sentence "For God [**ELO.HIM'**] himself will certainly scatter the bones..." the **ELO.HIM'** seems to be well supported except in two Hebrew manuscripts which read "Yahweh." Evidence for scribal changes of **YHWH** throughout Book II of the Psalms is plentiful: 44:23; 51:15; 53:1, 2, 4, 5, 6; 54:4; 55:9; 57:9; 59:11; 62:12; 66:18; 68:11, 17, 19, 22, 26, 32. Hence, in view of the above, a scribal change at Psalm 45:6 is certainly a strong possibility.

## The Apostle Paul's View of Psalm 45:6

However, when the apostle Paul quoted from this Psalm in his divinely inspired letter to the Hebrews, he saw no difficulty in reconciling the Greek Septuagint rendering (which he quoted almost word-for-word) with Christian teachings. To him, the Messiah was not the same person as the One who did the blessing and anointing, but was given the *authority of rulership,* or the "throne," by this One.

The correct understanding of Paul's words can be obtained from biblical context, and from the Scriptural use of "throne" in a metaphorical sense.

For example, Pharaoh of Egypt imparted great authority to Joseph when he said:

> "You will personally be over my house, and all my people will obey you implicitly. ONLY AS TO THE THRONE [the seat of ruling authority] shall I be greater than you." — Genesis 41:40.

After Darius the Mede had received the Kingdom of Babylon in 539 BC it is said that the prophet Daniel "was steadily distinguishing himself over the high officials and the satraps." Then it is said that the king "was intending to elevate him *over all the kingdom.*" (Daniel 5:31-6:3). This kind of authority was obviously not absolute, but was relative to Darius' own authority (which, incidentally, was relative to the overall rulership of Cyrus the Great). The relative authority of Christ as compared to the absolute authority of God is clearly brought out by the apostle Paul at 1 Corinthians 15:24, 27.

The metaphorical use of "throne" can also be seen from 1 Kings 16:11:

> "And it came about that when he [i.e. Zimri] began to reign, as soon as he sat down upon his throne, he struck down all the house of Baasha."

He clearly did not strike down the house of Baasha literally sitting on his throne! Nor would he approach and seat himself on his throne — in a literal sense — for the purpose of immediately going out into battle. The 'sitting down upon the throne' is, of course, a way of saying "he began to rule," or "he began to use his authority as king." Similarly, it is God who possesses the power and the authority behind Jesus' rule as king, as Scriptural context bears out. — Compare Exodus 17:16; Deuteronomy 17:18; 1 Samuel 2:8; 2 Samuel 3:10; 7:13, 16; 14:9; Esther 3:1; Psalm 89:44; Hebrews 4:16; in which texts "throne" is used metaphorically.

Concerning the kingship of David (through whom the Messiah was to come), Yahweh said:

> "I will cause him to stand in my house and in my kingship to time indefinite, and his throne will itself become one lasting to time indefinite." — 1 Chronicles 17:14.

The importance ascribed to the Judean throne is highlighted at 1 Chronicles 29:23 where it is said that "Solomon began to sit on *Yahweh's throne.*" Prior to this, at 1 Chronicles 28:5, it is called "the throne *of* *the kingship* of Yahweh.*" Judean kings from David on were seen to be sitting on the seat of rulership representing the Universal Sovereignty of Almighty God himself, particularly in its relationship to our earth. Therefore, the kings of the Davidic line ruled with the express permission, the will, the prescribed authority of God.

That the above view applies also to Jesus Christ and his having *received* authority to rule from God, can be seen from the following scriptures which confirm the rendering of "God is your throne" for Hebrews 1:8 and Psalm 45:6:

> "He will be great, and will be called the Son of the Most High; and the Lord God *will give to him* the throne of his father David." — Luke 1:32; *Revised Standard Version.*

> "And Jesus came and said to them [i.e. his disciples]: 'All authority in heaven and on earth has been *given to me.*"— Matthew 28:18; *Revised Standard Version.* [Compare Daniel 6:3 and the above discussion concerning delegated/relative authority.]

> "Those who prove victorious I will allow to share my throne, just as I was victorious myself and took my place *with my Father* on his throne." — Revelation 3:21; *Jerusalem Bible.*

The above "authority" translates the Greek word **EX.OU.SI'A**. Concerning this word W. E. Vine's *Expository Dictionary of New Testament Words,* Volume 1, p. 89, says:

> "**EX.OU.SI'A** denotes authority (from the impersonal verb **EX.ESTI'**, "it is lawful". From the meaning of leave or permission, or liberty of doing as one pleases, it passed to that of the ability or strength with which one is endued, then to the power of authority, the right to exercise power, e.g., Matt. 9:6; 21:23; 2 Cor. 10:8."

So Jesus has been *given,* or granted, this "all authority" by his Father, and his rulership is thus by

God's leave or permission. As Revelation 3:21 also bears out, Jesus does not exercise absolute authority inasmuch as he has been granted to sit down *with his Father* on His throne thus exercising delegated authority — rulership relative to that of Yahweh's absolute power — which Jesus in turn shares with those anointed to be kings and priests with him in the heavenly kingdom. — Revelation 5:9,10.

The translation of Hebrews 1:8, "Your throne, O God, is forever and ever," is a claim that the Trinity is a biblical teaching; as if it were taught by the apostle Paul. But within the carefully constructed framework of "the pattern of healthful words" (or the "pattern of truth" — *The Living Bible*), the Scriptures nowhere teach that Jesus is God. (2 Timothy 1:13) The relatively few controversial scriptures that Trinitarians point to, when seen in the light of biblical context, do not support this view.

# 15 The Humility and the Exaltation of Christ

Paul, at Philippians 2:5-11, admonishes the Philippian congregation to cultivate the quality of humility, lowliness of mind using the superlative example of Christ and the humility he demonstrated in willingly coming to earth and adopting a "slave's form."

The passage contains carefully chosen contrasts and synonyms in order to portray Christ as the supreme example of humility and loyalty; for which reason he was exalted to a "superior position." The lesson is followed up with encouragement to remain obedient (Greek: **THE'LO**: "to be willing," v. 13). Hence Paul begins verse 12 with the word **HO'STE**, "consequently"; that is, '*because* of this consideration of Christ's humility...' be obedient, be blameless and innocent, etc.

Keep "this *mental attitude* in you," Paul says. This translates **PHRO.NEI'TE** ("be you minding"), a verb in the imperative mood. We are not to passively retain this thought in mind, but must *actively generate* and maintain this thought; cultivate this mental attitude or mental inclination. **PHRO.NEI'TE** implies the intent of the mind, the directing of one's mind to a thing.

## Christ's Existence in the "Form" of God

Christ existed "in God's form." (Philippians 2:6) 'Form' translates the Greek **MOR.PHE'** which occurs again in verse 7, and elsewhere only at the spurious ending to Mark's gospel (v. 12). **MOR.PHE'** means "the form by which a person or thing strikes the vision; the external appearance." (*Greek-English Lexicon of the New Testament* — Grimm-Thayer) The idea that creatures of heaven have form is borne out by 1 Corinthians 15:44, where spirit creatures are spoken of as having bodies: "If there is a physical body, there is also a spiritual one." However, **MOR.PHE'** also means more than simply "the external appearance," as *A Dictionary of New Testament Greek Synonyms* (p. 30), by G. R. Berry, says in dealing with three synonyms **I.DE'A**, **MOR.PHE'** and **SCHE'MA** (the latter is used at Philippians 2:8):

> "**I.DE'A** denotes merely *outward appearance*. Both **MOR.PHE'** and **SCHE'MA** express something more than that. They too denote outward form, but as including one's habits, activities and modes of action in general. In **MOR.PHE'** it is also implied that the outward form expresses the inner essence, an idea which is absent from **SCHE'MA**. **MOR.PHE'** expresses the form as that which is intrinsic and essential, **SCHE'MA** signifies the figure, shape, as that which is more outward and accidental. Both **SCHE'MA** and **I.DE'A** therefore deal with externals, **SCHE'MA** being more comprehensive than **I.DE'A**, while **MOR.PHE'** deals with externals as expressing that which is internal."

In view of this, some Bible translations use the word "nature" instead of form. That Christ was in the *nature of god* also has Scriptural confirmation. In his letter to the Colossians (written at about the same time as Philippians), Paul says that in Christ "all the fullness of the divine quality [**THE.O'TETOS**] dwells bodily." (Colossians 2:9) At Hebrews 1:3, Christ is described as the impress (**CHA'RAK.TER**) of God's "very being" (**HU.PO.STA'SEOS**). This word **HU.PO'STA.SIS** relates to the substructure or foundation of a building. It also refers to "that which settles at the bottom, sediment." (*Liddell & Scott*) Hence it is rendered "very being" (*New English Bible*) "nature" (*Revised Standard Version*) "character" (*Moffat*) and "substance" (*American Standard Version*; *Douay*). The *King James Bible* renders it "person" here, but concerning this, W. E. Vine, in his *Expository Dictionary of New Testament Words*, says (Vol. III, p. 88):

"The A.V., [*King James*] 'person' is an anachronism; the word was not so rendered till the 4th cent."

**HU.PO'STA.SIS**, then, is an interesting comparison to **MOR.PHE'**. The former refers to the inner essence, the true nature, the very being; whilst the latter refers to the outward manifestation of a thing as expressive of its inner nature. — Compare also John 1:1; Colossians 1:15.

Paul contrasts the heavenly form of Christ (the likeness of God) with "a slave's form" — "the likeness of men." The two statements are in direct opposition. This required, on Christ's part, an emptying of himself, depriving himself of all that he was and had in his heavenly form in order to take on the likeness of an earthling man and become the Son of man. But he did more than this, he humbled himself, made himself lowly, "and became obedient as far as death."

## No Consideration to a Seizure

Paul says that Christ, "although he was existing in God's form, gave no consideration to a seizure, namely, that he should be equal to God." This passage is variously rendered:

did not count equality with God a thing to be grasped — *Revised Standard Version*

did not think to snatch at equality with God —*New English Bible*

counted not the being on an equality with God a thing to be grasped —*American Standard Version*

being in very nature God, did not consider equality with God something to be grasped —*New International Version* had the nature of God, but he did not think that by force he should try to become equal with God —*Good News Bible*

though being in God's Form, yet did not meditate a Usurpation 'to BE like God —*Emphatic Diaglott*

did not think it a matter to be earnestly desired —C*larke*

did not earnestly affect —*Cyprian*

did not regard as an object of solicitous desire —*Stuart*

thought not ... a thing to be seized —*Sharpe*

did not eagerly grasp —*Kneeland*

did not violently strive —*Dickinson*

An interlinear reading sets out the sentence like this:

| **OUKH** | **HARPAGMON'** | **E.GE'SATO** |
|---|---|---|
| Not | snatching | he considered |

| **TO EI'NAI** | **I'SA** | **THE.O'** |
|---|---|---|
| the to be | equal (things) | to God |

The subject (Jesus) is implied by the verb **E.GE'SATO**, which is negated by **OUKH**: he *did not* consider. **HARPAG.MON'** is the predicate: he did not consider snatching. *EI'NAI*, "to be," is an infinitive verb with the article, together they constitute the direct object: he did not consider snatching in order TO BE. **I'SA** is an adverbial noun, "equal things," and **THE.O'** the dative form of **THE.OS'**, "God," being the indirect object:

*He did not consider snatching in order to be equal to God.*

This literal rendering is similar to the *Hebrew New Testament* of Delitzsch:

| **LO-CHA.SHAV' LO** | **LE SHA.LAL' HEYO.THO'** |
|---|---|
| did not consider | to plunder |

| **SHA.WEH'** | **LE'LO.HIM'** |
|---|---|
| being equal | to God |

Some translations, however, present a slightly different view. For example, the *Jerusalem Bible* says:

"He did not *cling to* his equality with God." — Philippians 2:6.

(See also the *Living Bible*, and the footnote to the *Good News Bible*.) Says *The Greek-English Lexicon of the New Testament*, (p. 418) by Grimm-Thayer:

"Phil. ii. 6; ... this whole passage ... is to be explained as follows: who, although (formerly when he was **LO'GOS A'SARKOS** [the word without flesh]) he bore the form (in which he appeared to the inhabitants of heaven) of God (the sovereign, as opposed to **MOR.PHEN' DOU'LOU** [a slave's form]), yet did not think that this equality with God was to be eagerly clung to or retained ... but emptied himself of it ... so as to assume the form of a servant, in that he became like unto men (for angels also are **DOU'LOI TOU THE.OU'**, [slaves of God] Rev. xix. 10; xxii. 8 sq.) and was found in fashion as a man."

Advocates of the doctrine of the Trinity see Christ as being equal to God but as not wanting to hold on to or retain this right in his taking on human form. They thus overstep the boundaries of exegesis and enter the realm of *eisegesis* (literally: "to guide in"), putting ideas *into* the text which were not present formerly. They begin a study of this passage with the idea that Christ is equal to God — a statement in the Trinity dogma. Based upon this assumption they conclude that the Greek word **HARPAG.MOS'** is to be understood in the sense of 'hold fast; retain,' rather than the sense of 'a thing to be seized; a seizure.' This would give rise to the meaning that Christ, though equal to God, gave up the right to his 'prize,' did not 'retain' his equality, in taking on human form.

However, *never* does **HARPAG.MOS'**, nor the root word **HAR.PA'ZO**, mean 'holding; retaining' in any of the 14 occurrences in the New Testament. Note these few examples: the English word "harpoon" is taken from **HAR.PA'ZO** (through **HAR.PE'**); an instrument which *snatches* its victim's flesh. The Harpies of Greek mythology (as seen in the film "Jason and the Argonaughts") were evil winged monsters who *snatched away* food from the table. The Greek word **HARPE.DO'NE** (also taken from **HAR.PA'ZO**) was a rope or cord used for snaring game.

It is thus abundantly clear that **HARPAG.MOS'** demands the rendering 'seizure, snatching' rather than the weaker 'holding; retaining.' In harmony with this, note what *The Expositor's Greek Testament*, edited by W. Robertson Nicoll, says (Vol. III, pp. 436, 437):

> "We cannot find any passage where **HAR.PA'ZO** or any of its derivatives has the sense of 'holding in possession,' 'retaining'. It seems invariably to mean 'SEIZE,' 'SNATCH VIOLENTLY'. Thus it is not permissible to glide from the true sense 'grasp at' into one which is totally different, 'hold fast'."

For comparison, the 13 occurrences of **HAR.PA'ZO** are as follows: Matthew 11:12; 13:19; John 6:15; 10:12, 28, 29; Acts 8:39; 23:10; 2 Corinthians 12:2, 4; 1 Thessalonians 4:17; Jude 23; Revelation 12:5.

One reason for the aforementioned interpretation (Christ's equality with God) is the idea that Christ's being "in God's form" is equivalent to the idea of the "equal things" (**I'SA**) which he refused to seize (or, hold on to, according to Trinitarians). *Thus, one assumption has led to another!* The first is the Trinitarian concept of Christ's equality with God; the second is that the "equal things" belonged to Christ whilst in his heavenly form. After making these assumptions, Trinitarians set about interpreting the passage in harmony with the pagan concepts of the doctrine.

## Is Christ Equal to God?

In order to resolve the question of Philippians 2:6, we must first ask:

Was Christ equal to God even when in his heavenly form? Once we have found the Scriptural answer to this question we can then return to a consideration of the text with the correct, Scriptural view.

So, then, what do the Scriptures teach?:

> "But I want you to know that the head of every man is the Christ; ... in turn the head of the Christ is God." — 1 Corinthians 11:3.

Paul makes no distinction between Christ's earthly form and his heavenly; merely that "the *head* of Christ is God." A little later Paul says:

> "For the scripture says, 'God put ALL things under his feet.' It is clear, of course, that the words 'all things' do not include God himself, who puts all things under Christ. But when all things have been placed under Christ's rule, then he himself, the Son, will place himself under God, who placed all things under him; and God will rule completely over all." — 1 Corinthians 15:27, 28; *Good News Bible.*

Jesus referred to the Father as "my Father" and as "my God" whilst in his fleshly form on earth. (John 20:17) Years later — in fact decades after his ascension to his Father — whilst in his heavenly glory, he used this same expression "my God" four times at Revelation 3:12.

Moreover, Jesus himself said:

> "The Father is greater than I am." — John 14:28.

Exponents of the Trinity doctrine, when shown this scripture, often explain it away by saying that Jesus meant, "the Father is greater than the Son when in earthly form." But where does that idea occur at John 14:28 or the surrounding verses? Jesus said that he was returning to his Father in heaven *"because* the

Father is greater than I am." His Father was dwelling in heaven during Jesus' earthly ministry.

The Christian writer Irenaeus said, concerning this scripture:

> "We may learn through Him [Christ] that the Father is above all things. For 'the Father,' says He, 'is greater than I.' The Father, therefore, has been declared by our Lord to excel with respect to knowledge." — *Against Heresies,* Book II, chapter 28.8.

References that Jesus makes to God indicate, not the three persons of the Trinity, but "the Father." This is why the Scriptures repeatedly make reference to the "one God" as being "the Father," not three "divine persons."

The only reference to any 'equality' of Christ in Scripture outside of Philippians 2:6 is the erroneous conclusion of the Pharisees in the gospel of John:

> "He had said that God was his own Father and in this way had made himself equal with God." — John 5:18; *Good News Bible.*

That this was an erroneous view is seen from two things:

1. In the same verse the conclusion is drawn that Jesus was "breaking the sabbath" — never did Jesus break God's Law (Matthew 5:17, 18), but he *did* overstep the *traditions* of the Pharisees (Matthew 15:6); and:

2. Jesus' answer to this false conclusion in verse 19 reversed this view: "the Son can do nothing on his own: he does only what he sees his Father doing."

Exponents of the Trinity often turn to John 5:18 in support of the teaching. But surely does not the reply of Jesus count more than the opinion of the Pharisees? Verse 19 is an utter refutation of the Pharisees' view.

Elsewhere in this book, consideration is given to four scriptures (Proverbs 8:22, Micah 5:2; Colossians 1:15, and Revelation 3:14) that prove Jesus was *created*. No created being can be equal to God.

All things considered, then, the Scriptural teaching is that Christ neither was, nor is, nor ever will be equal to his Father.

The passage under consideration (Philippians 2:6) must therefore mean that Christ, though existing in the form of God — a mighty spirit possessing divine qualities and attributes — nonetheless refused to give consideration to a seizure, a violent snatching, so that he should be equal to God. Thus, the 'being on an equality with God' has nothing to do with Christ's being "in God's form." Even the angels are referred to as "heavenly beings" *(New International Version)*; Hebrew: **ELO.HIM'**; Greek: **AN'GELOS** "angels") at Psalm 8:5. Though angels can be considered as being godlike ones, yet they are certainly not equal to God.

Furthermore, Paul's lesson here concerns *humility, lowliness of mind.* If we are to accept the *King James* and *Douay* versions' view of this passage, are we to understand that Paul is actually urging us to consider it "not robbery," but our *right*, "to be equal with God"? Absurd!

## Summary

Jesus was in the form and likeness of God as a spirit created in God's image (Colossians 1:15) and manifesting the "exact imprint of [God's] very substance," the perfect reflection of God's very nature and qualities. (Hebrews 1:3) In him dwelt "the fullness of the divine quality." (Colossians 2:9) The apostle John referred to him as "a god" or as "divine." (John 1:1; *Moffat*) Although existing in this form, he provided a superb example in humility and lowliness of mind, by his *not even giving consideration* to any kind of seizure that he should be equal to God. This echoes the words of Jesus himself who said: "The Father is greater than I am." (John 14:28) He willingly submitted to his Father's will, not only in the days of his flesh, but also as a mighty spirit existing in an exalted nature at his Father's side in heaven.

In harmony with this, Jesus prayed to his Father, in the hearing of his faithful apostles: "Father, glorify me alongside yourself with the glory that I had alongside you before the world was." (John 17:5) Jesus gave up his heavenly existence in order to come to earth, and was granted a resurrection back to that same existence following his faithful earthly course.

For his faithfulness and willing obedience, "God exalted him [yes gave him greater glory than he had *once enjoyed* in heaven] to a superior position ['higher than the heavens' — Hebrews 7:26] and kindly gave him the name that is above every name, so that in the name of Jesus every knee should bend of those in heaven and those on earth and those under the ground [Daniel 12:2], and every tongue should openly acknowledge that Jesus Christ is Lord to the glory of God the Father." — Philippians 2:9-11.

So then, note how great was the glory conferred upon Jesus, how high the superior position granted to him, how great the name given to him. But note especially, it is all *"to the glory* [or, *the greater glory] of God the Father."*

# 16 Jesus Christ — Firstborn of all Creation

## COLOSSIANS 1:15

### Non-Trinitarian Renderings

| | |
|---|---|
| the firstborn of every creature | — *King James* |
| the first-born of all creation | — *Revised Standard Version* |
| Firstborn of All Creation | — *Benjamin Wilson* |
| the firstborn of all creation | — *American Standard Version* |
| firstborn of all creation | — *Byington* |

### Trinitarian Renderings

| | |
|---|---|
| his is the primacy over all created things | — *New English Bible* |
| superior to all created things | — *Good News Bible* |
| born first, before all the creation | — *Moffatt* |
| the firstborn over all creation | — *New International Version* |

## REVELATION 3:14

### Non-Trinitarian Renderings

| | |
|---|---|
| the beginning of the creation of God | — *King James* |
| the beginning of God's creation | — *Revised Standard Version* |
| the beginning of the creation of God | — *Benjamin Wilson* |
| the beginning of the creation of God | — *American Standard Version* |
| the beginning of God's creation | — *Byington* |

### Trinitarian Renderings

| | |
|---|---|
| the prime source of all God's creation | — *New English Bible* |
| the origin of all that God has created | — *Good News Bible* |
| the origin of God's creation | — *Moffatt* |
| the ruler of God's creation | — *New International Version* |

It is clear from the above references that the "Trinitarian Renderings" (among other Bible translations) present Jesus as one who is not a part of God's creation; one who is not created by God. The former renderings present the opposite view, that Christ is a part of creation, that he is the "beginning" of God's creation, and holds the position as of a firstborn son amongst the rest of God's creatures. A closer examination of the above scriptures in the light of Bible context will demonstrate which view harmonises with the rest of Scripture.

## Support Sought from Extra-Biblical Sources

In a footnote to Colossians 1:15, the *Douay* Bible says:

> "THE FIRSTBORN. That is, first begotten; as the Evangelist [John] declares, *the only begotten* of his Father. Hence, St. Chrysostom explains *firstborn*, not first created, as he was not created at all, but born of his Father before all ages; that is, coequal with the Father and with the Holy Ghost."

Rather than seek support from within the Bible, reference is made instead to a church writer of the fourth century — the century in which the aforementioned "controversies" finally brought the Trinity, along with its pagan concepts, into Christian teachings. However, the Greek word for "first-created" is **PRO.TO'KTIS.TOS**, which would make the clause read, "first-created of creation." Not only would this introduce tautology, but would, more importantly, detract from the pre-eminence Paul is here ascribing to Christ. In using the term **PRO.TO'TO.KOS** Paul is making deliberate reference to the biblical laws of primogeniture, the rights of the firstborn son in the father's household. Nevertheless, it is clear that Paul is assigning the creatorship to God and the position of a creature, a created one, to the Son, as the following arguments will demonstrate.

## Primogenitureship, The Rights of Firstborn

The firstborn (Greek: **PRO.TO'TO.KOS**; Hebrew: **BE.KHO.RAH'**) held an honoured position in the family of the biblical Jews, and was the one who succeeded to the headship of the household. The patriarch Jacob's firstborn was Reuben. According to the Greek Septuagint translation of the Old Testament, this is how Genesis 49:3 reads:

> "Ruben, thou art my first-born (**PRO.TO'TO.KOS**), thou my strength, and the first [**AR.KHE'**: *beginning*] of my children." — *The Septuagint Version of the Old Testament* (Samuel Bagster & Sons Limited, London).

Similarly, at Deuteronomy 21:17, the double-portion of the inheritance was to go to the firstborn (**PRO.TO'TO.KOS**) "because he is the *first* (**AR.KHE'**: 'beginning')" of the children.

Likewise, Jesus had the rights of firstborn conferred upon him as the first one in God's family of sons. The firstborn son was the first (Greek: **AR.KHE'**) of the father's generative power, he was not considered equal to the father. Moreover, the title of firstborn is never applied either to God or to the Holy Spirit.

## Wisdom Personified — the Earliest of God's Achievements

This understanding of Colossians 1:15 harmonises with Proverbs 8:22, where wisdom personified (according to the apostle Paul, Christ "has *become* to us wisdom from God," hence he is wisdom personified — 1 Corinthians 1:30) says that:

> "Yahweh himself *produced* me [Hebrew: **QA.NA'NI**] as the beginning [from Hebrew: **RE.SHITH'** and Greek: **AR.KHE'**] of his way, the earliest of his achievements of long ago." — Proverbs 8:22.

A minority of Bible versions render the above as, not "produced me," but as "possessed me." But this rendering is without any reasonable support. The Hebrew Masoretic text (reproduced, for instance, in Kittel's *Biblia Hebraica*), the *Aramaic Targums*, the *Greek Septuagint* (**E'KTI.SEN' ME**) and the *Syriac Peshitta* all read, "produced" or, "formed" or, "created." In order to fit "possessed me" into their Bible versions, these translators alter the Hebrew text's **RE.SHITH'** to "*in* the beginning," which, as found in the very opening word of Genesis, is actually **BE.RE.SHITH'**. In Greek, "in the beginning," if it occurred here, would be **EN AR.KHEI'** (see Genesis 1:1, *Greek Septuagint*), but, at Proverbs 8:22, the *Greek Septuagint* reads **AR.KHEN'** giving the following rendering:

> "The Lord made me the beginning of his ways for his works." — *Bagster's Septuagint.*

In order to harmonise Proverbs 8:22, Colossians 1:15, and Revelation 3:14 with the extra-biblical doctrine of the Trinity, then, requires altering the texts of the original God-inspired Bible writers, so that they are *out of harmony* with the rest of Scripture. — Note Galatians 1:8, 9 and Revelation 22:18, 19.

## The Partitive Genitive: 'Firstborn AMONG all Creation'

In the clause "firstborn of all creation," Paul made use of a grammatical device known as the *partitive genitive.* This is a noun placed in the genitive case following words that denote a part; such as "some of..." "part of..." "among..." etc. There are examples in the New Testament:

SOME OF the sons of Israel
    Matthew 27:9
the scribes OF the Pharisees
    Mark 2:16
the poor OF the holy ones
    Romans 15:26
I am no PART OF the body
    1 Corinthians 2:15, 16
Hymenaeus and Alexander BELONG TO these ones
    1 Timothy 1:20
throwing SOME OF you into prison
    Revelation 2:10

It is also seen in the Greek Septuagint:

you have eaten OF the tree
Genesis 3:12 (LXX)
Abel brought SOME OF the firstlings
Genesis 4:4
I will leave SOME OF the people
Genesis 33:15
SOME OF the older men
Exodus 17:5

Though some scholars doubt whether Paul was here using a partitive genitive, a comparison of the clause "firstborn from the dead" at Colossians 1:18, which is also partitive genitive, makes the point clear.

## Jesus is the "firstborn from the dead"

Upon his resurrection, Jesus became the firstborn *from among* those raised to heavenly life; Jesus was thus the first one to be raised to heavenly life (see John 3:13). To employ the reasoning that some apply to the clause "firstborn of all creation" (saying that Jesus is *apart from* creation) we would now say, about Colossians 1:18, that Jesus is *not* actually from among those of the resurrection, that he was *not* in reality one of those resurrected to heavenly life. Such a statement would be clearly absurd. Obviously the 'dead ones' mentioned here are the *whole* of a class, and Jesus is described as the first one from among this class, a *part of* this class.

A similar use of the partitive genitive is found in Luke 14:33 where the Greek **PAS EX HUMON'** ("everyone out of you") occurs. Here the use of **EK** (or, **EX**), "out of," is similar to its use at Colossians 1:18. The individuals Jesus is here addressing are a whole, a *class*, and certain ones *out of* them will "say good-bye to all" their belongings and become Jesus' followers. Similarly, the 'dead ones' are the *whole*, the *class*, and Jesus is the first member *out of* this group, the "firstfruits." — 1 Corinthians 15:23; compare Luke

11:15; John 7:40; 16:17 for further examples of the above use.

Accordingly, the clause "firstborn of all creation" is also unquestionably a partitive genitive. The *whole*, or *class*, is the creation of God, and the firstborn, or pre-eminent one, is a part of that creation; he is *among* creation.

## Instrumental Use of Greek: EN, "By Means of Him"

The first clause of Colossians 1:16 literally reads: "in him all things were created." Some versions render this: "by him all things were created" (for example, *Moffatt*, *New International Version*). However, a consideration of the so-called instrumental use of the Greek word **EN** ("in") will bring out the full meaning.

**EN** is sometimes used, along with a noun in the dative case, to describe the instrument *by means of* which something is accomplished. Examples are:

It is BY MEANS OF the ruler of the demons [as the instrument] that he expels demons
Matthew 9:34
(Matthew 12:24, 27)
it is BY MEANS OF God's spirit that I expel the demons
Matthew 12:28
By [i.e. BY MEANS OF] what authority do you do these things?
Matthew 21:23
all those who take the sword will perish BY [as the instrument] the sword
Matthew 26:52
whether he is able WITH [or, BY MEANS OF] ten thousand troops to win
Luke 14:31
WITH WHAT [i.e. BY WHAT MEANS] will the salt be seasoned?
Luke 14:34

he [Jesus] became known to them BY MEANS OF the
breaking of the loaf
> Luke 24:35

nearly all things are cleansed WITH [as the instrument]
blood according to the law
> Hebrews 9:22

A notable example of the instrumental **EN** occurs
at Acts 17:31 where Jesus is again referred to by Paul
as the *instrument* of God's purposes. He explains that
God "has set a day in which he purposes to judge the
inhabited earth in righteousness *by* [Greek: **EN**; i.e. *by
means of*; Christ as the instrument] a man whom he
has appointed."

Consequently, in Colossians 1:16, 17 Jesus is
described as the instrument *by means of* which God
accomplishes his works of creation. (Compare the
expression of wisdom personified at Proverbs 8:30,
namely, "I came to be beside him [God] as a master
worker," and Genesis 1:26, "Let *us* make man in our
image.") To translate this, "all things were created *by*
him," would imply that Jesus is, not the instrument,
but the *originator*, the *cause* of creation. Since
nowhere in Scripture is Jesus Christ ever spoken of as
being the Creator, such a rendering would be, not only
inconsistent, but misleading. It would not fit in with
the internal harmony of the Scriptures.

## PANTA, "All Things," Allowing for Exceptions

If, as has been maintained by the above
arguments, Jesus Christ is indeed a *part of* creation
and is not himself the Creator, the question now
arises, How do we harmonise this statement, at
Colossians 1:16, that "all things" were created by
means of him? Is it possible from a grammatical point
of view to consider Jesus as being *excluded from* these
"all things" even though he himself is not the Creator?

The Greek in question here is the word **PANTA**
which comes from **PAS** meaning, literally, "all."

However, that this word (and its inflections) can be used with exceptions to the "all" being *understood* can be seen from the following:

At 1 Corinthians 15:24, Paul speaks of the end of Christ's reign at which time he will have "brought to nothing *all government* and *all authority* and *power.*" The question may arise in his readers' minds, Does this mean that Christ will eventually usurp the position, the authority, and the power of Almighty God himself? Could *all* existing power and authority be included in this statement *without exceptions*? Paul himself provides the answer:

> "But when he says that 'all things (**PANTA**) have been subjected,' *it is evident* [or, "it is plain" *Revised Standard Version*] that it is with the *exception* of the one who subjected all things to him [God]." — 1 Corinthians 15:27.

Thus, the "all things" are considered by Paul to have an obvious, or "evident," exception. Note the *Good News Bible*:

> "It is clear, of course, that the words 'all things' **[PANTA]** do not include God himself."

Moreover, this is no isolated use of **PAS** in the Scriptures, as the following passages demonstrate:

> give as gifts the things on the inside and ALL [OTHER] things are clean about you
> Luke 11:41
> you give the tenth of the mint and the rue [themselves vegetables] and of EVERY [OTHER] vegetable
> Luke 11:42
> Do you imagine that these Galileans were proved worse sinners than ALL [OTHER] Galileans?
> Luke 13:2
> Note the fig tree and ALL the [OTHER] trees
> Luke 21:29
> Through one man [Adam] sin entered into the world and death through sin, and thus death spread to ALL MEN [excluding Adam to whom death did not "spread," even though Adam was himself a man]          Romans 5:12

Flee from fornication. EVERY [OTHER] sin [fornication
is, of course, itself a sin]
  1 Corinthians 6:18
God kindly gave him the name that is above EVERY
[OTHER] name [excluding, of course, the giver's name]
  Philippians 2:9
For ALL the [OTHERS] [other than Timothy] are
seeking their own interests
  Philippians 2:21

Comparing the above references with the Greek
text it will be found that Luke and Paul do not actually
use the word "other" in those places. But by
examining the sense it is plain that the word is
*understood*; or, as Paul might have put it, "*it is evident
that 'all other' is to be understood.*"

So the Bible at times uses the word "all" in a way
that allows for exceptions. Likewise with the five uses
of **PAS** in Colossians 1:16, 17 & 20.

## God reconciles "by means of" Christ

Equally strong evidence is found in the immediate
context of the scripture in question which will show
that the inclusion of the word "other" is not only
required but is, in fact, *demanded*. Note carefully
Paul's use of "all things" (**PANTA**) in verse 20. Christ
does not need to be 'reconciled again' to God
inasmuch as he himself is the redeemer of all *other
things*. He is the one "*through whom*" God is
performing the reconciliation. He is thus naturally
assumed to be *excepted* from the "all things" by Paul.

This harmonises with 2 Corinthians 5:19 where,
incidentally, we find another use of the instrumental
**EN**: "God was *by means of* [**EN**, instrumental] Christ,
reconciling a world to himself."

So Christ was not *himself* being reconciled to God,
but was the instrument used *by* God in reconciling *all
other* creation to Him. This being the case, it is

imperative to the full sense of verse 20 to render **PANTA** as "all other." It is likewise imperative to render the remaining four instances as "all other." Notice how Paul uses the expression "*the* all things" in verse 20. Hence, it is "*the* all things" previously referred to, excluding Christ. The correct understanding of **PANTA** harmonises with its use in the immediate context.

## DI.A' With Genitive of Agency, "Through Him"

Paul goes on to say that "all other things have been created through" Jesus.

"Through" here translates the Greek word **DI.A'**. This word is often used with a noun in the genitive case as a means of expressing the *agency through which* (or, whom) something is accomplished, and is close in application to the instrumental **EN** previously discussed.

It occurs, for instance, in the following scriptures: Matthew 18:7; 26:24; John 1:7, 17; 11:4; 17:20; Acts 1:16; 2:43; 3:18; 10:36; 11:29, 30; 1 Corinthians 1:9 (where God himself is the agent); 12:8 (where the Holy Spirit is the agent); Galatians 1:1; Philemon 7 (here Philemon is the agent); Hebrews 2:10; 13:11 (here the high priest is the agent); 1 Peter 2:14.

Note, also, the following examples:

All things came into existence *through him* (i.e. through the agency of the Word)
John 1:3
God sent his Son for the world to be saved *through him*
John 3:17
No one comes to the Father except *through me*
John 14:6
He [Moses] supposed they would grasp God was giving them salvation *by* his hand
Acts 7:25
from him [Jesus] and *by* him and for him are all things
Romans 11:36

What are Apollos & Paul? ministers *through whom* you
became believers
1 Corinthians 3:5

Thus, as the agency used throughout the creation
of all other things Jesus himself is not the Creator.

## AR.KHE' — The Beginning of God's Creation

Jesus' occupying the pre-eminent position in
creation, and the same position amongst the class of
'dead ones,' is such that "he might become the one
who is first [**AR.KHE'**] in all things." (Colossians 1:15,
18) We thus come to Revelation 3:14.

As the aforementioned quotations show, some
versions render the Greek word **AR.KHE'** with the
idea of "origin," "primary source," or, "ruler." One who
maintains the above view is Greek scholar Henry
Alford, but he nevertheless concedes concerning the
word:

"The mere word **AR.KHE'** would admit the meaning
that Christ is the first created being: see Gen. xlix. 3;
Deut. xxi. 17; and Prov. viii. 22. And so the Arians
here take it, and some who have followed them: e.g.
Castalio, 'chef d' oeuvre:' 'omnium Dei operum
excellentissimum atque primum: · [meaning, "the
first and most excellent of all God's works"] and so
Ewald and Zullig."

As has been remarked above, support for the
Trinitarian belief is sought from non-biblical sources.
For example, *Jerome's Commentary* claims that Paul
(at Colossians one) was making reference to the
apocryphal books of the Old Testament (e.g. Wisdom
7). However, never did any inspired Bible writer quote
from any of the apocryphal writings. Nor did they
quote from any Greek philosophy, except to show the
contrast between it and Christian truth, or to quote
from reliable sources to show some agreement with
fundamental Christian teachings. (Acts 17:16-34)
There are, however, hundreds of references made in

the New Testament to the pre-Christian Old Testament, showing the close-knit internal harmony of the inspired Scriptures.

On the subject of **AR.KHE'** (beginning), *The Expositor's Greek Testament* says that to understand Revelation 3:14 as meaning that Jesus is "the active source" of creation, rather than the first created person, one must interpret **AR.KHE'** "as in Greek philosophy and [non-biblical] Jewish wisdom-literature, **AITI'A**, or origin." But if one desires to preserve the harmony of the Scriptures, it is essential to refrain from attempting to harmonise extra-biblical teachings! — 2 Peter 2:1.

Anaximander, a Greek philosopher of the 8th century BCE, is said to have been the first to use **AR.KHE'** in the sense of *first cause*. But nowhere does this idea prevail in the Scriptures.

On the other hand, the word **AR.KHE'** occurs 56 times in the New Testament (according to the Westcott and Hort text) providing an abundance of source material by means of which it is possible to see the precise meaning the Bible writers ascribe to the word. Of the 56 occurrences, **AR.KHE'** is used in the pure sense of "beginning" no less than 42 times. As for the remaining 14 times it is variously rendered "principalities" "governments" "corners" "extremities" and "original" at the following places: Luke 12:11; 20:20; Acts 10:11; 11:5; Romans 8:38; 1 Corinthians 15:24; Ephesians 1:21; 3:10: 6:12; Colossians 1:16; 2:10; 2:15; Titus 3:1; Jude 6.

Notably, the apostle John consistently uses **AR.KHE'** in the purest sense of "beginning" in each of its 21 occurrences in his books and letters: John 1:1, 2; 2:11; 6:64; 8:25, 44; 15:27; 16:4; 1 John 1:1; 2:7, 13, 14, 24, 24; 3:8, 11; 2 John 5, 6; Revelation (3:14); 21:6; 22:13. There would need to be solid biblical support in order to suddenly switch meanings at

Revelation 3:14 and infer that Jesus is the "principal one" of creation rather than the beginning. — Compare "beginning," Hebrew: **RE.SHITH'**, Greek: **AR.KHE'**, at Proverbs 8:22 and notes on this text above.

Nevertheless, nowhere in the Bible does the use of **AR.KHE'** allow for the meaning of one who is not a *part of* the order of things, as is implied by the "Trinitarian renderings" of Revelation 3:14. A careful analysis of the list of the 14 uses of this word as above (starting with Luke 12:11) will show this secondary meaning of **AR.KHE'** is based on the sense of "beginning": "first ones", "those in the *first*, or principal position within the order of things", "principalities." Consider the expression "extremities" or "corners" (**AR.KHAIS'**) as applied to the great linen sheet seen by Peter in vision. (Acts 10:11; 11:5) Peter obviously saw the sheet being carried by its "end" parts, its four extremities, or four corners. The *Emphatic Diaglott's* interlinear reading says "four ends."

At Jude 6, **AR.KHE'** is used to describe the "original" position the fallen angels occupied. Here the King James says: "And the angels which kept not their *first estate.*"

It is clear, then, that translating Revelation 3:14 as "ruler" or, "prime source," is an attempt to put Jesus *outside* of creation. But biblical context does not allow for such a view.

At Revelation 3:14 Jesus is also referred to as "the Amen." This could be rendered, "the so-be-it." Here we harmonise Paul's words to the Corinthians where there occurs a further use of the aforementioned INSTRUMENTAL **EN**, and **DI.A'** with the GENITIVE OF AGENCY; please note:

> "For no matter how many the promises of God are, they have become Yes *by means of* [**EN**] him.

Therefore also *through him* [**DI.A'** with the genitive] is the 'Amen' said to God for glory through us." — 2 Corinthians 1:20.

Thus, Christ is the means by which God's promises are, and shall be, accomplished. It is through Jesus that all of God's promises find fulfilment. Because of his faithful life course and obedience even to a sacrificial death he is called "the faithful and true witness." He has made possible the bringing to reality all of God's promises and declarations.

The Greek expression for "the faithful witness," (Revelation 1:5; 3:14) namely, **HO MAR.TUS' PIS.TOS'** (or, **HO PIS.TOS'** with the definite article "the") occurs in the Greek Septuagint at Psalm 88:37 (89:37 in modern Bibles) where the seed of David is spoken of prophetically as being firmly established "as a faithful witness."

This passage of the Psalms (89), which abounds in Messianic prophecies, records the words of God, as can be seen from verses 18-37. Interestingly, verse 27 of this Psalm ties us into Colossians 1:18 again when Yahweh says concerning this one: "I myself shall place him as firstborn." He was thus prophesied to become "the firstborn among many brothers," (Romans 8:29) namely, "*among*" the 'dead ones' referred to at Colossians 1:18; the class that share with Christ in the "likeness of his resurrection" (Romans 6:5), Christ being the "firstfruits" of this class. — 1 Corinthians 15:23.

### Jesus Had an "Origin"

Another scripture that proves Jesus' subordination to the Father, and that he was created, is Micah 5:2. This reads:

"But you, (Bethlehem) Ephrathah, the least of the clans of Judah, out of you will be born for me the one who is to rule over Israel; his origin goes back to the distant past." — Micah 5:2; *Jerusalem Bible*.

This was the scripture the Pharisees failed to take account of when they asked Jesus:

"You are not fifty yet, and you have seen Abraham?" — John 8:57.

It was Jesus' pre-human existence that puzzled the Pharisees. To them the Christ was simply "the son of David." — Luke 20:41-44.

However, Jesus lived before his fleshly manifestation. He had his "origin" in the heavens, as a spirit son of God. He was the first of God's creation.

## Summary of Colossians 1:15-18

Consequently, it can be seen from the above references how scriptures are carefully knitted together forming a pure fabric of "healthful words." (2 Timothy 1:13) We have come full circle from a discussion of Colossians 1:15-18 describing the exalted position of Christ among creation, as well as among those anointed by Holy Spirit who constitute the 'dead ones,' to his position as the "beginning of God's creation" and his role as the Amen and the faithful witness. This took us to the Psalms where Jesus is spoken of prophetically as both "the faithful witness" and as the "firstborn," he being placed in such position by God.

There is clearly a profound simplicity in the way the above truths have been woven into the Scriptures by the Supreme Author. How different from the philosophical mysticism of the Trinity doctrine!

## PLE'ROMA: Fullness, Full Measure

At Colossians 1:19 "all fullness" is said to dwell in Christ. "Fullness" translates the Greek word **PLE'ROMA**. According to *Bagster's Lexicon*, 1977 edition, edited by H. K. Moulton, **PLE'ROMA** means, "that which fills up; full measure, entire contents, full extent, full number, that which fills up a deficiency, full development, plenitude."

A comparison of the word's 17 occurrences in the New Testament will further clarify its meaning:

its FULL STRENGTH would pull from the garment
    Matthew 9:16
its FULL STRENGTH pulls from it
    Mark 2:21
they took up fragments, 12 baskets FULL
    Mark 6:43
provision baskets FULL of fragments
    Mark 8:20
we all received out of his FULLNESS
    John 1:16
the FULL NUMBER of them
    Romans 11:12
the FULL NUMBER of people of the nations
    Romans 11:25
love is the law's FULFILMENT
    Romans 13:10
I shall come with a FULL MEASURE of blessing from Christ
    Romans 15:29
to Yahweh belong the earth and THAT WHICH FILLS it
    1 Corinthians 10:26
when the FULL LIMIT of the time arrived
    Galatians 4:4
for an administration at the FULL LIMIT of the appointed times
    Ephesians 1:10
the FULLNESS of him who fills up all things in all
    Ephesians 1:23
that you may be filled with all the FULLNESS that God gives
    Ephesians 3:19
the measure of stature that belongs to the FULLNESS of the Christ
    Ephesians 4:13
he [God] saw good for all FULLNESS to dwell in him

[Christ]
Colossians 1:19
in him [Jesus] all the FULLNESS of the divine quality
dwells bodily
Colossians 2:9

At John 1:16, the apostle says that we have "all received from out of his [Christ's] fullness, even undeserved kindness upon undeserved kindness [grace upon grace]." Out of the fullness of Jesus' superlative qualities we have received God's "indescribable free gift" of undeserved kindness. Accordingly, this has come "to be *through* Jesus Christ." — 2 Corinthians 9:15; John 1:17.

Paul spoke of his yearning to see the Roman Christians in order that he may "impart some spiritual gift" to them that they may be "made firm." He thus explained: "I know that when I do come to you I shall come with a full measure **(PLE'ROMA)** of blessing from Christ." Therefore, his spiritual gifts to them would be in a complete, or full measure; Paul being the one *through whom* this blessing would be imparted. — Romans 1:11; 15:29.

That **PLE'ROMA** is akin to **TE'LEI.OS** (meaning: complete, fully developed, perfect, fully realised) can be seen from a comparison of the use of **PLE'ROMA** at Ephesians 4:13 with the use of **TE'LEI.OS** in the same verse and at Colossians 1:28. Paul spoke, at Ephesians 4:13, of "a full-grown man (or, a perfect man)" attaining to the "measure of stature (or, growth) that belongs to the fullness **(PLE.RO'MATOS)** of the Christ"; and, in the latter reference he explains how he is "admonishing every man" in order that by teaching them "all wisdom, we may present every man complete **[TE'LEI.ON**: mature, perfect] in union with the Christ."

Thus, the "fullness" of the Christ in Ephesians 1:23, Colossians 1:19 and 2:9 refers to his qualities which are in *full measure* as those of God

(**THE.O'TETOS**: divine quality — note Vincent's, *Word Studies in the New Testament*, Vol. III, p. 16, and Goodspeed's translation, which renders this as "divine character" — Colossians 2:9). The fullness, or the **PLE'ROMA**, of Christ's love is highlighted at Ephesians 3:19 where Paul describes the "love of the Christ which surpasses knowledge, that you may be filled with all the fullness (**PLE'ROMA**) that God gives."

According to the wording of Colossians 1:19, it was *God* who "saw good for all fullness (**PLE'ROMA**) to dwell in" Christ. It thus cannot be said that the very *person* of God, or the "*being* of God" (note the *New English Bible*) was by God's choice made to dwell in Christ. It is the *qualities* of God, his personality, his attributes, which dwell in full measure in Christ. The *Good News Bible* renders this:

> "For it was by God's own decision that the Son has in himself the *full nature* of God." — Colossians 1:19.

If we are to understand **THE.O'TES** (Colossians 2:9) as the *essence* of God rather than his qualities then how is it possible to harmonise 2 Peter 1:4 where faithful anointed Christians (the aforementioned class of 'dead ones') are promised, by "divine power," that they "may become *sharers in divine nature*"? Thus, these anointed Christians share with Christ the "divine nature," the qualities of God.

Further clarification is seen in Colossians 2:10 where, after describing the *fullness* that dwells in Christ, Paul goes on to say that the Colossian Christians themselves are "possessed of a fullness by means of" Christ. Thus, if it is maintained that the *person* of God, or as some translations endeavour to show, the "godhead" dwells in Christ, then it also dwells in all anointed Christians.

Finally, Paul says, at Colossians 2:9, that this "divine quality dwells *bodily*" in Christ. "Bodily" here translates the Greek word **SOMA.TIKOS'**. An investigation of its use at Colossians 2:17 will demonstrate its use here where **SO'MA** (body) is placed in contrast with **SKI.A'** (shadow). At Hebrews 10:1, Paul said that the "Law has a shadow (**SKI.AN'**) of the good things to come, but not the *very substance* of the things." (Compare Hebrews 8:5) So the Law of Moses is being compared to that which is shadowy, unreal; whereas the *very substance*, the reality, belongs to the Christ: "for those things are a shadow (**SKI.A'**) of the things to come, but the *reality* (**SO'MA**) belongs to Christ." — Colossians 2:17.

Thus, the very qualities of God, the "divine quality" or, "godship," are not merely symbolically represented in Christ, but they are present "bodily," in *reality*, in *substance*. Jesus has the true personality of his Father.

So, in summary, we may say of Colossians 1:19:

"God saw good for a completeness, a fullness, a perfect degree of love, wisdom, knowledge and goodness to dwell in Christ."

Compare also John 1:16, Ephesians 3:19, and Colossians 2:3, where these qualities are described in Christ.

In summarising Colossians 2:9 we may say:

"It is in Christ that a perfect degree, a full limit, of the very substance of the divine qualities and attributes dwells."

## Final Summary

In order to further confirm the accuracy of the above arguments, a final panoramic view of the book of Colossians will show how these points are in full harmony with the entire book.

In the introduction to Colossians, Paul provides a picture of the subordinate position of Jesus Christ to God when he says:

"We thank God the Father of our Lord Jesus Christ always when we pray for you." — Colossians 1:3.

Jesus is not described as being God, but God is "the Father of our Lord Jesus Christ." In the Revelation to John, written some 63 years after Jesus' ascension to heaven, God is referred to as "his God and Father" when speaking of Jesus.

It is God who has "delivered us from the authority of the darkness and transferred us into the kingdom of the Son of his love." — v. 13.

The INSTRUMENTAL **EN** is used again by Paul in verse 22 when he says that God "has again reconciled *by means of* [**EN**, instrumental] that one's [Christ's] fleshly body through his death."

In verse 27, it was God's own pleasure to make known the "sacred secret among the nations." This was, of course, Christ. — Compare Ephesians 3:8-11.

Colossians 2:12 explains that it was God who raised Jesus up from the dead. This agrees with the following texts: Psalm 16:10; Isaiah 38:17; Acts 2:24, 31, 32; 3:15; 10:40; 13:33, 37; 17:31; Romans 1:4 (notice here that the word **DU'NAMIS** — "power" — occurs, as opposed to the use of **EX.OU.SI'A** — "authority" — at John 10:18); 4:24; 6:4; 8:11; 1 Corinthians 6:14; 2 Corinthians 4:14; Ephesians 1:20; Hebrews 13:20; 1 Peter 1:21.

Finally, Paul counsels the Colossian Christians to "do everything in the name of the Lord Jesus, thanking God the Father *through him.*" Thus, Jesus, as the Firstborn of all creation, is seen to be the first of God's creation, and remains eternally subordinate to the Father. — Colossians 3:17.

# 17 Immanuel — "With Us Is God"

A scripture commonly used in support of the Trinity is found at Matthew 1:23 which refers to the name Immanuel; taken from Hebrew, this has the meaning, "with us is God," in connection with Christ Jesus.

As the apostle Matthew explained, the birth of Jesus fulfilled the prophecy of Isaiah:

> "Behold, a virgin shall conceive, and bear a son, and shall call his name Immanuel." — Isaiah 7:14; *King James.*

Matthew's gospel reads:

> "Thou shalt call his name JESUS: for he shall save his people from their sins. Now all this was done, that it might be fulfilled which was spoken of the Lord by the prophet, saying: Behold, a virgin shall be with child, and shall bring forth a son, and they shall call his name Emmanuel, which being interpreted is, God with us." — Matthew 1:22, 23.

The inference drawn by Trinitarians is that, because the name Immanuel (or Emmanuel) is applied to Jesus, meaning "With us is God," then this proves that he *was* God. As if the text means, "With us is God himself."

However, there are two major reasons why this does not fit in with the harmony of the Scriptures. One involves a comparison of the original meaning of the prophecy in Isaiah's day, and the other involves a comparison of the expression "God is with us" with other texts in the Scriptures.

## Appeal to Context — the 'Pattern of Sound Words'

As has often been stated, appeal to context is the foremost way of understanding a given scripture. Just as the proverbial jig-saw puzzle can be reassembled in a multitude of misshapen ways, so the text of the Bible can be "reassembled" into almost any fashion the writer or speaker chooses — but only by taking one of the pieces out and casting it in a different light, contrary to its position in the overall puzzle. The Bible is a closely knit "pattern" of interrelated words. — 2 Timothy 1:13 (*Revised Standard Version*).

## The Prophecy in Isaiah's Day

The context of Isaiah 7:14 provides the answer as to the meaning of the expression "God is with us." Verse 1 begins:

"When King Ahaz, the son of Jotham and grandson of Uzziah, ruled Judah, war broke out. Rezin, king of Syria, and Pekah son of Remaliah, king of Israel, attacked Jerusalem, but were unable to capture it." — *Good News Bible*.

This event took place somewhere between 762 and 759 BC. Syria and the northern kingdom of Israel combined to attack King Ahaz of Judah from the north, the Edomites from the south-east, and the Philistines from the west. The kings of Israel and Syria intended to place a man, the son of a so-called Tabeel, on the throne in his stead. — 2 Chronicles 28:5-15, 17-19; 2 Kings 16:5, 6; Isaiah 7:1-6.

However, God had made a covenant with King David, and He purposed to protect Judah from this attack. He said:

"But I, the Lord, declare that this will never happen." — Isaiah 7:7; *Good News Bible*.

Ahaz was even offered a sign from God, guaranteeing that He would help him. But Ahaz refused, saying that he would never put God to the test. (Isaiah 7:10, 11). Nevertheless, God was determined to give Ahaz a sign. Isaiah scolded Ahaz for 'wearing out the patience of God.' And then said: "Well, then the Lord himself *will* give you a sign: a young woman who is pregnant will have a son and will name him 'Immanuel'."

So Immanuel was born, not in the 1st century AD, but in the 8th century BC. He was, in fact, one of Isaiah's sons. As Isaiah later put it:

> "Here I am with the children the Lord has given me. The Lord Almighty, whose throne is on Mount Zion, has sent us as living messages to the people of Israel." — Isaiah 8:18; *Good News Bible.*

Or, as the *New English Bible* puts it:

> "I and the sons whom the Lord has given me are to be signs and portents in Israel."

Isaiah, along with his sons, were *themselves* "signs and portents" in Israel! Their very presence ought to have been an encouragement to the Israelites, as Isaiah's sons were born as *proof* of God's protection and blessing.

This begs the question: Was Immanuel, Isaiah's son, God himself? Did Almighty God enter the womb of this maiden and bring himself to birth as a baby boy? Surely not! The birth of Immanuel was a *sign*, proof that God was with Ahaz, and that the threats against him from Israel and Syria were baseless. It was said regarding Immanuel that "by the time he is old enough to make his own decisions, people will be drinking milk and eating honey." (Isaiah 7:15) The promise of milk and honey would no doubt remind the people of Judah of God's promises to his people through Moses. The land they were to inherit was a good land, "a land flowing with milk and honey." (Numbers 13:27) So the boy, Immanuel, would provide a reminder to God's people that the threat of military defeat was not real, and that it would be swept away "by the time he is old enough to make his own decisions."

The *Living Bible* puts it this way:

"By the time this child is weaned and knows right from wrong, the two kings you fear so much—the kings of Israel and Syria—will both be dead." — Isaiah 7:15.

The birth of Isaiah's second son, Mahershalalhashbaz, provided additional proof that God's protection was there. (Isaiah 8:1-4) This time, before the boy could even call the names of his parents, the mighty Assyrian power would defeat Judah's enemies, taking away spoils from Syria and Israel.

This attack by Assyria is poetically described in Isaiah 8:9, 10 in the following words:

"Do your worst, O Syria and Israel, our enemies, but you will not succeed—you will be shattered. Listen to me, all you enemies of ours: Prepare for war against us—and perish! Yes! Perish! Call your councils of war, develop your strategies, prepare your plans of attacking us, and perish! For God is with us." — *Living Bible.*

The land of Judah is to be protected. The armies of Syria and Israel would not enter into it. Verse 8 of Isaiah chapter 8 refers to this land as belonging to Immanuel!

"The stretching out of his wings shall fill the breadth of thy land, O Immanuel." — *King James.*

The people of Judah ought to have had complete confidence in salvation by their God, for, as Isaiah 8:9, 10 put it, their enemies would surely perish, for "God is with us."

Consequently, Immanuel's birth in Isaiah's day did not mean that God had been physically born onto the earth. It clearly meant that, by means of the birth of

Isaiah's son, Immanuel, God was "with" his people, he had turned his attention to them and was acting for them. Likewise, the birth of Jesus proved that God had turned his attention once again to his people, that he was "with them."

## In What Sense is God "With" His People?

This expression "God is with us," or its equivalent meaning thereof, occurs in similar forms throughout the Scriptures. In each case it refers to the same thing. Not a *physical* manifestation of God himself, but a turning of His attention toward his people. An assurance that he is on their side, supporting them, providing them comfort.

When the angels visited Abraham and Sarah, speaking with the authority of God they foretold the birth of their son, Isaac, saying:

> "At the time appointed I will return unto thee, according to the time of life, and Sarah shall have a son." — Genesis 18:14; *King James.*

A year later, Sarah did indeed have a son. But did the angel actually return? The *New English Bible* says:

> "The Lord showed favour to Sarah as he had promised, and made good what he had said about her." — Genesis 21:1.

The *Revised Standard Version* has here:

> "The LORD visited Sarah as he had said, and the LORD did to Sarah as he had promised."

For God to have "visited" Sarah, does not necessitate his coming down from the heavens and being bodily present. He turned his *attention* toward her, he "showed favour to Sarah," by fulfilling his promise and giving her a son.

When the Israelites set out to drive the Canaanites from the Promised Land, the record states:

"And the house of Joseph, they also went up against Bethel: and the Lord was with them." — Judges 1:22; *King James.*

Did God go with them *physically* into battle? Or, rather, did he not help them to achieve victory? The *Good News Bible* simply says: "The Lord helped them," at this place.

Jeremiah felt assured of God's help when he said:

"But the Lord is with me as a mighty terrible one: therefore my persecutors shall stumble." — Jeremiah 20:11; *King James.*

The *Living Bible* has here:

"But the Lord stands beside me like a great warrior, and before him, the Mighty, Terrible One, they shall stumble."

This would clearly not require God to stand physically alongside Jeremiah. The prophet felt assured of God's care and protection when facing his enemies.

The Psalms extol God's virtues in poetic form:

"The Lord of hosts is with us; the God of Jacob is our refuge." — Psalm 46:7.

This is repeated in verse 11. The "Lord of hosts" is paralleled by the "God of Jacob," and His being "with" his people, is paralleled by his being a "refuge." God is not *physically* with them. He is on their side. He supports, comforts, and protects them.

## God Visited Them in Giving Them Bread

Another example of this is in the book of Ruth:

"She [Naomi] had heard in the country of Moab how that the Lord had visited his people in giving them bread." — Ruth 1:6; *King James.*

But had God actually come down from the heavens and "visited" his people? No. It says that he visited them "in giving them bread." The *New English Bible* says:

"The Lord had cared for his people and given them food."

Jesus' concluding words to his disciples in Matthew 28:20, "I am with you always, even unto the end of the world," demonstrate the above points. Did Jesus continue with them physically? Clearly not, as the comparative text in Acts 1:9 shows, not long after saying these words he ascended to heaven and was separated, physically, from them. But he was not separated spiritually. He was *with them* in that his attention was constantly turned towards them, and he continued to assist them from his lofty position in the heavens.

## Summary

There is, though, a third reason that proves Matthew 1:23 does not support the teaching of the Trinity. And that is the aforementioned "harmony of the Scriptures." For this scripture to support any doctrine, then that doctrine would need to be supported elsewhere in the Bible. As has been consistently demonstrated, each of the scriptures proffered by Trinitarians is unable to support the doctrine of "three persons in one God," when examined in the light of biblical context. There are, on the contrary, an abundance of Bible texts that refer to the subordinate position of Christ, showing that Jesus was subject to his Father *before* his coming to earth, *upon* coming to earth, and *after* returning to heaven; the fact of Jesus' having been *created* by God; the Holy Spirit's operation as an invisible active force rather than a person; the "one God" consisting only of "the Father," *not* Father, Son, and Holy Spirit; and so on.

Additionally, the wise young man, Elihu, who counselled Job during his tribulation, was clearly not God himself. Yet his name means "God is he." Immanuel's name meaning "With us is God," does not make Immanuel God himself. Interestingly, why does Matthew make a point of giving us the *meaning* of the name Immanuel? Because the emphasis is on the *role* Jesus is playing as the Deliverer promised by God. Never is he referred to by that name anywhere else in the gospels.

So Jesus' being called "Immanuel," prophetically, proves that God's attention was once again turned toward his people Israel. It does not prove that Jesus was God. The birth of Jesus was a *sign* of God's protection and care, just as the original birth of Immanuel, Isaiah's son, proved that God was "with" his people (caring for them, protecting them) in Isaiah's day.

# 18  Jesus Christ —
## In Existence before Abraham

"'I am telling you the truth,' Jesus replied. 'Before Abraham was born, "I Am!"'"

This is how the *Good News Bible* reads at John 8:58. Many other versions use a similar rendering.

The above statement will no doubt appear very odd to those unacquainted with the doctrine of the Trinity. The "I Am" seems out of place, out of context, as if part of the sentence is missing.

Actually the "I Am" is quite deliberate. It is a literal rendering of the Greek **E.GO' EI.MI'** which does occur in Greek manuscripts (from which translations of the New Testament are made) at John 8:58. Trinitarians claim a connection between this expression and that recorded at Exodus 3:14. This reads (from the *Good News Bible*): "God said, 'I am who I am. This is what you must say to them: "The one who is called I AM has sent me to you."'" They thus establish, by their choice of rendering, a connection between God's personal revelation of himself to Israel and the statement by Jesus Christ.

| A COMPARISON OF THE TWO VERSES ||
|---|---|
| **Statement by God** | **Statement by Jesus** |
| Exodus 3:14 | John 8:58 |
| "I AM that I AM" | "Before Abraham was born, I AM" |

However, this "connection" only appears in Bible *translations*. The translators render both Exodus 3:14 and John 8:58 with the same expression. But can this connection be sustained through an analysis of the original Bible languages, and a comparison of the expressions chosen by the inspired writers, as well as a close examination of the context? Jesus certainly didn't speak English, so we need to compare the original languages to see if there is a connection. Only the original Bible writers were inspired by God's Holy Spirit. No modern-day Bible translator can claim to be inspired.

In the Hebrew Masoretic Text (from which translations of the Old Testament are made), the expression at Exodus 3:14 is **EH.YEH' A.SHER' EH.YEH'**. However, Hebrew versions of the New Testament do not choose to render Jesus' words (at John 8:58) using this Hebrew expression. Instead they choose **A.NI' HU'**, "I am he," and **A.NI' HA.YI'THI**, "I have been." Had Jesus been making some kind of reference to Exodus 3:14, he would surely have used the same expression!

The Greek Septuagint (a Greek translation of the Old Testament made in the second century before Christ) renders Exodus 3:14 **E.GO' EI.MI' HO ON'** meaning, "I am The Being." However, the Greek text of the New Testament merely has **E.GO' EI.MI'** at John 8:58. In fact, the Greek versions by Theodotion and Aquila both choose to render Exodus 3:14 as: **E'SO.MAI HOS E'SO.MAI**, meaning, "I will be who I will be." **E'SO.MAI** is the future tense form of the present tense **EI.MI'** ("I am").

Therefore, one is compelled to ask: *Where is the Trinitarian support for the idea that there is a "connection" between Exodus 3:14 and John 8:58?*

It can be readily seen, then, that the only connection between Exodus 3:14 and John 8:58 is found in a translation, the Greek Septuagint. However, even this connection is impossible to sustain. According to Bagster's Septuagint, **E.GO' EI.MI' HO ON'** means "I am THE BEING." If the expression **E.GO' EIMI'** was of significance, why does the subsequent statement read: "THE BEING [**HO ON'**] has sent me to you," and not "The I AM [**E.GO' EI.MI'**] has sent me to you"? (Exodus 3:14) Clearly, even the Septuagint translators considered **HO ON'**, "THE BEING," to be the significant part of the statement. The **E.GO' EI.MI'** is merely a vehicle to convey this idea in the form of a sentence. Yet some erroneously translate this as "The I AM."

However, even *if* the Septuagint reading had been, "The I AM has sent me to you," there are still considerable difficulties using the Septuagint as a basis for Christian doctrine, as the following demonstrates.

## The Septuagint and Greek Philosophy

To what extent can we rely on the Septuagint translators' interpretation of God's declaration? Ernst Wurthwein, in his book *The Text of the Old Testament* (pages 63-66), says on this:

> "Today we recognize that [the Septuagint] neither was nor was intended to be a precise scholarly translation... Often the Hebrew text demanded more lexical and grammatical knowledge of the early translators than they possessed. They were apparently unaware of the precise meaning of such a common word as **DE'BHER** ("pestilence"), for they rendered it either in the general meaning of **THA'NATOS** ["death"], or read it as **DA.BHAR'** ["word" or "thing"] (Hos. 13:14 **DI'KE** ["punishment"]; Hab. 3:5; Ps. 90:3 [91:3 in our Bibles] **LO'GOS** ["a word" "a saying"]; Ps. 90:6 **PRAG'MA** ["a deed" "a thing"]). Ziegler's verdict on the translator of Isaiah is that 'he was not scrupulously concerned to translate his original precisely, word for word. He does not hesitate to omit difficult or rare words if it does not disturb the meaning of a sentence, or to reconstrue the parts of a sentence if he has difficulty understanding the original. Sometimes he seems dominated by a particular idea which he permits to influence his translation of a passage. Thus in Isaiah

we find a great number of examples of what we must strictly call 'free' translations.

"The differences between the Jews of the Greek diaspora and the people who wrote the Hebrew Old Testament were not restricted to matters of their language alone. They lived in a world of different social conditions, with different ways of thinking, and not least with differences of [religious] belief. Their environment affected them, 'hellenized' them. They spoke more abstractly and philosophically about God than the 'Hebrews,' and they avoided the anthropomorphic [the ascribing of human characteristics to God] and anthropopathic [the ascribing of human emotions to God] expressions which are so characteristic of the Hebrew Old Testament: Exod. 19:3, Moses does not ascend to God, but to the mountain of God; Exod. 24:10, the elders do not see God, but the place where God stands; Josh. 4:24, [the Hebrew expression **YADH YAH'WEH** [*hand of God*]] is translated [by the Greek **DU'NAMIS TOU KU.RI'OU**, "power of the Lord"]. The statement that 'God repented' is avoided by circumlocution.

"Of particular significance is the expansion of the concept of God implied by the consistent translation of the divine name [in Hebrew: **YAH'WEH**] by [Greek: **KU'RI.OS**]: 'The Bible whose God is Yahweh is a national Bible; the Bible whose God is **KU'RI.OS** is a universal Bible' [a quotation from A. Deissman].

"In other instances the translators eliminated possible theological misunderstandings by avoiding literal translations. For example, they did not adopt the common Old Testament image of God as 'the Rock' ([Hebrew **TSOHR**]), but substituted other expressions ... The efforts of translators to make the Old Testament intelligible to their compatriots in Egypt led them to use terms native to their Egyptian and Alexandrian environment which were not the exact equivalents of Hebrew expressions."

It is important to understand the purpose and background of the Greek Septuagint if we wish to determine how its rendering of Exodus 3:14 has influenced the rendering "I am" in many modern Bible versions. Note from the above quotation how the Greek translators spoke "more abstractly and philosophically about God" than the Hebrews. If we also take into consideration that the Septuagint translator of Isaiah "was not scrupulously concerned to translate his original precisely word for word," then how can a Christian use the Septuagint to support a doctrine which the Hebrew Masoretic text does not support? Moreover, it is clear that **E.GO' EI.MI' HO ON'** ("I am THE BEING," or "I am The Existing One") is really only a paraphrase of the Hebrew **EH.YEH' A.SHER' EH.YEH'** and points merely to God's self-existence whilst failing to convey the true force of the Hebrew expression. It is an example of the Septuagint translators using words which were "not the exact equivalents of Hebrew expressions." It echoes the philosophical ideas concerning God, but is sadly unfaithful to the original inspired Hebrew text. Thus, the Septuagint "neither was nor was intended to be a precise scholarly translation."

The apostle Paul contrasted the mystical philosophies of the Greeks with the pure truth of God's Word when he said:

> "For Jews demand signs and Greeks seek wisdom, but we preach Christ crucified, a stumbling block to Jews and folly to Gentiles." — 1 Corinthians 1:22, 23; *Revised Standard Version.*

The Greeks inhabiting the city of Colossae were known for their indulgence in speculation and in philosophical arguments. To the Christians in Colossae Paul wrote:

> "See to it, then, that no one enslaves you by means of the worthless deceit of human wisdom, which comes from the teachings handed down by men and from the ruling spirits of the universe, and not from Christ." — Colossians 2:8; *Good News Bible.*

The Greek Septuagint's rendering of Exodus 3:14 is based on "human wisdom" and is no reliable basis for an interpretation of Scripture.

## EH.YEH' — "I Will Be"

What is the true sense conveyed by the Hebrew **EH.YEH'**, three times repeated in Exodus 3:14?

**EH.YEH'** is a verb in the imperfect state. This means that the verb signifies incomplete, or continuous, developing, progressive action. Though it is not strictly correct to speak of the Hebrew language as having tenses (Hebrew has two verb "states" perfect and imperfect) nevertheless the Hebrew verb can convey the full range of our English tenses. Regarding the imperfect, Gesenius' *Hebrew Grammar* (second English edition, page 125) says:

> "The Imperf. denotes, on the other hand, the beginning, the unfinished, and the continuing, that which is just happening, which is conceived as in process of coming to pass, and hence, also that which is yet future; likewise also that which occurs repeatedly or in a continuous sequence in the past (Latin imperf.)."

The context is the best guide in determining the precise rendering of a given verb in the imperfect. The use of the same word in other scriptures is also of help. Additionally, a translator must consider carefully the lexicology of the word — its history, etymology, and primary meaning.

The word **EH.YEH'** comes from the root **HA.YAH'** (from which the divine name, **YAH'WEH**, is also drawn), which does not simply mean "to exist" as the rendering "I am" (=**EH.YEH'**) would suggest. **HA.YAH'** means: *to come into existence, to come to pass, to become, to happen, occur, take on* (an attribute), *enter upon* (a state), *constitute*.

Thus, when God used the imperfect of **HA.YAH'** in addressing Moses, namely **EH.YEH'**, he was referring to something abundantly more profound than the mere fact of his existence! It is not logical to render this word in the present tense ("I am," that is, *I am at present existing*) and then to attach to it philosophical meanings which the Hebrew cannot convey. Note what Professor Benjamin Davidson, the "one whom the best judges have pronounced to be a leader in Old Testament learning" (Bookman), says in his *Theology of the Old Testament* (pages 46, 55, 56) regarding Exodus 3:14:

"In the Pentateuch the [divine name] is brought into connection with the verb to be. This, however, is not an account of the actual origin of the name, but only a play at most referring to its significance, or perhaps more probably connecting a significance with it. But the significance thus connected with it is of extreme importance, because it expresses, if not the original meaning of the name, which probably had been lost, the meaning which it suggested to the mind of Israel during their historic period.

"And this, not its primary sense, is, of course, what is important for us. As connected with the verb to be, it is the third singular imperfect. When spoken by Jehovah Himself this is the first person [**EH.YEH'**], or in a longer form, which merely makes more absolute the simple form, [**EH.YEH' A.SHER' EH.YEH'**]. The verb to be in Hebrew hardly expresses the idea of absolute or self-existence; it rather expresses what is or will be historically, and the imperfect tense must mean not I am, but I will be. In Ex. iii. 11-14 the revelation of the name [**YAH'WEH**] is described — 'And Moses said unto God, Who am I, that I should go unto Pharaoh?' And God said, 'I will be with thee, [**KI EH.YEH' 'IM.MAKH'**] ... And Moses said unto God, Behold, when I come unto the children of Israel, and shall say unto them, The God of your fathers hath sent me unto you; and they shall say unto me, What is His name? what shall I say unto them? And God said unto Moses, [**EH.YEH' A.SHER' EH.YEH'**]: and he said, 'Thus shalt thou say unto the children of Israel, Ehyeh hath sent me unto you.' ...

"To the Israelites of history the covenant name Jahweh has a meaning which may be expressed by the first singular imperfect Qal of [**HA.YAH'**], to be. Now, two things must be premised about this verb. First, the imperfect of such a stative verb [a verb which refers to a state as opposed to an action] as [**HA.YAH'**] must be taken in the sense of a future. I do not think there is in the Hebrew Bible a case of the imperfect of this verb having the sense of the English present. This is expressed by the perfect. The word means to fall, fall out, become; hence its perfect is equivalent to *to be*. The imperfect must be rendered, *I will be*. Second, [**HA.YAH'**] does not mean to be essentially, but to be phenomenally; it is not [Greek, **EI'NAI**], but [**GIN'ES.THAI**]. It cannot be used ordinarily to express 'being' in the sense of existence. Now these two facts regarding [**HA.YAH'**] exclude a large number of conjectures as to the meaning of Jahweh. In the first place, the translation I am is doubly false: the tense is wrong, being present; and the idea is wrong, because am is used in the sense of essential existence. All those interpretations which proceed upon the supposition that the word is a name of God as the self-existent, the absolute, of which the Septuagint's [**HO ON'**] is the most conspicuous illustration, must be set aside. Apart from the fact that such abstract conceptions are quite out of keeping with the simplicity and concreteness of Oriental thought, especially in the most early times, the nature of the verb and the tense peremptorily forbid them.

Second, the translation I will be, or I will be what I will be, while right as to tense, must be guarded also against having a metaphysical sense imported into the words will be. Some have supposed that the expression denoted the eternity of God, or the self-consistence of God, or His absolute freedom and His inviolability from all sides of the creature universe; but these constructions also put a sense upon

[**HA.YAH'**] which it cannot bear. The expression I will be is a historical formula; it refers, not to what God will be in Himself; it is no predication regarding His nature, but one regarding what He will approve Himself to others, regarding what He will show Himself to be to those in covenant with Him. The name is not a name like Elohim, which expresses God on the side of His being, as essential, manifold power; it is a word that expresses rather relation — Elohim in relation to Israel is Jahweh. In this respect the word has almost the same signification as the term [**QA.DHOSH'**] holy; the [**QE'OSH'**] and Jahweh are one. It is in this sense that Hosea says to Israel: [**LO' A.SHER' LA.KHEM'**] I will not be to you; but I 'will save them by the Lord their God' ([**BAH.OWAH'**]) — i.e. as Jahweh their God (i. 7, 9).

"In Exodus the formula appears in two shapes — the simple [**EH.YEH'**], I will be, and the larger [**EH.YEH A.SHER' EH.YEH'**] I will be that I will be. But it is evident that the lesser formula is a full expression of the name — 'say unto the children of Israel that [**EH.YEH'**] hath sent me unto you.' The name is, I will be. Thus it is equivalent almost to [Greek, **HO ER.CHO'MENOS**] — he who is to come; it premises God, a God known; it promises His fuller manifestation, His ever closer nearness, His clearer revelation of His glory. And the burden of all the Old Testament prophets is: The Lord shall come: — 'Say unto the cities of Judah, Behold your God! Behold, the Lord God will come with strong hand;' 'the glory of the Lord God shall be revealed, and all flesh shall see it together' (Isa. xl. 9, 5). I will be, or, I will be it; but what He will be has to be filled up by a consciousness of God already existing, and always receiving from every new manifestation of Him new contents."

Let us summarise Professor Davidson's discussion:

(a) the root verb **HA.YAH'** ("to be") does not express the idea of self-existence.

(b) **EH.YEH'** (as used at Exodus 3:14 and other places) does not mean "I am," but "I will be."

(c) **HA.YAH'** does not mean to be *essentially* (Greek, **EI'NAI**), but to be *phenomenally* (Greek, **GIN'ES.THAI**).

(d) The translation "I am" (of **EH.YEH'**) is doubly false — the tense is wrong and the interpretation is wrong.

\*          \*          \*          \*

Those who argue in favour of the rendering "I am" are only able to appeal to Greek philosophy, the abstract conceptions of which "are quite out of keeping with the simplicity and concreteness of Oriental thought" (Professor Davidson). It is a fallacious appeal. Not only is the rendering devoid of Scriptural support, it is at variance with the true meaning of **EH.YEH'**, and with the context (compare verse 12).

There is a further consideration regarding this "appeal to Greek philosophy": The Greek Septuagint itself provides the correct rendering of **EH.YEH'** in almost every occurrence except Exodus 3:14! The most popular rendering of the Hebrew **EH.YEH'** by Greek translators is **E'SO.MAI**: I will be. It will be remembered that the Greek versions of Theodotion and Aquila chose this word in rendering Exodus 3:14:

| Hebrew: | | |
|---|---|---|
| **EH.YEH'** | **A.SHER'** | **EH.YEH'** |
| Greek: | | |
| **E'SO.MAI** | **HOS** | **E'SO.MAI** |
| I will be | who | I will be |

Note the following list which compares most of the occurrences of **EH.YEH'** with the Septuagint and the *Revised Standard Version*. (In the table below, the Septuagint does not always have an equivalent translation, this is due to the aforementioned paraphrasing so prevalent in the Septuagint).

## Table Showing Occurrences of Hebrew EH.YEH'

| | Hebrew Masoretic Text | Greek Septuagint Translation | Revised Standard Version |
|---|---|---|---|
| Genesis 26:3 | EH.YEH' | E'SO.MAI | I will be |
| Genesis 31:3 | EH.YEH' | E'SO.MAI | I will be |
| Exodus 3:12 | EH.YEH' | E'SO.MAI | I will be |
| Exodus 3:14 | EH.YEH' | HO ON | I AM |
| Exodus 4:12 | EH.YEH' | (I will open) | I will be |
| Exodus 4:15 | EH.YEH' | (I will open) | I will be |
| Deuteronomy 31:23 | EH.YEH' | (he will be) | I will be |
| Joshua 1:5 | EH.YEH' | E'SO.MAI | I will be |
| Joshua 3:7 | EH.YEH' | E'SO.MAI | I will be |
| Judges 6:16 | EH.YEH' | (he will be) | I will be |
| Judges 11:9 | EH.YEH' | E'SO.MAI | I will be |
| 2 Samuel 7:14 | EH.YEH' | E'SO.MAI | I will be |
| 2 Samuel 15:34 | EH.YEH' | E.GO (I) | I will be |
| 2 Samuel 16:18 | EH.YEH' | E'SO.MAI | I will be |
| 2 Samuel 16:19 | EH.YEH' | E'SO.MAI | I will (serve) |
| 1 Chronicles 17:13 | EH.YEH' | E'SO.MAI | I will be |
| 1 Chronicles 28:6 | EH.YEH' | E'SO.MAI | I will be |
| Isaiah 3:7 | EH.YEH' | E'SO.MAI | I will be (not) |
| Jeremiah 11:4 | EH.YEH' | E'SO.MAI | I will be |
| Jeremiah 24:7 | EH.YEH' | E'SO.MAI | I will be |
| Jeremiah 30:22 | EH.YEH' | E'SO.MAI | I will be |
| Jeremiah 31:1 | EH.YEH' | E'SO.MAI | I will be |
| Jeremiah 32:38 | EH.YEH' | E'SO.MAI | I will be |
| Ezekiel 11:20 | EH.YEH' | E'SO.MAI | I will be |
| Ezekiel 14:11 | EH.YEH' | E'SO.MAI | I may be |
| Ezekiel 34:24 | EH.YEH' | E'SO.MAI | I will be |
| Ezekiel 36:28 | EH.YEH' | E'SO.MAI | I will be |
| Ezekiel 37:23 | EH.YEH' | E'SO.MAI | I will be |
| Hosea 13:7 | EH.YEH' | E'SO.MAI | I will be |
| Zechariah 8:8 | EH.YEH' | E'SO.MAI | I will be |

**"I do not think there is in the Hebrew Bible a case of the imperfect of this verb having the sense of the English present."**
**— Professor Benjamin Davidson.**

We can glean several important points from this list. The most outstanding, of course, is the inconsistency of the Septuagint and many modern translations (the *Revised Standard Version* is merely representative of the "I am" versions) which find no difficulty giving **EH.YEH'** a future connotation *except at the disputed scripture.* It will be seen that in most of these passages God is the speaker. At Genesis 31:3, Deuteronomy 31:23, Joshua 1:5, 3:7 and Judges 6:16 the formula **EH.YEH' 'IM.MAKH'**, *I will be with you,* occurs. This serves to underscore the correct rendering ("I will be") of **EH.YEH'** at Exodus 3:14.

The example at Exodus 3:12 is particularly notable, for if the context of verse 14 points to a present tense (*I am*) rendering of **EH.YEH'**, why translate the same word in the future tense (*I will be*) in verse 12? Are the translators trying to force a connection with John 8:58?

Incidentally, the Greek word **E'SO.MAI** ("I will be") occurs 13 times in the New Testament at the following places: <u>Matthew 17:17</u>; <u>Mark 9:19</u>; <u>Luke 9:41</u>; <u>John 8:55</u>; <u>1 Corinthians 14:11</u>; 2 Corinthians 6:16, 18; 12:6; <u>Hebrews 1:5</u>; 2:13; 8:10, 12; <u>Revelation 21:7</u>. The underlined scriptures represent occasions where the Hebrew **EH.YEH'** translates the Greek **E'SO.MAI** in Hebrew versions of the New Testament.

The verb **HA.WAH'**, related to **HA.YAH'**, is the root from which the divine name is drawn. Concerning this the Lexicon of *Brown, Driver, and Briggs* (based on Gesenius' Lexicon) says concerning Exodus 3:14, under the main heading **HA.WAH'** and subheading **YAH'WEH** (pages 217, 218):

> "Many recent scholars explain **YAH'WEH** as Hiph. [i.e. the causative form] of **HA.WAH'** (=**HA.YAH'**) the one bringing into being, life-giver (cf. **CHA.WAH'** Gn 3:20) Schr HSch; giver of existence, creator, Kue Tiele; he who brings to pass (so already Le Clerc), performer of his promise ... Ex. 3:12-15 ... **EH.YEH'**

**'IM.MAKH'** I shall be with thee (v.12), which is then implied in **EH.YEH' A.SHER' EH.YEH'** I shall be the one who will be it, v.14a (i.e. with thee v.12) and then compressed into **EH.YEH'** v.14b (i.e. with thee v.12), which then is given the nominal form **YHWH** He who will be it, v.15 (i.e. with thee v.12)."

Notice the repeated references to verse 12. Appeal to context is the most powerful argument in favour of a given interpretation of a scripture. Compare the Revised Standard Version's use of the future tense in the verses cited in the above list:

"He [God] said, 'But I *will be* with you.'" — Exodus 3:12.

"Now therefore go, and I *will be* with your mouth and teach you what you *shall* speak." — Exodus 4:12.

"And you *shall* speak to him and put the words in his mouth; and I *will be* with your mouth and with his mouth, and *will* teach you what you *shall* do." — Exodus 4:15.

**EH.YEH'** is, then, properly rendered "I will be" at Exodus 3:14.

## The Meaning of The Name at Exodus 3:14

*The Living World of the Old Testament* (published in America under the name *Understanding the Old Testament*) by Bernhard W. Anderson, Professor of Old Testament Theology at Princeton Theological Seminary, presents three views concerning this passage. The first takes the divine name as being the causative form (Hiphil — see the quotation from *Brown, Driver, and Briggs*, above) of the verb "to be," giving rise to the rendering: "I cause to be what I cause to be," or, "I create what I create." Concerning the second view, namely, translating **EH.YEH'** as "I am," he says (on pages 54, 55):

"To this interpretation the objection may be raised that it introduces a philosophical notion of God's eternal being that seems alien to the Israelite mentality. The ancient Greeks, who struggled philosophically with the problem of the changing and the Changeless, would have favored the view that God, in his eternal being, is not affected by the flux and flow of time. But in Israel, on the other hand, there was concern about God's historical activity and the disclosure of his will — not about God's being in himself."

This view finds Scriptural support in Exodus 3:6-10 where God declares that he has favourably heard Israel's outcry. God's words begin (verse 7): **RA.O' RA.I'THI**, literally "seeing I have seen," a use of the infinitive absolute for the purpose of intensifying the sense: hence, "Unquestionably I have seen ..." This is God's reply to the outcries of his people. Since the latter days of Joseph (more than a hundred and fifty years earlier), the people of Israel knew that deliverance from Egypt was inevitable. (Genesis 50:25) This was God's answer in the form of an assurance that (a) he was the same One who had appeared to Abraham, Isaac, and Jacob, (b) that he had seen their affliction, and heard their outcry, and (c) that he was going to deliver them. The future deliverance is the issue. Clearly, the Greek philosophy ("I am") is totally out of place here.

Hence, Professor Anderson presents his third view:

"A third view, one that is favored by probability, is also based on the present reading of the text, though the simple form of the verb is translated in the future tense ('I will be'). According to this interpretation, the declaration in verse 14 must be understood in the immediate context, where the God of the fathers promises to be with and to go with Moses: 'I will be with you' (3:12); 'I will be with your mouth' (4:12, 15), or 'I will be your God' (6:7). Thus the name of God signifies God whose being is turned toward his people, who is present in their midst as deliverer, guide, and judge, and who is accessible in worship. And yet in putting himself at the disposal of his people, so to speak, Yahweh retains his freedom to be present as he will be present, and to show mercy upon whom he will show mercy (Ex. 33:19)."

Likewise, the *Analytical Concordance to the Bible*, by Robert Young, LL.D. (7th edition, page 506), says of this expression:

"A name indicating rather the unsearchableness of God than his mere existence, as commonly supposed."

The *Twenty-Four Books of the Holy Scriptures* by Rabbi Isaac Leeser renders Exodus 3:14 thus: "I WILL BE THAT I WILL BE." *Rotherham's* translation says: "I will become whatsoever I please." *Byington's* has: "I will be what I will be." The footnotes to the *New English Bible* and the *Good News Bible* say: "I will be who I will be." The footnotes to the *Revised Standard Version* and the *New International Version* read: "I will be what I will be," as does the main text of *Moffatt's* translation. The *American Standard Version* offers "I WILL BE THAT I WILL BE," as one alternative to its main text. The footnote to *Rotherham's* translation says:

"**HA.YAH'** does not mean 'to be' essentially or ontologically, but phenomenally... What he will be is left unexpressed — He will be with them, helper, strengthener, deliverer."

Compare this comment with the words of Professor Davidson quoted earlier.

Additionally, *The Pentateuch and Haftorahs*, edited by Dr. J. H. Hertz, C. H., says (on page 215):

"I AM THAT I AM. Heb. Ehyeh ASHER ehyeh ... I am that I am is, however, not merely a philosophical phrase; the emphasis is on the active manifestation of the Divine existence; ... To the Israelites in bondage, the meaning would be, 'Although He has not yet displayed His power towards you, He will do so; He is eternal and will certainly redeem you.'

"Most moderns follow Rashi in rendering 'I will be what I will be'; i.e. no words can sum up all that He will be to His people, but His everlasting faithfulness and unchanging mercy will more and more manifest themselves in the guidance of Israel. The answer which Moses receives in these words is thus equivalent to, 'I shall save in the way that I shall save.' It is to assure the Israelites of the fact of deliverance, but does not disclose the manner. It must suffice the Israelites to learn that, 'Ehyeh, I WILL BE (with you), hath sent me unto you.'"

Interestingly, though Trinitarians appeal to the Greek Septuagint, their choice of words (at Exodus 3:14) takes their translations even further away from the original inspired writings than the Septuagint's rendering does. For the **E.GO' EI.MI'** ("I am") is not repeated in the Septuagint. It does not say: **E.GO' EI.MI' HOS E.GO' EI.MI'**, i.e. "I am who I am." It says: **E.GO' EI.MI' HO ON'**, "I am The Existing One." Only in the Hebrew Masoretic Text does repetition occur, namely: **EH.YEH' A.SHER' EH.YEH'**. This serves to emphasise that there is no connection with Jesus' statement. In addition, there is no known Hebrew version which inserts **EH.YEH'** at John 8:58.

Note what the *Journal of Biblical Literature* says regarding Exodus 3:14 (Vol. 23, 1904, page 126):

"The Hebrew equivalent of I exist, if the occasion for such a declaration could be conceived of by the Hebrew mind, would be not **EH.YEH'** but **HA.YI'THI** (Perfect [tense]), I have come into existence and so am here. On the other hand, I am (something) as distinguished from I exist, would not make use of the verb **HA.YAH'** at all. *I am* can only be expressed by means of a nominal sentence [a sentence made up of names or words without a verb]. The Hebrew for I am (so and so) is **A.NI'** followed by the predicate noun (or adverb) [not by a verb]. Thus the Hebrew for *I am that I am* is not **EH.YEH' A.SHER' EH.YEH'**, nor does it differ from that clause only in the matter of the tense of the verb. A nominal instead of a verbal sentence is required ...

"**EH.YEH'** in this sentence can only mean I will be or become (something); for of course I will be or become (somebody) is not a sensible alternative. Not merely the most natural, then, but the necessary construction of **EH.YEH' A.SHER' EH.YEH'** is I will be what I will be. So much for the literal meaning of the Hebrew clause."

Before leaving the Hebrew expression at Exodus, observe what Professor Davidson says in his book *The Theology of the Old Testament,* on pages 69-71 under the subheading "The Historical Occasion of the Application of the Name Jehovah":

"The reply of the Lord to [Moses] is significant, and the phraseology of it of great importance: 'Surely I will be with thee' **KI EH.YEH' 'IM.MAKH'** — **EH.YEH'** — I will be. And in token of this great promise of His presence with him the Lord proposes to Moses a sign. Now, as I have said, it is of consequence to notice the phraseology used, **EH.YEH'**, I will be, because it recurs immediately. Moses is still reluctant to undertake what seemed to him so hazardous an enterprise; he pictures to himself not only the dangers he might encounter from the Egyptians, but the incredulity with which he is likely to be met on the part of the Hebrews — 'Behold, when I come unto the children of Israel, and shall say unto them, The God of your fathers hath sent me unto you; and they shall say unto me, What is his name? what shall I say unto them?' And God said unto him **EH.YEH' A.SHER' EH.YEH'**; 'and he said thus shalt thou say unto the children of Israel, **EH.YEH'** hath sent me unto you.' And God added finally: 'Thus shalt thou say unto the children of Israel, Jahweh, the God of your fathers, the God of Abraham, the God of Isaac, and the God of Jacob, hath sent me unto you: this (i.e. Jahweh) is My name for ever, and this is My memorial unto all generations.' Then follows an amplified form of the promise to deliver the people, and work great signs and wonders in Egypt, and do great judgments upon that people.

"Now, here the name appears in three forms: **EH.YEH' A.SHER' EH.YEH'**, the simple **EH.YEH'**, and Jahweh. Jahweh is merely the third person, of which Ehyeh is the first; He who says Ehyeh when speaking of Himself is Jahweh when spoken about. But does it not seem manifest, as has already been indicated, that the name Ehyeh or Ehyeh ASHER Ehyeh cannot be translated differently from that former expression: 'Certainly I will be with thee,' **EH.YEH' 'IM.MAKH'**; that it is nothing else but that promise raised into a title, and that we must render I will be, and I will be that I will be, and, in the third person, He will be? It is evident that the whole meaning of the larger phrase, 'I will be that I will be,' **EH.YEH' A.SHER' EH.YEH'**, may be expressed by the shorter phrase I will be **EH.YEH'**, or, in the third person, **YAH'WEH**. The addition, 'that which I will be,' or as it might be rendered: 'I who I will be,' only adds emphasis to the preceding I will be. The expression resembles the other declaration: 'I will have mercy on whom I will have mercy,' the meaning of which would be clearer if put in this order: 'On whom I will have mercy I will have mercy.' That is to say, when He has mercy, then, indeed, He has mercy; and so, 'that which I will be, I will indeed be.' But the point of the phrase lies in the circumstances of misery and bondage on the part of the people in which it was spoken, in the very vagueness of the promise of interference and presence, and in the continuousness of that presence which is suggested. The name is a circumference the contents of which cannot be expressed. He who relies on the same has the assurance of One, the God of his fathers, who will be with him. What He shall be to him when with him the memory of what He has been to those that have gone before him may suggest; or his own needs and circumstances in every stage and peril of his life will tell him. Or his conception of God as reposing on the past and on his own experience, and looking into the future, may project that before his mind."

In summary, then, Exodus 3:14 contains a promise of God's future blessing upon Israel, and has no reference to God's self-existence.

Thus, the translation "I am" is in error.

## The Name at Hosea 1:9

Another occurrence of **EH.YEH'** in the Old Testament is at Hosea 1:9. From the *New International Version*, this reads: "Then the LORD said, 'Call him Lo-Ammi, for you are not my people, and I am not your God.'"

This is how an interlinear rendering of the last clause looks:

| **WE.ANO.KHI'** | **LO-EH.YEH'** | **LA.KHEM'** |
|---|---|---|
| and I | not will be | for you |

Some translators see an implication of the divine name in this verse due to the use of the verb **EH.YEH'**. Hence some render it "I am." (New International Version, *Good News Bible*, The Bible In Living English, Revised Standard Version, etc.) The Greek Septuagint chooses: **E.GO' OUK EI.MI'**, literally, "I not am." However, others have the future tense, "I will be" (*The American Standard Version, New English Bible, Douay, King James Version*). Professor Davidson in his book (quoted earlier) chose the future tense for this verb at Hosea 1:9. The context leads to this conclusion:

The prophet Hosea was commanded to take "an adulterous wife"; that is, after bearing a child to Hosea, she would thereafter be unfaithful to him, and would become an adulterous wife. His first child was named Jezreel, which means "God will sow seed." This was prophetic of God's future blessings upon Israel (compare Zechariah 10:8-10) as well as an accounting with the house of Jehu (2 Kings 15:8-10). These future blessings were revealed in Hosea's later words (2:23):

"And I will sow her unto me in the earth; and I will have mercy upon her that had not obtained mercy; and I will say to them that were not my people, Thou art my people; and they shall say, Thou art my God." (*American Standard Version*)

The two other children, born to Hosea's wife, were also prophetic: Lo-ruhamah means "She was not shown mercy," and Lo-ammi means "Not my people." Hence, all three children are alluded to in Hosea 2:23.

These children were prophetic of God's future dealings with, and attitude towards his people. They served as signs. It was similar with Isaiah the prophet, who said:

"I and the children God has given me have symbolic names that reveal the plans of the Lord of heaven's armies for his people." — Isaiah 8:18; *The Living Bible*.

Hosea's reference to future events serves to underline the rendering "I will be (not)" for **LO-EH.YEH'** at Hosea 1:9, as opposed to "I am (not)." Notice the above quotation, Hosea 2:23; God said "I will sow her", "I will have mercy", "I will say to them", "and they shall say." (Compare Romans 9:25, 26.) Hosea 1:6, 7 also contains references to future events. Observe this interlinear reading of part of these verses:

| **QE.RA'** | **SHE.MAH'** | | **LO-RU.CHA'MAH** |
| Call | her name | | Lo-ruhamah |
| **KI** | **LO** | **O.SIPH'** | **ODH** |
| for | not | more | continue |
| **ARA.CHEM'** | | **ETH-BETH'** | **YISRA.EL'** |
| I will show mercy | | [to the] house | [of] Israel |
| **KI-NA.SO'** | **ES.SA'** | | **LA.HEM'** |
| for to lead astray | I will lead astray | | to them |
| **WE.ETH-BETH'** | | **YEHU.DHAH'** | **ARA.CHEM'** |
| and [to the] house | | [of] Judah | I will show mercy |

| **WE.HO.SHA'TIM'** | **BAH.WAH'** | **ELO.HE.HEM'** |
|---|---|---|
| and I will save them | by Yahweh | their God |

This too contains future verbs: "*will* show mercy," "*will* lead astray," "*will* save them."

All of this, of course, is to be expected, since prophecies, by their own self-designation, relate to future events. But why should some choose to render **EH.YEH'**, at Hosea 1:9, in the present tense, namely "I am [not]"? Even the Revised Standard Version, though favouring "I will be" at the 26 places cited earlier, has "I am [not]" at this place. Clearly, it is because of the similarity to Exodus 3:14, or the 'allusion' to the divine name that many refer to. Having committed themselves to the paraphrastic Greek Septuagint and its "I am ..." at Exodus, they are compelled to follow it here also. There is, though, a further consideration with regard to the Greek Septuagint at Hosea 1:9. The Masoretic Text omits **ELO.HE.KHEM'**, "your God," giving: *and I will not be for you,* or *and I will not be yours.* However, some would render the Greek equivalent **KAI E.GO' OUK EI.MI' HU.MON'** (literally *and I not am yours*), into "not your AM" as if the **EI.MI'** was a title, and thus establishing a further "connection" with John 8:58. But this could also mean "and I am not yours." The Hebrew text omits "God" at the beginning of verse 9 when it says: and said ___ 'Call his name Lo-ammi.' The underscore after the word "said" indicates that an expression is implied in the text, but does not actually occur there. The implication is that "your God" is to be read at the end of the verse: "and I will not be your God." The *Revised Standard Version, King James Version, The Bible In Living English,* the *New International Version,* the *American Standard Version,* the *Living Bible,* the *Good News Bible,* and the *New English Bible* all place "your God" at the end of the verse. Others say "I will not be yours," or similar.

To consider **EI.MI'** ("am") a title here is an incredible suggestion. Clearly it is the title "God" which is significant, whether it is written (Origen) or implied. Moreover, as has been mentioned, the Masoretic Text is obviously more faithful than the Greek Septuagint and must be followed, generally, if the translator encounters a disagreement. Even if the divine name is alluded to at Hosea 1:9, still it fails to provide Trinitarians with a link with John 8:58.

## The One Who Is and Who Was and Who Is Coming

At Revelation 1:4, God is referred to as "The One who is and who was and who is coming," — Greek **HO ON' KAI HO EN' KAI HO ER.KHO'MENOS**. This is repeated at Revelation 1:8. At Revelation 4:8 it is placed in chronological order, and at 11:17 and 16:5 it is abbreviated to "the One who is and who was."

Only here can a successful claim be made of a "connection" with Exodus 3:14, "I will be who I will be." But to whom are all these expressions applied? To Jesus Christ? No! Note John's Revelation:

"Grace to you and peace from him who is and who was and who is to come, and from the seven spirits who are before his throne, and from Jesus Christ." — Revelation 1:4, 5; *Revised Standard Version.*

Revelation 1:8 is applied to "the Almighty," **HO PAN.TO.KRA'TOR**. Some Hebrew versions even include the divine name, **YHWH**, in this verse, further clarifying the Bearer of the title as being God, not Jesus Christ.

Revelation 4:8 is a doxology addressed to the God, **HO THE.OS'**, (Hebrew, **HA'ELO.HIM'**). Here again, instead of Lord (Greek: **KU'RI.OS**), eleven Hebrew versions use the divine name. Jesus appears in the vision a little later, in chapter 5 verse 6.

Both Revelation 11:17 and 16:5 are addressed to "Almighty God" (see 16:7), some Hebrew versions including the divine name at both places. John's Revelation distinguishes between the Owner of this title and Jesus Christ, when it says:

> "The power to rule over the world belongs now to our Lord and his Messiah." — Revelation 11:15; *Good News Bible.*

This title fittingly describes Almighty God, who always "was" (Psalm 90:2; 93:2), he is the "king of eternity" (1 Timothy 1:17; 1 Chronicles 29:10; Revelation 15:5), and he will yet exist for all future time (Genesis 21:33; Deuteronomy 33:27; Psalm 9:7; 102:12, 27; Isaiah 40:28; Jeremiah 10:10; Lamentations 5:19; Habakkuk 1:12).

Interestingly, the Greek **HO ON'** does occur elsewhere in the Greek text — at <u>Matthew 12:30</u>; <u>Luke 11:23</u>; John 1:18; 3:13 (Received Text); <u>3:31</u>; 6:46; <u>8:47</u>; <u>12:17</u>; 18:37; <u>Romans 9:5</u>; 2 Corinthians 11:31. However, it is not used here as a title but merely as an expression, as a 'vehicle,' just as **E.GO' EI.MI'** is a vehicle as used at John 8:58. Comparing the above list is quite instructive; the underlined scriptures refer to occasions where **HO ON'** is applied to individuals other than Almighty God and Jesus Christ. Of the rest, Romans 9:5 and 2 Corinthians 11:31 are applied to God, the others to Jesus Christ.

A comparison of John 1:18 and 6:46 further underscores the fallacy of the Trinitarian argument. For here, **HO ON'**, as a simple expression — a 'vehicle' — is applied to Jesus Christ: the one being (**HO ON'**) in the "bosom of the Father." (John 1:18) This emphasises the fact that **HO ON'** does not constitute a title of itself. It is only the context which can determine whether it is used as a title — as in the five instances in Revelation. John 6:46 says similarly: no one has seen the Father, except 'the one being (**HO ON'**) beside of the God.' This is merely saying "the one who is from God". It would be absurd to claim that **HO ON'** was here used as a title. It is likewise absurd to claim that **E.GO' EI.MI'** at John 8:58 is a title when the context clearly shows that it is used as part of a sentence, as a 'vehicle.'

## Hebrew: A.NI' HU' — I Am He

In view of the foregoing facts, some seek to find support for the Trinity in the Hebrew expression **A.NI' HU'** ("I am he") which occurs in Hebrew versions of John 8:58 in the statement by Jesus, and many times in the Old Testament in statements by God. (Deuteronomy 32:39; Isaiah 41:4; 43:10, 13; 46:4) However, this view cannot be sustained for the reason that **A.NI' HU'** is also used by man. It occurs at 1 Chronicles 21:17 where king David says: I am he [**A.NI' HU'**] 'who sinned in ordering the illegal census.' Would righteous king David have claimed a divine title? Would he have made use of a title reserved only for Almighty God? Or, on the contrary, would you not agree that he merely made use of a common expression, a 'vehicle' used to express a more important idea?

In Hebrew versions of the New Testament it occurs in John's account where the once-blind man said:

"I am he [Hebrew: **A.NI' HU'**; Greek: **E.GO' EI.MI'**]."
— John 9:9.

What did he mean? He was simply responding to the question: 'Is this the man that used to sit and beg?' Some would say: 'This is he.' Others would say: 'No, but he is like him.' The man then said: 'I am he.' They did not take this to be a divine title, nor an expression used exclusively by God. Their response manifested no surprise, no hint that the man had used anything more than a common, everyday expression. They said: 'How, then, were your eyes opened?' They understood the man as simply claiming to be "he," that is, the once-blind man.

Another example of the use of the Greek **E.GO' EI.MI'** as a simple expression is at Acts 22:3 in the statement of the apostle Paul: I am [**E.GO' EI.MI'**] a Jew. It would be absurd to read into this any more than the simple fact that Paul was claiming to be a Jew. **E.GO' EI.MI'** is just a vehicle used to convey this thought.

If Trinitarians maintain that by the use of the particular expression **E.GO' EI.MI' (A.NI HU'** in Hebrew) Jesus was claiming the divine title, then what does the same use of that expression by David, the once-blind man, the apostle Paul, etc., tell us?

The following is a list of all the occurrences of **E.GO' EI.MI'** in the Greek text of the New Testament. The scriptures underlined represent occasions when individuals other than Jesus used the expression, such as Jesus' disciples, Judas Iscariot, Zechariah, the angel Gabriel, John the Baptist, Pontius Pilate, Peter, etc.

Matthew 14:27; 22:32; 24:5; 26:22; 26:25; Mark 6:50; 13:6; 14:62; Luke 1:18; 1:19; 21:8; 22:70; 24:39; John 1:20; 3:28; 4:26; 6:20; 6:35; 6:41; 6:48; 6:51; 8:12; 8:18 [Note this use: "I am the one that bears witness about myself, and the Father who sent me bears witness about me," thus making a clear distinction between the Father and the Son]; John 8:23; 8:23; 8:24; 8:28; 8:58; 9:9; 10:7; 10:9; 10:11; 10:14; 11:25; 13:19; 14:3; 14:6; 15:1; 15:5; 18:5; 18:6; 18:8; 18:35; Acts 9:5; 10:21; 13:25; 18:10; 22:3; 22:8; 26:15; 26:29; 27:23; Romans 11:13; 1 Corinthians 1:12; 3:4; 15:9; 1 Timothy 1:15; Revelation 1:8; 1:17; 2:23; 22:16.

This makes a total of 61 occurrences, 23 of which were not by Jesus!

In view of the above arguments, even those who adhere to the doctrine of the Trinity are impelled to admit the lack of support the "I am" statements provide. Note what Arthur Wainwright says in his book, *The Trinity in the New Testament* (page 91):

"The 'I AM' sayings, however, in the fourth gospel do not directly imply that Jesus is linked with Yahweh. It is rather a case of undefined suggestion."

The author does not even claim that the 'I am' sayings are an implication of this connection. The matter is relegated to something as remote as "undefined suggestion." Surely the Bible either teaches the Trinity, or it does not. It is not going to vaguely suggest it and then leave the matter to a time when those who wrote the scriptures, and also those who knew the Bible writers personally, were long dead, and the Man of Sin (2 Thessalonians 2:3) began to be revealed. — Compare Acts 20:27 and 2 Timothy 2:2.

## Jesus' Statement in its Context

The best way of determining the meaning of a given scripture, as has been consistently pointed out, is to examine the context. We can establish from the question posed by the Jews (at John 8:57): "How can you have seen Abraham?" that, because they did not accept Jesus to be the Christ (nor even a true prophet), they failed to fully understand his claim to a pre-human existence (verse 56): "Abraham rejoiced that he was to see my day; he saw it," Jesus said, that is, with eyes of faith. (Hebrews 11:13) In his reply Jesus pointed, not only to the time of Abraham, but to the time before Abraham, in his statement: **PRIN ABRA.AM' GE.NES'THAI E.GO' EI.MI'**. Following this the Jews attempted to stone Jesus, but he hid from them and went out of the temple (v. 59).

Some look to the Jews' reaction for support in their opinion that Jesus was laying claim to a divine title. Does this mean, then, that each time the Jews attempted to do away with Jesus it was because of his claiming to be God? Or, on the contrary, were there not many occasions when they attempted to kill him for many and various reasons? At Luke 4:24-30, Jesus made the claim merely of being a prophet, and yet the Jews became incensed and attempted to do away with him. And this was at the beginning of his earthly ministry, long before his "controversial" teachings became known to the Jews, particularly the deeply religious Pharisees.

At John 10:31-39, after the Jews attempted to stone Jesus, he defended his claim of being the "Son of God," not God! In fact, during this defence, Jesus quoted from Psalm 82:1, 6 where God calls human judges "gods" (Hebrew: **E.LO.HIM'**). Here was another opportunity for Jesus to clarify matters as to his divinity. However, far from claiming to be an **E.LO.HIM'** as these unrighteous men had been, he merely claimed *son*ship not *god*ship, asking the Pharisees how it was possible for him to be accused of blasphemy on those grounds?

During the mock trial for Jesus' life, his opponents had an excellent opportunity of accusing him of claiming to be God. Did they? No, they complained to Pilate:

> "We have a law, and by that law he ought to die, because he has made himself the Son of God." — John 19:7; *Revised Standard Version.*

What a powerful argument against Jesus it would have been to assert that he claimed to be God! Yet nowhere throughout the trial is this assertion made. — See also Mark 14:55-58; Matthew 12:14; Mark 3:6; John 7:19; 8:37, 40 and John 12:10, 11.

## Unless You Believe That "I Am He"

In the immediate context of John 8:58 there occurs a use of **E.GO' EI.MI'** which further underscores the fallacy of the Trinitarian argument. In verse 24 of the same chapter Jesus says:

"I told you that you would die in your sins, for you will die in your sins unless you believe that I am he [Greek: **E.GO' EI.MI'**; Hebrew: **A.NI' HU'**]." — John 8:24.

The Greek does not include the word **AU.TOS'**, "he," in the text. But this does not create ambiguity. The singular masculine pronoun is implied after **E.GO' EI.MI'**, namely, I am *he.*

Many versions choose the simple "I am he" here. *Moffatt's* translation says: "Unless you believe who I am, you will die in your sins." The Living Bible says: "Unless you believe that I am the Messiah, the Son of God." The New International Version has: "If you do not believe that I am the one I claim to be," and in its footnote says: "Or I am he."

But others, mindful of the popular rendering of verse 58, prefer either "I am" or something even more closely linked with the statement by God at Exodus 3:14 (as rendered by the Greek Septuagint). The New English Bible says: "If you do not believe that I am what I am." The *Good News Bible* goes a stage further, putting the key words within quotation marks and using capitals: "And you will die in your sins if you do not believe that 'I Am Who I Am.'" Later, in verse 28, it has: "When you lift up the Son of Man, you will know that 'I Am Who I Am.'" Here again, though, the Greek text merely has **E.GO' EI.MI'**, with the meaning "I am he." They clearly transgress the bounds of a translator, not only into the field of exegesis (textual interpretation), but into the field of eisegesis (reading foreign ideas into the text without authority from the context). Nor is the addition of the Greek word **HO'TI** ("that"), preceding **E.GO' EI.MI'**, of any help to the Trinitarian idea, for this is also used of the once-blind man's statement: "he said that I am he." — John 9:9.

Where is the support for the *Good News Bible*'s rendering of John 8:24? More accurately, where is the Scriptural support? The next verse, in fact, refutes it. For, instead of replying with shock or even surprise at a "clear reference" to the revelation of God to Moses (at Exodus 3:14), the Jews simply replied:

"Who are you?" — John 8:25.

Curious! That is, curious if one looks for support for the Trinity in this text.

Jesus identified himself in the hearing of the Jews in the context of his statement at John 8:58, not as God, but as the "son of man" (verse 28). This no doubt reminded the Jews of the prophecy at Daniel 7:13, 14 where the individual seen approaching the throne of God is referred to as a "son of man." — Compare Revelation 5:6, 7.

## John 8:58 and Greek Grammar

Is **E.GO' EI.MI'** at John 8:58 used in the way Trinitarians believe? Do we understand: "Before Abraham came to be born, I am he"? Let us put the final clause at the beginning of the sentence: "I am he before Abraham came to be born." This is clearly lacking something. Looking from the Trinitarians' point of view, for a moment, their appeal to the use of **E.GO' EI.MI'** in verses 24 & 28 at very best establishes the identity of the "he" as "the son of man," for it was belief in him as the son of man which would allow for forgiveness of sins. This would then give: "I am the son of man before Abraham came to be born."

It must be obvious even to the most casual observer that the above considerations cannot present accurately the true sense of John 8:58.

Clearly Jesus is referring to his existence, his pre-human existence. Robertson's *Grammar of the Greek New Testament in the Light of Historical Research* says (on page 394) regarding the verb **EI.MI'**:

> "Sometimes it does express existence as a predicate like any other verb, as in **E.GO' EI.MI'** (Jo. 8:58)."

So then, **E.GO' EI.MI'**, "I am," *could* be rendered: I exist. How does this shed light on Jesus' statement?: "Before Abraham came to be born, I exist." But it would make more sense grammatically to say: "Before Abraham came to be born, I did exist," or, "Before Abraham came to be born, I have existed."

However, "I have existed" is in the perfect tense; **E.GO' EI.MI'** is in the present tense. Does this mean we are forced to return to the Trinitarians' view of considering **E.GO' EI.MI'** a title? On the contrary, the statement makes perfect sense as it stands: **E.GO' EI.MI'**, *though normally a present tense verb, is not understood as a simple present at this place.*

This use of the Greek verb is quite common. Moulton's *Grammar of New Testament Greek* (Vol. III, page 62), discusses the Perfective Present of verbs such as **HE'KO** (meaning, "I am arriving") which, although present tense in form (i.e. they are normally understood in the present tense) are rendered in the perfect tense. (A verb in the perfect tense describes an action — to sleep, to eat, to bring, to do — as complete, finished, brought to an appropriate conclusion, perfected — have slept, have eaten, have brought, have done.) An example of the Perfective Present occurs at John 8:42 where the Greek literally reads:

> "For out of God I CAME OUT [perfect tense, completed action] and I AM ARRIVING [present tense, implying continuous action]." — John 8:42.

But notice how this is properly rendered:

> "For from God I came out and am here."

To render **HE'KO** at this place in its apparent present continuous tense "I am arriving," would be nonsense. It would then be saying that Jesus had already come to earth (perfect tense), and yet at the very same time was still on his way, still in the process of arriving. Thus, the present tense verb **HE'KO** is understood here in the perfect (completed action) tense. — Compare **HE'KO**, "I am come," at Hebrews 10:7, 9.

Moulton's *Grammar* goes on to explain:

"The Present which indicates the continuance of an action during the past and up to the moment of speaking is virtually the same as Perfective, the only difference being that the action is conceived as still in progress (Burton 17). It is frequent in the NT: Lk 2:48 13:7 (["these three years I have come seeking"]) 15:29 (["these many years I have served you"], and I still do), Jn 5:6 8:58 ([**EI.MI'**]) 14:9 (["I have been with you so long"]) 15:27 (["you have been with me from the beginning"]), Ac 15:21 (["Moses has had in every city those who preach him"], and still has) 26:31 (["This man has done nothing to deserve death"], his manner of life still continues), 2 Co 12:19, 2 Ti 3:15 (["he has strongly opposed our message"]), 2 Pt 3:4, 1Jn 2:9 3:8."

This use of the verb is different from the Perfective in that the action expressed by the verb is understood, not only as beginning in the past, but continuing up to and including the present and, in some cases, beyond, into the future. The scriptures in the above list could be over-translated in order to bring out the meaning of the perfective-present of the verb more fully: Here it is so many years that I have slaved and am continuing to slave for you. (Luke 15:29) The 'slaving' began some time in the past and was still continuing at the time of the boy's speaking.

Notably, the John 8:58 verb **EI.MI'** is included in the above list at John 14:9. Although **EI.MI'** is in the present tense (*I am at present* ...) it is obvious from the context that it is meant as a perfective-present. Otherwise it would read:

> "I am [at present] with you all this time and yet you HAVE not COME [perfect tense] to know me."

Which would be a bad rendering. Although Jesus was including the present (he was, of course, present with his disciples at the time of his speaking), the context informs us that he was also referring to the past, to the time since Philip first came to know him.

The verb **EI.MI'** is used at John 3:28 in the words of John the Baptist. The reference is again to past time, to the time before the beginning of Christ's ministry. John was declaring that he had been sent forth **(A.PES.TAL.ME'NOS)** in front of Jesus, in advance of him. Note this interlinear rendering:

| | |
|---|---|
| **A.PES.TAL.ME'NOS** | **EI.MI'** |
| Sent forth | I am |
| **EM'PROS.THEN** | **E.KEI'NOU** |
| in front | of that one |

The word **A.PES.TAL.ME'NOS** ("sent forth") is in the perfect tense, whereas the **EI.MI'**, as has been established, is a present tense verb. The correct rendering, then, is: "I have been sent as his forerunner" (*New English Bible*), despite the present tense **EI.MI'**.

A *Grammar of the Idiom of the New Testament*, by G. B. Winer (7th edition, page 267), says regarding this use of the present tense:

> "Sometimes the Present includes also a past tense (Mdv. 108), viz. when the verb expresses a state which commenced at an earlier period but still continues — a state in its duration; as, Jno xv. 27 **AP' AR.KHES' MET' E.MOU' E.STE'** ["from the beginning with me you are"], viii. 58 **PRIN' ABRA.AM' GE.NES'THAI E.GO' EI.MI'**."

The Greek Septuagint also makes use of this verb form. At Jeremiah 1:5, the expression "Before I formed you in the womb, I was acquainted with you," uses a present tense verb: **E.PI'STA.MAI**, "am acquainted with." But the context clearly indicates a past tense. Psalm 89 (90 in our Bibles) verse 2 in the Septuagint reads: "Before the mountains existed, and is being formed [**PLAS.THE'NAI**] the land and the inhabited earth ..." Here again the perfect tense is necessary in translating **PLAS.THE'NAI**.

Winer's Grammar (referred to above) compares also 2 Peter 3:4 ("from the day our forefathers fell asleep, all things are [at present] continuing ..."), and 1 John 3:8 ("from the beginning the Devil is sinning"). Though these verbs refer to the present, they also include a reference to the past.

It is always made clear from the context whether a present tense verb is used in a perfective sense. Regarding the statement in question (John 8:58), **PRIN' ABRA.AM' GE.NES'THAI E.GO' EI.MI'**, there are several considerations which help to prove that the verb **EI.MI'**, in this instance, is a perfective-present and not a pure present tense. For example, Jesus himself places the action of the verb (in point of time) "before Abraham," that is, many centuries prior to the time of speaking.

Thus, the "action" of the verb (i.e. Jesus' existence) began before the birth of Abraham and continued up to that time (and, of course, continued on). To translate **E.GO' EI.MI'** in the present tense, "I am," is very bad grammar.

Putting the "I am" first in the sentence further clarifies the point. If we write, "I am before Abraham was born," we then get a statement similar to the above-mentioned "bad rendering" of John 14:9: "I am with you all this time and yet you HAVE not COME [perfect tense] to know me."

The perfect tense "I have existed," or "I have been," is essential in order to supply the proper aspect of time "before Abraham" and up to the time of Jesus' speaking:

"Before Abraham was born, I have existed."

Or,

"I have existed [since] before Abraham was born."

Trinitarians respond to the above rendering (and other similar versions) by suggesting that Jesus could have said, "I was," Greek **E.GO' EN'**, if he had wanted to refer to his past existence. However, **EN** is merely the imperfect tense of **EI.MI'** (that is, **EN** means "was," whilst **EI.MI'** means "am"). Had Jesus said: "Before Abraham was born, I was," he would not have conveyed the idea of his continuing existence from the time before Abraham *up to and beyond* the time of his speaking. Only the perfective-present of **EI.MI'** adequately conveys this thought. In other words, Jesus was not simply referring to his having existed before Abraham, but to his continuing existence from before the time of Abraham, up to the present time, and beyond into the future. The imperfect tense **EN** does not convey this idea.

Thus, in conclusion, the action of the verb **EI.MI'** at John 8:58 started "before Abraham was born" and is to be regarded as still in progress — the perfective-present. Jesus did not declare that he was in existence merely at the time of his speaking, but was referring, in addition, to past time, to the time before Abraham's existence. This sense agrees with the immediate context of the verse ("how can you have seen Abraham?" — verse 57), and with the perfective-present use of **EI.MI'** at John 14:9 and at John 3:28, as well as with other references to Jesus' pre-human existence. — Proverbs 8:22; John 1:1; 17:5; Philippians 2:6; Colossians 1:15-17; 1 John 2:3; Revelation 3:14.

## Summary

Trinitarians claim a connection between Exodus 3:14 and John 8:58. However, as the above arguments demonstrate, this view is not sustained under close scrutiny. Exodus does not refer simply to God's existence but to his future purposes, what he intends to do and to become on behalf of his people. The expression in John, by contrast, does refer to existence, that of Jesus Christ; an existence which began "before Abraham" and still continues.

Consequently, the only connection that can be sustained between Exodus 3:14 and John 8:58 is by using *erroneous translations*. There is no connection either in the original Hebrew or Greek languages!

Note how various translations render John 8:58:

"I have been when there had as yet been no Abraham."

Salkinson & Ginsburg (in Hebrew: **A.NI' HA.YI'THI**)

"I have existed before Abraham was born."

Moffatt; Schonfield, and *An American Translation*

"Before Abraham came to be, I was."

Stage *The Old Georgian Version of the Gospel of John*

"Before there was an Abraham, I was already there!"

Pfaefflin

"Before Abraham was born, I was."

George M. Lansa, from the Syriac Peshitta

*The New Testament ... in Ethiopic by Thomas Pell Platt*

"Before Abraham existed, I was."

Dr. James Moffatt, also from the Syriac Peshitta

*The Syriac New Testament Translated into English from the Peshitta Version* by James Murdock

"Before Abraham existed, I was existing."

*The Brazilian 'Sacred Bible'* published by the

Catholic Bible Center of Sao Paulo
"Before Abraham was, I have been."
*A Translation of the Four Gospels from the
Syriac of the Sinaitic Palimpsest* by
Agnes Smiti Lewis
Delitzsch (in Hebrew: **A.NI' HA.YI'THI**)
"Before ever Abraham came to be, I was."
*The Curetonian Version of the Four Gospels*

# 19 Jesus Christ — A Divine One, An E.LO.HIM'

"In the beginning was the Word and the Word was with God, and the Word was God." — John 1:1.

The above rendering of the opening verse of John's gospel presents the most popular view of John's words as contained in many modern Bible versions.

However, did John intend his readers to understand that Jesus, the Word or Logos, was *the* God? This is the Trinitarian view. Let us, though, examine the implications of that concept:

If, within the 'one God,' there are three persons, and one of those persons is Jesus, the Word, then why does John say that Jesus is both *with* God and at the same time *is* God? Why does he use the word "God" in two subtly distinct ways — one which *excludes* the Logos and one which *includes* him? How can the Word, himself 'God,' be with the three persons of the Trinity?

It must be clear to any rational person that John's second use of "God" is distinct from the first. So what was John's meaning? One thing that both Trinitarians and Unitarians can agree upon is this:

John does not *simply* say that Jesus is God!

Today there is no-one who speaks New Testament Greek as a mother-tongue. True, there are scholars and theologians who study the language and make judgements based upon their findings. But that is very different from a mother-tongue! The *lingua franca* (common language) of the first century was Hellenistic, or **KOI.NE'** (common), Greek. The majority of John's readers had first-hand knowledge of this language.

Was John introducing the philosophical concept of 'three persons in one God' as taught by the Classical writers? His first century readers had available to them an important device that we today can make use of in answering this question — contextual comparison. How do the surrounding verses and other scriptures enlighten us?

We have already mentioned the fact that the Word, or Logos, was "with" God. "With" translates the Greek preposition **PROS**. This can have various meanings: *by, near, towards, with, in relation to,* etc. Its use at John 1:1 can be illustrated by comparison with the following texts:

I was *with* **[PROS]** you in the temple
Mark 14:49
how long must I be *with* **[PROS]** you
Luke 9:41
my presence again *with* **[PROS]** you
Philippians 1:26
when we were *with* **[PROS]** you
1 Thessalonians 3:4
while I was yet *with* **[PROS]** you
2 Thessalonians 2:5
when we were *with* **[PROS]** you
2 Thessalonians 3:10

Regarding this, observe what *The Four Gospels Harmonized and Translated*, by Professor Leo Wiener says (p. 30, para. 2):

"If it says that in the beginning was the *comprehension*, or *word*, and that the *word was* to God, or *with God*, or for God, it is impossible to go on and say that it was God."

The Word was in close proximity to the Father. They had a close, intimate, Father-Son relationship. In verse 18, the apostle elucidates on this:

"Nobody has ever seen God, but God has been unfolded by the divine One, the only Son, who lies upon the Father's breast." — John 1:18; *Moffatt*.

Giving his reasons for including "the only Son" here, Moffatt says in a footnote to John 1:18:

"Although **THE.OS'** ('the divine One') is probably more original than the variant reading **HUI.OS'** ['son'], **MONOGE.NES'** [only-begotten] requires some such periphrasis in order to bring out its full meaning here."

Moffatt's decision is somewhat of a compromise between two distinct views on this verse. Many ancient manuscripts read "only-begotten *Son*," and many others read "only-begotten *God.*" It is an interesting study to inquire as to the *reason* why some translators (*Revised Standard Version, King James, Good News Bible, New English Bible, American Standard Version, New International Version*, for example) have chosen "Son" rather than "God" (*Byington's, Rotheram's*).

Could it be that the rendering "only-begotten God who is in the bosom of the Father" helps to clarify the meaning of John's opening verse?

Let us divide the manuscripts between those which contain **HUI.OS'**, "Son," and those which have **THE.OS'**, "God":

"Son": —

Alexandrine
5th cent.
Codex Ephraemi (corrector)
5th cent.
Old Latin Versions
2nd-4th cent.
Latin Vulgate
c. 400 AD
Syriac Peshitta (corrector)
5th cent.
Philoxenian—Harclean Syriac
6th & 7th cent.

"God": —

> Vatican No. 1209
> 4th cent.
> Sinaitic (original)
> 4th cent.
> Syriac Peshitta (original)
> 5th cent.
> Codex Ephraemi (original)
> 5th cent.
> Papyrus Bodmer 2 (P66)
> c. 200 AD
> Papyrus Bodmer 14, 15 (P75)
> c. 200 AD

The older and hence more reliable manuscripts, then, have the reading "God" rather than "Son."

Regarding John 1:18, *The Gospel According to S. John, with Introduction and Notes*, edited by A. Plummer, says (on p. 75):

> "**MONOGE.NES' THE.OS'** [Only-begotten God]. The question of reading here is of much interest. Most MSS and versions read **HO MONOGE.NES' HUI.OS'** [only-begotten son]. But the three oldest and best MSS. and two others of great value read **MONOGE.NES' THE.OS'**. The test of the value of a MS., or group of MSS., on any disputed point, is the extent to which it admits false readings on other points not disputed. Judged by this test, the group of MSS. reading **MONOGE.NES' THE.OS'** is very strong, while the far larger group of MSS. reading **HUI.OS'** [son] for **THE.OS'** [God] is comparatively weak, for the same group might be quoted in favour of a multitude of readings which no one would think of defending. Again, the revised Syriac, which is among the minority of versions supporting **THE.OS'**, is here of special weight, because it agrees with MSS from which it usually differs. The inference is that the very unusual expression **MONOGE.NES' THE.OS'** is the original one, which has been changed into the usual **HO MONOGE.NES' HUI.OS'** (iii. 16, 18; 1 John iv. 9); a change easily made, as **OC** (=**THE.OS'**) is very like (=**YIOC** [Son]). Both

readings can be traced back to the second century, which again is evidence that the Gospel was written in the first century. Such differences take time to spread themselves so widely."

It is a matter of speculation to determine why the 'correctors' altered the text from **THE.OS'**, *God*, to **HUI.OS'**, *Son*. But why is it that translators of modern versions should "think of defending" the inferior reading "Son"? Translators ought to feel an obligation toward the original text and endeavour to achieve the greatest accuracy, rather than choose a reading which does not embarrass Church dogma as much as the true reading.

Observe the following comparison between v. 1 and v. 18:

| v. 1 | the Word; a divine one | was with | the God |
|------|------------------------|----------|---------|
| v. 18 | the only-begotten God | was in the bosom | of the Father |

## An Object of Reverence, an E.LO.HIM', a God

It should be no surprise to students of God's Word that the title of God (Hebrew: **E.LO.HIM'**) is applied to Jesus Christ. (Isaiah 9:6; John 20:28) After all, *God* is a designation, a descriptive term. It means: an *object of reverence*, an *object of devotion*.

Did the apostle John mean that the Logos was an object of reverence, a Divine One, a Mighty One? Note what Ernst Haenchen's *Commentary on the Gospel of John* Chapters 1-6, (which translates John 1:1 "and divine was the Logos") translated by Professor F. W. Funk, says on pp. 108-110:

"John 1:1, however, tells of something that was in existence already in time primeval; astonishingly, it is not 'God.' ... The Logos (we have no word in German or English that corresponds to the range of meaning of the Greek term) is thereby elevated to such heights that it almost becomes offensive. The expression is made tolerable only by virtue of the continuation in 'and the Logos was in the presence of God,' viz., in intimate, personal union with God."

The Logos was with God at this "beginning," just as he was with God throughout the creation of the material universe. (Proverbs 8:22, 30, 31; Colossians 1:15, 16) He was *with* God ... but was he that *same God?*

Haenchen's *Commentary* continues:

"In order to avoid misunderstanding, it may be inserted here that **THE.OS'** and **HO THE.OS'** ('god, divine' and 'the God') were not the same thing in this period. Philo has therefore written: the **LO'GOS** means only **THE.OS'** ('divine') and not **HO THE.OS'** ('God') since the logos is not God in the strict sense. ... In a similar fashion, Origen, too, interprets: the Evangelist does not say that the logos is 'God,' but only that the logos is 'divine.' In fact, for the author of the hymn [in John 1:1], as for the Evangelist, only the Father was 'God' (**HO THE.OS'**; cf. 17:3); 'the Son' was subordinate to him (cf. 14:28). But that is only hinted at in this passage because here the emphasis is on the proximity of the one to the other.

"It was quite possible in Jewish and Christian monotheism to speak of divine beings that existed alongside and under God but were not identical with him. Philippians 2:6-10 proves that. In that passage Paul depicts just such a divine being, who later became man in Jesus Christ. ... Thus, in both Philippians and John 1:1 it is not a matter of a dialectical relationship between two-in-one, but of a personal union of two entities."

It is important to look at texts such as John 1:1 through the eyes of the Christianized-Jew as opposed to that of the 'philosophical' Greek. The scriptures apply the designation 'god; a divine one' to individuals other than the One true God and Jesus Christ. For example, at 2 Corinthians 4:4, even the arch-enemy of God, Satan, is referred to as "the god." The Greek text has the article ("the") merely because Satan is the only one who occupies this particular position. He is *the* god-of-this-age, or world. (1 John 5:19) However, it serves to illustrate the use of the term 'god.' How could Satan be called a god? Because he is a mighty, spirit creature, one who was formerly an angelic son of God. Moreover, he is a ruler; Jesus called him the "prince of this world" (lit, *ruler*, Gr. **AR'CHON**). — John 12:31; 14:30; 16:11; *New International Version.*

With the meaning, an *object of reverence* or *veneration* in mind, the apostle Paul said concerning some who were "enemies of the cross of Christ":

"They are heading for destruction, appetite is their god, and they glory in their shame." — Philippians 3:19; *New English Bible.*

How could one's appetite be termed a god? By excessive greed, obesity, becoming a 'servant of one's own appetite.' Food becomes the object of one's attention to the extent that the desire for it consumes one's entire being. — Romans 16:18.

## E.LO.HIM' ("Divine") Applied to Angels

A notable example of the use of **E.LO.HIM'** occurs at Psalm 8:5, where the Hebrew text says:

"And you made him (Christ) a little less than **E.LO.HIM'** [god]."

Many translations have "God" here:

"You made him less than God."

However, the *Aramaic Targums*, the *Septuagint*, the *Syriac Peshitta* and the *Latin Vulgate* all have "angels; messengers." The *King James* follows this, giving: "thou hast made him a little lower than the angels," in order that it may agree with Hebrews 2:7. The apostle Paul must have been in agreement with the *Septuagint* translators' opinion of the use of **E.LO.HIM'** at Psalm 8:5. He used the term "angels" for **E.LO.HIM'**. He was obviously aware of the original Hebrew using the term

**E.LO.HIM'**, but found no difficulty with the *Septuagint's* reference to "angels."

> You made him a little less than *gods.*
> Psalm 8:5
> You made him a little less than *angels.*
> Hebrews 2:7

This calls into serious question the translations which render **E.LO.HIM'** as "God."

As the Scriptures are clearly one harmonious whole (2 Timothy 3:16, 17), there must be another view of **E.LO.HIM'** which accounts for the apparent difficulty.

Obviously, **E.LO.HIM'** is here used in a collective sense with respect to the angels. *Moffatt's* translation has:

> "Yet thou hast made him little less than divine." — Psalm 8:5.

Regarding **E.LO.HIM'**, *Gesenius' Hebrew Grammar,* p. 418, para. 2, says:

> "There is another use of **BEN-** or **BE.NE'** to denote membership of a guild or society (or of a tribe, or any definite class). Thus **BE.NE' E.LO.HIM' or BE.NEI HA.ELO.HIM'** Gn 6:2, 4, Jb 1:6, 2:1, 38:7 (cf. also **BENEI E.LIM'** Ps 29:1, 89:7) properly means not *sons of god(s),* but beings of the class of **E.LO.HIM'** or **E.LIM'**."

The *Grammar* continues with other examples such as, *belonging to the guild of the prophets; one of the guild of apothecaries.* This helps to explain the use of **E.LO.HIM'** at Psalm 8:5 as applying to angels, that is, divine beings. The *Lexicon for the Old Testament Books,* by Koehler and Baumgartner (p. 134, col. 1), says:

> "**BE.NE' E.LO.HIM'** (*individual*) *divine beings, gods.*
> **BE.NE' HA.ELO.HIM'** *the (single) gods* Genesis 6:2;
> Job 1:6; 2:1; 38:7."

**E.LO.HIM'** is used in a similar way of supernatural beings at 1 Samuel 28:13 where the witch of Endor referred to the 'ghost' of Samuel as "a god." In fact, what she actually said was:

"I saw **E.LO.HIM'** coming up out of the earth." — 1 Samuel 28:13.

**E.LO.HIM'** being, of course, "a god."

On this use the *Theological Dictionary of the Old Testament* (Vol. 1, p. 282) says:

"Finally, we may mention certain passages in which *'elohim* has a somewhat irregular meaning. In 1 S. 28:13, the medium at Endor calls the spirit of Samuel which had come up an *'elohim*, i.e., a nonhuman or 'supernatural' being. The same idea appears in Isa. 8:19: 'Should not a people consult their *'elohim*, the dead on behalf of the living?' In Ps. 8:6(5) ('Thou hast made him (man) little less than *'elohim'*), the most natural meaning of *'elohim* is 'divine being' (cf. the LXX *par' ange'lous* 'than angels'): the critical thing here is the similarity with the divine in general."

The Hebrew word for God, **E.LO.HIM'**, then, can be a generalised term that means far less than "*the supreme being.*" On this, the book *Theology of the Old Testament* (Vol. 1, translated by J. A. Baker, p. 186), by Walther Eichrodt, says:

"Finally **E.LO.HIM'** is used in an extremely generalised sense to mean the 'divine essence' or 'nature'. [Footnote:] The term is applied to the spirits of the dead; I Sam. 28.13. The angels, however, are also called *bene elo.him*, Gen. 6.2,4; Job 1.6 etc., here the word *bene* is not to be taken in a genealogical sense, but is an expression connoting 'congruence' or 'belonging together'. Analogous is the use of *ruach elohim* to mean the 'spirit of divinity': Gen. 41.38; Dan. 4.5f., 15; 5.11."

## E.LO.HIM' — Exceedingly Great

At Jonah 3:3, **E.LO.HIM'** ("God") is even used to denote *exceeding greatness*. The phrase **'IR GEDHO.LAH' E.LO.HIM'** is rendered: "an exceedingly great city" by the *Revised Standard Version*; others are comparable. Some consider **CHOKH.MATH' E.LO.HIM'**, "wisdom of God," at 1 Kings 3:28 to belong to this use, namely: "exceedingly great wisdom." Note these further examples:

you are a *mighty* **[E.LO.HIM']** prince
   Genesis 23:6
with *mighty* **[E.LO.HIM']** wrestlings
   Genesis 30:8
will be no *might* **[EL]** in your hand
   Deuteronomy 28:32
it became a *very great* **[E.LO.HIM']** quaking
   1 Samuel 14:15
the *mighty* **[E.LIM']** are afraid
   Job 41:25 (v.17 in MT)
you *sons of the mighty* **[BE.NE' E.LIM']**
   Psalm 29:1
like the *great* **[EL]** mountains
   Psalm 36:6
the *Divine One* **[EL]** God, the LORD
   Psalm 50:1
God **[E.LO.HIM']** in the congregation
   of the *mighty* **[E.LIM']**
   Psalm 82:1
the *sons of the mighty* **[BHE.NE' E.LIM']**
   Psalm 89:6
the *mighty* **[E.LE']** of the land
   Ezekiel 17:13

This use of **E.LO HIM'** is carried over to the New Testament where the Greek word for God, **THE.OS'**, is used: Acts 7:20 and 2 Corinthians 10:4. At Acts 7:20, the disciple Stephen describes Moses as "a divinely beautiful child" (*Moffatt*). The *Good News Bible* says: "a very beautiful child." The *American Standard Version* has: "and was exceeding fair." Other translations have "and was beautiful before God"

(*Revised Standard Version*) or similar. The Greek text says literally: **A.STEI'OS TO THE.O'**, "beautiful to the God."

At 2 Corinthians 10:4, *The Bible in Living English* has: "divinely powerful." *The New English Bible* has: "divinely potent."

In these texts, "God" (Greek: **THE.OS'**) is in the dative case. This use of the dative of **THE.OS'** is regarded as an *intensive* or *elative*. Says *An Idiom-Book of New Testament Greek*, (p. 184) by C. F. D. Moule:

> "**TO THE.O** *as an Intensive* is a well-known Hebraism. In Gen. x. 9, **GI'GAS KUNE.GOS' ENAN.TI'ON KU.RI'OU** [a great hunter against the LORD] represents probably a merely intensive use of God's name; and even more clearly Jonah iii. 3 **PO'LIS ME.GA'LE TO THE.O'** means simply *a very great city*. Accordingly Acts vii. 20 **A.STEI'OS TO THE.O** may well be a Semitism of the same sort. Cf. II Cor. x. 4 **DUNA.T.A' TO THE.O** powerful to the God ." ... Is II Cor. xi. 2 **THE.OU' ZE'LO** [of God jealousy] to be interpreted as a *divine* (i.e. supernaturally great) eagerness, or is it nearer to the meaning *an eagerness which is God's own eagerness* (or *which springs from God Himself*)?"

For this latter text (2 Corinthians 11:2) *Moffatt* has: "I feel a divine jealousy on your behalf." The *American Standard Version* and *New International Version* say: "a godly jealousy"; the *Revised Standard Version* and *New English Bible* have: "a divine jealousy." At 2 Corinthians 10:4 the "divinely strong" (*Moffatt*) weapons are those belonging to the spirit, godly weapons, as opposed to fleshly, carnal weapons of warfare.

The above arguments are important for our discussion of John 1:1. Why should Christ, the Word, not be given the title **E.LO.HIM'**, a divine one? Is he not greater than the angels, the other *divine beings*?

The Hebrew word **EL** ("God") is used in the book of Ezekiel where it is applied to human rulers:

"I will give it into the hand of a mighty one [**EL**] of the nations." — Ezekiel 31:11.

In Deuteronomy the same word, **EL**, is used in the sense of "power":

"It shall not be in the power [**EL**] of your hand to prevent it." — Deuteronomy 28:32.

The apostle John must have been fully aware of the above considerations, and, moreover, would not by any means have introduced teachings foreign to the "pattern of the sound words." (2 Timothy 1:13; *Revised Standard Version*; compare Galatians 1:8, 9) Why, then, look for an explanation of John's opening words in the complexities of Greek philosophy when the explanation lies in this divine "pattern," this Grand Jig-saw Puzzle of divine making?

As was discussed earlier, **ELO.HIM'** is a title applied many times though not exclusively, to the Father. However, the title **HA.E.LO.HIM'**, meaning *the One true God*, occurs 376 times in the Hebrew Masoretic Text, and all but eight of these are applied to the Father. If we now take into consideration the uses of **E.LO.HIM'** under discussion, namely, *a divine one, a divine being*, we may apply this to John's opening verse. In harmony with the use of the Greek article **HO** ("the"), let us include the Hebrew article (**HA**, "the") where **HO THE.OS'** (*the God*) occurs in the Greek text:

"In the beginning was the Word, and the Word was with **HA.E.LO.HIM'**, and **E.LO.HIM'** was the Word. The Word was in the beginning with **HA.E.LO.HIM'**." — John 1:1.

The article, **HA** ("the), before **E.LO.HIM'** serves to determine the application of the word to the One individual, the Father. It is thus rendered "the one true God." (See *The Hebrew and Aramaic Lexicon of the*

*Old Testament*, by F. Zorrell, p. 54; and *Gesenius Hebrew Grammar*, section 126(e)). Taking this into account, let us look at John 1:1 from another perspective:

> "In the beginning was the Word, and the Word was with *the one true God*, and a *divine being* was the Word. The Word was in the beginning with *the one true God*."

The *Hebrew New Testament* of Delitzsch conveys this idea (see also the *Hebrew New Testament* of the United Bible Societies). Observe this interlinear rendering of John 1:1 using Delitzsh's Hebrew text:

| **BERE.SHITH'** | **HA.YAH'** | **HAD.DA.BHAR'** |
|---|---|---|
| In beginning | was | the Word |
| **WE.HAD.DA.BHAR'** | **HA.YAH'** | **'ETH** |
| and the Word | was | [with] |
| **HA.E.LO.HIM'** | **WE'LO. HIM'** | |
| the one true God, | and a divine being | |
| **HA.YAH'** | **HAD.DA.BHAR'** | |
| was | the Word. | |

The first **E.LO.HIM'** has the article (**HA**, "the"), the second does not. The Hebrew text does not say that the Word was *with* **HA.E.LO.HIM'** and at the same time the Word *was* **HA.E.LO.HIM'**; it merely says that the Word was **E.LO.HIM'** a Mighty One, a Divine One, a divine being. Likewise the Greek text does not say that the Logos was *with* **HO THE.OS'** and yet was **HO THE.OS'**; merely that the Word was **THE.OS'**, of the class of divine, a divine being.

## "Mighty God" and Thomas' Exclamation

No doubt it was with these ideas in mind that Isaiah, writing under inspiration, gave Jesus the title of "Mighty God" (Isaiah 9:6), and that Thomas exclaimed before Jesus: "My Lord and my God!" — John 20: 28.

Interestingly, just as there are many who consider the lack of the article ("the") before the second **THE.OS'** of John 1:1 to be significant (namely, denoting the *nature* of the Logos), so too there are some in the opposing camp who consider the *presence* of the article at John 20:28 to be significant. Thomas said, quoting literally from the Greek: "*the* Lord of me and *the* God of me." However, the nominative case is used here in a vocative (i.e. form of address) sense and is followed by a possessive, and it is for this reason that the article is used. Professor Moule, in his *Idiom-Book of New Testament Greek* (pp. 116, 117), says on this:

> "In John xx. 28 **HO KU'RI.OS MOU KAI HO THE.OS' MOU** [the Lord of me and the God of me], it is to be noted that a substantive in the Nominative case used in a vocative sense and followed by a possessive *could not be anarthrous* (see Hoskyns and Dewey, *Commentary*, in 1cc.); the article before **THE.OS'** may, therefore, not be significant. ... the use of the article with a virtual *Vocative* (cf. John xx. 28 referred to above, and I Pet. ii. 18, Col. iii. 18ff.) may also be due to Semitic idiom."

Moreover, could an emotional statement by Thomas be used as a basis for teaching theological dogma? After denying that the women had indeed seen the resurrected Jesus, it would certainly have been an emotional moment when Jesus appeared to Thomas.

Concerning Jesus' title "Mighty God" (Isaiah 9:6; Hebrew: **EL GIB.BOR'**), the point is raised by Trinitarians that this same title is applied to the Father at Isaiah 10:21. However, what is it that those who proffer such argumentation are actually saying?: That because the Father and the Son share this title, both being called Mighty God, this means that Jesus is the *one true God*.

That there is no basis for this view can be seen from the following:

The expression **EL GIB.BOR'** is a title meaning "Mighty Divine One." **EL** means "God" (the singular form of **E.LO.HIM'**). The **GIB.BO.RIM'** (plural of **GIB.BOR'**, "mighty") were the mighty warriors of King David. (2 Samuel 23:18) It was the "mighty men of valour" the **GIB.BO.RE' HA.CHA'YIL**, who crossed the Jordan with Joshua and dispossessed the Canaanites. (Joshua 1:14) As discussed above, **E.LO.HIM'** and its related forms are often used to mean "mighty, strong, great." At Exodus 15:15, **E.LE'** ("God") is applied to the men of Moab, where the *King James* has "*mighty men* of Moab."

Yet these same expressions, **EL** and **GIB.BOR'**, are used of the *one true God*, the Father, at Jeremiah 32:10:

| **HA.EL'** | **HAG.GA.DHOL'** | **HAG.GIB.BOR'** |
|---|---|---|
| the Divine One | the Great | the Mighty One |

| **YEH.WAH'** | **TSE.BHA.OTH'** |
|---|---|
| Yahweh | [of] armies |

Do we consider *the one true God* to be a lesser one, a lesser being, simply because he happens to bear a title which is also given to men? Or should we consider men to be equal to God simply because they are called "gods," **E.LO.HIM'**, (Psalm 82:1, 6) and "mighty ones," the **GIB.BO.RIM'** (Genesis 6:4; Joshua 6:2)? Or, rather, is not the title in itself descriptive of a person's role, one's designation as a warrior and a leader?

Why, then, should some find it unusual that no less a person than the Son of God bears the title, not only of a Mighty One, a **GIB.BOR'**, but a *divine* Mighty One, a Mighty God? This does not identify who he is, it does not say he *is* the one true God; it is a descriptive title explaining his power, his exalted nature, his authority and position as a leader of heavenly armies — a position granted him by God.

181

Moreover, Isaiah did not identify the **EL GIB.BOR'** of 9:6 with the **EL GIB.BOR'** of 10:21! The first one, the "son," is given exalted titles *by the very zeal of God*, his Father. The fact that Isaiah later describes the Father as also being a Mighty Divine One does not identify the two as the same individual — merely that they share a particular designation.

If the repetition of a title can in itself teach that one individual is identified with another, then why is it that Jesus shares the title "King of kings" (Revelation 17:14) with Nebuchadnezzar (Daniel 2:37)? Why are Jesus' disciples called "the light of the world" (Matthew 5:14) when this expression is also used of Christ (John 8:12)? Clearly this is because a title is descriptive of the role played or the position occupied by the person bearing it, a descriptive designation, and is not necessarily an exclusive title.

As was covered earlier, there are indeed titles used exclusively of God. One such title is **EL SHAD.DAI'**, God Almighty. Note the *superlative* nature of this title: *Al*mighty. Only the Father can rightly and authentically bear this title. It refers to absolute power, absolute authority. (See the discussion regarding *delegated authority* in Chapter 14: 'Your Throne, O God' or 'Your Throne is God,' Which?) Never is the title **SHAD.DAI'**, Almighty, applied to the Son. Though the Father *can* properly be referred to as Mighty, as can the Son, yet the Son does not have absolute dominion, he is not Almighty! (See also the discussion on Titus 2:13 and the title 'Saviour.')

Also, throughout the Scriptures Jesus is never referred to as "God of gods." Only the Father bears this designation:

> the Lord your God is God of gods and LORD of lords
> > Deuteronomy 10:17
> your God is God of gods and Lord of kings
> > Daniel 2:47

speak astonishing things against the God of gods
Daniel 11:36

## E.LO.HIM', Pagan Deities, and Human Judges

In support of the above application of **E.LO.HIM'** to John 1:1 is the common use of the word when referring to pagan deities. For, if false gods who were considered in the Old Testament to be "no gods" (Isaiah 37:19) were nonetheless attributed the title E.LO.HIM' — the plural of excellence — then surely the Son of God has a right to authentically bear this title.

The apostle Paul said that the gods of the nations were not gods "by nature." (Galatians 4:8) That is, by their very origin and production they did not actually achieve the status of gods; they were not gods intrinsically, they were merely pieces of stone or wood. Yet they were venerated by the nations, each of which considered their god to be **E.LO.HIM'**, a divine being. Even the inspired Bible writers did not deny them this title inasmuch as their devotees venerated their gods as such.

Psalm 82:1, 6 has been referred to above where **EL** is rendered "mighty." However, these verses render further assistance in our discussion by (a) applying **E.LO.HIM'** to unrighteous men, and (b) it is quoted by no less an authority than Christ Jesus who used it in response to an accusation of the Jews, namely, that he was making himself **THE.OS'** or **E.LO.HIM'** (Delitzsch's *Hebrew New Testament*). — John 10:33.

Firstly, let us consider an interlinear reading of Psalm 82:1:

**E.LOHIM'**      **NITS.TSABH'**
God                   stations himself

**BA'A.DHA.THE-EL'**
in [the] assembly [of the] mighty,

**BE.QE'REBH**          **E.LO.HIM'**       **YISH.POT'**
In [the] middle        [of the] gods       he is judging

That this is applied to men, to mere humans, can be seen from the rest of the psalm where God commands these judges to be impartial and to consider the afflicted and needy. In verse 6, God again takes up the offensive:

"I say, 'You are gods **[E.LO.HIM']** sons of the Most High **[EL.YON']**, all of you'." — Psalm 82:6; *Revised Standard Version.*

This consideration of **E.LO.HIM'** creates an embarrassment for Trinitarians who find difficulty reconciling Jesus' use of this Psalm, as recorded at John 10:33-36, with the teaching of the Trinity. One problem involves the Jews' accusation that Jesus was making himself "God" (v. 33). This could also be rendered: 'making yourself *a god.*' However, both "God" and "god" prove awkward for Trinitarians. If we take the former to be the Jews' meaning, that Jesus was making himself *the* God, **HA.E.LO.HIM'**, or **HO THE.OS'** (Greek), then Jesus' subsequent reply to this must be taken as a denial. If, however, the latter is correct, "a god," then not only did the Jews merely have in mind the meaning of **E.LO.HIM'** as discussed above (under the heading *An Object of Reverence, an* **E.LO.HIM'**, *a God*), but Jesus' reply even went *beyond* this ...

Not only did Jesus displace the designation of **E.LO.HIM'**, a Mighty One, a divine being, from himself, but impressed upon the Jews that claiming to be "the Son of God" cannot be blasphemy if the Scriptures themselves apply exalted titles, even divine titles, to unrighteous human judges.

"'In your own Law it says that men are gods,' Jesus replied. 'So if the Scripture, which cannot be untrue, speaks of those as gods to whom the message of God came, do you call it blasphemy when the one sanctified and sent into the world by the Father says, "I am the Son of God"?'" — John 10:34-36; *The Living Bible.*

The fact that Jesus responds to the Jews' charge by referring to gods (**E.LO.HIM'**), indicates that the correct rendering of John 10:33 is:

"... because you, being a man, are making yourself a god."

Neither "man" nor "god" has the definite article ("the") in the Greek text here. Moreover, Hebrew versions of the New Testament have **E.LO.HIM'** here, meaning "a god," not **HA.E.LO.HIM'**, "the God." The contrast is between the state of being human, a man, with the state of being divine, a god. The reference is not to a particular man, "the man," in contrast with the true God, "the God," but to *a* man in contrast with *a* god. Jesus did not attempt to answer any incredible suggestion that he was the *one true God*, **HA.E.LO.HIM'**, the Father. The accusation was that Jesus was making himself a *divine being*, an **E.LO.HIM'**. This is what Jesus treated.

This bears a resemblance to the *Septuagint* usage at 1 Kings 18:27 (*3 Kings* in the Septuagint) and Ezekiel 28:2, 9. The former scripture relates Elijah's mocking of the servants of Baal. Here is a Greek interlinear reading of part of Elijah's words:

| **EPIKA.LEI'STHE** | **EN** | **PHO.NE'** | **ME.GA'LE,** |
|---|---|---|---|
| Call out | with | voice | loud |

| **HO'TI THE.OS'** | **ESTIN** | | |
|---|---|---|---|
| for god | he is | | |

Elijah was referring to the false god Baal. But did he say: "he is God," that is, **HO THE.OS'** (Greek), or **HA.ELO.HIM'** (Hebrew)? Both the *Septuagint* and the Hebrew *Masoretic Text* omit the article ("the"). Clearly the clause is best rendered: "for he is a god." Elijah was under no misapprehension that Baal was the true God, or even that his worshippers considered him to be such. Elijah mocked Baal, 'surely he can hear your cries, for he is a divine one, a god?' (Check 1 Kings 18:27 with *Bagster's Septuagint*, the *King James*, *The*

*Good News Bible, The New English Bible,* the *Revised Standard Version,* the *Douay,* the *New International Version, The Bible in Living English,* etc.)

It is obvious that the omission of the article ("the") here is significant.

## The King of Tyre was E.LO.HIM', a God

Ezekiel 28:2, 9 contains the words of the ruler (Greek **AR'CHON**; Hebrew **NA.GHIDH'**) of Tyre. A Hebrew interlinear reads:

**EL      A'NI**
god     I am

A Greek interlinear reading of the *Septuagint* has:

**THE.OS'      EIMI' E.GO'**
god            am I

Did the King of Tyre claim to be *the only true God?* Or did he claim to be *a god,* **E.LO.HIM'**? Modern translations are a little divided. The Catholic *Douay* says: "I am God," in both verses. The *King James* adds the indefinite article ("a") in verse 2, but still capitalises "God." In v. 9 it has: "I am God," without the "a." The *American Standard Version* has "a god" followed by "I sit in the seat of God" for verse 2; then for verse 9 has: "I am God." Bagster's *Septuagint* also has "God."

However, the *Revised Standard Version, The New English Bible, The Good News Bible,* the *New International Version* and *The Bible in Living English,* and others, all have "a god" for each occurrence here. They all use the indefinite article ("a") and they all use a lower-case 'g' for "god". Note how *The Bible in Living English* renders verses 2 & 9, and observe how the translator (Steven Byington) renders the Hebrew forms:

"Says the Lord Jehovah, Since your thoughts go high and you say 'I am a divinity [**EL**] I occupy a god's [**E.LO.HIM'**] station in the heart of the ocean,' when you are human and not divine [**EL**] but you feel as if you were a god [**E.LO.HIM'**]; ... Will you say 'I am a god [**E.LO.HIM'**]' before him who is killing you? but you are human [**A.DHAM'**] and not divine [**EL**]' but you feel as if you were a god [**E.LO.HIM'**]; ... Will you say 'I am a god [**E.LO.HIM'**]' before him who is killing you? But you are human [**A.DHAM'**], and not divine [**EL**]."

The *Jerusalem Bible* renders Ezekiel 28:2 thus:

"Though you are a man and not a god, you consider yourself the equal of God."

Nowhere does the text use the definite article **HA** ("the") before **E.LO.HIM'** or **EL** here. Also, note the comparison with **A.DHAM'** "human," or "man." The state or condition of being human, or a man, is contrasted with the state or condition of being divine, a god. The word **A.DHAM'** is not an adjective, it is a noun; nevertheless it is used for the *quality* of being human, the *nature* of humanity. The King of Tyre claimed to have the nature of *a god*, the qualities and attributes of E.LO.HIM'. However, Ezekiel was to prophesy against him and condemn him for his haughtiness; to inform him that he was merely human, he had the nature of man. He was *a* man, not *a* god.

There is a further example in the New Testament at Acts 28:6. The Maltese people observed a poisonous snake hanging from Paul's hand. At first they imagined he was a murderer and that justice had caught up with him. However, after a long time "and seeing nothing unusual happen to him, they changed their minds and *said he was a god*." (*New International Version*) All the above-mentioned Bible versions have "a god" here. The *Hebrew New Testament* of Delitzsch has **E.LO.HIM'**, and the *Hebrew New Testament* of the United Bible Societies has **EL**, both without the article (**HA**, "the"). — Compare also 2 Thessalonians 2:4.

It is obvious to any enquirer that the Maltese were not assuming Paul to be Almighty God, the Creator.

They simply felt, because Paul survived the bite of a poisonous snake, that he was *divine.*

## John 1:1 and Greek Grammar

We have examined the use of **E.LO HIM'** (without the article — *the*) and its various applications to supernatural beings, pagan deities, and even to men. In comparing 1 Kings 18:27, Ezekiel 28:2, 9 and Acts 28:6, it is clear that on each occasion "a divine being," "a god," is the intended meaning. However, what of John 1:1? Note what J. W. Wenham says in a footnote (on p. 35) in his book *The Elements of New Testament Greek*:

> "In ancient manuscripts which did not differentiate between capital and small letters, there would be no way of distinguishing between Theos ('God') and theos ('god'). Therefore as far as grammar alone is concerned, such a sentence could be printed: **THEOS ESTIN HO LOGOS**, which would mean either, 'The Word is a god', or, 'The Word is the god'. The interpretation of John 1.1 will depend upon whether or not the writer is held to believe in only one God or in more than one god. It will be noticed that the above rules for the special uses of the definite article are none of them rigid and without exceptions. It is wiser not to use them as a basis for theological argument until the student has reached an advanced stage in the knowledge of the language."

Mr. Wenham puts the clause into the present tense no doubt to divorce his readers from the controversies connected with John 1:1 and to isolate the elements of the problem. Let us put it back into its correct tense — the imperfect — and observe the two alternatives:

The Word was *a* god
The Word was *the* god

It is somewhat poignant that the many controversies surrounding this verse revolve around just these two alternatives. There are grammatical principles which support both renderings. However, bear in mind that it is merely *grammar*, the science of linguistics, which supports both versions. The correct alternative can only be ascertained by appeal to context, both immediate and Scripture as a whole.

Professor C. H. Dodd, director of *The New English Bible* project, offers this possible rendering of John 1:1:

"A possible translation ... would be, 'The Word was a god'. As a word-for-word translation it cannot be faulted."

However, *The New English Bible* renders the verse:

"When all things began, the Word already was. The Word dwelt with God, and what God was, the Word was."

Trinitarians look for support in grammatical principles such as that mentioned in Green's *Handbook to the Grammar of the Greek Testament* (p. 178). Here it says regarding the article ("the"):

"Hence arises the general rule, that in the simple sentence the Subject takes the article, the Predicate omits it. The subject is definitely before the mind, the predicate generally denotes the class to which the subject is referred, or from which it is excluded."

In the third clause of John 1:1, "the Word" is the subject, while the expression **THE.OS' EN**, "god was," constitutes the predicate — the part of a sentence which says something about the subject. What the above grammar seems to be saying is that the article before the second **THE.OS'** ought to be *understood*, as if the sentence meant: *the* god was the Word. However, the grammar goes on to list a number of sentences as an illustration of its meaning, such as: "thy word is truth," "the Word was God," "God is love." Now note what it goes on to say:

"Had the article been employed with the Predicate in the above case, the sentences would have read thus:

... *Word* is the *Truth*, and nothing else can be so described; the Word was the *entire Godhead*, and God and Love are *identical*, so that in fact Love is God."

Hence the above-mentioned "general rule" is by no means universal. Nor can it be applied to John 1:1. The **LO'GOS** and **HO THE.OS'** (the God) are not interchangeable. Though God is said to be love, love is not God. Though *a* god was the Word, yet the Word was not *the* God.

Professor Moule, in *An Idiom-Book of New Testament Greek*, deals with the definite article in chapter ten. On p. 115 he quotes E. C. Colwell's rules for the definite article. One rule (2(b)) says that "definite predicate nouns which precede the verb usually lack the article". In John 1:1, the predicate noun **THE.OS'** precedes the verb **EN**, "was." Colwell's "rule" says that these nouns *usually* lack the article, even though they are actually definite (as if the article is understood). Moule then says, on p. 116:

"More striking still is the application of this canon to the much debated John i. I. Is the omission of the article in **THE.OS' EN HO LO'GOS** nothing more than a matter of idiom? Middleton had already taken it as an instance of the article being omitted simply because **THE.OS'** is 'the Predicate of a Proposition which does not reciprocate'. ... On the other hand it needs to be recognized that the Fourth Evangelist need not have chosen this word-order, and that his choice of it, though creating some ambiguity, may in itself be an indication of his meaning; and Westcott's note (in loc.), although it may require the addition of some reference to idiom, does still, perhaps, represent the writer's [John's] theological intention: 'It is necessarily without the article (**THE.OS'** not **HO THE.OS'**) inasmuch as it describes the nature of the Word and does not identify His Person. It would be pure Sabellianism to say "the Word was **HO THE.OS'**". No idea of inferiority of nature is suggested by the form of expression, which simply affirms the true deity of the Word. Compare the converse statement of the true humanity of Christ v. 27 (**HO'TI HUI.OS' AN.THRO'POU ESTIN'** ['for son of man he is'])."

The above-mentioned "ambiguity" only arose after the Church adopted the teaching of the Trinity in the 4th century. Had the apostle John wished to say that the Word was *the one true God*, **HA.E.LO.HIM'** he would surely not have left the matter to ambiguity. His first and second century readers could not have seen ambiguity in John's expression. They understood John to mean — as Westcott pointed out —the divine *nature*, the *deity* of the Word, and not the identification of the Word as the *one true God*. This is also what Philip P. Harner wrote in the *Journal of Biblical Literature* (Vol. 92, 1973):

> "Perhaps the clause could be translated, 'the Word had the same *nature* as God'."

## The Word was THE.OS' — One of a Kind

This is how *A Manual Grammar of the Greek New Testament*, by Dana and Mantey, explains the use of anarthrous nouns (nouns which are not preceded by the definite article *the*), as indicating a *quality* about someone or something. On page 148, paragraph 3, the Grammar explains that in a copulative sentence (i.e. one which makes use of a conjunction such as "and") sometimes the article makes the subject distinct from the predicate. It then refers to Xenophon's *Anabasis*, 1:4:6, **EM.PO'RION D'EN TO KHO.RI'ON**, which is translated *but the place was a market*. The "market" was not *the* market, it was only one of a kind. Correspondingly the **LO'GOS** was not *the* God, but was one of a kind, of the class of divine being. Dana and Mantey's *Grammar* could have rendered John 1:1 the same way, in accord with the same principle.

Dr. A. T. Robertson considered John's omission of the article to be intentional. In *A Grammar of the Greek New Testament*, p. 768, he says:

"'God' and 'love' are not convertible terms any more than 'God' and 'Logos' or 'Logos' and 'flesh.' ... The absence of the article here is on purpose and essential to the true idea."

These 'unconvertible terms' agree with the comment of Middleton, as quoted from Moule above.

An example of *convertible* terms occurs at 1 John 3:4. Notice how this contrasts with the use at John 1:1:

| **KAI** | **HE** | **HAMAR.TI'A** | **ES.TIN'** |
|---------|--------|----------------|-------------|
| and | the | sin | is |

| **HE** | **ANO.MI'A** |
|--------|--------------|
| the | lawlessness |

John is making the point that everyone doing sin is guilty of lawlessness; hence sin and lawlessness are one and the same; they are convertible terms. Sin is lawlessness, and lawlessness is sin. Notice how both nouns take the article ("the").

The *Grammar* of Dana and Mantey makes reference to Robertson's *Grammar* (p. 140), where it says:

"Surely when Robertson says that **THE.OS'**, as to the article, 'is treated like a proper name and may have it or not have it' (R. 761), he does not mean to intimate that the presence or absence of the article with **THE.OS'** has no special significance. We construe him to mean that there is no definite rule governing the use of the article with **THE.OS'**, so that sometimes the writer's viewpoint is difficult to detect, which is entirely true. But in the great majority of instances the reason for the distinction is clear. The use of **THE.OS'** in John 1:1 is a good example."

If the apostle John had wanted to teach the difficult and complex doctrine of the Trinity, would he have used words in which "the writer's viewpoint is difficult to detect"? Or rather, would you not agree that the doctrine of the Trinity was far away from John's mind when he penned those words, and that his use of the Greek **THE.OS'** was in line with the above discussion of the Hebrew equivalent **E.LO.HIM'**?

The non-use of the article (anarthrous use) before the second **THE.OS'** is clearly distinctive. There are many instances in John alone where the article is used with a predicate noun:

| Clause | Scriptures in John |
|---|---|
| *the* life was the light of men | 1:4 |
| *the* Prophet are you? | 1:21 |
| that one was *the* lamp | 5:35 |
| *the* prophet that was to come | 6:14 |
| this is *the* bread that comes down | 6:50 |
| I am *the* bread that came down | 6:51, 58 |
| *the* flesh is of no use | 6:63 |
| *the* fine shepherd surrenders his soul | 10:11 |
| *the* Jews encircled him | 10:24 |
| he called *the* Jesus and said | 18:33 |

This proves that it is a *general* rule which says that predicate nouns preceding the verb are anarthrous (without the article "the"). Note what *A Greek Grammar of the New Testament and Other Early Christian Literature* (p. 143, para. 273), by Blass-Debrunner-Funk, says:

> "Predicate nouns *as a rule* are anarthrous. Nevertheless the article is inserted if the predicate noun is presented as something well known or as that which alone merits the designation (the only thing to be considered)."

If the article *is* sometimes used with a predicate noun, for example one which is "well known," then there is no basis for saying that the article is understood at John 1:1. Dr. N. Turner, in Moulton's

*Grammar of New Testament Greek (Vol.* III, p. 183), has this to say regarding the article:

> "Although predicate nouns are usually anarthrous, the art. thus distinguishing the subject from the complement, the art. may be inserted if the predicate noun is supposed to be a unique or notable instance (e.g. Mt 6:22 *the eye* alone is *the light* of the body)."

There can be no doubt that the apostle John knew nothing of the so-called Christology, a doctrine which antedates John's gospel by some two centuries. This in itself helps to settle the question of the anarthrous **THE.OS'**. For, had John been aware of any questions regarding Jesus' "godship," his identification *as* God, he would surely have included the definite article, *definitely* stating that Jesus is God: **KAI HO LO'GOS EN HO THE.OS'**, and the Word was *the* God. Note what Bible translator William Barclay says on this point:

> "Now normally, except for special reasons, Greek nouns always have the definite article in front of them, ... When a Greek noun has not got the article in front of it, it becomes rather a description than an identification, and has the character of an *adjective* rather than of a noun. We can see exactly the same in English. If I say: "James is THE man", then I identify James with some definite man whom I have in mind; but, if I say: "James is man", then I am simply describing James as human, and the word has become a description and not an identification. If John (at 1:1) had said **HO THEOS EN HO LOGOS** ["the God was the Word"], using a definite article in front of both nouns, then he would definitely have identified the **LOGOS**, with God, but because he has no definite article in front of **THEOS** it becomes a description, and more of an adjective than a noun. The translation then becomes, to put it rather clumsily, "The Word was in the same class as God, belonged to the same order of being as God" . . . John is not here identifying the Word with God. To put it very simply, he does not say that Jesus was

God." — *Many Witnesses, One Lord* (1963), pp. 23, 24.

Compare Barclay's explanation with the above discussion of Ezekiel 28:2, 9.

In a similar vein, observe what Dr. G. B. Winer's *Grammar of New Testament Greek* (translated and enlarged by W. F. Moulton) says on p. 151:

> "In Jo. i.1 (**THE.OS' EN HO LO'GOS**), the article could not have been omitted if John had wished to designate the **LO'GOS** as **HO THE.OS'**, because in such a connexion **THE.OS'** without the article would be ambiguous. It is clear, however, both from the distinct antithesis **PROS TON THE.ON'** ver. 1 , 2, and from the whole description (Characterisirung) of the **LO'GOS**, that John wrote **THE.OS'** designedly. Similarly, in 1 P. iv. 19 we find **PIS.TOS' KTI'STES** without the article."

The ambiguity Dr. Winer refers to would indeed by present if John had understood Jesus to be *the one true God*. But he wrote **THE.OS'** without the article to purposely distinguish the two individuals. This is at variance with Dr. Turner's comment in Moulton's *Grammar* (loc. cit.), where he says that "there need be no doctrinal significance in the dropping of the art., for it is simply a matter of word-order". It must be noted he said "there *need* be" no significance. There are many of the opinion that the omitting of the article is significant. Furthermore, as has been mentioned, such a view harmonises with John 1:18.

Interestingly, there is yet another view of John 1:1. *The Patristic Gospels — An English Version of the Gospels as they existed in the Second Century*, by Roslyn D'Onston, contains a Critical Note to the verse on p. 156 which supports the suggested reading **KAI THE.OU' EN HO LO'GOS**: *and of God was the Logos*:

> "There are three distinct reasons for believing "of God" to be the true reading. First, the manuscripts as stated in that note; secondly, the logical

argument, because if the Evangelist meant "was God," there would have been no occasion for the next verse; thirdly, the grammatical construction of the sentence: for "was God," would he not have written ho *logos en theos,* which would at any rate, have been more elegant? But if we read it, *kai theou en ho logos* [and of *God* was the Logos], the *theou* ["of God"] is in its proper place in the sentence. I have refrained from correcting the text of this passage at the express desire of the late Bishop Westcott."

There is, though, no real difficulty with the text as it is, which simply states that the Word was an **E.LO.HIM'** *a divine one, a god.*

Finally, it is because of the above considerations that the following translations render John 1:1 thus:

"And what God was, the Word was"
*New English Bible*
"The Word was divine"
*Smith-Goodspeed*
"The Logos was divine"
*Moffatt*
"It was tightly bound up with God, yes itself of divine being"
*Beohmer* (German)
"The Word was itself of divine being"
*Stage* (German)
"And god (=of divine being) the Word was"
*Menge* (German)
"And was of divine weightiness"
*Pfaefflin* (German)
"And god of a sort the Word was"
*Thimme* (German)
"And the Word was a god"
*The New Testament, in An Improved Version*
"And a god was the Word"
*Emphatic Diaglott* (interlinear reading)
"And a god (or, of a divine kind) was the Word"
*Siegfried Schulz* (German)
"And godlike sort was the Logos"

*Johannes Schneider* (German)
"And the Word was a God"
*New World Translation*
"And a god was the Logos"
*Jurgen Becker* (German)
"And the Word was a divine being"
*Dictionary of the Bible*, by John McKenzie

# 20   God Forever Blessed!

A text which many believe provides strong proof of the Trinity is Romans 9:5. In *The Jerusalem Bible,* this verse reads:

> "Christ who is above all, God for ever blessed!" — Romans 9:5.

However, note the punctuation used by the *Revised Standard Version:*

> "According to the flesh, is the Christ. God who is over all be blessed for ever."

In its footnote it offers the alternative rendering:

> "Christ, who is God over all, blessed for ever."

Clearly, the matter of punctuation is paramount in a consideration of this verse. The original Greek manuscripts had no punctuation, and therefore the translation can be largely a matter of choice.

Note an interlinear reading of part of this verse:

| KA.TA' SAR'KA | HO 'ON | E.PI' |
|---|---|---|
| According to flesh | the one who is | upon |

| PAN'TON | THE.OS' | EULOGE.TOS' | EIS |
|---|---|---|---|
| all | God | blessed | into |

| TOUS'AI.O'NAS | AMEN |
|---|---|
| the ages | amen |

Note how this extract begins with "according to the flesh." This appears to lend weight to the conclusion that "the one who is" "according to the flesh" is God. But observe how choosing an earlier extract of the same verse puts a different slant on the matter:

| KAI | EX | 'HON | HO | CHRIS.TOS' TO |
|---|---|---|---|---|
| and | out of | whom | the | Christ |

| KATA | SAR'KA |
|---|---|
| the | according to flesh |

If the logical break, where in English we would put the full stop, occurs after the word "flesh," then a new sentence ascribes glory to "God who is blessed forever." Therefore, from the point of view of grammar, the clause "the one who is over all" can apply *either* to God, *or* to Christ.

Even a Catholic Dictionary admits:

"There is no reason in grammar or in the context which forbids us to translate 'God, who is over all, be blessed for ever, Amen.'"

Compare Romans 9:5 in the Catholic *New American Bible* and the Protestant *New English Bible*.

Vincent Taylor points out the differences of opinion on this text, but adds:

"I think the balance of opinion falls on this side, and that Christ is not addressed as God."

Thus most translations make a clear distinction between God and Christ and punctuate the sentence before referring to God.

## The Context of Romans 9:5

Romans chapter nine discusses the outworking of God's purposes which depends, not on flesh, but on the will of God. Verses 14-18, referring back to God's dealings with Pharaoh of Egypt, highlight the mercy and justice of God. In verses 19-24, the illustration of the potter and the clay manifestly illustrates the superiority of God over his creation. How appropriate, then, that Romans 9:5 praises God who is "supreme above all" and who is "blessed for ever!" — *New English Bible*.

*The New International Dictionary of New Testament Theology* says:

"Rom. 9:5 is disputed ... It would be easy, and linguistically perfectly possible to refer the expression to Christ. The verse would then read,

'Christ who is God over all, blessed for ever. Amen.'
Even so, Christ would not be equated absolutely with
God, but only described as a being of divine nature,
for the word *theos* has no article. ... The much more
probable explanation is that the statement is a
doxology directed to God." — (Grand Rapids, Mich.;
1976), translated from German, Vol. 2, p. 80.

Note these renderings of Romans 9:5:

| | |
|---|---|
| "and from whom by physical descent the Christ came. God who is over all be blessed through the ages! Amen." | *The Riverside New Testament,* Boston and New York (1935) |
| "and theirs too (so far as natural descent goes) is the Christ. (Blessed for evermore be the God who is over all! Amen.)" | *A New Translation of the Bible,* by James Moffatt, New York and London. |
| "and of their race, according to the flesh, is the Christ. God who is over all be blessed for ever. Amen." | *Revised Standard Version,* New York. |
| "and from them, in natural descent, sprang the Messiah. May God, supreme above all, be blessed for ever! Amen." | *The New English Bible,* Oxford and Cambridge. |
| "and Christ, as a human being, belongs to their race. May God, who rules over all, be praised for ever! Amen." | *Today's English Version,* American Bible Society, New York. |
| "and from them came the Messiah (I speak of his human origins). Blessed forever be God who is over all! Amen." | *The New American Bible,* New York and London. |

## Titus 2:13 — Our Great God and Our Saviour

In a few other Bible verses, the proximity of
"Christ" or "Jesus" to statements about God has led to
some confusion, due to the already existing doctrine of
the Trinity in the minds of the Bible translators. When

a scripture text can be translated one of two ways, the Trinitarian will choose the method which conforms to his belief. But does it conform to Bible context?

For example, Titus 2:13 reads, from the *Good News Bible*:

"The great God and Saviour Jesus Christ."

Any unsuspecting reader would immediately take this to be proof of the Trinity. It clearly refers to Jesus Christ as "the great God." However, this is not the only way of rendering this verse, and flies against the grain of the most respected scholarly views on the text, as we will see later.

The main text of the *New English Bible* agrees with the above rendering when it says, "our great God and Saviour Christ Jesus," but in its footnote it offers the following alternative:

"*Or* of the great God and our Saviour ..." — Titus 2:13.

The addition of the word "our" makes all the difference. Suddenly there are distinctly two individuals referred to. Alternative renderings are usually subtly distinct in their meanings. For example, 2 Timothy 2:26, in the *New English Bible*, says, in part:

"And thus they may come to their senses and escape from the devil's snare, in which they have been caught and held at his will." — 2 Timothy 2:26.

In its footnote, the translators offer the following alternative:

"*Or*, escape from the devil's snare, caught now by God and made subject to his will."

In the former, one has been snared by the devil and held by his will but has escaped. In the latter, one has been snared by the devil and escaped, and is now held by God's will. The distinction does not alter matters drastically. The choice hinges on the identity of the one Paul specifies in saying "his will."

The situation with Titus 2:13, however, is quite different. One rendering quite categorically states that Jesus is God, whilst the other maintains his distinctness as a separate individual.

The critical question is whether the scripture should be rendered 'the glory of our great God and Saviour, Jesus Christ,' identifying Christ as God, or 'the glory of the great God, and of our Saviour Jesus Christ,' separating the identities of God and Christ. Vincent Taylor says on this:

"The grammarians range themselves on both sides."

So if grammar is of little help, what about the context? Titus 3:4-6 helps. Verse 4 begins by describing the kindness and love for man on the part "of our Saviour, God." Then verse 6 explains that the Holy Spirit has been poured out "through Jesus Christ our Saviour." But the Greek clearly says it is "he," God, who poured out the Holy Spirit through Christ. Is Paul providing a clear distinction between God and Christ in one scripture, and then referring to them as being the same individual in another? Indeed, the apostle Paul opens up the book of Titus (verse 4) with the salutation:

"May there be grace and peace from God the Father and Christ Jesus our Saviour." — Titus 1:4.

Could there be a clearer distinction? Paul would surely be consistent in his terminology if he wanted to state that the "great God" was also our "Saviour Christ." So the lack of the definite article ("the") in front of "Saviour" at Titus 2:13 cannot be significant.

Note the same salutation that Paul uses during the opening verses of the following Bible books (extracted from *The Jerusalem Bible*):

"May God our Father and the Lord Jesus Christ
1 Corinthians 1:3

send you grace and peace."
   2 Corinthians 1:2

   Galatians 1:3
   Ephesians 1:2
   Philippians 1:2

"To the Church in Thessalonika which is in God
the Father and the Lord Jesus Christ."
   1 Thessalonians 1:1

"Wishing you grace and peace from God the Father
and the Lord Jesus Christ."
   2 Thessalonians 1:1

"From Paul, apostle of Christ Jesus appointed by the
command of God our saviour and of Christ Jesus."
   1 Timothy 1:1

"Mercy and peace from God the Father and from Christ
   1 Timothy 1:2
Jesus our Lord."
   2 Timothy 1:2

"Grace and peace from God the Father and from Christ
Jesus our saviour."
   Titus 1:4

In all the above cases, Paul makes a clear
distinction between God and Christ. The context,
then, bears out the correct rendering of Titus 2:13 as:

"The great God and our Saviour Jesus Christ."

Turning to other New Testament writers, the
disciple James opens his book in the following way:

"James, a slave of God and of the Lord Jesus Christ."
— James 1:1.

If Titus 2:13 truly referred to "our God and Saviour
Jesus Christ," then why does James not take the
opportunity of making the same point?

The apostle Peter makes an even clearer distinction
when he says:

"Blessed be the God and Father of our Lord Jesus
Christ." — 1 Peter 1:3.

This helps when we turn to the opening verse of 2 Peter. Here it says:

"The righteousness of our God and [the] Saviour Jesus Christ." — 2 Peter 1:1.

Here the same difficulty as Titus 2:13 arises. The *Jerusalem Bible* says here:

"The righteousness of our God and saviour Jesus Christ."

Without the definite article ("the"), and without other scriptures to serve as guides, the reader would be forgiven for concluding that only one individual is being spoken about, the "God and Saviour Jesus Christ." But the immediate context makes the matter clear:

"A knowledge of God and of Jesus our Lord." — 2 Peter 1:2.

If in one breath Peter is stating that Jesus is God, why, in the next breath, does he make this distinction? Surely the article ("the") must be included to make the sense clear: "our God and *the* Saviour Jesus Christ."

The apostle John, who penned the words of John 1:1 about which so much has been written, offers assistance in the opening words of his first letter:

"This sharing of ours is with the Father and with his Son Jesus Christ." — 1 John 1:3.

How clear the meaning would be if he had said: "This sharing of ours is with our God Jesus Christ." But, again, a clear distinction between God and Christ is made. — See also 2 John 3; Jude 1, 25; Revelation 1:1.

This distinction was carried over by the Christian writer Polycarp, who wrote early in the 2nd century:

"Peace from God Almighty, and from the Lord Jesus Christ, our Saviour." — The Ante-Nicene Fathers, Volume I, page 33.

The Revelation to John speaks of "the kingdom of our God and the authority of his Christ." (Revelation 12:10) The seventh angel announces the "kingdom of our Lord [God] and of his Christ." How, then, can Christ be God?

A similar difficulty occurs over Ephesians 5:5. Here, the *King James Bible* has:

"The kingdom of Christ and of God."

The original Greek text has:

| **TE** | **BA.SI.LEI'A** | **TOU** | **CHRIS.TOU'** |
|--------|-----------------|---------|----------------|
| the | kingdom | of | Christ |

| **KAI** | **THE.OU'** |
|---------|-------------|
| and | of God |

This seems to be a clear distinction between God and Christ. But Nigel Turner, in his *Grammatical Insights Into the New Testament*, p. 16, suggests that ...

"we must also seriously consider the possibility of departing from all our English versions by translating Eph. 5⁵, 'in the kingdom of Christ who is God'."

But why depart from all English versions, not to mention the rest of the Scriptures, just to force agreement with a doctrine which is not taught in the Bible? He also suggests that 2 Thessalonians 1:12 ought to be, "Our lord and God Jesus Christ." But this is not how most versions render it. Nor is it in harmony with the rest of the Holy Scriptures.

\*              \*              \*              \*

Returning to Romans 9:5, comments by leading bible scholars shed light on the accurate rendering of the text. For example, in *A Grammar of the Idiom of the New Testament*, p. 551, by G. B. Winer says that...

"...when the subject constitutes the principal notion, especially when it is antithetical to another subject, the predicate may and must be placed after it, cf. Ps. lxvii. 20 Sept [Ps 67:19 LXX]. And so in Rom. ix. 5, if the words [**HO ON E.PI' PAN'TON THE.OS' EU.LO.GE.TOS'** "the one being upon all God blessed"] are referred to God, the position of the words is quite appropriate, and even indispensable."

The "subject" in question is God. He is the "principal notion."

A detailed study of Romans 9:5 is found in *The Authorship of the Fourth Gospel and Other Critical Essays,* by Ezra Abbot. On pp. 345, 346 and 432 the author says:

"But here [**HO ON** "*the being*"] is separated from [**HO KHRI.STOS'** "*the Christ*"] by [**TO KA.TA' SAR'KA** "*according to the flesh*"], which in reading *must* be followed by a pause,—a pause which is lengthened by the special emphasis given to the κατὰ σάρκα [**KA.TA' SAR'KA** "*according to flesh*"] by the τό [**TO** "*the*"]; and the sentence which precedes is complete in itself grammatically, and requires nothing further logically; for it was only as to the flesh that Christ was from the Jews. On the other hand, as we have seen (p. 334), the enumeration of blessings which immediately precedes, crowned by the inestimable blessing of the advent of Christ, naturally suggests an ascription of praise and thanksgiving to God as the Being who rules over all; while a doxology is also suggested by the 'Αμήν [**A.MEN'**] at the end of the sentence. From every point of view, therefore, the doxological construction seems easy and natural ... The naturalness of a pause after σάρκα [**SAR'KA** "*flesh*"] is further indicated by the fact that we find a point after this word in all our oldest MSS. that testify in the case,—namely, A, B, C, L, ... I can now name, besides the uncials A, B, C, L, ... at least twenty-six cursives which have a stop after σάρκα [**SAR'KA** "*flesh*"], the same in general which they have after αἰῶνας [**AI.O'NAS**] or 'Αμήν [**A.MEN'**]."

So the sentence stating, "Christ who is according to the flesh" is complete in itself. It is therefore logical to begin a new sentence with "God who is blessed forever," thus separating the identities of God and Christ.

In conclusion, then, Romans 9:5 clearly ascribes praise and thanksgiving to God. This scripture does not identify Almighty God with Jesus Christ.

# 21  Did God Die at Calvary?

A problem fundamental to the issue of Jesus' godship is: "If Jesus actually died a sacrificial death, who resurrected him?" Of course, the answer is usually offered along the lines of, "He is God and therefore resurrected himself." However, the problems are much deeper and more serious than this simple question would imply.

Paul referred to Jesus as the "last Adam" and also as a "corresponding ransom." (1 Corinthians 15:45; 1 Timothy 2:6) Jesus had to be a perfect man, the equivalent of Adam. His body had to be offered in sacrifice, he had to actually *die*. If Jesus were God, he would be more than the equivalent of Adam. Moreover, God *cannot* die, he possesses immortality, "deathlessness" (from the Greek: **A.KA.THAR.SI'A**). Jesus "put on" immortality upon his resurrection (1 Corinthians 15:54), and thereafter remains "deathless," being eternally beyond the reach of death. This is why, in the Revelation to John, he said of himself ...

> "I am the First and Last, the living one who died, who is now alive for evermore." — Revelation 1:18; *The Living Bible*.

Although he has died, he is now living forever, deathless, immortal. But this cannot be said of God. He has always been immortal. Death could never possibly have claimed Him. — Psalm 90:2; Jeremiah 10:10; Habakkuk 1:12; 1 Timothy 1:17.

## God Purchased the Congregation With The Blood of His Own

Related to the question of the sacrifice of Christ is the somewhat difficult scripture at Acts 20:28. This reads:

"Shepherd the congregation of God, which he purchased with the blood of his own."

Some translations render this, "which he purchased with his own blood." This clearly implies that God himself died at Calvary, and that God's own blood was offered in sacrifice. But this is not the way all versions translate this text. For example:

with the blood of His own Son
*The Holy Bible in Modern English*

through the death of his own Son
*Good News Bible*

Some Greek manuscripts escape the difficulties of this text by translating "the congregation of the Lord," instead of "the congregation of God." But the major manuscripts (Sinaitic, Vatican manuscript No. 1209, and the Latin Vulgate) all have the latter, indicating that this was the original text.

J. Moulton says on this, in *A Grammar of New Testament Greek*, Vol. 1, p. 90:

"Before leaving **I'DI.OS** [*one's own*] something should be said about the use of **HO I'DI.OS'** without a noun expressed. This occurs in Jn $1^{11}$ $13^1$, Ac $4^{23}$ $24^{23}$. In the papyri we find the singular used thus as a term of endearment to near relations: *e.g.* **HO DEI'NA TO I.DI'O KAI'REIN** [*The certain one my own. Greetings!*]. In *Expos.* VI. iii. 277 I ventured to cite this as a possible encouragement to those (including B. Weiss) who would translate Ac $20^{28}$ "the blood of one who was his own.""

C. F. D. Moule remarks, in *An Idiom-Book of New Testament Greek*, p. 120:

"Note that **I'DI.OS**, *one's own*, is sometimes practically no more than a possessive adjective; e.g. in John i. 41, Matt. xxii. 5 it seems to be quite unemphatic ... In the famous *crux* of Acts xx. 28, **TOU I.DI'OU** is possibly used as a noun=*his own (Son)*; cf. John i. 11, xiii. 1, etc."

And the master Greek text of Westcott and Hort, *The New Testament in the Original Greek*, in the Appendix on pp. 99, 100, states:

> "It is by no means impossible that **HUI.OU'** [*of the Son*] dropped out after **TOU I.DI'OU** [*of his own*] at some very early transcription affecting all existing documents. Its insertion leaves the whole passage free from difficulty of any kind."

Furthermore, there are a plenitude of scriptures that refer to the death of Christ, but not one that speaks of the death of God:

Christ died for ungodly men
  Romans 5:6
Christ died for us
  Romans 5:8
reconciled to God by the death of his Son
  Romans 5:10
Christ is the one who died
  Romans 8:34
Christ both died and came to life
  Romans 14:9
Christ died for our sins
  1 Corinthians 15:3
We believe that Jesus died and rose again
  1 Thessalonians 4:14
Christ died once for sins
  1 Peter 3:18

So, in line with the title of this section, God *did* purchase the congregation with "his blood"; not his own blood, but that of his Son, Jesus Christ.

It is noteworthy that, of all the scriptures that make reference to the one who was offered in sacrifice, Acts 20:28 is the only one that presents a measure of difficulty. All the rest clearly state that it was Jesus, not God, who died.

# 22 Now You Have Tasted the Lord's Goodness

The apostle Peter admonished us to become "hungry for nothing but milk." (1 Peter 2:3) This, he said, would help us to "grow up to salvation—now that you have tasted the goodness of the Lord." — *Jerusalem Bible.*

The *Jerusalem Bible* puts the words "tasted the goodness of the Lord" in italics to indicate that the wording is borrowed from the Old Testament, namely the Psalms:

"How good Yahweh is—only taste and see!
Happy the man who takes shelter in him." — Psalm 34:8; *Jerusalem Bible.*

This quotation is pointed out by Trinitarians, in that the Psalmist was referring to Yahweh, but Peter was talking about Jesus. The discussion on Psalm 110:1 earlier (Chapter 10) explained the problems caused by translating the divine name as "Lord." It could be *either* the Lord God (Yahweh), or the Lord Jesus Christ. The Trinitarian point of view is that they are one and the same.

However, note what F. J. A. Hort wrote in *The First Epistle of St Peter:*

"In the Psalm [Psalm 34:8] **HO KU'RI.OS** stands for Jehovah, as it very often does, the LXX. inserting and omitting the article with **KU'RI.OS** on no apparent principle. On the other hand the next verse shews St Peter to have used **HO KU'RI.OS** in its commonest though not universal N[ew] T[estament] sense, of Christ. It would be rash however to conclude that he meant to identify Jehovah with Christ. No such identification can be clearly made out in the N[ew] T[estament]. St Peter is not here making a formal quotation, but merely borrowing O[ld] T[estament] language, and applying it in his own manner. His use, though different from that of the Psalm, is not at variance with it, for it is through the χρηστότης [**CHRE.STO'TES**, "kindness"] of the Son that the **CHRE.STO'TES** of the Father is clearly made known to Christians: 'he that hath seen me hath seen the Father.'"

The same argument applies to Philippians 2:10, where Paul asserts that every knee should bend at the name of Jesus. The "language" of the Old Testament is borrowed, but the application does not prove that God and Christ are one and the same. (Note the concluding paragraphs of Chapter 15.)

## All God's Angels Must Worship Him

Hebrews 1:6 is often used to support the teaching that Christ must be worshipped as God. The scripture says:

"All God's angels must worship him." — Hebrews 1:6; *Good News Bible*.

Paul was here quoting from the Greek Septuagint version, from Psalm 97:7. In the *Revised Standard Version*, this says:

"All gods bow down before him."

The Psalm is evidently talking about God. But Paul uses the same wording and applies it to Christ.

The *Good News Bible* quotation above uses the word "worship." But this is not the only translation of the Greek word **PROS.KU.NE'O**. The *Greek-English Lexicon of the New Testament* by Grimm-Thayer, explains **PROS.KU.NE'O** to mean the following:

"*to kiss the hand to (towards) one*, in token of reverence: ... *to fall upon the knees and touch the ground with the forehead* as an expression of profound reverence ... hence in the N[ew] T[estament] *by kneeling or prostration to do homage* (to one) or *make obeisance*, whether in order to express respect or to make supplication." — p. 548.

It then explains two main uses of the word. (1) homage shown to men of superior rank, and (2) homage rendered to God, the ascended Christ, to heavenly beings, and to demons.

Clearly, the Greek **PROS.KU.NE'O** has a much broader meaning than the English "worship." For example, if we wish to express the meaning that an individual "kissed the hand" of the Queen, we would not say they "worshipped." But this is the expression used in Greek.

Homage due to Christ is not equal to that rendered to Almighty God. Nor is the word **PROS.KU.NE'O** used exclusively of God and Christ. For example, the Hebrew equivalent **SE.GHADH'** is used at Daniel 2:46, where Nebuchadnezzar "did homage to Daniel" (*Revised Standard Version*). — Note also the following references 1 Samuel 25:23, 24; 2 Samuel 14:4-7; 1 Kings 1:16; 2 Kings 4:36, 37.

## The Speakers in Revelation

The above discussion brings us to the concluding chapter of the book of Revelation. There are several participants in the concluding remarks: God, Jesus, the apostle John, the angel, and the bride.

One point of interest to Trinitarians is that it appears to be God who begins to speak in verse 10, who refers to himself as "the Alpha and the Omega, the First and the Last." However, verse 16 begins "I, Jesus." This would appear, at first reading, to identify Jesus with the Alpha and the Omega. According to Revelation 1:8, the Alpha and Omega is "the Lord God." This also occurs at Revelation 21:6, where the speaker is identified as God (see v. 7).

Note, however, how the speakers are not clearly identified throughout chapter 22. For example, if we were to argue that, because the speaker in verse 16 is clearly identified as Jesus, then should we not also conclude that the speaker in verse 9 is also Jesus? But this cannot be the case, because here, just after John had fallen down at the speaker's feet, the speaker says:

> "Don't do it! I am a fellow-servant of yours and of your brothers the prophets and of all those who obey the words in this book. Worship God!" — Revelation 22:9; *Good News Bible.*

So the one speaking is clearly "the angel" from verse 6. But there is no announcement of a change of speaker in verse 10. The change however must have been made because he is identified as the Alpha and the Omega, a definite reference to Almighty God.

So, then, this passage of Revelation cannot be used to teach the doctrine of the Trinity either; because the characters speaking are separate individuals, including God and Jesus.

In the Introduction to this book, it was stated:

> "This book reveals that scriptures which support the teaching of the Trinity in some Bible versions are incorrectly translated. The student can be forgiven for readily accepting the Trinity when his or her own Bible clearly teaches it!"

And in Revelation 22:12 there is a case in point. Compare this text with most versions, and you will not find the name of the speaker mentioned. From the above arguments, we have deduced that he must be Almighty God. However, the *Good News Bible* has taken liberties with the text and added the words, "Listen! Says Jesus." These words do not occur in any Greek manuscripts. Nor is there any authority from the context to add the words.

## Thrice is All?

In the Fourth Century B.C. Aristotle wrote:

"All things are three, and thrice is all: and let us use this number in the worship of the gods; for, as the Pythagoreans say, everything and all things are bound by threes, for the end, the middle, and the beginning have this number in everything, and these compose the number of the Trinity."

This predilection towards the number three has been carried to extremes. Trinitarians quote almost any scripture where something is mentioned three times, or where "God" is repeated three times. One such scripture is the following:

"The LORD bless you and keep you:
The LORD make his face to shine upon you, and be gracious to you:
The LORD lift up his countenance upon you, and give you peace." — Numbers 6:24-26; *Revised Standard Version.*

In the Hebrew text, the Masoretic text, the divine name, Yahweh, occurs here instead of LORD.

If you were new to the Bible, and someone read this scripture to you, would you have any idea that such words could be used to teach the complex doctrine of the Trinity? Why should the fact that *three* blessings are spoken have any significance, other than a repetition for emphasis? Note Jesus' words in the book of Revelation:

"Those who prove victorious I will make into pillars in the sanctuary of *my God*, and they will stay there for ever; I will inscribe on them the name of *my God* and the name of the city of *my God*, the new Jerusalem which comes down from *my God* in heaven, and my own new name as well." — Revelation 3:12; *Jerusalem Bible.*

Who is the one Jesus refers to as "my God"? Is it not the Father? Notice too, that he repeats this, not three, but *four* times. This also agrees with other scriptures where Jesus refers to his Father as "my God." — Matthew 27:46; John 20:17; Revelation 3:2.

# PART FOUR:

# HOLY SPIRIT —
# PERSON OR ENTITY?

# 23  The Spirit and The Comforter

The idea that the Holy Spirit is a person was adopted late in the theological controversies of the first four centuries. The central ideas of the personality of the spirit were defined first at the Council of Alexandria in 362 AD and finally by the Council of Constantinople of 381 AD. The church initially dealt only with the doctrine of the deity of Christ.

Today, it is common to refer to the Holy Spirit as "he." But the Scriptures generally use the impersonal pronoun "it." The problem arises in the passage in the gospel of John (14:16, 26; 16:13), where Jesus refers to the paraclete, or Comforter. In the Greek language, this is **PA.RA'KLE.TOS**, a word in the masculine gender. The more widely used term, though, is **PNEU'MA**, "spirit," a word in the neuter gender, neither masculine nor feminine.

## He Will Guide You ...

Though inanimate things are often given personality in the Scriptures, do we ever find humans or spirit creatures referred to by the impersonal pronoun "it"? In other words, it is not unusual to read certain references which appear to attribute personality to the spirit: "he will guide you," "he will teach you." But these are few compared to the many references which treat the spirit as an entity, as an "it." There are no scriptures which use the impersonal pronoun "it" in reference to God or Christ.

The Catholic *New American Bible* admits regarding John 14:17:

> "The Greek word for 'Spirit' is neuter, and while we use personal pronouns in English ['he,' 'his,' 'him'], most Greek MSS [manuscripts] employ 'it.'"

It is easy to see how the doctrine of the personality of the spirit was developed. The triads and trinities of ancient pagan nations consisted exclusively of three personalities. When the Trinitarian controversies of the 3rd and 4th centuries raged, the problem of applying personality to the Holy Spirit was a difficult one. The masculine references to the *paraclete* (Greek: **PA.RA'KLE.TOS**) were used as a lever to reinforce the ideas. But the harmony of the Scriptures does not allow for this interpretation. The use of the masculine pronoun ("he") can be easily explained in light of other scriptures which attribute personality to inanimate objects. For example:

is not sin at the door like a crouching beast
　　Genesis 4:7
your brother's blood, crying out to me from the ground
　　Genesis 4:10
this stone shall be a witness against us
　　Joshua 24:27
death will herd them to pasture
　　Psalm 49:14
wisdom has been proved right by all her children
　　Luke 7:35
death reigned over all from Adam to Moses
　　Romans 5:15
blood for purification which pleads more insistently
　　Hebrews 12:24
the Spirit, the water and the blood, ... agree
　　1 John 5:8
and I heard the altar say ...
　　Revelation 16:7

The impersonal pronoun ("it") would never have been used if the Holy Spirit was understood to be a person.

Furthermore, the Bible itself appears to have been given personality in the following scripture:

"The word of God is alive and active, sharper than any double-edged sword. It cuts all the way through, to where soul and spirit meet, to where joints and marrow come together." — Hebrews 4:12; *Good News Bible.*

Do we assume that God's Word, the Bible, is a person? Of course not. This is explaining the power that the impersonal, written word of God has in the lives of those who put its words into practise. Likewise the use of the personal pronoun, "he," in respect to the Holy Spirit, does not mean that it must be a person.

## The Holy Spirit Says

Other scriptures which Trinitarians use to support the teaching use expressions such as "the Holy Spirit says" and "the Holy Spirit spoke" and "the spirit told me," etc. (Acts 1:16; 11:12; 13:2; 15:28; 16:6, 7; 20:23, 28; 21:11) However, rather than looking for an explanation of these expressions in the "personality" of the spirit, the Scriptures themselves explain the usage. For example, notice this reference in the book of Acts, where the apostles said:

> "Who by the mouth of our father David, thy servant, didst say by the Holy Spirit." — Acts 4:25; *Revised Standard Version.*

After the expression "didst say by the Holy Spirit," the apostles then proceed to quote from the second Psalm. So instead of quoting the *spoken* word, they quoted the *written* word. The Holy Spirit did not speak *literally*, it spoke *figuratively* through the pages of the Bible! This is just the same in modern language usage. We use the expression, "Look what the papers say," when referring to the *written* word of the daily paper.

This is borne out later in the book of Acts, where the apostle Paul said:

> "The Holy Spirit was right in saying to your fathers through Isaiah the prophet." — Acts 28:25; *Revised Standard Version.*

The speaking was not literal. The message was expressed by the hand of Isaiah the prophet who wrote under the "inspiration" of the spirit. Paul expresses it this way in the second book of Timothy:

> "All scripture is inspired by God and can profitably be used for teaching." — 2 Timothy 3:16.

The Greek text has here **THE.OP'NEU.STOS**, which literally means "God-breathed." The spirit of God thus directed the minds and pens of the Bible writers. In this way God speaks, He being the author of the Bible. In this way also, it could be said that the Holy Spirit "speaks," inasmuch as it was God's spirit that directed the Bible's writing. — See also Acts 11:28; 21:4; Hebrews 3:7; 9:8; 10:15.

The prophet Nehemiah bears the above out when he says:

> "Many years thou didst bear with them, and didst warn them by thy Spirit through thy prophets." — Nehemiah 9:30; *Revised Standard Version.*

God did indeed use his spirit to warn his people, but he did so "through" his prophets. This also explains such texts as Hebrew 3:7 where the apostle Paul uses the expression, "the Holy Spirit says." He then proceeds to quote from the Psalms. No spoken words can be heard coming from the document. Pedants would probably insist on using the expression "it *reads* here" rather than "*says.*"

This is also borne out in the words of Jesus, when he said:

> "It is not you who will be speaking; the Spirit of your Father will be speaking in you." — Matthew 10:20; *Jerusalem Bible.*

The spirit energises the minds of the disciples, guiding their thinking, enabling them to make a defence of their faith before the authorities. It is God's invisible spirit which does this. It is as if it "speaks."

At Acts 10:19, the Spirit "speaks" to Peter:

"And while Peter was pondering the vision, the Spirit said to him, 'Behold, three men are looking for you.'" — Acts 10:19; *Revised Standard Version.*

However, on other occasions this "speaking" is done by others. For example:

"Agabus, seized by the Spirit, stood up and predicted that a famine would spread over the whole empire." — Acts 11:28; *Jerusalem Bible.*

So the speaking was done by Agabus, who was prophesying under the power of the Holy Spirit. In Peter's case, the speaking was no doubt done by an angel (compare Acts 12:7).

## It Has Been Decided By The Holy Spirit

The expression "it has been decided by the Holy Spirit" occurs at Acts 15:28 (*Jerusalem Bible*). This gives the immediate impression of personality, for how could an inanimate object make decisions? But how does it harmonise with other scriptures on the Holy Spirit? Paul's statement to the Roman Christians is of interest here:

"And in the same way the Spirit too takes hold to help our weakness; for we do not know what prayers to make as we need to, but the Spirit itself intercedes by groans which cannot be put into words." — Romans 8:26; *The Bible in Living English.*

When prayer becomes difficult, and choosing the right words is a problem, the Holy Spirit can help us to "put into words" the ideas and feelings we wish to convey to God, reorienting our thinking. The "groans" (or "sighs" — *Revised Standard Version*) of the Spirit assist with the innermost thoughts and feelings to guide the words of the prayer, perhaps by bringing appropriate scriptures to mind. In like manner, the apostles, during the debate on circumcision (Acts 15) were assisted by the spirit to locate applicable scriptures which were brought to bear on the issue.

Thus, it was as if the Holy Spirit had "decided" the matter. This is why, later, the letter that the brothers sent out to the congregations remarked that it "seemed good to the Holy Spirit and to us" to render the decision.

An experience of Bible translator Robert Moffatt proves interesting here. Whilst on a mission he had set up amongst the Tswana-speaking people of southern Africa, he told of an African man who saw some people reading the Gospel of Luke. When he asked them what they were holding, they responded, "It is the Word of God." The man asked, "Does it speak?" The people replied, "Yes, it speaks to the heart."

Is it not also similar to the words of the Psalmist, who said:

> "Day to day pours forth speech, and night to night declares knowledge.
> There is no speech, nor are there words; their voice is not heard; yet their voice goes out through all the earth, and their words to the end of the world." —
> Psalm 19:2, 3; *Revised Standard Version.*

To assert that something 'speaks' or 'makes decisions,' then, does not by itself prove that something has personality.

*A Catholic Dictionary* agrees with this, saying:

> "On the whole, the New Testament, like the Old, speaks of the spirit as a divine energy or power."

\*          \*          \*          \*

Ephesians 4:4-6, though often used by Trinitarians, offers a refutation of the doctrine. For verse 6 speaks again of the "one God" as the "Father," and not as the three "persons." *The Bible in Living English*, by Steven T. Byington, says that there is "one God and Father of all."

At Matthew 28:19 reference is made to "the name ... of the Holy Spirit." But the word "name" does not always mean a personal name. When someone says, "in the name of the law," they are not referring to a person. They mean that which the law stands for, its authority. Robertson's *Word Pictures in the New Testament* says:

> "The use of name **ON.OMA'** here is a common one in the Septuagint and the papyri for power or authority."

So baptism 'in the name of the Holy Spirit' recognises the authority of the spirit, that it is from God and functions by divine will.

## The True Nature of the Holy Spirit

The references to the Holy Spirit in Trinitarian writings imply that the Bible writers were divided, or even confused, about the true nature of the Spirit. For example, the references to the paraclete (comforter) above, are used to imply that the Spirit has personality. But when other scriptures are encountered which clearly indicate that the Spirit is an impersonal force, there is no attempt to "harmonise" the scriptures. It is as if one Bible writer believed one thing, and another believed something in diametric opposition.

That the personal pronoun "he" is used of the spirit is explained above by the *masculine* word **PA.RA'KLE.TOS**. But when the *neuter* word **PNEU'MA** is used, the Greek text has the impersonal "it." And this agrees with other scriptures:

Note for example the use in the second chapter of the book of Acts. Here, the disciples are gathered in the upper room. Then the account says:

> "They were all filled with the Holy Spirit and began to talk in other languages, as the Spirit enabled them to speak." — Acts 2:4; *Good News Bible*.

It is clear from this description that the Spirit is not a person. As the word "spirit" itself implies, it is an invisible force used by God to accomplish a purpose. In this case it "enabled them to speak" in different tongues. Other translations use expressions such as "the Spirit gave them the gift of speech" (*Jerusalem Bible*), and "the Holy Spirit gave them this ability" (*The Living Bible*). By means of the power of this God-given Spirit, the disciples had this remarkable ability.

This also harmonises with Paul's use at 2 Corinthians. Here he stated:

> "By purity, knowledge, forbearance, kindness, the Holy Spirit, genuine love." — 2 Corinthians 6:6; *Revised Standard Version.*

The *Revised Standard Version* puts the definite article ("the") in front of Holy Spirit here, but the Greek text does not. An alternative rendering therefore is:

> "In integrity, in knowledge, in patience, in kindness, in Holy Spirit, in unfeigned love." — 2 Corinthians 6:6; *The Bible in Living English.*

The Holy Spirit, though obviously not a quality, is here included with qualities such as patience, kindness, and integrity. This has presented difficulties in the minds of those who regard the Holy Spirit as a person. And to this extent they have departed from the pure Greek text of the New Testament. For example:

> "By our purity, knowledge, patience, and kindness we have shown ourselves to be God's servants—by Holy Spirit, by our true love." — 2 Corinthians 6:6; *Good News Bible.*

But this is a major departure from the original Greek:

| **EN CHRE.STO'TE.TI** | **EN PNEU'MA.TI** |
|---|---|
| in kindness | in spirit |
| **HA.GI'O** | **EN MA.KROTH.U.MI'A** |
| holy | in long spirit |

The seven faithful men of Acts 6:3 were said to be "wise and full of the Holy Spirit." (*The Living Bible*) Barnabas, Paul's faithful travelling companion, was referred to as "full of the Holy Spirit and of faith." And the disciples continued to be "filled with joy and with the Holy Spirit."

How, then, can the Holy Spirit be a person? It is clearly, as its name implies, a "spirit." As it comes from God himself, it is pure, sanctified, holy. It can fill a person, energise their mind to recall Scriptural principles, guide their hand to make faithful written records, and provide them with miraculous oratory gifts. And all of this is gleaned from the harmony of the Holy Scriptures.

In Matthew 3:11, John the Baptist said that Jesus would baptise his disciples "with Holy Spirit and fire." Paul urged his fellow Christians, not to "get drunk with wine," but to "be filled with the Spirit." (Ephesians 5:18) Peter, when quoting from the book of Joel, said that God would "pour out my Spirit upon all flesh" enabling them to prophecy. (Acts 2:17) Later, because Peter was "filled with Holy Spirit," he was able to make a thorough defence before the rulers of the people. (Acts 4:8) Still later, the disciples were praying when "the place in which they were gathered together was shaken; and they were all filled with the Holy Spirit and spoke the word of God with boldness." The disciple Stephen, just prior to his martyrdom, was "full of Holy Spirit." (Acts 7:55) And Ananias, when he came into Saul, who later became Paul, prayed that he be "filled with Holy Spirit." — Acts 9:17.

There are many scriptures that use expressions similar to those above, where the Holy Spirit is not preceded by the definite article "the." For example, note the following: Acts 6:3, 5; 7:55; 8:15, 17, 19; 9:17; 11:24; 13:9, 52; 19:2; Romans 9:1; 14:17; 15:13, 16, 19; 1 Corinthians 12:3. The lack of the article, "the," indicates the impersonal nature of the Holy Spirit.

At 2 Corinthians 3:3 "written with spirit of a living God," the Greek word for spirit, **PNEU'MA**, is here not preceded by the definite article, "the." It does not say "written with *the* spirit of God," but simply "written with spirit." Likewise verse 6, Paul says "not in a written code but in spirit," again without the article, "the." Similarly, at Ephesians 2:22, it is not "the" spirit which inhabits us, but we have become "built up into a place for God to inhabit by spirit." This agrees with Ephesians 3:5 where the sacred secret has been revealed "by spirit." In both occurrences the INSTRUMENTAL **EN** is used (see the discussion on page 108). — See also Ephesians 6:18; 2 Thessalonians 2:13; Hebrews 2:4; 6:4; 2 Peter 1:21; Jude 20.

## The Holy Spirit in the Old Testament

In Old Testament references to the Holy Spirit, it is clearly an impersonal force. It is first mentioned in the book of Genesis in the following words:

> "And the Spirit of God was moving over the face of the waters." — Genesis 1:2; *Revised Standard Version.*

The Hebrew word here translated "Spirit" is **RU'ACH**. *The Analytical Hebrew and Chaldee Lexicon* by Benjamin Davidson, defines this as:

> "I. *air, breeze* ... II. *breath*; metaph[orically] *vanity, folly.*—III. *spirit, soul.*—IV. *mind, spirit, disposition* ... V. *the spirit of God.*—VI. *wind*; also *tempest, hurricane.*—VII. *wind, side, quarter* of the heavens.— VIII. *anger, wrath*, from the idea of breathing, snuffing."

The root from which **RU'ACH** is drawn literally means *"to smell, touch, scent, perceive."* It is variously translated in modern Bible versions: blast, breath, wind, tempest. After the Noachian flood, "God sent a wind across the earth and the waters subsided." (Genesis 8:1; *Jerusalem Bible*) God sent a **RU'ACH** across the earth, an invisible force.

Adam talked to God during "the cool of the day." The Hebrew text has **RU'ACH** here, referring to the wind or the breeze. (Genesis 3:8; *Revised Standard Version.*) At the back of Young's *Analytical Concordance of the Bible* is a list of the words based on the Hebrew **RU'ACH**. These include the following:

air
anger
blast
breath
cool
courage
mind
quarters
side
spirit
tempest
wind
vain
windy

And so the references continue, over and over again the same idea:

flesh in which there was the breath [**RU'ACH**] of life
    Genesis 7:15
Lord brought an east wind [**RU'ACH**] upon the land
    Exodus 10:13
the Lord turned a very strong west wind [**RU'ACH**]
    Exodus 10:19
a strong east wind [**RU'ACH**] all night
    Exodus 14:21
the blast [**RU'ACH**] of thy nostrils the waters piled up
    Exodus 15:8
and there was no courage [**RU'ACH**] left in any man
    Joshua 2:11
he was seen upon the wings of the wind [**RU'ACH**]
    2 Samuel 22:11

at the blast of the breath [**RU'ACH**] of his nostrils
   2 Samuel 22:16
remember that my life is a breath [**RU'ACH**]
   Job 7:7

Note what the *Catholic Encyclopedia* says:

"Nowhere in the Old Testament do we find any clear indication of a Third Person."

The Hebrew **RU'ACH** is consistently an invisible force, never a personality, as the above selections demonstrate.

Catholic theologian Edmund Fortman agrees, saying:

"The Jews never regarded the spirit as a person; nor is there any solid evidence that any Old Testament writer held this view. ... The Holy Spirit is usually presented in the Synoptics [Gospels] and in Acts as a divine force or power."

And the *New Catholic Encyclopedia* has this to say:

"The O[ld] T[estament] clearly does not envisage God's spirit as a person ... God's spirit is simply God's power. If it is sometimes represented as being distinct from God, it is because the breath of Yahweh acts exteriorly. ... The majority of N[ew] T[estament] texts reveal God's spirit as *something,* not *someone;* this is especially seen in the parallelism between the spirit and the power of God."

So nowhere in the Scriptures is the idea found that the Holy Spirit has personality, or is the third person of the Trinity. The teaching is a clear addition to the sacred writings, and only after the affirmation of the church in the 4th century has the doctrine of the third person been fully developed.

# 24   Another Helper —
## The Holy Spirit

"And I will pray the Father, and he will give you another Counselor, to be with you for ever." — John 14:16; *Revised Standard Version.*

It is claimed by some that Jesus' use of the word "another" (Greek: **A'LLOS**) in the above scripture supports the doctrine of the Trinity and the belief that the Holy Spirit is a person. This is because there are, in Biblical Greek, two words for "another"; namely, **A'LLOS** and **HE'TEROS**. In many contexts **HE'TEROS** is translated by the word "different."

Greek scholar W. E. Vine (in his *Expository Dictionary of New Testament Words*), whilst maintaining the above view, admits that the difference in the meaning of **A'LLOS** and **HE'TEROS** has a "tendency to be lost." (Vol. I, p. 60) However, W. Graham Scroggie makes an enormous claim, writing in the foreword to Vine's first volume:

"This Dictionary indicates the doctrinal bearing which the use of chosen words has. A case in point will be found on page 60, under ANOTHER. The use of **A'LLOS** and **HE'TEROS** in the New Testament should be carefully examined, for *another numerically* must not be confounded with *another generically.* Mr. Vine points this out in John 14:16. When Christ said, "I will make request of the Father, and He shall give you another Helper (**ALLON PARA'KLE.TON**)" He made a tremendous claim both for Himself and for the Spirit, for **A'LLOS** here implies the personality of the Spirit, and the equality of both Jesus and the Spirit with the Father."

This is clearly a very deep implication drawn from a grammatical principle that is, in its own turn, by no means clearly defined. It is the obligation of every sincere Bible student to read *out from* the meaning of the Bible's words *(exegesis)* and not to read *into* them *(eisegesis)* doctrines that are not taught elsewhere in the Scriptures! — 2 Timothy 1:13; 3:16, 17.

The determining factors for the Bible writers which governed the choice between **A'LLOS** and **HE'TEROS** are sufficiently fluid (indeed, frequently confused) as to cause sincere Bible students to be extremely cautious in attempting to find support for any teaching on the basis of the presence of the words in various contexts.

If the rules determining the choice of **A'LLOS** and **HE'TEROS** were always so subtle, or were of any doctrinal significance, they would not have been used arbitrarily and interchangeably at texts such as 1 Corinthians 12:8-10 and 14:17, 19.

Obviously it would be superfluous to attempt to introduce some teaching based on the alternating use of these words in the above scriptures, or to separate their meanings here by some peculiarly exact definition. Consequently, it is only *because* of the already existing doctrine of the Trinity that many refer to **A'LLOS** at John 14:16 in an attempt to support the doctrine (a case of *eisegesis*). Had the doctrine never occurred in the writings and words of Christendom over the centuries, the presence of **A'LLOS** at John 14:16 would have been unable to teach something as complex as the Trinity doctrine. For example, J. W. Wenham, in a footnote to page 35 of his book *The Elements of New Testament Greek*, says regarding the controversial John 1:1:

> "In ancient manuscripts which did not differentiate between capital and small letters, there would be no way of distinguishing between Theos ('God') and theos ('god'). Therefore as far as grammar alone is concerned, such a sentence could be printed: **THE.OS' ESTIN HO LO'GOS**, which would mean *either*, 'The word is a god,' or, 'The Word is the god.'

"The interpretation of John 1:1 will depend upon whether or not the writer is held to believe in only one God or in more than one god."

So, supporters of the Trinity will prefer "The Word was the god," whereas those who deny the Trinity will prefer "The Word was a god".

Consequently, this statement alone cannot be used by *either* party in support of their beliefs without reference to the context (both immediate context and Scripture as a whole). And the immediate context (the second clause of John 1:1) says that the Word was "with God"; therefore the Word cannot at one and the same time be the God. So the conclusion is as obvious as the rendering of "a god" at Acts 28:6. Here the people of Malta thought that the apostle Paul was a **THE.OS'** (God), not **HO THE.OS'** (*the* God). Bible translators have no problem inserting the "a" at this place, to read "*a* God," since "*the* God" is obviously not meant. Likewise at John 1:1, *the* God is already mentioned in the verse as the one who is with the Word.

Regarding the use of **A'LLOS** and **HE'TEROS**, the above Moulton's *Grammar of New Testament Greek* (Vol. III, page 197) explains that **HE'TEROS** is not widely used in the New Testament and that **A'LLOS** at times even usurps the province of **HE'TEROS** (when it denotes the one or the other *of two*, such as cheeks, hands etc.) The grammar quotes Matthew 5:39; Luke 6:29; Matthew 12:13; John 18:16; 19:32; 20:3 where one would expect to see **HE'TEROS** rather than **A'LLOS**. The writer then notes the classical use of the expression **ALLOI ALLO** (*one thing … one another*). In a footnote he also points to two classical writers who consider the two words to be equal.

Bible scholars often express caution concerning references to Classical Greek grammar. After all, the Bible was written in **KOI'NE** (*common*) Greek, not Classical. Classical references are sometimes misleading from a Biblical viewpoint. For example, J. W. Wenham says regarding these two words (**A'LLOS** and **HE'TEROS**) in his above-mentioned book (p.62):

> "In classical Greek **HE'TEROS** is the correct word when speaking of 'the other two,' but in the New Testament this distinction between the two words has almost disappeared."

However, the above illustrates (still further) that to attempt to apply *eisegesis* in the extreme opposite direction (toward a more clearly defined doctrinal application of **A'LLOS**) in support of a non-Scriptural teaching is to go against the spirit of the apostle Paul's counsel at 1 Corinthians 4:6:

> "Do not go beyond the things that are written."

That is, beyond the complete, inspired Word of God which is "beneficial for teaching, for reproving, for setting things straight." — 2 Timothy 3:16; compare Galatians 1:8.

# PART FIVE:

# APPENDIX

The following questions are all answered in this book. Use the index at the back to locate the answers.

1. Does the scripture at John 10:30 ("I and the Father are one?") support the teaching of the Trinity?

2. How does this verse harmonise with John 17:22, where Jesus says, "in order that they [that is, the disciples] may be one *just as* we are one"?

3. In what sense, then, are the Father and the Son "one"?

4. What is the meaning of Jesus' words, "He that has seen me has seen the Father"?—John 14:9.

5. How does the above scripture harmonise with Hebrews 1:3, where Jesus is referred to as the "exact *likeness*" of his Father (*Today's English Version*)?

6. How do the following scriptures—as read from the Authorised (*King James*) Bible—support the Trinity: Philippians 2:6; 1 Timothy 3:16; 1 John 5:7?

7. Why do most other Bible versions not agree with the above renderings?

8. Why did the Jews say to Jesus (John 8:57) "You are not yet fifty years old, and still you have seen Abraham?"

9. What was the meaning of Jesus' reply at verse 58, "Before Abraham was, I am"? (*King James*)

10. Is the expression translated "I am" in this verse the equivalent of the expression found at Exodus 3:14?

11. Why do the following versions render John 8:58 thus:

"I have existed before Abraham was born."
        *Moffatt, Schonfield,* and *An American Translation*
"Before Abraham came to be, I was."
        *Stage*
"Before there was an Abraham, I was already there!"
        *Pfaefflin*
"Before Abraham was born, I was."

George M. Lansa, from the *Syriac Peshitta*
"Before Abraham existed, I was existing."
'*Sacred Bible*', Catholic Bible Center?

12. Consequently, was Jesus not referring to the fact of his having existed since before the time of Abraham?

13. In Daniel 7:13, 14, who is the "Ancient of Days," and also, who is the "son of man"?

14. Was the vision of an *earthly*, or a *heavenly* scene?

15. From whom did the "son of man" receive kingship?

16. Why was the Holy Spirit not mentioned?

17. In Psalm 110:1, two "lords" are referred to (*King James*). What is the identify of each "lord"?

18. How can God and Christ be "coequal" when Jesus said that his Father was *greater* than he is?—John 14:28.

19. At Proverbs 8:22, 23, who is the "Creator" and who is the one "created" as the beginning of God's works?

20. Does the above scripture harmonise with Colossians 1:15, 16 and Revelation 3:14 concerning Jesus' being the *first* of God's creation?

21. Mark 13:32 says that "no-one knows" the day or the hour of God's coming judgement, not even the son "but only the Father." How is this possible?

22. Further, why is it that the Holy Spirit does not know the day or hour?

23. The 144,000 bear the name of the Father and the Son on their forehead, why not also the name of the Holy Spirit?—Revelation 14:1.

24. Just before the disciple Stephen was stoned to death, he saw a vision of Christ standing at God's right hand. Why didn't he also see the Holy Spirit?—Acts 7:56.

25. How did Jesus cause the disciples to receive Holy Spirit by *blowing* upon them?—John 20:22 (see Genesis 1:2).

26. Does the use of a masculine pronoun ("he") by itself prove that something is a person?—Joshua 24:27; Luke 7:35; Romans 5:14, 21; Revelation 16:7.

27. Can a person be called "it"?—John 14:17; Romans 8:26.

28. Which scriptures show that Jesus Christ was subject to his Father *before* his coming to earth, *upon* his coming to earth and lastly, *after* returning to heaven?

29. The Bible repeatedly says that Jehovah is *one God*. How is this possible if he consists of three persons?

30. Is Jesus also this *one God?*

31. Does this one God consist of Father, Son, *and* Holy Spirit?

32. Why, then, did Paul speak of the one who is *one God* as being "the Father"? — 1 Corinthians 8:5, 6.

33. Why, in the above scripture, is the *one God* separate from the *one Lord*, Jesus Christ?

34. Why does Jesus refer to the Father as "my God" even *after* his return to heaven? — Revelation 3:2, 12.

35. Why does the much-used expression "God the son" not occur even once throughout the Bible?

36. Though some translations use John 1:1 to support the Trinity, why do the following versions render it thus:

"The Logos [Word] was Divine."
*Dr. James Moffatt*
"The Word was Divine."
*Smith-Goodspeed*
"The Word was itself of Divine Being."
*Stage*
"And God [=of Divine Being] the Word was."
*Menge*
"And God of a sort the Word was."
*Thimme?*

37. Can a human be called a god? — Psalm 82:1, 6; Acts 28:6.

38. Can an angel be called a god?— Psalm 8:5.

39. Can Satan be called a god? — 2 Corinthians 4:4.

40. If the Hebrew word for God (**E.LO.HIM'**) can be used to mean something *less than* a god (for example, "great," "mighty"), why is it so unusual that Christ is referred to as an **E.LO.HIM'** at John 1:1 (using the Greek **THE.OS'**)?

41. What reason does Bible Translator William Barclay give for the absence of the definite article ["the"] before the "Word" at John 1:1?

42. How does John 1:1 harmonise with John 1:18, where "the only-begotten god", Jesus, is in the bosom position *with* the Father?

43. If Jesus and his apostles had taught the Trinity, why did *unbelieving Jews*, who bitterly and passionately opposed Christianity, not attack a doctrine that to them would have been abhorrent?

44. If the Father and the Son are said to be co-eternal and co-equal, why are there many references to the subordination of the Son to the Father (John 14:28; 1 Corinthians 15:28; 1 Timothy 2:5, etc.) but no references to the subordination of the Father to the Son?

45. Why, when a certain ruler called Jesus "Good Teacher," did Jesus refuse the title, saying that "nobody is good, except one, God"? — Mark 10:17, 18.

# 25 Bibliography

The following bibliography provides the basis for much of the research conducted in preparation of this volume, and enables further reading on the subject of the Trinity:

*The Septuagint Version* — Samuel Bagster and Sons Limited

*The New Bible Dictionary* — J. D. Douglas, The Inter-Varsity Fellowship

*Davidson's Introductory Hebrew Grammar* — John Mauchline, T. & T. Clark

*Hebrew and Aramaic Dictionary of the Old Testament* — Georg Fohrer, SCM Press Ltd

*An Idiom-Book of New Testament Greek* — C. F. D. Moule, Cambridge University Press

*Greek Grammar* — William W. Goodwin, St. Martin's Press

*Lexical Aids for Students of New Testament Greek* — Bruce M. Metzger, Basil Blackwell

*Introduction to the Literature of the Old Testament* — S. R. Driver, T. & T. Clark

*Grammatical Insights Into The New Testament* — Nigel Turner, T. & T. Clark

*The Text of the Old Testament – An Introduction to the Bible Hebraica* — Ernst Würthwein, SCM Press Ltd

*Gesenius' Hebrew Grammar* — As Edited and enlarged by the late E. Kautzsch, Revised in accordance with the 28th German edition by A. E. Cowley, Clarendon Press

*A Greek Grammar of the New Testament and Other Early Christian Literature* — A revision of F. Blass and A. Debrunner, Translated and edited by Robert W. Funk, Cambridge University Press

*The Pentateuch and Haftorahs* — Dr. J. H. Hertz, Soncino Press

*The Analytical Hebrew and Chaldee Lexicon* — Benjamin Davidson, Zondervan

*The Analytical Greek Lexicon Revised 1978 Edition* — Harold K. Moulton, Zondervan

*The Oxford English–Hebrew Dictionary* — Oxford University Press

*The Theology of the Old Testament* — A. B. Davidson, T. & T. Clark

*Grammar of New Testament Greek* — Vols. I–III, James Hope Moulton & Nigel Turner, T. & T. Clark

*New Testament Greek, An Introductory Grammar* — Eric G. Jay, S.P.C.K.

*Grammar of New Testament Greek* — Dr. G. B. Winer, T. & T. Clark

*Greek-English Lexicon of the New Testament*, Grimm's Wilke's Clavis Novi Testamenti, Translated and enlarged by Joseph Henry Thayer — Fourth Edition, T. & T. Clark

*The Living World of the Old Testament, Third Edition* — Bernard W. Anderson, Longman

*A Concordance to the Greek Testament* — W. F. Moulton, A. S. Geden, T. & T. Clark

*The Strongest Strong's Exhaustive Concordance of the Bible* — James Strong, Zondervan

*Analytical Concordance to the Holy Bible* — Robert Young, The Religious Tract Society

*The Development of Christian Doctrine* — Cardinal Newman

*The Two Babylons* — S. W. Partridge & Co, Alexander Hislop

*The Trinity in the New Testament* — Arthur W. Wainwright, S.P.C.K.

*Dictionary of the Bible* — Bruce Publishing Co, John L. McKenzie

*The Triune God* — Edmund Fortman, The Westminster Press

*The Paganism in Our Christianity* — Arthur Weigall, Gordon Press

*The Influence of Greek Ideas on Christianity* — Edwin Hatch, Harper

*The Formation of Christian Dogma* — Dr. Martin Werner, Harper

*The Divinity of Jesus Christ* — John Martin Creed, Cambridge

*The Search for the Christian Doctrine of God* — R. P. C. Hanson, Baker Academic

*Grammar of the Greek New Testament in the Light of Historical Research* — A. T. Robertson, Broadman Press

# 26  Index

Printed in the United Kingdom by
Lightning Source UK Ltd., Milton Keynes
139329UK00001B/85/A